The Real
Thomas
Jefferson

"I have sworn upon the altar of God eternal hostility against
every form of tyranny over the mind of man."

Th: Jefferson

Virginia
Jefferson's Country

Drawn by Julianne S. Kimber

Volume 1 of the
AMERICAN CLASSIC SERIES

The Real Thomas Jefferson

Part I
Thomas Jefferson: Champion of Liberty
(A History of His Life)
By *Andrew M. Allison*

Part II
Timeless Treasures from Thomas Jefferson
(Selections from His Writings)
Prepared by *M. Richard Maxfield,*
K. DeLynn Cook, and W. Cleon Skousen

Second Edition, Revised and Enlarged

National Center for Constitutional Studies

Library of Congress Cataloging-in-Publication Data

The Real Thomas Jefferson.
    (Vol. 1 of the American Classic Series)
    Includes bibliographical references.
    Contents: Part 1. Thomas Jefferson, champion of libery/ by Andrew M. Allison. Part 2. Timeless treasures from Thomas Jefferson (selections from his writings) / prepared by M. Richard Maxfield, K. DeLynn Cook, and W. Cleon Skousen.
    Includes index.
    1. Jefferson, Thomas, 1743-1826.   2. Presidents—United States—Biography. 3. Jefferson, Thomas, 1743-1826—Quotations.   I. Jefferson, Thomas, 1743-1826 II. Allison, Andrew M., 1949–   Thomas Jefferson, champion of liberty. 1983.   III. Jefferson, Thomas, 1743-1826. Selections. 1983   IV. Series: American Classic Series (National Center for Constitutional Studies (U.S.)); v.1.
E332.R33 1983
973.4'6'0924   83-17404
[B]   CIP

ISBN 10: 0-88080-006-2
ISBN 13: 978-0-88080-006-8

National Center for
Constitutional Studies
www.nccs.net

Contents

Illustrations

Preface

As the English novelist Samuel Butler once noted, "Though God cannot alter the past, historians can."[1] His observation is especially applicable to our changing perceptions of great historical personalities, most of whom are relentlessly "reinterpreted" by each new generation of biographers. It is doubtful whether many of these renowned characters of yesteryear would even recognize themselves in some of the publications devoted to them today.

There is no better example of this kind of metamorphosis than Thomas Jefferson, author of the American Declaration of Independence and third President of the United States. Since his death in 1826 he has been alternately vilified and deified in numerous forms by writers of varying motivations. In fact, so wildly has his image fluctuated in the national consciousness over the years that an extensive scholarly study has been conducted to investigate this phenomenon.[2]

During the first five decades of this nation's history, Jefferson was preeminent among his peers as an advocate of the rights of man. The inspiring appeal of his philosophy and the eloquent force of his expression have made him a powerful symbol of freedom throughout the Western world, and his influence has been even

---

1. *Erewhon Revisited*, The Works of Samuel Butler, ed. Henry Festing Jones and A.T. Bartholomew, vol. 16 (1925; reprint ed., New York: AMS Press, Inc., 1968), p. 132.

2. Merrill D. Peterson, *The Jefferson Image in the American Mind* (New York: Oxford University Press, 1960).

greater in death than in life. Because of this tremendous influence, hosts of "experts" have predictably come forward and altered the Jeffersonian image to accommodate partisan political objectives.

Some have chosen to dwell on Jefferson's personal character. He has been variously portrayed as either a scoundrel or a demigod, depending on the author's purpose. One recent product of the vilification school, for instance, is a popular "psychobiography" which has now found its way into most American libraries.[3] Claiming to be an "intimate history" of Jefferson's private life, the book focuses largely on his alleged lust for an enchanting slave mistress. It has Jefferson suffering from a near-schizophrenic condition as he desperately struggles to conceal his scandalous immorality in order to retain the esteem of the country he loves. As the following pages will demonstrate, this bizarre tale—like so many others about notable figures of the past—bears no resemblance to historical fact.[4]

Others have preferred to explore Jefferson's system of ideas on government, economics, education, or some other subject. But whatever side of him is treated, the standard approach among today's writers is to "analyze" and "interpret" him for the reader. We are not permitted to look at Jefferson directly, but rather through the eyes

---

3. Fawn M. Brodie, *Thomas Jefferson: An Intimate History* (New York: W.W. Norton & Co., Inc., 1974). Distributed widely in both the United States and England, it was reportedly "the best-selling hardcover historical work to appear in 1974." Virginius Dabney, *The Jefferson Scandals: A Rebuttal* (New York: Dodd, Mead & Company, 1981), pp. 2–3.

4. See chapter 18 herein, "A Season of Slander," especially the note beginning on page 231.

of various authors who summarize what he did and paraphrase what he said, then carefully explain *why* he did and said those things. Every few years another author comes along with still one more "fresh interpretation." As these pile up, one on top of another, the thoughtful reader begins to wonder who in the world Thomas Jefferson really was.

That is precisely why *The Real Thomas Jefferson* has been published. The title may seem presumptuous at first glance, but it is not meant to suggest that those of us who prepared the book are gifted with superior insight. Indeed, we have made a conscious effort to keep ourselves out of the picture. By allowing Jefferson to explain his life and ideas in his own words, we have tried to ensure that his spirit, not ours, will breathe in these pages—so that all who read them will become acquainted with Jefferson himself, not another second-hand interpretation of him.

For reasons already noted, Jefferson's life and thought have been misrepresented and misconstrued by Americans of the twentieth century. Yet before we can appreciate and utilize his magnificent vision of a free republic, we must correctly understand both his life *and* his ideas. Thus the two-part format of this volume: the biography in Part I and the selected quotations in Part II are complementary elements, each making the other more meaningful and providing a fuller portrait of the real Jefferson. As we have indicated, the book consists mostly of Jefferson's own words; even the biography is drawn chiefly from his writings. In both sections the passages quoted are carefully documented from original sources.

This volume is part of a series being published by the National Center for Constitutional Studies, which has been established to help restore Constitutional principles in the tradition of America's Founding Fathers. The AMERICAN CLASSIC SERIES is designed to revive an intelligent appreciation of the Founders and the remarkable system of free government which they gave us. The nation these men built is now in the throes of a political, economic, social, and spiritual crisis that has driven many to an almost frantic search for "modern solutions." Ironically, the solutions have been readily available for nearly two hundred years in the writings of our Founding Fathers. An honest examination of twentieth-century American history reveals that virtually every serious problem which has developed in our society can be traced to an ill-conceived departure from the sound principles taught by these great men. The citizen of today who turns back to the Founders' writings is often surprised by their timeless relevance—and perhaps equally dismayed that we have permitted ourselves to stray so far from such obvious truths.

It is our earnest hope that the AMERICAN CLASSIC SERIES will prove to be an inspiration and a valuable resource to those who believe that this nation can yet fulfill its "manifest destiny" as a bulwark of freedom in the world.

Andrew M. Allison, Editor
AMERICAN CLASSIC SERIES

Acknowledgments

We are indebted to many persons for their contributions to the preparation of this volume. The staffs of the J. Willard Marriott Library at the University of Utah and the Harold B. Lee Library at Brigham Young University, both of which house excellent collections in American history and biography, have been helpful and cooperative in identifying and making available many of the sources cited in Part I. Sammie Lane Thornton, librarian at the National Center for Constitutional Studies, has assisted in researching the quotations found in Part II, while Andrew and Mabel Mitchell have kindly volunteered many hours in arranging and preparing these quotations for typesetting. Other staff members at the National Center have also provided valuable help: Bryan W. Neville and Harold Skousen have ably supervised the various phases of the production process, Glen Fairclough has assisted with copy editing and proofreading, and Jean Marshall and Ken Neff have handled the typesetting and layout of the book.

We also express thanks to the many devoted Americans who have contributed financially to support the work of the National Center for Constitutional Studies, thus making this and other publications possible. Finally, each of us owes a debt of gratitude to a patient and loving wife and to other family members who have encouraged us and sacrificed to help us complete this endeavor.

Thomas Jefferson: Biographical Highlights

1743, April 13   Born at Shadwell, Albemarle County, Virginia.

1745   Moved with his family to the Tuckahoe estate in nearby Goochland County (age 2).

1748   Began studying under the direction of his cousin's tutor (age 5).

1752   Placed in the care of the Reverend William Douglas, under whom he studied Latin, Greek, and French (age 9).

1757, August 17   His father died at the age of 49; soon afterward he enrolled in a school run by the Reverend James Maury, where he studied classical literature and additional languages (age 14).

1760, January   Entered the College of William and Mary in Williamsburg, Virginia (age 16).

1762, April 25   Graduated from William and Mary, then began an intensive five-year study of the law and many other disciplines under George Wythe (age 19).

1767, February   Moved back to Shadwell and began a successful law career (age 23).

1768, December   Elected to represent Albemarle County in the 1769 session of the Virginia House of Burgesses (age 25).

1769, July   Began building his new home at Monticello (age 26).

1772, January 1   Married Martha Wayles Skelton (age 28).

1774   His *Summary View of the Rights of British America* was printed and distributed throughout England and America; retired from his law practice to devote more attention to political matters (age 31).

1775, June 20   Arrived in Philadelphia as a delegate to the Second Continental Congress (age 32).

1776, March 31   His mother died at the age of 57 (age 32).

1776, June 11–28   Wrote the Declaration of Independence (age 33).

1776, October   Returned to the Virginia legislature and began a three-year project of revising the state's legal code (age 33); his labors in this period, including a public education bill and the Statute of Virginia for Religious Freedom, eventually wielded a major influence on the liberties of American citizens.

1779, June 1 Elected as the second Governor of Virginia, succeeding Patrick Henry (age 36); served for two difficult years during the Revolutionary War.

1781-82 Authored *Notes on the State of Virginia* (age 38).

1782, September 6 His wife died at the age of 33 (age 39).

1783-84 Served in Congress and drafted several important state papers (age 40-41).

1784, August 6 Reached Paris, France, to join Benjamin Franklin and John Adams in negotiating commercial treaties with the European nations (age 41).

1785, March 10 Succeeded Franklin as the American minister to France (age 41); while in Europe, influenced the American Constitutional Convention of 1787 through his friend James Madison, and witnessed the early stages of the French Revolution.

1789, November 23 Upon returning to the United States after five years abroad, learned that President George Washington had appointed him as the first Secretary of State in the new federal government (age 46); sworn in the following March, he served in this position for four years, often opposing the measures of Secretary of the Treasury Alexander Hamilton.

1794, January Resigned as Secretary of State and went back to Virginia to farm his plantations (age 50); remained there the next three years.

1797, March 2 Arrived again in Philadelphia to begin a four-year term as Vice President of the United States (age 53), during which he compiled a *Manual of Parliamentary Practice* still in use today; later in the same year, he was elected as president of the American Philosophical Society.

1798, September Secretly drafted the Kentucky Resolutions, which declared the Alien and Sedition Acts unconstitutional; decided to become the active head of the Republican party (age 55).

1801, March 4   Became the third President of the United States
                  and delivered his famous First Inaugural Address
                  in the new federal city of Washington (age 57).

1803, December 20 The historic Louisiana Purchase, which Presi-
                  dent Jefferson had initiated, resulted in the
                  transfer of a vast territory from France to the
                  United States, more than doubling the nation's
                  land mass (age 60).

1805, March 4   Sworn in for his second term as President
                  (age 61), during which he prevented war with
                  Great Britain by means of an unpopular Em-
                  bargo Act.

1809, March 4   Attended the inauguration of his successor,
                  James Madison; a week later, left Washington
                  for the last time and retired to Monticello
                  (age 65).

1823   In response to inquiries from President James
                  Monroe, shared views that helped shape the
                  Monroe Doctrine (age 80).

1825, April 1   The University of Virginia, which Jefferson
                  had virtually created single-handedly in Char-
                  lottesville, opened for classes; he served as the
                  first president of the university (age 81).

1826, July 4   Died peacefully at Monticello, on the fiftieth
                  anniversary of the signing of the Declaration of
                  Independence (age 83).

PART I

Thomas Jefferson:
Champion of Liberty

Andrew M. Allison

Chapter 1

"If He Were Here
We Might Rebuild..."

W ashington, D.C., with its classical architecture,
broad avenues, and graceful landscapes, is regarded today as one of the most beautiful
cities in the world. But at the opening of the nineteenth
century it was still a rude village, recently cut out of the
Potomac's thick forests and sitting on a swampland that
often turned its few ungraveled "streets" into miry pits
of mud. In those days the nation's new seat of government
consisted of several crowded boardinghouses, a tavern,
and two unfinished federal buildings—the Capitol and the
Executive Mansion (later called the White House). [1]

---

1. Jefferson estimated the population of the Washington area in 1802 to
be about six thousand people. Letter to Joel Barlow (3 May 1802), Albert Ellery
Bergh, ed., *The Writings of Thomas Jefferson*, 20 vols. (Washington: The Thomas
Jefferson Memorial Association, 1907), 10:321. Hereafter cited as Bergh.

Every afternoon about one o'clock, a plainly dressed
gentleman near sixty years of age whose appearance was
"very much like that of a tall, large-boned farmer"[2] could
be seen striding out of the Executive Mansion, mounting
his thoroughbred stallion, and riding off alone toward the
river or into the surrounding hills. He would be gone
about two hours, exploring the countryside. Almost
always he would return with some new botanical
specimen.[3]

This became a familiar sight to the townspeople of
Washington, but foreign dignitaries and other visitors
were often surprised to discover that this ordinary-
looking horseman was actually the President of the United
States. He was also, in this case, an agriculturalist, an
author, a musician, a paleontologist, an architect, an
inventor, and a hundred other things. He was Thomas
Jefferson.

An Embarrassing Introduction

One day, as President Jefferson was riding along one of
the highways leading into Washington, he overtook a
stranger who was making his way toward the city on foot.
He drew up his horse and greeted the man, as was his
custom. The traveler returned his greeting, and they
immediately launched into a political discussion. (People

2. Sir Augustus John Foster, *Jeffersonian America: Notes on the United States of
America Collected in the Years 1805-6-7 and 11-12*, ed. Richard Beale Davis (San
Marino, Cal.: The Huntington Library, 1954), p. 10.

3. See William Eleroy Curtis, *The True Thomas Jefferson* (Philadelphia: J.B.
Lippincott Company, 1901), p. 187; Sarah N. Randolph, *The Domestic Life of
Thomas Jefferson* (New York: Harper and Bros., 1871), p. 289; Margaret Bayard
Smith, *The First Forty Years of Washington Society in the Family Letters of Margaret Bayard
Smith*, ed. Gaillard Hunt (New York: Charles Scribner's Sons, 1906), p. 393.

talked as freely about politics then as we do about the weather now.)

Not realizing whom he was addressing, the man indulged in some unkind remarks about the President, referring to several indecent and slanderous accusations which his political opponents had recently printed in the newspapers. Jefferson's first impulse was to bid the fellow a good day and ride on, but he was held by his amusement at the situation. After listening a few more minutes, he asked the stranger whether he knew the President personally.

"No," said the man, "nor do I wish to."

"But do you think it fair," Jefferson asked, "to repeat such stories about a man whom you dare not face?"

"I will never shrink from meeting Mr. Jefferson should he ever come my way."

"Will you go to his house tomorrow at ten o'clock and be introduced to him, if I promise to meet you there at that hour?"

"Yes, I will," he decided after a moment's thought. Jefferson then excused himself, touched his hat to the traveler, and rode away toward Washington.

When the man appeared at the Executive Mansion the next morning, a servant answered the door and escorted him down a hall to President Jefferson's office. As he came face to face with the President, he suddenly realized what had happened. Greatly embarrassed, but with gentlemanly bearing, he managed to say, "I have called, Mr. Jefferson, to apologize for having said to a stranger—"

"Hard things of an imaginary being who is no relation of mine," interrupted Jefferson, as he gave the man his hand and a warm, good-natured smile.

The red-faced visitor turned out to be a merchant of high standing from Kentucky, and Jefferson insisted that he stay for dinner so they could become better acquainted. He did stay, and was quickly won over to the President he had unknowingly insulted the day before.

From that day forward the merchant and his family were "fiery Jeffersonians."⁴ Like so many other Americans, they quickly acquired a sincere affection for this tall, soft-spoken statesman from Virginia—and a deep commitment to the principles of freedom that he advocated.

"I Am Your Friend"

Many former detractors were quickly disarmed upon first meeting Jefferson. Margaret Bayard Smith, an early resident of Washington whose husband was active in political circles, had believed for some time that Jefferson was "an ambitious and violent demagogue, coarse and vulgar in his manners, awkward and rude in his appearance, for such had the public journals and private conversations of the [Federalist] party represented him to be."⁵ But then something occurred which radically changed her opinion.

In December 1800, a few days after Congress had for the first time met in our new metropolis, I was one morning sitting alone in the parlor when the servant opened the door and showed in a gentleman who wished to see my husband.... [We] entered into conversation

---

4. From Randolph, pp. 289–90; Curtis, pp. 199–200; Henry S. Randall, *The Life of Thomas Jefferson*, 3 vols. (New York: Derby & Jackson, 1858), 3:233–34. According to the last of these sources, the Kentuckian afterward made it a habit "to laughingly caution young people not to be *too* free in talking with strangers."

5. Smith, p. 6.

on the commonplace topics of the day, from which, before I was conscious of it, he had drawn me into observations of a more personal and interesting nature....

I knew not who he was, but the interest with which he listened to my artless details induced the idea he was some intimate acquaintance or friend of Mr. Smith's and put me perfectly at ease. In truth, so kind and conciliating were his looks and manners that I forgot he was not a friend of my own until, on the opening of the door, Mr. Smith entered and introduced the stranger to me as *Mr. Jefferson.*

I felt my cheeks burn and my heart throb, and not a word more could I speak while he remained. Nay, such was my embarrassment I could scarcely listen to the conversation carried on between him and my husband. ... [Because of] my previously conceived ideas of the coarseness and vulgarity of his appearance and manners, [I] was ... equally awed and surprised on discovering the stranger whose deportment was so dignified and gentlemanly, whose language was so refined, whose voice was so gentle, whose countenance was so benignant, to be no other than Thomas Jefferson.

How instantaneously were all these preconceived prejudices dissipated, and in proportion to their strength was the reaction that took place in my opinions and sentiments. I felt that I had been the victim of prejudice, that I had been unjust. The revolution of feeling was complete, and from that moment my heart warmed to him with the most affectionate interest, and I implicitly believed all that his friends and my husband believed, and which the after experience of many years confirmed. Yes, not only was he great, but a truly good man!...

He shook hands cordially with us both when he departed, and in a manner which said as plain as words could do, "I am your friend."[6]

"The Central Figure in American History"

Others who met Jefferson were awed by his genius and versatility. For almost two decades he presided over the most distinguished scientific organization in the United States, and he achieved international recognition for his scholarly endeavors in a surprisingly broad range of disciplines. Reflecting the admiration of many of Jefferson's contemporaries, one modern writer has noted that the scope of his interests was "breathtaking" and "nearly incredible.... There has probably never been anything like it since the Italian Renaissance."[7]

Jefferson continues to be widely respected throughout the Western world, both for his character and for his contributions to the arts and sciences. But he is remembered most for his profound influence on man's institutions of self-government. "The principles of Jefferson," wrote Abraham Lincoln, "are the definitions and axioms of free society."[8] Not only did he eloquently proclaim the principles of justice and liberty; as the following pages will demonstrate, the life he lived was the very epitome of the precepts he preached. Because of his unstinting devotion to those precepts, the famed French

---

6. Ibid., pp. 6–8.

7. Saul K. Padover, ed., *The Complete Jefferson* (New York: Tudor Publishing Company, 1943), p. x.

8. Abraham Lincoln to H. L. Pearce and others (6 Apr. 1859), Roy P. Basler, ed., *The Collected Works of Abraham Lincoln*, 8 vols. (New Brunswick, N. J.: Prentice-Hall, Inc., 1971), 3:375.

jurist Alexis de Tocqueville considered him "the most powerful advocate democracy has ever had."[9]

As President Woodrow Wilson once said, "The immortality of Thomas Jefferson does not lie in any one of his achievements, or in the series of his achievements, but in his attitude towards mankind."[10] Jefferson himself best described that attitude when he wrote the words now inscribed on his memorial in the city of Washington: "I have sworn upon the altar of God eternal hostility against every form of tyranny over the mind of man."[11] His thinking, his writing, and virtually his entire adult life were dedicated to the overthrow of tyranny and the protection of individual freedom.

In many respects, Thomas Jefferson was the embodiment of the American ideal. James Truslow Adams called him "the most intensely 'American' of all the great figures of his time."[12] And historian Henry Steele Commager took a still larger view: "Jefferson is the central figure in American history, and—if freedom and democracy survive in our generation—he may yet prove to be the central figure in modern history."[13] Even among that remarkable group of men known as the Founding Fathers, Jefferson was truly a giant.

---

9. Alexis de Tocqueville, *Democracy in America*, 2 vols. (1840; New York: Vintage Books, 1945), 1:280.

10. From a Jefferson Day address delivered in Washington, D.C. (13 Apr. 1916), Arthur S. Link, ed., *The Papers of Woodrow Wilson*, 37 vols. by 1981 (Princeton, N.J.: Princeton University Press, 1966–), 36:472.

11. TJ to Dr. Benjamin Rush (23 Sept. 1800), Bergh 10:175.

12. James Truslow Adams, *The Living Jefferson* (New York: Charles Scribner's Sons, 1936), p. vi.

13. Quoted in *New York Times*, 21 May 1950, sec. 7, p. 17.

"If He Were Here We Might Rebuild..."

All these and many similar expressions illustrate a deeply rooted disposition, especially among Americans, to revere the memory of Jefferson. His political philosophy and public services were a guiding force in the early years of the Republic, and some have openly expressed the wish that he could somehow return to steer the nation through its present difficulties. Nearly half a century ago, during another national crisis, an American poet penned six brief lines which he entitled "The Tomb of Thomas Jefferson." Many share his feelings today.

> This is an ignorant year
> Within a cruel time.
> If he were here
> We might rebuild
> The firm wall raised by him,
> The column felled. [14]

Jefferson, of course, cannot come back to solve the problems of this generation. But he did foresee those problems with almost prophetic accuracy, and he consciously left behind the tools that would enable us to "rebuild the firm wall raised by him"—if we have the wisdom to do so. While he was here, he saw and recorded and implemented the enduring principles by which a people can become genuinely free, prosperous, and secure. His noble life and his magnificent writings are the legacy he left to his countrymen. By reexamining that legacy and putting his principles to work once again, we may yet breathe the Jeffersonian spirit back into the nation he helped create.

---

14. Lawrence Lee, "The Tomb of Thomas Jefferson" (1940), in Dixon Wecter, *The Hero in America* (New York: Charles Scribner's Sons, 1941), p. 148.

Chapter 2

"An Inquisitive Youth"

On April 13, 1743, Thomas Jefferson was born at Shadwell, his father's estate on the Rivanna River in Albermarle County, Virginia.[1] He was the third child and eldest son of Peter Jefferson and Jane Randolph.

His mother, described as "a woman of a clear and strong understanding," bore ten children between 1740 and 1755.[2] It was through her that the family acquired its social standing among Virginia's wealthy aristocrats, as

---

1. According to the "Old Style" Julian calendar, in use throughout the British empire at that time, his birthdate was actually April 2, 1743. But the adoption of the Gregorian system in 1752 shifted the calendar by eleven days.

2. Randolph, *The Domestic Life of Thomas Jefferson*, pp. 21–22; Dumas Malone, *Jefferson the Virginian*, Jefferson and His Time, vol. 1 (Boston: Little, Brown and Company, 1948), p. 430.

the Randolphs were among the most prominent families
in the "Old Dominion."

Peter, on the other hand, was a "self-made" man. "My
father's education had been quite neglected," Jefferson
later wrote, "but being of a strong mind, sound judgment,
and eager after information, he read much and improved
himself."[3] After Peter Jefferson established his home in
Albemarle, an area then considered Virginia's frontier, his
"strong mind" and "sound judgment" were quickly recognized by his neighbors as he filled one leadership post after
another.

While employed as deputy surveyor, he helped survey
and draw the first accurate map of Virginia. He was also
appointed a lieutenant colonel in the county militia, a
justice of the peace, and later a member of the Virginia
House of Burgesses.

Not only was Peter's mind strong; his physical prowess
was almost legendary. It was said that he could up-end two
tobacco hogsheads at the same time, each weighing over
five hundred pounds.[4] On one occasion he "directed three
able-bodied slaves to pull down a ruinous shed by means of
a rope. After they had again and again made the effort, he
bade them stand aside, seized the rope, and dragged down
the structure in an instant."[5] His son Tom inherited a

---

3. Autobiography (1821), Bergh 1:2. The works of Addison, Swift, Pope,
and Shakespeare were among the well-worn volumes in his modest library.
Colonel Peter Jefferson was said to be "a staunch Whig, and he adhered to
certain democratic... notions and maxims which descended to his son."
Randall, *The Life of Thomas Jefferson*, 1:14.
4. Randolph, p. 20; Randall, 1:13.
5. Randall, 1:13.

Still standing today is this large home on the Tuckahoe estate, where Jefferson spent many of his boyhood years.

good measure of this strength, as well as his enthusiasm for horses and the outdoors.

The Tuckahoe Years

Thomas Jefferson's "earliest recollection in life was of being...handed up to a servant on horseback, by whom he was carried on a pillow for a long distance."[6] He was only two years old at the time, too young to understand that the family was journeying from Albemarle to a place called Tuckahoe in neighboring Goochland County. A relative there had died earlier that year, leaving a will which appointed Peter Jefferson the executor of his estate

6. Randolph, p. 23.

and the guardian of his surviving son.[7] Peter moved his whole family to Tuckahoe to fulfill this charge, and they ended up staying for seven years.

Young Tom was five when his schooling began in Goochland. He later recalled sneaking impatiently out of a classroom that first year and kneeling behind the building to repeat the Lord's Prayer, hoping thereby to hasten the hour of dismissal.[8]

"His Inquisitiveness Was Proverbial"

But as he grew, so did his eagerness to learn. Early acquaintances remembered the boy's insistence on seeing and understanding everything around him. "He was an inquisitive youth," according to one account:

> When he discovered a neighbor or a stranger doing something he did not understand, he asked questions and observed the proceedings until his curiosity was fully gratified, and then usually made notes of his observations in a memorandum book. His inquisitiveness was proverbial in the neighborhood, and [one] woman . . . remarked that she "never knew anyone to ask so many questions as Thomas Jefferson."[9]

When the Jefferson family returned to Shadwell in 1752, Tom—now nine years old—remained in Goochland under the care of the Reverend William Douglas, an Anglican minister from Scotland who served as his tutor.

---

7. The relative was Colonel William Randolph, Jane Randolph's first cousin and Peter Jefferson's best friend. His son was Thomas Mann Randolph, called "Tuckahoe Tom" by the Jefferson family. Years later the oldest daughter of Thomas Jefferson would marry the son of Tuckahoe Tom.

8. Randolph, p. 23.

9. Curtis, *The True Thomas Jefferson*, p. 24.

He learned quickly: within five years he could read Latin, Greek, and French (to which he soon added Spanish, Italian, and Anglo-Saxon).

His Beloved Father Dies

Not long after he turned fourteen in April 1757, Tom finally left Goochland County and moved back to the farm where he was born. He was happy to be with his family once again, but within a few short weeks tragedy struck his young life. On August 17, at the age of forty-nine, Peter Jefferson died of an unknown malady. This was a heartwrenching blow to Tom, who loved and admired his father greatly. He now inherited the estate at Shadwell and became the "man of the family," but his schooling was soon to take him away from home again. Indeed, he would be absent most of the time for several years to come. He later reminisced about the challenges and temptations he faced as a teenager after his father's death:

> When I recollect that at fourteen years of age the whole care and direction of myself was thrown on myself entirely, without a relation or friend qualified to advise or guide me, and recollect the various sorts of bad company with which I associated from time to time, I am astonished I did not turn off with some of them and become as worthless to society as they were. [10]

But thanks to a certain provision in his father's will, young Jefferson's mind was also exposed to nobler influences which helped mold the future course of his life.

---

10. TJ to Thomas Jefferson Randolph (24 Nov. 1808), Bergh 12:197. Spelling, capitalization, and punctuation have been modernized here and in other quotations in this biography.

In his mature years he repeatedly declared that if he were forced to choose between "the classical education which his father had given him, and the estate left him, he would decide in favor of the former."[11]

A Curious Proposition

In early 1758 Tom enrolled as a student of the Reverend James Maury, who officiated in the Fredericksville Parish of Albemarle County. The student from Shadwell considered his new instructor "a correct classical scholar."[12] He boarded with Maury for two years, usually returning home only on weekends.

Among Jefferson's young classmates was a fellow named Dabney Carr, destined to become his intimate friend and eventually his brother-in-law. One midwinter day after school was out, some of the boys prodded Dabney and Tom to come together for a horse race. A convenient place was designated, and Tom—realizing that his slow pony stood little chance against Dabney Carr's swift mare—cleverly suggested that the event be held on February 30. All the boys looked forward to the race with excitement, and not until the last day of the month did it dawn on them that they had been duped![13]

---

11. These words are from Thomas Jefferson Randolph (Jefferson's grandson), quoted in Randall, 1:18. In 1800 Jefferson wrote: "To read the Latin and Greek authors in their original is a sublime luxury.... I thank on my knees him who directed my early education for having put into my possession this rich source of delight, and I would not exchange it for anything which I could then have acquired." TJ to Joseph Priestley (27 Jan. 1800), Bergh 10:146–47.

12. Autobiography (1821), Bergh 1:3.

13. Malone, *Jefferson the Virginian*, p. 42.

"Deciding on My Conduct"

As noted earlier, Jefferson's teenage years sometimes found him in "various sorts of bad company." With his father now gone and his mother living far away, he was frequently faced with choices that proved to be important in the development of his character. As he gained experience in making these choices, he settled on a method that showed him to be wise beyond his years:

I had the good fortune to become acquainted very early with some characters of very high standing, and to feel the incessant wish that I could ever become what they were. Under temptations and difficulties I would ask myself, what would Dr. Small, Mr. Wythe, [or] Peyton Randolph do in this situation? What course in it will ensure me their approbation? I am certain that this mode of deciding on my conduct tended more to correctness than any reasoning powers I possessed. 14

He met most of these "characters of very high standing" at the College of William and Mary in Williamsburg, Virginia, where he was enrolled as an advanced student in January 1760.

---

14. TJ to Thomas Jefferson Randolph (24 Nov. 1808), Bergh 12:197. Peyton Randolph, his mother's cousin, was a member of the Virginia House of Burgesses. He later became speaker of that body, and in 1774 he was unanimously elected president of the First Continental Congress. William Small and George Wythe will be introduced in the next chapter.

Chapter 3

College Days

Williamsburg was the capital of the province when sixteen-year-old Thomas Jefferson arrived there to continue his education. Though a small town, it was the center of culture and high society in colonial Virginia. Men and women strolled down the Duke of Gloucester Street in the most elegant fashions of the day, and the popular Raleigh Tavern was always the scene of intense and exciting political discussion.

But if the young man from Albemarle was impressed by his new environment, the residents of Williamsburg were soon impressed by him also. He was already approaching his full height of six feet, two-and-a-half inches—at a time when the average height of American men was at least half a foot shorter. His eagerness to learn and his early accomplishments also set him apart in other ways from the rest of the new students who enrolled with him that winter at the College of William and Mary. The following description, taken from the accounts of those who knew him, provides a mental picture of young Jefferson in early 1760:

> He was a fresh, bright, healthy-looking youth, with large feet and hands, red hair, freckled skin, ... hazel-gray eyes, prominent cheekbones, and a heavy chin. His form "was as straight as a gun barrel, sinewy and alert," and he cultivated his strength "by familiarity with saddle, gun, canoe, and minuet." He early showed ... perfect self-reliance, and had a strong taste for mathematics and mechanics.[1]

Plunging right into his studies, he often spent fifteen hours a day trying to satisfy his ever-growing passion for knowledge.[2] His friend and classmate John Page, who later became a Congressman and then Governor of Virginia, recalled that Jefferson "could tear himself away from his dearest friends to fly to his studies."[3]

Soon after his arrival at William and Mary, young Jefferson developed a relationship with one of his instructors that greatly accelerated his intellectual development:

> It was my great good fortune, and what probably fixed the destinies of my life, that Dr. William Small of

---

1. Curtis, *The True Thomas Jefferson*, p. 24.

2. "During the most closely occupied days of his college life, it was his habit to study until two o'clock at night and rise at dawn. The day he spent in close application—the only recreation being a run at twilight to a certain stone which stood at a point a mile beyond the limits of the town." Randolph, *The Domestic Life of Thomas Jefferson*, p. 31. See also Randall, *The Life of Thomas Jefferson*, 1:24.

3. Quoted in Malone, *Jefferson the Virginian*, p. 58.

Scotland was then professor of mathematics, a man profound in most of the useful branches of science, with a happy talent of communication, correct and gentlemanly manners, and an enlarged and liberal mind. He, most happily for me, became soon attached to me and made me his daily companion when not engaged in the school, and from his conversation I got my first views of the expansion of science and of the system of things in which we are placed.[4]

Jefferson's college days were not filled entirely with books, however. At the end of his first year, he wrote one of the executors of his father's estate to acknowledge that he had spent too much money on clothes and horses.[5] He also enjoyed weekend dances in the Apollo Room of the Raleigh Tavern, concerts and stage plays, horse races and shooting matches, and an occasional fox hunt. And not the least of his interests at William and Mary was a pretty young miss named Rebecca Burwell.

A Frustrated Romance

We have no record of Jefferson's first acquaintance with Rebecca Burwell, but at some point she favored him with a little remembrance—a silhouette of herself to adorn his pocket watch. He took it with him when he went home for Christmas in 1762, but the "watch paper" became an object of misfortune when Jefferson stayed overnight at a friend's plantation en route to Shadwell. He described the sorry incident in a tongue-in-cheek letter to John Page:

You must know, dear Page, that I am now in a house surrounded with enemies who take counsel together

4. Autobiography (1821), Bergh 1:3.
5. Randolph, p. 37; Randall, 1:22.

against my soul; and when I lay me down to rest they say among themselves, come let us destroy him. I am sure if there is such a thing as a Devil in this world, he must have been here last night and have had some hand in contriving what happened to me.

Do you think the cursed rats (at his instigation, I suppose) did not eat up my pocketbook, which was in my pocket within a foot of my head? And not contented with plenty for the present, they carried away my jemmy-worked silk garters and half a dozen new minuets I had just got, to serve, I suppose, as provision for the winter. But of this I should not have accused the Devil (because you know rats will be rats, and hunger, without the addition of his instigations, might have urged them to do this) if something worse, and from a different quarter, had not happened.

You know it rained last night, or if you do not know it I am sure I do. When I went to bed I laid my watch in the usual place, and going to take her up after I arose this morning, I found her in the same place, it's true, but *Quantum mutatus ab illo!* [How changed from what it was!] All afloat in water, let in at a leak in the roof of the house, and as silent and still as the rats that had eaten my pocketbook. Now, you know if chance had had anything to do in this matter, there were a thousand other spots where it might have chanced to leak as well as this one, which was perpendicularly over my watch. But I'll tell you, it's my opinion that the Devil came and bored a hole over it on purpose....

And now, although the picture be defaced, there is so lively an image of her imprinted in my mind that I shall think of her too often, I fear, for my peace of mind. [6]

---

6. TJ to John Page (25 Dec. 1762), Bergh 4:1-3.

"She Never Gave Me Reason to Hope"

And he did think of her often. Whether Miss Burwell ever became serious about Jefferson is unknown, but there is no doubt that he hoped to marry "Belinda," as he often called her. In January he wrote Page that he wanted to return to Williamsburg and ask for Rebecca's hand. "Inclination tells me to go, receive my sentence, and be no longer in suspense; but reason says if [I] go, and [my] attempt proves unsuccessful, [I] will be ten times more wretched than ever."[7] When summer arrived he was still in a quandary:

> If I am to meet with a disappointment, the sooner I know it, the more of life I shall have to wear it off.... If Belinda will not accept of my service, it shall never be offered to another. That she may, I pray most sincerely; but that she will, she never gave me reason to hope.[8]

By early October, now back in Williamsburg, he apparently thought he had gathered enough courage to approach Miss Burwell with his proposal of marriage. But when the strategic moment arrived, he failed miserably. Once again he shared his woe with John Page:

> In the most melancholy fit that ever any poor soul was, I sit down to write to you. Last night, as merry as agreeable company and dancing with Belinda in the Apollo could make me, I never could have thought the succeeding sun would have seen me so wretched as I now am! I was prepared to say a great deal; I had dressed up, in my own mind, such thoughts as occurred to me, in as moving a language as I knew how, and expected to

---

7. TJ to John Page (20 Jan. 1763), Bergh 4:7.
8. TJ to John Page (15 July 1763), Bergh 4:9.

have performed in a tolerably creditable manner. But . . .
when I had an opportunity of venting them, a few broken
sentences, uttered in great disorder and interrupted
with pauses of uncommon length, were the too visible
marks of my strange confusion![9]

Jefferson made another attempt several months later. "I
then opened my mind more freely, and more fully," he
wrote afterward. [10] But while the second approach may
have been more polished, it was certainly no more
successful: within a few weeks Rebecca announced her
marriage to one of Jefferson's friends, Jacquelin Ambler.
To give the knife a final twist, Ambler—not knowing
about Jefferson's feelings for his fiancee—asked him to
serve as best man at the wedding![11]

Visits to the Governor's Palace

Sometime during Jefferson's enrollment at the College
of William and Mary, Professor Small introduced him to
George Wythe, an attorney who was practicing in
Williamsburg, and to Francis Fauquier, then the royal
Governor of Virginia. Small, Wythe, and Fauquier
frequently met over dinner for philosophical discussions,
and their circle now included Thomas Jefferson.

---

9. TJ to John Page (7 Oct. 1763), Bergh 4:12.

10. TJ to John Page (19 Jan. 1764), Bergh 4:13.

11. Gilbert Chinard, *Thomas Jefferson: The Apostle of Americanism*, 2nd ed. rev.
(Ann Arbor: The University of Michigan Press, 1964), p. 17. John Marshall, a
distant cousin of Jefferson who later became his political foe while serving as
Chief Justice of the Supreme Court, married a daughter of Jacquelin and
Rebecca Ambler. Also of interest is that Jacquelin's brother, Edward Ambler,
married a young lady who had rejected another famous Virginia suitor—
George Washington. See Bishop William Meade, *Old Churches, Ministers and
Families of Virginia*, 2 vols. (Philadelphia: J. B. Lippincott & Co., 1861), 1:101,
108–9.

It was unusual for such an honor to come to a young student, for these three men were among the most outstanding intellects in the province. "At these dinners," Jefferson later recalled, "I have heard more good sense, more rational and philosophical conversations, than in all my life besides."[12] He admired Governor Fauquier's accomplishments as a former protege of Sir Isaac Newton, an economist of some repute, a student of physics, and a fellow of the Royal Society. And the admiration seems to have been reciprocal. Fauquier apparently respected Jefferson's talents as well as his intellect, because he made arrangements for his young friend to play the violin at weekly concerts in the Governor's Palace.

Student of the Law

After completing his second year at William and Mary, Jefferson was graduated. He remained in Williamsburg, however, to become a law student under George Wythe. For the next five years he worked and studied in Wythe's law office, devouring one book after another in an incredibly intensive course of self-education.

He studied not only the law, but also languages, physics, agriculture, mathematics, philosophy, chemistry, anatomy, zoology, botany, religion, politics, history, literature, rhetoric, and virtually every other subject imaginable—always recording quotations and observations in his personal notebooks. Jefferson called this "a time of life when I was bold in the pursuit of knowledge, never fearing to follow truth and reason to whatever

---

12. TJ to L.H. Girardin (15 Jan. 1815), Bergh 14:231.

George Wythe, under whom Jefferson studied law for five years. Wythe later became a signer of the Declaration of Independence when the two served together in Congress.

results they led."[13] He was laying a solid foundation for his future career as an eminent American statesman.

Wythe (later a member of Congress and a signer of the Declaration of Independence) became a giant influence in Jefferson's life during this period. Jefferson penned the following tribute to this brilliant man, whom he sometimes called "my second father":

No man ever left behind him a character more venerated than George Wythe. His virtue was of the purest tint, his integrity inflexible, and his justice exact; of warm patriotism and devoted as he was to liberty and the natural and equal rights of man, he might truly be called the Cato of his country.[14]

It is not difficult to see the reflection of Wythe's teachings in his student's own lifelong devotion to "liberty and the natural and equal rights of man." After becoming President, Jefferson referred to George Wythe as "my

---

13. TJ to Dr. Thomas Cooper (10 Feb. 1814), Bergh 14:85.

14. TJ to John Saunderson (31 Aug. 1820), Bergh 1:169. Marcus Porcius Cato (234–149 B.C.) was a renowned Roman statesman and orator who wrote the first Latin history of Rome.

ancient master, my earliest
and best friend; and to him I
am indebted for first im-
pressions which have had
the most salutary influence
on the course of my life."[15]
Even in old age he could still
say, "Mr. Wythe continued
to be my faithful and be-
loved mentor in youth, and
my most affectionate friend
through life."[16]

Patrick Henry

Jefferson's thinking in
these early years was further influenced by an even
more illustrious character—
Patrick Henry. The two had
first met just after Christmas in 1759, when Jefferson

Patrick Henry, whose fiery oratory
held Jefferson spellbound during a
1765 speech in the Virginia House of
Burgesses. Jefferson succeeded him as
Governor of the state in 1779.

was traveling across Virginia to enter the College of
William and Mary. He later described his initial view
of Mr. Henry, who was seven years his senior: "His

15. TJ to William DuVal (14 June 1806), quoted in Dumas Malone, *Jefferson the President: Second Term, 1805–1809*, Jefferson and His Time, vol. 5 (Boston: Little, Brown and Company, 1974), p. 137.

16. Autobiography (1821), Bergh 1:4. At the time of Wythe's death in 1806, his neighbor and executor wrote to President Jefferson that "Mr. Wythe loved you as sincerely as if you had been his son." And in another letter he said, "You were dearer to him than any relation he had." William DuVal to TJ (29 June and 21 Nov. 1806), quoted in Malone, *Jefferson the President: Second Term, 1805–1809*, p. 138.

passion was fiddling, dancing, and pleasantry. He excelled in the last, and it attached everyone to him."[17] Henry entered the legal profession the same year Jefferson enrolled in college, and he usually shared Jefferson's apartment when he came to Williamsburg to argue court cases. Although political differences were to come between them afterward, they formed a friendship in the 1760s which left an indelible impression on the young law student.

It was not Henry's fiddling and dancing, but rather his uncompromising devotion to his countrymen's freedom and his unsurpassed power as a public speaker that aroused Jefferson. While studying law he often attended sessions of the Virginia House of Burgesses, and he was present on May 29, 1765, when Henry—then a new member of the assembly—offered a series of strongly worded resolutions against the infamous Stamp Act.

These resolutions, which Henry himself had written, were destined to ignite in the American colonies a spirit of fierce resistance to British oppression.[18] On their first reading, however, many of the legislators thought them too daring for presentation to the Crown. As Henry rose from his chair and defended the document with his famous "If this be treason, make the most of it" speech, Jefferson fastened his eyes on the scene and listened with wonder to every emotion-charged phrase:

---

17. TJ to William Wirt (5 Aug. 1815), Bergh 14:341.

18. Due largely to the force of Henry's eloquent appeal to his colleagues, the resolutions were passed by a narrow margin in the House of Burgesses. Their subsequent publication throughout the American provinces led to the passage of similar petitions in other colonies and to the formation of the Stamp Act Congress in New York the following October. The Stamp Act was repealed by Parliament in March 1766.

> I attended the debate . . . at the door of the lobby of the House of Burgesses, and heard the splendid display of Mr. Henry's talents as a popular orator. They were great indeed; such as I have never heard from any other man. He appeared to me to speak as Homer wrote. [19]

He was completely spellbound by Henry's passionate oratory. Many years later he declared that he had "never heard anything that deserved to be called by the same name with what flowed from him; and where he got that torrent of language is inconceivable. . . . He was truly a great man." [20]

Something remarkable happened to Thomas Jefferson as he witnessed this fateful debate. As he stood listening in the crowded doorway, electrified by Patrick Henry's fiery discourse, a flame was kindled in his soul—a flame of liberty and patriotism that would burn brighter and ever brighter, until he himself would feel compelled to take up the banner of the great American cause. It has been said that Jefferson later referred to this as the most important day of his life. [21]

First Trip Outside Virginia

During the summer of 1766, which was the final year of his legal apprenticeship, Jefferson took his first journey outside his native colony. His chief purpose was to travel to Philadelphia for an inoculation against smallpox—a

---

19. Autobiography (1821), Bergh 1:5. Homer was a Greek epic poet who is thought to have flourished around 850 B.C.; according to tradition, he authored both the *Iliad* and the *Odyssey*. These references to Greek and Roman characters reflect Jefferson's familiarity with classical literature.

20. Spoken by Jefferson to Leavit Harris (11 Oct. 1824), recorded by Nicholas P. Trist and quoted in Randall, 1:40.

21. Curtis, p. 123.

fairly new practice in those days. But he also took the opportunity to see many sights along the way, and to satisfy his curiosity about a portion of the world around him. It was clear from his writings that he considered this trip, like most of his experiences, a part of his education.

He stopped in Annapolis to observe the Maryland General Assembly in session, but was appalled by the careless manner in which they conducted their legislative business. (By this time he had gained a thorough knowledge of correct parliamentary procedure.) He must have marveled at Philadelphia, which at that time was among the largest cities in the British empire. And he extended his journey in order to visit the city of New York, finally returning to Virginia by ship after an absence of three months.

Jefferson Ponders His Future

Back in Williamsburg, Jefferson continued to mingle with Virginia's young aristocrats while finishing his preparations for the upcoming law examination. Having seen and learned much during his twenty-three years, he now contemplated the future direction of his life. Almost a half century later he wrote to his grandson Thomas Jefferson Randolph, describing the crossroads of decision he faced during this period:

> From the circumstances of my position I was often thrown into the society of horse racers, card players, fox hunters, scientific and professional men, and of dignified men; and many a time have I asked myself in the enthusiastic moment of the death of a fox, the victory of a favorite horse, the issue of a question eloquently argued at the bar or in the great council of the nation,

well, which of these kinds of reputations should I prefer?
That of a horse jockey? a fox hunter? an orator? or the
honest advocate of my country's rights? Be assured, my
dear Jefferson, that these little returns into ourselves,
this self-catechizing habit, is not trifling nor useless, but
leads to the prudent selection and steady pursuit of what
is right.[22]

For the time being, at least, Jefferson made up his mind
to enter the legal profession.

---

22. TJ to Thomas Jefferson Randolph (24 Nov. 1808), Bergh 12:198.

Chapter 4

The Law, Monticello, and Martha

In early 1767, under George Wythe's sponsorship, Jefferson was brought before the General Court of Virginia to be examined for admission to the bar. His examiners must have been astounded at the breadth and depth of his knowledge. Whereas many young men at that time were spending less than a year in preparation to practice law (Patrick Henry boasted that he had studied "not more than six weeks"!),[1] Jefferson had been systematically acquiring knowledge about the law and all related subjects for over half a decade. Perhaps no

---

1. TJ to William Wirt (5 Aug. 1815), Bergh 14:341. However, other sources indicate that Henry may have studied law up to "six or eight months" before his examination. See Norine Dickson Campbell, *Patrick Henry: Patriot and Statesman* (Old Greenwich, Conn.: The Devin-Adair Company, 1975), p. 23.

American had ever entered the profession so superbly equipped; there was no question about his readiness.

A Young and Successful Attorney

Jefferson was to spend the next seven years as a Virginia lawyer, dividing his time between his estate and the city of Williamsburg, where court sessions were held. His success surprised some of the more seasoned practitioners; within two or three years he was responsible for several hundred cases. In addition to the income from his lands, which then came to about $2,000 a year, his law practice produced earnings of nearly $3,000—a sizable sum in those days. One writer has described his exceptional performance as an attorney:

> Jefferson was a laborious and painstaking lawyer; nothing was slighted, big or little. It was his thorough preparation of cases both as to law and facts, the discriminating way in which he handled them in court, and his influence over judges and juries by virtue of his early reputation as a learned jurist that secured him a clientage among all classes, including some of the most prominent citizens of Virginia and of neighboring colonies.
>
> The few briefs which have come down to us show great thoroughness and erudition; he took nothing for granted, he was a searcher for the origin and reason of every rule of law involved in a case, and he shows a familiarity with the civil and ecclesiastical as well as the common law. [2]

---

2. G. A. Finkelnberg, quoted in Henry F. Graff, *Illustrious Americans: Thomas Jefferson* (Morristown, N.J.: Silver Burdett Company, 1968), p. 17.

"He Always Took the Right Side"

Many years later one of Jefferson's grandsons met an elderly gentleman who, as a young man, had often heard Jefferson deliver legal arguments in Williamsburg. Naturally curious, the grandson inquired about his famous progenitor's performance as a courtroom advocate. "Well," said the old gentleman, "it is hard to tell, because he always took the right side."[3] Jefferson's clientele increased with his reputation, and before long he was being sought out "by the first men in the colonies, and even in the mother country."[4] His surviving records show that he handled close to a thousand cases between 1767 and 1774.

There were also some drawbacks to the occupation. Finding that he was able to collect only about one-third of the fees he earned, Jefferson had to place a notice in the *Virginia Gazette* declaring that at least partial payment would have to be received in advance for cases accepted in the future.[5] And the endless lawsuits over land and property rights must have become tiresome after a while to a mind as brilliant as Jefferson's. "I was bred to the law," he said, "and that gave me a view of the dark side of humanity. Then I read poetry to qualify it with a gaze upon its bright side."[6]

His comments on an item he once drafted and sent to a member of the Virginia legislature give us an amusing

---

3. Quoted in Randolph, *The Domestic Life of Thomas Jefferson*, p. 40.
4. Ibid., p. 39.
5. See Malone, *Jefferson the Virginian*, pp. 123–24.
6. Quoted in Joseph L. Gardner et al., eds., *Thomas Jefferson: A Biography in His Own Words* (New York: Newsweek, Inc., 1974), p. 35.

insight into Jefferson's attitude toward the cryptic language of the legal profession:

> I should apologize, perhaps, for the style of this bill. I dislike the verbose and intricate style of the English statutes.... You, however, can easily correct this bill to the taste of my brother lawyers by making every other word a "said" or "aforesaid," and saying everything over two or three times, so that nobody but we of the craft can untwist the diction and find out what it means; and that, too, not so plainly but that we may conscientiously divide, one half on each side.[7]

"The Favorite Passion of My Soul"

Jefferson also found other activities more to his liking during these seven years. For example, he spent a good deal of time improving the Shadwell estate through agricultural experimentation, which was one of his most satisfying pastimes. His peaceful domestic life was suddenly upset, however, by a tragedy that occurred in February 1770. While he was away on business early that month, the family home at Shadwell was destroyed by fire. When a servant found him and delivered the bad news, Jefferson's first inquiry was about his books. "They were all burnt," said the servant, "but ah! we saved your fiddle."[8] After surveying the ruins of his house, Jefferson lamented to John Page that he had lost "every paper I had in the world, and almost every book."[9]

Nevertheless, he was grateful that the "fiddle" had been rescued from the conflagration. For some years he had

---

7. TJ to Joseph Cabell (9 Sept. 1817), Bergh 17:417–18.
8. Quoted in Randolph, p. 43.
9. TJ to John Page (21 Feb. 1770), Bergh 4:18.

practiced an hour or more every day on this instrument. "Music," he wrote to a friend, "is the favorite passion of my soul."[10] He played both the violin and the cello from his youth, and he eventually owned a large music library. When the Revolutionary War broke out in 1775, Jefferson paid a departing Englishman thirteen pounds for a well-made Italian violin, and it remained with him the rest of his life. In Philadelphia as a Congressman, in France as a foreign minister, and even as President of the United States, he continued to sharpen his musical skills on the instrument.[11]

Jefferson's "Little Mountain"

Another of Jefferson's interests during this period was architecture. Studying the sixteenth-century neoclassical style, he made and revised elevation drawings of a mansion he planned to build on a mountaintop near his home at Shadwell. The name he had chosen for this future residence was Monticello, the Italian word for "little mountain." Its design and construction were to become virtually a lifelong project for Jefferson.

As early as 1768, Jefferson contracted to pay a Mr. Moore 180 bushels of wheat and 24 bushels of corn to "level 250 feet square on the top of the mountain . . . by

---

10. TJ to [Francis Alberti?] (8 June 1778), Bergh 4:40–41. He later told a relative that in his young manhood he "took [violin] lessons for several years. I suppose that during at least a dozen years of my life, I played no less than *three hours* a day." Quoted by Nicholas P. Trist in Randall, *The Life of Thomas Jefferson*, 1:131.

11. Curtis, *The True Thomas Jefferson*, p. 26.

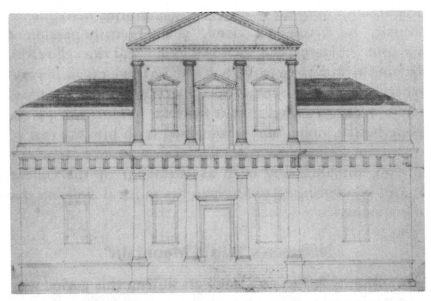

Jefferson's 1771 elevation drawing of the first version of Monticello. The appearance of the home underwent many changes over the next forty years as a result of Jefferson's fascination with architecture.

Christmas."[12] The idea of building a home on a mountain-top was unprecedented in Virginia, where plantation owners consistently lived along the river valleys in order to have access to commercial waterways. After Jefferson's death, his oldest daughter was asked by a family friend why Monticello had been built in such an unlikely place. She replied:

> I have heard my father say that when [he was] quite a boy, the top of this mountain was his favorite retreat. Here he would bring his books to study, here [he] would pass his holiday and leisure hours. . . . He never wearied

---

12. Contract (15 May 1768), in Edwin Morris Betts, ed., *Thomas Jefferson's Garden Book, 1766–1824, with Relevant Extracts from His Other Writings* (Philadelphia: The American Philosophical Society, 1944), p. 12.

of gazing on the sublime and beautiful scenery that spread around, bounded only by the horizon or the far-off mountains, and ... the indescribable delight he here enjoyed so attached him to that spot that he determined, when arrived at manhood, he would here build his family mansion.[13]

The fire at Shadwell accelerated Jefferson's construction plans, and by the following November the workers had completed enough of the new home for him to take up residence there.

Martha and Marriage

In 1770 Jefferson began paying visits to the home of John Wayles, a fellow attorney who lived on an estate called "The Forest," near Williamsburg. But he did not go there to discuss legal matters: Wayles had a daughter named Martha, who was quite talented on the pianoforte and the harpsichord, and she was the object of Jefferson's visits.

Martha Wayles Skelton was a young, attractive widow whose first husband had died in 1768, before she was twenty years old. She

Martha Wayles Skelton, who became Jefferson's wife in 1772 and brought him "ten years [of] uncheckered happiness." He never married again after her death in 1782.

---

13. Martha Jefferson Randolph, quoted in Smith, *The First Forty Years of Washington Society*, p. 387.

welcomed Jefferson's attentions and frequently accompanied him in musical duets when he came to see her. A description of Martha by one of her descendants helps us understand the attraction she must have held for her suitor:

> She is described as having been very beautiful. A little above middle height, with a lithe and exquisitely formed figure, she was a model of graceful and queenlike carriage. Nature, so lavish with her charms for her, to great personal attractions added a mind of no ordinary calibre. She was well educated for her day, and a constant reader; she inherited from her father his method and industry, as the accounts, kept in her clear handwriting and still in the hands of her descendants, testify. Her well-cultivated talent for music served to enhance her charms not a little in the eyes of such a musical devotee as Jefferson.[14]

One interesting anecdote from the young couple's courtship has been preserved in family tradition. According to the story, two of Jefferson's rivals appeared simultaneously on the Wayles doorstep one day, each of them intending to call on Martha. Both were shown into the front hallway, but before either could enter the drawing room they caught the strains of "a touching song" from behind the door. In addition to the harpsichord and violin, "the accompanying voices of Jefferson and his lady-love were soon recognized, and the two disconcerted lovers, after exchanging a glance, picked up their hats and left."[15]

Sometime in the next year Jefferson asked Martha to be his wife. She agreed, and the marriage took place at her

14. Randolph, pp. 43–44.
15. Randolph, p. 44; Randall, 1:64.

father's estate on New Year's Day, 1772. After several days of festivities, the newlyweds left for Monticello, over a hundred miles distant.

Arriving in a blizzard, they had to abandon their carriage and travel the last eight miles on horseback in about two feet of snow. When they finally reached Monticello and entered the small brick building—the only part of the mansion which was finished at that

The "honeymoon cottage" at Monticello, where the Jeffersons spent the first few months of their marriage. This was the only building on the mountaintop estate that had been completed by early 1772.

time—it was "late at night, the fires all out, and the servants retired to their own houses for the night."

Too happy in each other's love, however, to be long troubled by the "dreariness" of a cold and dark house, and having found a bottle of wine "on a shelf behind some books," the young couple refreshed themselves with its contents and startled the silence of the night with song and merry laughter.[16]

Mr. and Mrs. Jefferson worked hard to turn their mountaintop home into a comfortable haven. Before the end of the year, new sounds were heard at Monticello: their first child, a baby girl, was welcomed into the family. She was named Martha after her mother.

---

16. Randolph, pp. 44–45; see also Curtis, pp. 32–33.

The Jefferson Estate Is Doubled

Just over a year after the marriage, Martha's father died. Her inheritance practically doubled the size of Jefferson's estate, adding several thousand acres to the land he had inherited from his father and acquired through purchases.

Included among his holdings was an area containing the now-famous Natural Bridge, about eighty miles west of Monticello. Jefferson, a lover of beautiful sites, called this formation "the most sublime of nature's works."[17] He often went there for relaxation.

Unfortunately, a large debt was attached to the land which Martha inherited from her father. This indebtedness was a burden to Jefferson for a long time thereafter, as was the condition of his lands. Many years later his plantation overseer complained, "It was not a profitable estate; it was too uneven and hard to work."[18]

Jefferson also inherited many Negro slaves. Through most of his adult years he owned about ten thousand acres of land and between one and two hundred slaves.[19] This became a sensitive matter for Jefferson. Although his own economic circumstances, the Virginia plantation system,

---

17. *Notes on the State of Virginia* (1782), Bergh 2:30.

18. Captain Edmund Bacon, quoted in James A. Bear, Jr., ed., *Jefferson at Monticello* (Charlottesville: The University Press of Virginia, 1967), p. 51. Jefferson noted in 1798 that the problem was not peculiar to his own lands: "The unprofitable condition of Virginia estates in general leaves it now next to impossible for the holder of one to avoid ruin." TJ to Mary Jefferson Eppes (7 Jan. 1798), Edwin Morris Betts and James Adam Bear, Jr., eds., *The Family Letters of Thomas Jefferson* (Columbia, Mo.: University of Missouri Press, 1966), p. 152.

19. Dumas Malone, "Thomas Jefferson," *Dictionary of American Biography*, ed. Allen Johnson and Dumas Malone, 20 vols. (New York: Charles

and the colonial attitude toward blacks made it a practical necessity for him to keep the slaves on his estate, he detested the institution of slavery and tried many times during his life to bring it to an end.

Scribner's Sons, 1928–36), 10:18. See also Malone, *Jefferson the Virginian*, Appendix II, "The Jefferson Estate," pp. 435–46.

Chapter 5

"The Reputation of a Masterly Pen"

Jefferson's political career began even before he was married. At the age of twenty-five, he was elected to represent Albermarle County in the Virginia House of Burgesses. The politicians of that era were renowned for their oratorical skills—but Jefferson was very different. He seldom spoke in a public gathering, mostly because his vocal cords were not up to it: when he raised his voice above a conversational level for any length of time, his throat tightened severely and he became hoarse and almost inaudible.[1] However, even his political

---

1. Jefferson's biographer Dumas Malone observed: "He'd have a lot of trouble running for office today. He might not be good on TV. So far as I know, he never made a political speech." Quoted in Mike W. Edwards, "Thomas Jefferson: Architect of Freedom," *National Geographic*, February 1976, p. 236.

enemies acknowledged that he was a brilliant and captivating conversationalist.

"Subordinate to the Mother Country"

His Albemarle neighbors greatly respected his personal integrity and his powerful legal mind. Beginning in 1769, they elected him to the colonial legislature every year until he became a member of the Continental Congress in 1775. Jefferson commented on his first efforts in the House of Burgesses, revealing the attitude under which he and his colleagues then worked:

> In 1769 I became a member of the legislature by the choice of the county in which I live, and so continued until it was closed by the Revolution. I made one effort in that body for the permission of the emancipation of slaves, which was rejected; and indeed during the regal government nothing liberal could expect success.
>
> Our minds were circumscribed within narrow limits by an habitual belief that it was our duty to be subordinate to the mother country in all matters of government, to direct all our labors in subservience to her interests, and even to observe a bigoted intolerance for all religions but hers.[2]

Things were about to change, however. Within a few years this "habitual belief" would give way to a fervent movement for American independence. Among those standing at the forefront of this movement would be Thomas Jefferson.

---

2. Autobiography (1821), Bergh 1:4. It is significant that Jefferson's first act as a legislator was an attempt to allow slaveowners to legally free their slaves.

Deepening Studies in Governmental Theory

The Townshend duties and other acts of British oppression during this time raised serious questions in the minds of many colonial leaders, causing them to take up a concentrated study of political philosophy. It is doubtful that any of them studied with more ardor than Jefferson. By now he had rebuilt his library to more than a thousand volumes, and his book orders after he entered the House of Burgesses reflected an increasing interest in the theory of government. [3]

For Jefferson this was a continuation of his earlier studies under George Wythe, and he now added to his notebooks many passages from Lord Kames, Blackstone, Bolingbroke, Montesquieu, John Locke, and other political philosophers. (Some of these notes were copied in French, as he always preferred to study the original writings rather than English translations.) Many of Jefferson's own ideas about government can be traced to the works he examined during this period. [4]

Revolutionary Leader

As the relationship between England and the colonies worsened, some of the Virginia legislators sensed an urgent need for the American people to unite themselves and decide on a common course. In the early part of 1773, Jefferson and a few of his colleagues initiated an effort which contributed to the eventual formation of the First Continental Congress.

---

3. See Marie Kimball, *Jefferson: The Road to Glory, 1743–1776* (New York: Coward-McCann, Inc., 1943), pp. 209–10.

4. See Malone, *Jefferson the Virginian,* pp. 173–79; Chinard, *Thomas Jefferson: The Apostle of Americanism,* pp. 28–32.

Not thinking our old and leading members up to the point of forwardness and zeal which the times required, Mr. [Patrick] Henry, Richard Henry Lee, Francis L. Lee, Mr. [Dabney] Carr, and myself agreed to meet in the evening, in a private room of the Raleigh, to consult on the state of things. There may have been a member or two more whom I do not recollect.

We were all sensible that the most urgent of all measures was that of coming to an understanding with all the other colonies, to consider the British claims as a common cause to all, and to produce a unity of action; and, for this purpose, that a committee of correspondence in each colony would be the best instrument for inter-communication; and that their first measure would probably be to propose a meeting of deputies from every colony, at some central place, who should be charged with the direction of the measures which should be taken by all. [5]

They drew up resolutions to that end and submitted them to the legislature, which voted its unanimous approval. The royal Governor, Lord Dunmore, promptly dissolved the assembly, but they simply moved down the street and reconvened in the Apollo Room of the Raleigh Tavern. (This had become almost a routine procedure, as the Governor had a habit of dismissing the House of Burgesses whenever they proposed measures that displeased him.) Copies of the resolutions were sent to the other colonies, and each one soon organized a correspondence committee.

A Day of Fasting and Prayer

The next steps were taken in May 1774. Some of the

---

5. Autobiography (1821), Bergh 1:7.

younger legislators, including Jefferson, proposed a day of fasting and prayer throughout Virginia "to implore Heaven to avert from us the evils of civil war, to inspire us with firmness in support of our rights, and to turn the hearts of the King and Parliament to moderation and justice."[6] The proposal was approved, again without opposition, and with the expected result:

> The Governor dissolved us, as usual. We retired to the Apollo, as before, agreed to an association, and instructed the committee of correspondence to propose to the corresponding committees of the other colonies to appoint deputies to meet in Congress at such place, *annually*, as should be convenient, to direct from time to time the measures required by the general interest; and we declared that an attack on any one colony should be considered as an attack on the whole....
>
> We further recommended to the several counties to elect deputies to meet at Williamsburg the 1st of August ensuing, to consider the state of the colony, and particularly to appoint delegates to a general Congress, should that measure be acceded to by the committees of correspondence generally. It was acceded to; Philadelphia was appointed for the place, and the 5th of September for the time of the meeting.[7]

When news of these latest resolutions reached the citizens of Virginia and they assembled in each county to observe the fast day, Jefferson said they reacted "with anxiety and alarm in their countenances, and the effect of the day through the whole colony was like a shock of

6. Ibid., pp. 9–10.
7. Ibid., p. 10.

electricity, arousing every man and placing him erect and solidly on his center."[8]

"Mr. Jefferson's Bill of Rights"

Upon being appointed by his county to attend the convention which would select delegates for the new Congress, Jefferson sat down and prepared a draft of instructions for the delegates, hoping it might serve to guide them at Philadelphia. The paper, much of which was written in the form of an open letter to King George III, was not adopted by the Williamsburg conventioneers, who thought it "too bold for the present state of things." A few excerpts from the closing paragraphs will show why.

> Kings are the servants, not the proprietors, of the people. Open your breast, Sire, to liberal and expanded thought. Let not the name of George the Third be a blot on the page of history. You are surrounded by British counselors, but remember that they are parties. You have no minister for American affairs, because you have none taken from among us, nor amenable to the laws on which they are to give you advice. It behooves you, therefore, to think and act for yourself and your people....
>
> No longer persevere in sacrificing the rights of one part of the empire to the inordinate desires of another; but deal out to all equal and impartial right. Let no act be passed by any one legislature [i.e., the British Parliament] which may infringe on the rights and liberties of another [any of the colonial assemblies]....
>
> This, Sire, is the advice of your great American council, on the observance of which may perhaps

8. Ibid., p. 11.

depend your felicity and future fame and the preservation of that harmony which alone can continue, both to Great Britain and America, the reciprocal advantages of their connection.

It is neither our wish nor our interest to separate from her. We are willing, on our part, to sacrifice everything which reason can ask to the restoration of that tranquility for which all must wish. On their part, let them [the British ministers and Parliament] be ready to establish union on a generous plan. Let them name their terms, but let them be just. . . . Still less let it be proposed that our properties, within our own territories, shall be taxed or regulated by any power on earth but our own. The God who gave us life gave us liberty at the same time; the hand of force may destroy but cannot disjoin them.

This, Sire, is our last, our determined resolution. And that you will be pleased to interpose with that efficacy which your earnest endeavors may insure, to procure redress of these our great grievances, to quiet the minds of your subjects in British America against any apprehensions of future encroachment, to establish fraternal love and harmony through the whole empire, and that that may continue to the latest ages of time, is the fervent prayer of all British America. [9]

Although the members of the convention prepared more moderate instructions for the congressional delegates, they were so much impressed by Jefferson's

---

9. *A Summary View of the Rights of British America* (Aug. 1774), Bergh 1:209–11. The entire text is reprinted in Bergh 1:184–211. Jefferson later observed that if this composition "had any merit, it was that of first taking our true ground, and that which was afterwards assumed and maintained." TJ to John W. Campbell (3 Sept. 1809), Bergh 12:308.

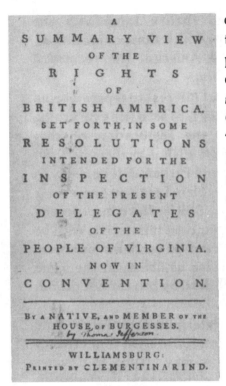

A

S U M M A R Y   V I E W

OF THE

R I G H T S

OF

BRITISH AMERICA.

SET FORTH IN SOME

R E S O L U T I O N S

INTENDED FOR THE

I N S P E C T I O N

OF THE PRESENT

D E L E G A T E S

OF THE

PEOPLE OF VIRGINIA.

NOW IN

C O N V E N T I O N.

By a NATIVE, and MEMBER of the
HOUSE of BURGESSES.
by Thomas Jefferson

WILLIAMSBURG:
PRINTED BY CLEMENTINA RIND.

Title page of *A Summary View of the Rights of British America*, the 1774 pamphlet that established Jefferson's reputation as a forceful political writer.

eloquent and forceful appeal to the King that they printed it as a pamphlet entitled *A Summary View of the Rights of British America.* Quickly winning fame as "Mr. Jefferson's Bill of Rights," it ran through several editions and was circulated widely among the colonies and in Great Britain, making Jefferson's name a household word on both sides of the Atlantic. The pamphlet even "procured me the honor," he later wrote, "of having my name inserted in a long list of proscriptions [and] enrolled in a bill of attainder commenced in one of the houses of Parliament."[10]

"The Reputation of a Masterly Pen"

In August 1774, Jefferson retired from his law practice in order to devote more time to political matters (he turned his clients over to a distant cousin and fellow attorney, Edmund Randolph, in return for one-third of their future fees). The timing was probably fortunate: within a few months he was elected a member of the Continental Congress, and in the meantime he was called upon with

10. Autobiography (1821), Bergh 1:13.

increasing frequency to take up his pen in defense of the American position.

Among the writings Jefferson produced during these months was his pointed reply to Lord North's "conciliatory propositions." Lord North, then the British Prime Minister, offered to exempt from imperial taxation any colony which would voluntarily grant contributions for the defense of the empire and would provide for the support of its own civil government. Parliament, of course, would retain the right to determine whether such provisions were adequate. But Jefferson had argued for more than a year that the Americans owed allegiance to the King only, not to Parliament, and that Parliament had no power to tax the colonies under any circumstances—a position in which he "had never been able to get anyone to agree with me but Mr. Wythe."[11] In his answer to Lord North, which was adopted by the Virginia House of Burgesses and later by Congress, he boldly called upon the British government for either a complete redress of grievances or war.[12]

---

11. Ibid., p. 11. Jefferson first articulated his views on the nature of Anglo-American relations in a series of resolutions he drafted in July 1774 for a meeting of citizens in his own Albemarle County. The Albemarle Resolutions were similar in many respects to the more famous Fairfax Resolutions, adopted in another county assembly over which Colonel George Washington presided that same summer. The Albemarle Resolutions are reprinted in Julian P. Boyd, ed., *The Papers of Thomas Jefferson*, 20 vols. by 1982 (Princeton, N. J.: Princeton University Press, 1950–), 1:117–18. (Hereafter cited as Boyd.) It should be noted that Benjamin Franklin had developed virtually the same ideas as early as 1754. See Andrew M. Allison et al., *The Real Benjamin Franklin* (Salt Lake City: The Freemen Institute, 1982), pp. 101–3, 160–61. However, there is no evidence that Jefferson was aware of Franklin's writings on this subject before 1775.

12. For the text of Jefferson's reply as adopted by the Virginia legislature (10 June 1775), see Boyd 1:170–74; the later version adopted by Congress (31 July 1775) is in Boyd 1:225–33.

There were other papers as well, and Jefferson's skill increased with each new effort. His popularity also increased as more of his writings circulated among the colonists. John Adams, a Congressman from Massachusetts, noted that he "had the reputation of a masterly pen."[13] On another occasion Adams recorded: "Mr. Jefferson came into Congress in June 1775, and brought with him a reputation for literature, science, and a happy talent of composition. Writings of his were handed about, remarkable for the peculiar felicity of expression."[14]

When Jefferson reached Philadelphia that summer to make his quiet entry onto the stage of intercolonial politics, he already enjoyed great respect among his fellow American statesmen. Little did he know what the years ahead held in store for his country—and the part he would be called upon to play in those great events. "When he ferried across the Potomac on his way to the Continental Congress," wrote one historian, "he crossed his Rubicon. . . . There could be no turning back, and from this date onward his story becomes an integral part of the history of the Republic."[15]

Virginia Congressman

At the age of thirty-two, Jefferson was one of the youngest members of Congress—only John Jay of New

13. Autobiography of John Adams (1802–7), Lyman H. Butterfield, ed., *Diary and Autobiography of John Adams,* 4 vols. (Cambridge, Mass.: Harvard University Press, The Belknap Press, 1961), 3:335.

14. John Adams to Timothy Pickering (6 Aug. 1822), Charles Francis Adams, ed., *The Works of John Adams,* 10 vols. (Boston: Little, Brown and Company, 1850–56), 2:513–14n.

15. Malone, *Jefferson the Virginian,* p. 201.

York was his junior. As had been his practice in the Virginia legislature, he seldom if ever spoke to the entire assembly.[16] He preferred to remain in the background, exercising his well-honed legal skills to influence committee decisions and drafting official papers when so appointed (for example, he helped John Dickinson prepare a "Declaration of the Causes and Necessity for Taking Up Arms").[17]

Another statement by John Adams suggests the kind of impression Jefferson made on his colleagues at the outset of the Revolutionary period: "Though a silent member in Congress, he was so prompt, frank, explicit, and decisive upon committees and in conversation—not even Samuel Adams was more so—that he soon seized upon my heart."[18]

Grief at Home

When Congress adjourned in August 1775, Jefferson was happy to return to his family at Monticello. But his gladness soon turned to sorrow: the very next month his second child, Jane Randolph Jefferson, died. Her life had been short, only a year and a half, and her parents were deeply shaken by this unexpected tragedy.

Reappointed to Congress, Jefferson left his grief-stricken wife and their three-year-old daughter in the care of a brother-in-law, then dutifully set out again for

---

16. John Adams later wrote of Jefferson, "During the whole time I sat with him in Congress, I never heard him utter three sentences together." Autobiography of John Adams (1802–7), Butterfield, 3:335.

17. The extent of Jefferson's authorship of this declaration has been a matter of some controversy among historians. See Boyd 1:187–92.

18. John Adams to Timothy Pickering (6 Aug. 1822), C.F. Adams, 2:514*n*.

Philadelphia toward the end of September. Martha's health had not been promising in recent months, and Jefferson was increasingly distracted from the business of Congress by his deep concern for her physical and emotional state. Several weeks went by without a letter from home, and on November 7 he wrote his brother-in-law: "I have never received the scrip of a pen from any mortal in Virginia since I left it, nor been able by any inquiries I could make to hear of my family.... The suspense under which I am is too terrible to be endured. If anything has happened, for God's sake let me know it."[19]

A few days before the opening of 1776, he obtained permission to leave his post and travel back to Virginia to be with his family. To his great relief, he arrived to find that all was well with Martha. They enjoyed the remainder of the winter together at Monticello, turning their thoughts away from the war which had begun at Lexington and Concord several months earlier. But as the Anglo-American crisis worsened and Jefferson gained assurance that his wife's health was not in danger, he knew that he must return to his public station. Just as he was making preparations to depart, however, another tragedy intervened.

On March 31 Jefferson's mother suddenly passed away. She was fifty-seven years old and had been in relatively good health. But that morning she suffered an apoplectic stroke, and within an hour she was gone. This must have been a painful and trying experience for Jefferson. Although he left no record of his feelings, we know that

---

19. TJ to Francis Eppes (7 Nov. 1775), Boyd 1:252.

he was incapacitated by severe migraine headaches for the next five weeks.[20]

By May he had recovered, so he rode once more to Philadelphia and took his seat in Congress—quite unaware of the momentous assignment that awaited him. It was unfortunate that Jefferson's mother died when she did. Only four months longer and she would have lived to see her son fashion the immortal document which gave birth to the United States of America.

---

20. Malone, *Jefferson the Virginian*, p. 216.

Chapter 6

The Declaration
of Independence

Despite the boldness of their rhetoric, most Americans were not eager to separate from Great Britain—even after hostilities broke out at Lexington and Concord in April 1775. Even Thomas Jefferson, one of the most forward leaders of the Revolution, hoped for reconciliation with England long after the war began. But as much as he hated the fighting, he considered the suppression of his countrymen's liberty far worse.

"I hope the returning wisdom of Great Britain will ere long put an end to this unnatural contest," he wrote in August 1775.

> I... would rather be in dependence on Great Britain, properly limited, than on any nation on earth, or than on no nation. But I am one of those, too, who, rather than

submit to the rights of legislating for us assumed by the British Parliament, and which late experience has shown they will so cruelly exercise, would lend my hand to sink the whole island in the ocean.[1]

"I Will Cease to Exist Before I Yield"

Three months later Jefferson's determination to resist tyranny was growing even stronger, and his thoughts were moving more and more toward American independence.

> In an earlier part of this contest our petitions told him [George III] that from our King there was but one appeal. The admonition was despised, and that appeal forced on us. To undo his empire, he has but one truth more to learn—that after colonies have drawn the sword there is but one step more they can take. That step is now pressed upon us by the measures adopted, as if they were afraid we would not take it.
>
> Believe me, dear sir, there is not in the British empire a man who more cordially loves a union with Great Britain than I do. But by the God that made me, I will cease to exist before I yield to a connection on such terms as the British Parliament propose; and in this I think I speak the sentiments of America.[2]

Little did he know at that moment that Congress was soon to call upon him to express again "the sentiments of America"—this time in words which would forever alter the history of mankind.

---

1. TJ to John Randolph (25 Aug. 1775), Bergh 4:30.
2. TJ to John Randolph (29 Nov. 1775), Bergh 4:32-33.

An Enticement Back Home

Thomas Jefferson almost missed his appointment with destiny. Many of the colonial delegates had already received instructions to vote for independence by the time Jefferson returned to Congress in May of 1776, and he was therefore absent from a number of important discussions on the subject.

Besides that, once he reached Philadelphia and learned that his own colony was forming a new government (the royal Governor had fled in the face of mounting hostilities), he did his best to get himself recalled home so that he could help write a Virginia constitution. At the time, he considered the framing of orderly republican institutions even more important than the business facing Congress. "It is the whole object of the present controversy," he felt, "for should a bad government be instituted for us in [the] future, it had been as well to have accepted at first the bad one offered to us from beyond the water, without the risk and expense of contest."[3]

But Jefferson was not permitted this opportunity to implement his governmental theories. Lacking an invitation to join the Virginia convention, he remained dutifully in Philadelphia. He did prepare a draft constitution and sent it to Williamsburg for consideration, but it arrived too late to have much impact on the proceedings there.[4]

---

3. TJ to Thomas Nelson, Jr. (16 May 1776), Bergh 4:254.

4. Jefferson actually prepared three versions of a proposed constitution for Virginia, each differing from the others in some respects. These documents are historically valuable because they clearly reveal Jefferson's fundamental political ideas in this early period. They are published together in Boyd 1:329–65.

"I Will Do As Well As I Can"

On June 7 Richard Henry Lee, a fellow delegate from Virginia, introduced a formal resolution in Congress calling for complete separation from Great Britain.[5] The motion was seconded by George Wythe and John Adams. Debate on the issue was taken up the next day, and Jefferson kept notes on the arguments of both sides. After recording the discussions at some length, he entered the following in his notes:

> It appearing in the course of these debates that the colonies of New York, New Jersey, Pennsylvania, Delaware, Maryland, and South Carolina were not yet matured for falling from the parent stem, but that they were fast advancing to that state, it was thought most prudent to wait awhile for them, and to postpone the final decision to July 1st; but, that this might occasion as little delay as possible, a committee was appointed to prepare a Declaration of Independence. The committee were John Adams, Dr. Franklin, Roger Sherman, Robert R. Livingston, and myself.[6]

The committee's first step, of course, was to appoint one of their number to prepare a draft of the document. Benjamin Franklin, though the oldest and most experienced, was confined to his home at the time due to illness. Both Adams and Jefferson had achieved recognition as writers, so it seemed likely that one of them would be selected.

---

5. Lee had been so instructed by the Virginia legislature. Virginia, the oldest of the colonies, was also the largest, the richest, and the most centrally located, so it played a very significant role in colonial affairs.

6. Autobiography (1821), Bergh 1:25–26.

Jefferson simply noted that "the committee...desired me to do it." But John Adams left a more interesting account:

Jefferson proposed to me to make the draft. I said, "I will not. You should do it."

"Oh, no! Why will you not? You ought to do it."

"I will not."

"Why?"

"Reasons enough."

"What can be your reasons?"

"Reason first—You are a Virginian, and a Virginian ought to appear at the head of this business. Reason second—I am obnoxious, suspected, and unpopular. You are very much otherwise. Reason third—You can write ten times better than I can."

"Well," said Jefferson, "if you are decided, I will do as well as I can."[7]

Writing the Declaration of Independence

A twentieth-century scholar has observed that when Thomas Jefferson accepted the assignment to write the Declaration of Independence, "he stepped across the threshold of 'The Old Dominion' to enter the world stage as an American founder."[8] In the summer of 1776, however, his undertaking may not have seemed quite so glorious. Most Americans did not learn who had authored the Declaration until months or even years later, and while drafting it Jefferson labored under great personal

---

7. John Adams to Timothy Pickering (6 Aug. 1822), Charles Francis Adams, ed., *The Works of John Adams*, 10 vols. (Boston: Little, Brown and Company, 1850–56), 2:514*n*.

8. Adrienne Koch, ed., *Jefferson* (Englewood Cliffs, N.J.: Prentice-Hall, Inc., 1971), p. 4.

Jefferson wrote the Declaration of Independence in a rented second-floor suite in this building on the corner of Seventh and Market streets in Philadelphia.

On this portable writing desk, which Jefferson himself designed, he penned the original draft of the Declaration of Independence.

stress. His mother and one of his daughters had recently died, and the state of his wife's health was now a matter of increasing concern.

Yet he spared no effort in setting his "masterly pen" to this task. Every evening after Congress adjourned, the townspeople of Philadelphia could see him hurrying back to his rented suite at Seventh and Market streets. There he closed the door behind him, sat in a large armchair in the parlor, and placed another sheet of foolscap paper on his portable writing desk. For seventeen days he composed and revised his rough draft of the Declaration, usually working from about six o'clock to midnight. [9] The surviving original manuscript shows that he

9. See Mike W. Edwards, "Thomas Jefferson: Architect of Freedom," *National Geographic*, February 1976, pp. 243-44. Jefferson himself had designed the portable writing desk he was using at this time. See Silvio A. Bedini, *Declaration of Independence Desk: Relic of Revolution* (Washington: Smithsonian Institution Press, 1981).

took great care in his expression, repeatedly altering words and phrases to give them more strength and rhetorical beauty. [10]

"We Hold These Truths to Be Self-Evident"

Many citizens of the United States have considered it providential that Jefferson was appointed to write the Declaration of Independence. It is safe to say that no other man in the country was so well equipped to do so, both in political philosophy and in literary talent. This is amply demonstrated in the document's now famous opening lines:

> When, in the course of human events, it becomes necessary for one people to dissolve the political bands which have connected them with another, and to assume, among the powers of the earth, the separate and equal station to which the laws of nature and of nature's God entitle them, a decent respect to the opinions of mankind requires that they should declare the causes which impel them to the separation.
>
> We hold these truths to be self-evident, that all men are created equal, that they are endowed by their Creator with certain unalienable rights, that among these are life, liberty, and the pursuit of happiness. That, to secure these rights, governments are instituted among men, deriving their just powers from the consent of the governed. That, whenever any form of government becomes destructive of these ends, it is the right of the people to alter or abolish it, and to institute new government, laying its foundations on such principles, and organizing its powers in such form, as to

---

10. A facsimile of Jefferson's rough draft of the Declaration is reproduced on the pages following Bergh 1:28.

The first page of Jefferson's original rough draft of the Declaration of Independence, showing his own interlined changes and a few others by Benjamin Franklin and John Adams.

them shall seem most likely to effect their safety and happiness.[11]

As he turned to an explanation of the "necessity" which had constrained the colonists "to alter their former systems of government," Jefferson declared, "The history of the present King of Great Britain is a history of repeated injuries and usurpations, all having in direct object the establishment of an absolute tyranny over these states."[12] Then came a spirited recounting of the "long train of abuses and usurpations" practiced by George III, after which the Declaration closed with these moving words:

We, therefore, the representatives of the United States of America, in general Congress assembled, appealing to the Supreme Judge of the world for the rectitude of our intentions, do, in the name and by authority of the good people of these colonies, solemnly publish and declare, that these united colonies are, and of right ought to be, free and independent states; that

---

11. Mortimer J. Adler et al., eds., *The Annals of America*, 18 vols. (Chicago: Encyclopaedia Britannica, Inc., 1968), 2:447.

12. Ibid., p. 448.

The Declaration of Independence, painted by contemporary artist John Trumbull. Jefferson, flanked by other members of the writing committee, is shown placing the finished document on the desk of John Hancock (then serving as president of Congress).

they are absolved from all allegiance to the British Crown, and that all political connection between them and the state of Great Britain is and ought to be totally dissolved; and that, as free and independent states, they have full power to levy war, conclude peace, contract alliances, establish commerce, and to do all other acts and things which independent states may of right do. And for the support of this declaration, with a firm reliance on the protection of Divine Providence, we mutually pledge to each other our lives, our fortunes, and our sacred honor.[13]

13. Ibid., p. 449.

"The Colossus of That Congress"

After presenting his work to Franklin and Adams, who made only a few minor changes in the wording, Jefferson submitted the draft to Congress on Friday, June 28. It was tabled until a final vote could be taken on Richard Henry Lee's earlier motion for independence. When the vote was called the following Tuesday morning (July 2), it was found that the formerly reluctant colonies had now "matured for falling from the parent stem." The momentous resolution was passed.

Now that the decision to separate from England was sealed, Jefferson sat anxiously through almost three days of debate as his fellow Congressmen tried to improve on the work he had so carefully produced. He remained silent through the whole painful process, believing it "a duty to be on that occasion a passive auditor of the opinions of others, more impartial judges than I could be of its merits or demerits."[14] Doctor Franklin, who was sitting beside Jefferson and noticed that he was "writhing a little under the acrimonious criticisms" made against part of the document, offered some friendly words of comfort.[15]

John Adams, speaking on behalf of the committee to whom the writing task had been assigned, took up the defense for the paper. He "supported the Declaration with zeal and ability," wrote Jefferson, "fighting fearlessly for every word of it."[16] Jefferson gratefully dubbed Adams "the Colossus of that Congress."[17]

---

14. TJ to James Madison (30 Aug. 1823), Bergh 15:463.
15. Ibid. This anecdote is recounted in Bergh 18:168–70.
16. TJ to James Madison (30 Aug. 1823), Bergh 15:463.
17. Quoted in Bergh 13:xxiv. "John Adams," he wrote, "was the pillar of

"The Bells Rang All Day and Almost All Night"

The revised Declaration was approved in the late afternoon of July 4, 1776. Its language had been altered in some places, and a fervent denunciation of Great Britain's role in the Negro slave trade had been "struck out in complaisance to South Carolina and Georgia, who had never attempted to restrain the importation of slaves, and who, on the contrary, still wished to continue it. Our

John Adams, who "fearlessly" defended the Declaration of Independence during Congressional debates in early July 1776.

northern brethren also, I believe, felt a little tender under those censures; for though their people had very few slaves themselves, yet they had been pretty considerable carriers of them to others."[18]

But in all, Jefferson's colleagues had made relatively few changes in his composition. When the debate concluded, John Hancock signed the paper as president of Congress and Charles Thomson attested as secretary. At that moment the United States of America was quietly born. (An

its [the Declaration's] support on the floor of Congress, its ablest advocate and defender against the multifarious assaults it encountered." TJ to William P. Gardner (19 Feb. 1813), Paul Leicester Ford, ed., *The Writings of Thomas Jefferson*, 10 vols. (New York: G.P. Putnam's Sons, 1892–99), 9:377. Hereafter cited as Ford.

18. Autobiography (1821), Bergh 1:28.

engrossed parchment copy of the Declaration was later prepared, and the other delegates affixed their signatures on August 2.)[19]

Over the weekend, news of the great event quickly spread throughout Philadelphia. Printed copies of the Declaration were off the press by Monday morning, July 8, and "a great crowd of people" gathered excitedly at the Pennsylvania State House (later named Independence Hall) to witness the historic proclamation.

An appointed herald rose to his feet on the small stage in the State House yard. All eyes turned to the paper he lifted, and a sudden hush came upon the throng. "When, in the course of human events," the crier began, and his hearers listened breathlessly as the words all America awaited were proclaimed in public for the first time. John Adams recorded what happened in the city after the last sentence was read: "Three cheers rended the welkin [sky]. The battalions paraded on the common and gave us the *feu de joie*, notwithstanding the scarcity of powder. The bells rang all day and almost all night. Even the chimers chimed away."[20]

"An Expression of the American Mind"

There are some who have attempted to criticize the text of the Declaration of Independence on the basis that its

---

19. Jefferson later spoke of a general signing of the approved paper copy on July 4 (see entries under "DECLARATION OF INDEPENDENCE, Signers of the" in Part II of this book), but this differs from the standard historical interpretation. The matter, still unsettled, is discussed in Boyd 1:305–8. A full analysis of the various textual changes made in the document can be found in Julian P. Boyd, *The Declaration of Independence: The Evolution of the Text* (Princeton, N.J.: Princeton University Press, 1945).

20. John Adams to Samuel Chase (9 July 1776), C.F. Adams, 9:420.

ideas were borrowed from other writers. But Jefferson never claimed otherwise; he readily acknowledged the influence on his own thinking of the many theorists he had studied up to that time. "The object of the Declaration of Independence," he explained, was

> not to find out new principles or new arguments never before thought of, not merely to say things which had never been said before; but to place before mankind the common sense of the subject, in terms so plain and firm as to command their assent, and to justify ourselves in the independent stand we [were] compelled to take.
>
> Neither aiming at originality of principle or sentiment, nor yet copied from any particular and previous writing, it was intended to be an expression of the American mind, and to give to that expression the proper tone and spirit called for by the occasion. All its authority rests, then, on the harmonizing sentiments of the day, whether expressed in conversation, in letters, printed essays, or in the elementary books of public right, as Aristotle, Cicero, Locke, Sidney, etc.[21]

On another occasion he wrote: "Whether I had gathered my ideas from reading or reflection I do not know. I know only that I turned to neither book nor pamphlet while writing it. I did not consider it as any part of my charge to invent new ideas."[22] But while Jefferson was only one among many writers of his time who believed in the principles contained in the Declaration of Independence, surely no one before him or since has expressed those ideas with such inspired force and eloquence.

---

21. TJ to Henry Lee (8 May 1825), Bergh 16:118–19.
22. TJ to James Madison (30 Aug. 1823), Bergh 15:462.

For the rest of his life, Jefferson remained deeply
grateful for the honor of having written the Declaration
of Independence, which he once called the "holy bond of
our Union."[23] Nearly half a century after 1776, he
expressed to his old friend James Madison the hope that
Americans would always remember the Declaration and
cherish its ideals, "and it is a heavenly comfort to see that
these principles are yet so strongly felt. . . . I pray God that
these principles may be eternal."[24]

---

23. TJ to Dr. James Mease (26 Sept. 1825), Bergh 16:123.
24. TJ to James Madison (30 Aug. 1823), Bergh 15:464.

Chapter 7

Laying a Foundation for Free Government

After the Declaration of Independence was adopted on July 4, 1776, Jefferson continued to serve on important Congressional committees through the remainder of the summer. An effort resulting from one of these committee assignments has special significance for Americans of today because of what it reveals about the all-but-forgotten origins of our system of Constitutional government.

"That Happy System of Our Ancestors"

Together with Benjamin Franklin and John Adams, Jefferson was appointed to draw up a proposal for the Great Seal of the United States. Although Congress later adopted a simpler design, Jefferson took this occasion to emphasize the historical influence of two earlier civilizations on the liberties of his countrymen. One side of his proposed seal depicted the Anglo-Saxon leaders Hengist and Horsa, while the other side portrayed the ancient Israelites being led through the wilderness by God's pillar of fire. [1]

Like others of the American Founding Fathers, Jefferson had studied the various forms of government which had operated throughout recorded history. [2] Along with the Greek democracies, the Roman republic, and the numerous monarchies, aristocracies, and other political systems of Europe, he had examined with great interest the governmental institutions established by the ancient Israelites and the very similar forms later used among the Anglo-Saxons. [3] In these he saw the model for free government in his own era.

Now that the United States had declared itself an independent nation, the members of Congress were responsible to devise a system of government that would most effectively serve the American people. Jefferson attended the first two months of debate on this great issue. He said very little on the floor of Congress, as usual, but there was no question in his mind about the direction that the new national government should take. "Has not

<hr/>

1. See Richard S. Patterson and Richardson Dougall, *The Eagle and the Shield: A History of the Great Seal of the United States* (Washington: U.S. Department of State, 1976), pp. 16–18.

2. See Malone, *Jefferson the Virginian,* pp. 173–79; Chinard, *Thomas Jefferson: The Apostle of Americanism,* pp. 28–32.

3. For a discussion of the origins and similarities of Anglo-Saxon and Israelitish political institutions, see the Constitutional study course by W. Cleon Skousen, *The Miracle of America,* 2nd ed. rev. (Salt Lake City: The Freemen Institute, 1981), Lesson 2, "The Founders' Search for an Ideal Society," pp. 16–21.

every restitution of the ancient Saxon laws had happy effects?" he asked a friend that summer. "Is it not better now that we return at once into that happy system of our ancestors, the wisest and most perfect ever yet devised by the wit of man, as it stood before the eighth century?"[4] One of Jefferson's biographers has written of him:

> Jefferson's great ambition at that time was to promote a renaissance of Anglo-Saxon primitive institutions on the new continent. Thus presented, the American Revolution was nothing but the reclamation of the Anglo-Saxon birthright of which the colonists had been deprived by "a long train of abuses." ... This is the true foundation of Jefferson's political philosophy.[5]

The system hammered out by the Congressional delegates over the following months was known as the Articles of Confederation, and it suffered from several fatal weaknesses that would eventually lead to the Constitutional Convention of 1787. On that occasion Jefferson's political studies would prove even more useful than in 1776. But in the meantime he turned his attention once again to the state of Virginia, where he soon found plenty of opportunity to put into practice his lofty concept of free government.

Back to the Virginia Legislature

In September 1776 Jefferson resigned from Congress and returned to Monticello because of his deep concern over his wife's ill health. Shortly afterward he was offered a post as commissioner to France, where he was to assist

---

4. TJ to Edmund Pendleton (13 Aug. 1776), Boyd 1:492.
5. Chinard, pp. 86–87.

Benjamin Franklin and Silas Deane in negotiating trade and friendship treaties with the European powers, but he turned down this appointment for the same reason.

He also had another motive for staying in Virginia, however. Having been denied a voice in the formation of the new state constitution, he was very eager to take part in what he considered a much-needed revision of Virginia's legal code. "I knew that our legislation, under the regal government, had many very vicious points which urgently required reformation," he wrote, "and I thought I could be of more use in forwarding that work."[6] He was easily reelected, of course, to his old seat in the Williamsburg assembly (now called the Virginia House of Delegates).

"A Foundation Laid for a Government Truly Republican"

Jefferson's efforts in the Virginia legislature over the next three years were essentially a continuation of his work in Congress. He believed that the principles of liberty contained in the Declaration of Independence could not become reality until specific laws were passed to protect the rights of individual citizens.

Now that American independence had opened the way for each state to create its own system of government, Jefferson welcomed the opportunity to help establish a

---

6. Autobiography (1821), Bergh 1:53. He also wrote that he had returned to Virginia "in the persuasion that our whole code must be reviewed [and] adapted to our republican form of government. And now that we had no negatives [vetoes] of councils, governors, and kings to restrain us from doing right, it should be corrected in all its parts with a single eye to reason and [to] the good of those for whose government it was framed." Ibid., p. 62.

model republic in Virginia. His intent was to form "a system by which every fiber would be eradicated of ancient or future aristocracy, and a foundation laid for a government truly republican."[7] He also saw the necessity of striking while the iron was hot, as shown in a statement he wrote a few years afterward:

> It can never be too often repeated that the time for fixing every essential right on a legal basis is while our rulers are honest, and ourselves united. From the conclusion of this war we shall be going downhill. It will not then be necessary to resort every moment to the people for support. They will be forgotten, therefore, and their rights disregarded. They will forget themselves, but in the sole faculty of making money, and will never think of uniting to effect a due respect for their rights. The shackles, therefore, which shall not be knocked off at the conclusion of this war will remain on us long, will be made heavier and heavier, till our rights shall revive or expire in a convulsion.[8]

Many of the freedoms we take for granted in American society today can be traced to the laws initiated by Jefferson during these three years; this was in some respects the most important period of his public career. "He deserves the chief credit," wrote biographer Dumas Malone, "for legislative achievements that have rarely been equaled in American history.... His plans for his state were never fully carried out, but he may properly be termed the architect of Virginia government."[9] And much of his work in Virginia provided a pattern for similar

---

7. Ibid., p. 73.

8. *Notes on the State of Virginia* (1782), Bergh 2:225.

9. Malone, *Dictionary of American Biography*, 10:20.

legislative reforms in other states throughout the new nation.

Dismantling the Old Aristocracy

Jefferson moved into action as soon as he reached Williamsburg. His first step was a controversial one because it placed him in the position of turning on his own class—the landed aristocracy.

Five days after the House of Delegates convened in early October 1776, he introduced a Bill to Abolish Entails. The entail laws, which were relics from the days of European feudalism, prohibited the partition of large estates into smaller parcels; they also required that the property of a wealthy landholder be passed, undivided, to one of his lineal descendants. This practice ensured the perpetuation of the nobility and prevented the peasant class from acquiring land.

"The Aristocracy of Virtue and Talent"

Usually accompanying the entail laws was a provision known as primogeniture, which gave the exclusive right of property inheritance to the eldest son (whether he was competent to manage an estate or not). Because this condition prevailed in Virginia, Jefferson also introduced a measure to abolish primogeniture. He explained what motivated him to propose these fundamental changes in the state's inheritance laws:

> In the earlier times of the colony, when lands were to be obtained for little or nothing, some provident individuals procured large grants; and, desirous of founding great families for themselves, settled them on their descendants in fee tail. The transmission of this

property from generation to generation, in the same name, raised up a distinct set of families who, being privileged by law in the perpetuation of their wealth, were thus formed into a patrician order, distinguished by the splendor and luxury of their establishments. . . .

To annul this privilege and, instead of an aristocracy of wealth, of more harm and danger than benefit to society, to make an opening for the aristocracy of virtue and talent, which nature has wisely provided for the direction of the interests of society and scattered with equal hand through all its conditions, was deemed essential to a well-ordered republic. To effect it, no violence was necessary, no deprivation of natural right, but rather an enlargement of it by a repeal of the law. For this would authorize the present holder to divide the property among his children equally, as his affections were divided; and would place them, by natural generation, on the level of their fellow citizens. [10]

The two bills were approved, but not without opposition. Many of Virginia's aristocrats, though united with Jefferson in the struggle for American independence, did not share his views regarding the equality of all men. Nor were they eager to relinquish their position in society.

The opposition was led by Edmund Pendleton, Speaker of the House, whom Jefferson called "the ablest man in debate I have ever met with."[11] But there were equally able men who came to the defense of the measures. Among these were George Mason, chief draftsman of the new Virginia constitution; George Wythe, who had instructed Jefferson in the law and served with him in

---

10. Autobiography (1821), Bergh 1:54.
11. Ibid., pp. 54–55.

Congress; and a newly elected member of the legislature—
a young man named James Madison.

A New Legal Code for Virginia

On October 12, 1776, Jefferson proposed to the House
of Delegates a revision of Virginia's entire legal structure.
The bill was soon approved, and a small but distinguished
committee was appointed to accomplish this monumental
work. Jefferson served as chairman.

Beginning in earnest the next January, the committee
reviewed "all the British statutes from Magna Charta to
the present day, and all the laws of Virginia."[12] They spent
over two years at their task, selecting and updating those
laws which they felt should be retained, then drafting new
bills to further safeguard the rights and liberties of the
people. On June 18, 1779, they submitted "one hundred
and twenty-six bills, making a printed folio of ninety
pages," to the assembly in Williamsburg. Jefferson
commented on the results of their efforts:

> Some bills were taken out occasionally, from time to
> time, and passed; but the main body of the work was not
> entered on by the legislature until after the general
> peace, in 1785, when, by the unwearied exertions of Mr.
> Madison, in opposition to the endless quibbles,
> chicaneries, perversions, vexations, and delays of law-
> yers and demi-lawyers, most of the bills were passed by
> the legislature, with little alteration.[13]

"Saids and Aforesaids"

Jefferson personally devoted a great deal of time and

---

12. Ibid., p. 66.
13. Ibid.

energy to this project. One of his objectives was simply to make the laws understandable to the average citizen, a condition he considered essential to free government.

> I thought it would be useful... to reform the style of the later British statutes and of our own acts of assembly, which from their verbosity, their endless tautologies, their involutions of case within case and parenthesis within parenthesis, and their multiplied efforts at certainty by *saids* and *aforesaids*, by *ors* and by *ands*, to make them more plain, are really rendered more perplexed and incomprehensible, not only to common readers but to the lawyers themselves. [14]

He was not interested only in form, however; he was also aiming at the substance of the legal code. He personally drafted a complete revision of the criminal laws, a bill to establish a system of judicial courts, and several other measures which eventually brought about major social changes—not only in Virginia, as noted before, but throughout the United States. Three of these reform efforts deserve particular consideration in this chapter because of their central position in Jefferson's political philosophy: (1) a "Bill for the More General Diffusion of Knowledge," (2) the Statute of Virginia for Religious Freedom, and (3) a proposal to end the importation of slaves.

"Illuminate...the Minds of the People"

In the eighteenth century, most Americans believed that only property owners or "freeholders" should be permitted to vote. (This was sometimes referred to as the

---

14. Ibid., p. 65.

"stake in society" principle.) Although Jefferson accepted this notion, he did not agree with those who wanted to limit political power to a wealthy aristocracy. In keeping with his vision of broader citizen participation in government, he advocated that cheap land be made available in the western territories to all who would till it. And to further extend the right of suffrage, he proposed extremely low property qualifications for voting. Jefferson always believed that "cultivators of the earth" were "the most virtuous and independent citizens,"[15] and he was therefore of the opinion that an agrarian society of many "small landholders" was the safest foundation for republican government.

But while he felt that "the influence over government must be shared among all the people,"[16] he was equally convinced that the exercise of political power must be based on knowledge, not ignorance. "If a nation expects to be ignorant and free," he once declared, "it expects what never was and never will be."[17] In another place he wrote:

> Experience has shown that even under the best forms [of government], those entrusted with power have in time, and by slow operations, perverted it into tyranny; and . . . the most effectual means of preventing this would be to illuminate, as far as practicable, the minds of the people at large. . . .

---

15. *Notes on the State of Virginia* (1782), Bergh 2:241. "Those who labor in the earth," Jefferson wrote, "are the chosen people of God, if ever He had a chosen people." Ibid., p. 229.

16. Ibid., p. 207. On the same page he observed: "Every government degenerates when trusted to the rulers of the people alone. The people themselves, therefore, are its only safe depositories. And to render even them safe, their minds must be improved to a certain degree."

17. TJ to Colonel Charles Yancey (6 Jan. 1816), Bergh 14:384.

Laws will be wisely formed and honestly administered in proportion as those who form and administer them are wise and honest; whence it becomes expedient for promoting the public happiness that those persons whom nature hath endowed with genius and virtue should be rendered by liberal education worthy to receive, and able to guard, the sacred deposit of the rights and liberties of their fellow citizens, and that they should be called to that charge without regard to wealth, birth, or other accidental condition or circumstance. [18]

Jefferson's Plan of Education

It was for this reason that Jefferson submitted to the House of Delegates a "Bill for the More General Diffusion of Knowledge," which would commit public funds to help educate young people in Virginia whose parents lacked the means to provide for their schooling. He called it "by far the most important bill in our whole code," and urged its passage by asserting that "no other sure foundation can be devised for the preservation of freedom and happiness." [19]

The measure called for "three distinct grades of education, reaching all classes. First, elementary schools for all children generally, rich and poor. Second, colleges for a middle degree of instruction, calculated for the common purposes of life.... And third, an ultimate grade for teaching the sciences generally, and in their highest degree." [20]

---

18. Preamble to a Bill for the More General Diffusion of Knowledge (June 1779), Boyd 2:526-27.

19. TJ to George Wythe (13 Aug. 1786), Bergh 5:396.

20. Autobiography (1821), Bergh 1:70-71.

This bill proposes to lay off every county into small districts of five or six miles square, called hundreds, and in each of them to establish a school for teaching reading, writing, and arithmetic. The tutor [is] to be supported by the hundred, and every person in it entitled to send their children three years gratis, and as much longer as they please, paying for it. These schools [are] to be under a visitor who is annually to choose the boy of best genius in the school, of those whose parents are too poor to give them further education, and to send him forward to one of the grammar schools, of which twenty are proposed to be erected in different parts of the [state] for teaching Greek, Latin, geography, and the higher branches of numerical arithmetic.

Of the boys thus sent in one year, trial is to be made at the grammar schools one or two years, and the best genius of the whole selected and continued six years, and the residue dismissed. By this means twenty of the best geniuses will be raked from the rubbish annually, and be instructed at the public expense so far as the grammar schools go. At the end of six years' instruction, one half are to be discontinued (from among whom the grammar schools will probably be supplied with future masters); and the other half, who are to be chosen for the superiority of their parts and disposition, are to be sent and continued three years in the study of such sciences as they shall choose at William and Mary College. [21]

This bold proposal, like the others Jefferson introduced during the same period, was a reflection of his democratic

21. *Notes on the State of Virginia* (1782), Bergh 2:203–4. At the same time, Jefferson proposed an expansion of the College of William and Mary into a full-fledged university, and the establishment of a public library in Richmond.

principles. The basic purpose of his plan, he later explained, was to qualify the people "to understand their rights, to maintain them, and to exercise with intelligence their parts in self-government."[22]

> By that part of our plan which prescribes the selection of the youths of genius from among the classes of the poor, we hope to avail the state of those talents which nature has sown as liberally among the poor as the rich, but which perish without use if not sought for and cultivated. But of the views of this law none is more important, none more legitimate, than that of rendering the people the safe, as they are the ultimate, guardians of their own liberty.[23]

"A Crusade Against Ignorance"

When the bill finally came up for debate in 1786, Jefferson was in Paris as the American minister to the French government. Yet his interest in the proposal had not waned; he wrote to his friend George Wythe, then Speaker of the House in the Virginia legislature: "Preach, my dear sir, a crusade against ignorance; establish and improve the law for educating the common people. Let our countrymen know... that the tax which will be paid for this purpose is not more than the thousandth part of what will be paid to kings, priests, and nobles who will rise up among us if we leave the people in ignorance."[24]

It should be understood that Jefferson never advocated public schools like those operating in the nation today. The grammar schools under his plan were still largely

---

22. Autobiography (1821), Bergh 1:73–74.
23. *Notes on the State of Virginia* (1782), Bergh 2:206.
24. TJ to George Wythe (13 Aug. 1786), Bergh 5:397.

supported by tuition, and his primary concern was simply to provide educational opportunities for children whose parents were unable to afford private tutors. As one modern scholar has noted, "Jefferson expressed both fear and scorn when contemplating a centralized state authority in education."[25] And while serving as President of the United States he observed in a message to Congress that the "ordinary branches" of education should not be taken "out of the hands of private enterprise, which manages so much better all the concerns to which it is equal."[26]

Many believe that Jefferson's educational ideas— particularly with regard to the relationship between certain kinds of knowledge and responsible self-government—deserve renewed consideration in our day.[27] In any event, it is certain that the plan he submitted to the legislature in Williamsburg was far ahead of its own time. Virginia was not yet ready to provide any public funds to help enlighten its citizens, and the measures

---

25. James Bryant Conant, *Thomas Jefferson and the Development of American Public Education* (Berkeley: University of California Press, 1962), pp. 30–31.

26. Sixth Annual Message to Congress (2 Dec. 1806), Bergh 3:423.

27. In this regard, Jefferson's curricular proposals are quite interesting. For students in the earlier years he recommended instruction in morality and history. Instilling into their minds "the first elements of morality," he said, "may teach them how to work out their own greatest happiness by showing them that it does not depend on the condition of life in which chance has placed them, but is always the result of a good conscience, good health, occupation, and freedom in all just pursuits." He believed that the pupils' reading assignments should be "chiefly historical. History, by apprising them of the past, will enable them to judge of the future; it will avail them of the experience of other times and other nations; it will qualify them as judges of the actions and designs of men; it will enable them to know ambition under every disguise it may assume and, knowing it, to defeat its views." *Notes on the State of Virginia* (1782), Bergh 2:204–5, 207.

Jefferson proposed in 1779 were not implemented during his lifetime. Nevertheless, the seed he planted would ultimately contribute to significant advances in American education.

"Almighty God Hath Created the Mind Free"

After the separation from Great Britain in 1776, many Virginians hoped that state support of the Anglican church would come to an end. "To compel a man to furnish contributions of money for the propagation of opinions which he disbelieves," wrote Jefferson, "is sinful and tyrannical."[28] But he went even further, declaring that any attempt by a government to enforce adherence to particular religious beliefs or practices violated the rights of free citizens.

> Our rulers can have no authority over [our] natural rights, only as we have submitted to them. The rights of conscience we never submitted, we could not submit. We are answerable for them to our God. The legitimate powers of government extend to such acts only as are injurious to others. But it does me no injury for my neighbor to say there are twenty gods, or no God. It neither picks my pocket nor breaks my leg.[29]

Ironically, Jefferson's political enemies later used the last part of this statement against him in an attempt to prove he was an atheist. But he was no disbeliever; the point he was making was that "Almighty God hath created the mind free," and that "all attempts to influence it by temporal punishments or burdens, or by civil incapacitations, tend only to beget habits of hypocrisy and meanness,

---

28. A Bill for Establishing Religious Freedom (June 1779), Boyd 2:545.
29. *Notes on the State of Virginia* (1782), Bergh 2:221.

and are a departure from the plan of the Holy Author of our religion."[30]

Jefferson was confident that religious truth would prosper in an atmosphere of freedom. "Reason and free inquiry are the only effectual agents against error. Give a loose to them," he said, and "they will support the true religion."[31]

Religious Freedom Established in Virginia

With these convictions in mind, Jefferson introduced in the legislature in 1779 his Bill for Establishing Religious Freedom:

> We, the General Assembly of Virginia, do enact that no man shall be compelled to frequent or support any religious worship, place, or ministry whatsoever, nor shall be enforced, restrained, molested, or burdened in his body or goods, nor shall otherwise suffer on account of his religious opinions or belief; but that all men shall be free to profess, and by argument to maintain, their opinions in matters of religion, and that the same shall in no wise diminish, enlarge, or affect their civil capacities.[32]

The measure was passed, after long and heated debates, in 1786. (Jefferson was in France at the time.) A few years later, this principle of protecting religion from the state would become part of the Constitution of the United States. When Jefferson wrote the epitaph for his tombstone shortly before he died, he listed the Statute of Virginia for Religious Freedom alongside the Declaration

---

30. A Bill for Establishing Religious Freedom (June 1779), Boyd 2:545.
31. *Notes on the State of Virginia* (1782), Bergh 2:221.
32. A Bill for Establishing Religious Freedom (June 1779), Boyd 2:546.

of Independence as one of the most important accomplishments of his life.

Jefferson on Slavery

The first act of Jefferson's political career, as noted earlier, was an attempt to make it legal for slaveowners in Virginia to emancipate their slaves. That bill was rejected, as was the condemnation of slavery in his original draft of the Declaration of Independence.

His labors in this cause finally met with some success in 1778, when he introduced a bill in the Virginia House of Delegates to prevent the further importation of slaves into the state. The proposal was approved, but he recognized that it only "stopped the increase of the evil by importation, leaving to future efforts its final eradication."[33]

It was Jefferson's desire to open the way for this "final eradication" the very next year, when his committee submitted their proposals for the revision of Virginia's legal code. However, he ascertained through conversations with his colleagues that the legislature was not yet prepared to consider such a progressive step—so he calculated another strategy.

> The bill on the subject of slaves was a mere digest of the existing laws respecting them, without any intimation of a plan for a future and general emancipation. It was thought better that this should be kept back, and attempted only by way of amendment whenever the bill should be brought on.[34]

---

33. Autobiography (1821), Bergh 1:56.
34. Ibid., p. 72.

But when the bill did come up for debate, Jefferson was unable to get his amendment passed. "It was found that the public mind would not yet bear the proposition.... Yet the day is not distant when it must bear and adopt it," he wrote, "or worse will follow. Nothing is more certainly written in the book of fate than that these people are to be free."[35]

Jefferson would be heard from again on the issue of slavery.

_____

35. Ibid.

Chapter 8

Wartime Governor
of Virginia

I n June 1779, the same month in which Jefferson introduced his historic legislative reforms, the Virginia House of Delegates elected him to succeed Patrick Henry as Governor. This was a most difficult time to assume the reins of Virginia government. The state's finances were in a disastrous condition due to the failure of many to pay their taxes and the economic impact of the Revolutionary War, and the British military forces—having lately undertaken a major campaign in the southern states—were gradually closing in on Virginia.

"The Greatest Man on the Continent"

The new Governor was generally held in high esteem by his fellow citizens. At the time of his election, one prominent Virginian wrote to another: "I wish [his] excellency's activity may be equal to the abilities he possesses in so eminent a degree. In that case we may boast of having the greatest man on the continent at the helm." But, recognizing the tremendous challenge confronting Jefferson, the same writer lamented, "Never was a country in a more shabby situation."[1] Virginia was virtually defenseless, he said, and it seemed doubtful whether any leader could successfully bring the "Old Dominion" through the awful crisis it now faced.

Moving into the Governor's Palace in Williamsburg, Jefferson spent the first part of his administration battling serious economic problems. For four years Virginia's resources had been flowing northward to meet the heavy demands of the New England states, which had borne the early brunt of the war. After Jefferson took office in 1779, this continuing exportation combined with a severe blight on Virginia crops to threaten the state's food supply.

Under these conditions, the young statesman from Monticello reacted with his usual resourcefulness—and also with an unexpected degree of versatility. At the age of thirty-six he had already acquired "the reputation of a masterly pen," as John Adams had said, and he had achieved some renown as a political philosopher. But his activities as Governor demonstrated that he also possessed the practical abilities which enabled him to attend effectively to the daily requirements of his office. As one biographer has written, it appears from the surviving records that "he was diligence itself in official

---

1. St. George Tucker to Theodorick Bland, Jr. (6 June 1779), Charles Campbell, ed., *The Bland Papers*, 2 vols. (Petersburg, Va., 1840–43), 2:11; quoted in Malone, *Jefferson the Virginian*, p. 304.

business.... Throughout his administration he gave the impression of unfailing zeal and incessant labor."[2]

Jefferson's powers as Governor were severely limited under the constitution Virginia had adopted in 1776. He was expected to carry out the express will of the Assembly, by whom he had been elected, and he could exercise no veto over their legislative acts. In his administrative decisions he was to be guided by an eight-man Council of State, also appointed by the legislature.[3] However, in spite of these limitations and the added difficulties imposed by the war, he performed admirably during his term of service as Virginia's chief executive.

Benedict Arnold Attacks Richmond

In April 1780 the seat of state government was moved from Williamsburg to Richmond, which was more centrally located and was thought to be less vulnerable to the enemy. But it was not safe enough. The following January, Richmond was raided by British forces under Benedict Arnold, an American general who had deserted to the enemy.

Virginia's defenses consisted of an inexperienced and untrained militia, which was further hampered by a gross deficiency in arms and munitions, and several hundred Continental soldiers led by the Frenchman Lafayette. Seeing that the situation in Richmond was beyond hope,

---

2. Malone, *Jefferson the Virginian*, p. 307.

3. One member of Jefferson's Council of State was James Madison, and it was during this period that the two future Presidents developed the famous friendship which lasted throughout their lives. Another member was Jacquelin Ambler—the husband of Jefferson's college flame, Rebecca Burwell.

Jefferson arranged for some of the public stores and state records to be moved out of the city. He stayed behind so long to personally supervise the transfer that many feared for his safety, but as the Redcoats approached he hurried away on horseback.

After Arnold's troops left sections of the new state capital in flames, the Governor considered a plan to capture their treasonous leader and bring him to justice:

> It is above all things desirable to drag him from those under whose wing he is now sheltered.... Having peculiar confidence in the men from the western side of the mountains, I meant, as soon as they should come down, to get the enterprise proposed to a chosen number of them, such whose courage and whose fidelity would be above all doubt,...and engage them to undertake to seize and bring off this greatest of all traitors. [4]

A Call for Help

But the Governor, back in Richmond after the departure of the British, could not legally act on his own; and it was impossible to gather a quorum of the Assembly to conduct business because most of the elected officials had fled to other parts of the state. As Virginia's government came to a standstill, Jefferson was unable to carry out his plan to apprehend "this greatest of all traitors."

Some of the legislators finally assembled on May 10 and voted to move temporarily to Charlottesville, a small town in Virginia's western mountains near Jefferson's home. Arnold, who was now on his way toward Richmond once more, was soon to be joined by Lord Cornwallis from the south. As the British forces continued inland with very

---

4. TJ to [George Rogers Clark?] (31 Jan. 1781), Bergh 4:154–55.

little organized resistance, the plight in Virginia was becoming desperate.

Jefferson, who had been "knocking at the door of Congress for aids of all kinds"[5] since the previous summer, now sent a plea to General George Washington in New York to lead his Continental troops to the defense of his home state:

> Were it possible for this circumstance to justify in your excellency a determination to lend us your personal aid, it is evident from the universal voice that the presence of their beloved countryman, whose talents have so long been successfully employed in establishing the freedom of kindred states, to whose person they have still flattered themselves they retained some right, and have ever looked up as their *dernier resort* in distress—that your appearance among them, I say, would restore full confidence of salvation, and would render them equal to whatever is not impossible.[6]

Later that summer Washington responded to Jefferson's plea and began marching his army southward to meet Cornwallis at Yorktown. As it turned out, this movement decided the outcome of the war.

Governor Jefferson Steps Aside

During the American Revolution, the Virginia constitution allowed the Governor of that state to serve a maximum of three consecutive one-year terms. Jefferson's second term ended on Saturday, June 2, 1781. He was

---

5. TJ to General Horatio Gates (17 Feb.1781), Bergh 4:162. This was at a time when men and supplies were still being requested from Virginia for the southern campaign.

6. TJ to General George Washington (28 May 1781), Bergh 4:183.

eligible to be reelected for one more year, but he informed the General Assembly that he believed another course would better meet Virginia's needs during the present crisis.

> From a belief that under the pressure of the invasion...the public would have more confidence in a military chief, and that, the military commander being invested with the civil power also, both might be wielded with more energy, promptitude, and effect for the defense of the state, I resigned the administration at the end of my second year. [7]

He further recommended that General Thomas Nelson, Jr., ranking officer of the state militia, be appointed to succeed him. The legislators resolved to cast ballots for a new Governor on June 2, the last day of Jefferson's term. When the day came, however, they postponed the action until Monday, June 4. Over the weekend the outgoing Governor remained in Charlottesville, the temporary seat of government, to finish up some official business. He then returned to Monticello, considering himself a private citizen.

A Narrow Escape

Hoping to destroy what remained of Virginia's government, Cornwallis ordered his cavalry commander,

---

7. Autobiography (1821), Bergh 1:75. In another place Jefferson wrote: "Unprepared by [my] line of life and education for the command of armies, [I] believed it right not to stand in the way of talents better fitted than [my] own to the circumstances under which [Virginia] was placed. [I] therefore proposed...that General Nelson...should be appointed Governor, believing that the union of the civil and military power in the same hands at this time would greatly facilitate military measures." Diary of Arnold's invasion and notes on subsequent events in 1781, Boyd 4:260–61.

Banastre Tarleton, to execute a surprise attack on
Charlottesville and to capture Jefferson. On the evening of June 3, Tarleton's
250 men were spotted on
the road by an American
captain named Jack Jouett,
who "was even taller than
Jefferson and weighed
more than two hundred
pounds."[8]

Jouett, who later came
to be called "Virginia's Paul
Revere," immediately headed into the woods and rode
all night to warn Jefferson
of the approaching Red-
coats. "He knew the back
trails and bypaths," one
writer informs us, "and
through the night he fol-
lowed them. It is said that

Silhouette of Captain Jack Jouett,
"Virginia's Paul Revere," whose all-
night ride enabled Governor Jefferson
and members of the state legislature
to avoid being captured in a secret raid
by British cavalrymen in 1781.

the scars made on his face by the lashing branches of
the undergrowth remained with him all his life."[9] He
reached Monticello before dawn on Monday, June 4. Upon
hearing the news, Jefferson arranged for his family to be
taken to a friend's estate, then stayed behind to secure

8. Malone, *Jefferson the Virginian*, p. 356.
9. Ibid.

some of his belongings. Jouett rode on to warn the sleeping legislators in Charlottesville. [10]

Meanwhile, the British troops pulled into a place called
Castle Hill, just eight miles from Monticello, where Jouett
had obtained a fresh horse earlier that morning. The
owner of the plantation, a man named Thomas Walker,
now gave Jefferson a little more time by detaining
Tarleton's men with breakfast and mint juleps.

Another American officer rode up to Monticello at full
speed and shouted that the British cavalrymen were
ascending the mountain, so Jefferson mounted his horse
and galloped into the surrounding forest with only
minutes to spare. As Tarleton and his troops appeared,
Jefferson's servants were lowering his silver and other
valuables into a hiding place beneath the porch. They
quickly dropped the plank, leaving below one man named
Great George who was unable to get out in time. The
faithful servant remained there for the next eighteen
hours, in darkness and without food, to avoid betraying
the location of his master's belongings. [11]

Cornwallis Destroys Jefferson's
Elk Hill Plantation

Tarleton was civil enough to order his men not to

---

10. "Jack Jouett's ride...was obviously more difficult than the far more
famous one by Paul Revere. It came toward the end of the Revolution rather
than at the beginning, and the ensuing events were less heroic, but the chief
difference between the two rides lies in the fact that no poet immortalized
Jouett." Ibid. The best account of this episode is in Virginius Dabney, "Jouett
Outrides Tarleton," *Scribner's Magazine*, June 1928, pp. 690–98.

11. These details are from Anne Revis, "Mr. Jefferson's Charlottesville,"
National Geographic, May 1950, pp. 556–59; see also Jefferson's diary of
Arnold's invasion and notes on subsequent events in 1781, Boyd 4:261, 265.

damage anything at Monticello, but not all of Jefferson's properties met with such good fortune. Cornwallis himself had raided another of his plantations, a place called Elk Hill. Jefferson later discovered that the British general had lived up to his reputation for wanton destruction.

> He destroyed all my growing crops of corn and tobacco; he burned all my barns containing the same articles of the last year, having first taken what he wanted; he used, as was to be expected, all my stocks of cattle, sheep, and hogs for the sustenance of his army, and carried off all the horses capable of service; of those too young for service he cut the throats; and he burned all the fences on the plantation so as to leave it an absolute waste.

> He carried off also about thirty slaves. Had this been to give them freedom, he would have done right; but it was to consign them to inevitable death from the smallpox and putrid fever then raging in his camp. This I knew afterwards to have been the fate of twenty-seven of them. [12]

But this was Cornwallis's last offensive move in the war. Soon afterward the Marquis de Lafayette combined his troops with reinforcements from Pennsylvania and began pushing the British back toward the sea. Then Washington's army and a large French force arrived in September, and the historic siege of Yorktown began. Lord Cornwallis surrendered on October 19, 1781, ending the last great battle of the Revolutionary War.

---

12. TJ to Dr. William Gordon (16 July 1788), Bergh 7:68–69.

Jefferson's Governorship Is Vindicated

However, at the time of Tarleton's raid the previous summer, Virginia's political leaders could not foresee this fortuitous event. When Jack Jouett rode into Charlottesville with his alarming news on the morning of June 4, the legislators fled in panic to an even more remote location in the western mountains. It was not until June 12 that they elected the new Governor. They chose Thomas Nelson, the man Jefferson had recommended.

On the same day, a young member of the House of Delegates named George Nicholas proposed an official inquiry into the former Governor's administration. Several legislators rumored that Jefferson had been guilty of malfeasance in office and personal cowardice during the recent difficulties. Some charged that he had abandoned his post in a critical moment, and a few even criticized him for fleeing from Tarleton's cavalry! (He later joked that it had been "sung in verse, and said in humble prose, that forgetting the noble example of the hero of La Mancha and his windmills, I declined a combat singly against a troop, in which victory would have been so glorious.") [13]

The resolution to investigate Jefferson's governorship apparently sprang from the desire of some officials to find a scapegoat for the humiliation they had suffered at the hands of the British army. But better sense prevailed when the legislators reconvened in the fall. Jefferson appeared before the House of Delegates to defend his administration—Nicholas did not even attend the session—and the two houses of the legislature unanimously responded as follows:

---

13. Diary and notes, Boyd 4:265.

> *Resolved,* That the sincere thanks of the General Assembly be given to our former Governor, Thomas Jefferson, Esquire, for his impartial, upright, and attentive administration whilst in office. The Assembly wish in the strongest manner to declare the high opinion which they entertain of Mr. Jefferson's ability, rectitude, and integrity as Chief Magistrate of this Commonwealth, and mean, by thus publicly avowing their opinion, to obviate and to remove all unmerited censure. [14]

Jefferson's political enemies never let the issue die, however, and there are still a few writers today who accuse him of abdicating his responsibility as Governor. But as one Jefferson biographer has noted, "It would be nearer the truth to say that the government abandoned him than that he abandoned the government." [15]

Another endorsement of Jefferson's labors as chief executive came from the Commander-in-Chief of the American armies, General George Washington. It was written in June 1781.

> Give me leave, before I take leave of your excellency in your public capacity, to express the obligations I am under for the readiness and zeal with which you have always forwarded and supported every measure which I have had occasion to recommend through you, and to assure you that I shall esteem myself honored by a continuance of your friendship and correspondence

---

14. Reprinted in Boyd 6:135–36. This resolution was adopted in December 1781.

15. Malone, *Jefferson the Virginian,* p. 358.

should your country permit you to remain in the private walk of life. [16]

Jefferson's "readiness and zeal" in forwarding the cause of the war, especially in view of the severe economic conditions of the times, contrasted sharply with the slackness of many American governors during that period. According to the eminent Jefferson scholar Julian Boyd, "The mass of [Jefferson's] papers for 1779-1781 . . . shows that no war governor worked more devotedly than he against odds more completely insuperable." [17] His leadership in Virginia was one of the few bright spots in a very dark and difficult segment of the nation's history.

---

16. George Washington to TJ (8 June 1781), John C. Fitzpatrick, ed., *The Writings of George Washington*, 39 vols. (Washington: United States Government Printing Office, 1931-44), 22:190.

17. Boyd 4:257.

Chapter 9

Rising Above Tragedy

The early 1780s were not a particular happy time in Jefferson's life. Besides his frustrating governorship and the bitter accusations that followed, he witnessed another tragedy in his family—the death of a five-month-old daughter in April 1781—and worried about the worsening illness of his dear wife. Following Cornwallis's destruction of his Elk Hill plantation in June, he was thrown from a horse and disabled for several weeks. In September 1781, he wrote to a friend in Congress that he had taken his "final leave" from political affairs and had "retired to my farm, my family, and books, from which I think nothing will ever more separate me."[1]

---

1. TJ to Edmund Randolph (16 Sept. 1781), Bergh 4:187.

This supposed "retirement" did not find him idle, however. As soon as he recovered from the injuries sustained in his riding accident, he immersed himself in his favorite activities at home. Some of these are mentioned in a brief account recorded by the Marquis de Chastellux, a noted Frenchman who visited Monticello in the spring of 1782:

> Let me... describe to you a man, not yet forty, tall, and with a mild and pleasing countenance, but whose mind and attainments could serve in lieu of all outward graces; an American who, without ever having quitted his own country, is [a] musician, draftsman, surveyor, astronomer, natural philosopher, jurist, and statesman....
>
> A gentle and amiable wife, charming children whose education is his special care, a house to embellish, extensive estates to improve, and the arts and sciences to cultivate—these are what remain to Mr. Jefferson, after having played a distinguished role on the stage of the New World....
>
> At... times natural philosophy was the subject of our conversations, and at... others politics or the arts, for no object had escaped Mr. Jefferson; and it seems indeed as though ever since his youth he had placed his mind, like his house, on a lofty height whence he might contemplate the whole universe. [2]

Notes on the State of Virginia

It was also during this period that Jefferson prepared the manuscript for the only full-length book he ever

---

2. Marquis de Chastellux, *Travels in North America in the Years 1780, 1781 and 1782*, rev. ed., trans. Howard C. Rice, Jr., 2 vols. (Chapel Hill: The University of North Carolina Press, 1963), 2:391-92.

published, his *Notes on the State of Virginia*. The effort was prompted by a series of questions he had received during his governorship from a French diplomat in Philadelphia. The man had been instructed by his superiors in Paris to learn all he could about the laws, customs, history, physical features, and economic conditions of the thirteen states, so he sent a long list of inquiries to all the American governors.

Jefferson took the request more seriously than any of his contemporaries. He spent several months studying and writing about "my country," as he often called Virginia. The initial draft was completed by the end of 1781, then revised and enlarged substantially the next year. His interest in the project continued, and by mid-1784 his manuscript was almost three times its original size.

NOTES on the state of VIRGINIA;
written in the year 1781, somewhat corrected and enlarged in the winter of 1782, for the use of a Foreigner of distinction, in answer to certain queries proposed by him respecting

1. Its boundaries - page 1
2. Rivers - 3
3. Sea ports - 27
4. Mountains - 28
5. Cascades and caverns - 33
6. Productions mineral, vegetable and animal - 41
7. Climate - 134
8. Population - 151
9. Military force - 161
10. Marine force - 165
11. Aborigines - 166
12. Counties and towns - 171
13. Constitution - 173
14. Laws - 135
15. Colleges, buildings, and roads - 275
16. Proceedings as to tories - 283
17. Religion - 287
18. Manners - 298
19. Manufactures - 302
20. Subjects of commerce - 304
21. Weights, Measures and Money - 317
22. Public revenue and expences - 313
23. Histories, memorials, and state-papers - 322

MDCCLXXXII.

Title page of Jefferson's only full-length book, *Notes on the State of Virginia*. The subjects listed here reveal the breadth of his interests and knowledge.

"The Most Important Scientific Work Published in America"

Though he did not intend to publish the work at large, Jefferson did have two hundred copies printed privately in

1785 for some friends and scholars with whom he corresponded. The book soon aroused great interest, especially
in Europe, and wider publication became inevitable.

A European copy, by the death of the owner, got into
the hands of a bookseller, who engaged its translation,
and when [it was] ready for the press [he] communicated
his intentions and manuscript to me, suggesting that I
should correct it, without asking any other permission
for the publication.

I never had seen so wretched an attempt at
translation. Interverted, abridged, mutilated, and often
reversing the sense of the original, I found it a blotch of
errors from beginning to end. I corrected some of the
most material, and in that form it was printed in French.
A London bookseller, on seeing the translation,
requested me to permit him to print the English original.
I thought it best to do so, to let the world see that it was
not really so bad as the French translation had made it
appear.[3]

Despite his modest appraisal, Jefferson's *Notes*
eventually gained wide popularity and saw numerous
editions in both English and French. The book was also
translated into German. In addition to several important
expressions of Jefferson's political philosophy, the volume
contained many useful observations on natural history
and other scientific subjects. It has been called "the most
important scientific work published in America up to
[that] time,"[4] and one writer noted that it "placed
Jefferson's name to the forefront in virtually all learned

3. Autobiography (1821), Bergh 1:91-92.

4. Austin H. Clark, "Thomas Jefferson and Science," *Washington Academy
of Sciences Journal*, 15 July 1943, pp. 197-98.

circles" and "drew world-wide attention to him as a true scientist as well as a statesman."[5]

"He Nursed My Poor Mother"

In the early months of 1782, while Jefferson was revising his first draft of the *Notes on Virginia*, he became increasingly alarmed about the fragile health of his wife Martha. After giving birth in the late spring to their sixth child, Lucy Elizabeth, she failed rapidly. In May Jefferson declined his recent reelection to the Virginia House of Delegates, even though he was criticized for it by friends and neighbors who were unaware of the circumstances. He felt his place was at Martha's side. Jefferson's oldest daughter wrote of him:

> As a nurse no female ever had more tenderness nor anxiety. He nursed my poor mother . . . sitting up with her and administering her medicines and drink to the last. For four months that she lingered, he was never out of calling; when not at her bedside, he was writing in a small room which opened immediately at the head of her bed.[6]

The Death of Mrs. Jefferson

September 6, 1782, was the darkest day in Thomas Jefferson's life. In his daily account book he could manage only these words: "My dear wife died this day at 11:45 a.m." As when his mother had passed away in 1776, he wrote almost nothing to reveal the extent of his grief. But his daughter left this deeply moving description of her

---

5. Edwin T. Martin, *Thomas Jefferson: Scientist* (New York: Henry Schuman, 1952), pp. 140, 257. Jefferson's book is reprinted in Bergh 2:1-261.

6. Randolph, *The Domestic Life of Thomas Jefferson*, p. 63.

father's emotional struggle during the weeks after Mrs. Jefferson's death:

> A moment before the closing scene, he was led from the room in a state of insensibility by his sister, Mrs. Carr, who, with great difficulty, got him into the library, where he fainted, and remained so long insensible that they feared he never would revive. The scene that followed I did not witness, but the violence of his emotion when, almost by stealth, I entered his room by night, to this day I dare not describe to myself.
>
> He kept his room three weeks, and I was never a moment from his side. He walked almost incessantly night and day, only lying down occasionally, when nature was completely exhausted, on a pallet that had been brought in during his long fainting fit. My aunts remained constantly with him for some weeks—I do not remember how many.
>
> When at last he left his room, he rode out, and from that time he was incessantly on horseback, rambling about the mountain in the least frequented roads, and just as often through the woods. In those melancholy rambles I was his constant companion—a solitary witness to many a burst of grief.[7]

In the preceding seven years Jefferson had buried his mother, two young daughters, and an infant son; and his wife's repeated illnesses during this period had certainly not offered much promise. But in spite of it all, he seemed quite unprepared for this latest and most devastating event. Martha was only thirty-three years old at the time of her passing.

------

7. Ibid.

The Tenderness of Family Ties

Decades later, as an old man, Jefferson reflected that in 1782 he had "lost the cherished companion of my life, in whose affections...I had lived the last ten years in uncheckered happiness."[8] He never married again,[9] and his remaining children became more important to him than anything else in his life. Still another tragedy occurred in 1784 when two-year-old Lucy Elizabeth died, leaving him with only two daughters. His emotional attachment to them is revealed in a touching passage from a 1787 letter he wrote to his fourteen-year-old, named Martha after her mother:

> Nobody in this world can make me so happy, or so miserable, as you.... To your sister and yourself I look to render the evening of my life serene and contented. Its morning has been clouded by loss after loss, till I have nothing left but you.[10]

Jefferson once said, "It is in the love of one's family only that heartfelt happiness is known,"[11] and he called children "the keystone of the arch of matrimonial happiness."[12] To the end of his life he remained a devoted family man, giving helpful instruction and warm affection to his daughters and grandchildren.

---

8. Autobiography (1821), Bergh 1:76.

9. According to the house servants who were in the room at the time of Mrs. Jefferson's death, she secured a promise from her husband that he would not marry again. Bear, *Jefferson at Monticello*, pp. 99–100.

10. TJ to Martha Jefferson (28 Mar. 1787), Betts and Bear, *The Family Letters of Thomas Jefferson*, p. 35.

11. TJ to Mary Jefferson Eppes (26 Oct. 1801), Betts and Bear, p. 210.

12. TJ to Martha Jefferson Randolph (9 Feb. 1791), Betts and Bear, p. 71.

"A Single Event Wiped Away All My Plans"

One of the few allusions Jefferson ever made to the death of his wife was contained in a letter he wrote in November 1782 to the Marquis de Chastellux, the Frenchman who had visited Monticello the previous spring. Recent correspondence from Chastellux, he said, had found him "a little emerging from the stupor of mind which had rendered me as dead to the world as she was whose loss occasioned it."

> Your letter recalled to my memory that there were persons still living of much value to me. If you should have thought me remiss in not testifying to you sooner how deeply I had been impressed with your worth in the little time I had the happiness of being with you, you will, I am sure, ascribe it to its true cause, the state of the dreadful suspense in which I had been kept all the summer and the catastrophe which closed it.
>
> Before that event, my scheme of life had been determined. I had folded myself in the arms of retirement, and rested all prospects of future happiness on domestic and literary objects. A single event wiped away all my plans and left me a blank which I had not the spirits to fill up. [13]

A Fortuitous Change of Mind

But it would not take long to fill the void. Jefferson's loss was a source of deep sorrow to him personally, but it also brought him to a decision which altered the course of his life and proved very fortunate for the American nation. A few months earlier he had forever renounced all political affairs in favor of his family, his farm, and his books; but

---

13. TJ to the Marquis de Chastellux (26 Nov. 1782), Bergh 4:199–200.

by the end of 1782 he had made up his mind to return to public service.

Some of Jefferson's friends in Congress, anticipating this change of heart when they heard of his wife's death, secured for him an appointment to join Benjamin Franklin and John Adams as a peace commissioner in Europe. He spent the winter in Philadelphia and Baltimore, waiting for the ice to clear in Chesapeake Bay so he could sail across the Atlantic. But in February he learned that a preliminary treaty with England had already been signed, and Congress decided soon afterward that there was no need to send him overseas.

Back in Virginia, Jefferson tried to initiate a convention to revise the Virginia constitution of 1776, but he was unsuccessful. As it turned out, this was his last effort in state politics for many years; in the summer of 1783 the Virginia legislature reelected him to Congress for the 1783–84 session, and that was to be followed by a series of national leadership positions which eventually led him to the highest office in the land.

"The Morbid Rage of Debate"

Congress had decided to meet that fall in Annapolis, Maryland, and Jefferson arrived in November to take his seat. He later recalled his impressions of the long and heated debates he sat through during the next several months:

> Our body was little numerous, but very contentious. Day after day was wasted on the most unimportant questions. A member, one of those afflicted with the morbid rage of debate...who heard with impatience any logic which was not his own, sitting near me on

some occasion of a trifling but wordy debate, asked me how I could sit in silence, hearing so much false reasoning which a word should refute.

I observed to him that to refute indeed was easy, but to silence was impossible; that in measures brought forward by myself I took the laboring oar, as was incumbent on me; but that in general I was willing to listen; that if every sound argument or objection was used by some one or other of the numerous debaters, it was enough; if not, I thought it sufficient to suggest the omission without going into a repetition of what had been already said by others.... I believe that if the members of deliberative bodies were to observe this course generally, they would do in a day what takes them a week....

I served with General Washington in the legislature of Virginia before the Revolution and, during it, with Dr. Franklin in Congress. I never heard either of them speak ten minutes at a time, nor to any but the main point which was to decide the question. They laid their shoulders to the great points, knowing that the little ones would follow of themselves.

If the present Congress errs in too much talking, how can it be otherwise in a body to which the people send one hundred and fifty lawyers, whose trade it is to question everything, yield nothing, and talk by the hour? That one hundred and fifty lawyers should do business together ought not to be expected. [14]

A Leader in Congress

But Jefferson did not spend all of his time sitting and listening. He was a member—and usually the chairman—

---

14. Autobiography (1821), Bergh 1:86–87.

of every important committee, and he wrote practically all the significant state papers which came out of that session of Congress.

Among his most important duties was chairing the committee appointed to examine the Treaty of Paris, which officially ended the war and granted recognition to American independence. In accordance with the committee's recommendation, Congress ratified the historic treaty in January 1784. During the same session Jefferson submitted his "Notes on the Establishment of a Money Unit, and of a Coinage for the United States." This farsighted proposal eventually resulted in the adoption of a decimal monetary system throughout the nation. (It also earned for its author the title "father of the dollar.")

Government in the Western Territories

The vast area between the Appalachians and the Mississippi River had long been claimed by several of the original states, but the recent cession of these claims placed the area under the control of Congress. In early 1784, Jefferson was appointed chairman of a committee to settle the many land disputes which had arisen and to prepare a plan for the government of this western region. Jefferson himself drafted the report, known to history as the Ordinance of 1784.[15]

According to one scholar, the plan "ranked second in importance only to the Declaration of Independence among Jefferson's state papers."[16] This document, which

15. Reprinted, together with preliminary drafts, in Boyd 6:603-15.

16. Malone, *Dictionary of American Biography,* 10:21; see also Chinard, *Thomas Jefferson: The Apostle of Americanism,* p. 147. Julian P. Boyd called it "the foundation stone of American territorial policy." Boyd 6:581.

became the basis for the famous Northwest Ordinance of 1787, provided for the creation of self-governing territories that would eventually be admitted to the Union on terms of full equality with the original states. It was a bold and brilliant concept, one that would ultimately have a tremendous influence on the westward expansion of the United States.[17]

"Heaven Was Silent in That Awful Moment!"

But Congress rejected a very significant element in Jefferson's report on the western territories. He had included in his bill a clause barring slavery in any of these territories after the year 1800—a measure which might have averted the Civil War[18]—but this proposal was defeated by one vote. Jefferson lamented:

> The voice of a single individual...would have prevented this abominable crime from spreading itself over the new country. Thus we see the fate of millions unborn hanging on the tongue of one man, and Heaven was silent in that awful moment! But it is to be hoped it will not always be silent, and that the friends to the rights of human nature will in the end prevail.[19]

Yet he worried about what might have to take place before this victory for "the rights of human nature" could be secured.

---

17. Jefferson had actually advocated this idea eight years earlier. His proposed new Virginia constitution contained a provision that any future colonies established from Virginia's western domain would be "free and independent of this colony and of all the world." Boyd 1:353, 363.

18. Malone, *Jefferson the Virginian*, p. 414; Richard B. Morris, *The American Revolution Reconsidered* (New York: Harper & Row, 1967), p. 73.

19. TJ to Jean Nicolas Demeunier (22 June 1786), Boyd 10:58.

I tremble for my country when I reflect that God is just; that His justice cannot sleep forever; that considering numbers, nature, and natural means only, a revolution of the wheel of fortune, an exchange of situation, is among possible events; [and] that it may become probable by supernatural interference! The Almighty has no attribute which can take side with us in such a contest. [20]

Always an optimist in the end, however, Jefferson noted the next year that the cause of emancipation was "gaining daily recruits from the influx into office of young men, grown and growing up. These have sucked in the principles of liberty, as it were, with their mother's milk; and it is to them I look with anxiety to turn the fate of this question." [21]

---

20. *Notes on the State of Virginia* (1782), Bergh 2:227.
21. TJ to Dr. Richard Price (7 Aug. 1785), Bergh 5:56.

Chapter 10

American Minister
to France

I n May 1784, after Jefferson had played a leading role in Congress for nearly six months, his colleagues in Annapolis renewed an earlier request that he join Benjamin Franklin and John Adams in Paris to help them negotiate commercial treaties with the nations of Europe.[1] This time there was nothing to prevent his assuming the post, and soon his baggage was packed for the journey.

After an instructive tour of the New England states, Jefferson and his daughter Martha, then eleven years of age, sailed from Boston in July. For the time being he

---

1. Interestingly enough, the official instructions which Jefferson carried with him to Europe had been drafted by himself during that year's session of Congress.

decided to leave five-year-old Mary and two-year-old Lucy behind in the care of their aunt and uncle, Elizabeth and Francis Eppes (Elizabeth was the sister of Jefferson's deceased wife). Following a "pleasant voyage of nineteen days from land to land,"[2] father and daughter reached Paris on August 6.

Diplomatic Negotiations at the Court of Versailles

Jefferson entered almost immediately into his duties as the new minister plenipotentiary. With Franklin and Adams he formulated plans to obtain commercial rights from the European powers that would enable the United States to begin paying off the immense debt incurred during the Revolutionary War. These early diplomatic efforts produced mixed results.

We sounded the ministers of the several European nations at the court of Versailles on their dispositions towards mutual commerce, and the expediency of encouraging it by the protection of a treaty. Old Frederic of Prussia met us cordially and without hesitation, and [a treaty with his country] was soon concluded. Denmark and Tuscany entered also into negotiations with us.

Other powers appearing indifferent, we did not think it proper to press them. They seemed, in fact, to know little about us but as rebels who had been successful in throwing off the yoke of the mother country. They were ignorant of our commerce, which had been always monopolized by England, and of the exchange of articles it might offer advantageously to both parties. They were inclined, therefore, to stand aloof until they could

2. Autobiography (1821), Bergh 1:90.

see better what relations might be usefully instituted with us.[3]

"I Am Only His Successor"

In the summer of 1785, the aging Dr. Franklin was called home after having served most of the last thirty years in diplomatic posts abroad. Jefferson was appointed to replace him as the American minister to France, while John Adams was assigned to the court of George III in London. Franklin had been very popular among the French people during his nine-year stay in Paris, and

Benjamin Franklin, whom Jefferson succeeded in 1785 as American minister to France.

especially among his local neighbors in the suburban village of Passy. At the time of his departure, Jefferson later recalled with amusement, "the ladies smothered him with embraces, and on his introducing me to them as his successor, I told him I wished he would transfer these privileges to me, but he answered, 'You are too young a man.'"[4]

Although Jefferson was only kidding about this transfer of "privileges," he did experience some anxiety about

3. Ibid., p. 93.
4. Quoted in Smith, *The First Forty Years of Washington Society,* p. 59.

being able to fill the shoes of a man so deeply admired by the French nation as was Benjamin Franklin:

> There appeared to me more respect and veneration attached to the character of Dr. Franklin in France than to that of any other person in the same country, foreign or native. I had opportunities of knowing particularly how far these sentiments were felt by the foreign ambassadors and ministers at the court of Versailles....
>
> The succession to Dr. Franklin at the court of France was an excellent school of humility. On being presented to anyone as the minister of America, the commonplace question used in such cases was *"C'est vous, Monsieur, qui remplace le Docteur Franklin?"*—"It is you, sir, who replace Dr. Franklin?" I generally answered, "No one can replace him, sir; I am only his successor."[5]

Despite his initial feeling that he was standing in Franklin's shadow, Jefferson proved himself a very able diplomat in his own right. During the four years he served as minister to France, he won a number of valuable concessions to American trade. "On these occasions," he wrote, "I was powerfully aided by all the influence and the energies of the Marquis de Lafayette, who proved himself equally zealous for the friendship and welfare of both nations. And, in justice, I must also say that I found the [French] government entirely disposed to befriend us on all occasions, and to yield us every indulgence not absolutely injurious to themselves."[6]

A Father's Loving Counsel

A few months after reaching France in 1784, Jefferson

---

5. TJ to [the Reverend William Smith ?] (19 Feb. 1791), Bergh 8:129–30.
6. Autobiography (1821), Bergh 1:96.

received word that his youngest daughter, Lucy Elizabeth, had died from whooping cough. This unhappy event drew him even closer to the two girls who remained, and his frequent letters to them show a tender concern for their welfare and development. In late 1785 he began making arrangements to have Mary (whom he often called "Maria" or "Polly") join him in France, and he wrote her about his intentions:

> I wish so much to see you that I have desired your uncle and aunt to send you to me. I know, my dear Polly, how sorry you will be, and ought to be, to leave them and your cousins; but your sister and myself cannot live without you, and after a while we will carry you back again to see your friends in Virginia. In the meantime, you shall be taught here to play on the harpsichord, to draw, to dance, to read and talk French, and such other things as will make you more worthy of the love of your friends....
>
> I hope you are a very good girl, that you love your uncle and aunt very much, and are very thankful to them for all their goodness to you; that you never suffer yourself to be angry with anybody, that you give your playthings to those who want them, that you do whatever anybody desires of you that is right, that you never tell stories, never beg for anything, mind your books and your work when your aunt tells you, never play but when she permits you, nor go where she forbids you....
>
> We shall hope to have you with us next summer, to find you a very good girl, and to assure you of the truth of our affection for you. [7]

_____

7. TJ to Mary Jefferson (20 Sept. 1785), Betts and Bear, *The Family Letters of Thomas Jefferson*, pp. 29–30.

Martha "Patsy" Jefferson, who accompanied her father to France. She was seventeen years old when this miniature portrait was painted in 1789, shortly before their return to the United States.

"Do What Is Right"

Jefferson also offered fatherly advice to his oldest daughter, Martha, who was staying at a boarding school in Paris. When he was away from Paris, he kept in touch with her through the mails and monitored her progress. On one such occasion she wrote him that she was unable to get through a Latin history of Rome without the constant help of an instructor, and he replied with classic Jeffersonian philosophy:

I do not like your saying that you are unable to read the ancient print of your Livy but with the aid of your master. We are always equal to what we undertake with resolution. A little degree of this will enable you to decipher your Livy. If you always lean on your master, you will never be able to proceed without him. It is a part of the American character to consider nothing as desperate, to surmount every difficulty by resolution and contrivance. [8]

When the time of Polly's arrival finally drew near in 1787, after several delays, Jefferson counseled Martha

---

8. TJ to Martha Jefferson (28 Mar. 1787), Betts and Bear, p. 35.

("Patsy") about her heavy responsibility to help train her younger sister.

When she arrives, she will become a precious charge on your hands. The difference of your age, and your common loss of a mother, will put that office on you. Teach her above all things to be good, because without that we can neither be valued by others nor set any value on ourselves. Teach her to be always true; no vice is so mean as the want of truth, and at the same time so useless. Teach her never to be angry; anger only serves to torment ourselves, to divert others, and alienate their esteem. And teach her industry and application to useful pursuits. I will venture to assure you that if you inculcate this in her mind, you will make her a happy being in herself, a most inestimable friend to you, and precious to all the world.

In teaching her these dispositions of mind, you will be more fixed in them yourself and render yourself dear to all your acquaintances. Practice them, then, my dear, without ceasing. If ever you find yourself in difficulty and doubt how to extricate yourself, do what is right, and you will find it the easiest way of getting out of the difficulty. Do it for the additional incitement of increasing the happiness of him who loves you infinitely, and who is, my dear Patsy, yours affectionately. [9]

The Barbary Pirates

Jefferson had many opportunities to travel while he was in Europe. The first of these came in early 1786, when Adams urgently requested that he come to London to assist in negotiations with Great Britain, Portugal, and the Barbary states. Jefferson reached England on March 1 and

---

9. TJ to Martha Jefferson (7 Apr. 1787), Betts and Bear, pp. 36–37.

assisted Adams in drafting treaty proposals. He was especially eager to establish a trade agreement with the Barbary states. These small nations along the northern coast of Africa had long been pirating "tribute" money from European shippers entering the Mediterranean, and American vessels would be treated no differently. The Europeans seemed willing to suffer this humiliation, but the American minister had a very different attitude:

> We have taken some pains to find out the sums which the nations of Europe give to the Barbary states to purchase their peace. They will not tell this, yet from some glimmerings it appears to be very considerable, and I do expect that they would tax us at one, two, or perhaps three hundred thousand dollars a year. Surely our people will not give this. Would it not be better to offer them an equal treaty; if they refuse, why not go to war with them? . . .
>
> We ought to begin a naval power if we mean to carry on our own commerce. Can we begin it on a more honorable occasion, or with a weaker foe? I am of opinion [John] Paul Jones with half a dozen frigates would totally destroy their commerce. [10]

Unfortunately, the Barbary pirates were not amenable to such negotiation, and the United States was unable at that time to furnish even a single warship to protect her commercial vessels in the Mediterranean. Consequently, the Americans paid more than $2,000,000 over the next fifteen years in tribute to the Barbary states. Jefferson did not forget this injustice, however. He would eventually attack the problem again—and not through diplomatic channels—after he became President.

---

10. TJ to James Monroe (11 Nov. 1784), Boyd 7:511-12.

George III and the English Gardens

Jefferson and Adams continued their discussions in London, but they were no more successful with Portugal or Great Britain than they had been with the Barbary states. When they were introduced to George III at the royal court, the reception was hardly cordial.

> On my presentation ... to the King and Queen at their levees, it was impossible for anything to be more ungracious than their notice of Mr. Adams and myself. I saw at once that the ulcerations in the narrow mind of that mulish being left nothing to be expected on the subject of my attendance.[11]

The King was apparently still smarting from the reprimand Jefferson had sent him years earlier in his *Summary View of the Rights of British America*—and in the Declaration of Independence.

After several weeks of fruitless work, Adams and Jefferson decided to take a break. They set out on April 2, 1786, to visit the famous English gardens along the Thames River west of London. This was

King George III, who received Jefferson and John Adams impolitely in London in 1786.

11. Autobiography (1821), Bergh 1:94.

a real treat for Jefferson, who had avidly studied gardening back home while landscaping Monticello. A few days after leaving England he wrote: "The gardening in that country is the article in which it surpasses all the earth. I mean their pleasure gardening. This indeed went far beyond my ideas."[12]

Having concluded his efforts in London, Jefferson returned to Paris at the end of April.

"A One-Man Information Bureau"

While serving as minister to France, Jefferson maintained his lifelong habit of increasing his knowledge about the sciences and the arts. Always one who enjoyed tinkering with mechanical devices, he brought back from England "a box containing small tools for wooden and iron work, for my own amusement."[13] He often met with European inventors to examine and discuss their latest projects. Responding to a request from the Virginia legislature, he commissioned the famed artist Jean Antoine Houdon to sculpt a statue of George Washington (Houdon also completed a bust of Jefferson himself in 1789). And in order to settle a scholarly dispute with a French natural historian, he had the entire skeleton of an American moose shipped from New Hampshire to Paris!

Wherever he traveled in his diplomatic duties—in France, England, Italy, Holland, Germany—he carefully observed anything that was new to him, hoping to find in it some useful application for his own country. As one

---

12. TJ to John Page (4 May 1786), Bergh 5:304.

13. Quoted in Edward Dumbauld, *Thomas Jefferson, American Tourist* (Norman, Okla.: University of Oklahoma Press, 1946), p. 72.

writer put it, "While abroad, Jefferson served as a one-man information bureau to keep America abreast of European science."[14]

He purchased and sent across the Atlantic many mechanical inventions (or sketches of them with detailed descriptions of their operation), recent scientific journals, seeds, plants, agricultural products, and even birds and small animals. In 1787 he smuggled out samples of Italian rice seed to be planted in South Carolina and Georgia. When he returned to the United States two years later, he brought with him a pair of bulldogs, the first of their breed in America. He also encouraged several European scholars and scientists to move to the United States.[15]

Jefferson the Architect

Among the most important contributions Jefferson made in this period was his design for a new capitol building at Richmond, Virginia. The design was based on the remains of the Roman temple Maison Carree in southern France, which he visited several times and called "the most precious, the most perfect model of ancient architecture remaining on earth."[16] Construction of the Virginia capitol closely followed Jefferson's plans and sketches, and this building soon exerted a major influence

---

14. Edwin T. Martin, *Thomas Jefferson: Scientist* (New York: Henry Schuman, 1952), p. 55.

15. See Martin, pp. 53–60; Malone, *Dictionary of American Biography,* 10:22; Henry F. Graff, *Illustrious Americans: Thomas Jefferson* (Morristown, N.J.: Silver Burdett Company, 1968), p. 49. Many years later, as the founder and first president of the University of Virginia, Jefferson would employ a number of European professors as members of the university faculty.

16. TJ to Dr. James Currie (28 Jan. 1786), Boyd 9:240.

The Real Thomas Jefferson

The Roman temple Maison Carree in southern France. Jefferson called this structure "the most perfect model of ancient architecture remaining on earth."

The Virginia State Capitol, which Jefferson designed in 1786 after the Maison Carree. This building sparked a revival of classical architecture in America.

on the development of architectural styles throughout the nation. According to one writer, Jefferson "did more than any other man to stimulate the classical revival in America."[17]

Jefferson's interest in architecture persisted until his death. He sought to establish formal architectural instruction in the United States, and he personally designed—either wholly or in part—numerous public buildings and Virginia mansions. It has been observed in this century that he "may truly be called the father of our national architecture."[18]

Europe and America Contrasted

Jefferson greatly admired the European arts. "Were I to...tell you how much I enjoy their architecture, sculpture, painting, [and] music," he wrote to a friend, "I should want words."[19] But he was disgusted with the preoccupations and morals of the wealthy class in France. In a 1787 letter to an acquaintance in America, he provided this humorous description of a day in the life of a Parisienne:

> At eleven o'clock it is day, *chez madame*. The curtains are drawn. Propped on bolsters and pillows, and her head scratched into a little order, the bulletins of the sick are read, and the billets of the well. She writes to some of her acquaintance, and receives the visits of others. If the morning is not very thronged, she is able to get out and hobble round the cage of the Palais Royal; but she must

17. Malone, *Dictionary of American Biography*, 10:33–34.

18. Fiske Kimball, ed., *Thomas Jefferson, Architect* (1916; reprint ed., New York: Da Capo Press, 1968), p. 89.

19. TJ to Charles Bellini (30 Sept. 1785), Bergh 5:154.

hobble quickly, for the *coiffeur's* turn is come, and a tremendous turn it is! Happy if he does not make her arrive when dinner is half over!

The torpitude of digestion a little passed, she flutters half an hour through the streets by way of paying visits, and then to the spectacles. These finished, another half hour is devoted to dodging in and out of the doors of her very sincere friends, and away to supper. After supper, cards; and after cards, bed; to rise at noon the next day and to tread, like a mill horse, the same trodden circle over again.

Thus the days of life are consumed, one by one, without an object beyond the present moment; ever flying from the ennui of that, yet carrying it with us; eternally in pursuit of happiness, which keeps eternally before us. If death or bankruptcy happens to trip us out of the circle, it is matter for the buzz of the evening and is completely forgotten by the next morning.

In America, on the other hand, the society of your husband, the fond cares for the children, the arrangements of the house, the improvements of the grounds, fill every moment with a healthy and a useful activity. [20]

While in France Jefferson often contrasted the fashionable hubbub of Paris with "the tranquil, permanent felicity with which domestic society in America blesses most of its inhabitants." [21] To the aged Dr. Franklin he may have seemed still a young man, but at forty-two he considered himself "now of an age which does not easily accommodate itself to new manners and new modes of living; and I am savage enough to prefer the

---

20. TJ to Mrs. William Bingham (7 Feb. 1787), Bergh 6:81–82.
21. TJ to Charles Bellini (30 Sept. 1785), Bergh 5:153.

woods, the wilds, and the independence of Monticello to all the brilliant pleasures of this gay capital."[22]

A Caution Against "European Luxury and Dissipation"

Jefferson was mature enough to benefit from the advantages of French culture while rejecting its unwholesome elements, but he worried about the American youths then living in Europe who were exposed to that environment in their tender years. Many parents in the United States who could afford to do so preferred to send their children across the Atlantic to obtain an education. But Jefferson warned against this practice. A young man coming to Europe for his schooling, he said,

> acquires a fondness for European luxury and dissipation, and a contempt for the simplicity of his own country; he is fascinated with the privileges of the European aristocrats, and sees with abhorrence the lovely equality which the poor enjoy with the rich in his own country; he contracts a partiality for aristocracy or monarchy. . . .
>
> He is led by the strongest of all the human passions into a spirit for female intrigue, destructive of his own and others' happiness, or a passion for whores, destructive of his health, and in both cases learns to consider fidelity to the marriage bed as an ungentlemanly practice, and inconsistent with happiness; he recollects the voluptuary dress and arts of the European women, and pities and despises the chaste affections and simplicity of those of his own country. . . .

22. TJ to Baron de Geismer (6 Sept. 1785), Bergh 5:128–29.

It appears to me, then, that an American coming to Europe for education loses in his knowledge, in his morals, in his health, in his habits, and in his happiness. I had entertained only doubts on this head before I came to Europe; what I see and hear since I came here proves more than I had even suspected. [23]

Jefferson and Maria Cosway

Much has been written in recent years about Jefferson's alleged "love affair" with Maria Cosway, a twenty-seven-year-old Englishwoman who came to France with her husband in the fall of 1786. The Cosways were both artists of some renown, and they had traveled to the Continent to further their professional careers. Richard Cosway was a small, foppish, worldly man in his forties whose "marriage of convenience" was eclipsed by his passion for his work and by a long string of illicit romantic intrigues. Maria, on the other hand, was a woman of deep religious convictions. Having been born in Italy, she had seen much of Europe and could speak several languages. She had read widely and was skilled on the harp as well as with the paintbrush.

A mutual friend in Paris introduced the Cosways to Jefferson. He admired Maria's beauty, talents, and accomplishments, and on at least two occasions during her short stay in the city he accompanied her on sightseeing tours. She visited France a second time for a few weeks in the late summer of 1787, but Jefferson saw very little of her at that time. There is no evidence that they were ever alone together, and we know nothing about their relation-

---

23. TJ to John Banister, Jr. (15 Oct. 1785), Bergh 5:186-88.

ship except what appears in the sporadic letters they exchanged after the Cosways' departure from Paris in October 1786.

It is clear that Jefferson and Maria acquired a sincere friendship toward each other, and certain passages in their early correspondence suggest that they may have briefly felt something even deeper—although it is difficult to be sure when the exuberant expressions typical of eighteenth-century letters of friendship are discounted.[24] In any event, despite the fertile imaginations of

Self-portrait by Maria Cosway, an English artist whom Jefferson befriended in Paris. Some modern writers have made much of their supposed "love affair."

some modern writers, responsible historians have demonstrated that "there is absolutely no evidence nor reason to believe that the relation became anything but platonic."[25]

24. Jefferson's best-known letter to Maria Cosway (12 Oct. 1786), including his fascinating "dialogue . . . between my Head and my Heart," is found in Bergh 5:430–48. The most complete record of their correspondence is Helen Duprey Bullock, *My Head and My Heart: A Little Chronicle of Thomas Jefferson and Maria Cosway* (New York: G.P. Putnam's Sons, 1945).

25. Nathan Schachner, *Thomas Jefferson: A Biography* (New York and London: Thomas Yoseloff, 1951), p. 317. See also Frank R. Donovan, *The Women in Their Lives: The Distaff Side of the Founding Fathers* (New York: Dodd, Mead & Company, 1966), p. 233; and John Chester Miller, *The Wolf by the Ears: Thomas Jefferson and Slavery* (New York: Macmillan Publishing Co., Inc.,

The two never saw each other again after 1787, but they did correspond infrequently over the years. Maria eventually entered a Catholic convent, and in her later life she founded and administered "establishments of education" for young ladies in France and Italy. "It has afforded me satisfaction unfelt before," she wrote Jefferson in 1819. "What comfortable feelings seeing children grow up accomplished, modest, and virtuous women!"[26] Jefferson, by then an old man, wrote back the following year and reminisced about the friends he and Maria had formerly known in Paris. They were all "dead, diseased, [or] dispersed," he said. "But... the religion you so sincerely profess tells us we shall meet again; and we have all so lived as to be assured it will be in happiness."[27]

Travels Among the French People

"Behold me at length on the vaunted scene of Europe!" wrote Jefferson to a friend after he had been in France about a year. He was grateful for the opportunity to see that part of the world, but he lamented for the wretched condition of the common people there. In the same letter he said: "You are perhaps curious to know how this new scene has struck a savage of the mountains of America. Not advantageously, I assure you. I find the general fate of

The Free Press, 1977), pp. 185-94. Contrasting starkly with these and other reliable studies is the popular but widely discredited "psychobiography" by Fawn M. Brodie, *Thomas Jefferson: An Intimate History* (New York: W.W. Norton & Co., Inc., 1974), which is typified by the unfounded and irresponsible statement (p. 223) that Mrs. Cosway "must certainly have been racked by fears of pregnancy." For further information about Brodie's book, see the note beginning on page 231 of this biography.

26. Maria Cosway to TJ (7 Apr. 1819), in Bullock, p. 174.
27. TJ to Maria Cosway (27 Dec. 1820), Bergh 18:309-10.

humanity here most deplorable. The truth of Voltaire's observation offers itself perpetually, that every man here must be either the hammer or the anvil.... The great mass of the people are thus suffering under physical and moral oppression."[28]

Although he did not admire the morals of Parisian society, he developed a great love for the French people, and whenever his official duties would permit he went out of his way to become acquainted with them. For example, he told the Marquis de Lafayette in 1787:

> I am constantly roving about to see what I have never seen before, and shall never see again. In the great cities I go to see what travelers think alone worthy of being seen; but I make a job of it, and generally gulp it all down in a day. On the other hand, I am never satiated with rambling through the fields and farms, examining the culture and cultivators with a degree of curiosity which makes some take me to be a fool, and others to be much wiser than I am.[29]

He wished Lafayette could be with him, for he thought it would be useful for his friend "to know, from your own inspection, the condition of all the provinces of your own country."

> And to do it most effectually you must be absolutely incognito; you must ferret the people out of their hovels as I have done, look into their kettles, eat their bread, loll on their beds under pretense of resting yourself, but in fact to find if they are soft. You will feel a sublime pleasure in the course of this investigation, and a sub-limer one hereafter when you shall be able to apply

---

28. TJ to Charles Bellini (30 Sept. 1785), Bergh 5:152.
29. TJ to the Marquis de Lafayette (11 Apr. 1787), Bergh 6:109.

your knowledge to the softening of their beds or the throwing a morsel of meat into their kettles of vegetables.[30]

The political unrest caused by the "physical and moral oppression" which Jefferson had observed in his travels was about to explode into the French Revolution. The American minister to France had high hopes for the outcome of that historic upheaval, and he himself was to play a small part in its earliest stages.

---

30. Ibid. On another occasion, Jefferson's compassion was aroused by a French peasant woman he met and conversed with while walking along a country road near Fountainebleau. As they parted he placed in her hand several coins—enough to equal three days' wages. He recorded that "she burst into tears of a gratitude which I could perceive was unfeigned, because she was unable to utter a word." TJ to James Madison (28 Oct. 1785), Boyd 8:681.

Chapter 11

A New Era Dawns on Two Continents

While the revolution was beginning to brew in Paris, an occurrence of even greater interest to the American minister to France was under way on the other side of the Atlantic. It is ironic that Thomas Jefferson, author of the Declaration of Independence and one of America's foremost political thinkers, was on another continent when the Constitutional Convention opened in Philadelphia in May 1787.

His influence, however, was certainly not absent. Many of the participants in this historic assembly had worked with Jefferson in Congress or had read from his political writings, and his constitutional and legislative proposals in Virginia had particularly impressed the delegates from that state. One of these delegates, James Madison, played such a prominent role in the convention that he has come to be known as "the father of the Constitution," and it was through him that Jefferson wielded his greatest influence on the new charter of national government.

Jefferson, Madison, and the United States Constitution

Jefferson and Madison had known each other since the fall of 1776, when they first served together in the Virginia House of Delegates. Madison, then only twenty-five years of age, soon acquired a deep and lasting respect for his older colleague. The affinity between them was strengthened when Madison served on Governor Jefferson's council a few years later, and the two corresponded regularly and collaborated in many public endeavors through the remainder of their lives.

Shortly before his death Jefferson wrote to Madison, "The friendship which has subsisted between us, now half a century, and the harmony of our political principles and pursuits, have been sources of constant happiness to me through that long period."[1] And these feelings were fully reciprocated. Madison said in 1826 that he had known Jefferson "for a period of fifty years, during which there has not been an interruption or diminution of mutual confidence and cordial friendship for a single moment in a single instance."[2] Certainly no member of the Constitutional Convention was closer to Jefferson personally, or more in agreement with his views on government, than James Madison.

---

1. TJ to James Madison (17 Feb. 1826), Bergh 16:158.
2. James Madison to Nicholas P. Trist (6 July 1826), Gaillard Hunt, ed., *The Writings of James Madison*, 9 vols. (New York: G.P. Putnam's Sons, 1900–1910), 9:247–48.

Like many other American leaders in the 1780s, Jefferson was seriously concerned about the weakness of the national government under the Articles of Confederation. At the end of his last term in Congress he told Madison that "nothing can preserve our confederacy unless the band of union, their common council, is strengthened."[3] Soon after arriving in France he began sending shipments of books to Madison. He sent nearly two hundred volumes altogether, many of them dealing with the various

James Madison, lifelong personal friend of Jefferson who came to be known as "the father of the Constitution" because of his important role in the Federal Convention of 1787. Jefferson influenced Madison's thinking through correspondence and by sending him many European books on governmental theory

forms of confederate governments attempted throughout history. According to one scholar, these had a "great and immediate effect... on Madison's constitutional studies."

On the strength of [these shipments of books] he plunged into a study of ancient and modern confederacies, using and citing authorities which previously he had not had access to. Jefferson was abroad during the fateful period when the American Constitution was

3. TJ to James Madison (1 July 1784), Bergh 4:458.

being framed and adopted, but by these indirect means he made a significant contribution to it. [4]

Another writer has described Madison's studies during this period as "probably the most fruitful piece of scholarly research ever carried out by an American." [5] His preparations now completed by the important works Jefferson had sent, Madison became the chief architect of the famous Virginia Plan, which in turn provided the basic framework for the magnificent charter of government forged by the Constitutional Convention.

After learning in late 1786 of the plan to devise a new national constitution, Jefferson was eager for all political news from America. Although his letter writing was hindered by a recent accident which had broken his right wrist (he used his left hand for several months thereafter), he wrote Madison and others to strongly urge the creation of an independent executive branch and the establishment of a "proper division of powers." One of these communications described his general views:

> To make us one nation as to foreign concerns, and keep us distinct in domestic ones, gives the outline of the proper division of powers between the general [federal] and particular [state] governments. But to enable the federal head to exercise the powers given it to best advantage, it should be organized as the particular ones are, into legislative, executive, and judiciary.

---

4. Dumas Malone, *Jefferson and the Rights of Man,* Jefferson and His Time, vol. 2 (Boston: Little, Brown and Company, 1951), p. 87.

5. From Douglass Adair's sketch of Madison in Willard Thorp, ed., *The Lives of Eighteen from Princeton* (Princeton, N.J.: Princeton University Press, 1946), p. 150.

... When last with Congress, I often proposed to members to do this. [6]

Jefferson continued to write, and as the months passed he became increasingly anxious for word from Philadelphia. It was not until November 1787, two months after the convention had adjourned, that he got his first look at the document they had produced.

The Fight for a Bill of Rights

As Jefferson studied the new Constitution, his reaction was mixed. Although he strongly favored most of its provisions, there were two features he disliked: the eligibility of the President to be reelected indefinitely, and the absence of a bill of rights. Madison was among the delegates who believed that the constitutional limitations on the power of the federal government made a specific listing of citizens' rights unnecessary, but Jefferson argued that the people deserved a better instrument of protection.

> To say... that a bill of rights was not necessary because all is reserved in the case of the general government which is not given, while in the particular ones all is given which is not reserved, might do for the audience to which it was addressed; but it is surely a *gratis dictum*, the reverse of which might just as well be said....
>
> Let me add that a bill of rights is what the people are entitled to against every government on earth, general

---

6. TJ to James Madison (16 Dec. 1786), Bergh 6:9. The following summer Jefferson wrote that the convention's guiding principle should be "to make the states one as to everything connected with foreign nations, and several as to everything purely domestic." TJ to Edward Carrington (4 Aug. 1787), Bergh 6:227. Compare TJ to John Blair (13 Aug. 1787), Bergh 6:273.

or particular, and what no just government should refuse or rest on inference. [7]

Despite its imperfections, Jefferson considered the Constitution "unquestionably the wisest ever yet presented to men." [8] Knowing that the probable alternative to its adoption was a break-up of the United States, he earnestly hoped that the document would be ratified. He was confident that its weaknesses would afterward be corrected through the amendment process. "We must take care," he wrote, "that [no] objection to the new form produces a schism in our Union. That would be an incurable evil, because near friends falling out never reunite cordially; whereas, all of us going together, we shall be sure to cure the evils of our new Constitution before they do great harm." [9]

Over the next several months he followed the ratification fight very closely. Also during this period he read *The Federalist*, a series of newspaper articles written by Madison, Alexander Hamilton, and John Jay to convince New York citizens and other Americans of the merits of

---

7. TJ to James Madison (20 Dec. 1787), Bergh 6:388–89. "By a declaration of rights," Jefferson explained to another correspondent, "I mean one which shall stipulate freedom of religion, freedom of the press, freedom of commerce against monopolies, trial by juries in all cases, no suspensions of the habeas corpus, no standing armies. These are fetters against doing evil which no honest government should decline." TJ to Alexander Donald (7 Feb. 1788), Bergh 6:425–26.

8. TJ to Colonel David Humphreys (18 Mar. 1789), Bergh 7:322.

9. TJ to Alexander Donald (7 Feb. 1788), Bergh 6:426. On another occasion he observed: "It will be more difficult, if we lose this instrument, to recover what is good in it than to correct what is bad after we shall have adopted it. It has, therefore, my hearty prayers." TJ to William Carmichael (27 May 1788), Bergh 7:29.

the Constitution. Jefferson called this work "the best commentary on the principles of government which ever was written."[10]

After the Constitution was ratified, Jefferson continued to press for a bill of rights. "Half a loaf is better than no bread," he pointed out to Madison in March 1789. "If we cannot secure all our rights, let us secure what we can."[11] Partly because he was persuaded by Jefferson's arguments, and partly to fulfill a promise made to several reluctant states during the ratification process, Madison himself sponsored the bill which resulted in the first ten amendments to the Constitution (all adopted in 1791).

Jefferson and the French Revolution

Jefferson was proud of the peaceful manner in which his countrymen had adopted their new Constitution. "We can surely boast," he said, "of having set the world a beautiful example of a government reformed by reason alone, without bloodshed." But at the same time he lamented that "the world is too far oppressed to profit by the example."[12] He had seen evidences of that oppression all around him since his arrival in France, and at first he attributed it to the "bad form of government" there.

> It is difficult to conceive how so good a people, with so good a King, so well-disposed rulers in general, so genial a climate, so fertile a soil, should be rendered so ineffectual for producing human happiness by one single curse—that of a bad form of government. But it is a fact, in spite of the mildness of their governors, the

---

10. TJ to James Madison (18 Nov. 1788), Bergh 7:183.
11. TJ to James Madison (15 Mar. 1789), Bergh 7:311.
12. TJ to Edward Rutledge (18 July 1788), Bergh 7:81.

people are ground to powder by the vices of the form of government. [13]

By 1786, however, he revised his earlier conclusion about "the mildness of their governors." He deplored the division of the French people into rigid economic and social classes, and he no longer doubted who was to blame. "If anybody thinks that kings, nobles, or priests are good conservators of the public happiness," he wrote, "send him here. It is the best school in the universe to cure him of that folly. He will see here, with his own eyes, that these descriptions of men are an abandoned confederacy against the happiness of the mass of the people."[14]

The American minister continued to observe political conditions in France as he carried out his diplomatic duties, and by August 1787 he was persuaded that "a spirit of this country is advancing towards a revolution in their constitution."[15] It was an accurate prediction, for within a few months he found himself witnessing the first stages of the French Revolution.

"Events Have Proved Their Lamentable Error"

Jefferson was widely known in France for his devotion to the rights of man, and he was highly respected among political figures there for his accomplishments as a statesman.[16] He was therefore befriended by several of

13. TJ to Mrs. Eliza House Trist (18 Aug. 1785), Bergh 5:81.

14. TJ to George Wythe (13 Aug. 1786), Bergh 5:396.

15. TJ to John Jay (6 Aug. 1787), Bergh 6:247.

16. For example, Jean-Joseph Mounier, a leader in the Patriot party, described Jefferson as a man "known for his lights and virtues, who had at

the early leaders of the French Revolution who felt that their cause could benefit from his advice. On occasion he did offer some insights to the Marquis de Lafayette and others, and in June 1789 he even prepared a "Charter of Rights for the King and Nation" for their consideration. But he was careful to avoid any direct or intimate involvement because of his position as an official representative of the American government. When invited to attend a meeting of the committee appointed by the National Assembly to draft a French constitution, he declined.

The Marquis de Lafayette, who had fought heroically for America during the Revolutionary War. He and other political leaders in France sought Jefferson's advice in the early stages of the French Revolution.

> I excused myself on the obvious considerations that my mission was to the King as chief magistrate of the nation, [and] that my duties were limited to the concerns of my own country and forbade me to intermeddle with the internal transactions of that in which I had been received under a specific character only. 17

---

the same time the experience and the theory of institutions proper for the maintenance of liberty." Quoted in Malone, *Jefferson and the Rights of Man*, p. 230.

17. Autobiography (1821), Bergh 1:154.

In later years, after the French Revolution had turned to violence and America's relations with France had deteriorated, Jefferson's political enemies depicted him as a wild-eyed Jacobin (French radical) who advocated anarchy and mobocracy. But his private communications to the French revolutionary leaders amply demostrate the falsity of these accusations. While he was in Paris, he repeatedly advised Lafayette and other heads of the Patriot party to proceed with moderation as the people gained more experience with self-rule. "Should they attempt more than the established habits of the people are ripe for," he believed, "they may lose all, and retard indefinitely the ultimate object of their aim."[18] His consistent recommendation was that they seek compromises with the King and achieve their political reforms a step at a time.

One such occasion arose in June 1789, just four months before his departure from France. Following a heated confrontation between certain members of the National Assembly and the ministers of Louis XVI, "the leading patriots of the Assembly" sought Jefferson's counsel.

> I urged, most strenuously, an immediate compromise to secure what the government was ready to yield, and trust to future occasions for what might still be wanting.... With the exercise of these powers they could obtain, in future, whatever might be further necessary to improve and preserve their constitution.

---

18. TJ to Madame la Comtesse de Tesse (20 Mar. 1787), Bergh 6:105. "The misfortune," wrote Jefferson, "is that they [the French people] are not yet ripe for receiving the blessings to which they are entitled." TJ to James Madison (18 Nov. 1788), Bergh 7:184.

They thought otherwise, however, and events have proved their lamentable error. [19]

"The Appeal to the Rights of Man ...Is Irresistible"

Jefferson had great hopes that the French Revolution would signal the ultimate expansion of republican forms of government throughout the Western world. "I look with great anxiety," he wrote, "for the firm establishment of the new government in France, being perfectly convinced that if it takes place there it will spread sooner or later all over Europe. On the contrary, a check there would retard the revival of liberty in other countries." [20]

He knew that victory in this noble cause would not come without a struggle; the French people, he said, should not "expect to be translated from despotism to liberty in a featherbed." [21] But he suffered bitter disappointment as he saw the movement degenerate into extremism and bloodshed after his departure from France. Years later, he admitted that John Adams had been right in predicting that the revolution would fail to produce a free republic— but even then he was not willing to give up hope for the future:

> Your prophecies [about the French Revolution] proved truer than mine.... The destruction of eight or ten millions of human beings has probably been the effect of these convulsions. I did not, in 1789, believe they would have lasted so long, nor have cost so much blood.

---

19. Autobiography (1821), Bergh 1:139.
20. TJ to Colonel George Mason (4 Feb. 1791), Bergh 8:123–24.
21. TJ to the Marquis de Lafayette (2 Apr. 1790), Bergh 8:13.

But although your prophecy has proved true so far, I hope it does not preclude a better final result. That same light from our West seems to have spread and illuminated the very engines employed to extinguish it [i.e., the nations of Europe]. It has given them a glimmering of their rights and their power. The idea of representative government has taken root and growth among them. Their masters feel it, and are saving themselves by timely offers of this modification of their own powers. Belgium, Prussia, Poland, Lombardy, etc. are now offered a representative organization—illusive, probably, at first, but it will grow into power in the end. Opinion is power, and that opinion will come. Even France will yet attain representative government. [22]

Five years before his death, Jefferson still maintained his faith that "the rights of man" would achieve an eventual victory in Europe.

The appeal to the rights of man which had been made in the United States was taken up by France first of the European nations. From her the spirit has spread. ...The tyrants...have allied against it; but it is irresistible,...and the conditions of man through the civilized world will be finally and greatly ameliorated. [23]

Farewell to France

Having been in France longer than he expected, Jefferson felt a need to return to America, at least for a few

---

22. TJ to John Adams (11 Jan. 1816), Bergh 14:395–96. See also TJ to John Adams (28 Oct. 1813), Bergh 13:402.

23. Autobiography (1821), Bergh 1:158. For an excellent discussion of Jefferson's early views on the French Revolution, see Malone, *Jefferson and the Rights of Man*, pp. 180–83, 192–96, 214–34; see also Chinard, *Thomas Jefferson: The Apostle of Americanism*, pp. 215–41.

months, in order to look into his personal affairs and "to place my daughters in the society and care of their friends."[24] In the summer of 1789 he requested a leave of absence from George Washington, who had recently been inaugurated as the first President of the United States, and word came in August that the request was approved.

After staying several more weeks to finish up official business in Paris, the American minister sailed from France with his two daughters in the early hours of October 8, 1789. Jefferson had now served overseas for five years, and as his ship pulled out of the harbor he may have wondered whether he would truly be coming back to Europe. He later reflected on his warm feelings toward the French nation:

> A more benevolent people I have never known, nor greater warmth and devotedness in their select friendships. Their kindness and accommodation to strangers is unparalleled, and the hospitality of Paris is beyond anything I had conceived to be practicable in a large city....
>
> So, ask the travelled inhabitant of any nation, in what country on earth would you rather live? Certainly in my own, where are all my friends, my relations, and the earliest and sweetest affections and recollections of my life. Which would be your second choice? France.[25]

---

24. Autobiography (1821), Bergh 1:159.
25. Ibid., pp. 159–60.

Chapter 12

First Secretary of State

Ajoyous reception greeted the Jeffersons when they finally reached home in December 1789, just two days before Christmas. The slaves from the various family plantations were anxiously gathered four miles down the road from Monticello. This account by Martha shows the deep love they felt for their master:

> The negroes discovered the approach of the carriage as soon as it reached Shadwell, and such a scene I never witnessed in my life. They collected in crowds around it, and almost drew it up the mountain by hand....
>
> When the door of the carriage was opened, they received him in their arms and bore him to the house, crowding around and kissing his hands and feet—some blubbering and crying, others laughing. It seemed

impossible to satisfy their anxiety to touch and kiss the very earth which bore him. [1]

An Unsettling Request from President Washington

Jefferson, too, was happy to be home again. The previous year he had written from France to a friend in Richmond:

There are minds which can be pleased by honors and preferments, but I see nothing in them but envy and enmity. It is only necessary to possess them to know how little they contribute to happiness, or rather how hostile they are to it. . . .

President George Washington, who appointed Jefferson to serve in his administration as the first Secretary of State.

I had rather be shut up in a very modest cottage with my books, my family, and a few old friends, dining on simple bacon and letting the world roll on as it liked, than to occupy the most splendid post which any human power can give. [2]

But it was not Jefferson's destiny to sit at home and eat bacon. Almost as soon as he stepped on the American shore in late November 1789, he was notified that President George

---

1. Quoted in Randolph, *The Domestic Life of Thomas Jefferson*, p. 152.
2. TJ to Alexander Donald (7 Feb. 1788), Bergh 6:427.

Washington had appointed him as the first Secretary of State in the newly formed government. Jefferson received this news "with real regret."

My wish had been to return to Paris, where I had left my household establishment as if there myself, and to see the end of the [French] Revolution, which I then thought would be certainly and happily closed in less than a year. I then meant to return home, to withdraw from political life, into which I had been impressed by the circumstances of the times, to sink into the bosom of my family and friends, and devote myself to studies more congenial to my mind. [3]

Even before reaching Monticello that December, he expressed his reluctance in a letter to President Washington.

I... am truly flattered by your nomination of me to the very dignified office of Secretary of State, for which permit me here to return you my very humble thanks. Could any circumstance induce me to overlook the disproportion between its duties and my talents, it would be the encouragement of your choice. But when I contemplate the extent of that office, embracing as it does the principal mass of domestic administration together with the foreign, I cannot be insensible to my inequality to it....

But it is not for an individual to choose his post. You are to marshal us as may be best for the public good.... If you think it better to transfer me to another post, my inclination must be no obstacle. [4]

---

3. Autobiography (1821), Bergh 1:160–61.

4. TJ to President George Washington (15 Dec. 1789), Boyd 16:34–35. It will be noted from Jefferson's letter that the duties of the Secretary of State were more comprehensive in that era than at present.

With the President's further encouragement, Jefferson accepted the appointment and made plans to move to New York City, which had been the seat of national government for the last five years.

Disturbing Symptoms of Monarchism

Jefferson stayed at Monticello long enough to attend to some personal business, including the marriage of his daughter Martha to her second cousin, Thomas Mann Randolph, Jr. [5] (According to a family tradition, the two first fell in love during the summer of 1788 when Randolph was visiting Paris.) [6] The wedding took place on February 23, 1790. Jefferson was pleased with the match, as he considered his new son-in-law "a young gentleman of genius, science, and honorable mind." [7]

On the first day of March Jefferson left for New York, arriving later that month to be sworn in as Secretary of State. "Here," he wrote, "I found a state of things which, of all I had ever contemplated, I the least expected."

> I had left France in the first year of her revolution, in the fervor of natural rights and zeal for reformation. My conscientious devotion to these rights could not be heightened, but it had been aroused and excited by daily exercise. The President received me cordially, and my colleagues and the circle of principal citizens apparently with welcome. The courtesies of dinner parties given

---

5. He was the son of "Tuckahoe Tom," with whom Jefferson had lived during several years of his childhood. See chapter 2 of this biography.

6. Randall, *The Life of Thomas Jefferson*, 1:558. There is some question about the authenticity of this tradition, however. See Malone, *Jefferson and the Rights of Man*, pp. 250–51 and *n*; Betts and Bear, *The Family Letters of Thomas Jefferson*, p. 7 and *n*.

7. Autobiography (1821), Bergh 1:161.

me, as a stranger newly arrived among them, placed me at once in their familiar society. But I cannot describe the wonder and mortification with which the table conversations filled me.

Politics were the chief topic, and a preference of kingly over republican government was evidently the favorite sentiment. An apostate I could not be, nor yet a hypocrite; and I found myself for the most part the only advocate on the republican side of the question, unless among the guests there chanced to be some member of that party from the legislative houses. [8]

As the weeks passed, Jefferson saw many more evidences of these "Anglican, monarchical, and aristocratical" leanings among government officials in New York City. He was deeply disturbed by "the levees, [the] birthdays, the pompous cavalcade to the State House on the meeting of Congress, the formal speech from the throne, the procession of Congress in a body to re-echo the speech in an answer, etc., etc."

I was much astonished, indeed, at the mimicry I found established of royal forms and ceremonies, and more alarmed at the unexpected phenomenon by the monarchical sentiments I heard expressed and openly maintained in every company, and among others by the high members of the government, executive and judiciary (General Washington alone excepted), and by a great part of the legislature [i.e., Congress]. . . .

I took occasion at various times of expressing to General Washington my disappointment at these symptoms of a change of principle, and that I thought them encouraged by the forms and ceremonies which

---

8. The Anas (1818), Bergh 1:270-71.

I found prevailing, not at all in character with the
simplicity of republican government, and looking as if
wistfully to those of European courts. [9]

"He Manifested Conspicuous Ability"

These tendencies may seem strange to Americans of
today. But at the beginning of President Washington's
first administration, the newly created executive branch
had no precedent to guide it in the development of official
forms and procedures. It was only natural under those
circumstances for federal officers to pattern their
ceremonies after the familiar British model. And the very
location of the government's headquarters gave added
impetus to these inclinations, as New York City had long
been a stronghold of British sympathizers.

But the new Secretary of State believed that "the
simplicity of republican government" should be upheld in
form as well as in principle. He certainly made no attempt
personally to imitate the polished courtiers of Europe.
When he first appeared before a committee of the Senate
in May 1790, one of the Senators in attendance recorded
these interesting observations: "Jefferson...sits in a
lounging manner on one hip, commonly, and with one of
his shoulders elevated much above the other.... His
whole figure has a loose, shackling air...and nothing
of that firm, collected deportment which I expected would
dignify the presence of a Secretary or Minister. I looked
for gravity, but a laxity of manner seemed shed about
him." [10]

9. TJ to Martin Van Buren (29 June 1824), Bergh 16:59–60.

10. *The Journal of William Maclay, United States Senator from Pennsylvania,
1789–1791* (New York: Albert & Charles Boni, 1927), pp. 265–66.

Very few attempted to criticize his performance as a member of the President's Cabinet, however. As indicated in this statement by Daniel Webster, who himself served as Secretary of State fifty years later, Jefferson was highly effective in carrying out the duties of his office:

> He was placed at the head of the Department of State. In this situation . . . he manifested conspicuous ability. His correspondence with the ministers of other powers residing here, and his instructions to our own diplomatic agents abroad, are among our ablest state papers. A thorough knowledge of the laws and usages of nations, perfect acquaintance with the immediate subject before him, [and] great felicity . . . in writing show themselves in whatever effort his official situation called on him to make. [11]

Accomplishments in the State Department

Jefferson played a very active role as Secretary of State, a position which in those days required him to be involved in many domestic matters as well as foreign relations. Even though he was allowed a staff of only five persons— the Treasury Department, by contrast, boasted about seventy employees—his accomplishments during his four-year term of office were remarkable.

Among his most permanent and far-reaching achievements was the establishment of the principle that the United States should recognize any foreign government "which is formed by the will of the nation substantially declared." [12]

---

11. "Adams and Jefferson," discourse delivered in Boston (2 Aug. 1826), *The Works of Daniel Webster*, 6 vols. (Boston: Little, Brown and Company, 1851), 1:140.

12. TJ to Gouverneur Morris (7 Nov. 1792), Bergh 8:437.

We surely cannot deny to any nation that right whereon our own government is founded, that every one may govern itself according to whatever form it pleases, and change these forms at its own will; and that it may transact its business with foreign nations through whatever organ it thinks proper, whether king, convention, assembly, committee, president, or anything else it may choose. The will of the nation is the only thing essential to be regarded.[13]

Despite his personal attachment to France, Jefferson advocated American neutrality during the wars then being waged in Europe. His efforts in this regard helped produce the Neutrality Proclamation of 1793, which laid the groundwork of the nation's foreign policy for the next century.[14] He also directed negotiations with Spain which provided American shippers with guaranteed rights of navigation on the Mississippi River.

After playing a prominent role in the decision to locate the future federal city of Washington on the banks of the Potomac, Jefferson helped prepare a plan for the layout of the city. (For example, today's "mall" near Pennsylvania Avenue resulted from his sketches.) He then produced architectural drawings which influenced the design of the

---

13. TJ to Gouverneur Morris (12 Mar. 1793), Bergh 9:36–37.

14. Some historians have stated that Jefferson resisted a neutral stance because of his sympathies for the French cause, and that he was "chagrined" by the issuing of the Neutrality Proclamation. This is not true. In fact, a month *before* the proclamation was adopted he was urging American diplomats abroad to "preserve the line of neutrality. We wish not to meddle with the internal affairs of any country, nor with the general affairs of Europe." TJ to C.W.F. Dumas (24 Mar. 1793), Bergh 9:56.

Capitol building and the Executive Mansion (later known as the White House).[15]

As Secretary of State, Jefferson was authorized by Congress to issue patents for new inventions submitted to the federal government. Already the "father" of so many things, he came to be called the "father of the Patent Office" because of the deep interest he took in this function. He conducted detailed examinations of the new devices and personally signed patents for many of them. One of these was given to Eli Whitney for an invention called the cotton gin.[16]

---

15. See Saul K. Padover, ed., *Thomas Jefferson and the National Capital* (Washington: United States Government Printing Office, 1946).

16. See TJ to Eli Whitney (16 Nov. 1793), Ford 6:448; Curtis, *The True Thomas Jefferson*, p. 377. See also Malone, *Jefferson and the Rights of Man*, pp. 281–85.

Chapter 13

Jefferson Versus Hamilton

J efferson proved himself an able and innovative
leader in the State Department, but he never felt
at home there. "I am sincerely mortified," he
wrote President Washington in 1791, "to be... brought
forward on the public stage, where to remain, to advance,
or to retire will be equally against my love of silence
and quiet, and my abhorrence of dispute."[1] Most of the
"dispute" he was alluding to resulted from his stormy
relationship with the Secretary of the Treasury, Alexander
Hamilton.

Hamilton repeatedly meddled in foreign affairs, which
were the province of the Department of State, and always
with an eye toward strengthening ties between the United

---

1. TJ to President George Washington (8 May 1791), Bergh 8:194.

States and Great Britain. But of even greater concern to Jefferson were his colleague's political principles. On one occasion, Jefferson noted, he had heard Hamilton state that the American Constitution "was a shilly-shally thing of mere milk and water, which could not last, and was only good as a step to something better."[2] Hamilton, believing in a strong central government, favored a very broad interpretation of the Constitution; Jefferson took the opposite position.

The philosophical distance between the two men soon became obvious, especially in Cabinet meetings. "In these discussions," wrote Jefferson, "Hamilton and myself were daily pitted in the Cabinet like two cocks."[3] They expressed opposing views on almost every major issue that came before the Washington administration.

The National Bank Controversy

In December 1790, Hamilton submitted to Congress a proposal calling for the repayment of foreign and domestic debts through the issuing of new federal loans. He also recommended that the state debts incurred during the Revolutionary War be assumed by the national government. (This proved to be a very controversial measure because it was designed to benefit primarily the wealthy speculators, mostly in New England, who were buying up the severely discounted promissory notes issued to soldiers and farmers during the war.)

---

2. The Anas (1 Oct. 1792), Bergh 1:318. According to Jefferson, Hamilton favored the adoption of a constitution very much like that of England, which he considered "the most perfect government which ever existed." The Anas (1818), Bergh 1:279.

3. TJ to Dr. Walter Jones (5 Mar. 1810), Bergh 12:371.

At the same time, Hamilton proposed the creation of a "Bank of the United States" to handle his funding system. Although this institution would act in behalf of the federal government, it would be owned and operated by private bankers and stockholders. The bank, wrote Hamilton, was to be established "under a *private*, not a *public*, direction—under the guidance of *individual interest*, not of *public policy*."[4] By introducing these plans, the Secretary of the Treasury was emerging as a powerful friend and spokesman of the nation's financial and commercial interests, some of which were based in Europe.

Alexander Hamilton, the first Secretary of the Treasury, whose political ideas differed greatly from Jefferson's. "Hamilton and myself were daily pitted in the Cabinet like two cocks," Jefferson later wrote.

Jefferson and several others were alarmed at this proposal because it delegated to the bankers the power to issue money for the United States—a function which the Constitution had reserved to Congress. This transfer of power would require the government to borrow its own money from the new privately owned bank.[5]

4. Second Report on the Further Provision Necessary for Establishing Public Credit (13 Dec. 1790), Harold C. Syrett, ed., *The Papers of Alexander Hamilton*, 26 vols. (New York: Columbia University Press, 1961–79), 7:331.

5. The Federal Reserve Act of 1913 created a very similar arrangement which has prevailed in this century. The Federal Reserve System has come

James Madison vigorously fought Hamilton's bill in the House of Representatives, but it passed both houses of Congress and was submitted for the President's signature in February 1791. Washington, uncertain about the constitutionality of the legislation, asked Madison to prepare a veto message for his consideration. He then requested the views of his Cabinet members.

Jefferson, who had acknowledged years before that he was "not a friend to a very energetic government,"[6] argued that the Constitution did not authorize the establishment of a national bank. Excerpts from his written opinion to President Washington provide important insights into his political philosophy:

> I consider the foundation of the Constitution as laid on this ground: that "all powers not delegated to the United States by the Constitution, nor prohibited by it to the states, are reserved to the states or to the people." . . . To take a single step beyond the boundaries thus specifically drawn around the powers of Congress is to take possession of a boundless field of power, no longer susceptible of any definition.
>
> The incorporation of a bank, and the powers assumed by this bill, have not, in my opinion, been delegated to the United States by the Constitution. They are not among the powers specially enumerated. . . .
>
> It has been urged that a bank will give great facility or convenience in the collection of taxes. Suppose this were true; yet the Constitution allows only the means which are "necessary," not those which are merely "conve-

---

under severe criticism in recent years, and some Congressmen are now calling for a repeal of the 1913 legislation.

6. TJ to James Madison (20 Dec. 1787), Bergh 6:391.

nient," for effecting the enumerated powers. If such a latitude of construction be allowed to this phrase as to give any non-enumerated power, it will go to every one, for there is not one which ingenuity may not torture into a convenience in some instance or other. [7]

But the President—deeply concerned over the desperate condition of national finances, and believing that the measure was only temporary—listened to Hamilton's arguments instead and decided to sign the bill. This action established the principle of "implied powers" and created the First Bank of the United States in Philadelphia.

"A System... for Deluging the States with Paper Money"

The Secretary of State continued to believe that the "national bank" was unconstitutional. [8] He also voiced other objections to Hamilton's financial program, which he said had been devised "as a machine for the corruption of the [Congress].... And with grief and shame it must be acknowledged that his machine was not without effect; that even in this, the birth of our government, some members were found sordid enough to bend their duty to their interests, and to look after personal rather than

---

7. Opinion against the constitutionality of a national bank (15 Feb. 1791), Bergh 3:146–52.

8. Over a decade later, during his first term as President, Jefferson declared that the Bank of the United States was an institution "of the most deadly hostility existing, against the principles and form of our Constitution.... I deem no government safe which is under the vassalage of any self-constituted authorities, or any other authority than that of the nation or its regular functionaries." TJ to Albert Gallatin (13 Dec. 1803), Bergh 10:437–38.

public good."[9] In a conversation with President Washington in February 1792, he explained how this corruption had manifested itself:

> I told him ... that it was a fact, as certainly known as that he and I were then conversing, that particular members of the [Congress], while those laws were on the carpet, had feathered their nests with paper, had then voted for the laws, and consistently since [had] lent all the energy of their talents, and instrumentality of their offices, to the establishment and enlargement of this system.[10]

Two elements in Hamilton's funding bill—the federal government's assumption of state debts, and the attractive interest rates of the "scrip" issued by the national bank—soon resulted in a widespread spirit of financial speculation. Observing this, Jefferson charged that the Treasury Department had contrived "a system ... for deluging the states with paper money instead of gold and silver, [and] for withdrawing our citizens from the pursuits of commerce, manufactures, buildings, and other branches of useful industry to occupy themselves and their capitals in a species of gambling."[11]

> Ships are lying idle at the wharves, buildings are stopped, capitals withdrawn from commerce, manufactures, arts, and agriculture to be employed in gambling; and the tide of public prosperity almost unparalleled in any country is arrested in its course, and suppressed by the rage of getting rich in a day. No mortal can tell where this will stop, for the spirit

---

9. The Anas (1818), Bergh 1:271.
10. The Anas (1 Mar. 1792), Bergh 1:290–91.
11. Ibid., p. 290.

of gaming, when once it has seized a subject, is incurable. The tailor who has made thousands in one day, though he has lost them the next, can never again be content with the slow and moderate earnings of his needle. [12]

When harsh economic reality descended suddenly upon New York City in early 1792, Jefferson was not surprised.

At length our paper bubble is burst.... In New York ...the bankruptcy is become general. Every man concerned in paper [is] broke, and most of the tradesmen and farmers who had been laying down money, having been tempted by these speculators to lend it to them at an interest of from 3 to 6 percent a month, have lost the whole. It is computed there is a dead loss at New York of about five millions of dollars, which is reckoned the value of all the buildings of the city; so that if the whole town had been burned to the ground it would have been just the measure of the present calamity. [13]

Finally, the Secretary of State was opposed to Hamilton's financial program because it increased the national debt while claiming to do just the reverse. The whole system was designed "as a puzzle," he said, "to exclude popular understanding and inquiry." [14] He was convinced that Hamilton had purposely complicated the system so that "neither the President nor Congress should be able to understand it, or to control him."

He succeeded in doing this, not only beyond their reach, but so that he at length could not unravel it

---

12. TJ to Edward Rutledge (25 Aug. 1791), Bergh 8:233.
13. TJ to Thomas Mann Randolph (19 Apr. 1792), Ford 5:509–10.
14. The Anas (1818), Bergh 1:271.

himself. He gave to the debt in the first instance, in funding it, the most artificial and mysterious form he could devise . . . until the whole system was involved in impenetrable fog; and while he was giving himself the airs of providing for the payment of the debt, he left himself free to add to it continually, as he did in fact, instead of paying for it. [15]

Beginnings of the Two-Party System

Jefferson and Hamilton disagreed on other national issues as well, both foreign and domestic. The opposing views of these two powerful Cabinet members, widely publicized and hotly debated in newspapers throughout the country, eventually became rallying points for the formation of two contending political parties.

Members of the "Federalist" party were concentrated primarily among the commercial and industrial interests of the northern states. They shared Hamilton's desire for a strong central government controlled by "the rich, the wise, and the well-born," and most of them advocated close relations with Great Britain. The "Republican" party, on the other hand, largely drew its strength from the agricultural populations of the southern states and the

---

15. TJ to Albert Gallatin (1 Apr. 1802), Bergh 10:306. This was written when Jefferson was President of the United States and Gallatin was his Secretary of the Treasury. In the same letter he said: "I think it an object of great importance . . . to simplify our system of finance and bring it within the comprehension of every member of Congress. . . . We might hope to see the finances of the Union as clear and intelligible as a merchant's books, so that every member of Congress, and every man of any mind in the Union, should be able to comprehend them, to investigate abuses, and consequently to control them." Ibid., pp. 306–8.

western territories.[16] Like Jefferson, the Republicans favored a limited government which respected states' rights and allowed for broad citizen participation. During the European conflicts of the time they generally sided with France, at least in the early part of that country's revolution.

The philosophical differences between the Federalists and the Republicans were destined to exert an immeasurable influence on American politics for many generations. But while Jefferson was Secretary of State he did not look upon these "parties" as formal organizations. Nor did he yet consider himself a party leader. His only intent was to further the cause of republicanism (spelled with a small "r"), to protect the Constitution, and to prevent the "monarchists" from consolidating power in the federal government.

Thoughts of Home

In late 1790, less than a year after Jefferson became Secretary of State, the federal government moved its headquarters from New York City to Philadelphia while awaiting construction of roads and public buildings in the future city of Washington. But Philadelphia was still far from Monticello, and Jefferson sorely missed the tranquil scenes of his mountaintop home. He never did enjoy the heat of political battles, and almost from the beginning of his present appointment he dreaded "the table piled with

16. It should be noted that the political movement known in the 1790s as the Republican party was later called the Democratic-Republican party, and eventually the Democratic party. Today's Republican party is of later origin.

papers and the eternal sound of the doorbell."[17] Soon after the State Department settled into its new offices in Philadelphia, he complained of having "not one moment's repose from business from the first to the last moment of the week."[18]

He especially missed his family. His thirteen-year-old daughter Mary came to live with him in the fall of 1791, but Martha and her husband remained at Monticello. And there was now another attraction to draw Jefferson's thoughts back to Virginia: his first grandchild, Anne Cary Randolph, had come into the world that year. As the months passed by, Jefferson began to consider when he might appropriately hand over the reins of the State Department to someone better suited to public life. In early 1792 he wrote Martha that he was

> always impressed with the desire of being at home once more, and of exchanging labor, envy, and malice for ease, domestic occupation, and domestic love and society, where I may once more be happy with you, with Mr. Randolph, and dear little Anne, with whom even Socrates might ride on a stick without being ridiculous. [19]

A few weeks later Jefferson decided to resign in March 1793, at the end of President Washington's first term. In another letter to his oldest daughter he said that it would be "a relief to be withdrawn from the torment of the scenes amidst which we are. Spectators of the heats and

---

17. TJ to David Rittenhouse (12 Aug. 1792), quoted in Malone, *Jefferson and the Rights of Man*, p. 458.

18. TJ to Martha Jefferson Randolph (23 Dec. 1790), Betts and Bear, *The Family Letters of Thomas Jefferson*, p. 67.

19. TJ to Martha Jefferson Randolph (15 Jan. 1792), Betts and Bear, p. 93.

tumults of conflicting parties, we cannot help partici-
pating of their feelings.... The ensuing year will be the
longest of my life, and the last of such hateful labors.
The next we will sow our cabbages together."[20]

"I Am Going to Virginia"

After learning of Jefferson's plans, the President tried
several times during 1792 to dissuade his Secretary of
State. He expressed the wish that he could be the
"mediator" to resolve the differences between Hamilton
and Jefferson, believing that these were partly responsible
for the latter's decision to resign. He also told Jefferson
that "he thought it important to preserve the check of my
opinions in the administration, in order to keep things
in their proper channel and prevent them from going
too far."[21]

As much as he longed to return home, Jefferson finally consented to stay in office until the end of 1793. This
turned out to be fortunate for the American government,
as the first year of Washington's second term presented
some very delicate problems in foreign relations.
Jefferson, characteristically, did not slacken in his attention to his public duties. But in private circles he made
no secret of his inclinations. That summer he shared his
feelings with James Madison:

> The motion of my blood no longer keeps time with the
> tumult of the world. It leads me to seek for happiness in
> the lap and love of my family, in the society of my
> neighbors and my books, in the wholesome occupations

---

20. TJ to Martha Jefferson Randolph (22 Mar. 1792), Betts and Bear, p. 96.
21. The Anas (1 Oct. 1792), Bergh 1:317.

of my farm and my affairs, in an interest or affection in every bud that opens, in every breath that blows around me, in an entire freedom of rest, of motion, of thought, owing account to myself alone of my hours and actions. [22]

At last the day came. On December 31, 1793, he submitted his formal resignation to President Washington. He had served in the Cabinet for four long years, and it was with a sense of great relief that he left Philadelphia in early January.

I am going to Virginia.... I am then to be liberated from the hated occupations of politics and to remain in the bosom of my family, my farm, and my books. I have my house to build, my fields to farm, and to watch for the happiness of those who labor for mine. [23]

"The length of my tether is now fixed for life from Monticello to Richmond," he told a friend after he got home. "My private business can never call me elsewhere, and certainly politics will not." [24]

---

22. TJ to James Madison (9 June 1793), Bergh 9:119.

23. TJ to Mrs. Angelica Church (27 Nov. 1793), Ford 6:455-56.

24. TJ to General Horatio Gates (3 Feb. 1794), in Gardner et al., *Thomas Jefferson: A Biography in His Own Words*, p. 250.

Chapter 14

"My Family, My Farm, and My Books"

Although governmental duties had kept him away from his plantations during much of his adult life, Jefferson had always thought of himself as a man of the soil. Several months before resigning as Secretary of State he had written, "When I first entered on the stage of public life (now twenty-four years ago), I came to a resolution never to . . . wear any other character than that of a farmer."[1] As soon as the weather permitted following his return to Monticello in early 1794, he completely immersed himself in agriculture. That spring he wrote to President Washington:

---

1. TJ to an unknown correspondent (18 Mar. 1793), Bergh 9:44–45. "Those who labor in the earth," he believed, "are the chosen people of God, if ever He had a chosen people." *Notes on the State of Virginia* (1782), Bergh 2:229.

I return to farming with an ardor which I scarcely knew in my youth, and which has got the better entirely of my love of study. Instead of writing ten or twelve letters a day, which I have been in the habit of doing as a thing in course, I put off answering my letters now, farmer-like, till a rainy day, and then find them sometimes postponed by other necessary occupations. [2]

"I find on . . . examination of my lands," he noted, "that a ten years' abandonment of them to the ravages of overseers has brought on them a degree of degradation far beyond what I had expected." [3] So he developed an elaborate six-year crop-rotation plan and experimented with various types of farm machinery. It was also during these years that he perfected his design for an improved plow—the "moldboard of least resistance"—which later brought international acclaim.

An eighteenth-century plow showing Jefferson's "moldboard of least resistance," which he designed and perfected during his farming years at Monticello. The greatly improved design was widely acclaimed in America and Europe.

2. TJ to President George Washington (25 Apr. 1794), Bergh 9:283–84.
3. TJ to President George Washington (14 May 1794), Bergh 9:287.

"I Found Him in the Midst of the Harvest"

In the summer of 1796 Monticello was visited by the Duc de la Rochefoucauld-Liancourt, formerly president of the French National Assembly. This notable statesman was surprised to discover that the former American minister to France worked in the fields alongside his servants:

> In private life Mr. Jefferson displays a mild, easy, and obliging temper, though he is somewhat cold and reserved. His conversation is of the most agreeable kind, and he possesses a stock of information not inferior to that of any other man.
>
> In Europe he would hold a distinguished rank among men of letters, and as such he has already appeared there; at present he is employed with activity and perseverance in the management of his farms and buildings; and he orders, directs, and pursues in the minutest detail every branch of business relative to them. I found him in the midst of the harvest, from which the scorching heat of the sun does not prevent his attendance....
>
> As he cannot expect any assistance from the two small neighboring towns, every article is made on his farm.... His superior mind directs the management of his domestic concerns with the same abilities, activity, and regularity which he evinced in the conduct of public affairs, and which he is calculated to display in every situation of life. [4]

4. The Duc de la Rochefoucauld-Liancourt, *Travels Through the United States of North America, the Country of the Iroquois, and Upper Canada in the Years 1795, 1796, and 1797,* 2 vols. (London: Printed for R. Phillips, 1799), 2:79–80.

As the Frenchman noted, virtually "every article" used at Monticello was produced at Monticello. Jefferson wanted each of his plantations to be as self-sustaining as possible. During his years at home he designed and set up a small nail factory, a flour mill, a blacksmith shop, a textile operation, and several other manufactories. Products not used on his estate were sold in Charlottesville, Richmond, and elsewhere.

Jefferson had an intimate knowledge of everything on his farms—the name of every tree, which trees were diseased, how many seeds were needed to plant an acre of ground—he even directed which pigs were to be killed for food. He always carried a small pocket ruler with him to measure the growth of tree trunks, flowers, crops, and domestic animals, and he kept meticulous records of all these measurements to assist him in his agricultural plans for the future. [5]

"Row for Your Lives!"

Among the best sources of information about Jefferson's life at Monticello are the recollections of Captain Edmund Bacon, chief overseer of the plantation for sixteen years. Although Bacon's service in this position occurred during a later period (he was hired in 1806), several of his reminiscences are quoted in this chapter because of what they reveal about Jefferson during his domestic years. For example, Bacon recalled that his employer never seemed to get upset or angry when things went wrong on the farm.

---

5. See Edwin T. Martin, *Thomas Jefferson: Scientist* (New York: Henry Schuman, 1952), pp. 20–21; Curtis, *The True Thomas Jefferson,* p. 107; Bear, *Jefferson at Monticello,* pp. 47, 51–57, 65–68.

His countenance was always mild and pleasant. You never saw it ruffled. No odds what happened, it always maintained the same expression....

I have rode over the plantation, I reckon, a thousand times with Mr. Jefferson, and when he was not talking he was nearly always humming some tune, or singing in a low tone to himself. [6]

He could get excited, however, when occasion required it. Once, when he and his daughter Martha were having some belongings ferried across a river, a fight broke out between the two ferrymen. "They ceased to use their oars or to steer the boat, which drifted swiftly towards some dangerous rapids. Mr. Jefferson spoke to them calmly, and then sternly, but they paid no attention to him." [7]

The next moment, with his eyes flashing, he had snatched up an oar and, in a voice which rang out above the angry tones of the men, flourished it over their heads and cried out, "Row for your lives, or I will knock you both overboard!" And they did row for their lives; nor . . . did they soon forget the fiery looks and excited appearance of that tall . . . figure brandishing the heavy oar over their offending heads. [8]

No Tobacco, No Profanity, No Cards

Captain Bacon also recorded other interesting observations on Jefferson's appearance, character, and activities during his years at Monticello. The following excerpts are taken from Bacon's account:

---

6. Bear, pp. 71, 83.
7. Randall, *The Life of Thomas Jefferson*, 3:510.
8. Randolph, *The Domestic Life of Thomas Jefferson*, p. 322.

Mr. Jefferson...was like a fine horse; he had no surplus flesh. He had an iron constitution and was very strong. He had a machine for measuring strength. There were very few men that I have seen try it that were as strong in the arms as his son-in-law, Colonel Thomas Mann Randolph; but Mr. Jefferson was stronger than he. He always enjoyed the best of health.

Mr. Jefferson was always an early riser—arose at daybreak or before. The sun never found him in bed. I used sometimes to think, when I went up there *very* early in the morning, that I would find him in bed; but there he would be before me, walking on the terrace.

He did not use tobacco in any form. He never used a profane word or anything like it. He never played cards. I never saw a card in the house at Monticello.

He never ate much hog meat. He often told me, as I was giving out meat for the servants, that what I gave one of them for a week would be more than he would use in six months.... He was very fond of vegetables and fruit and raised every variety of them.

Every day, just as regularly as the day came, unless the weather was very bad, he would have his horse brought out and take his ride. The boy who took care of his horse knew what time he started, and would bring him out for him, and hitch him in his place. He generally started about nine o'clock. He was an uncommonly fine rider—sat easily upon his horse and always had him in the most perfect control.

Mr. Jefferson was very liberal and kind to the poor.... People all about the country would...come in crowds to Monticello to beg him. He would give them notes to me directing me what to give them.... I could hardly get it hauled as fast as he would give it away. [9]

Another source of information about Jefferson's activities at Monticello was one of his slaves, a young man named Isaac. Many years after Jefferson died, when Isaac was in his sixties, he shared these recollections with an interviewer:

> Old Master had abundance of books; sometimes would have twenty of 'em down on the floor at once— read fust one, then tother. Isaac has often wondered how Old Master came to have such a mighty head; read so many of them books; and when they go to him to ax him anything, he go right staight to the book and tell you all about it.
>
> He kept three fiddles; played in the arternoons and sometimes arter supper.... Mr. Jefferson always singing when ridin' or walkin'; hardly see him anywhar outdoors but what he was a-singin'. Had a fine clear voice.
>
> Old Master very kind to servants. [10]

Jim Hubbard and the Stolen Nails

The overseer, Bacon, was more explicit about Jefferson's treatment of the slaves at Monticello.

---

9. Scattered excerpts from Bear, pp. 71–76.

10. Ibid., pp. 12–13. These reminiscences were dictated to a Virginia historian named Charles Campbell in the 1840s. Isaac, like many slaves in that era, eventually assumed the surname of his master. He was the son of Great George, the faithful servant who had saved Jefferson's silver and other valuables from a British cavalry unit in 1781. Douglass Adair, *Fame and the Founding Fathers: Essays by Douglass Adair*, ed. Trevor Colbourn (New York: W.W. Norton & Co., Inc., 1974), p. 171.

> Mr. Jefferson was always very kind and indulgent to his servants. He would not allow them to be at all overworked, and he would hardly ever allow one of them to be whipped. His orders to me were constant: that if there was any servant that could not be got along without the chastising that was customary, to dispose of him. He could not bear to have a servant whipped, no odds how much he deserved it. [11]

Bacon remembered an incident involving a young slave named Jim Hubbard who worked in the nail factory. One day, while Bacon was filling an order, he noticed that all the eightpenny nails were missing. He later discovered that Jim had stolen them and hidden them in a tree.

> Mr. Jefferson was at home at the time, and when I went up to Monticello I told him of it. He was very much surprised and felt very badly about it. Jim had always been a favorite servant. He told me to be at my house next morning when he took his ride, and he would see Jim there.
>
> When he came, I sent for Jim, and I never saw any person, white or black, feel as badly as he did when he saw his master. He was mortified and distressed beyond measure. He had been brought up in the shop, and we all had confidence in him. Now his character was gone. The tears streamed down his face, and he begged pardon over and over again. I felt very badly myself.
>
> Mr. Jefferson turned to me, and said, "Ah, sir, we can't punish him. He has suffered enough already." He then talked to him, gave him a heap of good advice, and sent him to the shop. Grady [supervisor of the nailery] had waited, expecting to be sent for to whip him, and he was

---

11. Ibid., p. 97.

astonished to see him come back and go to work after such a crime.

When he [Grady] came to dinner—he boarded with me then—he told me that when Jim came back to the shop, he said, "Well, I'se been a'seeking religion a long time, but I never heard anything before that sounded so, or made me feel so, as I did when master said, 'Go, and don't do so any more'; and now I'se determined to seek religion till I find it." And sure enough, he afterwards came to me for a permit to go and be baptized. I gave him one and never knew of his doing anything of the sort again. He was always a good servant afterwards. [12]

During the Civil War, when Bacon was a very old man, he recalled that Jefferson had given freedom to a number of the Monticello slaves in his will. "I think he would have freed all of them," he said, "if his affairs had not been so much involved that he could not do it." [13] (He was referring to the serious indebtedness of the estate at the time of Jefferson's death.)

No servants ever had a kinder master than Mr. Jefferson's. He did not like slavery. I have heard him talk a great deal about it. He thought it a bad system. I have heard him prophesy that we should have just such trouble with it as we are having now. [14]

"All My Wishes End, Where I Hope My Days Will End, at Monticello"

It is unlikely that anyone loved being home more than Thomas Jefferson. Several years earlier, when he was

12. Ibid., pp. 97–99.
13. Ibid., p. 102.
14. Ibid., p. 103.

living in France, he wrote a friend about the feelings he had for his little mountain in Virginia:

> I am as happy nowhere else, and in no other society, and all my wishes end, where I hope my days will end, at Monticello. Too many scenes of happiness mingle themselves with all the recollections of my native woods and fields to suffer them to be supplanted in my affection by any other. [15]

Especially appealing to him were the breathtaking scenes of beauty which the seasons produced on all sides as he gazed out from the heights of his elevated mansion. On one occasion he became almost poetic as he described the visual wonders surrounding his "own dear Monticello."

> Where has nature spread so rich a mantle under the eye? Mountains, forests, rocks, rivers. With what majesty do we there ride above the storms! How sublime to look down into the workhouse of nature, to see her clouds, hail, snow, rain, thunder, all fabricated at our feet! And the glorious sun, when rising as if out of a distant water, just gilding the tops of the mountains, and giving life to all nature! [16]

Jefferson started building his residence in 1769, and he finished it in 1782—the original version, that is. "Monticello house was pulled down in part and built up again some six or seven times," said his servant Isaac. "They was forty years at work upon that house before Mr. Jefferson stopped building." [17] The servants may have

---

15. TJ to Dr. George Gilmer (11 Aug. 1787), Bergh 6:265.
16. TJ to Maria Cosway (12 Oct. 1786), Bergh 5:436–37.
17. Bear, pp. 3–4.

A modern photograph of the west front of Monticello. Jefferson himself designed and built the unusual mountaintop home, and he often said that he was "as happy nowhere else."

grown weary of this never-ending project, but the builder himself certainly did not. He reportedly once stated that "architecture is my delight, and putting up and pulling down one of my favorite amusements."[18]

It was an impressive structure. Rochefoucauld-Liancourt, the French statesman who visited Jefferson in the summer of 1796, believed that Monticello was "infinitely superior to all other houses in America in point of taste and convenience;...and his new plan, the execution of which is already much advanced, will be accomplished before the end of next year, and then his

18. Quoted in B.L. Rayner, *Sketches of the Life, Writings, and Opinions of Thomas Jefferson* (New York: A. Francis and W. Boardman, 1832), p. 524.

house will certainly deserve to be ranked with the most pleasant mansions in France and England."[19]

Major structural changes were begun in early 1794, soon after Jefferson resigned as Secretary of State. Eventually the north and south wings were added, the east front was rebuilt, and a dome—inspired by the Hotel de Salm in Paris—was placed on top. The interior also was perpetually being remodeled. The house took its present form in 1809, although various minor alterations continued until Jefferson's death in 1826.

A Very Unusual House

The design of Jefferson's home was unprecedented. While other Virginia mansions were built along the lowland waterways and surrounded by ugly service buildings, Monticello sat on an airy hilltop whose beautiful landscaping was unmarred by any other structures. Jefferson had cleverly built the servants' quarters, stables, smokehouse, kitchen, and other outbuildings under the brow of a hill, on the back side of the main residence; they were hidden from public view beneath grassy terraces and were connected by tunnels to the basement of the house.

On one side of the mountain was a quiet park enclosed by a high fence, where Jefferson raised deer and other animals from the surrounding forest. The Marquis de

---

19. *Travels Through the United States of North America*, 2:70. The Marquis de Chastellux called Jefferson "the first American who has consulted the fine arts to know how he should shelter himself from the weather." *Travels in North America in the Years 1780, 1781 and 1782*, rev. ed., trans. Howard C. Rice, Jr., 2 vols. (Chapel Hill: The University of North Carolina Press, 1963), 2:391.

Chastellux, a French general who had spent several days at Monticello in 1782, recorded this interesting observation: "Mr. Jefferson having amused himself by raising a score of [deer] in a park, they soon become very tame.... He enjoys feeding them with Indian corn, of which they are very fond, and which they eat out of his hand."[20]

The home at Monticello contained thirty-five rooms behind a single-story front. There were actually four levels altogether (including the cellar), but the windows of the second-story bedrooms, extending from eye level down to the floor, appeared from the outside to be the upper portion of long first-floor windows. The highest rooms were illuminated by skylights in the ceiling.

Jefferson personally attended to every detail in the design and construction of Monticello, both inside and out. All of the stone, brick, lumber, and nails used to build the house came from the estate itself. Much of the furniture and other household articles were designed by Jefferson, who then instructed his servants to produce them (sometimes under his close supervision). He even drew up instructions for decorative items like window draperies.

One contemporary visitor to Monticello noted the "odd union" of fine art and "curiosities" displayed in the entrance hall.[21] Jefferson had purchased and imported one of the best collections of paintings and statuary in America, eventually including over sixty oils and many

---

20. *Travels in North America*, 2:394.

21. George Ticknor, quoted in Francis Coleman Rosenberger, ed., *Jefferson Reader: A Treasury of Writings About Thomas Jefferson* (New York: E.P. Dutton & Company, Inc., 1953), p. 81.

busts and figurines. Along with these he exhibited more
unusual things: the heads and horns of a moose, an elk, a
buffalo, and other large animals; antiquities and artwork
from Mexico and various Indian tribes; shell and mineral
collections; even ancient fossils and dinosaur bones.

Gadgets, Inventions, and Labor-Saving Devices

Some of the novelties which today's visitors can see at
Monticello illustrate Jefferson's curiosity and his skill as
an inventor. Examples include a clock with cannonball
weights which mark the days of the week as they descend
down a wall, a weather vane that can be read from under a
portico by means of a dial on the ceiling, and a machine for
measuring a person's strength. A few of his inventions are
quite familiar in our era: still on display in the home are his
swivel chair, his revolving tabletop, his folding campstool,
and his adjustable music stand.

Jefferson appreciated comfort and convenience. He
concealed a dumbwaiter in his fireplace mantel, and a
revolving door in the wall of his dining room, so that hot
meals could be served to his guests without the intrusion
of a servant. He installed a chain-and-sprocket assembly
under a set of double doors so that a tug on either handle
would open both doors simultaneously. His bed was
handily placed in an alcove that opened into his dressing
room on one side and his study on the other.[22]

---

22. The first edition of this biography erroneously stated, as do several
other current publications, that Jefferson's bed could be hoisted to the ceiling
to create a passageway between the adjoining rooms. We have since
consulted with historians and architects who have closely examined the
structure of Monticello, and they have assured us that this popular legend is
not true. Additional details about the home can be found in Frederick D.
Nichols and James A. Bear, Jr., *Monticello* (Monticello, Va.: Thomas Jefferson

Jefferson's bedroom and personal study at Monticello.

The Nation Beckons Again

Even before returning to Monticello in early 1794, Jefferson had vowed never to return to "the hated occupations of politics." When he was invited in the fall of that year to travel to Spain as a special envoy to negotiate a treaty for the United States, he replied to the new Secretary of State: "No circumstances, my dear sir, will ever more tempt me to engage in anything public. I thought myself perfectly fixed in this determination when

Memorial Foundation, 1967); also Joseph Judge, "Mr. Jefferson's Monticello," *National Geographic*, September 1966, pp. 426–44.

I left Philadelphia, but every day and hour since has added to its inflexibility."[23]

For a while the decision seemed to be irreversible. After he had been home nearly a year he wrote to James Madison, "I would not give up my ... retirement for the empire of the universe."[24] When Madison hinted to Jefferson the following spring that many Americans wished to see him become the next President, his response was not encouraging: "The little spice of ambition which I had in my younger days has long since evaporated, and I set still less store by posthumous than present fame. ... The question is forever closed with me."[25]

But Jefferson's peaceful world of farming and home building was destined to last only three years. During this period he became increasingly concerned about the measures of the Federalist party in Congress, and he repeatedly expressed his hope that Madison or some other strong Republican would win the next presidential election. No one in that party, however, could rival Jefferson in national popularity, and there was never any real question among Republican leaders about their preferred candidate. When President George Washington announced in 1796 that he would not serve a third term, it was Madison himself who led the movement to place Jefferson's name in nomination.

"I Shall ... Rejoice at Escaping"

While Jefferson allowed this much to be done, he

---

23. TJ to Edmund Randolph (7 Sept. 1794), Bergh 9:290.
24. TJ to James Madison (28 Dec. 1794), Bergh 9:297.
25. TJ to James Madison (27 Apr. 1795), Bergh 9:303.

certainly did not engage in any campaign. Knowing that a close vote was predicted, he confided to an old friend, "I shall, from the bottom of my heart, rejoice at escaping."[26] He never left Monticello, and practically the only political letter he wrote during these months was an unusual plea to Madison: in the unlikely event of a tie vote in both the electoral college and the House of Representatives, "I pray you and authorize you fully to solicit on my behalf that Mr. Adams [Vice President John Adams, the Federalist candidate] may be preferred."

> He [Adams] has always been my senior from the commencement of our public life, and the expression of the public will being equal, this circumstance ought to give him the preference.... Let those come to the helm who think they can steer clear of the difficulties. I have no confidence in myself for the undertaking.[27]

There was no tie, but the vote was indeed a close one: 71 for Adams, 68 for Jefferson. It is remarkable that Jefferson, after absenting himself from the national scene for three years, commanded such widespread popularity—especially when he made no effort to encourage his supporters.

Although the Federalists had chosen Thomas Pinckney of South Carolina as Adams's running mate, the system which then prevailed gave Jefferson the vice presidency

---

26. TJ to Edward Rutledge (27 Dec. 1796), Bergh 9:353.
27. TJ to James Madison (17 Dec. 1796), Bergh 9:351–52.

because he had received the second largest number of electoral votes. Now fifty-three years of age, he reluctantly accepted the voice of the people and made preparations to leave Monticello once again.

Chapter 15

Statesman and Scientist

Jefferson would have preferred to be quietly sworn in as Vice President somewhere outside Philadelphia, but he finally decided to come to the city "as a mark of respect to the public."[1] However, he said, "I hope I shall be made a part of no ceremony whatever. I shall escape into the city as covertly as possible."[2]

"Friend of the People"

As it turned out, his arrival was hardly "covert." He pulled into Philadelphia on March 2, 1797. As he stepped out of his carriage, he was greeted by an artillery salute

---

1. TJ to James Madison (22 Jan. 1797), Bergh 9:367.
2. TJ to James Madison (30 Jan. 1797), Bergh 9:376.

and a large banner proclaiming "Jefferson, the Friend of the People." Two days later at the inauguration ceremony, an incident occurred that was characteristic of Jefferson's modesty:

> After the oaths of office had been administered, the President (Mr. Adams) resumed his seat for a moment, then rose and, bowing to the assembly, left the hall. Jefferson rose to follow, but seeing General Washington also rise to leave, he at once fell back to let him pass out first. The General, perceiving this, declined to go before, and forced the new Vice President to precede him. The doors of the hall closed upon them both amid the tumultuous cheering of the assembly. [3]

Jefferson, whose political views differed considerably from those of the new administration, was very seldom consulted on executive decisions. Adams, having served as Washington's Vice President, retained most of the former President's council, and Jefferson was not invited to Cabinet meetings. Although Alexander Hamilton had resigned as Secretary of the Treasury in 1795, he continued to exert a strong influence on those who remained, so Jefferson was happy to be excluded.

> I cannot have a wish to see the scenes of 1793 revived as to myself, and to descend daily into the arena like a gladiator, to suffer martyrdom in every conflict. As to duty, the Constitution will know me only as the member of a legislative body. [4]

He was referring here to his responsibility to preside over the Senate, and that proved to be virtually his only

3. Randolph, *The Domestic Life of Thomas Jefferson*, p. 242.
4. TJ to James Madison (22 Jan. 1797), Bergh 9:368.

official function during the next four years. But he certainly fulfilled it with distinction, impartially conducting the proceedings of that body and compiling a *Manual of Parliamentary Practice* which serves even today as the basis of parliamentary action in both houses of Congress. [5]

"The Tranquil Pursuits of Science"

"Nature intended me for the tranquil pursuits of science by rendering them my supreme delight," Jefferson once wrote. "But the enormities of the times in which I have lived have forced me to take a part in resisting them, and to commit myself on the boisterous ocean of political passions." [6]

He never had enjoyed the rough-and-tumble of politics, and he winced at the hot party feelings to which he was constantly exposed since his return to public life. Less than a year after assuming the vice presidency he described Philadelphia as "a dreary scene where envy, hatred, malice, revenge, and all the worse passions of men are marshalled to make one another as miserable as possible." [7] So he turned to a segment of society more to his liking.

> Politics are such a torment that I would advise everyone I love not to mix with them. I have changed my circle here according to my wish, abandoning the rich

5. See Dumas Malone, *Jefferson and the Ordeal of Liberty*, Jefferson and His Time, vol. 3 (Boston: Little, Brown and Company, 1962), pp. 453–57. Jefferson's *Manual of Parliamentary Practice* is reprinted in Bergh 2:331–450.

6. TJ to Pierre Samuel Du Pont de Nemours (2 Mar. 1809), Bergh 12:260.

7. TJ to Martha Jefferson Randolph (8 Feb. 1798), Betts and Bear, *The Family Letters of Thomas Jefferson*, p. 155.

and declining their dinners and parties, and associating entirely with the class of science. [8]

President of the American Philosophical Society

Besides being the temporary seat of national government, Philadelphia was the home of the American Philosophical Society—at that time the leading scientific organization in the United States. Jefferson, who had become a member in 1780, relished his association with this distinguished group of men. They clearly admired him also: in 1797 Jefferson was elected president of the Society, succeeding the eminent astronomer David Rittenhouse. (Benjamin Franklin, who had founded the organization in 1743, served as its president before Rittenhouse.)

Jefferson was to continue as president of the American Philosophical Society for nearly two decades. He considered his election to this post "the most flattering incident of my life."[9] And well he might, for according to Dr. Samuel Latham Mitchill (physician, scientist, and later Senator from New York), it was "as high an honor as can be conferred upon a scientific man in our country."[10]

---

8. TJ to Martha Jefferson Randolph (11 Feb. 1800), Betts and Bear, p. 184.

9. Quoted by Samuel Harrison Smith in his *Memoir of the Life, Character, and Writings of Thomas Jefferson*, an address delivered to the Columbian Institute of Washington (Washington: S.A. Elliott, Printer, 1827), p. 28. Jefferson was also an active or honorary member of many other scientific and literary societies in Europe and America.

10. Quoted in Edwin T. Martin, *Thomas Jefferson: Scientist* (New York: Henry Schuman, 1952), p. 249.

"I Had Run Against a College Professor Who Knew Everything"

Few men could have come to this position so well qualified as Thomas Jefferson. "To catalogue the areas of his exploration," wrote historian Julian Boyd, "is to list most of the principal categories of knowledge—law, government, history, mathematics, architecture, medicine, agriculture, languages and literature, education, music, philosophy, religion, and almost every branch of the natural sciences from astronomy though meteorology to zoology."[11] He had already been awarded doctoral degrees by three universities, and he was often spoken of as a "walking library."[12]

This breadth of learning is illustrated by an anecdote involving a highly educated man from New England who chanced to meet Jefferson at a country inn one evening, not knowing who he was. The man repeatedly introduced new topics into their conversation, and he was so astounded at his dinner companion's knowledge that he afterward inquired of the innkeeper regarding Jefferson's identity. The surprised New Englander later described his impressions of the enlightened statesman-farmer from Virginia:

> When he spoke of law, I thought he was a lawyer; when he talked about mechanics, I was sure he was an engineer; when he got into medicine, it was evident that he was a physician; when he discussed theology, I was

---

11. From an introductory essay in Boyd 1:viii.

12. See Samuel Harrison Smith, p. 31; also Randolph, p. 37. The doctorates were awarded by William and Mary (1783), Yale (1786), and Harvard (1788).

convinced that he must be a clergyman; when he talked of literature, I made up my mind that I had run against a college professor who knew everything. [13]

A Bona Fide Scientist

Jefferson was so highly regarded by men of science in his own day that a plant was named in his honor in 1792, the *Jeffersonia diphylla;* the citation declared that "in botany and zoology, the information of this gentleman is equalled by that of few persons in the United States." [14] He was an extremely curious person: his diaries and budget books over the years list admission fees he paid to see new inventions, wild animals, human dwarfs, wax figures, and many other novelties. [15] And we have already noted that he was good with his hands. One of his servants, a trained tinsmith, admired Jefferson's ability to fashion keys, locks, and chains out of brass and iron. [16]

When he traveled to Philadelphia in 1797 his luggage included a box of large bones, which he introduced to his fellow scientists that March as the "megalonyx," a type of giant sloth. According to one scholar, this contribution fired the "signal gun of American paleontology." [17] He also took great interest in the origins, languages, and customs of American Indians, and amassed a large number of Indian vocabularies as a part of this study.

---

13. Curtis, *The True Thomas Jefferson*, pp. 358–59; compare Randolph, p. 38.

14. Quoted in Gardner et al., *Thomas Jefferson: A Biography in His Own Words*, p. 123.

15. Martin, p. 18.

16. Bear, *Jefferson at Monticello*, p. 18.

17. Malone, *Dictionary of American Biography*, 10:33.

Jefferson was the first to state that objects found in lower sediments of soil were of more ancient origin than those uncovered near the surface—long before this was an established archaeological principle. His inventions were numerous, as indicated in the previous chapter, but he did not seek a patent on any of these, "having never thought of monopolizing by patent any useful idea which happens to offer itself to me."[18]

The "Federalist Reign of Terror"

As Jefferson proceeded through his term as Vice President, serious political concerns increasingly overshadowed his interest in science. Foreign affairs were especially problematic during the presidency of John Adams. Relations with France had degenerated to such an extent that by mid-1798 the United States was engaged in an undeclared naval war with the French Republic, and anti-French sentiment was running very high in the Federalist-controlled Congress.

That summer Congress passed four laws, known collectively as the Alien and Sedition Acts, which were designed to suppress both "foreign" (French) influence in America and Republican party opposition to the Adams administration. The extreme measures in three of these laws made them subjects of controversy throughout the nation. The Naturalization Act extended from five to fourteen years the residency requirement for American citizenship, while the Alien Act gave the President unlimited authority to expel any aliens he considered "dangerous to the peace and safety of the United

18. TJ to Charles Willson Peale (13 June 1815), Bergh 18:288.

States."[19] The Sedition Act, by far the most notorious of the bunch, authorized imprisonment of persons who conspired "with intent to oppose any measure . . . of the government"—or who produced "any false, scandalous, and malicious writing" against the federal government or its officials.[20]

Jefferson called this legislation "an experiment on the American mind to see how far it will bear an avowed violation of the Constitution,"[21] and he considered the Sedition Act a direct violation of the First Amendment right to a free press. Indeed, the editors of several Republican newspapers were subsequently arrested and convicted for having questioned the policies of the Adams administration in their columns, and other citizens were jailed, fined, and persecuted because they dared to voice their opinions.

The Kentucky Resolutions of 1798

Upset over what he called the "Federalist reign of terror,"[22] Jefferson decided that something had to be done. The Republican minority in Congress were practically helpless until the next election, and he himself could not appropriately speak out in public because of his position in the administration. So he turned to what

---

19. Reprinted in Mortimer J. Adler et al., eds., *The Annals of America*, 18 vols. (Chicago: Encyclopaedia Britannica, Inc., 1968), 4:59.

20. Ibid., p. 61.

21. TJ to Stevens Thomson Mason (11 Oct. 1798), Bergh 10:61–62.

22. Quoted in Saul K. Padover, *Jefferson* (New York: Harcourt, Brace and Company, 1942), p. 258.

he regarded as the most effective check on the federal government: the state legislatures. [23]

That fall he secretly drafted a series of resolutions which he hoped to have introduced in one or more of the state assemblies. Through the agency of a friend who agreed not to divulge the author's identity, the document was adopted in November by both legislative houses in Kentucky. The Kentucky Resolutions of 1798 have since become a classic in American political thought. Quoted here are the opening lines:

> *Resolved*, that the several states composing the United States of America are not united on the principle of unlimited submission to their general government; but that, by a compact under the style and title of a Constitution for the United States, and of amendments thereto, they constituted a general government for special purposes [and] delegated to that government certain definite powers, reserving, each state to itself, the residuary mass of right to their own self-government; and that whensoever the general government assumes undelegated powers, its acts are unauthoritative, void, and of no force. [24]

Relying on his training as a legal scholar, Jefferson went on to demonstrate that the Alien and Sedition Acts were "altogether void and of no force" because they violated a host of provisions in the federal Constitution. The final section of his composition contained these now famous words:

---

23. Even after serving as President, Jefferson believed that "the true barriers of our liberty in this country are our state governments." TJ to Destutt de Tracy (26 Jan. 1811), Bergh 13:19.

24. Reprinted in Bergh 17:379–80.

It would be a dangerous delusion were a confidence in the men of our choice to silence our fears for the safety of our rights.... Confidence is everywhere the parent of despotism. Free government is founded in jealousy, and not in confidence; it is jealousy, and not confidence, which prescribes limited constitutions to bind down those whom we are obliged to trust with power.... Our Constitution has accordingly fixed the limits to which, and no further, our confidence may go....

In questions of power, then, let no more be heard of confidence in man, but bind him down from mischief by the chains of the Constitution.[25]

The Kentucky Resolutions advocated a repeal of the Alien and Sedition Acts, as did a similar paper drafted by James Madison and adopted by the Virginia legislature in December 1798. Numerous citizens and private groups from around the country petitioned for repeal as well. The Federalists in Congress refused to hear these pleas, and the controversial legislation remained in force until the end of John Adams's presidency. But within two years the public resentment created by this episode would begin to bring about the permanent dissolution of the Federalist party.

---

25. Ibid., pp. 388–89.

Chapter 16

"An Awful Crisis"

S oon after he wrote the Kentucky Resolutions of 1798, Jefferson made another important deci- sion. In response to the urgings of many friends and countrymen who were concerned about the direction of the national government, he finally consented to step forward and become the active head of the Republican party. He believed that the Federalist excesses could be overturned

> by the people confining their choice of Representatives and Senators to persons attached to republican government and the principles of 1776.... Such men are the true representatives of the great American interest,

and are alone to be relied on for expressing the proper American sentiments.[1]

Defending "The Principles of 1776"

The national elections in 1800 were to become the battleground for returning the government to these "principles of 1776." Jefferson characteristically kept himself out of the spotlight, preferring to wield his influence through Republican Congressional leaders and newspaper editors. But although his guiding hand was seldom visible, he played a very active role in the campaign. Throughout 1799 and 1800, he held numerous private meetings and wrote scores of letters to define the principles he felt should govern national policy. One of these communications, written to Elbridge Gerry of Massachusetts, sounded almost like a party platform.

> I do...with sincere zeal wish an inviolable pres-
> ervation of our present federal Constitution according
> to the true sense in which it was adopted by the states,
> that in which it was advocated by its friends and not
> that which its enemies apprehended, who therefore
> became its enemies; and I am opposed to the monar-
> chizing its features by the forms of its administration,
> with a view to conciliate a first transition to a President
> and Senate for life, and from that to a hereditary tenure
> of these offices, and thus to worm out the elective
> principle.
>
> I am for preserving to the states the powers not
> yielded by them to the Union, and to the legislature of
> the Union [i.e., Congress] its constitutional share in the
> division of powers; and I am not for transferring all the

1. TJ to Colonel Arthur Campbell (1 Sept. 1797), Bergh 9:420-21.

powers of the states to the general government, and all those of that government to the executive branch.

I am for a government rigorously frugal and simple, applying all the possible savings of the public revenue to the discharge of the national debt; and not for a multiplication of officers and salaries merely to make partisans, and for increasing by every device the public debt on the principle of its being a public blessing....

I am for free commerce with all nations, political connection with none, and little or no diplomatic establishment. And I am not for linking ourselves by new treaties with the quarrels of Europe, entering that field of slaughter to preserve their balance or joining in the confederacy of kings to war against the principles of liberty.

I am for freedom of religion, and against all maneuvers to bring about a legal ascendancy of one sect over another; for freedom of the press, and against all violations of the Constitution to silence by force and not by reason the complaints or criticisms, just or unjust, of our citizens against the conduct of their agents. [2]

Bitter Attacks by the Federalists

Jefferson would have ample opportunity to demonstrate his commitment to "freedom of the press." In spite of his well-known desire to return to private life, there was no doubt among either Republicans or Federalists about who would be nominated to oppose President Adams in the upcoming election. Through the summer and fall of 1800, Federalist newspapers and pamphlets waged a war of vindictiveness and slander against the Vice

---

2. TJ to Elbridge Gerry (26 Jan. 1799), Bergh 10:76–78.

President. He was depicted as a French agent, an immoral profligate, and an infidel. One Jefferson scholar has written of this period:

> The personal attacks on the chief Republican were the most vicious in any presidential campaign on record. One may doubt if a more distorted picture of a candidate for the first office has ever been presented by his foes....
>
> The charge of atheism was the most pressed in this campaign: it was not only made in the public press; it was hurled from pulpits in various places.... As the story goes, the time was approaching when Bibles were to be hidden in New England's wells. [3]

"Would you not rather be scourged with sword and famine and pestilence," read one tract, "than see your country converted into a den of atheism?"[4] A journalist in New York City asked, "Do you believe in the strangest of all paradoxes—that a spendthrift, a libertine, or an atheist is qualified to make your laws and govern you and your posterity?"[5]

"I Leave Them ... to the Reproof of Their Own Consciences"

But Jefferson chose not to defend himself against these vulgar accusations, at least not publicly. "As to the

3. Malone, *Jefferson and the Ordeal of Liberty,* pp. 479, 481.

4. John M. Mason, *The Voice of Warning to Christians, on the Ensuing Election of a President of the United States* (New York, 1800), quoted in Henry F. Graff, *Illustrious Americans: Thomas Jefferson* (Morristown, N.J.: Silver Burdett Company, 1968), p. 60.

5. New York *Commercial Advertiser* (9 Oct. 1800), quoted in Malone, *Jefferson and the Ordeal of Liberty,* p. 481.

calumny of atheism," he said to James Monroe, "I am so broken to calumnies of every kind...that I entirely disregard it.... It has been so impossible to contradict all their lies that I have determined to contradict none, for while I should be engaged with one they would publish twenty new ones. [My] thirty years of public life have enabled most of those who read newspapers to judge of one for themselves."[6] Three months later he wrote:

> From the moment that a portion of my fellow-citizens looked towards me with a view to one of their highest offices, the floodgates of calumny have been opened upon me.... I know that I might have filled the courts of the United States with actions for these slanders, and have ruined perhaps many persons who are not innocent. But this would be no equivalent to the loss of character. I leave them, therefore, to the reproof of their own consciences. If these do not condemn them, there will yet come a day when the false witness will meet a Judge who has not slept over his slanders.[7]

He then proceeded to answer, for his correspondent's "own satisfaction," a recently published charge that he had obtained part of his lands in Virginia by fraud—but even this defense he wanted kept from the newspapers, "into which I have made it a point to enter on no provocation."[8] Jefferson had already determined "very early" in his life "never to put a sentence into any newspaper.... I have thought it better to trust to the justice of my countrymen, that they would judge me by

6. TJ to James Monroe (26 May 1800), Ford 7:447–48.
7. TJ to Uriah McGregory (13 Aug. 1800), Bergh 10:171.
8. Ibid., pp. 172–73.

what they *see* of my conduct on the stage where they have placed me."[9]

A Republican Victory, But for Whom?

His faith in the people proved well founded: the election that year, which Jefferson later termed "the revolution of 1800,"[10] produced decisive Republican victories in both the executive and legislative branches of the federal government. "The nation at length passed condemnation on the political principles of the Federalists by refusing to continue Mr. Adams in the presidency," wrote Jefferson.[11] On the day that the results were made public, he had occasion to call on President Adams "on some official business."

> He was very sensibly affected, and accosted me with these words: "Well, I understand that you are to beat me in this contest, and I will only say that I will be as faithful a subject as any you will have."
>
> "Mr. Adams," said I, "this is no personal contest between you and me. Two systems of principles on the subject of government divide our fellow citizens into two parties. With one of these you concur, and I with the other. As we have been longer on the public stage than most of those now living, our names happen to be more

---

9. TJ to Samuel Smith (22 Aug. 1798), Bergh 10:58–59.

10. TJ to Spencer Roane (6 Sept. 1819), Bergh 15:212. As an old man Jefferson wrote, "The contests of that day were contests of principle between the advocates of republican and those of kingly government, and . . . had not the former made the efforts they did, our government would have been, even at this early day, a very different thing from what the successful issue of those efforts have made it." The Anas (1818), Bergh 1:266. He was confirmed in his optimism by the fact that the election of 1800 was followed by twenty-four unbroken years of Republican administrations.

11. TJ to Benjamin Rush (16 Jan. 1811), Bergh 13:5.

generally known. One of these parties, therefore, has put your name at its head, the other mine. Were we both to die today, tomorrow two other names would be in the place of ours, without any change in the motion of the machinery. Its motion is from its principle, not from you or myself."

"I believe you are right," said he, "that we are but passive instruments, and should not suffer this matter to affect our personal dispositions."[12]

However, there were still several weeks of uncertainty about who would actually become the new President. Aaron Burr of New York, the Republicans' vice-presidential candidate, naturally received the same number of votes as Jefferson did in the electoral college. So it became the duty of the House of Representatives to break the tie—even though there was no question in anyone's mind about the voters' intentions. (This procedural problem in the original Constitution was corrected by the Twelfth Amendment in 1804.)

"I Would Not Go into It with My Hands Tied"

The Federalists, of course, were quite bitter about the outcome of the election. They still had control of the House until inauguration day, and they saw in this tie vote an opportunity to either prevent Jefferson from taking office or force certain concessions from him before he assumed the presidency. Their greatest fears were that he would "turn all Federalists out of office" and would "wipe off the public debt," and several leaders of the Federalist

---

12. Ibid., pp. 5–6.

party approached him privately with assurances that he needed only "to declare, or authorize my friends to declare, that I would not take these steps, and instantly the event of the election would be fixed."[13] Jefferson wrote to a friend at that time: "Many attempts have been made to obtain terms and promises from me. I have declared to them unequivocally that I would not receive the government on capitulation, that I would not go into it with my hands tied."[14]

Seeing that he would not compromise his principles, the Federalists talked openly of what Jefferson later called "a very dangerous experiment... to defeat the presidential election by an act of Congress declaring the right of the Senate to name a president of the Senate, [and] to devolve on him the government."[15] But when the plan became public, Virginia and several other states announced that "the day such an act passed [they] would arm, and that no such usurpation, even for a single day, should be submitted to."[16] The majority members of the House quickly agreed to settle the tie vote in the manner prescribed by the Constitution.

The Nation Waits in Suspense

The historic battle opened on February 11, 1801. The federal government had very recently moved to its permanent home in the city of Washington, and the House

13. The Anas (15 Apr. 1806), Bergh 1:451.
14. TJ to James Monroe (15 Feb. 1801), Bergh 10:202.
15. The Anas (15 Apr. 1806), Bergh 1:452. This would have been a president *pro tempore*. The official president of the Senate at that time, of course, was Vice President Jefferson.
16. TJ to James Monroe (15 Feb. 1801), Bergh 10:201.

of Representatives convened that morning in the north wing of the Capitol building (the only portion of that structure which was close to completion). In spite of a bad snowstorm, the Congressmen arrived promptly to take their places in the hall—including one member of the Maryland delegation who had to be carried in because he was dangerously ill. One Washington resident described the tension that filled the city:

> It was an awful crisis. The people who with such an overwhelming majority had declared their will would never peaceably have allowed the man of their choice to be set aside, and the individual they had chosen as Vice President to be put in his place. A civil war must have taken place, to be terminated in all human probability by a rupture of the Union. Such consequences were at least calculated on, and excited a deep and inflammatory interest.
>
> Crowds of anxious spirits from the adjacent county and cities thronged to the seat of government and hung like a thundercloud over the Capitol, their indignation ready to burst on any individual who might be designated as President in opposition to the people's known choice. The citizens of Baltimore...were with difficulty restrained from rushing on with an armed force to prevent—or if they could not prevent, to avenge—this violation of the people's will. [17]

The Federalists, who deeply resented the popular Republican leader, had previously agreed in a party caucus to side with Aaron Burr. But the vote was to be taken by states, not individual delegates, and in that "lame duck"

---

17. Smith, *The First Forty Years of Washington Society,* p. 22.

Congress the states were equally divided between the two parties. So on the first ballot neither Jefferson nor Burr won a majority of votes. The second ballot was also deadlocked, as were several others which followed that day. The Representatives had agreed not to separate until they had elected a President, and the impasse persisted for an entire week through more than thirty ballots. This unnerving situation began to wear on the members of the House.

> The question on which hung peace or war, nay, the union of the states, was to be decided. What an awful responsibility was attached to every vote given on that occasion! The sitting was held with closed doors. It lasted the whole day, the whole night. Not an individual left that solemn assembly; the necessary refreshment they required was taken in rooms adjoining the hall.... Beds as well as food were sent for the accommodation of those whom age or debility disabled from enduring such a long, protracted sitting. The balloting took place every hour; in the interval men ate, drank, slept, or pondered over the result of the last ballot, compared ideas and persuasions to change votes, or gloomily anticipated the consequences. [18]

"The Storm Through Which We Have Passed"

As the days crept by and the ballots multiplied without any sign of resolution, some of the Federalists resorted to desperate tactics. One of the Republican Congressmen,

---

18. Ibid., p. 23.

Matthew Lyon of Vermont, reported being approached by members of the other party and strongly urged to switch his vote. What they offered in return was very generous: "What is it you want, Colonel Lyon? Is it office, is it money? Only say what you want, and you shall have it."[19]

Members of the Senate were invited into the closed session as witnesses, and as president of that body Jefferson could not have been unaware of the stormy scenes and passionate rhetoric that darkened the proceedings of the House. But as one observer noted, the Vice President "preserved through this trying period the most unclouded serenity, the most perfect equanimity. A spectator who watched his countenance would never have surmised that he had any personal interest in the impending event."[20] Had the vote gone for Burr he would have "acquiesced in a moment," he said, "because, however it might have been variant from the intentions of the voters, yet it would have been agreeable to the Constitution. No man would more cheerfully have submitted than myself."[21] He had only one real concern, and that was expressed in a letter he wrote to his daughter Mary on February 15:

> I feel no impulse from personal ambition to the office now proposed to me, but . . . I feel a sincere wish indeed to see our government brought back to its republican principles, to see that kind of government firmly fixed to which my whole life has been devoted. I hope we shall now see it so established as that when I retire it may be

19. Quoted by Jefferson in the Anas (31 Dec. 1803), Bergh 1:442.
20. Smith, p. 23.
21. TJ to Governor Thomas McKean (9 Mar. 1801), Bergh 10:221.

Federalist Congressman James A. Bayard of Delaware, whose courageous vote in February 1801 ended a long and suspenseful deadlock in the House of Representatives and resulted in Jefferson's election as President of the United States.

under full security that we are to continue free and happy. [22]

Two days later the deadlock was broken. Congressman James A. Bayard of Delaware, being the only delegate from his state, was in a position to turn the entire election with his vote. When he announced to his Federalist colleagues that he was no longer willing "to exclude Jefferson at the expense of the Constitution," [23] they vehemently rebuked him for disloyalty to the party. But he stood firm, and on the thirty-sixth ballot Thomas Jefferson was elected President of the United States. [24] A resident of the city recorded that when the decision of the House was officially declared, "the assembled crowds [outside] the

22. TJ to Mary Jefferson Eppes (15 Feb. 1801), Betts and Bear, *The Family Letters of Thomas Jefferson*, p. 197.

23. James A. Bayard to Samuel Bayard (22 Feb. 1801), Elizabeth Donnan, ed., *Papers of James A. Bayard, 1796–1815*, Annual Report of the American Historical Association for the Year 1913, Vol. II (Washington, 1915), p. 131.

24. Bayard had also converted several wavering members of his party to his point of view, so on the final ballot the Federalist delegates from three other states joined him in abstaining. Ironically, the outcome of the election may have been due in part to the influence of Alexander Hamilton, who wrote letters urging Bayard and other Federalist Congressmen to vote for

Capitol rent the air with their acclamations and gratulations, and the conspirators, as they were called, hurried to their lodgings under strong apprehensions of suffering from the just indignation of their fellow citizens."[25]

"The storm through which we have passed has been tremendous indeed," wrote Jefferson a few days later. He was referring not only to the recent struggle in the House of Representatives, but to what he considered a four-year period of national crisis under Federalist rule. "The tough sides of our argosy have been thoroughly tried. Her strength has stood the waves into which she was steered with a view to sink her. We shall put her on her republican tack, and she will now show by the beauty of her motion the skill of her builders.... A just and solid republican government maintained here will be a standing monument and example for the aim and imitation of the people of other countries."[26]

Jefferson himself had also weathered the storm, and his countrymen had approved his course by giving him the highest honor they could bestow. A new patriotic song was soon circulating throughout the land to honor the President-elect. Each of its fourteen stanzas was followed by this exultant chorus:

> Rejoice! Columbia's sons, rejoice!
> To tyrants never bend the knee,
> But join with heart and soul and voice
> For JEFFERSON and LIBERTY. [27]

Jefferson. He still disliked Jefferson; but he considered Aaron Burr far more dangerous.

25. Smith, p. 25.

26. TJ to John Dickinson (6 Mar. 1801), Bergh 10:217.

But the real test—to translate the Jeffersonian principles of freedom into living reality—still lay ahead. The man from Monticello had now come to his greatest challenge.

---

27. Philadelphia *Aurora* (24 Jan. 1801), quoted in Dumas Malone, *Jefferson the President: First Term, 1801–1805*, Jefferson and His Time, vol. 4 (Boston: Little, Brown and Company, 1970), p. 30.

Chapter 17

President of the United States

March 4, 1801, was the historic day on which the reins of national government were to pass into the hands of the Republican party, and Thomas Jefferson was the first President to be inaugurated in the new federal city of Washington. As the President-elect entered the dining hall at Conrad's Boardinghouse that morning, he greeted his fellow boarders and "took his usual place at the bottom of the table," farthest from the fire. [1] After breakfast he walked to the nearby Capitol building, where the inauguration ceremonies were about to begin in the nearly completed north wing. One of the citizens in attendance noted that "the Senate chamber was so crowded that I believe not

---

1. Smith, *The First Forty Years of Washington Society*, p. 12.

another creature could enter.... Every inch of ground was occupied. It has been conjectured by several gentlemen whom I've asked that there were near a thousand persons within the walls."[2]

"The Creed of Our Political Faith"

After he was sworn in by Chief Justice John Marshall (a Federalist kinsman from Virginia who was to become one of his strongest political foes), the new President pulled a manuscript from his coat pocket and calmly delivered one of his rare public speeches. Unfortunately, many in the throng were unable to hear him because of the chronic weakness of his vocal cords. But the eloquent words he spoke on that occasion have been proudly echoed by every generation of Americans since.

In his now famous First Inaugural Address, Jefferson sought to heal the wounds of the recent campaign and to outline what he considered the nation's political creed.

> Let us, then, fellow citizens, unite with one heart and one mind. Let us restore to social intercourse that harmony and affection without which liberty and even life itself are but dreary things.... We have called by different names brethren of the same principle. We are all Republicans, we are all Federalists.... Let us, then, with courage and confidence, pursue our own federal and republican principles, our attachment to union and representative government....
>
> A wise and frugal government, which shall restrain men from injuring one another, which shall leave them otherwise free to regulate their own pursuits of industry and improvement, and shall not take from the

2. Ibid., p. 26.

mouth of labor the bread it has earned—this is the sum of good government....

About to enter, fellow citizens, on the exercise of duties which comprehend everything dear and valuable to you, it is proper you should understand what I deem the essential principles of our government and, consequently, those which ought to shape its administration....

Equal and exact justice to all men, of whatever state or persuasion, religious or political; peace, commerce, and honest friendship with all nations, entangling alliances with none; the support of the state governments in all their rights, as the most competent administrations for our domestic concerns and the surest bulwarks against anti-republican tendencies; the preservation of the general government in its whole Constitutional vigor, as the sheet anchor of our peace at home and safety abroad; a jealous care of the right of election by the people—a mild and safe corrective of abuses which are lopped by the sword of revolution where peaceable remedies are unprovided; absolute acquiescence in the decisions of the majority—the vital principle of republics, from which is no appeal but to force, the vital principle and immediate parent of despotism; a well-disciplined militia, our best reliance in peace and for the first moments of war till regulars may relieve them; the supremacy of the civil over the military authority; economy in the public expense, that labor may be lightly burdened; the honest payment of our debts, and sacred preservation of the public faith; encouragement of agriculture, and of commerce as its handmaid; the diffusion of information and arraignment of all abuses at the bar of the public reason; freedom of religion, freedom of the press, and freedom of person under the

protection of the habeas corpus and trial by juries
impartially selected.

These principles form the bright constellation which
has gone before us and guided our steps through an age
of revolution and reformation. The wisdom of our sages
and blood of our heroes have been devoted to their
attainment. They should be the creed of our political
faith, the text of civil instruction, the touchstone by
which to try the services of those we trust; and should
we wander from them in moments of error or alarm, let
us hasten to retrace our steps and to regain the road
which alone leads to peace, liberty, and safety.

I repair, then, fellow citizens, to the post you have
assigned me.... And may that Infinite Power which
rules the destinies of the universe lead our councils to
what is best and give them a favorable issue for your
peace and prosperity.[3]

"Is This the Violent Democrat?"

Jefferson had been a resident of the new federal city for
only a few weeks, and many of his Washington neighbors
did not become acquainted with him until after his
inauguration. Most were greatly impressed, and a few
were pleasantly surprised, when they met their new
President. "Is this the violent democrat, the vulgar
demagogue, the bold atheist and profligate man I have so
often heard denounced by the Federalists?" asked one
woman after her first introduction to Jefferson.

Can this man so meek and mild, yet dignified in his
manners, with a voice so soft and low, with a
countenance so benignant and intelligent, can he be that

3. First Inaugural Address (4 Mar. 1801), Bergh 3:318–23.

daring leader of a faction, that disturber of the peace, that enemy of all rank and order?...

I felt that I had been the victim of prejudice, that I had been unjust.... Not only was he great, but a truly good man![4]

One of his most inveterate political opponents, Justice William Paterson of the Supreme Court, acknowledged after he came to know the President: "Though we differed on many points, he displayed an impartiality [and] a freedom from prejudice that...were unusual. There was a mildness and amenity in his voice and manner that at once softened any of the asperities of party spirit that I felt.... No man can be personally acquainted with Mr. Jefferson and remain his personal enemy."[5] And a member of the New York delegation in the House of Representatives recorded this interesting description:

I have had several opportunities of seeing and conversing with [President Jefferson] since my arrival at Washington. He is tall in stature and rather spare in flesh. His dress and manners are very plain; he is grave, or rather sedate, but without any tincture of pomp, ostentation, or pride, and occasionally can smile, and both hear and relate humorous stories as well as any other man of social feeling.... He is more deeply versed in human nature and human learning than almost the whole tribe of his opponents and revilers.[6]

---

4. Smith, pp. 5-6, 8.

5. Quoted in Smith, pp. 406-7.

6. Dr. Samuel Latham Mitchill to his wife (10 Jan. 1802), in *Harper's Magazine*, April 1879, pp. 743-44.

One of the many Federalist cartoons depicting President Jefferson as a would-be destroyer of the federal government. This one, in which "Mad Tom" is assisted by the devil and a bottle of brandy, appeared in 1802.

Introducing Republican Simplicities

Some reacted less favorably, however. Believing that American political leaders too closely resembled European royalty in their extremes of fashion and etiquette, Jefferson deliberately reduced the pomp and ceremony surrounding his own office. Besides dispensing with excessive formality at the social events he hosted, he often dressed much more plainly than his predecessors had. A Senator from New Hampshire "thought [he] was a servant" until properly introduced,[7] and the secretary of the British legation in Washington observed that the President's appearance was "very much like that of a tall, large-boned farmer."[8]

---

7. William Plumer to Jeremiah Smith (9 Dec. 1802), in Lynn W. Turner, *William Plumer of New Hampshire, 1759–1850* (Chapel Hill: The University of North Carolina Press, 1962), p. 94. In the same letter he described Jefferson as "a tall, high-boned man" and complained that at their first meeting he was "dressed, or rather *undressed*, with an old brown coat, red waistcoat, old corduroy small clothes, much soiled, woolen hose, and slippers without heels." He also noted, however, that the President was "easy of access, and conversed with great ease and freedom." Ibid., pp. 94–95.

8. Sir Augustus John Foster, *Jeffersonian America: Notes on the United States of America Collected in the Years 1805–6–7 and 11–12,* ed. Richard Beale Davis (San Marino, Cal.: The Huntington Library, 1954), p. 10.

When the newly appointed minister from Great Britain appeared in full uniform at the Executive Mansion to present his credentials, he was highly incensed to find the Chief Executive of the United States wearing house slippers!

Still disdaining the "monarchical and aristocratical" forms he had spoken against years earlier while serving as Secretary of State, Jefferson now simplified official relations between the executive and legislative branches of the federal government. One of the changes he introduced afforded a significant savings of time among the partisans in Congress:

> By sending a [written] message instead of making a speech at the opening of the session, I have prevented the bloody conflict to which the making an answer would have committed them. They consequently were able to set into real business at once, without losing ten or twelve days in combatting an answer. [9]

An amusing anecdote from this period illustrates the adjustment that Washington's high society had to make when Jefferson entered the presidency. It seems that his predecessor had reserved Tuesday evenings for formal receptions in the Executive Mansion, and these had become regular social gatherings which gave the fashionable guests a place to exchange the latest gossip and parade their latest costumes. Jefferson's decision to abolish these British-style "levees" was not well received by certain local citizens.

> Many of the ladies at Washington, indignant at being cut off from the pleasure of attending them, and

9. TJ to Dr. Benjamin Rush (20 Dec. 1801), Bergh 10:303-4.

thinking that their discontinuance was an innovation on former customs, determined to force the President to hold them. Accordingly, on the usual levee day they resorted in full force to the White House.

The President was out taking his habitual ride on horseback. On his return, being told that the public rooms were filled with ladies, he at once divined their true motives for coming on that day. Without being at all disconcerted, all booted and spurred and still covered with the dust of his ride, he went in to receive his fair guests.

Never had his reception been more graceful or courteous. The ladies, charmed with the ease and grace of his manners and address, forgot their indignation with him and went away feeling that, of the two parties, they had shown most impoliteness in visiting his house when not expected. The result of their plot was for a long time a subject of mirth among them, and they never again attempted to infringe upon the rules of his household. [10]

Entertaining at the Executive Mansion

Although he did away with the pompous receptions and most of the elaborate state dinners, Jefferson was by no means opposed to social enjoyment. Nearly every day he invited ten or twelve guests to a luncheon at the Executive Mansion, and the President's table became quite famous because of his fascinating conversation and extraordinary menus. The meals, prepared by a French chef named Monsieur Julien, featured such European treats as

---

10. Randolph, *The Domestic Life of Thomas Jefferson,* pp. 282–83.

macaroni and ice cream.[11] Being a widower, Jefferson often invited Dolley Madison (the charming wife of his friend James Madison, whom he had appointed as Secretary of State) to serve as the official hostess on these and other social occasions.

In keeping with his lifelong practice, Jefferson never used public funds to entertain his guests, even when they came as official representatives of foreign governments. These social expenses and other public obligations, all paid out of his own pocket, finally saddled him with about $10,000 of indebtedness by the time he left the presidency.[12] The one "consolation" he could claim was that of "having added nothing to my private fortune during my public service, and of retiring with hands as clean as they are empty."[13]

A Mockingbird, a Mastodon, and a "Mammoth Cheese"

The elegant French recipes were not all that made the Executive Mansion a place of curiosity during Jefferson's administration. The room he used as his office and library was filled with interesting items that reflected the broad range of his personal interests: books, maps, globes, and scientific instruments were mingled with potted plants, a

---

11. See Bernard Mayo, "A Peppercorn for Mr. Jefferson," *Virginia Quarterly Review*, Spring 1943, pp. 228–29; Henry F. Graff, *Illustrious Americans: Thomas Jefferson* (Morristown, N.J.: Silver Burdett Company, 1968), pp. 66, 72, 113.

12. See his letter to Martha Jefferson Randolph (27 Feb. 1809), Betts and Bear, *The Family Letters of Thomas Jefferson*, p. 386; also Malone, *Jefferson the President: Second Term, 1805–1809*, p. 666.

13. TJ to Comte Diodati (29 Mar. 1807), Bergh 11:182.

violin, carpentry tools, gardening implements, a drafting board, and a palette and paints.

Suspended in a window recess between his roses and geraniums was the cage of his favorite mockingbird, who reportedly could sing popular American, French, and Scottish melodies as well as mimicking other birds of the woods. Sometimes Jefferson would open the cage to let this bird fly around the room, and it developed a habit of perching on the President's shoulder to peck a crumb of food from his lips.[14]

Down the hall in the unfinished East Room, Jefferson kept a huge fossil collection and the bones of a mastodon. After inviting a fellow member of the American Philosophical Society to examine this "precious collection,"[15] he donated it to the National Institute of France. This same room had already been the depository of a "Mammoth Cheese" (1,235 pounds!) delivered by well-wishers from Massachusetts on New Year's Day of 1802.[16] And outside on the lawn were two young grizzly bears brought back from the far west by Meriwether Lewis.[17]

"A Noiseless Course"

As for his administration of the government, Jefferson did his best to follow the principles he had set forth in his inaugural address. Working with the new Republican-dominated Congress which convened in the fall of 1801,

---

14. These details are from Smith, pp. 384–85, and Mayo, "A Peppercorn for Mr. Jefferson," p. 233.

15. TJ to Dr. Caspar Wistar (20 Mar. 1808), Bergh 12:15–16.

16. Mayo, "A Peppercorn for Mr. Jefferson," pp. 222–26.

17. Smith, p. 393.

he pardoned everyone who had been prosecuted under the Sedition Act, reduced the size of the army and the navy, reduced the number of federal officials, reduced taxes, and began paying off the national debt. He was pleased with the situation he observed after nearly two years in office:

> The path we have to pursue is so quiet that we have nothing scarcely to propose to [Congress]. A noiseless course, not meddling with the affairs of others, unattractive of notice, is a mark that society is going on in happiness. If we can prevent the government from wasting the labors of the people under the pretense of taking care of them, they must become happy. [18]

But Jefferson's presidency was not to remain tranquil for long.

---

18. TJ to Dr. Thomas Cooper (29 Nov. 1802), Bergh 10:342.

Chapter 18

A Season of Slander

The Republican administration, despite its popularity with the masses, was subjected to a steady
barrage of criticism by the Federalist press throughout Jefferson's two terms. The vilest attacks on the
President himself, however, came from an unexpected
source.

Callender's Calumnies

One of the victims of the Sedition Act who was
pardoned by President Jefferson in 1801 was James
Thomson Callender, a Republican journalist who had
been an unrelenting critic of the Federalists during the last
presidential campaign. But Callender wanted more than
a pardon: later that year he plainly told James Madison,
the new Secretary of State, that he hoped to be appointed
postmaster in Richmond, Virginia.

When it became clear that he was not going to be offered any government post, the embittered Callender sought revenge by going to work for a Federalist newspaper in Richmond. In March 1802, he began publishing various charges against Republican leaders in Congress and certain members of the Cabinet. By autumn he was training his guns on the President.

Callender has been described as "the most unscrupulous scandalmonger of the day, . . . a journalist who stopped at nothing and stooped to anything. . . . [He] was not an investigative journalist; he never bothered to investigate anything. For him, the story, especially if it reeked of scandal, was everything; truth, if it stood in his way, was summarily mowed down."[1] True to his style, he fabricated a series of scandalous stories about Jefferson's personal life, the ugliest of which charged him with having fathered several children by a mulatto slave at Monticello, a young woman named Sally Hemings. Although Callender had never gone near Jefferson's estate, he alleged that this was common knowledge in the neighboring area. He included many lurid details of this supposed illicit relationship among the "entertaining facts"[2] he created for his readers, even inventing the names of children whom "Dusky Sally" had never borne.

---

1. John Chester Miller, *The Wolf by the Ears: Thomas Jefferson and Slavery* (New York: Macmillan Publishing Co., Inc., The Free Press, 1977), pp. 153–54. Another historian has noted that "almost every scandalous story about Jefferson which is still whispered or believed" can be traced to Callender. James Truslow Adams, *The Living Jefferson* (New York: Charles Scribner's Sons, 1936), p. 315.

2. From an article by Callender in the Richmond *Recorder* (8 Dec. 1802), quoted in Malone, *Jefferson the President: First Term, 1801–1805*, p. 213. For a thorough account of Callender's attacks, see ibid., pp. 206–23.

Other Federalist editors took up these accusations with glee, and Callender's stories spread like wildfire from one end of the country to the other—sometimes expanded and embellished by subsequent writers. The President was charged with other evils as well; the torrent of slander never seemed to let up. As one biographer has written, "He suffered open personal attacks which in severity and obscenity have rarely if ever been matched in presidential history in the United States."[3]

"Why Are These Libels Allowed?"

Like other men, Jefferson was sensitive to these false accusations. Years earlier he had written, "My great wish is to go on in a strict but silent performance of my duty, to avoid attracting notice, and to keep my name out of newspapers, because I find the pain of a little censure, even when it is unfounded, is more acute than the pleasure of much praise."[4] Even before entering the presidency he felt he was being "used as the property of the newspapers, a fair mark for every man's dirt."[5] And now that he was subjected almost daily to fresh doses of venom from Federalist penmen, he sorely lamented "the malignant perversions of those who make every word from me a text for new misrepresentations and calumnies."[6]

Publicly, however, he made no response to these unscrupulous attacks. "I should have fancied myself half

---

3. Malone, *Jefferson the President: First Term, 1801–1805*, p. 206.
4. TJ to Francis Hopkinson (13 Mar. 1789), Bergh 7:302.
5. TJ to Peregrine Fitzhugh (23 Feb. 1798), Bergh 10:1.
6. TJ to Dr. Benjamin Rush (21 Apr. 1803), Bergh 10:380.

guilty," he said, "had I condescended to put pen to paper in refutation of their falsehoods, or drawn to them respect by any notice from myself."[7] Nor did he use the channels of civil authority to silence his accusers. True to the declarations he had made in his inaugural address and elsewhere, he defended his countrymen's right to a free press. The Baron Alexander von Humboldt, a famous German explorer and scientist, learned the depth of Jefferson's commitment to this principle when he visited the city of Washington in the summer of 1804. Calling at the Executive Mansion one morning, Humboldt was invited to meet with the President in the Cabinet room.

As he sat by the table, among the newspapers that were scattered about he perceived one that was always filled with the most virulent abuse of Mr. Jefferson, calumnies the most offensive, personal as well as political. "Why are these libels allowed?" asked the Baron, taking up the paper. "Why is not this libelous journal suppressed, or its editor at least fined and imprisoned?"

Mr. Jefferson smiled, saying, "Put that paper in your pocket, Baron, and should you hear the reality of our liberty [or] the freedom of our press questioned [in Europe], show this paper and tell where you found it."[8]

Jefferson's grandson, Thomas Jefferson Randolph,

---

7. TJ to Dr. George Logan (20 June 1816), Ford 10:27.

8. Smith, *The First Forty Years of Washington Society*, pp. 396–97. Despite the libelous treatment to which he himself was subjected by the newspapers, Jefferson always believed that a free press was essential to free government. "Were it left to me," he once wrote, "to decide whether we should have a government without newspapers, or newspapers without a government, I should not hesitate a moment to prefer the latter." TJ to Edward Carrington (16 Jan. 1787), Boyd 11:49.

described the calm perspective with which the President viewed these slanders:

> In speaking of the calumnies which his enemies had uttered against his public and private character with such unmitigated and untiring bitterness, he said that he had not considered them as abusing him; they had never known *him*. They had created an imaginary being clothed with odious attributes, to whom they had given his name; and it was against that creature of their imaginations they had levelled their anathemas. [9]

Not only did Jefferson remain silent about the sensational accusations of James Callender and like-minded journalists, but he also instructed the members of his Cabinet to do the same. The Federalist press continued its harassment throughout Jefferson's presidency, but this unsavory effort lost much of its momentum after July 1803—the month Callender drowned himself in the James River.

A Defense of Jefferson's Moral Integrity

Although Jefferson chose not to defend himself against Callender's lies, the question of his alleged intrigue with Sally Hemings deserves brief consideration here because a number of recent authors, incredibly enough, have resurrected this vulgar tale under the guise of "modern scholarship." [10] The twentieth century has brought forth a

---

9. Thomas Jefferson Randolph to Henry S. Randall (n.d.), in Randall, *The Life of Thomas Jefferson*, 3:544.

10. The most widely distributed of these works in recent years is Fawn M. Brodie's *Thomas Jefferson: An Intimate History* (New York: W. W. Norton & Co., Inc., 1974), which relies on slight circumstantial evidence and amateur psychoanalysis. The book has received very poor reviews by scholars who are familiar with the life and times of Jefferson. David Herbert Donald, the

rash of sensational and poorly researched publications designed to discredit America's Founding Fathers, and those which purport to "reveal" the clandestine Jefferson-Hemings affair are typical of this trend.

As for Callender's original accusations, they are immediately suspect because of his avowed hatred for Jefferson; and his stories about "Dusky Sally" are as incapable of proof today as they were when he wrote them. Indeed, many of the "facts" he dished up are known to be false. Douglass Adair, one of the most highly

---

Charles Warren Professor of American History at Harvard University, observed that Mrs. Brodie did not seem to be troubled by "the fact that she can adduce only slim factual support for her tales of what she primly calls Jefferson's 'intimate life.' ... Such absence of evidence would stop most historians, but it does not faze Mrs. Brodie. Where there are documents, she knows how to read them in a special way.... Where documents have been lost, Mrs. Brodie can make much of the gap.... Mrs. Brodie is masterful in using negative evidence too.... But Mrs. Brodie is at her best when there is no evidence whatever to cloud her vision. Then she is free to speculate." ("By Sex Obsessed," *Commentary*, July 1974, pp. 97-98.) Historian and author Garry Wills, after noting the abundance of obvious historical errors in the book—"one can only be so intricately wrong by deep study and long effort"—remarked that Brodie's writing "involves heroic feats of misunderstanding and a constant labor at ignorance. This seems too high a price to pay when the same appetites can be more readily gratified by those Hollywood fan magazines, with their wealth of unfounded conjecture on the sex lives of others, from which Ms. Brodie has borrowed her scholarly methods." ("Uncle Thomas's Cabin," *New York Review of Books*, 18 April 1974, pp. 26-28.) One other representative comment comes from the Pulitzer Prize-winning Jefferson biographer, Dumas Malone: "This determined woman carries psychological speculation to the point of absurdity. The resulting mishmash of fact and fiction, surmise and conjecture, is not history as I understand the term.... To me the man she describes in her more titillating passages is unrecognizable." Quoted in Virginius Dabney, *The Jefferson Scandals: A Rebuttal* (New York: Dodd, Mead & Company, 1981), p. 132. It is interesting to note that Brodie's three earlier biographies of historical figures also dwelt on their supposed sexual misconduct and were written in a similar vein.

respected historians of our era, concluded after examining all of the evidence on this matter which has now come to light: "Today, it is possible to *prove* that Jefferson was innocent of Callender's charges."[11]

One of the recently discovered documents to which Adair referred was a letter written by the nineteenth-century biographer Henry Randall, recounting a conversation at Monticello between himself and Jefferson's oldest grandson, Thomas Jefferson Randolph. In this conversation Randolph confirmed what others close to the family had already disclosed: that Sally Hemings was actually the mistress of Jefferson's nephew, Peter Carr, and that "their connection... was perfectly notorious at Monticello." He also pointed out that "there was not the shadow of suspicion that Mr. Jefferson in this or any other instance had commerce with female slaves."

> He said Mr. Jefferson never locked the door of his room by day, and that he (Colonel Randolph) slept within [the] sound of his breathing at night. He said he had never seen a motion or a look or a circumstance which led him to suspect for an instant that there was a particle more of familiarity between Mr. Jefferson and Sally Hemings than between him and the most repulsive servant in the establishment—and that no person ever living at Monticello dreamed of such a thing....
>
> Colonel Randolph said that he had spent a good share of his life closely about Mr. Jefferson, at home and on

---

11. "The Jefferson Scandals" (written in 1960), *Fame and the Founding Fathers: Essays by Douglass Adair*, ed. Trevor Colbourn (New York: W.W. Norton & Company, Inc., 1974), p. 169. See the entire essay, pp. 160–91, for a thorough presentation and skillful analysis of recent evidence touching on the Jefferson-Hemings legend. See also Dabney, *The Jefferson Scandals: A Rebuttal* (cited in the preceding note).

journeys, in all sorts of circumstances, and he fully believed him chaste and pure—as "immaculate a man as God ever created."[12]

As Randolph implied, the most conclusive argument against Callender's attacks—or those of today's writers—is Jefferson's own character. According to Professor Dumas Malone, whose monumental six-volume biography of Jefferson was awarded the Pulitzer Prize for History in 1975, the notion that such charges could be true is "virtually unthinkable in a man of Jefferson's moral standards and habitual conduct."

> To say this is not to claim that he was a plaster saint and incapable of moral lapses. But his major weaknesses were not of this sort. . . . It is virtually inconceivable that this fastidious gentleman whose devotion to his dead wife's memory and to the happiness of his daughters and grandchildren bordered on the excessive could have carried on through a period of years a vulgar liaison which his own family could not have failed to detect. It would be as absurd as to charge this consistently temperate man with being, through a long period, a secret drunkard.[13]

After these slanders had been widely circulated, Jefferson wrote privately that he "feared no injury which any man could do me; . . . I never had done a single act or been concerned in any transaction which I feared to have fully laid open, or which could do me any hurt if truly

12. Henry S. Randall to James Parton (1 June 1868), in Milton E. Flower, *James Parton: The Father of Modern Biography* (Durham, N.C.: Duke University Press, 1951), pp. 236–37.

13. Malone, *Jefferson the President: First Term, 1801–1805*, p. 214. See also Miller, *The Wolf by the Ears*, pp. 148–76.

stated."[14] And shortly before the end of his presidency he said, "I can conscientiously declare that, as to myself, I wish that not only no *act* but no *thought* of mine should be unknown."[15]

It was probably fortunate for the American people that their President chose to ignore his enemies' ravings in the newspapers, as mounting difficulties at home and abroad soon proved more than enough to engage his full time and attention.

---

14. The Anas (15 Apr. 1806), Bergh 1:449–50.
15. TJ to James Main (19 Oct. 1808), Bergh 12:175; italics added.

Chapter 19

Public Achievements and Private Adversity

J efferson had long resented the fact that American and European vessels entering the Mediterranean were forced to pay tribute to the Barbary states along the northern coast of Africa. The demands and the tactics of these pirates were becoming increasingly intolerable, and in May 1801 the President decided to send four warships to the Mediterranean to protect American commerce in that region. The result was a prolonged naval war with the small nation of Tripoli.

As the fighting grew fiercer, ten more warships were sent to the area. The hostilities dragged on for four years. Although this was America's first experience in naval warfare, her squadron eventually took the offensive. Finally, in 1805, Tripoli was forced to make peace and to respect American trade in the Mediterranean. Jefferson's popularity was greatly enhanced by this military triumph.

A Danger Closer to Home

But a far more serious threat to the security of the United States was lurking within the borders of its own continent. Jefferson learned during the first year of his presidency that Spain had secretly ceded Louisiana to France. (At that time, Louisiana was a name used to designate a vast tract of land stretching between the Mississippi River and the Rocky Mountains.) This was disturbing news because Napoleon was making no secret of his desire to establish a French empire in the New World. To make matters still worse, the port of New Orleans was suddenly closed to American shipping, and Western farmers—now unable to export their produce— began crying for war with France.

Though he saw the danger and the urgency of this situation, the President was determined to solve the problem through diplomatic negotiation if possible. In April 1802, he instructed Robert R. Livingston, the American minister to France, to try to induce Napoleon to cede New Orleans to the United States. Otherwise, he said, this "embryo of a tornado" would turn into war, and "we must [then] marry ourselves to the British fleet and nation"[1] in order to fight the French and their Spanish allies.

The Louisiana Purchase

Early in 1803 Jefferson sent James Monroe to assist

---

1. TJ to Robert R. Livingston (18 Apr. 1802), Bergh 10:313.

Livingston in these negotiations, and he persuaded Congress to appropriate money for a possible purchase of New Orleans. Then came the surprise. Napoleon, anticipating a renewal of his costly campaign against Great Britain and disappointed by the recent defeat of French troops occupying Haiti (which was supposedly the foothold from which he would launch his New World empire), offered to sell to the American government, not just the port city, but the entire Louisiana Territory!

A price of $15 million was agreed upon, and Jefferson received word of the deal in July. Despite his initial concerns about the Constitutional questions posed by such an acquisition, he called an early session of Congress that fall in order to obtain ratification of the purchase treaty before France backed out. Jefferson's insistence on diplomacy had paid off: nearly 512 million acres were added to the United States in a single stroke, more than doubling the nation's geographical area. The President, who had long been an advocate of American expansion, was delighted with the outcome.

> While the property and sovereignty of the Mississippi and its waters secure an independent outlet for the produce of the western states, and an uncontrolled navigation through their whole course, free from collision with other powers and the dangers to our peace from that source, the fertility of the country, its climate and extent, promise in due season important aids to our treasury, an ample provision for our posterity, and a widespread field for the blessings of freedom and equal laws. [2]

---

2. Third Annual Message to Congress (17 Oct. 1803), Bergh 3:353.

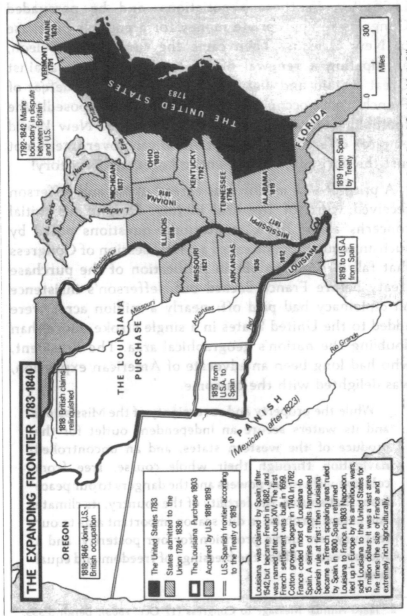

THE EXPANDING FRONTIER 1783–1840

The United States 1783

States admitted to the Union 1784–1836

The Louisiana Purchase 1803

Acquired by U.S. 1818–1819

U.S.–Spanish frontier according to the Treaty of 1819

Louisiana was claimed by Spain after 1542, but became French in 1682, and was named after Louis XIV. The first French settlement was built in 1699. Cotton growing began in 1740 in the first France ceded most of Louisiana to Spain. A series of revolts hampered Spanish rule at first; then Louisiana became a "French speaking area" ruled by Spain. In 1800 Spain returned Louisiana to France. In 1803 Napoleon, tied up in Europe by his ambitious wars, sold Louisiana to the United States for 15 million dollars. It was a vast area, five times the size of France and extremely rich agriculturally.

OREGON

1818–1846 Joint U.S.–British occupation

1818 British claims relinquished

THE LOUISIANA PURCHASE

1819 from U.S.A. to Spain

SPANISH (Mexican after 1823)

Rio Grande

Red

Arkansas

Missouri

1792–1842 Maine boundary in dispute between Britain and U.S.

MAINE 1820

VERMONT 1791

L. Ontario

L. Erie

L. Huron

L. Michigan

L. Superior

MICHIGAN 1837

OHIO 1803

INDIANA 1816

ILLINOIS 1818

KENTUCKY 1792

TENNESSEE 1796

MISSISSIPPI 1817

ALABAMA 1819

MISSOURI 1821

ARKANSAS 1836

LOUISIANA 1812

THE UNITED STATES 1783

FLORIDA

1819 from Spain by Treaty

1819 to U.S.A. from Spain

Mississippi

0   300
Miles

The Lewis and Clark Expedition

Jefferson had been interested in the territory west of the Mississippi before anyone had even thought of buying or selling Louisiana. As early as January 1803 he had sent a confidential message to the House of Representatives proposing that an expedition be sent to follow the Missouri River to its source and then proceed to the Pacific Ocean. The project was approved, and President Jefferson named his private secretary, Meriwether Lewis, to lead the group.

Meriwether Lewis, who was appointed by President Jefferson in 1803 to lead an expedition across the American continent to the Pacific Ocean.

With the President's permission, Lewis persuaded Captain William Clark (a friend and fellow Virginian) to share the command of the expedition, and they began to recruit young men and make other preparations for their journey. Jefferson himself drew up the instructions for Lewis and Clark, outlining their general route and directing them to observe Indian customs and to provide detailed records of the plant and animal life, minerals and geological formations, and climatic conditions they found along the way.

Meanwhile, the purchase of Louisiana was finalized—the United States took formal possession on December 20,

Captain William Clark, who joined Meriwether Lewis and shared command of the historic western expedition.

1803—and Jefferson became increasingly eager for the expedition to get under way. The group of about forty men wintered in St. Louis, then departed in May 1804. After finding the Missouri's source and crossing the Great Divide, they followed the Columbia River to the Pacific, finally reaching the coast in November of 1805. Lewis and Clark returned triumphantly to St. Louis the next September, concluding an adventurous journey which provided valuable information about the American wilderness and helped prepare the way for further westward expansion. President Jefferson, one of the earliest proponents of America's "manifest destiny," now began to speak of "our continent."[3]

The Death of the President's Daughter

Jefferson could point with pride to the achievements of his administration thus far. With the exception of the Federalist slanders, which actually had very little effect on most Americans of that day, his first term in the presidency had met with few real difficulties. But for

---

3. Sixth Annual Message to Congress (2 Dec. 1806), Bergh 3:420.

Jefferson himself, these years of tranquility were suddenly shattered by a wrenching tragedy which the nation was largely unaware of: the untimely death of his twenty-six-year-old daughter, Mary.

Even as President, Jefferson still considered his family the most important part of his life. The year before his election he had written to Mary, "[My] feelings of love for you and our dear connections...constitute the only real happiness of my life."[4] Mary and her older sister, Martha, the only two of Jefferson's children to survive childhood, returned their father's love and did their best to meet his high expectations of them. The two young ladies were quite different in both appearance and temperament; Mary was said to resemble her mother, while Martha took after her father.[5]

Also like her mother, Mary was never physically strong. Jefferson had frequently worried about her health. She seemed to improve, however, during their three years together at Monticello following his retirement from the Washington administration. In 1797 she married a distant relative named John Wayles Eppes, and her father declared his "inexpressible pleasure" that she had found such a worthy companion. He said that the choice "could not have been more...to my wishes if I had had the whole earth free to have chosen a partner for her."[6]

---

4. TJ to Mary Jefferson Eppes (7 Feb.1799), Betts and Bear, *The Family Letters of Thomas Jefferson*, pp. 173–74.

5. See Smith, *The First Forty Years of Washington Society*, p. 34, for a description of Mary and Martha by an acquaintance in 1802.

6. TJ to Martha Jefferson Randolph (8 June 1797), Betts and Bear, p. 146. Both of Jefferson's sons-in-law, Jack Eppes and Thomas Mann Randolph, served in Congress during his presidency.

Then came the children. Mary's first infant was born in December 1799 and died less than a month later. A son, Francis, was born in 1801; the birth had been difficult for Mary, but the boy proved to be strong (he lived to his eightieth year). The third and last pregnancy left Mary in a severely weakened condition. In February 1804 she gave birth to a daughter, Maria, who was destined to survive only three years. But the mother would not last nearly so long: she passed away on April 17, 1804.

"I . . . Have Lost Even the Half of All I Had"

Jefferson had now lost his father, his mother, his wife, and five of his six children. He turned to Governor John Page of Virginia, his boyhood friend, and vented his deep sorrow:

> Others may lose of their abundance, but I, of my want, have lost even the half of all I had. My evening prospects now hang on the slender thread of a single life. Perhaps I may be destined to see even this last cord of parental affection broken! The hope with which I had looked forward to the moment when, resigning public cares to younger hands, I was to retire to that domestic comfort from which the last great step is to be taken, is fearfully blighted.
>
> When you and I look back on the country over which we have passed, what a field of slaughter does it exhibit! Where are all the friends who entered it with us, under all the inspiring energies of health and hope? As if pursued by the havoc of war, they are strewed by the way, some earlier, some later, and scarce a few stragglers remain to count the numbers fallen. . . .

But whatever is to be our destiny, wisdom as well as duty dictates that we should acquiesce in the will of Him whose it is to give and take away, and be contented in the enjoyment of those who are still permitted to be with us. [7]

Jefferson Is Reelected by a Wide Margin

The bereaved President may have taken some comfort from the immense popularity he enjoyed among his countrymen in 1804. At the opening of that year, he had reason to believe that the accomplishments of his first term were softening even some of his opponents:

To do without a land tax, excise, stamp tax, and the other internal taxes, [and] to supply their place by economies so as still to support the government properly and to apply $7,300,000 a year steadily to the payment of the public debt; to discontinue a great portion of the expenses on armies and navies, yet protect our country and its commerce with what remains; to purchase a country as large and more fertile than the one we possessed before, yet ask neither a new tax nor another soldier to be added, but to provide that that country shall by its own income pay for itself before the purchase money is due; to preserve peace with all nations, and particularly an equal friendship to the two great rival powers, France and England; and to maintain the credit and character of the nation in as high a degree as it has ever enjoyed—[these] are measures which I think must reconcile the great body of those who thought themselves our enemies. [8]

---

7. TJ to Governor John Page (25 June 1804), Bergh 11:31-32.
8. TJ to Timothy Bloodworth (29 Jan. 1804), Bergh 10:444.

There was still a determined corps of die-hard Federalists, of course, who continued to vent their bitterness in the press. But Jefferson likened this to "the chimneys to our dwellings; it carries off the smoke of party which might otherwise stifle the nation."[9] These attacks made little if any difference in the 1804 campaign: the President was reelected by a wide margin, receiving 162 electoral votes (against Charles C. Pinckney's 14) and carrying every state except Connecticut and Delaware.[10]

---

9. Quoted in Bernard Mayo, "A Peppercorn for Mr. Jefferson," *Virginia Quarterly Review,* Spring 1943, p. 227. Compare TJ to General Thaddeus Kosciusko (2 Apr. 1802), Bergh 10:310.

10. Malone, *Jefferson the President: First Term, 1801–1805,* p. 433. George Clinton of New York was elected Vice President, replacing Aaron Burr (see page 255 of this biography).

Chapter 20

"A Splendid Misery"

On March 4, 1805, President Jefferson delivered his Second Inaugural Address in the city of Washington. After mentioning his efforts of the last four years to maintain peace and friendship with foreign powers, he spoke with justifiable pride of the domestic achievements of his first term.

At home, fellow citizens, you best know whether we have done well or ill. The suppression of unnecessary offices, of useless establishments and expenses, enabled us to discontinue our internal taxes.... The remaining revenue, on the consumption of foreign articles, is paid cheerfully by those who can afford to add foreign luxuries to domestic comforts. Being collected on our seaboard and frontiers only, and incorporated with the transactions of our mercantile citizens, it may be the pleasure and pride of an American to ask, what farmer, what mechanic, what laborer ever sees a tax-gatherer of the United States?[1]

He then discussed briefly the Louisiana Purchase, which he considered one of the greatest accomplishments of his administration. To those who had not approved of the acquisition for fear that "the enlargement of our territory would endanger its union," he answered: "Who can limit the extent to which the federative principle may operate effectively? The larger our association, the less will it be shaken by local passions."[2]

Jefferson also referred to "the artillery of the press" which, during his first administration, had been "levelled against us, charged with whatsoever its licentiousness could devise or dare." He was gratified that the outcome of this unhappy "experiment" had vindicated his faith in the good judgment of the American people.

> The experiment has been tried; you have witnessed the scene; our fellow citizens have looked on, cool and collected; they saw the latent source from which these outrages proceeded; they gathered around their public functionaries, and when the Constitution called them to the decision by suffrage, they pronounced their verdict, honorable to those who had served them....

1. Second Inaugural Address (4 Mar. 1805), Bergh 3:376.

2. Ibid., pp. 377–78. Actually, there were very few Americans who did not strongly favor the Louisiana Purchase. Almost all of its critics were staunch New England Federalists who feared a further deterioration of their political power in Congress.

The public judgment will correct false reasonings and opinions, on a full hearing of all parties; and no other definite line can be drawn between the inestimable liberty of the press and its demoralizing licentiousness. [3]

A Prayer for Enlightenment and Peace

The President closed his address with an acknowledgment of his own limitations and his dependence on Divine Providence for the years ahead.

I shall now enter on the duties to which my fellow citizens have again called me, and shall proceed in the spirit of those principles which they have approved. I fear not that any motives of interest may lead me astray. I am sensible of no passion which could seduce me, knowingly, from the path of justice; but the weaknesses of human nature and the limits of my own understanding will produce errors of judgment sometimes injurious to your interests. I shall need, therefore, all the indulgence I have heretofore experienced; the want of it will certainly not lessen with increasing years.

I shall need, too, the favor of that Being in whose hands we are; who led our forefathers, as Israel of old, from their native land and planted them in a country flowing with all the necessaries and comforts of life; who has covered our infancy with His providence, and our riper years with His wisdom and power; and to whose goodness I ask you to join with me in supplications, that He will so enlighten the minds of your servants, guide their councils, and prosper their

3. Ibid., pp. 380–82.

measures that whatsoever they do shall result in your good, and shall secure to you the peace, friendship, and approbation of all nations. [4]

Jefferson and the American Indians

In one respect, at least, President Jefferson's second term did live up to his hopes for continuing peace and friendship with other sovereign powers. Relations between the federal government and the various Indian nations living within the boundaries of the United States were more peaceful during his presidency than at any other time during the first hundred years following American independence. This was in some measure due to Jefferson's personal interest in the history, culture, and languages of the native Americans—and the sympathy he felt as he witnessed their sufferings under the relentless advance of the white man.

Even as a boy, Jefferson had had frequent contact with the Indian tribes living near his family home in Albemarle County, then on the Virginia frontier. He particularly remembered "the great Ontassete, the warrior and orator of the Cherokees; he was always the guest of my father on his journeys to and from Williamsburg."[5] An incident involving this noble chief which occurred in the spring of 1762, when young Thomas was attending the College of William and Mary, left an indelible impression on his mind that remained with him throughout life. As an old man he recorded the experience:

I was in his camp when he made his great farewell

---

4. Ibid., p. 383.
5. TJ to John Adams (11 June 1812), Bergh 13:160.

oration to his people, the evening before his departure for England. The moon was in full splendor, and to her he seemed to address himself in his prayers for his own safety on the voyage, and that of his people during his absence. His sounding voice, distinct articulation, animated action, and the solemn silence of his people at their several fires filled me with awe and admiration, although I did not understand a word he uttered.[6]

As he matured, Jefferson became an ardent student of the Indian people. "Few of his American contemporaries," noted one biographer, "were so deeply interested in the Indians over so long a period as he, if indeed anybody was."[7] Jefferson firmly believed that the Indian tribes were sovereign nations whose territorial rights should be respected equally with those of the American settlers. When he became Secretary of State, he stated this position in very strong terms:

I am of opinion that ... the Indians have a right to the occupation of their lands, independent of the states within whose chartered lines they happen to be; that until they cede them by treaty or other transaction equivalent to a treaty, no act of a state can give a right to such lands; that neither under the present Constitution, nor the ancient confederation, had any state or person a right to treat with the Indians without the consent of the general government; ... that the government is determined to exert all its energy for the patronage and protection of the rights of the Indians, and the preservation of peace between the United States and them; and that if any settlements are made on lands not

6. Ibid.

7. Malone, *Jefferson the President: Second Term, 1805–1809*, p. 6.

ceded by them, without the previous consent of the
United States, the government will think itself bound,
not only to declare to the Indians that such settlements
are without the authority or protection of the United
States, but to remove them also by public force. [8]

"Truly One People with Us"

As President, Jefferson declared that the white settlers
should obtain land from the Indians only by "all *honest* and
peaceable means, and I believe that the honest and peaceable
means adopted by us will obtain them as fast as the
expansion of our settlements, with due regard to
compactness, will require."[9] He was further convinced
that "nothing ought more to be avoided than the
embarking ourselves in a system of military coercion on
the Indians. If we do this, we shall have general and
perpetual war."[10]

> Our system is to live in perpetual peace with the
> Indians [and] to cultivate an affectionate attachment
> from them by everything just and liberal which we can
> do for them within the bounds of reason, and by giving
> them effectual protection against wrongs from our own
> people. [11]

He deplored the practice of those who "liquored up" the
Indians to gain unreasonable concessions from them. "I
have not filled you with whiskey as the English do," he told

8. TJ to General Henry Knox (10 Aug. 1791), Bergh 8:226–27.
9. TJ to General Andrew Jackson (16 Feb. 1803), Bergh 10:359.
10. TJ to Governor Meriwether Lewis (21 Aug. 1808), Bergh 12:142.
11. TJ to Governor William Henry Harrison (27 Feb. 1803), Bergh 10:369.

a group of tribal leaders, "to make you promise or give up what is against your interest when out of your senses."[12]

It was not Jefferson's intent to stem the inevitable westward flow of his countrymen. But he did seek to encourage a peaceful removal of the Indians from their former lands, always through the negotiation of treaties, and early enough to prevent the tragic depredations he had seen in the past. At the same time, knowing that farming and herding would enable the Indians to live much more prosperously within their diminishing geographical boundaries than would their traditional practice of hunting wild game, he took steps to provide them with instruction in "agriculture and the domestic arts." His Second Inaugural Address reflected his attitude toward the Indian people and outlined what he regarded as the proper policy of the federal government toward the native Americans:

> The aboriginal inhabitants of these countries I have regarded with the commiseration their history inspires. Endowed with the faculties and the rights of men, breathing an ardent love of liberty and independence, and occupying a country which left them no desire but to be undisturbed, the stream of overflowing population from other regions directed itself on these shores. Without power to divert or habits to contend against, they have been overwhelmed by the current or driven before it.
>
> Now reduced within limits too narrow for the hunter

---

12. TJ to the Chiefs of the Ottawas, Chippewas, Powtewatamies, Wyandots, and Shawanese (31 Jan. 1809), Bergh 16:472. In response to requests from several Indian leaders, President Jefferson urged Congress to pass legislation against the sale or distribution of liquor among the Indians.

state, humanity enjoins us to teach them agriculture and the domestic arts, to encourage them to that industry which alone can enable them to maintain their place in existence and to prepare them, in time, for that state of society which to bodily comforts adds the improvement of the mind and morals. We have, therefore, liberally furnished them with the implements of husbandry and household use; we have placed among them instructors in the arts of first necessity; and they are covered with the aegis of the law against aggressors from among ourselves. [13]

During the last year of his presidency, Jefferson said to a visiting delegation of tribal chiefs: "I shall rejoice to see the day when the red men, our neighbors, become truly one people with us, enjoying all the rights and privileges we do, and living in peace and plenty as we do, without anyone to make them afraid, to injure their persons, or to take their property without being punished for it according to fixed laws." [14]

Hamilton Is Killed in a Duel with Vice President Burr

But if Indian relations were peaceful during Jefferson's second term, little else was. His last four years in the presidency proved to be much more complex and troublesome than the first four. One of the most controversial problems to erupt during this period originated with the man who almost plucked the presidency away from Jefferson in 1801: Aaron Burr.

---

13. Second Inaugural Address (4 Mar. 1805), Bergh 3:378-79.
14. TJ to the Chiefs of the Upper Cherokees (4 May 1808), Bergh 16:434.

While serving as Vice President during Jefferson's first term, Burr had embarrassed the administration several times by using his tie-breaking vote in the Senate to aid the Federalists. When he decided to run for Governor of New York in late 1803, he sought Federalist backing because Republicans in the state no longer supported him. Having alienated the Republican leaders in Congress also, Burr was replaced by George Clinton as their vice-presidential candidate during the 1804 campaign.

Aaron Burr, who served as the Vice President in Jefferson's first administration. During the last months of his term he shot and killed Alexander Hamilton in a duel. Afterward he became involved in a plot to divide the Union, but was apprehended and tried for treason.

Burr's defeat in the New York gubernatorial election was due in large measure to the efforts of Alexander Hamilton, who was still a very powerful force in the Federalist party. Bitter over some of the charges made during the campaign, Burr challenged Hamilton to a duel. The challenge was accepted, and the fateful contest took place at Weehawken, New Jersey, on July 11, 1804. Hamilton fired the first shot, apparently missing on purpose; but Burr's gun found its target, and Hamilton died the next day. Warrants for the arrest of Vice President Aaron Burr were posted in both New Jersey and

New York, so he fled the area and lived out the last few months of his term in disgrace and exile.

The Burr Conspiracy

Having been denied political office at both the state and the national level, Burr later developed a scheme for gaining power in another way. There is still some mystery surrounding the details of his plan, but it appears that he intended to gather dissidents from the western territories and to lead them in an attack on Mexico, hoping eventually to set up a Napoleonic-type empire with himself at the head. The plan also called for the secession of some parts of the United States. President Jefferson, who had begun to hear rumors of this plot in late 1806, noted that the border dispute then taking place between Spain and the United States helped lend credibility to Burr's efforts.

> He collected ... all the ardent, restless, desperate, and disaffected persons who were ready for any enterprise analogous to their characters. He seduced good and well-meaning citizens, some by assurances that he possessed the confidence of the government and was acting under its secret patronage, a pretense which obtained some credit from the state of our differences with Spain. [15]

But Jefferson issued a proclamation against the expedition in November, and Burr was captured several months later as he led his force down the Mississippi toward New Orleans. He was eventually brought to trial in Richmond, Virginia, where Chief Justice John Marshall

---

15. Special Message to Congress (22 Jan. 1807), Bergh 3:431–32.

presided over the proceedings. When the trial began on August 3, 1807, Jefferson was sure that his former Vice President would "unquestionably be convicted."[16] But he expressed great dismay several weeks later when he learned that Justice Marshall, by creating a very narrow definition of treason and by making use of certain legal technicalities, had managed to acquit Burr of the charges brought against him.

> The scenes which have been acted at Richmond are such as have never before been exhibited in any country where all regard to public character has not yet been thrown off. They are equivalent to a proclamation of impunity to every traitorous combination which may be formed to destroy the Union.... However, they will produce an amendment to the Constitution which, keeping the judges independent of the executive, will not leave them so of the nation.[17]

Problems with the Federal Judiciary

This was not the President's first run-in with the judiciary. Before Jefferson was inaugurated in 1801, the Federalists in Congress passed a law which substantially increased the number of federal judges, and President Adams spent the final hours of his term filling these positions with members of his party. When Jefferson became President, he prevented these "midnight judges" from taking office by instructing his Secretary of State, James Madison, not to deliver the last-minute appointments Adams had signed. The new Republican

16. TJ to the Marquis de Lafayette (26 May 1807), Ford 9:65–66.
17. TJ to General James Wilkinson (20 Sept. 1807), Bergh 11:375.

Congress later abolished many of the judgeships created by the Federalists.

But the national courts remained a stronghold of Federalism throughout Jefferson's presidency, frustrating many efforts of the elected officials. "It is unfortunate," wrote Jefferson in 1807, "that Federalism is still predominant in our judiciary department, which is consequently in opposition to the legislative and executive branches, and is able to baffle their measures often."[18]

He was especially concerned about the absence of any effective controls on the federal judiciary, and the resultant likelihood that power would gradually be transferred by judicial decisions from the states to the national government. Speaking of the federal judges themselves, he noted that it was "their peculiar maxim and creed that 'it is the office of a good judge to enlarge his jurisdiction.'"

> We have seen, too, that, contrary to all correct example, they are in the habit of going out of the question before them, to throw an anchor ahead and grapple further hold for future advances of power. They are then, in fact, the corps of sappers and miners, steadily working to undermine the independent rights of the states and to consolidate all power in the hands of [the federal] government.[19]

What Jefferson advocated was a Constitutional amendment to place the national judiciary under the control of Congress and the state legislatures.

> Our judges are effectually independent of the nation.

---

18. TJ to James Bowdoin (2 Apr. 1807), Bergh 11:186.
19. Autobiography (1821), Bergh 1:121-22.

But this ought not to be. I would not, indeed, make them dependent on the executive authority;... but I deem it indispensable to the continuance of this government that they should be submitted to some practical and impartial control, and that this, to be imparted, must be compounded of a mixture of state and federal authorities....

I do not charge the judges with wilful and ill-intentioned error; but honest error must be arrested where its toleration leads to public ruin.... Judges should be withdrawn from their bench whose erroneous biases are leading us to dissolution. It may, indeed, injure them in fame or in fortune; but it saves the Republic, which is the first and supreme law. [20]

Jefferson Warns Against "Judicial Review"

The leader of the judiciary's opposition to the Republican administration was John Marshall, a distant cousin of Jefferson and a staunch Federalist who had served as Secretary of State under President Adams. Shortly before his term expired, Adams appointed Marshall as Chief Justice of the Supreme Court, a position he retained until his death in 1835. By a decision rendered during Jefferson's first administration, Marshall established the concept of "judicial review," enabling the

---

20. Ibid. Jefferson wrote that his proposed amendment was one "of which none of us thought at the time [during ratification debates after the Constitutional Convention], and in the omission of which lurks the germ that is to destroy this happy combination of national powers in the general government for matters of national concern, and independent powers in the states for what concerns the states severally." Ibid., p. 120. Similarly, a Judicial Reform Amendment which has been advocated in recent years would allow any Supreme Court decision to be overturned by two-thirds of both houses of Congress or by resolutions from three-fourths of the state legislatures.

Chief Justice John Marshall, who became one of President Jefferson's strongest political foes.

federal courts to void Congressional laws by declaring them unconstitutional. [21]

President Jefferson was opposed to this notion, believing that it endangered the separation-of-powers principle. In 1804 he wrote, "The opinion which gives to the judges the right to decide what laws are constitutional and what not, not only for themselves in their own sphere of action, but for the legislative and executive also in their spheres, would make the judiciary a despotic branch." [22] In his later years he declared that the practice of judicial review, which made the courts "the ultimate arbiters of all constitutional questions," was "a very dangerous doctrine indeed, and one which would place us under the despotism of an oligarchy."

> Our judges are as honest as other men, and not more so. They have, with others, the same passions for party, for power, and the privilege of their corps; . . . and their power [is] the more dangerous as they are in office for

---

21. This decision, from the famous *Marbury* v. *Madison* case, was handed down in February 1803. The significant portions are reprinted in Mortimer J. Adler et al., eds., *The Annals of America,* 18 vols. (Chicago: Encyclopaedia Britannica, Inc., 1968), 4:165–70.

22. TJ to Mrs. Abigail Adams (11 Sept. 1804), Bergh 11:51.

life, and not responsible, as the other functionaries are, to the elective control. The Constitution has erected no such single tribunal, knowing that to whatever hands confided, with the corruptions of time and party, its members would become despots. It has more wisely made all the departments co-equal and co-sovereign within themselves....

When the legislative or executive functionaries act unconstitutionally, they are responsible to the people in their elective capacity. The exemption of judges from that [i.e., from elections] is quite dangerous enough. I know of no safe depository of the ultimate powers of the society but the people themselves; and if we think them not enlightened enough to exercise their control with a wholesome discretion, the remedy is not to take it from them, but to inform their discretion by education.

This is the true corrective of abuses of constitutional power.... If the three powers maintain their mutual independence of each other, [the government] may last long, but not so if either can assume the authorities of the other. [23]

Provocations on the High Seas

During Jefferson's second term, the dangers posed by foreign powers overshadowed most domestic concerns. Soon after Napoleon sold Louisiana to the United States, he reopened hostilities with Great Britain. President Jefferson regretted the French leader's lust for conquest, and he feared that some unfortunate turn of events might eventually draw America into the conflict. But he was determined to prevent it if possible. "Peace is our passion,"

23. TJ to William Charles Jarvis (28 Sept. 1820), Bergh 15:277–78.

A political cartoon that appeared during Jefferson's second term in the presidency. Here the United States (represented by Jefferson) is being robbed by both France and Great Britain.

he wrote. "We prefer trying *ever* other just principles, right and safety, before we would recur to war."[24]

American merchants were also eager to remain neutral because the wartime demand for goods could bring increased trade with both England and France. But by 1807 both nations had declared naval blockades against each other's seaports, thus endangering the vessels of any country involved in European coastal trade—and particularly those of the United States, whose merchant marine was the largest of all the neutral powers.

---

24. TJ to Sir John Sinclair (30 June 1803), Bergh 10:397.

Of even greater concern was the British practice of searching American merchant ships, whether in port or at sea, under the pretext of locating deserters. Several thousand American sailors were forcefully taken and made to serve in the Royal Navy by means of this outrageous injustice, known as "impressment." British warships even patrolled the coasts and harbors of the United States for this purpose.

The *Chesapeake* Incident

On June 22, 1807, the American frigate *Chesapeake* pulled out of Norfolk, Virginia, to sail for the Mediterranean. Just a few miles off the coast it was hailed by a British naval vessel, the *Leopard,* whose commander insisted that he be allowed to search the American ship for deserters. When he was refused, he ordered his men to fire on the *Chesapeake.* The American sailors were unprepared for this attack; three of their number were killed, eighteen were wounded, and their ship was now disabled. As soon as the commander of the *Chesapeake* surrendered, the British boarded and carried away four men.

News of the incident spread quickly, and the country went wild with war fever. "Never since the battle of Lexington," observed Jefferson, "have I seen this country in such a state of exasperation as at present, and even that did not produce such unanimity."[25] He said afterward, "I had only to open [my hand] and let havoc loose."[26]

But the President decided on a more moderate course:

25. TJ to Pierre Samuel Du Pont de Nemours (14 July 1807), Bergh 11:274.

26. TJ to James Maury (25 Apr. 1812), Bergh 13:148.

he issued a proclamation banning British ships from American waters, ordered defensive preparations along the seacoast, and demanded reparations from Great Britain and an end to all impressments. Jefferson later recalled with amusement that this was the "single act of my whole administration" which the Federalists approved of.

> And when I found they approved of it, I confess I began strongly to apprehend I had done wrong, and to exclaim with the Psalmist, "Lord, what have I done that the wicked should praise me!"[27]

The Embargo Act

Although they eventually disavowed the attack on the *Chesapeake*, the British leaders refused to put a stop to impressments. As increasing numbers of American seamen were seized to man the Royal Navy, and as more and more American vessels were confiscated in European ports as a result of the British and French decrees, Jefferson saw his nation drifting rapidly into the conflict. But he believed there was still one possible alternative.

> The whole world is...laid under interdict by these two nations [England and France], and our vessels, their cargoes and crews, are to be taken by the one or the other, for whatever place they may be destined out of our own limits. If, therefore, on leaving our harbors we are certainly to lose them, is it not better, as to vessels, cargoes, and seamen, to keep them at home?[28]

On December 17, 1807, the President recommended to Congress a total embargo on American shipping abroad.

---

27. TJ to Elbridge Gerry (11 June 1812), Bergh 13:162.
28. TJ to General John Mason (Dec. 1807), Bergh 11:402.

As he expressed it, this was "the last card we have to play, short of war."[29] The Embargo Act was passed four days later.

Jefferson had two objects in mind with this measure. He knew that the nation's military forces were not yet ready for combat, and he hoped the embargo would buy time for further preparations. But his overriding hope was that France and England would suffer so much without imports from the United States that they would be forced to stop violating her neutral rights.

Outcry from New England Federalists

After the signing of the Embargo Act, enthusiastic letters of approval poured in from many parts of the country. These came from private citizens, religious organizations, and various public assemblies, including nearly every state legislature. Unfortunately, however, the new law seemed to hurt the United States more than it affected England or France. Or at least it hurt a very vocal segment of the American population—the Federalist merchants of New England. Their stores of cotton and tobacco piled up on the wharves while their ships rotted at the docks, and prices plummeted almost overnight. Some were driven out of business.

Despite the fact that the only apparent alternative was war, the New England Federalists hurled vicious criticisms at the President and his embargo policy. They also established a large-scale smuggling operation in defiance of the law, and many of them spoke openly of seceding from the Union. (Ironically, the same Federalist leaders

29. TJ to Levi Lincoln (23 Mar. 1808), Bergh 12:21.

threatened secession again in 1814, after a repeal of the embargo had helped push the country into war with Great Britain.) A few months after signing the act, Jefferson wrote to a member of his Cabinet: "This embargo law is certainly the most embarrassing one we have ever had to execute. I did not expect a crop of so sudden and rank growth of fraud and open opposition by force could have grown up in the United States."[30]

Repeal of the Embargo

In any event, Jefferson had never considered the embargo anything but a temporary measure. He wrote in March 1808, "If peace does not take place in Europe, and if France and England will not consent to withdraw the operation of their decrees and orders from us, when Congress shall meet in December they will have to consider at what point of time the embargo, continued, becomes a greater evil than war."[31]

Shortly after Congress convened in December 1808, John Quincy Adams (the son of President John Adams and a former Senator from Massachusetts) met privately with President Jefferson to express his grave concern over the extent of the secessionist movement in New England. He shared "information of the most unquestionable certainty" about secret negotiations then under way between certain Federalists and British agents, and he

---

30. TJ to Albert Gallatin (11 Aug. 1808), Bergh 12:122. Jefferson has been criticized by some historians because of his rigid enforcement of the Embargo Act. But he believed that the Constitution required him, as the chief executive officer of the federal government, to vigorously uphold the law as long as it was in force.

31. TJ to Levi Lincoln (23 Mar. 1808), Bergh 12:21.

urged that the danger of secession was real and imminent. "The repeal of the embargo," he told the President, "was absolutely necessary." Jefferson thanked Adams for this disclosure, observing that it was important "to the safety and even the salvation of our country."

> And, however reluctant I was to abandon the measure (a measure which, persevered in a little longer, we had subsequent and satisfactory assurance would have effected its object completely), from that moment, and influenced by that information, I saw the necessity of abandoning it.... I then recommended [to my friends in Congress] to yield to the necessity of a repeal of the embargo, and to endeavor to supply its place by the best substitute in which they could procure a general concurrence. [32]

By the following February Congress had repealed the Embargo Act and replaced it with a law which allowed American merchants to trade with all nations except England and France. One of Jefferson's last official acts as President was the signing of this new legislation, which he feared would ultimately lead to war. His fears were confirmed only three years later, when the War of 1812 erupted between England and the United States.

---

32. TJ to William Branch Giles (25 Dec. 1825), Bergh 16:143–45.

Chapter 21

"I Return to the People"

Although he was urged by political friends, citizens' groups, and many of the state legislatures to run for a third term, Jefferson had already made up his mind not to do so. As early as January 1805 he had decided "to withdraw at the end of my second term."

The danger is that the indulgence and attachments of the people will keep a man in the chair after he becomes a dotard, that re-election through life shall become habitual, and election for life follow that. General Washington set the example of voluntary retirement after eight years. I shall follow it. And a few more precedents will oppose the obstacle of habit to anyone after a while who shall endeavor to extend his term.

Perhaps it may beget a disposition to establish it by an amendment of the Constitution.[1]

As the 1808 campaign approached, he reaffirmed this decision to his solicitous friends. "That I should lay down my charge at a proper season," he told them, "is as much a duty as to have borne it faithfully."[2]

Jefferson had once called the presidency "a splendid misery,"[3] and he complained to an old friend during his turbulent second term that it seemed to bring him "nothing but unceasing drudgery and daily loss of friends."[4] As the day of his retirement drew near, he looked forward to his final return to Monticello:

> Within a few days I retire to my family, my books, and [my] farms; and having gained the harbor myself, I shall look on my friends still buffeting the storm with anxiety indeed, but not with envy. Never did a prisoner released from his chains feel such relief as I shall on shaking off the shackles of power.[5]

America Expresses Its Gratitude

During the last weeks of Jefferson's presidency, he received addresses from every corner of the Union, praising the accomplishments of his administration and congratulating him personally for a long and illustrious

---

1. TJ to John Taylor (6 Jan. 1805), Bergh 11:57. Jefferson's hope was finally realized when the Twenty-second Amendment was adopted in 1951, a few years after Franklin D. Roosevelt died during his fourth term in the presidency.

2. TJ to Isaac Weaver, Jr. (7 June 1807), Bergh 11:219.

3. TJ to Elbridge Gerry (13 May 1797), Bergh 9:381.

4. TJ to John Dickinson (13 Jan. 1807), Bergh 11:137.

5. TJ to Pierre Samuel Du Pont de Nemours (2 Mar. 1809), Bergh 12:259–60.

public career. As one writer noted, these communications "came from legislatures and popular bodies; from state, city, county, and town conventions and meetings; from political, ecclesiastical, military, industrial, and almost all other associations."[6] One characteristic example, a resolution passed by the Virginia legislature, makes it plain why Jefferson's presidency had met with such favor among most of his countrymen.

We have to thank you for the model of an administration conducted on the purest principles of republicanism; for pomp and state laid aside; patronage discarded; internal taxes abolished; a host of superfluous officers disbanded; the monarchic maxim that "a national debt is a national blessing" renounced, and more than thirty-three millions of our debt discharged;... and, without the guilt or calamities of conquest, a vast and fertile region added to our country, far more extensive than her original possessions, bringing along with it the Mississippi and the port of Orleans, the trade of the West to the Pacific Ocean, and in the intrinsic value of the land itself a source of permanent and almost inexhaustible revenue.

These are points in your administration which the historian will not fail to seize, to expand, and teach posterity to dwell upon with delight. Nor will he forget our peace with the civilized world, preserved through a season of uncommon difficulty and trial; the good will cultivated with the unfortunate aborigines of our country [the American Indians], and the civilization humanely extended among them; the lesson taught the inhabitants of the coast of Barbary, that we have the

6. Randall, *The Life of Thomas Jefferson,* 3:303.

means of chastising their piratical encroachments and awing them into justice; and that theme on which, above all others, the historic genius will hang with rapture— the liberty of speech and of the press preserved inviolate....

From the first brilliant and happy moment of your resistance to foreign tyranny until the present day, we mark with pleasure and with gratitude the same uniform, consistent character, the same warm and devoted attachment to liberty and the Republic, the same ... love of your country, her rights, her peace, her honor, her prosperity....

That your retirement may be as happy as your life has been virtuous and useful, that our youth may see in the blissful close of your days an additional inducement to form themselves on your model, is the devout and earnest prayer of your fellow citizens.[7]

"The Holy Cause of Freedom"

Such outpourings must have been deeply gratifying to President Jefferson, who had devoted virtually his entire adult life to what he called "the holy cause of freedom."[8] The American people were now returning their heartfelt gratitude for his lifetime of service to the Republic. One address, presented by the citizens of Washington, contained a more intimate note and revealed the feelings of Jefferson's neighbors as he prepared to leave their city.

We have ... beheld you, with parental solicitude and with a vigilance that never sleeps, watching over the

7. Resolution of the General Assembly of Virginia (7 Feb. 1809), Bergh 17:398–400.

8. TJ's response to address of welcome by the citizens of Albemarle County (12 Feb. 1790), Boyd 16:179.

fairest offspring of liberty, and by your unremitted labors in upholding, explaining, and vindicating our system of government, rendering it the object of love at home and respect abroad....

The world knows you as a philosopher and philanthropist; the American people know you as a patriot and statesman. We know you, in addition to all this, as a *man*. And ... there is not one among us whose predominant feeling at this moment is not that of affection for the mild and endearing virtues that have made everyone here your friend, and you his....

With a grateful nation we pray that you may be happy, and if the just Being that presides over the universe [will] insure to you but a portion of that felicity you have conferred on others, our prayers will be fulfilled![9]

"This Day I Return to the People"

In the election of 1808 the nation had chosen Jefferson's Secretary of State, James Madison, as his successor. Jefferson could not have been happier about this outcome. Madison, besides being a very close friend, was his personal preference for the office. Moreover, the fact that Madison had captured over two-thirds of the electoral votes indicated wide public approval of the Republican policies implemented over the past eight years.

The inauguration ceremonies were held on March 4, 1809. President-elect Madison invited his predecessor to sit beside him en route to the Capitol building that morning, but Jefferson declined. When asked afterward

9. Committee of Washington citizens to TJ (4 Mar. 1809), reprinted in Saul K. Padover, ed., *Thomas Jefferson and the National Capital* (Washington: United States Government Printing Office, 1946), pp. 458–60.

A portrait of James Madison at about the time he succeeded Jefferson as President of the United States.

why he had not accepted his old friend's invitation, he explained, "I wished not to divide with him the honors of the day; it pleased me better to see them all bestowed on him."[10] Accompanied only by his grandson, Jefferson mounted his horse and joined the "large procession of citizens" who were following Madison's carriage.

He had heard that a body of cavalry and infantry were preparing to escort him to the Capitol, and, still anxious to avoid all kinds of display, hurried off with his grandson. As they rode along Pennsylvania Avenue, Mr. Jefferson caught a glimpse of the head of the column coming down one of the cross streets. He touched his hat to the troops and, spurring his horse, trotted past them.[11]

When he reached the Capitol, Jefferson "dismounted, . . . hitched his own horse to a post, and followed the multitude into the Hall of Representatives. Here a seat had been prepared for him near that of the new President. This he declined, and when urged by the committee of

---

10. Quoted in Smith, *The First Forty Years of Washington Society*, p. 410.
11. Randolph, *The Domestic Life of Thomas Jefferson*, p. 323.

arrangement he replied, 'This day I return to the people, and my proper seat is among them.'"[12] At the conclusion of the ceremony he slipped quietly away on horseback and began to pack his personal belongings.

One week later, after bidding farewell to the Madisons and other friends, Thomas Jefferson headed toward his beloved home in Virginia. This was the last time he ever saw the city of Washington, and he was happy to leave it behind.

---

12. Smith, p. 410. For other interesting occurrences later in the same day see ibid., pp. 411–12.

Chapter 22

The Sage of Monticello

J efferson was sixty-five years old when he retired from the presidency in 1809, and the first
desire of his heart was to return to the amiable
companionship of his remaining family members. More
than a decade earlier he had spoken of his family circle as
"the only scene where, for me, the sweeter affections of
life have any exercise."[1] Although his daughter Mary had
died during his first term, he still had Martha and several
grandchildren, and they now lived with him on his little
mountain. "I am retired to Monticello," he rejoiced,

1. TJ to Martha Jefferson Randolph (17 May 1798), Betts and Bear, *The Family Letters of Thomas Jefferson,* p. 161.

"where, in the bosom of my family, and surrounded by my books, I enjoy a repose to which I have been long a stranger."[2]

No one could be more proud of his progeny than Jefferson. He boasted in 1813 that he had "ten and one-half grandchildren, and two and three-fourths great-grandchildren, and these fractions will ere long become units."[3] He loved each of them without reserve, and these feelings were fully reciprocated. One of his grand-daughters, writing in later years, recalled that she "loved and honored him above all earthly beings."

> And well I might. From him seemed to flow all the pleasures of my life. To him I owed all the small blessings and joyful surprises of my childish and girlish years. His nature was so eminently sympathetic that, with those he loved, he could enter into their feelings, anticipate their wishes, gratify their tastes, and surround them with an atmosphere of affection....
>
> Our grandfather seemed to read our hearts, to see our invisible wishes, to be our good [genie], to wave the fairy wand, to brighten our young lives by his goodness and his gifts.[4]

She also remembered his careful efforts to cultivate proper attitudes and manners in the youngsters at Monticello.

> He talked with us freely, affectionately, [and] never lost an opportunity of giving a pleasure or a good lesson.

2. TJ to General Thaddeus Kosciusko (26 Feb. 1810), Bergh 12:369.

3. TJ to Mrs. Abigail Adams (22 Aug. 1813), Bergh 19:194.

4. Ellen W. Coolidge to Henry S. Randall (n.d.), in Randall, *The Life of Thomas Jefferson*, 3:348–49; also in Randolph, *The Domestic Life of Thomas Jefferson*, pp. 344–45.

He reproved without wounding us, and commended without making us vain. He took pains to correct our errors and false ideas, checked the bold, encouraged the timid, and tried to teach us to reason soundly and feel rightly. Our smaller follies he treated with good-humored raillery, our graver ones with kind and serious admonition. He was watchful over our manners, and called our attention to every violation of propriety. [5]

Foot Races and Reading Circles

Jefferson often invited his grandchildren to join him while he worked in his flower gardens, and in the evenings he played games with them. Another granddaughter reminisced about some of these happy scenes:

One of our earliest amusements was in running races on the terrace or around the lawn. He placed us according to our ages, giving the youngest and smallest the start of all the others by some yards, and so on; and then he raised his arm high, with his white handkerchief in his hand, on which our eager eyes were fixed, and slowly counted three, at which number he dropped the handkerchief, and we started off to finish the race by returning to the starting place and receiving our reward of dried fruit—three figs, prunes, or dates to the victor, two to the second, and one to the lagger who came in last. These were our summer sports with him....

On winter evenings, when it grew too dark to read, in the half hour that passed before candles came in, as we all sat round the fire, he taught us several childish games, and would play them with us. I remember that

_____

5. Ibid.

"cross questions" and "I love my love with an A" were two I learned from him; and we would teach some of ours to him.

When the candles were brought, all was quiet immediately, for he took up his book to read; and we would not speak out of a whisper lest we should disturb him, and generally we followed his example and took a book; and I have seen him raise his eyes from his own book, and look round on the little circle of readers, and smile and make some remark to Mamma about it.[6]

On other occasions he delighted in taking up his violin to play for his grandchildren while they gleefully danced around him. He never tired of being with his family.

Occupations of Old Age

"The whole of my life has been a war with my natural taste, feelings, and wishes," Jefferson told a friend the summer after he left the presidency. "Domestic life and literary pursuits were my first and latest inclinations; circumstances and not my desires led me to the path I have trod. And like a bow, though long bent, which when unstrung flies back to its natural state, I resume with delight the character and pursuits for which nature designed me."[7] In a letter written several months later, he described the activities that now occupied his time:

My mornings are devoted to correspondence. From breakfast to dinner I am in my shops, my garden, or on horseback among my farms; from dinner to dark I give to society and recreation with my neighbors and friends;

---

6. Virginia J. Trist to Nicholas P. Trist (26 May 1839), in Randall, 3:349–50; also in Randolph, pp. 346–47.

7. Quoted in Smith, *The First Forty Years of Washington Society,* pp. 80–81.

and from candlelight to early bedtime I read. My health is perfect, and my strength considerably reinforced by the activity of the course I pursue; perhaps it is as great as usually falls to the lot of near sixty-seven years of age.

I talk of plows and harrows, of seeding and harvesting with my neighbors—and of politics too, if they choose, with as little reserve as the rest of my fellow citizens, and feel, at length, the blessing of being free to say and do what I please without being responsible for it to any mortal. [8]

Jefferson had given a lifetime of service to his country, and his career had certainly been an illustrious one. Now, having retired at last to his unique mountaintop home in the backwoods of Virginia, he was admired throughout the Western world as the "Sage of Monticello." The esteem in which he was held among the people of the United States and other nations is reflected in many writings of that era. This representative statement was made by a British officer who visited Monticello in 1817:

While he dedicates the evening of his glorious days to the pursuits of science and literature, [he] shuns none of the humbler duties of private life; but, having filled a seat higher than that of kings, succeeds with graceful dignity to that of the good neighbor, and becomes the friendly adviser, lawyer, physician, and even gardener of his vicinity. . . .

What monarch would venture thus to exhibit himself in the nakedness of his humanity? On what royal brow would the laurel replace the diadem? [9]

---

8. TJ to General Thaddeus Kosciusko (26 Feb. 1810), Bergh 12:369.

9. Lieutenant Francis Hall, *Travels in Canada and the United States in 1816 and 1817* (London: Printed for Longman, Hurst, Rees, Orme, & Brown, 1818), pp. 384–85.

But Jefferson simply regarded himself as a farmer who had finally come back to his native element. "I have often thought," he mused, "that if heaven had given me [the] choice of my position and calling, it should have been on a rich spot of earth, well watered.... No occupation is so delightful to me as the culture of the earth."[10] Having escaped the unpleasant world of politics, he now surrounded himself with the people and things he loved most. "I have withdrawn myself from all political intermeddlings," he said, "to indulge the evening of my life with what have been the passions of every portion of it— books, science, my farms, my family and friends. To these every hour of the day is now devoted."[11]

"Drudging at the Writing Table"

As his retirement years wore on, however, they were increasingly disrupted by still another obligation to the public—one which Jefferson had not anticipated. "I am oppressed by a general and revolting correspondence," he complained to one of his grandsons in 1820, "wearing me down with incessant labor instead of leaving me to the tranquil happiness with which reading and lighter occupations would fill pleasantly what remains to me of life."[12]

Although he had been "chained to a writing table" during his presidency, he thought that after leaving Washington in 1809 he would be free to choose his own pursuits.[13] But the Sage of Monticello was soon receiving

---

10. TJ to Charles Willson Peale (20 Aug. 1811), Bergh 13:79.

11. TJ to James Maury (25 Apr. 1812), Bergh 13:148–49.

12. TJ to Francis Wayles Eppes (6 Oct. 1820), Betts and Bear, p. 434.

13. TJ to Martha Jefferson Randolph (23 Nov. 1807), Betts and Bear, pp. 315–16.

letters from thousands of Americans and others who were eager to learn his views on matters of current interest. He noted that in a single year, 1820, he had received "one thousand two hundred and sixty-seven" communications, "many of them requiring answers of elaborate research, and all of them to be answered with due attention and consideration."[14]

Responding to these inquiries consumed more and more of his time. "From sunrise to one or two o'clock," he wrote in 1817, "and often from dinner to dark, I am drudging at the writing table. All this to answer ... strangers and others who, in the most friendly dispositions, oppress me with their concerns, their pursuits, their projects, inventions, and speculations, political, moral, religious, mechanical, mathematical, historical, etc., etc., etc."[15]

"The Finest Invention of the Present Age"

It has been said that "Jefferson probably wrote more letters with his own hand than any other public man that ever lived."[16] About 19,000 of these have been preserved, thanks largely to the "polygraph" he began using during his first term as President. The polygraph, invented by

---

14. TJ to John Adams (27 June 1822), Bergh 15:387.

15. TJ to John Adams (11 Jan. 1817), Bergh 15:97–98.

16. Curtis, *The True Thomas Jefferson*, p. 348. This was all the more remarkable in Jefferson's retirement years because of the physical difficulty he experienced in answering correspondence. In 1819 he noted that "a stiff wrist, the consequence of an early dislocation, makes writing both slow and painful." TJ to Dr. Vine Utley (21 Mar. 1819), Bergh 15: 187–88. Also in this period he prepared a history of his life through March 1790 (the "Autobiography") and revised the many notes he had written during his years of service as Secretary of State, Vice President, and President (the "Anas").

The "polygraph," a mechanical device which Jefferson used after 1804 to make file copies of his many letters.

John Hawkins of Philadelphia, was a desk-top mechanism which suspended two or more writing pens in such a way that any mark produced by one pen was simultaneously duplicated by the others.

Jefferson considered this device "the finest invention of the present age."[17]

He used one with two pens attached, and after about 1804 he produced a file copy of almost every letter he wrote. To demonstrate the quality of the instrument, he sometimes sent his friends the duplicates of his letters rather than the originals. He personally made several improvements on the polygraph in his later years.

Renewal of an Historic Friendship

One of Jefferson's frequent correspondents was Dr. Benjamin Rush, a Philadelphia physician and fellow member of the American Philosophical Society. Dr. Rush also communicated with John Adams, and in the fall of 1811 he was instrumental in healing the rift which political differences had created between Adams and Jefferson.

Rush had already written to the two former Presidents, urging them to put aside past differences and renew their correspondence. Both of them had indicated a willingness

---

17. TJ to James Bowdoin (10 July 1806), Bergh 11:118.

to do so; they were waiting only for a favorable occasion to present itself. The opportunity came in the summer of 1811. Two of Jefferson's neighbors, taking a tour of the northern states, happened to visit John Adams at his home in Massachusetts. During their conversation Adams made some reference to his successor in the presidency and said, "I always loved Jefferson, and still love him."[18]

When this was reported to Jefferson some months later, he openly expressed his feelings to Dr. Rush: "This is enough for me. I only needed this knowledge to revive towards him all the affections of the most cordial moments of our lives.... I have thus, my friend, laid my heart open to you, because you were so kind as to take an interest in healing again Revolutionary affections which have ceased in expression only, but not in their existence."[19] Rush forwarded this message to Adams, who then sat down and penned a letter to Monticello. Jefferson replied immediately with these touching lines:

> A letter from you calls up recollections very dear to my mind. It carries me back to the times when, beset with difficulties and dangers, we were fellow laborers in the same cause, struggling for what is most valuable to man, his right of self-government....
>
> No circumstances have lessened the interest I feel...respecting yourself; none have suspended for one moment my sincere esteem for you, and I now salute you with unchanged affection and respect.[20]

18. Quoted in Jefferson's letter to Dr. Benjamin Rush (5 Dec. 1811), Bergh 13:115–16.

19. Ibid., pp. 116–17.

20. TJ to John Adams (21 Jan. 1812), Bergh 13:123–25.

A portrait of John Adams in later life. After a political estrangement of several years, Adams and Jefferson renewed their old friendship and corresponded frequently until their deaths in 1826.

After the ice was broken Adams told his old friend, "You and I ought not to die before we have explained ourselves to each other."[21] And they spent the next fourteen years, until their deaths, doing just that. The letters which resulted from this exchange, covering an unusually broad range of topics, are among the most valuable and interesting in American history. One recent scholar has called them "a priceless gift to posterity."[22]

Jefferson and the Monroe Doctrine

Although Jefferson claimed to have withdrawn himself from "all political intermeddlings," he naturally continued to take an interest in important issues of the day. He frequently wrote to Adams and others to share his views on current domestic and foreign affairs. He never attempted to impose his ideas on government leaders during his retirement years, but Presidents Madison and Monroe—both having been close friends and political

21. John Adams to TJ (15 July 1813), in Bergh 13:315.

22. Dumas Malone, *The Sage of Monticello,* Jefferson and His Time, vol. 6 (Boston: Little, Brown and Company, 1981), p. 95. See Lester J. Cappon, ed., *The Adams-Jefferson Letters: The Complete Correspondence Between Thomas Jefferson and John and Abigail Adams,* 2 vols. (Chapel Hill: University of North Carolina Press, 1959).

disciples of Jefferson for many years—sometimes requested his counsel when they approached difficult decisions. Especially notable in this connection was Jefferson's influence on the formation of the Monroe Doctrine in 1823.

Jefferson had written during his presidency that the objective of the United States and its neighbors should be "to exclude all European influence from this hemisphere."[23] In 1820 he expressed the hope that he might see "all the American nations ... coalescing in an American system of policy totally independent of and unconnected with that of Europe."[24] When President Monroe asked for his advice in October 1823, at a time when European interference in Latin America was widely feared, he responded:

> The question presented by the letters you sent me is the most momentous which has ever been offered to my contemplation since that of Independence. That made us a nation; this sets our compass and points the course which we are to steer through the ocean of time opening on us.... Our first and fundamental maxim should be never to entangle ourselves in the broils of Europe. Our second, never to suffer Europe to intermeddle with cis-Atlantic affairs.[25]

Jefferson's ideas on this subject finally bore fruit when

---

23. TJ to Governor William Claiborne (29 Oct. 1808), Bergh 12:187. Five years later he declared: "America has a hemisphere to itself. It must have its separate system of interests, which must not be subordinated to those of Europe." TJ to Baron Alexander von Humboldt (6 Dec. 1813), Bergh 14:22.

24. TJ to William Short (4 Aug. 1820), Bergh 15:262-63.

25. TJ to President James Monroe (24 Oct. 1823), Bergh 15:477. Besides exchanging several letters on the matter, Jefferson and Monroe had discussed it at Monticello earlier that year.

the historic Monroe Doctrine was announced in the President's annual message to Congress six weeks later.

"The Hour of Emancipation ... Will Come"

Another of Jefferson's continuing political concerns was the evil of slavery. He wrote in 1814 that his views on the matter had "long since been in the possession of the public, and time has only served to give them stronger root."

> The love of justice and the love of country plead equally the cause of these people, and it is a moral reproach to us that they should have pleaded so long in vain.... Yet the hour of emancipation is advancing in the march of time. It will come.[26]

Jefferson has been criticized by some modern historians for favoring in 1820 the proposed admission of Missouri as a slave state. He did so reluctantly, fearing that the spreading threats of secession by the southern states placed the survival of the Union in jeopardy.

> The Missouri question, ... like a fire-bell in the night, awakened and filled me with terror. I considered it at once as the knell of the Union.... I can say, with conscious truth, that there is not a man on earth who would sacrifice more than I would to relieve us from this heavy reproach [i.e., slavery] in any *practicable* way. ... But as it is, we have the wolf by the ears, and we can neither hold him nor safely let him go. Justice is in one scale, and self-preservation in the other.[27]

He had not abandoned his commitment to the cause of freeing the slaves. Later in the same year he expressed

---

26. TJ to Edward Coles (25 Aug. 1814), Ford 9:477-78.

27. TJ to John Holmes (22 Apr. 1820), Bergh 15:249. The so-called Missouri Compromise did not involve the importation of new slaves from

unqualified approval when his son-in-law Thomas Mann Randolph, then Governor of Virginia, proposed "a plan of general emancipation" to the state legislature. "Although this is not ripe to be immediately acted on," he said, "it will, with the Missouri question, force a serious attention to this object by our citizens."[28] Eleven months before his death, "with one foot in the grave and the other uplifted to follow it," he still spoke of emancipation as the enterprise "of my greatest anxieties." As always, he refused to abandon hope on this issue.

> The march of events has not been such as to render its completion practicable within the limits of time allotted to me; and I leave its accomplishment as the work of another generation.... The abolition of the evil is not impossible; it ought never, therefore, to be despaired of. Every plan should be adopted, every experiment tried, which may do something towards the ultimate object.[29]

"Swarms of Impertinent Gazers"

As if the flood of letters were not enough, Jefferson's retirement years were also imposed upon by countless tourists who came to meet the "Sage of Monticello." Because there were few inns in the region, most of these people were invited to stay overnight at Jefferson's estate.

---

outside the country. In the same letter Jefferson noted that "as the passage of slaves from one state to another would not make a slave of a single human being who would not be so without it, so their diffusion over a greater surface would make them individually happier and [would] proportionally facilitate the accomplishment of their emancipation by dividing the burden on a greater number of coadjutors." Ibid., pp. 249–50. See also John Chester Miller, *The Wolf by the Ears: Thomas Jefferson and Slavery* (New York: Macmillan Publishing Co., Inc., The Free Press, 1977), pp. 221–52.

28. TJ to David Bailey Warden (26 Dec. 1820), Ford 10:173.

29. TJ to Miss Frances Wright (7 Aug. 1825), Bergh 16:119–20.

One of his granddaughters wrote that "they came of all nations, at all times, and paid longer or shorter visits."

> We had persons from abroad, from all the states of the Union, from every part of the state—men, women, and children. In short, almost every day for at least eight months of the year brought its contingent of guests.

> People of wealth, fashion, men in office, professional men, military and civil, lawyers, doctors, Protestant clergymen, Catholic priests, members of Congress, foreign ministers, missionaries, Indian agents, tourists, travellers, artists, strangers, friends. Some came from affection and respect, some from curiosity, some to give or receive advice or instruction, some from idleness, [and] some because others [had] set the example.[30]

Although Jefferson welcomed these visitors cheerfully and graciously, they often proved a burden to him and to his daughter Martha, who always served as hostess at Monticello. A friend once asked her "what was the largest number of persons for whom she had been called upon unexpectedly to prepare accommodations for the night, and she replied *fifty!*"[31]

But the overnight guests were not the only ones who invaded Monticello. Along with them, we learn from one biographer, came "swarms of impertinent gazers who, without introduction, permission, or any ceremony whatever, thrust themselves into the most private of Mr. Jefferson's out-of-door resorts, and even into his house, and stared about as if they were at a public show."

---

30. Ellen W. Coolidge to Henry S. Randall (1856), in Randall, 3:330; also in Randolph, pp. 401-2.

31. Dr. Robley Dunglison, quoted in Randolph, p. 403.

This nuisance increased as years advanced.... Groups of utter strangers, of both sexes, planted [themselves] in the passage between his study and dining room, consulting their watches and waiting for him to pass from one to the other to his dinner, so that they could momentarily stare at him. A female once punched through a window pane of the house with her parasol to get a better view of him.

Martha Jefferson Randolph in 1821. The oldest of Jefferson's six children and the only one to outlive him, she served as hostess at Monticello during his retirement years and bore him twelve grandchildren.

When [he sat] in the shade of his porticoes to enjoy the coolness of the approaching evening, parties of men and women would sometimes approach within a dozen yards and gaze at him point-blank until they had looked their fill, as they would have gazed on a lion in a menagerie. ... They wanted to tell their children, and have it told to their grandchildren, that they had seen Thomas Jefferson.[32]

Such intrusions must have been irksome to Jefferson, who had always placed great value on personal privacy. To escape the constant influx of strangers, he retreated three

---

32. Randall, 3:331.

or four times a year to his home at Poplar Forest, about ninety miles southwest of Monticello. Usually taking two of his grandchildren and a load of books with him, he stayed there "from a fortnight to a month at a time ... in the solitude of a hermit."[33]

An Emotional Reunion

Among the many visitors to Monticello were certain ones whom Jefferson was very happy to see. One of these was the Marquis de Lafayette, the famed French general who had fought heroically for the United States during the Revolutionary War. He had defended Virginia against the British when Jefferson was Governor of the state, and the two had developed a close friendship when Jefferson lived in Paris as the American minister to France. They had corresponded often following Jefferson's departure from Europe, but thirty-five years had passed since their last meeting.

When Jefferson learned in 1824 that Lafayette was sailing across the Atlantic for a tour of the United States, he wrote his old friend and urged that he come to Monticello. The memorable reunion took place on the morning of November 4. Jefferson's grandson, who was present, recorded what happened after Lafayette's carriage reached the summit of the little mountain.

> His escort—one hundred and twenty mounted men— formed on one side in a semicircle extending from the carriage to the house. A crowd of about two hundred

---

33. TJ to Dr. Benjamin Rush (17 Aug. 1811), Bergh 13:75. The house at Poplar Forest was also designed by Jefferson and built under his direction. For interesting details of these visits, as told by the grandchildren, see Randall, 3:341–45.

men, who were drawn together by curiosity to witness the meeting of these two venerable men, formed themselves in a semicircle on the opposite side.

As Lafayette descended from the carriage, Jefferson descended the steps of the portico. The scene which followed was touching. Jefferson was feeble and tottering with age—Lafayette permanently lamed and broken in health by his long confinement in the dungeon of Olmutz. As they approached each other, their uncertain gait quickened itself into a shuffling run, and exclaiming "Ah, Jefferson!" "Ah, Lafayette!" they burst into tears as they fell into each other's arms.

Among the four hundred men witnessing the scene there was not a dry eye—no sound save an occasional suppressed sob. The two old men entered the house as the crowd dispersed in profound silence.[34]

---

34. Account by Thomas Jefferson Randolph, quoted in Randolph, pp. 390–91. This brief mention of the "dungeon of Olmutz" was a reference to Lafayette's five-year imprisonment by the Austrians during a war between Austria and France in the 1790s.

Chapter 23

"The Hand of Age Is Upon Me"

D uring the closing years of his life, Jefferson devoted most of his energies to the establishment of a state university in Virginia—the capstone of a comprehensive system of public education which he had conceived many years earlier. His first proposal for a university supported by state funds was introduced in 1779, and he repeatedly expressed interest in the idea during the next three decades.[1] Upon his retirement from the presidency in 1809, the Sage of Monticello found that "a part of my occupation, and by no

---

1. See Roy J. Honeywell, *The Educational Work of Thomas Jefferson* (1931; reprint ed., New York: Russell & Russell, Inc., 1964); James Bryant Conant, *Thomas Jefferson and the Development of American Public Education* (Berkeley: University of California Press, 1962).

means the least pleasing, is the direction of the studies of such young men as ask it."

> They place themselves in the neighboring village [Charlottesville], and have the use of my library and counsel, and make a part of my society.... I endeavor to keep their attention fixed on the main objects of all science [i.e., knowledge], the freedom and happiness of man. So that, coming to bear a share in the councils and government of their country, they will keep ever in view the sole objects of all legitimate government.[2]

He believed that these two great purposes—"the freedom and happiness of man"—should serve as the polestars of all educational programs throughout the Republic.

In the spring of 1814 Jefferson was asked to serve on the board of trustees of the recently formed Albemarle Academy, and later that year he drafted a proposal urging the state legislature to transform the academy into a respectable institution of higher learning. After Central College was established in 1816, he vigorously pushed for further improvements. In January 1819 the legislators voted to create the University of Virginia in Charlottesville.

Jefferson was appointed the first president of the university, and he plunged wholeheartedly into the task of bringing it into existence. "The university will give employment to my remaining years," he wrote, "and quite enough for my senile faculties. It is the last act of

---

2. TJ to Thaddeus Kosciusko (26 Feb. 1810), Bergh 12:369-70.

usefulness I can render, and could I see it open I would not ask an hour more of life."[3]

"The Last Service I Can Render My Country"

He left nothing undone in his efforts to reach this goal. He regarded the university as "the last of my mortal cares, and the last service I can render my country,"[4] so it became the great passion of his final years. Though weakened by age, he personally surveyed the sites and laid off the foundations with pegs and twine; designed and supervised the construction of every building; hired carpenters, bricklayers, and stonemasons; planned the landscaping; fought for funds from the legislature; devised the curriculum and administrative policies of the university; and directed the assembling of its faculty (he even recruited professors from Europe to teach certain subjects in which he felt American scholars were deficient).

Jefferson's architectural concept for the school was unique in that era. "The plan of building," he wrote, "is not to erect one single magnificent building to contain everybody and everything, but to make of it an academical village in which every professor should have his separate house, containing his lecturing room with ... kitchen, garden, etc., [and] distinct dormitories for the students."[5] This "academical village" has since attained wide renown; in 1976, for example, the American Institute of Architects voted it "far and away in first place" among the "proudest

---

3. TJ to Judge Spencer Roane (9 Mar. 1821), Bergh 15:326.
4. TJ to J. Correa de Serra (24 Oct. 1820), Bergh 15:285.
5. TJ to Nathaniel Bowditch (26 Oct. 1818), Bergh 19:265.

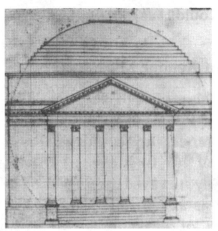

Jefferson's elevation drawing of the Rotunda of the University of Virginia.

achievements of American architecture over the past 200 years."[6]

But that was long afterward. During its initial construction, the University of Virginia was merely "an object of curiosity for the traveler" which also provided "frequent exercise" for its planner and builder.[7] Edmund Bacon, the chief overseer at Monticello, recalled that Jefferson rode to Charlottesville "every day while the university was building, unless the weather was very stormy."

> I don't think he ever missed a day unless the weather was *very* bad. Company never made any difference. When he could not go on account of the weather, he would send me if there was anything he wanted to know. He looked after all the materials and would not allow any poor materials to go into the building if he could help it. He took as much pains in seeing that everything was done right as if it had been his own house.[8]

In 1820, at the advanced age of seventy-seven, he shared with a friend his vision of the university—the dream which drove him on at such a demanding pace:

---

6. *AIA Journal*, July 1976, p. 91.

7. TJ to John Adams (15 Aug. 1820), Bergh 15:269.

8. Bear, *Jefferson at Monticello*, pp. 33–34.

"This institution of my native state, the hobby of my old age, will be based on the illimitable freedom of the human mind to explore and to expose every subject susceptible of its contemplation."[9] His ardent desire to see the university open was fulfilled when the first classes were held in 1825, the year before his death.

The Rotunda of the University of Virginia at Charlottesville, as it appears today.

"I Am a Real Christian"

Another of Jefferson's projects during his last years was a compilation, in several languages, of all the New Testament passages which he understood to be the actual utterances of Jesus Christ. He referred to this "wee little book" as "the Philosophy of Jesus."

A more beautiful or precious morsel of ethics I have never seen. It is a document in proof that I am a *real Christian*, that is to say, a disciple of the doctrines of Jesus—very different from the Platonists, who call *me* infidel and *themselves* Christians and preachers of the gospel, while they draw all their characteristic dogmas from what its Author never said nor saw. [10]

9. TJ to A.C.V.C. Destutt de Tracy (16 Dec. 1820), Ford 10:174.
10. TJ to Charles Thomson (9 Jan. 1816), Bergh 14:385–86.

Jefferson very seldom spoke with anyone, even those who were closest to him, about his religious beliefs. His grandson, Thomas Jefferson Randolph, noted that "his codification of the morals of Jesus was not known to his family before his death, and they learned from a letter addressed to a friend that he was in the habit of reading nightly from it before going to bed."[11]

It was partly because of his reticence on the subject of religion that Jefferson's political enemies had been able in earlier years to convince some voters that he was an atheist who would endanger their God-fearing republic. But his references to "our Savior" in his private letters prove that he was no atheist.[12] This fact is further evidenced in a personal statement he had written to Dr. Benjamin Rush during his presidency:

> My views of [the Christian religion] are the result of a life of inquiry and reflection, and very different from that anti-Christian system imputed to me by those who know nothing of my opinions. To the corruptions of Christianity I am indeed opposed; but not to the genuine precepts of Jesus himself. I am a Christian, in the only sense in which he wished anyone to be—sincerely attached to his doctrines in preference to all others.[13]

On another occasion he wrote, "I hold the precepts of Jesus, as delivered by himself, to be the most pure,

---

11. Thomas Jefferson Randolph to Henry S. Randall (n.d.), in Randall, *The Life of Thomas Jefferson*, 3:672.

12. For example, see his letter to Martin Van Buren (29 June 1824), Bergh 16:55.

13. TJ to Dr. Benjamin Rush (21 Apr. 1803), Bergh 10:379-80.

benevolent, and sublime which have ever been preached to man."[14]

Sharing a hope nurtured by many Americans in the early nineteenth century, Jefferson anticipated a re-establishment of the Christian religion in its "original purity" in the United States. Although he believed it would not take place until after his death, he had no doubt that it would eventually be accomplished. "Happy in the prospect of a restoration of primitive Christianity," he said, "I must leave to younger athletes to encounter and lop off the false branches which have been engrafted into it by the mythologists of the middle and modern ages."[15] His own Statute of Virginia for Religious Freedom, and later the First Amendment to the Constitution, had already prepared the way. The rest was simply a matter of time.

> If the freedom of religion guaranteed to us by law *in theory* can ever rise *in practice* under the overbearing inquisition of public opinion, truth will prevail over fanaticism, and the genuine doctrines of Jesus, so long perverted by his pseudo-priests, will again be restored to their original purity. This reformation will advance with the other improvements of the human mind, but too late for me to witness it.[16]

---

14. TJ to Jared Sparks (4 Nov. 1820), Bergh 15:288. "Had the doctrines of Jesus been preached always as pure as they came from his lips," Jefferson believed, "the whole civilized world would now have been Christian." TJ to Dr. Benjamin Waterhouse (26 June 1822), Bergh 15:385.

15. TJ to Dr. Benjamin Waterhouse (19 July 1822), Bergh 15:391.

16. TJ to Jared Sparks (4 Nov. 1820), Bergh 15:288.

"His Moral Character Was of the Highest Order"

While Jefferson's family members may not have understood all the intricacies of his theological opinions, they certainly had no doubts about his personal commitment to religion and morality. These recollections also come from his grandson:

> I never heard from him the expression of one thought, feeling, or sentiment inconsistent with the highest moral standard, or the purest Christian charity in its most enlarged sense. His moral character was of the highest order, founded upon the purest and sternest models of antiquity, [but] softened, chastened, and developed by the influences of the all-pervading benevolence of the doctrines of Christ—which he had intensely and admiringly studied....
>
> In his contemplative moments his mind turned to religion, which he studied thoroughly. He had seen and read much of the abuses and perversions of Christianity; he abhorred those abuses and their authors, and denounced them without reserve.
>
> He was regular in his attendance [at] church, taking his prayer book with him. He drew the plan of the Episcopal church in Charlottesville, was one of the largest contributors to its erection, and contributed regularly to the support of its minister. I paid, after his death, his subscription of $200 to the erection of the Presbyterian church in the same village.
>
> A gentleman of some distinction calling on him and expressing his disbelief in the truths of the Bible, his

reply was, "Then, sir, you have studied it to little purpose."[17]

"The Hand of Age Is Upon Me"

In April 1816, responding to a query from John Adams, Jefferson declared that he would certainly be willing to live his seventy-three years over again. "I think, with you, that it is a good world on the whole; that it has been framed on a principle of benevolence, and more pleasure than pain dealt out to us.... My temperament is sanguine. I steer my bark with hope in the head, leaving fear astern."[18]

He knew, of course, that the passage of time would eventually take its toll. In 1812 he had written: "The hand of age is upon me. All my old friends are nearly gone."[19] But the years were kind to him, and his vigorous health enabled him to remain active far longer than most of his contemporaries. A European traveler who came to Virginia in 1825, the year before Jefferson passed away, recorded his impressions of the elderly Sage of Monticello:

He was an old man of eighty-six [actually eighty-two] years of age, of tall stature, plain appearance, and long white hair. In conversation he was very lively, and his spirits, as also his hearing and sight, seemed not to have decreased at all with his advancing age. I found in him a man who retained his faculties remarkably well in his old age, and one would have taken him for a man of sixty. [20]

17. Thomas Jefferson Randolph to Henry S. Randall (n.d.), in Randall, 3:671–72.

18. TJ to John Adams (8 Apr. 1816), Bergh 14:467.

19. TJ to James Maury (25 Apr. 1812), Bergh 13:149.

20. Bernhard, Duke of Saxe-Weimar Eisenach, *Travels Through North America During the Years 1825 and 1826* (Philadelphia, 1828), quoted in Rosenberger, *Jefferson Reader*, p. 93.

Jefferson himself noted a few years before this that "except on a late occasion of indisposition, I enjoy good health; too feeble, indeed, to walk much, but riding without fatigue six or eight miles a day, and sometimes thirty or forty."[21] He had always been "a bold and fearless rider," according to his grandson, and "he retained to the last his fondness for riding on horseback."[22] In spite of his daughter's fears for his safety, he continued to ride alone. "So delightful and so necessary is this daily revival to me," he wrote, "that I would wish to lose that and life together."[23] Even when he was so weak that he could mount only by stepping down from a terrace, his servants obediently led "Old Eagle" up to the house so that Jefferson could take his regular afternoon ride over his farms. This occurred to within three weeks of his death.

He also retained his sense of humor to the end, as reflected in the following description of an incident that took place in October 1825. The sculptor John Henri Isaac Browere had come to Monticello to produce a plaster life mask of Jefferson, and the result was a near disaster.

> I was taken in by Mr. Browere. He said his operation would be of about twenty minutes, and less unpleasant than [French sculptor Jean Antoine] Houdon's method. I submitted without inquiry.
>
> But it was a bold experiment on his part on the health of an octogenarian worn down by sickness as well as age. Successive coats of grout plastered on the naked head

---

21. TJ to Dr. Vine Utley (21 Mar. 1819), Bergh 15:188.

22. Thomas Jefferson Randolph to Henry S. Randall (n.d.), in Randall, 3:675.

23. TJ to William Short (10 Apr. 1824), in Edwin M. Betts, ed., *Thomas Jefferson's Farm Book* (Princeton, N.J.: Princeton University Press, 1953), p. 87.

and kept there an hour would have been a severe trial of a young and hale man. He suffered the plaster also to get so dry that separation became difficult and even dangerous. He was obliged to use freely the mallet and chisel to break it into pieces and get off a piece at a time. These strokes of the mallet would have been sensible almost to a loggerhead. The family became alarmed and he confused till I was quite exhausted, and there became real danger that the ears would tear from the head sooner than from the plaster.

I now bid adieu forever to busts and even portraits.[24]

Gloomy Struggle with Indebtedness

The peace and happiness of Jefferson's last years were clouded by serious financial concerns. As noted in an earlier chapter, he was already about $10,000 in debt when he entered retirement. This was due to several causes: the neglect of his plantations during his forty years of public service; his insistence on personally paying for all social expenses during his presidency; and his enormous generosity to his grandchildren, to local beggars, and to various charitable organizations. As one biographer has written, "His contributions to religious, educational, and charitable objects through his life would have made his old age opulent!"[25]

He had hoped to put his finances back in good order through a successful farming operation after returning to private life, but the demands of others got in the way. In fact, the incessant throng of overnight guests gradually sank him further into indebtedness. "They almost ate him

24. TJ to James Madison (18 Oct. 1825), Bergh 19:287.
25. Randall, 3:334.

out of house and home," remembered the chief overseer of his estate. [26]

A potential source of relief presented itself during the War of 1812. When British troops burned the city of Washington two years after the outbreak of that conflict, Jefferson offered to sell his personal library to the federal government to serve as a nucleus for the new Library of Congress. [27] (His was the finest collection in America at the time, containing about ten thousand volumes gathered over a fifty-year period.) They eventually accepted his offer, but unfortunately paid him only $23,950 for the books—not even half their actual value. [28]

The difficulties continued to mount. He suffered devastating losses in the Panic of 1819, and the bankruptcy of a friend for whom he had countersigned loans plunged him another $20,000 into debt. In 1823 he calculated his personal liabilities, including the notes on which his friend had defaulted, to be more than $60,000. [29]

---

26. Captain Edmund Bacon, in Bear, *Jefferson at Monticello*, p. 113. One of Jefferson's servants, speaking of the many visitors accommodated at Monticello, later recalled that it took "the whole farm to feed them." Quoted in Randall, 3:332.

27. See his letter to Samuel H. Smith (21 Sept. 1814), Bergh 14:190–94. Historian Dumas Malone has noted that Jefferson "never claimed that he was the founder of the Library of Congress, but it was his virtual creation." *The Sage of Monticello*, p. xv.

28. Within weeks of this sale he had spent over $700 for the beginnings of another library, which eventually grew to about a thousand volumes. Malone, *The Sage of Monticello*, p. 185 and *n*. "I cannot live without books," he confessed to John Adams (10 June 1815), Bergh 14:301.

29. Statement of liabilities and resources (1 Apr. 1823), cited in Malone, *The Sage of Monticello*, p. 448.

At the opening of the year 1826, Jefferson's financial plight was such that he feared "a deadly blast of all my peace of mind during my remaining days."

> For myself, I should not regard a prostration of fortune. But I am overwhelmed at the prospect of the situation in which I may leave my family. My dear and beloved daughter, the cherished companion of my early life and nurse of my age, and her children, rendered as dear to me as if my own from having lived with them from their cradle, left in a comfortless situation, hold up to me nothing but future gloom....
>
> Perhaps, however, even in this case I may have no right to complain, as these misfortunes have been held back for my last days, when few remain to me. I duly acknowledge that I have gone through life with fewer circumstances of affliction than are the lot of most men.... And should this, my last request, be granted, I may yet close with a cloudless sun a long and serene day of life. [30]

The "Jefferson Lottery"

The "last request" to which he referred was a proposal then being considered by the General Assembly of Virginia. He had already attempted to raise money for his debts through the sale of some of his properties, but "the long succession of years of stunted crops, of reduced prices, [and] the general prostration of the farming business" had "glutted the land market" and reduced Virginia agricultural lands to about one-fifth of their original value. So he decided on another plan.

---

30. TJ to Thomas Jefferson Randolph (8 Feb. 1826), Betts and Bear, *The Family Letters of Thomas Jefferson*, pp. 469–70.

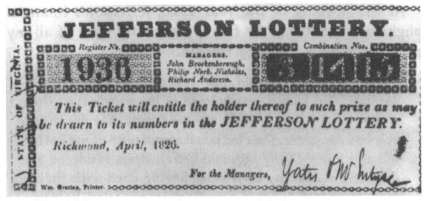

A ticket for the "Jefferson Lottery," which the Virginia legislature authorized in 1826 to enable Jefferson to overcome his indebtedness through the sale of his properties.

Reflecting on these things, the practice occurred to me of selling [my plantations] on fair valuation and by way of lottery, often resorted to before the Revolution to effect large sales, and still in constant usage in every state for individual as well as corporation purposes. If it is permitted in my case, my lands here alone, with the mills, etc., will pay everything and leave me Monticello and a farm free. If refused, I must sell everything here, perhaps considerably in Bedford, [and] move thither with my family, where I have not even a log hut to put my head into.[31]

In January 1826 he sent his oldest grandson, Thomas Jefferson Randolph, to Richmond in order to seek permission from the state legislature to conduct such a lottery. After extended and heated debate, the legislators finally passed the measure by a narrow margin.

---

31. TJ to James Madison (17 Feb. 1826), Bergh 16:157-58.

But as advertisements for the "Jefferson Lottery" began to appear in American newspapers, groups of concerned citizens all around the country offered to collect funds by private subscriptions and send these to Monticello. The initial results of these efforts appeared so promising that the lottery was promptly suspended. The inhabitants of New York City sent $8,500; then came $5,000 from Philadelphia, $3,000 more from Baltimore, and additional sums from other cities.

Jefferson was deeply moved by this "pure and unsolicited offering of love,"[32] which he gratefully received as an expression of thanks for his lifetime of service to his countrymen. In mid-March he wrote: "The necessity which dictated this expedient [i.e., the lottery] cost me...unspeakable mortification. The turn it has taken, so much beyond what I could have expected, has countervailed all I suffered and [has] become a source of felicity which I should otherwise never have known."[33] When he died several weeks later, he was happily unaware that the private contributions would prove woefully insufficient, and that his beloved Monticello would have to be sold after all to cover the debts which remained.

---

32. Quoted in Randall, 3:537.
33. TJ to Thomas Ritchie (13 Mar. 1826), Ford 10:382n.

Chapter 24

"I Have Done for My Country ...All That I Could Do"

As he felt the effects of rapidly declining health in the spring of 1826, Jefferson—now eighty-three years of age—fervently hoped he might survive long enough to see the fiftieth anniversary of the signing of the Declaration of Independence. Not only had he authored that immortal document, but he had spent virtually his entire life in defending its principles of freedom. "I will not believe our labors are lost," he wrote in 1821 to his old friend John Adams, who had also signed the Declaration. "I shall not die without a hope that light and liberty are on steady advance.... The flames kindled on the 4th of July, 1776, have spread over too much of the globe to be extinguished."[1] Two years later he told James

---

1. TJ to John Adams (12 Sept. 1821), Bergh 15:334.

Madison that it was a "heavenly comfort" to find that the ideals of the Declaration were "yet so strongly felt" by the American people. "I pray God," he said, "that these principles may be eternal."[2]

Jefferson's Last Letter

There were others, too, who earnestly hoped that Jefferson would live to see this special Independence Day of 1826. In June he was invited to travel to the city of Washington so that he could be honored there on the Fourth of July with other surviving signers of the Declaration. He regretted that his failing strength would not permit him to undertake the journey, but he did send a letter to the mayor of the city to express his gratitude for the invitation—and to offer some final reflections on the glorious event they would be celebrating.

> I should, indeed, with peculiar delight, have met and exchanged there congratulations personally with the small band, the remnant of that host of worthies, who joined with us on that day in the bold and doubtful election we were to make for our country, between submission or the sword; and to have enjoyed with them the consolatory fact that our fellow citizens, after half a century of experience and prosperity, continue to approve the choice we made.
>
> May it be to the world what I believe it will be (to some parts sooner, to others later, but finally to all), the signal of arousing men to burst the chains under which monkish ignorance and superstition had persuaded them to bind themselves, and to assume the blessings

2. TJ to James Madison (30 Aug. 1823), Bergh 15:464.

and security of self-government. That form which we have substituted restores the free right to the unbounded exercise of reason and freedom of opinion.

All eyes are opened, or opening, to the rights of man. The general spread of the light of science has already laid open to every view the palpable truth that the mass of mankind has not been born with saddles on their backs, nor a favored few booted and spurred, ready to ride them legitimately by the grace of God. These are grounds of hope for others. For ourselves, let the annual return of this day forever refresh our recollections of these rights, and an undiminished devotion to them. [3]

This remarkable letter, as it turned out, was Jefferson's last. He died on the day of the celebration.

The Closing Scenes of a Noble Life

Although he had lost none of his mental vigor, Jefferson knew that his physical body had pretty well run its course. "I am like an old watch," he said, "with a pinion worn out here and a wheel there, until it can go no longer." [4] During his last few days he was confined to his bed. "He suffered no pain," his grandson tells us, "but gradually sank from debility. His mind was always clear—it never wandered. He conversed freely, and gave directions as to his private affairs. His manner was that of a person going on a necessary journey." [5]

---

3. TJ to Roger C. Weightman (24 June 1826), Bergh 16:181–82.

4. Quoted by Thomas Jefferson Randolph in a letter to Henry S. Randall (n.d.), in Randall, *The Life of Thomas Jefferson,* 3:543.

5. Ibid. Three hours before Jefferson's death, another family member who was present wrote, "He has been to the last the same calm, clear-minded, amiable philosopher." Nicholas P. Trist, quoted in Randall, 3:546.

In addition to his parting words of affection and practical advice to family members, he prepared some written instructions to be opened after his death. Among them was the inscription for his gravestone:

Here was buried
Thomas Jefferson,
Author of the Declaration of American Independence,
Of the Statute of Virginia for Religious Freedom,
And Father of the University of Virginia

Characteristically, there was no mention of any of his public offices. He insisted on this brief epitaph "and not a word more . . . because by these as testimonials that I have lived I wish most to be remembered."[6]

"I Now Resign My Soul . . . to My God"

Toward the end Jefferson stated from his deathbed, "I have done for my country, and for all mankind, all that I could do; and I now resign my soul, without fear, to my God."[7] He had long believed that he would live on in another existence. Several years earlier he had written to John Adams: "The term is not very distant at which we are

6. Facsimile of Jefferson's notes regarding his tombstone inscription (1826), Bergh 1:262. It is significant that these brief lines reflect the three great liberties to which Jefferson had devoted his public career—political, religious, and educational freedom.

7. Quoted in B.L. Rayner, *Sketches of the Life, Writings, and Opinions of Thomas Jefferson* (New York: A. Francis and W. Boardman, 1832), p. 554. In a somewhat similar vein, Jefferson had modestly observed in 1790: "My feeble and obscure exertions in [my countrymen's] service, and in the holy cause of freedom, have had no other merit than that they were my best." TJ's response to address of welcome by the citizens of Albemarle County (12 Feb. 1790), Boyd 16:179.

to deposit in the same cerement our sorrows and suffering bodies, and to ascend in essence to an ecstatic meeting with the friends we have loved and lost, and whom we shall still love and never lose again."[8]

Just two days before he passed away, he told his daughter Martha that she would find his last words to her in a certain drawer, tucked into an old pocketbook. The closing lines of this touching message revealed his fondest and most intimate hope as he approached the final moment:

> Then farewell, my dear, my lov'd daughter, adieu!
> The last pang of life is in parting from you!
> Two seraphs await me long shrouded in death;
> I will bear them your love on my last parting breath. [9]

"Thomas Jefferson Still Survives!"

On the night of July 3, the family members who were gathered at Jefferson's bedside "anxiously desired that his death should be hallowed by the anniversary of Independence."[10] The husband of one of his grand-

---

8. TJ to John Adams (13 Nov. 1818), Bergh 15:174. Jefferson wrote this letter to console Adams on the recent death of his wife, Abigail. At the time of his daughter Mary's death in 1804 he had written: "Every step shortens the distance we have to go; the end of our journey is in sight, the bed wherein we are to rest, and to rise in the midst of the friends we have lost. 'We sorrow not, then, as others who have no hope,' but look forward to the day which 'joins us to the great majority.'" TJ to Governor John Page (25 June 1804), Bergh 11:31.

9. Quoted in Randolph, *The Domestic Life of Thomas Jefferson,* p. 429. The "two seraphs" were his beloved wife, Martha, and their daughter Mary. (Mary, the only one of Jefferson's other five children to live to adulthood, had been quite close to him until her death in 1804.)

10. Thomas Jefferson Randolph to Henry S. Randall (n.d.), in Randall, 3:544.

daughters reported that at one point he opened his eyes and asked, "This is the Fourth?" As the hands of the clock neared midnight, "an expression came over his countenance which said, 'Just as I wished.'"[11]

Fifty minutes past noon on July 4, 1826, the master of Monticello peacefully drew his last breath. Several hours later his old friend and fellow patriot John Adams also died, making that day one of the most memorable in the nation's history. Adams's last words have become perhaps the most famous ones he ever uttered: "Thomas Jefferson still survives!"[12] He spoke unwittingly, thinking that he was preceding Jefferson in death. But generations of Americans have attributed to his words a much deeper meaning. James Madison anticipated these sentiments when he learned of Jefferson's passing: "We are more than consoled for the loss ... by the assurance that he lives and will live in the memory and gratitude of the wise and good, as a luminary of science, as a votary of liberty, as a model of patriotism, and as a benefactor of humankind."[13]

In death as in life, Jefferson had wanted to avoid all public display. His grandson briefly recorded the burial scene:

> He desired that his interment should be private, without parade.... Our wish was to comply with his

---

11. Nicholas P. Trist, quoted in Randall, 3:546.

12. Quoted in John Quincy Adams and Charles Francis Adams, *The Life of John Adams*, rev. ed., 2 vols. (1871; reprint ed., New York: Haskell House Publishers, Ltd., 1968), 2:405.

13. James Madison to Nicholas P. Trist (6 July 1826), Gaillard Hunt, ed., *The Writings of James Madison*, 9 vols. (New York: G.P. Putnam's Sons, 1900–1910), 9:247–48. A related thought was expressed in the closing words of the first edition of this biography: "As long as a fervent passion for human liberty remains somewhere on the earth, Thomas Jefferson and the glorious principles for which he fought can never die."

request, and no notice of the hour of interment or invitations were issued. His body was borne privately from his dwelling by his family and servants, but his neighbors and friends, anxious to pay the last tribute of respect and affection to one whom they had loved and honored, waited for it in crowds at the grave.[14]

News of this sad event soon reached the public, and the nation's newspapers and lecture halls overflowed for months with eulogies to honor America's champion of liberty.[15] His countrymen of that day seemed to sense, as we do now, that the world is not likely ever to produce another Thomas

The monument over Jefferson's grave in the private family cemetery at Monticello.

---

14. Thomas Jefferson Randolph to Henry S. Randall (n.d.), in Randall, 3:544. Jefferson was buried "beneath his favorite oak" between his wife and his boyhood friend, Dabney Carr. Many years before Monticello was built on the wooded mountaintop, the two boys had often sat and conversed on this very spot. "On one occasion they mutually promised each other that whoever died first should be buried under this tree, and that the survivor, when his turn came, should lie by the side of his friend." Nicholas P. Trist, quoted in Smith, The First Forty Years of Washington Society, pp. 242-43.

15. Many declared publicly the same conviction that President John Quincy Adams recorded in his private journal—that there were "visible and palpable marks of Divine favor" in the passing of both John Adams and

Jefferson. Yet, as one American in that period of national mourning so eloquently declared, "The grief that such a man is dead may be well assuaged by the proud consolation that such a man has lived."[16]

Thomas Jefferson on the fiftieth anniversary of the signing of the Declaration of Independence. Charles Francis Adams, ed., *Memoirs of John Quincy Adams*, 12 vols. (Philadelphia: J.B. Lippincott & Co., 1874–77), 7:125. For examples of the public sentiment at that time, see *A Selection of Eulogies Pronounced in the Several States in Honor of Those Illustrious Patriots and Statesmen, John Adams and Thomas Jefferson* (Hartford, Conn.: D.F. Robinson & Co. and Norton & Russell, 1826).

16. Nicholas Biddle, *Eulogium on Thomas Jefferson*, delivered to the American Philosophical Society (11 Apr. 1827), quoted in Rosenberger, *Jefferson Reader*, p. 259.

Appendix: An Intimate View of Jefferson by His Grandson

The following undated letter was sent by Jefferson's oldest grandson, Thomas Jefferson Randolph, to the biographer Henry S. Randall. It was probably written in the 1850s, when Randall was preparing materials for his three-volume Life of Thomas Jefferson (New York: Derby & Jackson, 1858). The text of the letter is taken from the third volume of that work, pages 543–44 and 671–76. Punctuation and paragraphing have been altered somewhat for the sake of clarity, and topical subheadings have been inserted to facilitate reading.

DEAR SIR: In compliance with your request, I have committed to paper my reminiscences of Mr. Jefferson as they, still green and fresh in my memory, have occurred to me.

I was thirty-four years old when he died. My mother was his eldest and, for the last twenty-two years of his life, his only child. She lived with him from her birth to his death, except in his absence on public service at Philadelphia and Washington. Having lost her mother at ten years [of age], she was his inseparable companion until her marriage; he had sought to

supply her loss with all the watchful solicitude of a mother's
tenderness. Her children were to him as the younger members
of his family, having lived with him from their infancy.

"His Creditors Were All Paid"

I being fifteen years older than my brothers, the duty
devolved on me to place myself in the breach of his pecuniary
embarrassments and shield him, living and dead, from their
practical effects. He never failed to comply with a pecuniary
engagement; his creditors were all paid. It was unimportant to
them whether they were paid from the proceeds of the sales of
his property or the sacrifices and toil of his descendants.

"His Moral Character Was of the Highest Order"

I was more intimate with him than with any man I have ever
known. His character invited such intimacy—soft and feminine
in his affections to his family, he entered into and sympathized
with all their feelings, winning them to paths of virtue by the
soothing gentleness of his manner.

His private apartments were open to me at all times; I saw
him under all circumstances. While he lived, and since, I have
reviewed with severe scrutiny those interviews, and I must say
that I never heard from him the expression of one thought,
feeling, or sentiment inconsistent with the highest moral
standard, or the purest Christian charity in its most enlarged
sense. His moral character was of the highest order, founded
upon the purest and sternest models of antiquity, [but]
softened, chastened, and developed by the influences of the all-
pervading benevolence of the doctrines of Christ—which he
had intensely and admiringly studied.

As a proof of this, he left two codifications of the morals of
Jesus—one for himself, and another for the Indians. The first of
[these] I now possess, [namely] a blank volume, red morocco,

gilt, [and] lettered on the back "The Morals of Jesus," into which he pasted extracts in Greek, Latin, French, and English, taken textually from the four Gospels, and so arranged that he could run his eye over the readings of the same verse in four languages.

The boldness and self-confidence of his mind was the best guaranty of his truthfulness. He never uttered an untruth himself, or used duplicity, and he condemned it in others. No end, with him, could sanctify falsehood.

"He Detested Impiety"

In his contemplative moments his mind turned to religion, which he studied thoroughly. He had seen and read much of the abuses and perversions of Christianity; he abhorred those abuses and their authors, and denounced them without reserve.

He was regular in his attendance [at] church, taking his prayer book with him. He drew the plan of the Episcopal church in Charlottesville, was one of the largest contributors to its erection, and contributed regularly to the support of its minister. I paid, after his death, his subscription of $200 to the erection of the Presbyterian church in the same village. A gentleman of some distinction calling on him and expressing his disbelief in the truths of the Bible, his reply was, "Then, sir, you have studied it to little purpose."

He was guilty of no profanity himself, and did not tolerate it in others. He detested impiety, and his favorite quotation for his young friends, as a basis for their morals, was the 15th psalm of David.

He did not permit cards in his house; he knew no game with them.

Jefferson's Religious Opinions

Of his peculiar religious opinions, his family know no more than the world. If asked by one of them his opinion on any religious subject, his uniform reply was that it was a subject each was bound to study assiduously for himself, unbiased by the opinions of others. It was a matter solely of conscience; after thorough investigation, they were responsible for the righteousness, but not the rightfulness, of their opinions. [He believed] that the expression of his opinion might influence theirs, and he would not give it!

He held it to be an invasion of the freedom of religious opinion to attempt to subject the opinions of any man to the ordeal of public judgment; he would not submit to it in his own case, nor sanction it in another. He considered that religious opinions should be judged by the fruits they produced— if they produced good men, they must be good.

My mother was educated in a convent, the best school of the day in Paris. She took up a girlish desire to join the Catholic church, and wrote to her father to ask his permission. He called for her, took her home, and placed her in the gay society of the court of Louis XVI, where all such thoughts quickly vanished. His calling for her was the only intimation she ever had of the receipt of her letter; the subject was never alluded to by him.

His codification of the morals of Jesus was not known to his family before his death, and they learned from a letter addressed to a friend that he was in the habit of reading nightly from it before going to bed. . . .

"His Precepts Were Those of Truth and Virtue"

His family, by whom he was surrounded, and who saw him in all the unguarded privacy of private life, believed him to be the purest of men. His precepts were those of truth and virtue. "Be just, be true, love your neighbor as yourself, and your country more than yourself" were among his favorite maxims, and they recognized in him a truthful exemplar of the precepts he taught.

He said he had left the government of his country "with hands as clean as they were empty." His family circle knew that with calm serenity he had left the theatre of life, with a conscience as unsullied as his life had been just and upright.

"In the Bosom of His Family"

The beauty of his character was exhibited in the bosom of his family, where he delighted to indulge in all the fervor and delicacy of feminine feeling. Upon his death there were found carefully preserved, in a little sanctum sanctorum, locks of hair and other memorials of his wife and the children he had lost, with words of fond endearment written in his own hand upon the envelopes of the little mementos. Before he lost his taste for the violin, in winter evenings he would play on it, having his grandchildren dancing around him. In summer he would station them for their little races on the lawn, give the signal for the start, be the arbiter of the contest, and award the prizes.

"He Spoke Only of the Good Qualities of Men"

His manner was dignified, reserved with strangers, but frank and cordial with his friends; his conversation cheerful, often sportive, and illustrated by anecdotes. He spoke only of the good qualities of men, which induced the belief that he knew little of them; but no one knew them better. I had formed this opinion and, on hearing him speak very favorably of men with defects known to myself, stated them to him, when he asked if I supposed he had not observed them, adding others not noted by me and evincing much more accurate knowledge of the individual character than I possessed, observing, "My habit is to speak only of men's good qualities."

When he believed that either men or measures were adverse to republican institutions, he spoke of them with open and unqualified condemnation.

"The Friend of the Working Man"

Standing himself on an elevated position from his talents, education, fortune, and political station, he was emphatically the friend of the working man. On passing the home of a neighbor (Mr. Jesse Lewis), a blacksmith remarkable for his probity, his integrity, and his industry, and too wise when past the meridian of life to be ashamed to work at the trade that had made his fortune, he often remarked of him, "It is such men as that who constitute the wealth of a nation, not millionaires."

"His Powers of Conversation Were Great"

He never indulged in controversial conversation because it often excited unpleasant feeling, and [he] illustrated its inutility by the anecdote of two men who sat down candidly to discuss a subject, and each converted the other. His maxim was that every man had a right to his own opinion on all subjects, and others were bound to respect that right. Hence, in conversation, if anyone expressed a decided opinion differing from his own, he made no reply, but changed the subject. He believed men could always find subjects enough to converse on in which they agreed in opinion, omitting those upon which they differed. Unreserved and candid himself, he was a listener, encouraging others to converse.

His tact in the management of men was great. He inquiringly followed out adverse opinions to their results, leaving it to their friends to note the error into which it led them; taking up their doubts as important suggestions, [but] never permitting a person to place himself upon the defensive, or, if he did, changing the subject so as not to fix him in a wrong opinion by controverting it. With men of fertile and ingenious minds, fond of suggesting objections to propositions stated, he would sometimes suggest the opposite of the conclusion to which he desired them to come, then assent to the force of their objections and thus lead them to convert themselves.

If information was sought, he gave it freely; if doubts were suggested, he explained them without reserve, never objecting to the scrutiny or canvass of his own opinions. As a public man, his friends complained that he spoke too freely, communicating more than they thought prudent. His powers of conversation were great, yet he always turned it to subjects most familiar to those with whom he conversed, whether laborer, mechanic, or other; and if they displayed sound judgment and a knowledge of the subject, [he] entered the information they gave under appropriate heads for reference, embodying thus a mass of facts upon the practical details of everyday life.

"Methodical and Exact"

His capacity to acquire knowledge was of the highest order; his application intense and untiring; his system and arrangement for the preservation of and reference to the sources of his acquirements, most methodical and exact. The Honorable Littleton Waller Tazewell told me that when [he was] a young man, his father being in the Senate and Mr. Jefferson Vice President, [and] some case of impeachment coming on, he was sent with a note to Mr. Jefferson asking some references to authorities on the subject. On the delivery of the note, he took a notebook from a drawer and instantly copied the references. On [the young man's] delivering them to his father, the latter observed he believed [Mr. Jefferson] had sent him chapter and verse for everything written on the subject. Of his voluminous correspondence, embracing upwards of forty thousand letters written and received, and the private and public accounts of his whole life, he could in a moment lay his hand on any letter or receipt.

Shortly after his death, Mr. Madison expressed to me the opinion that Mr. Jefferson would be found to be the most learned man that had ever devoted so much time to public life.

He was economical, exact, and methodical in his expenses and accounts. The account books, now in my possession, of his maitre d'hotel at Paris and Washington show the minutest details of household expenditure, and notes and figures in his own handwriting exhibit the closest personal inspection by himself, and a monthly analysis in a tabularized form of the expenditures in each item. His own numerous account books show the entry at the time, in his own hand, of each expenditure, however minute.

"He Was a Gentleman Everywhere"

His manners were of that polished school of the colonial government, so remarkable in its day—under no circumstances violating any of those minor conventional observances which constitute the well-bred gentleman, courteous and considerate to all persons. On [my] riding out with him when a lad, we met a Negro who bowed to us. [My grandfather] returned his bow; I did not. Turning to me he asked, "do you permit a Negro [slave] to be more of a gentleman than yourself?"

There was a little emulation endeavored to be excited among the older gentlemen of the neighborhood in their gardening, and he who had peas first announced his success by an invitation to the others to dine with him. A wealthy neighbor, without children and fond of horticulture, generally triumphed. Mr. Jefferson on one occasion had them first, and when his family reminded him that it was his right to invite the company, he replied, "No, say nothing about it; it will be more agreeable to our friend to think that he never fails."

In his person he was neat in the extreme. In early life, his dress, equipage, and appointments were fastidiously appropriate to his rank. As he grew old, although preserving his extreme neatness, his dress was plainer and he was more indifferent to the appearance of his equipage. When at Paris, Philadelphia, and Washington, his furniture, table, servants, [and] equipage and the *tout ensemble* of his establishment were deemed highly appropriate to the position he held. He was a gentleman everywhere.

On entering the presidency he determined not to have

weekly levees, like his predecessors, and so announced. His political opponents determined that he should continue the custom. On the first levee day he rode out at his usual hour of one o'clock, returning at three, and on entering the President's house, booted, whip in hand, soiled with his ride, found himself in a crowd of ladies and gentlemen, fashionably dressed for the occasion. He greeted them with all the ease and courtesy of expected guests that he had been prepared to receive, exhibiting not the slightest indication of annoyance. They never again tried the experiment.

At home he desired to live like his neighbors, in the plain hospitality of a Virginia gentleman. It was a source of continued and deep regret to him that the number of strangers who visited him kept his neighbors from him; he said he had to exchange the society of his friends and neighbors for those whom he had never seen before, and never expected to see again.

Jefferson's Physical Appearance

Mr. Jefferson's hair, when [he was] young, was of a reddish cast, sandy as he advanced in years; his eye, hazel. Dying in his 84th year, he had not lost a tooth or had one defective. His skin [was] thin, peeling from his face on exposure to the sun, and giving it a tettered appearance; the superficial veins [were] so weak as upon the slightest blow to cause extensive suffusions of blood—in early life, upon standing to write for any length of time, bursting beneath the skin. It, however, gave him no inconvenience.

His countenance was mild and benignant, and attractive to strangers. While [he was] President, returning on horseback from court with company whom he had invited to dinner, and who were, all but one or two, riding ahead of him, on reaching a stream over which there was no bridge, a man asked him to take him up behind and carry him over. The gentlemen in the rear, coming up just as Mr. Jefferson had put him down and rode on, asked the man how it happened that he had permitted the others to pass without asking them. He replied, "From their looks I did not like to ask them—the old gentleman looked as if he would do it, and I asked him." He was very much surprised to hear that he had ridden behind the President of the United States.

Mr. Jefferson's stature was commanding, six feet two-and-a-half inches in height [and] well formed, indicating strength, activity, and robust health; his carriage, erect; [his] step firm and elastic, which he preserved to his death. His temper, naturally strong, [was] under perfect control; his courage, cool and impassive—no one ever knew him exhibit trepidation. His moral courage [was] of the highest order; his will, firm and inflexible. It was remarked of him that he never abandoned a plan, a principle, or a friend.

"A Bold and Fearless Rider"

A bold and fearless rider, you saw at a glance from his easy and confident seat that he was master of his horse, which was usually the fine blood horse of Virginia. The only impatience of temper he ever exhibited was with his horse, which he subdued to his will by a fearless application of the whip on the slightest manifestation of restiveness. He retained to the last his fondness for riding on horseback; he rode within three weeks of his death, when from disease, debility, and age he mounted with difficulty. He rode with confidence, and never permitted a servant to accompany him; he was fond of solitary rides and musing, and said that the presence of a servant annoyed him.

He held in little esteem the education that made men ignorant and helpless as to the common necessities of life; and he exemplified it by an incident which occurred to a young gentleman returned from Europe, where he had been educated. On riding out with his companions, the strap of his girth broke at the hole of the buckle; and they, perceiving it an accident easily remedied, rode on and left him. A plain man coming up and seeing that his horse had made a circular path in the road in his impatience to get on, asked if he could aid him. "Oh, sir," replied the young man, "if you could only assist me to get it up to the next hole." "Suppose you let it out a hole or two on the other side," said the man.

"He Was a Miser of His Time"

His habits were regular and systematic. He was a miser of his time. [He] rose always at dawn, wrote and read until breakfast, breakfasted early, and dined from three to four. After breakfast [he] read for half an hour in his public rooms, or [his] portico in summer; visited his garden and workshops; returned to his writing and reading till one, when he rode on horseback to three or half past; dined, and gave the evening to his family and company; retired at nine, and to bed from ten to eleven. He said in his last illness that the sun had not caught him in bed for fifty years. He always made his own fire.

He drank water but once a day, a single glass, when he returned from his ride. He ate heartily, and much vegetable food, preferring French cookery because it made the meats more tender. He never drank ardent spirits or strong wines— such was his aversion to ardent spirits that when, in his last illness, his physician desired him to use brandy as an astringent, he could not induce him to take it strong enough.

Summary of Jefferson's Financial Affairs

He inherited from his father 1,900 acres of land and some Negroes. He commenced the practice of the law soon after he came of age. When he married, in his 29th year, he had increased his estate to 5,000 acres, all paid for. His accounts show a receipt of $3,000 a year from his practice at the bar, and $2,000 from his farms, a large income at that day.

The death of his father-in-law ensuing soon after his marriage, he acquired a large addition to his estate, but the share of debt which fell to him was £3,749 12*s*. He sold property immediately to pay it. The payments for this property were made in paper money, which he deposited in the loan office, and received it back again at a depreciation out to him of one for forty. He sold again in 1785 and 1792 to discharge the debt with its accumulated interest. This swept nearly half of his estate.

He was absent from his estate as minister to France, Secretary of State, Vice President, and President from 1782 to 1809—27 years, with the exception of [three] years, from [1794] to 1797, which he devoted to his farms. He returned in his old age to be hunted down by the reputation he had won in the service of his country. Twelve years before his death, he remarked to me in conversation that if he lived long enough he would beggar his family—that the number of persons he was compelled to entertain would devour his estate. Many bringing letters from his ancient friends, and all coming with respectful feelings, he could not shut his door in their faces. A heavy loss by endorsing for a friend in 1819, and the extreme depression in the value of property when it became necessary to bring his into market, completed the catastrophe and verified his anticipations.

Jefferson's Last Illness

Mr. Jefferson had suffered for several years before his death from a diarrhea, which he concealed from his family lest it might give them uneasiness. Not aware of it, I was surprised, in conversation with him in March 1826, to hear him, in speaking of an event likely to occur about midsummer, say doubtingly that he *might* live to that time. About the middle of June, hearing that he had sent for his physician, Dr. Dunglison of the University of Virginia, I went immediately to see him and found him out in his public rooms. Before [I left] the house he sent a servant to me to come to his room, whereupon he handed me a paper which he desired me to examine, remarking, "Don't delay; there is no time to be lost."

He gradually declined, but would only have his servants sleeping near him; being disturbed only at nine, twelve, and four o'clock in the night, he needed little nursing. Becoming uneasy about him, I entered his room unobserved to pass the night. [When I came] round inadvertently to assist him, he chided me, saying that being actively employed all day, I needed repose. On my replying that it was more agreeable to me to be with him, he acquiesced, and I did not leave him again.

A day or two after, my brother-in-law (Mr. Trist) was admitted. His servants, ourselves, and the Doctor became his sole nurses. My mother sat with him during the day, but he would not permit her to sit up at night. His family had to decline for him numerous tenders of service from kind and affectionate friends and neighbors, fearing and seeing that it would excite him to conversation injurious to him in his weak condition.

Deathbed Reflections

He suffered no pain, but gradually sank from debility. His mind was always clear—it never wandered. He conversed freely, and gave directions as to his private affairs. His manner was that of a person going on a necessary journey, evincing neither satisfaction nor regret.

He remarked upon the tendency of his mind to recur back to the scenes of the Revolution. Many incidents he would relate, in his usual cheerful manner, insensibly diverting my mind from his dying condition. He remarked that the curtains of his bed had been purchased from the first cargo that arrived after the peace of 1782.

Upon my expressing the opinion on one occasion that he was somewhat better, he turned to me and said, "Do not imagine for a moment that I feel the smallest solicitude about the result; I am like an old watch, with a pinion worn out here and a wheel there, until it can go no longer." On another occasion, when he was unusually ill, he observed to the Doctor, "A few hours more, Doctor, and it will be all over."

Upon being suddenly aroused from sleep by a noise in the room, he asked if he had heard the name of Mr. Hatch mentioned—the minister whose church he attended. On my replying in the negative he observed, as he turned over, "I have no objection to see him, as a kind and good neighbor." The impression made upon my mind at the moment was that, his religious opinions having been formed upon mature study and reflection, he had no doubts upon his mind, and therefore did not desire the attendance of a clergyman; I have never since doubted the correctness of the impression then taken.

His parting interview with the different members of his family was calm and composed, impressing admonitions upon them, the cardinal points of which were to pursue virtue [and to] be true and truthful. My youngest brother, in his eighth year, seeming not to comprehend the scene, he turned to me with a smile and said, "George does not understand what all this means."

He would speculate upon the person who would succeed him as rector of the University of Virginia, and concluded that Mr. Madison would be appointed. With all the deep pathos of exalted friendship he spoke of his purity, his virtues, his wisdom, his learning, and his great abilities. The friendship of these great men was of an extraordinary character. They had been born, lived, and died within twenty-five miles of each other; they visited frequently through their whole lives. At twenty-three years [of age], Mr. Jefferson had been consulted on Mr. Madison's course of study—he then fifteen. Thus commenced a friendship as remarkable for its duration as it was for the fidelity and warmth of its feelings. The admiration of each for the wisdom, abilities, and purity of the other was unlimited. Their habit of reliance upon mutual counsel equalled the sincerity of their affection and the devotion of their esteem.

In speaking of the calumnies which his enemies had uttered against his public and private character with such unmitigated and untiring bitterness, he said that he had not considered them as abusing him; they had never known *him*. They had created an imaginary being clothed with odious attributes, to whom they had given his name; and it was against that creature of their imaginations they had levelled their anathemas.

"This Is the Fourth of July"

On Monday, the third of July, his slumbers were evidently those of approaching dissolution. He slept until evening, when upon awaking he seemed to imagine it was morning and remarked that he had slept all night without being disturbed— "This is the fourth of July." He soon sank again into sleep, and on being aroused at nine to take his medicine he remarked in a clear, distinct voice, "No, Doctor, nothing more." The omission of the dose of laudanum, administered every night during his illness, caused his slumbers to be disturbed and dreamy. He sat up in his sleep and went through all the forms of writing; [he] spoke of the Committee of Safety, saying it ought to be warned.

As twelve o'clock at night approached, we anxiously desired that his death should be hallowed by the anniversary of Independence. At fifteen minutes before twelve we stood noting the minute hand of the watch, hoping [for] a few minutes of prolonged life. At four A.M. he called the servants in attendance with a strong and clear voice, perfectly conscious of his wants. He did not speak again.

About ten he fixed his eyes intently upon me, indicating some want, which most painfully I could not understand, until his attached servant, Burwell, observed that his head was not so much elevated as he usually desired it, for his habit was to lie with it very much elevated. Upon [my] restoring it to its usual position, he seemed satisfied. About eleven, again fixing his eyes upon me and moving his lips, I applied a wet sponge to his mouth, which he sucked and appeared to relish. This was the last evidence he gave of consciousness.

"He Died a Pure and Good Man"

He ceased to breathe, without a struggle, fifty minutes past meridian—July 4th, 1826. I closed his eyes with my own hands. He was at all times during his illness perfectly assured of his approaching end, his mind ever clear, and at no moment did he evince the least solicitude about the result; he was as calm and composed as when in health. He died a pure and good man. It is for others to speak of his greatness.

He desired that his interment should be private, without parade, and our wish was to comply with his request, and no notice of the hour of interment or invitations were issued. His body was borne privately from his dwelling by his family and servants, but his neighbors and friends, anxious to pay the last tribute of respect and affection to one whom they had loved and honored, waited for it in crowds at the grave.

Very respectfully,

THOMAS J. RANDOLPH

PART II

Timeless Treasures
from
Thomas Jefferson

Prepared by

M. Richard Maxfield,
K. DeLynn Cook,
and
W. Cleon Skousen

Thomas Jefferson is sometimes spoken of as a modern-day Leonardo da Vinci, and the comparison seems very fitting. Those who examine his life are often astounded by the universality of his interests and abilities. As the biographer James Parton put it, Jefferson "could calculate an eclipse, survey an estate, tie an artery, plan an edifice, try a cause, break a horse, dance a minuet, and play a violin." He was an extremely curious and versatile person whose insatiable appetite for knowledge persisted as long as he lived. Many of his friends called him a "walking library," and indeed he had carefully studied virtually every important book written in the Western world since ancient times. The historian James Truslow Adams said he was "the most widely read man of his time in America."

Jefferson's thinking was probably more comprehensive in scope than that of any of the Founding Fathers. He moved easily from political theory to religion to the arts and sciences, from education to economics to human relations. And the value of his ideas is enhanced today by their surprising relevance to the problems of the present generation. Especially is this true of his philosophy of government. As a spokesman for the rights of man, Jefferson is without peer—even among the giants of his own illustrious era. Many agree with the Frenchman Alexis de Tocqueville that he is "the most powerful advocate democracy has ever had." Familiarity with his writings is therefore essential to a correct understanding of the principles of liberty underlying our democratic republic.

Reading Jefferson's public and private papers is a delightful and moving experience. Not only was he a man of far-ranging vision and deep philosophical insight, but he wrote with an almost inspired eloquence. Jefferson was a master craftsman of the English language. He combined his unusual breadth of information with a "peculiar felicity of expression" that has secured for him, to use the words of John Adams, "the reputation of a masterly pen." The Declaration of Independence, perhaps the most frequently quoted of all American documents, is but one example of the forceful Jeffersonian literary style that continues to captivate readers throughout the English-speaking world.

This section brings together the most significant passages from Jefferson's voluminous writings. For the convenience of the user, these excerpts are arranged alphabetically by subject matter and are extensively cross-referenced. Most of the selections are from Albert Ellery Bergh, ed., *The Writings of Thomas Jefferson*, 20 vols. (Washington: The Thomas Jefferson Memorial Association, 1907), and from Paul Leicester Ford, ed., *The Writings of Thomas Jefferson*, 10 vols. (New York: G.P. Putnam's Sons, 1892–99). Several quotations are taken from Edwin Morris Betts and James Adam Bear, eds., *The Family Letters of Thomas Jefferson* (Columbia, Mo.: University of Missouri Press, 1966), and Julian P. Boyd, ed., *The Papers of Thomas Jefferson*, 20 vols. by 1982 (Princeton, N.J.: Princeton University Press, 1950-). A few others are from additional sources which are cited fully where they appear in the text. John P. Foley, ed., *The Jeffersonian Cyclopedia*, 2 vols. (1900; reprint ed., New York: Russell & Russell, 1967), has been helpful in the selection and arrangement of part of this material. Spelling, capitalization, and punctuation have been modernized in some cases for the sake of clarity and readability.

Timeless Treasures
from
Thomas Jefferson

Prepared by

M. Richard Maxfield,
K. DeLynn Cook,
and
W. Cleon Skousen

A

ABOLITION. See SLAVERY.

ACCOUNTABILITY, Of Public Officials.—It should be remembered, as an axiom of eternal truth in politics, that whatever power in any government is independent is absolute also; in theory only at first, while the spirit of the people is up, but in practice as fast as that relaxes. Independence can be trusted nowhere but with the people in mass. They are inherently independent of all but moral law.—Ford 10:141. (1819.)

That there should be public functionaries independent of the nation, whatever may be their demerit, is a solecism in a republic, of the first order of absurdity and inconsistency.—Bergh 15:389. (1822.)

In truth, man is not made to be trusted for life if secured against all liability to account.—Bergh 15:487. (1823.)

ACCOUNTABILITY. See also PEOPLE; PUBLICITY; RESPONSIBILITY.

ADAMS (John), Character of.—He is vain, irritable, and a bad calculator of the force and probable effect of the motives which govern men. This is all the ill which can possibly be said of him. He is as disinterested as the Being who made him. He is profound in his views and accurate in his judgment, except where knowledge of the world is necessary to form a judgment. He is so amiable that I pronounce you will love him, if ever you become acquainted with him. He would be, as he was, a great man in Congress.—To James Madison. Bergh 6:68. (1787.)

ADAMS (John), Jefferson's Friendship for.—Mr. Adams's friendship and mine began at an early date. It accompanied us through long and important scenes. The different conclusions we had drawn from our political reading and reflections were not permitted to lessen personal esteem, each party being conscious they were the result of an honest conviction in the other. Like differences of opinion existing among our fellow citizens attached them to one or the other of us, and produced a rivalship in their minds which did not exist in ours. We never stood in one another's way; for if either had been withdrawn at any time, his favorers would not have gone over to the other, but would have sought for someone of homogeneous opinions. This consideration was sufficient to keep down all jealousy between us, and to guard our friendship from any disturbance by sentiments of rivalship. —To Abigail Adams. Bergh 11:28. (1804.)

ADAMS (John), Contrasted with Alexander Hamilton.—You know the perfect coincidence of principle and of action, in the early part of the Revolution, which produced a high degree of mutual respect and esteem between Mr. Adams and myself. Certainly no man was ever truer than he was, in that day, to those principles of rational republicanism which, after the necessity of throwing off our monarchy, dictated all our efforts in the establishment

of a new government. And although he swerved afterwards towards the principles of the English constitution, our friendship did not abate on that account. . . .

A collision of opinion arose between Mr. Adams and Colonel Hamilton on the merits of the British constitution, Mr. Adams giving it as his opinion that if some of its defects and abuses were corrected, it would be the most perfect constitution of government ever devised by man. Hamilton, on the contrary, asserted that with its existing vices it was the most perfect model of government that could be formed, and that the correction of its vices would render it an impracticable government. And this, you may be assured, was the real line of difference between the political principles of these two gentlemen.

Another incident took place on the same occasion which will further delineate Mr. Hamilton's political principles. The room being hung around with a collection of the portraits of remarkable men, among them were those of Bacon, Newton, and Locke. Hamilton asked me who they were. I told him they were my trinity of the three greatest men the world had ever produced, naming them. He paused for some time. "The greatest man," said he, "that ever lived was Julius Caesar." Mr. Adams was honest as a politician as well as a man; Hamilton honest as a man, but as a politician believing in the necessity of either force or corruption to govern men.—To Dr. Benjamin Rush. Bergh 13:2. (1811.)

ADAMS (John), And the Declaration of Independence.—John Adams was the pillar of its [the Declaration's] support on the floor of Congress, its ablest advocate and defender against the multifarious assaults it encountered.*—Ford 9:377. (1813.)

> *Daniel Webster visited Jefferson at Monticello toward the close of 1824. He quoted Jefferson as having then said in conversation: "John Adams was our Colossus on the floor. He was not graceful, nor elegant, nor remarkably fluent; but he came out, occasionally, with a power of thought and expression that moved us from our seats."—Ford 10:327.

ADAMS (John), Jefferson's Love for.—I love you with all my heart, and pray for the continuance of your life until you shall be tired of it yourself.—To John Adams. Bergh 15:276. (1820.)

ADAMS (John Quincy), Early Promise of.—This young gentleman is, I think, very promising. To a vast thirst after useful knowledge he adds a facility in acquiring it. What his judgment may be, I am not well enough acquainted with him to decide; but I expect it is good, and much hope it, as he may become a valuable and useful citizen.—Ford 4:42. (1785.)

ADAMS (John Quincy), Jefferson's Respect for.—I have never entertained for Mr. Adams any but sentiments of esteem and respect; and if we have not thought alike on political subjects, I yet never doubted the honesty of his opinions.—Bergh 16:154. (1826.)

ADAMS (Samuel), Patriarch of Liberty.—I addressed a letter to you, my very dear and ancient friend, on the 4th of March; not indeed to you by name, but through the medium of some of my fellow citizens, whom occasion called on me to address.* In meditating the matter of that address, I often asked myself, is this exactly in the spirit of the patriarch of liberty, Samuel Adams? Is it as he would express it? Will he approve of it? I have felt a great deal for our country in the times we have seen. But, individually, for no one so much as yourself. When I have been told that you were avoided, insulted, frowned on, I could but ejaculate, "Father, forgive them, for they know not what they do." I confess I felt an indignation for you which for myself I have been able, under every trial, to keep entirely passive.... How much I lament that time has deprived me of your aid! It would have been a day of glory which should have called you to the first office of the administration. But give us your counsel, my friend, and give us your blessing; and be assured that there exists not in the heart of man a more faithful esteem than mine to you, and that I shall ever bear you the most affectionate veneration and respect.—To Samuel Adams. Ford 8:38. (1801.)

> *Jefferson was here referring to his First Inaugural Address.—Editor.

ADAMS (Samuel), Services of.—I always considered him as more than any other member [in Congress] the fountain of our important measures. And although he was neither an eloquent nor easy speaker, whatever he said was sound and commanded the profound attention of the house. In the discussions on the floor of Congress he reposed himself on our main pillar in debate, Mr. John Adams. These two gentlemen were verily a host in our councils.—Ford 10:124. (1819.)

ADAMS (Samuel), Ability of.—He was truly a great man, wise in council, fertile in resources, immovable in his purposes, and had, I think, a greater share than any other member in advising and directing our measures, in the northern war especially.... Although not of fluent elocution, [he] was so rigorously logical, so clear in his views, abundant in good sense, and master always of his subject, that he commanded the most profound attention whenever he rose in an assembly.—Bergh 15:201. (1819.)

ADVICE, Giving of.—How easily we prescribe for others a cure for their difficulties, while we cannot cure our own.—Ford 10:187. (1821.)

ADVICE TO HIS DAUGHTER, On Caring for Her Younger Sister.—Our dear Polly will certainly come to us this summer. By the time I return it will be time to expect her. When she arrives, she will become a precious charge on your hands. The difference of your age, and your common loss of a mother, will put that office on you. Teach her above all things to be good, because without that we can neither be valued by others nor set any value on ourselves. Teach her to be always true. No vice is so mean as the want

of truth, and at the same time so useless. Teach her never to be angry. Anger only serves to torment ourselves, to divert others, and alienate their esteem. And teach her industry and application to useful pursuits. I will venture to assure you that if you inculcate this in her mind you will make her a happy being in herself, a most inestimable friend to you, and precious to all the world. In teaching her these dispositions of mind, you will be more fixed in them yourself, and render yourself dear to all your acquaintance. Practice them, then, my dear, without ceasing. If ever you find yourself in difficulty and doubt how to extricate yourself, do what is right, and you will find it the easiest way of getting out of the difficulty.—To Martha Jefferson. Betts & Bear, p. 36. (1787.)

ADVICE TO HIS GRANDSON, On the Development of Good Character.—While you endeavor, by a good store of learning, to prepare yourself to become a useful and distinguished member of your country, you must remember that this can never be without uniting merit with your learning. Honesty, disinterestedness, and good nature are indispensable to procure the esteem and confidence of those with whom we live, and on whose esteem our happiness depends. Never suffer a thought to be harbored in your mind which you would not avow openly. When tempted to do anything in secret, ask yourself if you would do it in public. If you would not, be sure it is wrong. In little disputes with your companions, give way rather than insist on trifles; for their love and the approbation of others will be worth more to you than the trifle in dispute. Above all things, and at all times, practice yourself in good humor. This, of all human qualities, is the most amiable and endearing to society. Whenever you feel a warmth of temper rising, check it at once and suppress it, recollecting it will make you unhappy within yourself and disliked by others. Nothing gives one person so great advantage over another as to remain always cool and unruffled under all circumstances. Think of these things, practice them, and you will be rewarded by the love and confidence of the world.—To Francis Wayles Eppes. Betts & Bear, p. 415. (1816.)

ADVICE TO A NAMESAKE.— This letter will, to you, be as one from the dead. The writer will be in the grave before you can weigh its counsels. Your affectionate and excellent father has requested that I would address to you something which might possibly have a favorable influence on the course of life you have to run, and I too, as a namesake, feel an interest in that course. Few words will be necessary, with good dispositions on your part. Adore God. Reverence and cherish your parents. Love your neighbor as yourself, and your country more than yourself. Be just. Be true. Murmur not at the ways of Providence. So shall the life into which you have entered be the portal to one of eternal and ineffable bliss.

And if to the dead it is permitted to care for the things of this world, every action of your life will be under my regard. Farewell....

A Decalogue of Canons for Observation in Practical Life

1. Never put off till tomorrow what you can do today.
2. Never trouble another for what you can do yourself.
3. Never spend your money before you have it.
4. Never buy what you do not want because it is cheap; it will be dear to you.
5. Pride costs us more than hunger, thirst, and cold.
6. We never repent of having eaten too little.
7. Nothing is troublesome that we do willingly.
8. How much pain have cost us the evils which have never happened.
9. Take things always by their smooth handle.
10. When angry, count ten before you speak; if very angry, an hundred.
—To Thomas Jefferson Smith. Bergh 16:110. (1825.)

AGRICULTURE, Ensures Prosperity and Morality.—Agriculture [is] the surest road to affluence and best preservative of morals.—Bergh 6:272. (1787.)

AGRICULTURE, Speculation vs.— Agriculture...is our wisest pursuit because it will in the end contribute most to real wealth, good morals, and happiness. The wealth acquired by speculation and plunder is fugacious in its nature, and fills society with the spirit of gambling. The moderate and sure income of husbandry begets permanent improvement, quiet life, and orderly conduct, both public and private.—To George Washington. Bergh 6:277. (1787.)

AGRICULTURE, Crop Rotation and.—I find...that a ten years' abandonment of [my lands] to the ravages of overseers has brought on them a degree of degradation far beyond what I had expected. As this obliges me to adopt a milder course of cropping, so I find that they have enabled me to do it by having opened a great deal of lands during my absence. I have therefore determined on a division of my farm into six fields, to be put under this rotation: first year, wheat; second, corn, potatoes, peas; third, rye or wheat, according to circumstances; fourth and fifth, clover where the fields will bring it, and buckwheat dressings where they will not; sixth, folding and buckwheat dressings. But it will take me from three to six years to get this plan under way.—To George Washington. Bergh 9:287. (1794.)

AGRICULTURE, Encouragement of.—I deem [one of] the essential principles of our government, and consequently [one] which ought to shape its administration, ... [the] encouragement of agriculture, and of commerce as its handmaid.—First Inaugural Address. Bergh 3:321. (1801.)

AGRICULTURE, The Most Useful Occupation.—The class principally defective is that of agriculture. It is the first in utility, and ought to be the first in respect. The same

artificial means which have been used to produce a competition in learning may be equally successful in restoring agriculture to its primary dignity in the eyes of men. It is a science of the very first order. It counts among its handmaids the most respectable sciences, such as chemistry, natural philosophy, mechanics, mathematics generally, natural history, [and] botany. In every college and university, a professorship of agriculture, and the class of its students, might be honored as the first. Young men closing their academical education with this as the crown of all other sciences, fascinated with its solid charms, and at a time when they are to choose an occupation, instead of crowding the other classes would return to the farms of their fathers, their own, or those of others, and replenish and invigorate a calling now languishing under contempt and oppression.—Bergh 10:429. (1803.)

AGRICULTURE, In Balance with Manufactures and Commerce.—An equilibrium of agriculture, manufactures, and commerce is certainly become essential to our independence.—Bergh 12:271. (1809.)

AGRICULTURE, Avoid Federal Regulation of.—Were we directed from Washington when to sow and when to reap, we should soon want bread.—Autobiography. Bergh 1:122. (1821.)

AGRICULTURE. See also FARMERS.

ALCOHOLIC BEVERAGES, Ale Preferable to Whiskey.—There is before the assembly [of Virginia] a petition of a Captain Miller, which I have at heart, because I have great esteem for the petitioner as an honest and useful man. He is about to settle in our country, and to establish a brewery, in which art I think him as skillful a man as has ever come to America. I wish to see this beverage become common instead of the whiskey which kills one-third of our citizens, and ruins their families. He is staying with me until he can fix himself, and I should be thankful for information from time to time of the progress of his petition.—Ford 10:2. (1815.)

ALCOHOLIC BEVERAGES. See also INTEMPERANCE; WINE.

ALEXANDER OF RUSSIA, Friendliness to U.S.—Of Alexander's sense of the merits of our form of government, of its wholesome operation on the condition of the people, and of the interest he takes in the success of our experiment, we possess the most unquestionable proofs; and to him we shall be indebted if the rights of neutrals, to be settled whenever peace is made, shall be extended beyond the present belligerents; that is to say, European neutrals, as George and Napoleon, of mutual consent and common hatred against us, would concur in excluding us. I thought it a salutary measure to engage the powerful patronage of Alexander at conferences for peace, at a time when Bonaparte was courting him; and although circumstances have lessened its weight, yet it is prudent for us to cherish his good dispositions, as those alone which

will be exerted in our favor when that occasion shall occur. He, like ourselves, sees and feels the atrociousness of both the belligerents. —Ford 9:287. (1810.)

ALIEN AND SEDITION ACTS, Tyrannical.—If the [Alien and Sedition Acts] should stand, these conclusions would flow from them: that the general government may place any act they think proper on the list of crimes, and punish it themselves whether enumerated or not enumerated by the Constitution as cognizable by them; that they may transfer its cognizance to the President, or any other person, who may himself be the accuser, counsel, judge, and jury, whose *suspicions* may be the evidence, his *order* the sentence, his *officer* the executioner, and his breast the sole record of the transaction; that a very numerous and valuable description of the inhabitants of these states being, by this precedent, reduced as outlaws to the absolute dominion of one man, and the barrier of the Constitution thus swept away from us all, no rampart now remains against the passions and the powers of a majority in Congress to protect from a like exportation, or other more grievous punishment, the minority of the same body, the legislatures, judges, governors, and counsellors of the states, nor their other peaceable inhabitants, who may venture to reclaim the Constitutional rights and liberties of the states and people, or who for other causes, good or bad, may be obnoxious to the views or marked by the suspicions of the President, or be thought dangerous to his or their election or other interests, public or personal; that the friendless alien has indeed been selected as the safest subject of a first experiment, but the citizen will soon follow, or rather has already followed, for already has a Sedition Act marked him as its prey; that these and successive acts of the same character, unless arrested at the threshold, necessarily drive these states into revolution and blood, and will furnish new calumnies against republican government, and new pretexts for those who wish it to be believed that man cannot be governed but by a rod of iron.—Kentucky Resolutions. Bergh 17:387. (1798.)

ALIEN AND SEDITION ACTS. See also SEDITION LAW.

ALLIANCES. See FOREIGN AFFAIRS; TREATIES.

AMERICA, Domestic Pursuits and Society in.—In America, ... the society of your husband, the fond cares for the children, the arrangements of the house, the improvements of the grounds fill every moment with a healthy and a useful activity. Every exertion is encouraging, because to present amusement it joins the promise of some future good. The intervals of leisure are filled by the society of real friends whose affections are not thinned to cobweb by being spread over a thousand objects. This is the picture, in the light it is presented to my mind.—Bergh 6:82. (1787.)

AMERICA, To Point the Way to Liberty for Other Nations.—Convinced that the republican is the only form of government which is not eternally at open or secret war with the rights of mankind, my prayers and efforts shall be cordially distributed to the support of that we have so happily established. It is indeed an animating thought that, while we are securing the rights of ourselves and our posterity, we are pointing out the way to struggling nations who wish, like us, to emerge from their tyrannies also. Heaven help their struggles and lead them, as it has done us, triumphantly through them.—Bergh 8:6. (1790.)

We are destined to be a barrier against the returns of ignorance and barbarism. Old Europe will have to lean on our shoulders, and to hobble along by our side under the monkish trammels of priests and kings as she can. What a colossus shall we be when the southern continent comes up to our mark! What a stand will it secure as a ralliance for the reason and freedom of the globe!—To John Adams. Bergh 15:58. (1816.)

AMERICA, An Asylum for Europeans.—America is now, I think, the only country of tranquility, and should be the asylum of all those who wish to avoid the scenes which have crushed our friends in Paris.—Ford 6:289. (1793.)

AMERICA, The Hope of All Mankind.—The station which we occupy among the nations of the earth is honorable, but awful. Trusted with the destinies of this solitary republic of the world, the only monument of human rights and the sole depository of the sacred fire of freedom and self-government, from hence it is to be lighted up in other regions of the earth, if other regions of the earth shall ever become susceptible of its benign influence. All mankind ought, then, with us, to rejoice in its prosperous and sympathize in its adverse fortunes, as involving everything dear to man. And to what sacrifices of interest, or convenience, ought not these considerations to animate us? To what compromises of opinion and inclination, to maintain harmony and union among ourselves, and to preserve from all danger this hallowed ark of human hope and happiness?—Bergh 16:347. (1809.)

The last hope of human liberty in this world rests on us. We ought, for so dear a stake, to sacrifice every attachment and every enmity.—Ford 9:313. (1811.)

When we reflect that the eyes of the virtuous all over the earth are turned with anxiety on us as the only depositories of the sacred fire of liberty, and that our falling into anarchy would decide forever the destinies of mankind and seal the political heresy that man is incapable of self-government, the only contest between divided friends should be who will dare farthest into the ranks of the common enemy.—Bergh 13:58. (1811.)

AMERICA, Conducive to Self-Government.—Before the establishment of the American states, nothing was known to history but the man of the old world, crowded within limits either small or overcharged, and steeped in the vices which that situation generates. A government adapted to such men would be one thing, but a very different one that for the man of these states. Here everyone may have land to labor for himself if he chooses; or, preferring the exercise of any other industry, may exact for it such compensation as not only to afford a comfortable subsistence, but wherewith to provide for a cessation from labor in old age. Everyone, by his property or by his satisfactory situation, is interested in the support of law and order. And such men may safely and advantageously reserve to themselves a wholesome control over their public affairs, and a degree of freedom which, in the hands of the *canaille* [rabble] of the cities of Europe, would be instantly perverted to the demolition and destruction of everything public and private. The history of the last twenty-five years of France, and of the last forty years in America, nay of its last two hundred years, proves the truth of both parts of this observation.—To John Adams. Bergh 13:401. (1813.)

AMERICA, Destined to Preserve Liberty in the Earth.—I shall not die without a hope that light and liberty are on steady advance.... Even should the cloud of barbarism and despotism again obscure the science and liberties of Europe, this country remains to preserve and restore light and liberty to them. In short, the flames kindled on the 4th of July,

1776, have spread over too much of the globe to be extinguished by the feeble engines of despotism; on the contrary, they will consume these engines and all who work them.— To John Adams. Bergh 15:334. (1821.)

AMERICA. See also COLONIES (American); MANIFEST DESTINY; POPULATION; UNION; UNITED STATES.

AMERICAN CONTINENT, Inhabited Very Early.—I suppose the settlement of our continent is of the most remote antiquity. The similitude between its inhabitants and those of the eastern parts of Asia renders it probable that ours are descended from them, or they from ours. The latter is my opinion, founded on this single fact: among the red inhabitants of Asia there are but a few languages radically different, but among our Indians the number of languages is infinite which are so radically different as to exhibit at present no appearance of their having been derived from a common source. The time necessary for the generation of so many languages must be immense.—Boyd 10:316. (1786.)

AMERICAN CONTINENT, Jefferson's First Proposal for an Expedition Across.—While I resided in Paris, John Ledyard of Connecticut arrived there, well known in the United States for energy of body and mind. He had accompanied Captain Cook in his voyage to the Pacific Ocean, and distinguished himself on that voyage by his intrepidity. Being of a roaming disposition, he was

now panting for some new enterprise. His immediate object at Paris was to engage a mercantile company in the fur trade of the western coast of America, in which, however, he failed. I then proposed to him to go by land to Kamchatka, cross in some of the Russian vessels to Nootka Sound, fall down into the latitude of the Missouri, and penetrate to and through that to the United States.

He eagerly seized the idea, and only asked to be assured of the permission of the Russian government. I [endeavored to obtain] that from M. de Simoulin, [minister plenipotentiary] of the Empress at Paris, but more especially the Baron de Grimm, [minister plenipotentiary] of Saxe-Gotha, her more special agent and correspondent there in matters not immediately diplomatic. Her permission was obtained, and an assurance of protection while the course of the voyage should be through her territories. Ledyard set out from Paris, and arrived at St. Petersburg after the Empress had left that place to pass the winter (I think) at Moscow.

His finances not permitting him to make an unnecessary stay at St. Petersburg, he left it with a passport from one of the ministers, and at two hundred miles from Kamchatka was obliged to take up his winter quarters. He was preparing in the spring to resume his journey when he was arrested by an officer of the Empress, who by this time had changed her mind and forbidden his proceeding. He was put into a closed carriage and conveyed day and night, without ever stopping, till they reached Poland, where he was set down and left to himself.

The fatigue of this journey broke down his constitution, and when he returned to Paris his bodily strength was much impaired. His mind, however, remained firm; and after this he undertook [a] journey to Egypt. I received a letter from him, full of sanguine hopes, dated at Cairo the 15th of November, 1788, the day before he was to set out for the head of the Nile, on which day, however, he ended his career and life; and thus failed the first attempt to explore the western part of our northern continent.—Bergh 18:143. (1813.)

AMERICAN CONTINENT, Jefferson's Second Proposal for an Expedition Across.—In 1792 I proposed to the [American Philosophical Society] that we should set on foot a subscription to engage some competent person to explore that region in the opposite direction, that is, by ascending the Missouri, crossing the Stony Mountains, and descending the nearest river to the Pacific. Captain [Meriwether] Lewis, being then stationed at Charlottesville on the recruiting service, warmly solicited me to obtain for him the execution of that object. I told him it was proposed that the person engaged should be attended by a single companion only, to avoid exciting alarm among the Indians. This did not deter him. But Mr. Andre Michaux, a professed botanist, author of the *Flora Boreali-Americana* and of the *Historie des chenes*

d'Amerique, offering his services, they were accepted. He received his instructions, and when he had reached Kentucky in the prosecution of his journey he was overtaken by an order from the minister of France, then at Philadelphia, to relinquish the expedition and to pursue elsewhere the botanical inquiries on which he was employed by that government; and thus failed the second attempt for exploring that region.—Bergh 18:144. (1813.)

AMERICAN CONTINENT, Third and Successful Attempt to Explore.—I had long deemed it incumbent on the authorities of our country to have the great western wilderness beyond the Mississippi explored, to make known its geography, its natural productions, its general character and inhabitants. Two attempts which I had myself made formerly, before the country was ours, the one from west to east, the other from east to west, had both proved abortive. When called to the administration of the general government, I made this an object of early attention and proposed it to Congress. They voted a sum of five thousand dollars for its execution, and I placed Captain [Meriwether] Lewis at the head of the enterprise. No man within the range of my acquaintance united so many of the qualifications necessary for its successful direction.—Bergh 15:342. (1821.)

AMERICAN CONTINENT. See also LEWIS AND CLARK EXPEDITION; LOUISIANA; LOUISIANA PURCHASE; MANIFEST

DESTINY; POPULATION; TERRITORY.

AMERICAN REVOLUTION, Canada and.—In a short time, we have reason to hope, the delegates of Canada will join us in Congress and complete the American union as far as we wish to have it completed.—To John Randolph. Bergh 4:32. (1775.)

AMERICAN REVOLUTION, Consequences of.—The inquiry which has been excited among the mass of mankind by our Revolution and its consequences will ameliorate the condition of men over a great portion of the globe.—To John Dickinson. Ford 8:8. (1801.)

AMERICAN REVOLUTION, Beginning of.—It would...be as difficult to say at what moment the Revolution began, and what incident set it in motion, as to fix the moment that the embryo becomes an animal, or the act which gives him a beginning.—Ford 10:107. (1818.)

AMERICAN REVOLUTION, New England and Virginia.—Throughout the whole of the Revolution, Virginia and the four New England states acted together; indeed they made the Revolution. Their five votes were always to be counted on; but they had to pick up the remaining two for a majority when and where they could.—Quoted by Daniel Webster from a conversation with Jefferson. Ford 10:329. (1824.)

AMERICAN REVOLUTION. See also COLONIES (American); DECLARATION OF INDEPENDENCE; FOURTH OF JULY; REVOLUTIONARY WAR.

ANARCHY, Suppress.—Let this be the distinctive mark of an American, that in cases of commotion he enlists himself under no man's banner, inquires for no man's name, but repairs to the standard of the laws. Do this and you need never fear anarchy or tyranny. Your government will be perpetual.—Ford 8:1. (1801?)

ANARCHY, Fatal.—Our falling into anarchy would decide forever the destinies of mankind, and seal the political heresy that man is incapable of self-government.—Bergh 13:58. (1811.)

ANGLO-SAXONS, American Government Based on Laws of.—Has not every restitution of the ancient Saxon laws had happy effects? Is it not better now that we return at once into that happy system of our ancestors, the wisest and most perfect ever yet devised by the wit of man, as it stood before the eighth century?—To Edmund Pendleton. Boyd 1:492. (1776.)

APPOINTMENT, The Power of.—The Constitution, having declared that the President shall *nominate* and, by and with the advice and consent of the Senate, shall *appoint* ambassadors, other public ministers, and consuls,...has taken care to circumscribe this [power] within very strict limits, for it gives the *nomination* of the foreign agents to the President, the *appointments* to him and the Senate jointly, and the *commissioning* to the President. This analysis calls our attention to the strict import of each term. To *nominate* must be to *propose*. *Appointment* seems that act of the will which constitutes or makes the agent, and the *commission* is the public evidence of it.—Ford 5:161. (1790.)

APPOINTMENT. See also PATRONAGE; POLITICAL OFFICES.

ARCHITECTURE, Ugliness of Virginia's Residential.—The private buildings [in Virginia] are very rarely constructed of stone or brick, much the greater portion being of scantling [wooden frame] and boards, plastered with lime. It is impossible to devise things more ugly, uncomfortable, and happily more perishable.—*Notes on Virginia.* Bergh 2:211. (1782.)

ARCHITECTURE, Virginia Capitol.—The designs for the [Virginia] Capitol are simple and sublime. More cannot be said. They are not the brat of a whimsical conception never before brought to light, but copied from the most precious, the most perfect model of ancient architecture remaining on earth, one which has received the approbation of near two thousand years, and which is sufficiently remarkable to have been visited by all travelers. —Ford 4:133. (1786.)

ARCHITECTURE, Importance of. —Architecture [is] worth great attention. As we double our number every twenty years, we must double our houses.... It is, then, among the most important arts, and it is desirable to introduce taste into an art which shows so much.—Bergh 17:292. (1788.)

ARISTOCRACY, Public Office and Natural.—It becomes expedient for promoting the public happiness that those persons whom nature hath endowed with genius and virtue should be rendered by liberal education worthy to receive, and able to guard, the sacred deposit of the rights and liberties of their fellow citizens; and that they should be called to that charge without regard to wealth, birth, or other accidental condition or circumstance.—Boyd 2:526. (1779.)

ARISTOCRACY, Artificial vs. Natural.—There is a natural aristocracy among men. The grounds of this are virtue and talents.... There is also an artificial aristocracy, founded on wealth and birth, without either virtue or talents; for with these it would belong to the first class. The natural aristocracy I consider as the most precious gift of nature for the instruction, the trusts, and government of society. And indeed, it would have been inconsistent in creation to have formed man for the social state, and not to have provided virtue and wisdom enough to manage the concerns of the society. May we not even say that that form of government is the best which provides the most effectually for a pure selection of these natural *aristoi* into the offices of government? The artificial aristocracy is a mischievous ingredient in government, and provision should be made to prevent its ascendancy.—To John Adams. Bergh 13:396. (1813.)

ARISTOCRACY. See also GENIUS; TALENTS.

ARMS, Right to Bear.—No freeman shall be debarred the use of arms within his own lands.—Proposed Virginia Constitution. Ford 2:27. (1776.)

ARMY, Increase of.—An act has passed for raising upon the regular establishment for the war 3,000 additional troops and a corps of 300 more, making in the whole about 5,000 men. To this I was opposed from a conviction they were useless, and that 1,200 or 1,500 woodsmen would soon end the [Indian] war, and at a trifling expense.—Ford 5:454. (1792.)

ARMY, Importance of State Militia. —The Greeks and Romans had no standing armies, yet they defended themselves. The Greeks by their laws, and the Romans by the spirit of their people, took care to put into the hands of their rulers no such engine of oppression as a standing army. Their system was to make every man a soldier, and oblige him to repair to the standard of his country whenever that was reared. This made them invincible, and the same remedy will make us so.— Bergh 14:184. (1814.)

ARMY. See also DEFENSE; DRAFT; MILITIA; NAVY.

ARTICLES OF CONFEDERATION, Weaknesses to Be Remedied.—The want of power in the federal head was early perceived, and foreseen to be the flaw in our constitution which might endanger its destruction. I have the pleasure to inform you that when I left America in July the people were becoming universally sensible of this, and a spirit to enlarge the powers of Congress was becoming general. Letters and other

information recently received show that this has continued to increase, and that they are likely to remedy this evil effectually. The happiness of governments like ours, wherein the people are truly the mainspring, is that they are never to be despaired of. When an evil becomes so glaring as to strike them generally, they arouse themselves and it is redressed. He only is then the popular man, and can get into office, who shows the best dispositions to reform the evil. This truth was obvious on several occasions during the late war, and this character in our governments saved us. Calamity was our best physician.—Boyd 7:630. (1785.)

ARTICLES OF CONFEDERATION, Fatal Weaknesses of.—Our first federal constitution, or Confederation, as it was called, was framed in the first moments of our separation from England, in the highest point of our jealousies of independence as to her, and as to each other. It formed, therefore, too weak a bond to produce a union of action as to foreign nations. This appeared at once on the establishment of peace, when the pressure of a common enemy which had hooped us together during the war was taken away. Congress was found to be quite unable to point the action of the several states to a common object. A general desire, therefore, took place of amending the federal constitution.—Ford 7:45. (1795.)

Our first essay in America to establish a federative government had fallen, on trial, very short of its object. During the War of Independence, while the pressure of an external enemy hooped us together, and their enterprises kept us necessarily on the alert, the spirit of the people, excited by danger, was a supplement to the Confederation, and urged them to zealous exertions, whether claimed by that instrument or not; but when peace and safety were restored, and every man became engaged in useful and profitable occupation, less attention was paid to the calls of Congress. The fundamental defect of the Confederation was that Congress was not authorized to act immediately on the people, and by its own officers. Their power was only requisitory, and these requisitions were addressed to the several [state] legislatures, to be by them carried into execution, without other coercion than the moral principle of duty. This allowed, in fact, a negative [i.e., veto] to every legislature on every measure proposed by Congress; a negative so frequently exercised in practice as to benumb the action of the federal government and to render it inefficient in its general objects, and more especially in pecuniary and foreign concerns. The want, too, of a separation of the legislative, executive, and judiciary functions worked disadvantageously in practice. Yet this state of things afforded a happy augury of the future march of our confederacy when it was seen that the good sense and good dispositions of the people, as soon as they perceived the incompetence of their first compact, instead of leaving its correction to insurrection and civil war, agreed with one voice to elect deputies to a general convention, who should peaceably meet and agree on such a constitution as "would ensure peace, justice, liberty, the common defense and general welfare."—Autobiography. Bergh 1:116. (1821.)

Among the debilities of the government of the Confederation, no one was more distinguished or more distressing than the utter impossibility of obtaining from the states the moneys necessary for the payment of debts, or even for the ordinary expenses of the government. Some contributed a little, some less, and some nothing; and the last furnished at length an excuse for the first to do nothing also.—Autobiography. Bergh 1:122. (1821.)

ARTICLES OF CONFEDERATION.
See also CONSTITUTION (U.S.).

ARTS, Enthusiasm for the.—I am an enthusiast on the subject of the arts. But it is an enthusiasm of which I am not ashamed, as its object is to improve the taste of my countrymen, to increase their reputation, to reconcile to them the respect of the world, and procure them its praise.—To James Madison. Bergh 5:137. (1785.)

ATTORNEYS. See LAWYERS.

B

BANJO, Origin of the.—The instrument proper to [the Negroes] is the Banjar [later corrupted to "banjo"], which they brought hither from Africa, and which is the original of the guitar, its chords being precisely the four lower chords of the guitar.—*Notes on Virginia.* Bergh 2:195. (1782.)

BANK OF THE UNITED STATES, Unconstitutional.—I consider the foundation of the Constitution as laid on this ground: that "all powers not delegated to the United States by the Constitution, nor prohibited by it to the states, are reserved to the states or to the people."... To take a single step beyond the boundaries thus specially drawn around the powers of Congress is to take possession of a boundless field of power, no longer susceptible of any definition. The incorporation of a bank, and the powers assumed by this bill, have not, in my opinion, been delegated to the United States by the Constitution.—Bergh 3:146. (1791.)

BANK OF THE UNITED STATES, Saddled and Bridled by.—We are completely saddled and bridled, and the bank is so firmly mounted on us that we must go where they will guide.—Ford 7:80. (1796.)

BANK OF THE UNITED STATES, Produced Ruin.—It was impossible the bank and paper mania should not produce great and extensive ruin. The President [Washington] is fortunate to get off just as the bubble is bursting, leaving others to hold the bag.—Ford 7:104. (1797.)

BANK OF THE UNITED STATES, Hostile to U.S. Government.—This institution is one of the most deadly hostility existing, against the principles and form of our Constitution.

The nation is, at this time, so strong and united in its sentiments that it cannot be shaken at this moment. But suppose a series of untoward events should occur, sufficient to bring into doubt the competency of a republican government to meet a crisis of great danger, or to unhinge the confidence of the people in the public functionaries. An institution like this, penetrating by its branches every part of the Union, acting by command and in phalanx, may, in a critical moment, upset the government. I deem no government safe which is under the vassalage of any self-constituted authorities, or any other authority than that of the nation or its regular functionaries.

What an obstruction could not this Bank of the United States, with all its branch banks, be in time of war? It might dictate to us the peace we should accept, or withdraw its aids. Ought we then to give further growth to an institution so powerful, so hostile? That it is so hostile we know, 1, from a knowledge of the principles of the persons composing the body of directors in every bank, principal or branch, and those of most of the stockholders; 2, from their opposition to the measures and principles of the government, and to the election of those friendly to them; and 3, from the sentiments of the newspapers they support.

Now, while we are strong, it is the greatest debt we owe to the safety of our Constitution to bring its powerful enemy to a perfect subordination under its authorities. The first measure would be to reduce them to an equal footing only with other banks, as to the favors of the government. But in order to be able to meet a general combination of the banks against us in a critical emergency, could we not make a beginning towards an independent use of our own money, towards holding our own bank in all the deposits where it is received, and letting the treasurer give his draft or note for payment at any particular place, which, in a well-conducted government, ought to have as much credit as any private draft, or bank note, or bill, and would give us the same facilities which we derive from the banks?—To Albert Gallatin. Bergh 10:437. (1803.)

BANK OF THE UNITED STATES, Opposition to Renewal of Its Charter.—The idea of creating [another] national bank I do not concur in, because it seems now decided that Congress has not that power (although I sincerely wish they had it exclusively), and because I think there is already a vast redundancy, rather than a scarcity, of paper medium. The rapid rise in the nominal price of land and labor (while war and blockade should produce a fall) proves the progressive state of the depreciation of our medium.—Ford 9:433. (1813.)

After the solemn decision of Congress against the renewal of the charter of the Bank of the United States [in 1811], and the grounds of that decision (the want of constitutional power), I had imagined that question at rest, and that no more applications would be made to them

for the incorporation of banks. The opposition on that ground to its first establishment, the small majority by which it was overborne, and the means practised for obtaining it cannot be already forgotten. The law having passed, however, by a majority, its opponents, true to the sacred principle of submission to a majority, suffered the law to flow through its term without obstruction. During this, the nation had time to consider the constitutional question, and when the renewal was proposed they condemned it, not by their representatives in Congress only, but by express instructions from different organs of their will.—Bergh 13:409. (1813.)

BANKS, Excess of.—That we are overdone with banking institutions, which have banished the precious metals and substituted a more fluctuating and unsafe medium, [and] that these have withdrawn capital from useful improvements and employments to nourish idleness, ... are evils more easily to be deplored than remedied.—Bergh 12:379. (1810.)

BANKS, Evils of.—Everything predicted by the enemies of banks, in the beginning, is now coming to pass. We are to be ruined now by the deluge of bank paper, as we were formerly by the old Continental paper. It is cruel that such revolutions in private fortunes should be at the mercy of avaricious adventurers who, instead of employing their capital, if any they have, in manufactures, commerce, and other useful pursuits, make it an instrument to burden all the interchanges of property with their swindling profits, profits which are the price of no useful industry of theirs. Prudent men must be on their guard in this game of *Robin's alive,* and take care that the spark does not extinguish in their hands. I am an enemy to all banks discounting bills or notes for anything but coin. But our whole country is so fascinated by this Jack-lantern wealth that they will not stop short of its total and fatal explosion.—Bergh 14:61. (1814.)

The evils they [the banks] have engendered are now upon us, and the question is how we are to get out of them? Shall we build an altar to the old paper money of the Revolution, which ruined individuals but saved the Republic, and burn on that all the bank charters, present and future, and their notes with them? For these are to ruin both Republic and individuals. This cannot be done. The mania is too strong. It has seized, by its delusions and corruptions, all the members of our governments, general, special, and individual.—To John Adams. Bergh 14:77. (1814.)

BANKS, Challenge to Government.—I hope we shall...crush in its birth the aristocracy of our moneyed corporations, which dare already to challenge our government to a trial of strength and bid defiance to the laws of our country. —Ford 10:69. (1816.)

BANKS, More Dangerous than Standing Armies.—I sincerely believe...that banking establishments are more dangerous than standing armies; and that the

principle of spending money to be paid by posterity, under the name of funding, is but swindling futurity on a large scale.—Bergh 15:23. (1816.)

BANKS. See also FRACTIONAL BANKING; MONEY; MONOPOLY.

BIBLE, Circulation of the.—I had not supposed there was a family in this state [Virginia] not possessing a Bible, and wishing without having the means to procure one. When, in earlier life, I was intimate with every class, I think I never was in a house where that was the case. However, circumstances may have changed, and the [Bible] Society, I presume, have evidence of the fact. I therefore enclose you cheerfully an order... for fifty dollars, for the purposes of the Society.—Bergh 14:81. (1814.)

BIBLE, Morality in the.—There never was a more pure and sublime system of morality delivered to man than is to be found in the four Evangelists.—Bergh 14:81. (1814.)

BIBLE. See also CHRISTIANITY; JESUS CHRIST; RELIGION.

BIGOTRY, A Disease.—Bigotry is the disease of ignorance, of morbid minds; enthusiasm of the free and buoyant. Education and free discussion are the antidotes of both. —To John Adams. Bergh 15:58. (1816.)

BIGOTRY, Self-Government and.—Ignorance and bigotry, like other insanities, are incapable of self-government.—Ford 10:84. (1817.)

BIGOTRY. See also INTOLERANCE.

BILL OF RIGHTS, The People and.—A bill of rights is what the people are entitled to against every government on earth, general or particular, and what no just government should refuse or rest on inference.—To James Madison. Bergh 6:388. (1787.)

BILL OF RIGHTS, Jefferson's Early Definition.—By a declaration of rights, I mean one which shall stipulate freedom of religion, freedom of the press, freedom of commerce against monopolies, trial by juries in all cases, no suspensions of the habeas corpus, no standing armies. These are fetters against doing evil which no honest government should decline.—Bergh 6:425. (1788.)

BILL OF RIGHTS, Demand for.—I sincerely rejoice at the acceptance of our new Constitution by nine states. It is a good canvas, on which some strokes only want retouching. What these are, I think are sufficiently manifested by the general voice from north to south, which calls for a bill of rights. It seems pretty generally understood that this should go to juries, habeas corpus, standing armies, printing, religion, and monopolies.... A declaration that the federal government will never restrain the presses from printing anything they please will not take away the liability of the printers for false facts printed. The declaration that religious faith shall be unpunished does not give impunity to criminal acts dictated by religious error. The saying there shall be no monopolies lessens the incitements to ingenuity, which is spurred on by the hope of a

monopoly for a limited time, as of fourteen years; but the benefit of even limited monopolies is too doubtful to be opposed to that of their general suppression. If no check can be found to keep the number of standing troops within safe bounds, while they are tolerated as far as necessary, abandon them altogether, discipline well the militia, and guard the magazines with them. More than magazine guards will be useless if few, and dangerous if many. No European nation can ever send against us such a regular army as we need fear, and it is hard if our militia are not equal to those of Canada or Florida. My idea, then, is that though proper exceptions to these general rules are desirable, and probably practicable, yet if the exceptions cannot be agreed on, the establishment of the rules in all cases will do ill in very few. I hope, therefore, a bill of rights will be formed to guard the people against the federal government, as they are already guarded against their state governments in most instances.—To James Madison. Bergh 7:96. (1788.)

BILL OF RIGHTS, Security in.—A general concurrence of opinion seems to authorize us to say [the Constitution] has some defects. I am one of those who think it a defect that the important rights, not placed in security by the frame of the Constitution itself, were not explicitly secured by a supplementary declaration. There are rights which it is useless to surrender to the government, and which governments have yet always been found to invade. These are the rights of thinking, and publishing our thoughts by speaking or writing; the right of free commerce; the right of personal freedom. There are instruments for administering the government so peculiarly trustworthy that we should never leave the legislature [i.e., Congress] at liberty to change them. The new Constitution has secured these in the executive and legislative departments, but not in the judiciary. It should have established trials by the people themselves, that is to say, by jury. There are instruments so dangerous to the rights of the nation, and which place them so totally at the mercy of their governors, that those governors, whether legislative or executive, should be restrained from keeping such instruments on foot, but in well-defined cases. Such an instrument is a standing army. We are now allowed to say such a declaration of rights, as a supplement to the Constitution where that is silent, is wanting to secure us in these points. The general voice has legitimated this objection.—To David Humphreys. Bergh 7:322. (1789.)

BIRTHDAY, Jefferson's.—Disapproving myself of transferring the honors and veneration for the great birthday of our Republic to any individual, or of dividing them with individuals, I have declined letting my own birthday be known, and have engaged my family not to communicate it. This has been the

uniform answer to every application of the kind.—Ford 8:246. (1803.)

BLACKSTONE (Sir William), Commentaries.—The exclusion from the courts of the malign influence of all authorities after the *Georgium Sidus* became ascendant would uncanonize Blackstone, whose book, although the most elegant and best digested of our law catalogue, has been perverted, more than all others, to the degeneracy of legal science.—Bergh 13:166. (1812.)

BORROWING. See DEBT; LOANS.

BOTANY, Value of.—Botany I rank with the most valuable sciences, whether we consider its subjects as furnishing the principal subsistence of life to man and beast, delicious varieties for our tables, refreshments from our orchards, the adornments of our flower borders, shade and perfume of our groves, materials for our buildings, or medicaments for our bodies. To the gentleman it is certainly more interesting than mineralogy (which I by no means, however, undervalue), and is more at hand for his amusement; and to a country family it constitutes a great portion of their social entertainment. No country gentleman should be without what amuses every step he takes into his fields.—Bergh 14:201. (1814.)

BRIBERY, Electoral.—No person shall be capable of acting in any office, civil, military, or ecclesiastical, who shall have given any bribe to obtain such office.—Proposed Virginia Constitution. Ford 2:28. (1776.)

BURR (Aaron), Treason of.—His conspiracy has been one of the most flagitious of which history will ever furnish an example. He meant to separate the western states from us, to add Mexico to them, place himself at their head, establish what he would deem an energetic government, and thus provide an example and an instrument for the subversion of our freedom. The man who could expect to effect this, with American materials, must be a fit subject for Bedlam.—Ford 9:113. (1807.)

C

CABINET, Advisers to President.— Our government, although in theory subject to be directed by the unadvised will of the President, is, and from its origin has been, a very different thing in practice. The minor business in each department is done by the head of the department, on consultation with the President alone. But all matters of importance or difficulty are submitted to all the heads of departments composing the Cabinet, sometimes by the President consulting them separately and successively as they happen to call on him, but in the gravest cases by calling them together, discussing the subject maturely, and finally taking the vote, in which the President counts himself but as one. So that in all important cases the executive is in fact a directory, which certainly the President might control, but of this there was never

an example, either in the first or present administration. I have heard, indeed, that my predecessor sometimes decided things against his council by dashing and trampling his wig on the floor. This only proves what you and I know, that he had a better heart than head.—Ford 9:69. (1807.)

CABINET OFFICERS, Public Confidence in.—It is essential to assemble in the outset persons to compose our administration whose talents, integrity, and Revolutionary name and principles may inspire the nation at once with unbounded confidence.... If I can obtain for the public the aid of those I have contemplated, I fear nothing. If this cannot be done, then we are unfortunate indeed! We shall be unable to realize the prospects which have been held out to the people, and we must fall back into monarchism for want of heads, not hands, to help us out of it. This is a common cause, my dear sir, common to all republicans.... The part which circumstances constrain us to propose to you is the Secretaryship of the Navy.... Come forward, then, my dear sir, and give us the aid of your talents and the weight of your character towards the new establishment of republicanism.—To Robert R. Livingston. Ford 7:464. (1800.)

CANADA, Expected to Join American Revolution.—In a short time, we have reason to hope, the delegates of Canada will join us in Congress and complete the American union, as far as we wish to have it completed.—Bergh 4:32. (1775.)

CAPITAL PUNISHMENT, Advocated for Murder or Treason.—The General Assembly [of Virginia] shall have no power to pass any law inflicting death for any crime excepting murder, and those offenses in the military service for which they shall think punishment by death absolutely necessary; and all capital punishments in ' other cases are hereby abolished.—Proposed Virginia Constitution. Ford 2:17. (1776.)

The punishment of death should be abolished except for treason and murder.—Autobiography. Bergh 1:64. (1821.)

CAPITAL PUNISHMENT, A Last Resource.—The reformation of offenders, though an object worthy the attention of the laws, is not effected at all by capital punishments, which exterminate instead of reforming, and should be the last melancholy resource against those whose existence is become inconsistent with the safety of their fellow citizens; which also weaken the state by cutting off so many who, if reformed, might be restored sound members to society, who, even under a course of correction, might be rendered useful in various labors for the public, and would be living and long-continued spectacles to deter others from committing the like offenses.—Ford 2:204. (1779.)

CAPITAL PUNISHMENT, Indians and.—It will be worthy the consideration of the [Congress] whether the provisions of the law inflicting on Indians, in certain cases, the punishment of death by hanging might not permit its commutation into death by military execution, the form of the punishment in the former way being peculiarly repugnant to their ideas, and increasing the obstacles to the surrender of the criminal.—Special Message to Congress. Bergh 3:349. (1802.)

CAPITAL PUNISHMENT, Substitutes for, Ineffective.—Beccaria and other writers on crimes and punishments had satisfied the reasonable world of the unrightfulness and inefficacy of the punishment of crimes by death, and hard labor on roads, canals, and other public works had been suggested as a proper substitute. The revisors [of the Virginia laws] had adopted these opinions, but the general idea of our country had not yet advanced to that point. The bill, therefore, for proportioning crimes and punishments was lost in the House of Delegates by a majority of a single vote. I learned afterwards that the substitute of hard labor in public was tried (I believe it was in Pennsylvania) without success. Exhibited as a public spectacle, with shaved heads and mean clothing, working on the high roads produced in the criminals such a prostration of character, such an abandonment of self-respect, as, instead of reforming, plunged them into the most desperate and hardened depravity of morals and character.—Autobiography. Bergh 1:67. (1821.)

CENSUS, Perfecting the.—For the articles of a statistical table, I think the last census of Congress presented what was proper, as far as it went, but did not go far enough. It required detailed accounts of our manufactures, and an enumeration of our people according to ages, sexes, and colors. But to this should be added an enumeration according to their occupations. We should know what proportion of our people are employed in agriculture, what proportion are carpenters, smiths, shoemakers, tailors, bricklayers, merchants, seamen, etc.—Bergh 14:429. (1816.)

CENTRALIZATION, Produces Despotism.—All the powers of government, legislative, executive, and judiciary, result to the legislative body [under the first Virginia constitution]. The concentrating these in the same hands is precisely the definition of despotic government. It will be no alleviation that these powers will be exercised by a plurality of hands, and not by a single one. One hundred and seventy-three despots would surely be as oppressive as one. Let those who doubt it turn their eyes on the republic of Venice.—*Notes on Virginia.* Bergh 2:162. (1782.)

CENTRALIZATION, Corrupts Government.—I do verily believe that...a single consolidated government would become the most corrupt government on the earth. —Ford 7:451. (1800.)

CENTRALIZATION, Destroys Liberty.—What has destroyed liberty and the rights of man in every government which has ever existed under the sun? The generalizing and concentrating all cares and powers into one body, no matter whether of the autocrats of Russia or France, or of the aristocrats of a Venetian senate.—Bergh 14:421. (1816.)

CENTRALIZATION, Eastern States and.—I fear our eastern associates wish for consolidation, in which they would be joined by the smaller states generally.—Ford 10:194. (1821.)

CENTRALIZATION, To Be Feared. —I scarcely know...which is most to be deprecated, a consolidation or dissolution of the states. The horrors of both are beyond the reach of human foresight.—Ford 10:225. (1822.)

CENTRALIZATION, Must Be Resisted.—Although I have little hope that the torrent of consolidation can be withstood, I should not be for giving up the ship without efforts to save her. She lived well through the first squall and may weather the present one.—Bergh 16:152. (1826.)

CENTRALIZATION. See also CONSTITUTION (U.S.); FEDERAL GOVERNMENT; GOVERNMENT; JUDICIARY; SEPARATION OF POWERS; STATES; STATES' RIGHTS; SUPREME COURT.

CHANCE, Games of, Not Inherently Immoral.—It is a common idea that games of chance are immoral. But what is chance? Nothing happens in this world without a cause. If we know the cause, we do not call it chance; but if we do not know it, we say it was produced by chance. If we see a loaded die turn its lightest side up, we know the cause, and that is not an effect of chance; but whatever side an unloaded die turns up, not knowing the cause, we say it is the effect of chance. Yet the morality of a thing cannot depend on our knowledge or ignorance of its cause. Not knowing why a particular side of an unloaded die turns up cannot make the act of throwing it, or of betting on it, immoral.

If we consider games of chance immoral, then every pursuit of human industry is immoral; for there is not a single one that is not subject to chance, not one wherein you do not risk a loss for the chance of some gain. The navigator, for example, risks his ship in the hope (if she is not lost in the voyage) of gaining an advantageous freight. The merchant risks his cargo to gain a better price for it. A landholder builds a house on the risk of indemnifying himself by a rent. The hunter hazards his time and trouble in the hope of killing game. In all these pursuits, you take some one thing against which you hope to win. But the greatest of all gamblers is the farmer. He risks the seed he puts into the ground, the rent he pays for the ground itself, the year's labor on it, and the wear and tear of his cattle and gear, to win a crop, which the chances of too much or too little rain, and general uncertainties of weather, insects, waste, etc., often make a total or partial loss. These, then, are games of chance. Yet so far from being immoral, they are indispensable to the existence of man; and everyone has a natural right to choose for his pursuit such one of

them as he thinks most likely to furnish him subsistence.

Almost all these pursuits of chance produce something useful to society. But there are some which produce nothing, and endanger the well-being of the individuals engaged in them, or of others depending on them. Such are games with cards, dice, billiards, etc. And although the pursuit of them is a matter of natural right, yet society, perceiving the irresistible bent of some of its members to pursue them, and the ruin produced by them to the families depending on these individuals, consider it as a case of insanity, *quoad hoc*, step in to protect the family and the party himself, as in other cases of insanity, infancy, imbecility, etc., and suppress the pursuit altogether, and the natural right of following it.

There are some other games of chance, useful on certain occasions, and injurious only when carried beyond their useful bounds. Such are insurances, lotteries, raffles, etc. These they [i.e., society] do not suppress, but take their regulation under their own discretion. The insurance of ships on voyages is a vocation of chance, yet useful, and the right to exercise it therefore is left free. So of houses against fire, doubtful debts, the continuance of a particular life, and similar cases.— Thoughts on Lotteries. Bergh 17:448. (1826.)

CHANCE. See also GAMBLING; LOTTERIES; SPECULATION.

CHARACTER, Strong American.— The order and good sense displayed in this recovery from delusions, and in the momentous crisis [i.e., the presidential election] which lately arose, really bespeak a strength of character in our nation which augurs well for the duration of our Republic, and I am much better satisfied now of its stability than I was before it was tried.—Ford 8:22. (1801.)

CHARACTER, Steady American.—The steady character of our countrymen is a rock to which we may safely moor.—Ford 8:43. (1801.)

CHARACTER, Evidence of.—The uniform tenor of a man's life furnishes better evidence of what he has said or done on any particular occasion than the word of any enemy, and of an enemy, too, who shows that he prefers the use of falsehoods which suit him to truths which do not.—Bergh 10:440. (1803.)

CHARITY, Not the Business of Government.—If we can prevent the government from wasting the labors of the people, under the pretense of taking care of them, they must become happy.—Bergh 10:342. (1802.)

CHARITY, Principles of Distributing.—I deem it the duty of every man to devote a certain portion of his income for charitable purposes, and that it is his further duty to see it so applied as to do the most good of which it is capable. This I believe to be best insured by keeping within the circle of his own inquiry and information the subjects of distress to whose relief his contributions

Jefferson in 1786 (age 43). Portrait by Mather Brown. Jefferson's contemporaries did not regard this as a good likeness of him. One of his friends, William Short, observed that "it has no feature like him."

shall be applied. If this rule be reasonable in private life, it becomes so necessary in my situation that to relinquish it would leave me without rule or compass.—Bergh 11:92. (1806.)

We are all doubtless bound to contribute a certain portion of our income to the support of charitable and other useful public institutions. But it is a part of our duty also to apply our contributions in the most effectual way we can to secure their object. The question, then, is whether this will not be better done by each of us appropriating our whole contributions to the institutions within our own reach, under our own eye, and over which we can exercise some useful control. Or would it be better that each should divide the sum he can spare among all the institutions of his state, or of the United States? Reason, and the interest of these institutions themselves, certainly decide in favor of the former practice.... If each portion of the state ... will apply its aids and its attentions exclusively to those nearest around them, all will be better taken care of. Their support, their conduct, and the best administration of their funds will be under the inspection and control of those most convenient to take cognizance of them, and most interested in their prosperity.—Bergh 12:341. (1810.)

CHARITY, A Duty.—Private charities, as well as contributions to public purposes in proportion to everyone's circumstances, are certainly among the duties we owe to society.—Bergh 13:134. (1812.)

CHARITY, Retain Local Control of.—It is a duty certainly to give our sparings to those who want, but to see also that they are faithfully distributed, and duly apportioned to the respective wants of those receivers. Why give through agents whom we know not, to persons whom we know not, and in countries from which we get no account, when we can do it at short

hand, to objects under our eye, through agents we know, and to supply wants we see?—Bergh 15:434. (1823.)

CHARITY. See also POOR; REDISTRIBUTION OF WEALTH; WELFARE.

CHILDREN. See FAMILY; GRAND-CHILDREN.

CHRISTIANITY, And Intolerance of Other Religions.—Why have Christians been distinguished above all people who have ever lived for persecutions? Is it because it is the genius of their religion? No, its genius is the reverse. It is the refusing *toleration* to those of a different opinion which has produced all the bustles and wars on account of religion.—Ford 2:103. (1776?)

CHRISTIANITY, Jefferson's Views on.—My views of [the Christian religion] ... are the result of a life of inquiry and reflection, and very different from that anti-Christian system imputed to me by those who know nothing of my opinions. To the corruptions of Christianity I am, indeed, opposed; but not to the genuine precepts of Jesus himself. I am a Christian, in the only sense in which he wished anyone to be—sincerely attached to his doctrines, in preference to all others; ascribing to himself every *human* excellence, and believing he never claimed any other.*—To Dr. Benjamin Rush. Bergh 10:379. (1803.)

*Toward the end of his life, Jefferson apparently changed his mind about the divinity of Jesus. The letters he wrote during his final years contain occasional references to "our Savior."— Editor.

I am a *real Christian*, that is to say, a disciple of the doctrines of Jesus— very different from the Platonists, who call *me* infidel and *themselves* Christians and preachers of the gospel, while they draw all their characteristic dogmas from what its Author never said nor saw. They have compounded from the heathen mysteries a system beyond the comprehension of man, of which the great Reformer of the vicious ethics and deism of the Jews, were He to return on earth, would not recognize one feature.—To Charles Thomson. Bergh 14:385. (1816.)

CHRISTIANITY, Corruption of Its Original Doctrines.—We must reduce our volume to the simple evangelists [and] select, even from them, the very words only of Jesus, paring off the amphibologisms into which they have been led by forgetting often, or not understanding, what had fallen from him.... There will be found remaining the most sublime and benevolent code of morals which has ever been offered to man. I have performed this operation for my own use by cutting verse by verse out of the printed book, and arranging the matter which is evidently his, and which is as easily distinguishable as diamonds in a dunghill. The result is an octavo of forty-six pages of pure and unsophisticated doctrines such as were professed and acted on by the unlettered Apostles, the Apostolic Fathers, and the Christians of the first century. Their Platonizing successors, indeed, in after times, in order to legitimate the corruptions which they had incorporated into the doctrines of Jesus, found it necessary to disavow the primitive Christians, who had taken their principles from the mouth of Jesus himself, of his Apostles, and the Fathers contemporary with them. They excommunicated their followers as heretics.—To John Adams. Bergh 13:389. (1813.)

The Christian priesthood, finding the doctrines of Christ levelled to every understanding and too plain to need explanation, saw in the mysticism of Plato materials with which they might build up an artificial system which might, from its indistinctness, admit everlasting controversy, give employment for their order, and introduce it to profit, power, and preeminence. The doctrines which flowed from the lips of Jesus himself are within the comprehension of a child; but thousands of volumes have not yet explained the Platonisms engrafted on them; and for this obvious reason, that nonsense can never be explained.—To John Adams. Bergh 14:149. (1814.)

No one sees with greater pleasure than myself the progress of reason in its advances towards rational Christianity. When we shall have done away the incomprehensible jargon of the Trinitarian arithmetic, that three are one and one is three; when we shall have knocked down the artificial scaffolding reared to mask from view the simple structure of Jesus; when, in short, we shall have unlearned everything which has been taught since His day, and got back to the pure and simple doctrines He inculcated, we shall then be truly and worthily His disciples; and my opinion is that if nothing had ever been added to what flowed purely from His lips, the whole world would at this day have been Christian.... The religion-builders have so distorted and deformed the doctrines of Jesus, so muffled them in mysticisms, fancies, and falsehoods, have caricatured them into forms so monstrous and inconceivable, as to shock reasonable thinkers, to revolt them against the whole, and drive them rashly to pronounce its Founder an impostor. —To Timothy Pickering. Bergh 15:323. (1821.)

The doctrines of Jesus are simple, and tend all to the happiness of man:

1. That there is one only God, and He all perfect.

2. That there is a future state of rewards and punishments.

3. That to love God with all thy heart, and thy neighbor as thyself, is the sum of religion.... But compare with these the demoralizing dogmas of Calvin.... The impious dogmatists, as Athanasius and Calvin, ... are the false shepherds foretold [in the New Testament] as to enter not by the door into the sheepfold, but to climb up some other way. They are mere usurpers of the Christian name, teaching a counter-religion made up of the *deliria* of crazy imaginations, as foreign from

Christianity as is that of Mahomet. Their blasphemies have driven thinking men into infidelity, who have too hastily rejected the supposed Author himself with the horrors so falsely imputed to Him. Had the doctrines of Jesus been preached always as pure as they came from his lips, the whole civilized world would now have been Christian.—To Dr. Benjamin Waterhouse. Bergh 15:383. (1822.)

CHRISTIANITY, Jefferson's Hope for Restoration of Primitive.—I hold the precepts of Jesus, as delivered by Himself, to be the most pure, benevolent, and sublime which have ever been preached to man. I adhere to the principles of the first age, and consider all subsequent innovations as corruptions of His religion, having no foundation in what came from Him.... If the freedom of religion guaranteed to us by law *in theory* can ever rise *in practice* under the overbearing inquisition of public opinion, truth will prevail over fanaticism, and the genuine doctrines of Jesus, so long perverted by His pseudo-priests, will again be restored to their original purity. This reformation will advance with the other improvements of the human mind, but too late for me to witness it.—To Jared Sparks. Bergh 15:288. (1820.)

Happy in the prospect of a restoration of primitive Christianity, I must leave to younger athletes to encounter and lop off the false branches which have been engrafted into it by the mythologists of the middle and modern ages.—To Dr.

Benjamin Waterhouse. Bergh 15:391. (1822.)

CHRISTIANITY. See also BIBLE; JESUS CHRIST; RELIGION.

CHURCH AND STATE. See RELIGION; RELIGIOUS FREEDOM.

CITIES, Corruption of Large.— When we get piled upon one another in large cities, as in Europe, we shall become corrupt as in Europe, and go to eating one another as they do there.—To James Madison. Bergh 6:392. (1787.)

I view great cities as pestilential to the morals, the health, and the liberties of man. True, they nourish some of the elegant arts, but the useful ones can thrive elsewhere, and less perfection in the others, with more health, virtue, and freedom, would be my choice.—Ford 7:459. (1800.)

CITIZENS, Protection of.—Every government [is obligated] to yield protection to [its] citizens as the consideration of their obedience.— To John Jay. Bergh 5:172. (1785.)

The persons and property of our citizens are entitled to the protection of our government in all places where they may lawfully go.—Bergh 3:244. (1793.)

CITIZENS, Naturalized.—Born in other countries, yet believing you could be happy in this, our laws acknowledge, as they should do, your right to join us in society, conforming ... to our established rules. That these rules shall be as equal as prudential considerations will admit will certainly be the aim of our legislatures, general and

particular [i.e., federal and state].— Bergh 10:258. (1801.)

CITIZENS, Fraudulent vs. Real.— [As to citizens] there is a distinction which we ought to make ourselves, and with which the belligerent powers [France and England] ought to be content. Where, after the commencement of a war, a merchant of either comes here and is naturalized, the purpose is probably fraudulent against the other, and intended to cloak their commerce under our flag. This we should honestly discountenance, and never reclaim their property when captured. But merchants from either, settled and made citizens before a war, are citizens to every purpose of commerce, and not to be distinguished in our proceedings from natives. Every attempt of Great Britain to enforce her principle of "once a subject, always a subject" beyond the case of *her own subjects* ought to be repelled.—Ford 8:251. (1803.)

CITIZENS, Exclusion of Dangerous.—Every society has a right to fix the fundamental principles of its association, and to say to all individuals that if they contemplate pursuits beyond the limits of these principles, and involving dangers which the society chooses to avoid, they must go somewhere else for their exercise; that we want no citizens, and still less ephemeral and pseudo-citizens, on such terms. We may exclude them from our territory, as we do persons infected with disease. We have most abundant resources of happiness within ourselves, which we may enjoy in peace and safety without permitting a few citizens, infected with the mania of rambling and gambling, to bring danger on the great mass engaged in innocent and safe pursuits at home.—Ford 10:34. (1816.)

CLARK (George Rogers), Greatness of.—I know the greatness of General Clark's mind, and am the more mortified at the cause which obscures it. Had not this unhappily taken place, there was nothing he might not have hoped; could it be surmounted, his lost ground might yet be recovered. No man alive rated him higher than I did, and would again, were he to become what I knew him. We are made to hope he is writing an account of his expeditions north of Ohio. They will be valuable morsels of history, and will justify to the world those who have told them how great he was.—Ford 5:295. (1791.)

CLAY (Henry), His Opposition to Jefferson.—It is true ... that a distance has taken place between Mr. Clay and myself. The cause I never could learn nor imagine. I had always known him to be an able man, and I believe him an honest one. I had looked to his coming into Congress with an entire belief that he would be cordial with the administration, and even before that I had always had him in my mind for a high and important vacancy which had been from time to time expected, but is only now about to take place. I feel his loss, therefore, with real concern, but it is

irremediable from the necessity of harmony and cordiality between those who are to manage together the public concerns. Not only his withdrawing from the usual civilities of intercourse with me (which even the Federalists, with two or three exceptions, keep up), but his open hostility in Congress to the administration, leave no doubt of the state of his mind as a fact, although the cause be unknown.— Bergh 11:353. (1807.)

CLERGY, Influence in New England.—The sway of the clergy in New England is indeed formidable. No mind beyond mediocrity dares there to develop itself. If it does, they excite against it the public opinion which they command, and, by little but incessant and tearing persecutions, drive it from among them. Their present emigrations to the western country are real flights from persecution, religious and political; but the abandonment of the country by those who wish to enjoy freedom of opinion leaves the despotism over the residue more intense, more oppressive.—Ford 10:13. (1816.)

COLONIES (American), Beginning of the.—America was conquered and her settlements made and firmly established at the expense of individuals, and not of the British public. Their own blood was spilt in acquiring lands for their settlement, their own fortunes expended in making that settlement effectual. For themselves they fought, for themselves they conquered, and for themselves alone they have right to hold. No shilling was ever issued from the public treasuries of his Majesty or his ancestors for their assistance till of very late times, after the colonies had become established on a firm and permanent footing.—*Summary View of the Rights of British America.* Bergh 1:186. (1774.)

COLONIES (American), Not Accountable to the British Parliament. —The British Parliament has no right to exercise authority over us. ... [One of its acts] must ever require peculiar mention. It is entitled "An Act [Suspending the Legislature of New York]." One free and independent legislature hereby takes upon itself to suspend the powers of another, free and independent as itself.... Not only the principles of common sense, but the common feelings of human nature must be surrendered up before his Majesty's subjects here can be persuaded to believe that they hold their political existence at the will of a British Parliament. Shall these governments be dissolved, their property annihilated, and their people reduced to a state of nature at the imperious breath of a body of men whom they never saw, in whom they never confided, and over whom they have no powers of punishment or removal, let their crimes against the American public be ever so great? Can any one reason be assigned why one hundred and sixty thousand electors in the island of Great Britain should give law to four millions in the states of America, every individual of whom is equal to every individual of them

in virtue, in understanding, and in bodily strength? Were this to be admitted, instead of [our] being a free people, as we have hitherto supposed, and mean to continue ourselves, we should suddenly be found the slaves, not of one, but of one hundred and sixty thousand tyrants; distinguished, too, from all others by this singular circumstance, that they are removed from the reach of fear, the only restraining motive which may hold the hand of a tyrant.—*Summary View of the Rights of British America.* Bergh 1:192. (1774.)

COLONIES (American), Relationship with Great Britain.—It is neither our wish nor our interest to separate from [Great Britain]. We are willing, on our part, to sacrifice everything which reason can ask to the restoration of that tranquility for which all must wish. On their part, let them [the British ministers and Parliament] be ready to establish union on a generous plan. Let them name their terms, but let them be just. Accept of every commercial preference it is in our power to give for such things as we can raise for their use, or they make for ours. But let them not think to exclude us from going to other markets to dispose of those commodities which they cannot use, nor to supply those wants which they cannot supply. Still less let it be proposed that our properties within our own territories shall be taxed or regulated by any power on earth but our own. The God who gave us life gave us liberty at the same time; the hand of force may destroy but cannot disjoin them. This, Sire [King George III], is our last, our determined resolution. And that you will be pleased to interpose with that efficacy which your earnest endeavors may insure, to procure redress of these our great grievances, to quiet the minds of your subjects in British America against any apprehensions of future encroachment, to establish fraternal love and harmony through the whole empire, and that that may continue to the latest ages of time, is the fervent prayer of all British America.—*Summary View of the Rights of British America.* Bergh 1:210. (1774.)

We have exhausted every mode of application which our invention could suggest as proper and promising. We have decently remonstrated with Parliament; they have added new injuries to the old. We have wearied our King with applications; he has not deigned to answer us. We have appealed to the native honor and justice of the British nation; their efforts in our favor have been hitherto ineffectual. What, then, remains to be done? That we commit our injuries to the even-handed justice of the Being who doth no wrong, earnestly beseeching Him to illuminate the councils and prosper the endeavors of those to whom America hath confided her hopes, that through their wise direction we may again see reunited the blessings of liberty, property, and harmony with Great Britain.—Ford 1:458. (1775.)

Looking with fondness towards a reconciliation with Great Britain, I cannot help hoping that you may be able to contribute towards expediting this good work. I think it must be evident to yourself that the ministry have been deceived by their officers on this side of the water, who (for what purpose I cannot tell) have constantly represented the American opposition as that of a small faction, in which the body of the people took little part. This, you can inform them of your own knowledge, is untrue. They have taken it into their heads, too, that we are cowards, and shall surrender at discretion to an armed force.... I wish they were thoroughly and minutely acquainted with every circumstance relative to America, as it exists in truth. I am persuaded this would go far towards disposing them to reconciliation.—To John Randolph. Bergh 4:28. (1775.)

I am sincerely one of those [who still wish for reconciliation with England], and would rather be in dependence on Great Britain, properly limited, than on any nation on earth, or than on no nation. But I am one of those, too, who, rather than submit to the rights of legislating for us assumed by the British Parliament, and which late experience has shown they will so cruelly exercise, would lend my hand to sink the whole island in the ocean.—To John Randolph. Bergh 4:30. (1775.)

There is not in the British empire a man who more cordially loves a union with Great Britain than I do. But by the God that made me, I will cease to exist before I yield to a connection on such terms as the British Parliament propose; and in this, I think I speak the sentiments of America. We want neither inducement nor power to declare and assert a separation. It is will alone which is wanting, and that is growing apace under the fostering hand of our King.—To John Randolph. Bergh 4:33. (1775.)

COLONIES (American), Reluctant to Separate from England.—In July 1775, a separation from Great Britain and establishment of republican government had never yet entered into any person's mind.... In April 1776, ... independence and the establishment of a new form of government were not even yet the objects of the people at large. One extract from the pamphlet called *Common Sense* had appeared in the Virginia papers in February, and copies of the pamphlet itself had got in a few hands. But the idea had not been opened to the mass of the people in April, much less can it be said that they had made up their minds in its favor.—*Notes on Virginia.* Bergh 2:165. (1782.)

Before the commencement of hostilities, I never had heard a whisper of disposition to separate from Great Britain. And after that, its possibility was contemplated with affliction by all.—Ford 10:188. (1821.)

COLONIES (American), Resistance to Unjust Taxation.—When Parliament proposed to consider us as objects of *taxation*, all the [colonies] took the alarm. Yet so little had we attended to this subject that our advocates did not know at first on what ground to take their stand. Mr. Dickinson, a lawyer of more ingenuity than sound judgment, and still more timid than ingenious, not daring to question the authority to regulate commerce so as best to answer their own purpose, to which we had long submitted, admitted that authority in its utmost extent. ... But sounder heads saw in the first moment that he who could put down the loom could stop the spinning wheel, and he who could stop the spinning wheel could tie the hands which turned it. They saw that this flimsy fabric could not be supported. Who were to be the judges whether duties were imposed with a view to burden and suppress a branch of manufacture or to raise a revenue? ... It was objected that this annihilated the Navigation Act. True, it does. The Navigation Act, therefore, becomes a proper subject of treaty between the two nations. —Ford 4:302. (1786.)

COLONIES (American). See also AMERICAN REVOLUTION; DECLARATION OF INDEPENDENCE; ENGLAND; REVOLUTIONARY WAR.

COMMERCE, Encouragement of International.—It should be our endeavor to cultivate the peace and friendship of every nation, even of that which has injured us most [i.e., England], when we shall have carried our point against her. Our interest will be to throw open the doors of commerce and to knock off all its shackles, giving perfect freedom to all persons for the vent of whatever they may choose to bring into our ports, and asking the same in theirs.—*Notes on Virginia.* Bergh 2:240. (1782.)

COMMERCE, International, A Natural Right.—It is impossible the world should continue long insensible to so evident a truth as that the right to have commerce and intercourse with our neighbors is a natural right. [For the European powers] to suppress this neighborly intercourse is an exercise of force, which we shall have a just right to remove when [we are] the superior force.—Bergh 8:33. (1790.)

COMMERCE, But No Alliance.—Commerce with all nations, alliance with none, should be our motto.—Ford 7:374. (1799.)

COMMERCE, In Balance with Agriculture and Manufactures.—I trust the good sense of our country will see that its greatest prosperity depends on a due balance between agriculture, manufactures, and commerce.—Ford 9:239. (1809.)

COMMERCE. See also FOREIGN AFFAIRS; FREE ENTERPRISE; MARKETS.

COMMON LAW, Origin of.—The term "common law," although it has more than one meaning, is perfectly definite, *secundum subjectam materiem.* Its most probable origin was on the conquest of the Heptarchy by Alfred, and the amalgamation of their several codes of law into one, which became *common* to them all. The authentic text of these enactments has not been preserved, but

their substance has been committed to many ancient books and writings, so faithfully as to have been deemed genuine from generation to generation, and obeyed as such by all. We have some fragments of them collected by Lambard, Wilkins, and others, but abounding with proofs of their spurious authenticity. Magna Charta is the earliest statute, the text of which has come down to us in an authentic form, and thence downward we have them entire. We do not know exactly when the *common* law and *statute* law, the *lex scripta et non scripta*, began to be contra-distinguished so as to give a second acceptation to the former term; whether before or after Prisot's day, at which time we know that nearly two centuries and a half of statutes were in preservation. In later times, on the introduction of the chancery branch of law, the term *common* law began to be used in a third sense, as the correlative of *chancery* law.—Bergh 16:82. (1824.)

COMMON SENSE, Safety in.—I can never fear that things will go far wrong where common sense has fair play.—To John Adams. Bergh 6:20. (1786.)

COMMON SENSE, Kings and.—No race of kings has ever presented above one man of common sense in twenty generations.—Ford 4:426. (1787.)

COMMON SENSE, Confidence in Mankind's.—I have great confidence in the common sense of mankind in general.—Ford 7:455. (1800.)

COMMON SENSE, Authority and.—Common sense [is] the foundation of all authorities, of the laws themselves, and of their construction.—Bergh 18:92. (1812.)

COMMUNAL SOCIETIES, Practicability of.—That, on the principle of a communion of property, small societies may exist in habits of virtue, order, industry, and peace, and consequently in a state of as much happiness as heaven has been pleased to deal out to imperfect humanity, I can readily conceive, and indeed have seen its proofs in various small societies which have been constituted on that principle. But I do not feel authorized to conclude from these that an extended society, like that of the United States or of an individual state, could be governed happily on the same principle. I look to the diffusion of light and education as the resource most to be relied on for ameliorating the condition, promoting the virtue, and advancing the happiness of man.—Bergh 15:399. (1822.)

COMPANIONS, Advice on Selecting.—Be very select in the society you attach yourself to; avoid taverns, drinkers, smokers, idlers, and dissipated persons generally, . . . and you will find your path more easy and tranquil.—Ford 9:233. (1808.)

COMPROMISE, Necessity of.—It is necessary to give as well as take in a government like ours.—Ford 5:184. (1790.)

CONFIDENCE. See PUBLIC CONFIDENCE.

CONGRESS, Authority of.—The authority of Congress can never be wounded without injury to the present Union.—Ford 2:286. (1779.)

CONGRESS, Training for Young Statesmen.—I see the best effects produced by sending our young statesmen [to Congress]. They see the affairs of the confederacy from a high ground; they learn the importance of the Union, and befriend federal measures when they return. Those who never come here see our affairs insulated, pursue a system of jealousy and self-interest, and distract the Union as much as they can.—Ford 3:403. (1784.)

Congress is a good school for our young statesmen. It gives them impressions friendly to the federal government instead of those adverse, which too often take place in persons confined to the politics of their state.—Ford 3:472. (1784.)

CONGRESS, Public Opinion and.—I think it a duty in those entrusted with the administration of [public] affairs to conform themselves to the decided choice of their constituents.—Ford 4:89. (1785.)

CONGRESS, Power of Self-Government.—Each house of Congress possesses this natural right of governing itself, and consequently of fixing its own times and places of meeting, so far as it has not been abridged by the law of those who employ them, that is to say, by the Constitution. . . .

The right of adjournment, then, is not given by the Constitution, and consequently it may be modified by law without interfering with that instrument. It is a natural right, and, like all other natural rights, may be abridged or regulated in its exercise by law; and the concurrence of the third branch in any law regulating its exercise is so efficient an ingredient in that law that the right cannot be otherwise exercised but after a repeal by a new law. The express terms of the Constitution itself show that this right may be modified *by law* when in Article I Section 4 (the only remaining passage on the subject not yet quoted) it says, "The Congress shall assemble at least once in every year, and such meeting shall be the first Monday in December, unless they shall, *by law,* appoint a different day." Then another day may be appointed *by law;* and the President's assent is an efficient ingredient in that law. Nay, further, they cannot adjourn over the first Monday of December but by *a law.* This is another Constitutional abridgment of their natural right of adjournment; and, completing our review of all the clauses in the Constitution which touch that right, authorizes us to say no part of that instrument gives it, and that the houses hold it, not from the Constitution, but from nature.

A consequence of this is that the houses may, by a joint resolution, remove themselves from place to place, because it is a part of their right of self-government.—Ford 5:205. (1790.)

CONGRESS, Political Corruption in.—I told [President Washington] ...that it was a fact, as certainly known as that he and I were then conversing, that particular members of the [Congress], while those laws [assumption, funding, etc.] were on

the carpet, had feathered their nests with paper, had then voted for the laws, and constantly since lent all the energy of their talents, and instrumentality of their offices, to the establishment and enlargement of this system.—The Anas. Bergh 1:290. (1792.)

It [is] a cause of just uneasiness when we [see] a legislature legislating for their own interests, in opposition to those of the people.—The Anas. Bergh 1:311. (1792.)

I told [President Washington] there was great difference between the little accidental schemes of self-interest, which would take place in every body of men and influence their votes, and a regular system for forming a corps of interested persons who should be steadily at the orders of the Treasury [Department].—The Anas. Bergh 1:318. (1792.)

The capital employed in paper speculation...has furnished effectual means of corrupting such a portion of the [Congress] as turns the balance between the honest voters, whichever way it is directed. ... This corrupt squadron, deciding the voice of the [Congress], have manifested their dispositions to get rid of the limitations imposed by the Constitution on the general legislature, limitations on the faith of which the states acceded to that instrument.... Of all the mischiefs objected to the system of measures before mentioned [i.e., public debt and speculation in paper money], none is so afflicting as the corruption of the [Congress]. As it was the earliest of these measures, it became the instrument for producing the rest, and will be the instrument for producing in future a king, lords and commons, or whatever else those who direct it may choose. Withdrawn such a distance from the eye of their constituents, and these so dispersed as to be inaccessible to public information, and particularly to that of the conduct of their own representatives, they will form the most corrupt government on earth if the means of their corruption be not prevented.—To President Washington. Bergh 8:344. (1792.)

I told [President Washington]... my wish was to see both houses of Congress cleansed of all persons interested in the bank or public stocks; and that a pure legislature being given us, I should always be ready to acquiesce under their determinations, even if contrary to my own opinions; for...I subscribe to the principle that the will of the majority, honestly expressed, should give law.—The Anas. Bergh 1:332. (1793.)

CONGRESS, Need for Businessmen in.—We want men of business [in Congress].... I am convinced it is in the power of any man who understands business, and who will undertake to keep a file of the business before Congress and press it, as he would his own docket in a court, to shorten the sessions a month one year with another, and to save in that way $30,000 a year. An ill-judged modesty prevents those from undertaking it who are equal to it.—Ford 8:187. (1802.)

CONGRESS, Need for Leaders in.—There never was a time when the services of those who possess talents, integrity, firmness, and sound judgment were more wanted in Congress. Someone of that description is particularly wanted to take the lead in the House of Representatives, to consider the business of the nation as his own business, to take it up as if he were singly charged with it, and carry it through.—Bergh 11:115. (1806.)

CONGRESS, Need for Full Representation in.—That every state should be represented in the great council of the nation is not only the interest of each, but of the whole united, who have a right to be aided by the collective wisdom and information of the whole in questions which are to decide on their future well-being.—Bergh 12:243. (1809.)

CONGRESS, Speeches Too Long.—I observe that the House of Representatives are sensible of the ill effects of the long speeches in their house on their proceedings. But they have a worse effect in the disgust they excite among the people, and the disposition they are producing to transfer their confidence from the legislature to the executive branch, which would soon sap our Constitution. These speeches, therefore, are less and less read, and if continued will soon cease to be read at all.—Ford 9:267. (1810.)

CONGRESS, Its Effectiveness Reduced by Endless Debate.—Our body [the Congress of 1783-84] was little numerous, but very contentious. Day after day was wasted on the most unimportant questions. A member, one of those afflicted with the morbid rage of debate, of an ardent mind, prompt imagination, and copious flow of words, who heard with impatience any logic which was not his own, sitting near me on some occasion of a trifling but wordy debate, asked me how I could sit in silence, hearing so much false reasoning which a word should refute.

I observed to him that to refute indeed was easy, but to silence was impossible; that in measures brought forward by myself I took the laboring oar, as was incumbent on me, but that in general I was willing to listen; that if every sound argument or objection was used by some one or other of the numerous debaters, it was enough; if not, I thought it sufficient to suggest the omission without going into a repetition of what had been already said by others; that this was a waste and abuse of the time and patience of the house which could not be justified. And I believe that if the members of deliberate bodies were to observe this course generally, they would do in a day what takes them a week; and it is really more questionable than may at first be thought whether Bonaparte's dumb legislature, which said nothing and did much, may not be preferable to one which talks much and does nothing.

I served with General Washington in the legislature of Virginia before the Revolution and, during it, with Dr. Franklin in Congress. I never heard either of them speak ten

minutes at a time, nor to any but the main point which was to decide the question. They laid their shoulders to the great points, knowing that the little ones would follow of themselves. If the present Congress errs in too much talking, how can it be otherwise in a body to which the people send one hundred and fifty lawyers, whose trade it is to question everything, yield nothing, and talk by the hour? That one hundred and fifty lawyers should do business together ought not to be expected.— Autobiography. Bergh 1:86. (1821.)

CONGRESS. See also CONTINENTAL CONGRESS; FEDERAL GOVERNMENT; LEGISLATURES; SENATE.

CONQUEST, Disavowed.—We did not raise armies for glory or for conquest.—Ford 1:475. (1775.)

CONQUEST, Un-American.— Conquest is not in our principles. It is inconsistent with our government.—Ford 5:230. (1790.)

If there be one principle more deeply rooted than any other in the mind of every American, it is that we should have nothing to do with conquest.—Ford 5:364. (1791.)

CONSCIENCE, Given by God, Should Be Followed.—If ever you are about to say anything amiss, or to do anything wrong, consider beforehand. You will feel something within you which will tell you it is wrong, and ought not to be said or done; this is your conscience, and be sure to obey it. Our Maker has given us all this faithful internal monitor, and if you always obey it, you will always be prepared for the end of the world; or for a much more certain event, which is death. This must happen to all; it puts an end to the world as to us, and the way to be ready for it is never to do a wrong act.—To Martha Jefferson. Betts & Bear, p. 21. (1783.)

CONSCIENCE, A Sure Guide.— Conscience is the only sure clue which will eternally guide a man clear of all doubts and inconsistencies.—Ford 5:96. (1789.)

CONSCIENCE, Moral Laws and.— The true fountains of evidence [are] the head and heart of every rational and honest man. It is there nature has written her moral laws, and where every man may read them for himself.—Ford 6:221. (1793.)

CONSCIENCE, Inquisition over.— I am averse to the communication of my religious tenets to the public because it would countenance the presumption of those who have endeavored to draw them before that tribunal, and to seduce public opinion to erect itself into that inquisition over the rights of conscience which the laws have so justly proscribed.—Ford 8:224. (1803.)

CONSCIENCE. See also MORAL LAW; MORAL SENSE.

CONSOLIDATION. See CENTRALIZATION.

CONSTITUTION (U.S.), Guiding Principles in Formation of.—To make us one nation as to foreign concerns, and keep us distinct in domestic ones, gives the outline of the proper division of powers between the [federal] and [state] governments. But to enable the federal head to exercise the powers given it to best advantage, it should be organized as the [state] ones are, into legislative, executive, and judiciary. The first and last are already separated. The second should be. When last with Congress, I often proposed to members to do this by making of the committee of the states an executive committee during the recess of Congress, and during its sessions to appoint a committee to receive and dispatch all executive business, so that Congress itself should meddle only with what should be legislative. But I question if any Congress (much less all successively) can have self-denial enough to go through with this distribution. The distribution, then, should be imposed on them.— To James Madison. Bergh 6:9. (1786.)

My general plan would be to make the states one as to everything connected with foreign nations, and several as to everything purely domestic.—Bergh 6:227. (1787.)

My idea is that we should be made one nation in every case concerning foreign affairs, and separate ones in whatever is merely domestic; that the federal government should be organized into legislative, executive, and judiciary, as are the state governments, and some peaceable means of enforcement devised for the federal head over the states.— Bergh 6:273. (1787.)

CONSTITUTION (U.S.), Jefferson's Initial Evaluation of.—I like much the general idea of framing a government which should go on of itself, peaceably, without needing continual recurrence to the state legislatures. I like the organization of the government into legislative, judiciary, and executive. I like the power given the [Congress] to levy taxes, and for that reason solely I approve of the greater house being chosen by the people directly. For though I think a house so chosen will be very far inferior to the present Congress, [and] will be very illy qualified to legislate for the Union, for foreign nations, etc., yet this evil does not weigh against the good of preserving inviolate the fundamental principle that the people are not to be taxed but by representatives chosen immediately by themselves. I am captivated by the compromise of the opposite claims of the great and little states, of the latter to equal and the former to proportional influence. I am much pleased, too, with the substitution of the method of voting by person, instead of that of voting by states; and I like the negative [i.e., veto] given to the executive, conjointly with a third of either house, though I should have liked it better had the judiciary been associated for that purpose, or invested separately with a similar power. There are other good things of less moment.

I will now tell you what I do not like. First, the omission of a bill of rights, providing clearly, and without the aid of sophism, for freedom of religion, freedom of the press, protection against standing armies, restriction of monopolies, the eternal and unremitting force of the habeas corpus laws, and trials by jury in all matters of fact triable by the laws of the land, and not by the laws of nations. To say, as Mr. Wilson does, that a bill of rights was not necessary because all is reserved in the case of the general government which is not given, while in the particular ones [i.e., in the state governments] all is given which is not reserved, might do for the audience to which it was addressed; but it is surely a *gratis dictum*, the reverse of which might just as well be said; and it is opposed by strong inferences from the body of the instrument, as well as from the omission of the cause of our present Confederation, which had made the reservation in express terms.... Let me add that a bill of rights is what the people are entitled to against every government on earth, general or particular, and what no just government should refuse or rest on inference. The second feature I dislike, and strongly dislike, is the abandonment in every instance of the principle of rotation in office, and most particularly in the case of the President. Reason and experience tell us that the first magistrate will always be reelected if he may be reelected. He is then an officer for life.—To James Madison. Bergh 6:386. (1787.)

CONSTITUTION (U.S.), Need for a Bill of Rights in.—I wish with all my soul that the nine first conventions may accept the new Constitution, because this will secure to us the good it contains, which I think great and important. But I equally wish that the four latest conventions, whichever they may be, may refuse to accede to it till a declaration of rights be annexed. This would probably command the offer of such a declaration, and thus give to the whole fabric, perhaps, as much perfection as any one of that kind ever had.—Bergh 6:425. (1788.)

CONSTITUTION (U.S.), Ratification Near.—With respect to the new government, nine or ten states will probably have accepted by the end of this month. The others may oppose it. Virginia, I think, will be of this number. Besides other objections of less moment, she will insist on annexing a bill of rights to the new Constitution, [that is], a bill wherein the government shall declare that, 1, religion shall be free; 2, printing presses free; 3, trials by jury preserved in all cases; 4, no monopolies in commerce; 5, no standing army. Upon receiving this bill of rights, she will probably depart from her other objections, and this bill is so much to the interest of all the states that I presume they will offer it, and thus our Constitution be amended and our Union closed by the end of the present year. In this way, there will have been opposition enough to do good, and not enough to do harm.—Bergh 6:430. (1788.)

I have seen with infinite pleasure our new Constitution accepted by eleven states, not rejected by the twelfth, and that the thirteenth happens to be a state of the least importance. It is true that the minorities in most of the accepting states have been very respectable; so much so as to render it prudent, were it not otherwise reasonable, to make some sacrifice to them. I am in hopes that the annexation of a bill of rights to the Constitution will alone draw over so great a proportion of the minorities as to leave little danger in the opposition of the residue; and that this annexation may be made by Congress and the assemblies without calling a convention, which might endanger the most valuable parts of the system.—To George Washington. Bergh 7:223. (1788.)

CONSTITUTION (U.S.), Ratify, Then Amend.—At first I wished that when nine states should have accepted the Constitution, so as to ensure us what is good in it, the other four might hold off till the want of the bill of rights, at least, might be supplied. But I am now convinced that the plan of Massachusetts is the best, that is, to accept and to amend afterwards. If the states which were to decide after her should all do the same, it is impossible but they must obtain the essential amendments. It will be more difficult, if we lose this instrument, to recover what is good in it than to correct what is bad after we shall have adopted it. It has, therefore, my hearty prayers.—Bergh 7:29. (1788.)

CONSTITUTION (U.S.), Wisdom of.—The Constitution...is unquestionably the wisest ever yet presented to men, and some of the accommodations of interest which it has adopted are greatly pleasing to me, who have before had occasions of seeing how difficult those interests were to accommodate.—To David Humphreys. Bergh 7:322. (1789.)

CONSTITUTION (U.S.), Tenth Amendment the "Foundation" of.—I consider the foundation of the Constitution as laid on this ground: that "all powers not delegated to the United States by the Constitution, nor prohibited by it to the states, are reserved to the states or to the people."... To take a single step beyond the boundaries thus specially drawn around the powers of Congress is to take possession of a boundless field of power, no longer susceptible of any definition.—Bergh 3:146. (1791.)

The capital and leading object of the Constitution was to leave with the states all authorities which respected their own citizens only, and to transfer to the United States those which respected citizens of foreign or other states; to make us several as to ourselves, but one as to all others.... Can it be believed that under the jealousies prevailing against the general government at the adoption of the Constitution, the states meant to surrender the authority of preserving order, of enforcing moral duties and restraining vice, within their own territory? ... Can any good be effected by taking from the states the moral rule of their citizens and subordinating it to the general authority, or to one of their corporations, which may justify forcing the meaning of words, hunting after possible constructions, and hanging inference on

inference, from heaven to earth, like Jacob's ladder? Such an intention was impossible, and such a licentiousness of construction and inference, if exercised by both governments, as may be done with equal right, would equally authorize both to claim all power, general and particular, and break up the foundations of the Union. Laws are made for men of ordinary understanding, and should therefore be construed by the ordinary rules of common sense. Their meaning is not to be sought for in metaphysical subtleties, which may make anything mean everything or nothing, at pleasure.... The states supposed that by their Tenth Amendment they had secured themselves against constructive powers. They were not ...yet...aware of the slipperiness of the eels of the law. I ask for no straining of words against the general government, nor yet against the states. I believe the states can best govern our home concerns, and the general government our foreign ones. I wish, therefore, to see maintained that wholesome distribution of powers established by the Constitution for the limitation of both; and never to see all offices transferred to Washington, where, further withdrawn from the eyes of the people, they may more secretly be bought and sold as at market.—Bergh 15:448. (1823.)

CONSTITUTION (U.S.), "Necessary and Proper" Clause.—[By] the ...general phrase..."to make all laws *necessary* and proper for carrying into execution the enumerated powers,"... the Constitution allows only the means which are *"necessary,"* not those which are merely "convenient" for effecting the enumerated powers. If such a latitude of construction be allowed to this phrase as to give any non-enumerated power, it will go to every one, for there is not one which ingenuity may not torture into a *convenience* in some instance *or other,* to *some one* of so long a list of enumerated powers. It would swallow up all the delegated powers and reduce the whole to one power. Therefore it was that the Constitution restrained them to the *necessary* means, that is to say, to those means without which the grant of power would be nugatory. —Bergh 3:149. (1791.)

CONSTITUTION (U.S.), Subverted by the Treasury Department. —I told [President Washington] that ...a system had there [in the Treasury Department] been contrived for deluging the states with paper money instead of gold and silver, for withdrawing our citizens from the pursuits of commerce, manufactures, buildings, and other branches of useful industry to occupy themselves and their capitals in a species of gambling, destructive of morality, and which had introduced its poison into the government itself. That it was a fact, as certainly known as that he and I were then conversing, that particular members of the [Congress], while those laws were on the carpet, had feathered their nests with paper, had then voted for the laws, and constantly since lent all the energy of their talents and instrumentality of their offices to the establishment and enlargement of this system; that they had chained it about our necks for a great length of time, and in order to keep the game in their hands had, from time to time, aided in making such legislative constructions of the Constitution as made it a very different thing from what the people thought they had submitted to; that they had now brought forward a proposition far beyond any one ever yet advanced, and to which the eyes of many were turned as the decision which was to let us know whether we live under a limited or an unlimited government. He asked me to what proposition I alluded. I answered, to that in [Hamilton's] Report on Manufactures which, under color of giving *bounties* for the encouragement of particular manufactures, meant to establish the doctrine that the power given by the Constitution to collect taxes to provide for the *general welfare* of the United States permitted Congress to take everything under their management which *they* should deem for the *public welfare,* and which is susceptible of the application of money; consequently, that the subsequent enumeration of their powers was not the description to which resort must be had, and did not at all constitute the limits of their authority.—The Anas. Bergh 1:290. (1792.)

CONSTITUTION (U.S.), And Assumed Powers.—Whensoever the general government assumes undelegated powers, its acts are unauthoritative, void, and of no force.—Kentucky Resolutions. Bergh 17:380. (1798.)

Where powers are assumed which have not been delegated, a nullification of the act is the rightful remedy. —Kentucky Resolutions. Bergh 17:386. (1798.)

If, wherever the Constitution assumes a single power out of many which belong to the same subject, we should consider it as assuming the whole, it would vest the general government with a mass of powers never contemplated. On the contrary, the assumption of particular powers seems an exclusion of all not assumed.—Ford 9:452. (1814.)

CONSTITUTION (U.S.), Confidence to Be Placed in It, Not in Men.—It would be a dangerous delusion were a confidence in the men of our choice to silence our fears for the safety of our rights.... Confidence is everywhere the parent of despotism. Free government is founded in jealousy, and not in confidence; it is jealousy, and not confidence, which prescribes limited constitutions to bind down those whom we are obliged to trust with power.... Our Constitution has accordingly fixed the limits to which, and no further, our confidence may go.... In questions of power, then, let no more be heard of confidence in man, but bind him down from mischief by the chains of the Constitution.—Kentucky Resolutions. Bergh 17:388. (1798.)

CONSTITUTION (U.S.), Original Meaning Should Be Preserved.— The Constitution on which our

Union rests shall be administered by me according to the safe and honest meaning contemplated by the plain understanding of the people of the United States at the time of its adoption—a meaning to be found in the explanations of those who advocated, not those who opposed it.... These explanations are preserved in the publications of the time.—Bergh 10:248. (1801.)

On every question of construction, [let us] carry ourselves back to the time when the Constitution was adopted, recollect the spirit manifested in the debates, and instead of trying what meaning may be squeezed out of the text, or invented against it, conform to the probable one in which it was passed.—Bergh 15:449. (1823.)

CONSTITUTION (U.S.), Should Be Interpreted Strictly.—When an instrument admits two constructions, the one safe, the other dangerous, the one precise, the other indefinite, I prefer that which is safe and precise. I had rather ask an enlargement of power from the nation, where it is found necessary, than to assume it by a construction which would make our powers boundless. Our peculiar security is in the possession of a written Constitution. Let us not make it a blank paper by construction.— Bergh 10:418. (1803.)

CONSTITUTION (U.S.), Makes Each Department Independent.— My construction of the Constitution is...that each department [of the federal government] is truly independent of the others, and has an equal right to decide for itself what is the meaning of the Constitution in the cases submitted to its action, and especially where it is to act ultimately and without appeal.—Bergh 15:214. (1819.)

CONSTITUTION (U.S.), Resolves Conflicts Between Governmental Departments.—The peculiar happiness of our blessed system is that in differences of opinion between these different sets of servants [in the three departments of the federal government], the appeal is to neither, but to their employers [i.e., the people], peaceably assembled by their representatives in convention. —Bergh 15:328. (1821.)

CONSTITUTION (U.S.), Limits Federal Jurisdiction.—It may be impracticable to lay down any general formula of words which shall decide at once, and with precision in every case, this limit of jurisdiction. But there are two canons which will guide us safely in most of the cases.

1st. The capital and leading object of the Constitution was to leave with the states all authorities which respected their own citizens only, and to transfer to the United States those which respected citizens of foreign or other states; to make us several as to ourselves, but one as to all others. In the latter case, then, constructions should lean to the general jurisdiction if the words will bear it; and in favor of the states in the former, if possible to be so construed. And, indeed, between citizens and citizens of the same state and under their own laws, I

know but a single case in which a jurisdiction is given to the general government. That is where anything but gold or silver is made a lawful tender, or the obligation of contracts is any otherwise impaired. The separate legislatures had so often abused that power that the citizens themselves chose to trust it to the general rather than to their own special authorities.

2nd. On every question of construction, carry ourselves back to the time when the Constitution was adopted, recollect the spirit manifested in the debates, and instead of trying what meaning may be squeezed out of the text, or invented against it, conform to the probable one in which it was passed.—Bergh 15:448. (1823.)

CONSTITUTION (U.S.), Importance of Preserving.—To preserve the republican form and principles of our Constitution and cleave to the salutary distribution of powers which that has established...are the two sheet anchors of our Union. If driven from either, we shall be in danger of foundering.—Bergh 15:452. (1823.)

CONSTITUTION (U.S.), Preservation of, a Central Issue in Presidential Elections.—I hope the choice [of the next President] will fall on some real republican, who will continue the administration on the express principles of the Constitution, unadulterated by constructions reducing it to a blank to be filled with what everyone pleases, and what never was intended.—Ford 10:264. (1823.)

CONSTITUTION (U.S.). See also ARTICLES OF CONFEDERATION; CENTRALIZATION; FEDERAL GOVERNMENT; GENERAL WELFARE CLAUSE; JUDICIAL REVIEW; JUDICIARY; SEPARATION OF POWERS; STATES; STATES' RIGHTS.

CONSTITUTIONAL CONVENTION, Consisted of Able Men.—The convention holding at Philadelphia...consists of the ablest men in America.—Bergh 6:128. (1787.)

It is really an assembly of demigods.—To John Adams. Bergh 6:289. (1787.)

A more able assembly never sat in America.—Bergh 6:295. (1787.)

CONSTITUTIONAL CONVENTION, Positive Example of.—The example of changing a constitution by assembling the wise men of the state, instead of assembling armies, will be worth as much to the world as the former examples we had given them.—To David Humphreys. Bergh 7:322. (1789.)

CONSTITUTIONAL CONVENTION, Historical Background of.—The want of some authority which should procure justice to the public creditors, and an observance of treaties with foreign nations, produced...the call of a convention of the states at Annapolis. Although, at this meeting, a difference of opinion was evident on the question of a republican or kingly government, yet so general through the states was the sentiment in favor of the former that the friends of the latter confined themselves to a course of obstruction only, and delay, to everything proposed. They hoped that, nothing being done, and all things going from bad to worse, a kingly government might be usurped, and submitted to by the people as better than anarchy and wars, internal and external, the certain consequences of the present want of a general government.

The effect of their maneuvers, with the defective attendance of deputies from the states, resulted in the measure of calling a more general convention, to be held at Philadelphia. At this, the same party exhibited the same practices, and with the same views of preventing a government of concord, which they foresaw would be republican, and of forcing through anarchy their way to monarchy. But the mass of that convention was too honest, too wise, and too steady to be baffled or misled by their maneuvers.

One of these was a form of government proposed by Colonel [Alexander] Hamilton, which would have been in fact a compromise between the two parties of royalism and republicanism. According to this, the executive and one branch of the legislature were to be during good behavior,[that is] for life, and the governors of the states were to be named by these two prominent organs. This, however, was rejected, on which Hamilton left the convention, as desperate, and never returned again until near its conclusion.—The Anas. Bergh 1:268. (1818.)

CONSTITUTIONS, Need for Amendments to.—Some men look at constitutions with sanctimonious reverence and deem them like the ark of the covenant, too sacred to be touched. They ascribe to the men of the preceding age a wisdom more than human, and suppose what they did to be beyond amendment.... I am certainly not an advocate for frequent and untried changes in laws and constitutions. I think moderate imperfections had better be borne with, because, when [these are] once known, we accommodate ourselves to them and find practical means of correcting their ill effects. But I know also that laws and institutions must go hand in hand with the progress of the human mind. As that becomes more developed, more enlightened, as new discoveries are made, new truths disclosed, and manners and opinions change with the change of circumstances, institutions must advance also, and keep pace with the times.—Bergh 15:40. (1816.)

CONSTITUTIONS, Amendment Process.—Whatever be the constitution, great care must be taken to provide a mode of amendment when experience or change of circumstances shall have manifested that any part of it is unadapted to the good of the nation. In some of our states it requires a new authority from the whole people, acting by their representatives, chosen for this express purpose and assembled in convention. This is found too difficult for remedying the imperfections which experience develops from time to time in an organization of the first impression. A greater facility of amendment is certainly

requisite to maintain it in a course of action accommodated to the times and changes through which we are ever passing.—Bergh 15:488. (1823.)

CONTINENTAL CONGRESS, History of Its Formation.—The legislature of Virginia happened to be in session in Williamsburg when news was received of the passage by the British Parliament of the Boston Port Bill, which was to take effect on the first day of June then ensuing. The House of Burgesses thereupon passed a resolution recommending to their fellow citizens that that day should be set apart for fasting and prayer to the Supreme Being, imploring him to avert the calamities then threatening us, and to give us one heart and one mind to oppose every invasion of our liberties.

The next day, May the 20th, 1774, the Governor dissolved us. We immediately repaired to a room in the Raleigh Tavern, about one hundred paces distant from the Capitol, formed ourselves into a meeting, Peyton Randolph in the chair, and came to resolutions declaring that an attack on one colony, to enforce arbitrary acts, ought to be considered as an attack on all, and to be opposed by the united wisdom of all. We therefore appointed a committee of correspondence to address letters to the Speakers of the several Houses of Representatives of the colonies, proposing the appointment of deputies from each to meet *annually in a general Congress*, to deliberate on their common interests and on the measures to be pursued in common. The members then separated to

Jefferson in 1787 (age 44). Detail from *The Declaration of Independence*, by John Trumbull.

their several homes, except those of the committee, who met the next day, prepared letters according to instructions, and dispatched them by messengers express to their several destinations.

It had been agreed also by the meeting that the Burgesses who should be elected under the writs then issuing should be requested to meet in convention on a certain day in August, to learn the results of these letters and to appoint delegates to a Congress, should that measure be approved by the other colonies. At the election, the people reelected every man of the former assembly as a proof of their approbation of what they had done.

Before I left home to attend the convention, I prepared what I thought might be given in instruction to the delegates who should be appointed to attend the general Congress proposed. They were drawn in haste, with a number of blanks, with some uncertainties and inaccuracies of historical facts, which I neglected at the moment, knowing they could be readily corrected at the meeting. I set out on my journey, but was taken sick on the road and was unable to proceed. I therefore sent on by express two copies, one under cover to Patrick Henry, the other to Peyton Randolph, who I knew would be in the chair of the convention. Of the former, no more was ever heard or known. Mr. Henry probably thought it too bold as a first measure, as the majority of the memberrs did. On the other copy being laid on the table of the convention by Peyton Randolph, as the proposition of a member who was prevented from attendance by sickness on the road, tamer sentiments were preferred, and I believe wisely preferred, the leap I proposed being too long as yet for the mass of our citizens.... They printed the paper, however, and gave it the title of *A Summary View of the Rights of British America*. In this form it got to London, where the opposition took it up [and] shaped it to opposition views, and in that form it ran rapidly through several editions.

Mr. [John] Marshall, in his history of General Washington, chapter 3, speaking of this proposition for committees of correspondence and for a general Congress, says, "This measure had already been proposed in town meeting in Boston," and some pages before he had said that "at a session of the General Court of Massachusetts in September 1770, that Court, in pursuance of a favorite idea of uniting all the colonies in one system of measures, elected a committee of correspondence to communicate with such committees as might be appointed by the other colonies." This is an error. The committees of correspondence elected by Massachusetts were expressly for a correspondence among the several *towns* of that province only. Besides the text of their prodeedings, his own note X proves this. The first proposition for a general correspondence between the several states, and for a general Congress, was made by our meeting of May 1774.—Bergh 1:181. (1821?)

CONTINENTAL CONGRESS. See also CONGRESS.

CORNWALLIS (Lord), Ravages of, in Virginia.—Lord Cornwallis... remained in this position [along the main James River] ten days, his own headquarters being in my house at that place [Elk Hill]. I had time to remove most of the effects out of the house. He destroyed all my growing crops of corn and tobacco; he burned all my barns, containing the same articles of the last year, having first taken what corn he wanted; he used, as was to be expected, all my stock of cattle, sheep, and hogs for the sustenance of his army, and carried off all the horses capable of service; of those too young for service he cut the throats; and he burned all the fences on the plantation, so as to leave it an absolute waste.

He carried off also about thirty slaves. Had this been to give them freedom, he would have done right; but it was to consign them to inevitable death from the smallpox and putrid fever, then raging in his camp. This I knew afterwards to be the fate of twenty-seven of them. I never had news of the remaining three, but presume they shared the same fate.

When I say that Lord Cornwallis did all this, I do not mean that he carried about the torch in his own hands, but that it was all done under his eye, the situation of the house in which he was, commanding a view of every part of the plantation, so that he must have seen every fire. I relate these things on my own knowledge in a great degree, as I was on the ground soon after he left it. He treated the rest of the neighborhood somewhat in the same style, but not with that spirit of total extermination with which he seemed to rage over my possessions. Wherever he went, the dwelling houses were plundered of everything which could be carried off. Lord Cornwallis's character in England would forbid the belief that he shared in the plunder; but that his table was served with the plate thus pillaged from private houses can be proved by many hundred eyewitnesses.

From an estimate I made at that time on the best information I could collect, I supposed the state of Virginia lost under Lord Cornwallis's hands that year about thirty thousand slaves; and that of these, about twenty-seven thousand died of the smallpox and camp fever. ... History will never relate the horrors committed by the British army in the southern states of America. They raged in Virginia six months only, from the middle of April to the middle of October, 1781, when they were all taken prisoners; and ... I suppose their whole devastations during those six months amounted to about three millions sterling.—Bergh 7:68. (1788.)

CORRESPONDENCE, A Natural Right.—A right of free correspondence between citizen and citizen on their joint interests, whether public or private, and under whatsoever laws these interests arise (to wit, of the state, of Congress, of France, Spain, or Turkey), is a natural right; it is not the gift of any municipal law, either of England, or of Virginia, or of Congress, but, in common with all our other natural rights, is one of the objects for the protection of which society is formed, and municipal laws established.—Ford 7:172. (1797.)

CORRESPONDENCE. See also LETTER WRITING.

CORRUPTION. See CONGRESS, Political Corruption in; POWER, Corrupts; VICE.

CREDIT, Sustaining.—I think nothing can bring the security of our continent and its cause into danger if we can support the credit of our paper. To do that, I apprehend, one of two steps must be taken. Either to procure free trade by alliance with some naval power able to protect it, or, if we find there is no prospect of that, to shut our ports totally, to all the world, and turn our colonies into manufactories. The former would be most eligible, because most conformable to the habits and wishes of our people.—Ford 2:132. (1777.)

CREDIT, Using.—I am anxious about everything which may affect our credit. My wish would be to possess it in the highest degree, but to use it little. Were we without credit, we might be crushed by a nation of much inferior resources, but possessing higher credit.—To George Washington. Bergh 6:453. (1788.)

Though I am an enemy to the using our credit but under absolute necessity, yet the possessing a good credit I consider as indispensable in the present system of carrying on war.—To James Madison. Bergh 6:455. (1788.)

CREDIT, Establishing.—I told [President Washington] all that was ever necessary to establish our credit was an efficient government and an honest one, declaring it would sacredly pay our debts, laying taxes for this purpose and applying them to it.—The Anas. Bergh 1:319. (1792.)

CREDIT, Taxation and.—It is a wise rule, and should be fundamental in a government disposed to cherish its credit, and at the same time to restrain the use of it within the limits of its faculties, "never to borrow a dollar without laying a tax in the same instant for paying the interest annually, and the principal within a given term; and to consider that tax as pledged to the creditors on the public faith." On such a pledge as this, sacredly observed, a government may always command, on a *reasonable interest*, all the lendable money of their citizens, while the necessity of an equivalent tax is a salutary warning to them and their constituents against oppressions, bankruptcy, and its inevitable consequence, revolution. But the term of redemption must be moderate, and at any rate within the limit of their rightful powers. But what limits, it will be asked, does this prescribe to their powers? What is to hinder them from creating a perpetual debt? The laws of nature, I answer. The earth belongs to the living, not to the dead. The will and the power of man expire with his life, by nature's law.—To John W. Eppes. Bergh 13:269. (1813.)

CRIME, Horse Stealing.—Whosoever shall be guilty of horse stealing shall be condemned to hard labor three years in the public works, and shall make reparation to the person injured.... The offense of horse stealing seems properly distinguishable from other larcenies here, where these animals generally run at large, the temptation being so great and frequent, and the facility of commission so remarkable.— Bergh 1:233. (1779.)

CRIME, Excessive Punishment Violates Laws of Nature.—It is not only vain but wicked in a legislator to frame laws in opposition to the laws of nature, and to arm them with the terror of death. This is truly creating crimes in order to punish them.—Bergh 1:236. (1779.)

CRIME, Principles of Punishing.— In forming a scale of crimes and punishments, two considerations have principal weight: 1, the atrocity of the crime; 2, the peculiar circumstances of a country which furnish greater temptations to commit it, or greater facilities for escaping detection. The punishment must be heavier to counterbalance this. Were the first the only consideration, all nations would form the same scale. But, as the circumstances of a country have influence on the punishment, and no two countries exist precisely under the same circumstances, no two countries will form the same scale of crimes and punishments. For example, in America the inhabitants let their horses go at large in the unenclosed lands, which are so extensive as to maintain them altogether. It is easy, therefore, to steal them, and easy to escape. Therefore, the laws are obliged to oppose these temptations with a heavier degree of punishment. For this reason, the stealing of a horse in America is punished more severely than stealing the same value in any other form. In Europe, where horses are confined so securely that it is impossible to steal them, that species of theft need not be punished more severely than any other. In some countries of Europe, stealing fruit from trees is punished capitally. The reason is that, it being impossible to lock fruit trees up in coffers, as we do our money, it is impossible to oppose physical bars to this species of theft. Moral ones are therefore opposed by the laws. This, to an unreflecting American, appears the most enormous of all the abuses of power, because he has been used to see fruits hanging in such quantities that if not taken by men they would rot.—Ford 4:169. (1786.)

The punishment of all real crimes is certainly desirable, as a security to society; the security is greater in proportion as the chances of avoiding punishment are less.—Ford 5:482. (1792.)

CRIME, Forgery.—There is one crime against property pressed by its consequences into more particular notice, to wit, forgery, whether of coin or paper; and whether paper of public or private obligation. But the fugitive for forgery is punished by exile and confiscation of the property he leaves. To which add by convention a civil action against the property he carries or acquires, to the amount of the special damage done by his forgery.—Ford 5:484. (1792.)

CRIME, Jurisdiction over.—The Constitution of the United States ... [has] delegated to Congress a power to punish treason, counterfeiting the securities and current coin of the United States, piracies and felonies committed on the high seas, and offenses against the law of nations, and no other crimes whatsoever; and it being true as a general principle, and one of the amendments to the Constitution having also declared that "the powers not delegated to the United States by the Constitution, nor prohibited by it to the states, are reserved to the states respectively, or to the people," therefore the act of Congress passed on the fourteenth day of July, 1798, and entitled "An Act in addition to the act entitled An Act for the punishment of certain crimes against the United States" [is] altogether void and of no force.... The power to create, define, and punish such other crimes is reserved, and of right appertains solely and exclusively to the respective states, each within its own territory.—Ford 7:292. (1798.)

CRIME. See also CAPITAL PUNISHMENT; MANSLAUGHTER; MURDER; PUNISHMENT; TREASON.

CRIMINALS, Reformation of.—A member of society committing an inferior injury does not wholly forfeit the protection of his fellow citizens, but, after suffering a punishment in proportion to his offense, is entitled to their protection from all greater pain, so that it becomes a duty in the legislature to arrange, in a proper scale, the crimes which it may be necessary for them to repress, and to adjust thereto a corresponding gradation of punishments. —Ford 2:204. (1779.)

CUBA, Acquisition by United States Favored.—The patriots of Spain have no warmer friends than the administration of the United States, but it is our duty to say nothing and to do nothing for or against either [party in the present European conflicts]. If they succeed, we shall be well satisfied to see Cuba and Mexico remain in their present dependence; but very unwilling to see them in that of either France or England, politically or commercially. We consider their interests and ours as the same, and that the object of both must be to exclude all European influence from this hemisphere.... These are sentiments which I would wish you to express to any proper characters of either of these two countries, and particularly that we have nothing more at heart than their friendship.—Bergh 12:186. (1808.)

I candidly confess that I have ever looked on Cuba as the most interesting addition which could ever be made to our system of states. The control which, with Florida Point, this island would give us over the Gulf of Mexico, and the countries and isthmus bordering on it, as well as all those whose waters flow into it, would fill up the measure of our political well-being.—To President James Monroe. Bergh 15:479. (1823.)

CURRENCY. See INFLATION; MONEY; PAPER MONEY.

D

DEATH, And a Future Life.—When you and I look back on the country over which we have passed, what a field of slaughter does it exhibit! Where are all the friends who entered it with us, under all the inspiring energies of health and hope? As if pursued by the havoc of war, they are strewed by the way, some earlier, some later, and scarce a few stragglers remain to count the numbers fallen, and to mark yet, by their own fall, the last footsteps of their party. Is it a desirable thing to bear up through the heat of the action, to witness the death of all our companions, and merely be the last victim? I doubt it. We have, however, the traveller's consolation. Every step shortens the distance we have to go; the end of our journey is in sight, the bed wherein we are to rest, and to rise in the midst of the friends we have lost.—To John Page. Bergh 11:31. (1804.)

DEATH, A Proper Time for.—There is a fulness of time when men should go, and not occupy too long the ground to which others have a right to advance.—Ford 9:329. (1811.)

To me every mail, in the departure of some contemporary, brings warning to be in readiness myself also, and to cease from new engagements. It is a warning of no alarm. When faculty after faculty is retiring from us, and all the avenues to cheerful sensation closing, sight failing now, hearing next, then memory, debility of body, torpitude of mind, nothing remaining but a sickly vegetation, with scarcely the relief of a little locomotion, the last cannot be but a *coup de grace*.— Bergh 14:219. (1814.)

With most of us, the powers of life are sensibly on the wane, sight becomes dim, hearing dull, memory constantly enlarging its frightful blank and parting with all we have ever seen or known, spirits evaporate, bodily debility creeps on palsying every limb, and so faculty after faculty quits us, and where then is life? . . . There is a ripeness of time for death, regarding others as well as ourselves, when it is reasonable we should drop off and make room for another growth. When we have lived our generation out, we should not wish to encroach on another. I enjoy good health; I am happy in what is around me, yet I assure you I am ripe for leaving all, this year, this day, this hour. . . . Bodily decay is gloomy in prospect, but of all human contemplations the most abhorrent is body without mind.—To John Adams. Bergh 15:57. (1816.)

Mine is the next turn, and I shall meet it with good will; for after one's friends are all gone before [him], and our faculties leaving us, too, one by one, why wish to linger in mere vegetation, as a solitary trunk in a desolate field, from which all its former companions have disappeared?—To Maria Cosway. Bergh 18:310. (1820.)

Charles Thomson [former secretary of Congress] still lives, . . . cheerful, slender as a grasshopper, and so much without memory that he scarcely recognizes the members of his household. An intimate friend of his called on him not long since; it was difficult to make him recollect who he was, and, sitting one hour, he told him the same story four

times over. Is this life? . . . It is at most but the life of a cabbage; surely not worth a wish. When all our faculties have left, or are leaving us, one by one, sight, hearing, memory, every avenue of pleasing sensation is closed, and athumy, debility, and malaise left in their places, when friends of our youth are all gone and a generation is risen around us whom we know not, is death an evil?—To John Adams. Bergh 15:371. (1822.)

DEATH. See also FUTURE LIFE; OLD AGE.

DEBATE. See CONGRESS.

DEBT, Fashion, Folly and.— Everything I hear from my own country fills me with despair. . . . Fashion and folly are plunging them deeper and deeper into distress; and the legislators of the country becoming debtors also, there seems no hope of applying the only possible remedy, that of an immediate judgment and execution. We should try whether the prodigal might not be restrained from taking on credit the gewgaw held out to him in one hand, by seeing the keys of a prison in the other.—Bergh 5:325. (1786.)

DEBT, Wisdom of Avoiding.—The maxim of buying nothing but what we [have] money in our pockets to pay for . . . lays the broadest foundation for happiness.—Bergh 6:188. (1787.)

The maxim of buying nothing without the money in our pockets to pay for it would make our country one of the happiest on earth. Experience during the war proved this; and I think every man will remember that, under all the privations it obliged him to submit to during that period, he slept sounder and awoke happier than he can do now.—Ford 4:414. (1787.)

Never [buy] anything which you have not money in your pocket to pay for. Be assured that it gives much more pain to the mind to be in debt than to do without any article whatever which we may seem to want.—To Martha Jefferson. Betts & Bear, p. 43. (1787.)

I know nothing more important to inculcate into the minds of young people than the wisdom, the honor, and the blessed comfort of living within their income; to calculate in good time how much less pain will cost them the plainest style of living, which keeps them out of debt, than after a few years of splendor above their income to have their property taken away for debt, when they have a family growing up to maintain and provide for.—To Martha Jefferson Randolph. Betts & Bear, p. 319. (1808.)

DEBT, Public, Should Not Be Passed from One Generation to Another.—The question, whether one generation of men has a right to bind another, seems never to have been started either on this or our side of the water. Yet it is a question of such consequences as not only to merit decision, but place also among the fundamental principles of every government. The course of reflection in which we are immersed here [France] on the elementary principles of society has presented this question to my mind; and that no

such obligation can be transmitted, I think very capable of proof. I set out on this ground, which I suppose to be self-evident: that the *earth belongs in usufruct to the living;* that the dead have neither powers nor rights over it.... If [one generation] could charge [another] with a debt, then the earth would belong to the dead and not to the living generation. Then, no generation can contract debts greater than may be paid during the course of its own existence.... A material difference must be noted between the succession of an individual and that of a whole generation. Individuals are parts only of a society, subject to the laws of a whole. These laws may appropriate the portion of land occupied by a decedent to his creditor rather than to any other, or to his child on condition he satisfies the creditor. But when a whole generation, that is, the whole society dies,... and another generation or society succeeds, this forms a whole, and there is no superior who can give their territory to a third society, who may have lent money to their predecessors beyond their faculties of paying. ... I suppose that the received opinion, that the public debts of one generation devolve on the next, has been suggested by our seeing habitually in private life that he who succeeds to lands is required to pay the debts of his predecessor; without considering that this requisition is municipal only, not moral, flowing from the will of the society, which has found it convenient to appropriate the lands of a decedent on the condition of a payment of his debts; but that between society and society, or generation and generation, there is no municipal obligation, no umpire but the law of nature.... Turn this subject in your mind, my dear sir, and particularly as to the power of contracting debts, and develop it with that cogent logic which is so peculiarly yours. Your station in the councils of our country gives you an opportunity of producing it to public consideration, of forcing it into discussion. At first blush it may be laughed at as the dream of a theorist; but examination will prove it to be solid and salutary. It would furnish matter for a fine preamble to our first law for appropriating the public revenue.—To James Madison. Bergh 7:454. (1789.)

It is a wise rule, and should be fundamental in a government disposed to cherish its credit, and at the same time to restrain the use of it within the limits of its faculties, "never to borrow a dollar without laying a tax in the same instant for paying the interest annually, and the principal within a given term; and to consider that tax as pledged to the creditors on the public faith." On such a pledge as this, sacredly observed, a government may always command, on a *reasonable interest*, all the lendable money of their citizens, while the necessity of an equivalent tax is a salutary warning to them and their constituents against oppressions, bankruptcy, and its inevitable consequence, revolution. But the term of redemption must be moderate, and at any rate within the limits of their rightful powers. But what limits, it will be asked, does this prescribe to their powers? What is to hinder them from creating a perpetual debt? The laws of nature, I answer. The earth belongs to the living, not to the dead. The will and the power of man expire with his life, by nature's law.... The generations of men may be considered as bodies or corporations. Each generation has the usufruct of the earth during the period of its continuance. When it ceases to exist, the usufruct passes on to the succeeding generation, free and unencumbered, and so on, successively, from one generation to another forever. We may consider each generation as a distinct nation, with a right, by the will of its majority, to bind themselves, but none to bind the succeeding generation, more than the inhabitants of another country.... The period of a generation, or the term of its life, is determined by the laws of mortality, which, varying a little only in different climates, offer a general average, to be found by observation.... At nineteen years... from the date of a contract, the majority of the contractors are dead, and their contract with them.... The laws of nature impose no obligation on [one generation] to pay [another's] debt. And although, like some other natural rights, this has not yet entered into any declaration of rights, it is no less a law, and ought to be acted on by honest governments. It is, at the same time, a salutary curb on the spirit of war and indebtment, which, since the modern theory of the perpetuation of debt, has drenched the earth with blood, and crushed its inhabitants under burdens ever accumulating. ... In seeking, then, for an ultimate term for the redemption of our debts, let us rally to this principle, and provide for their payment within the term of nineteen years at the farthest.—To John W. Eppes. Bergh 13:269. (1813.)

That we are bound to defray [the war's] expenses within our own time, and unauthorized to burden posterity with them, I suppose to have been proved in my former letter. I will place the question nevertheless in one additional point of view. The former regarded their independent right over the earth; this over their own persons. There have existed nations, and civilized and learned nations, who have thought that a father had a right to sell his child as a slave, in perpetuity.... We acknowledge that our children are born free; that that freedom is the gift of nature, and not of him who begot them; that though under our care during infancy, and therefore of necessity under a duly tempered authority, that care is confided to us to be exercised for the preservation and good of the child only; and his labors during youth are given as a retribution for the charges of infancy. As he was never the property of his father, so when adult he is ... entitled himself to the use of his own limbs and the fruits of his own exertions. So far we are advanced, without mind enough, it seems, to take the whole step. We

believe, or we act as if we believed, that although an individual father cannot alienate the labor of his son, the aggregate body of fathers may alienate the labor of all their sons, of their posterity in the aggregate, and oblige them to pay for all the enterprises, just or unjust, profitable or ruinous, into which our vices, our passions, or our personal interests may lead us. But I trust that this proposition needs only to be looked at by an American to be seen in its true point of view, and that we shall all consider ourselves unauthorized to saddle posterity with our debts, and morally bound to pay them ourselves; and consequently within what may be deemed the period of a generation, or the life of the majority. In my former letter I supposed this to be a little over twenty years. We must raise, then, ourselves the money for this war, either by taxes within the year or by loans; and if by loans, we must repay them ourselves, proscribing forever the English practice of perpetual funding.... Ought not, then, the right of each successive generation to be guaranteed against the dissipations and corruptions of those preceding, by a fundamental provision in our Constitution? And if that has not been made, does it exist the less, there being between generation and generation, as between nation and nation, no other law than that of nature? And is it the less dishonest to do what is wrong, because not expressly prohibited by written law? Let us hope our moral principles are not yet in that stage of degeneracy, and that in instituting the system of finance to be hereafter pursued we shall adopt the only safe, the only lawful and honest one, of borrowing on such short terms of reimbursement of interest and principal as will fall within the accomplishment of our own lives.— To John W. Eppes. Bergh 13:357. (1813.)

It is incumbent on every generation to pay its own debts as it goes; a principle which, if acted on, would save one-half the wars of the world. —Ford 10:175. (1820.)

DEBT, Public, Not a Public Blessing. —As the doctrine is that a public debt is a public blessing, so they [the supporters of state debt assumption] think a perpetual one is a perpetual blessing, and therefore wish to make it so large that we can never pay it off.—Ford 5:505. (1792.)

At the time we were funding our national debt, we heard much about "a public debt being a public blessing"; that the stock representing it was a creation of active capital for the aliment of commerce, manufactures, and agriculture. This paradox was well adapted to the minds of believers in dreams. . . . If the debt which the banking companies owe be a blessing to anybody, it is to themselves alone, who are realizing a solid interest of 8 or 10 percent on it. As to the public, these companies have banished all our gold and silver medium, which before their institution we had without interest, which never could have perished in our hands, and would have been our

salvation now in the hour of war; instead of which they have given us two hundred million of froth and bubble, on which we are to pay them heavy interest until it shall vanish into air. . . . The truth is that capital may be produced by industry, and accumulated by economy; but jugglers only will propose to create it by legerdemain tricks with paper. —Bergh 13:420. (1813.)

I . . . place economy among the first and most important of republican virtues, and public debt as the greatest of the dangers to be feared. —Bergh 15:47. (1816.)

DEBT, Discharging the National.— I am for . . . applying all the possible savings of the public revenue to the discharge of the national debt. —To Elbridge Gerry. Bergh 10:77. (1799.)

DEBT, Discharge of Public, Vital to Government's Survival.—I consider the fortunes of our republic as depending, in an eminent degree, on the extinguishment of the public debt before we engage in any war; because, that done, we shall have revenue enough to improve our country in peace and defend it in war, without recurring either to new taxes or loans. But if the debt should once more be swelled to a formidable size, its entire discharge will be despaired of, and we shall be committed to the English career of debt, corruption, and rottenness, closing with revolution. The discharge of the debt, therefore, is vital to the destinies of our government. —To Albert Gallatin. Bergh 12:324. (1809.)

DEBT, Posterity Swindled by Public.—The principle of spending money to be paid by posterity, under the name of funding, is but swindling futurity on a large scale.— Bergh 15:23. (1816.)

DEBT, Public, Results in Oppressive Taxation.—I am not among those who fear the people. They, and not the rich, are our dependence for continued freedom. And to preserve their independence, we must not let our rulers load us with perpetual debt. We must make our election between *economy and liberty* or *profusion and servitude.* If we run into such debts as that we must be taxed in our meat and in our drink, in our necessaries and our comforts, in our labors and our amusements, for our callings and our creeds, as the people of England are, our people, like them, must come to labor sixteen hours in the twenty-four, [and] give the earnings of fifteen of these to the government for their debts and daily expenses; and the sixteenth being insufficient to afford us bread, we must live, as they now do, on oatmeal and potatoes; have no time to think, no means of calling the mismanagers to account; but be glad to obtain subsistence by hiring ourselves to rivet their chains on the necks of our fellow sufferers.... This example reads to us the salutary lesson that private fortunes are destroyed by public as well as by private extravagance. And this is the tendency of all human governments. A departure from principle in one instance becomes a precedent for a second, that second for a third,

and so on, till the bulk of the society is reduced to be mere automatons of misery, to have no sensibilities left but for sinning and suffering. Then begins indeed the *bellum omnium in omnia* which some philosophers, observing [it] to be so general in this world, have mistaken...for the natural instead of the abusive state of man. And the forehorse of this frightful team is public debt. Taxation follows that, and in its train wretchedness and oppression.— Bergh 15:39. (1816.)

DEBT. See also ECONOMY; LOANS.

DECLARATION OF INDEPENDENCE, History of the.—On the 7th of June, 1776, the delegates from Virginia moved, in obedience to instructions from their constituents, that Congress should declare the thirteen united colonies to be independent of Great Britain, that a confederation should be formed to bind them together, and measures be taken for procuring the assistance of foreign powers. The house ordered a punctual attendance of all their members the next day at ten o'clock, and then resolved themselves into a committee of the whole and entered on the discussion.

It appeared in the course of the debates that seven states, [namely] New Hampshire, Massachusetts, Rhode Island, Connecticut, Virginia, North Carolina, and Georgia, were decided for a separation; but that six others still hesitated, to wit, New York, New Jersey, Pennsylvania, Delaware, Maryland, and South Carolina. Congress, desirous of unanimity, and seeing that the public mind was advancing rapidly to it, referred the further discussion to the first of July, appointing in the meantime a committee to prepare a Declaration of Independence, a second to form articles for the confederation of the states, and a third to propose measures for obtaining foreign aid.

On the 28th of June, the Declaration of Independence was reported to the house, and was laid on the table for the consideration of the members. On the first day of July, they resolved themselves into a committee of the whole and resumed the consideration of the motion of June 7th [declaring independence]. It was debated through the day, and at length was decided in the affirmative by the vote of nine states, [namely] New Hampshire, Massachusetts, Rhode Island, Connecticut, New Jersey, Maryland, Virginia, North Carolina, and Georgia. Pennsylvania and South Carolina voted against it. Delaware, having but two members present, was divided. The delegates from New York declared they were for it, and their constituents also; but that the instructions against it which had been given them a twelvemonth before were still unrepealed; that their convention was to meet in a few days, and they asked leave to suspend their vote till they could obtain a repeal of their instructions. Observe that all this was in a committee of the whole Congress, and that, according to the mode of their proceedings, the resolution of that

committee to declare themselves independent was to be put to the same persons reassuming their form as a Congress.

It was now evening, the members exhausted by a debate of nine hours, during which all the powers of the soul had been distended with the magnitude of the object—without refreshment, without a pause—and the delegates of South Carolina desired that the final decision might be put off to the next morning, that they might still weigh in their own minds their ultimate vote. It was put off, and in the morning of the second of July they joined the other nine states in voting for it. The members of the Pennsylvania delegation, too, who had been absent the day before came in and turned the vote of their state in favor of independence; and a third member of the state of Delaware, who, hearing of the division in the sentiment of his two colleagues, had travelled post to arrive in time, now came in and decided the vote of that state also for the resolution. Thus twelve states voted for it at the time of its passage, and the delegates of New York, the thirteenth state, received instructions within a few days to add theirs to the general vote, so that . . . there was not a dissenting voice.

Congress proceeded immediately to consider the Declaration of Independence which had been reported by their committee on the 28th of June. The several paragraphs of that were debated for three days, [namely] the second, third, and fourth of July. In the evening of the fourth they were finally closed, and the instrument approved by a unanimous vote and signed by every member except Mr. [John] Dickinson.—To the Editor of the *Journal de Paris*. Bergh 17:150. (1787.)

DECLARATION OF INDEPENDENCE, Signers of the.—Of the signers of the Declaration of Independence, I see now living not more than half a dozen on your side of the Potomac, and on this side, myself alone.—To John Adams. Ford 9:334. (1812.)

It was not till the 2nd of July that the Declaration itself was taken up, nor till the 4th that it was decided; and it was signed by every member present except Mr. [John] Dickinson. The subsequent signatures of members who were not then present, and some of them not yet in office, is easily explained if we observe who they were: to wit, that they were of New York and Pennsylvania. New York did not sign till the 15th because it was not till the 9th, five days after the general signature, that their convention authorized them to do so. The convention of Pennsylvania, learning that it had been signed by a minority only of their delegates, named a new delegation on the 20th, leaving out Mr. Dickinson, who had refused to sign, Willing and Humphreys, who had withdrawn, [and] reappointing the three members who had signed, Morris, who had not been present, and five new ones, to wit, Rush, Clymer, Smith, Taylor, and Ross; and Morris and the five new mem-

bers were permitted to sign because it manifested the assent of their full delegation and the express will of their convention, which might have been doubted on the former signature of a minority only. Why the signature of Thornton of New Hampshire was permitted so late as the 4th of November, I cannot now say; but undoubtedly for some particular reason which we should find to have been good, had it been expressed. These were the only post-signers, and you see, sir, that there were solid reasons for receiving those of New York and Pennsylvania, and that this circumstance in no wise affects the faith of this declaratory charter of our rights, and of the rights of man.—Bergh 15:199. (1819.)

I think Mr. Adams will outlive us all, I mean the Declaration men, although our senior since the death of Colonel Floyd. It is a race in which I have no ambition to win.—Ford 10:191. (1821.)

I have received the new publication of the secret journals of Congress, wherein is stated a resolution of July 19, 1776, that the Declaration passed on the 4th be fairly engrossed on parchment, and when engrossed be signed by every member; and another of August 2nd that, being engrossed and compared at the table, it was signed by the members; that is to say, the copy engrossed on parchment (for durability) was signed by the members, after being compared at the table, with the original one signed on paper as before stated.*—Ford 10:132. (1822.)

*Jefferson's recollection of a general signing on July 4 differs with the standard historical account. This matter, still unsettled, is discussed in Boyd 1:305-8.—Editor.

I observe your toast of Mr. [John] Jay on the 4th of July [1823], wherein you say that the omission of his signature to the Declaration of Independence was by *accident*. Our impressions as to this fact being different, I shall be glad to have mine corrected, if wrong. Jay, you know, had been in constant opposition to our laboring majority. Our estimate at the time was that he, Dickinson, and Johnson of Maryland, by their ingenuity, perseverance, and partiality to our English connection, had constantly kept us a year behind where we ought to have been in our preparations and proceedings. From about the date of the Virginia instructions of May 15th, 1776, to declare independence, Mr. Jay absented himself from Congress, and never came there again until December 1778. Of course, he had no part in the discussions or decision of that question. The instructions to their delegates by the convention of New York, then sitting, to sign the Declaration, were presented to Congress on the 15th of July only, and on that day the journals show the absence of Mr. Jay by a letter received from him, as they had done as early as the 29th of May by another letter. And I think he had been omitted by the convention on a new election of delegates when they changed their instructions. Of this last fact, however, having no

evidence but an ancient impression, I shall not affirm it. But whether so or not, no agency of *accident* appears in the case. This error of fact, however, whether yours or mine, is of little consequence to the public. But truth being as cheap as error, it is as well to rectify it for our own satisfaction.—To John Adams. Ford 10:271. (1823.)

DECLARATION OF INDEPENDENCE, Slavery Clause Deleted.— The clause...reprobating the enslaving the inhabitants of Africa was struck out in complaisance to South Carolina and Georgia, who had never attempted to restrain the importation of slaves, and who, on the contrary, still wished to continue it. Our northern brethren also, I believe, felt a little tender under those censures; for though their people had very few slaves themselves, yet they had been pretty considerable carriers of them to others.—Autobiography. Bergh 1:28. (1821.)

DECLARATION OF INDEPENDENCE, Where Written.—At the time of writing the Declaration, I lodged in the house of a Mr. Graff, a new brick house three stories high, of which I rented the second floor, consisting of a parlor and bedroom, ready furnished. In that parlor I wrote habitually, and in it wrote this paper particularly. So far I state from written proofs in my possession. The proprietor, Graff, was a young man, son of a German, and then newly married. I think he was a bricklayer, and that his house was on the south side of Market Street, probably between Seventh and Eighth streets, and if not the only house on that part of the street, I am sure there were few others near it. I have some idea that it was a corner house, but no other recollections throwing light on the question or worth communication.—Ford 10:346. (1825.)

DECLARATION OF INDEPENDENCE, Objects of the.—With respect to our rights, and the acts of the British government contravening those rights, there was but one opinion on this side of the water. All American Whigs thought alike on these subjects. When forced, therefore, to resort to arms for redress, an appeal to the tribunal of the world was deemed proper for our justification. This was the object of the Declaration of Independence. Not to find out new principles or new arguments never before thought of, not merely to say things which had never been said before; but to place before mankind the common sense of the subject, in terms so plain and firm as to command their assent, and to justify ourselves in the independent stand we [were] compelled to take. Neither aiming at originality of principle or sentiment, nor yet copied from any particular and previous writing, it was intended to be an expression of the American mind, and to give to that expression the proper tone and spirit called for by the occasion. All its authority rests, then, on the harmonizing sentiments of the day, whether expressed in conversation, in letters,

printed essays, or in the elementary books of public right, as Aristotle, Cicero, Locke, Sidney, etc.—Bergh 16:118. (1825.)

DECLARATION OF INDEPENDENCE, Semicentennial of the.—The kind invitation I received from you, on the part of the citizens of the city of Washington, to be present with them at their celebration on the fiftieth anniversary of American Independence, as one of the surviving signers of an instrument pregnant with our own [fate] and the fate of the world, is most flattering to myself, and heightened by the honorable accompaniment proposed for the comfort of such a journey. It adds sensibly to the sufferings of sickness to be deprived by it of a personal participation in the rejoicings of that day. But acquiescence is a duty under circumstances not placed among those we are permitted to control. I should, indeed, with peculiar delight, have met and exchanged there congratulations personally with the small band, the remnant of that host of worthies, who joined with us on that day in the bold and doubtful election we were to make for our country, between submission or the sword; and to have enjoyed with them the consolatory fact that our fellow citizens, after half a century of experience and prosperity, continue to approve the choice we made.

May it be to the world what I believe it will be (to some parts sooner, to others later, but finally to all), the signal of arousing men to burst the chains under which monkish ignorance and superstition had persuaded them to bind themselves, and to assume the blessings and security of self-government. That form which we have substituted restores the free right to the unbounded exercise of reason and freedom of opinion. All eyes are opened, or opening, to the rights of man. The general spread of the light of science has already laid open to every view the palpable truth that the mass of mankind has not been born with saddles on their backs, nor a favored few booted and spurred, ready to ride them legitimately by the grace of God. These are grounds of hope for others. For ourselves, let the annual return of this day forever refresh our recollections of these rights, and an undiminished devotion to them.

I will ask permission here to express the pleasure with which I should have met my ancient neighbors of the city of Washington and its vicinities, with whom I passed so many years of a pleasing social intercourse; an intercourse which so much relieved the anxieties of the public cares, and left impressions so deeply engraved in my affections, as never to be forgotten. With my regret that ill health forbids me the gratification of an acceptance, be pleased to receive for yourself, and those for whom you write, the assurance of my highest respect and friendly attachments.*—To Roger C. Weightman. Bergh 16:181. (1826.)

* This remarkable letter was evidently Jefferson's last. He died ten days later, on the day of the celebration.—Editor.

DECLARATION OF INDEPENDENCE. See also AMERICAN REVOLUTION; COLONIES (American); FOURTH OF JULY.

DEFENSE, Wars Prevented by Strong.—Justice ... on our part will save us from those wars which would have been produced by a contrary disposition. But how can we prevent those produced by the wrongs of other nations? By putting ourselves in a condition to punish them. Weakness provokes insult and injury, while a condition to punish often prevents them.—To John Jay. Bergh 5:95. (1785.)

DEFENSE, Proposed Measures for National.—Two measures have not been adopted which I pressed on Congress repeatedly at their meetings. The one, to settle the whole ungranted territory of Orleans by donations of land to able-bodied young men, to be engaged and carried there at the public expense, who would constitute a force always ready on the spot to defend New Orleans. The other was to class the militia according to the years of their birth, and make all those from twenty to twenty-five liable to be trained and called into service at a moment's warning. This would have given us a force of three hundred thousand young men, prepared by proper training, for service in any part of the United States; while those who had passed through that period would remain at home, liable to be used in their own or adjacent states. Those two measures would have completed what I deemed necessary for the entire security of our country. They would have given me, on my retirement from the government of the nation, the consolatory reflection that having found, when I was called to it, not a single seaport town in a condition to repel a levy of contribution by a single privateer or pirate, I had left every harbor so prepared by works and gunboats as to be in a reasonable state of security against any probable attack; the territory of Orleans acquired and planted with an internal force sufficient for its protection; and the whole territory of the United States organized by such a classification of its male force as would give it the benefit of all its young population for active service, and that of a middle and advanced age for stationary defense. But these measures will, I hope, be completed by my successor.—Bergh 12:367. (1810.)

DEFENSE. See also ARMY; MILITIA; NAVY; PEACE; WAR.

DEITY, Assistance of, Implored.— We commit our injuries to the even-handed justice of that Being who doth no wrong, earnestly beseeching Him to illuminate the councils and prosper the endeavors of those to whom America hath confided her hopes, that through their wise direction we may again see reunited the blessings of liberty, property, and harmony with Great Britain.—Ford 1:459. (1775.)

DEITY, Liberty and.—We...most solemnly, before God and the world, declare that...the arms we have been compelled to assume, we will use with perseverance, exerting to their utmost energies all those powers which our Creator hath given us, to preserve that liberty which He committed to us in sacred deposit.—Declaration of the Causes and Necessity for Taking Up Arms. Ford 1:476. (1775.)

DEITY, Inalienable Rights and.— All men are...endowed by their Creator with certain inalienable rights.—Declaration of Independence. Bergh 1:29. (1776.)

DEITY, Supplications to.—May that Infinite Power which rules the destinies of the universe lead our councils to what is best, and give them a favorable issue for your peace and prosperity.—First Inaugural Address. Bergh 3:323. (1801.)

I offer my sincere prayers to the Supreme Ruler of the Universe, that He may long preserve our country in freedom and prosperity.—Bergh 10:236. (1801.)

I join in addressing Him whose Kingdom ruleth over all, to direct the administration of [our citizens'] affairs to their own greatest good.—Bergh 10:293. (1801.)

I shall need...the favor of that Being in whose hands we are, who led our forefathers, as Israel of old, from their native land, and planted them in a country flowing with all the necessaries and comforts of life; who has covered our infancy with His providence, and our riper years with His wisdom and power; and to whose goodness I ask you to join with me in supplications, that He will so enlighten the minds of your servants, guide their councils, and prosper their measures, that whatsoever they do shall result in your good, and shall secure to you the peace, friendship, and approbation of all nations.—Second Inaugural Address. Bergh 3:383. (1805.)

DEITY, Gratitude to.—While we devoutly return thanks to the beneficent Being who has been pleased to breathe into [our sister nations] the spirit of conciliation and forgiveness, we are bound with peculiar gratitude to be thankful to Him that our own peace has been preserved.—First Annual Message to Congress. Bergh 3:327. (1801.)

DEITY, Goodness of.—When we assemble together . . . to consider the state of our beloved country, our just attentions are first drawn to those pleasing circumstances which mark the goodness of that Being from whose favor they flow, and the large measure of thankfulness we owe for His bounty.—Second Annual Message to Congress. Bergh 3:340. (1802.)

DEITY, Submission to.—Whatever is to be our destiny, wisdom as well as duty dictates that we should acquiesce in the will of Him whose it is to give and take away, and be contented in the enjoyment of those [loved ones] who are still permitted to be with us.—To John Page. Bergh 11:32. (1804.)

DEITY, An Overruling.—We are not in a world ungoverned by the laws and the power of a Superior Agent. Our efforts are in His hand, and directed by it, and He will give them their effect in His own time.—Ford 9:516. (1815.)

DEITY. See also GOD; PROVIDENCE; RELIGION.

DEMOCRACY. See GOVERNMENT; MAJORITY; PEOPLE; REPRESENTATION; REPUBLICAN GOVERNMENT; SELF-GOVERNMENT.

DEMOCRATS, Jefferson's Definition of.—Democrats consider the people as the safest depository of power in the last resort; they cherish them, therefore, and wish to leave in them all the powers to the exercise of which they are competent.—Ford 10:335. (1825.)

DICKINSON (John), Character of. —A more estimable man, or truer patriot, could not have left us. Among the first of the advocates for the rights of his country when assailed by Great Britain, he continued to the last the orthodox advocate of the true principles of our new government, and his name will be consecrated in history as one of the great worthies of the Revolution. We ought to be grateful for having been permitted to retain the benefit of his counsel to so good an old age. . . . A junior companion of his labors in the early part of our Revolution, it has been a great comfort to me to have retained his friendship to the last moment of his life.—Bergh 11:445. (1808.)

He was so honest a man, and so able a one, that he was greatly indulged even by those who could not feel his scruples.—Autobiography. Bergh 1:16. (1821.)

DIFFICULTIES, Should Be Endured Patiently.—When we see ourselves in a situation which must be endured and gone through, it is best to make up our minds to it. Meet it with firmness, and accommodate everything to it in the best way practicable. This lessens the evil, while fretting and fuming only serves to increase our own torment. —To Mary Jefferson Eppes. Betts & Bear, p. 151. (1798.)

DIPLOMATIC RECOGNITION. See FOREIGN AFFAIRS.

DIPLOMATS, Under President's Direction.—After mature consideration and consultation, I am of opinion that the Constitution has made the President the sole competent judge to what places circumstances render it expedient that ambassadors or other public ministers should be sent, and of what grade they should be; and that it has ascribed to the Senate no executive act but the single one of giving or withholding their consent to the person nominated. I think it my duty, therefore, to protest, and do protest against the validity of any resolutions of the Senate asserting or implying any right in that house to exercise any executive authority but the single one before mentioned. —Ford 5:415. (1792.)

DISPUTES, Avoidance of.—In stating prudential rules for our government in society, I must not omit the important one of never entering into dispute or argument with another. I never saw an instance of one of two disputants convincing the other by argument. I have seen many, on their getting warm, becoming rude and shooting one another. Conviction is the effect of our own dispassionate reasoning, either in solitude or weighing within ourselves, dispassionately, what we hear from others, standing uncommitted in argument ourselves. It was one of the rules which, above all others, made Doctor Franklin the most amiable of men in society, "never to contradict anybody." If he was urged to announce an opinion, he did it rather by asking questions, as if for information, or by suggesting doubts.

When I hear another express an opinion which is not mine, I say to myself, he has a right to his opinion, as I to mine; why should I question it? His error does me no injury, and shall I become a Don Quixote, to bring all men by force of argument to one opinion? If a fact be misstated, it is probable he is gratified by a belief of it, and I have no right to deprive him of the gratification. If he wants information he will ask it, and then I will give it in measured terms; but if he still believes his own story, and shows a desire to dispute the fact with me, I hear him and say nothing. It is his affair, not mine, if he prefers error.—To Thomas Jefferson Randolph. Bergh 12:199. (1808.)

DISPUTES. See also OPINION.

DOLLAR. See CURRENCY; MONEY; PAPER MONEY.

DRAFT, Unpopularity of a Military. —In Virginia a draft was ever the most unpopular and impracticable thing that could be attempted. Our people, even under the monarchical government, had learned to consider it as the last of all oppressions.

—To John Adams. Ford 2:129. (1777.)

DRUNKENNESS. See ALCOHOLIC BEVERAGES; INTEMPERANCE; WINE.

DUTY, Ability and Public.—A debt of service is due from every man to his country, proportioned to the bounties which nature and fortune have measured to him.—Ford 7:94. (1796.)

Some men are born for the public. Nature, by fitting them for the service of the human race on a broad scale, has stamped them with the evidences of her destination and their duty.—Ford 8:190. (1803.)

DUTY, Personal Comfort vs. Public.—Renounce your domestic comforts for a few months, and reflect that to be a good husband and good father at this moment, you must be also a good citizen.—To Elbridge Gerry. Ford 7:151. (1797.)

DUTY, And Natural Rights.—Man . . . has no natural right in opposition to his social duties.—Bergh 16:282. (1802.)

DUTY, Merit and.—If it be found that I have done my duty, as other faithful citizens have done, it is all the merit I claim.—Bergh 16:349. (1809.)

DUTY, Public Service a Natural.—Every man is under the natural duty of contributing to the necessities of the society; and this is all the laws should enforce on him.—Bergh 15:24. (1816.)

DUTY, To Pursue What Is Right.—Our part . . . is to pursue with steadiness what is right, turning neither to right nor left for the intrigues or popular delusions of the day, assured that the public approbation will in the end be with us.—Bergh 15:363. (1822.)

DUTY. See also ARISTOCRACY; GENIUS; MORAL LAW; TALENTS.

E

EARTH, Equal Rights in the.—The earth is given as a common stock for man to labor and live on.—Ford 7:36. (1785.)

EARTH, Theory of Creation.—I give one answer to all . . . theorists. That is as follows: They all suppose the earth a created existence. They must suppose a Creator, then, and that He possessed power and wisdom to a great degree.—To Charles Thomson. Bergh 6:12. (1786.)

EARTH, Belongs to the Living.—This ground . . . I suppose to be self-evident, that *the earth belongs in usufruct to the living;* that the dead have neither powers nor rights over it. The portion occupied by any individual ceases to be his when himself ceases to be, and reverts to the society. . . . The earth belongs always to the living generation. They may manage it, then, and what proceeds from it, as they please during their usufruct.—To James Madison. Bergh 7:454. (1789.)

EARTH, God's Gift.—The soil is the gift of God to the living.—Ford 9:391. (1813.)

ECONOMY, A Republican Virtue.—I am for a government rigorously frugal and simple, applying all the possible savings of the public revenue to the discharge of the national debt.—To Elbridge Gerry. Bergh 10:77. (1799.)

I ... place economy among the first and most important of republican virtues.—Bergh 15:47. (1816.)

ECONOMY, Insisting on.—We shall push [Congress] to the uttermost in economizing.—Bergh 10:261. (1801.)

ECONOMY, And Happiness.—If we can prevent the government from wasting the labors of the people, under the pretense of taking care of them, they must become happy.—Bergh 10:342. (1802.) Ford 8:187. (1802.)

ECONOMY, An Essential Principle. —To expend the public money with the same care and economy [that] we would practice with our own ... [is one of] the landmarks by which we are to guide ourselves in all our proceedings.—Ford 8:187. (1802).

The same prudence which in private life would forbid our paying our money for unexplained projects forbids it in the disposition of the public moneys.—Bergh 12:73. (1808.)

ECONOMY, Rigorous.—We are endeavoring ... to reduce the government to the practice of a rigorous economy, to avoid burdening the people and arming the magistrate with a patronage of money which might be used to corrupt and undermine the principles of our government.—Bergh 10:356. (1803.)

ECONOMY, Prodigality vs.—To reform the prodigalities of our predecessors is ... peculiarly our duty, and to bring the government

to a simple and economical course. —Ford 8:191. (1803.)

ECONOMY, And Liberty.—We must make our election between *economy and liberty* or *profusion and servitude.*—Bergh 15:39. (1816.)

ECONOMY, Evils of the Want of.— We see in England the consequences of the want of [economy]; their laborers reduced to live on a penny in the shilling of their earnings, to give up bread and resort to oatmeal and potatoes for food; and their landholders exiling themselves to live in penury and obscurity abroad, because at home the government must have all the clear profits of their land.... Our laborers and landholders must come to this also unless they severely adhere to the economy you recommend.—To Governor William Plumer. Bergh 15:47. (1816.)

ECONOMY, Household.—In household economy, the mothers of our country are generally skilled, and generally careful to instruct their daughters. We all know its value, and that diligence and dexterity in all its processes are inestimable treasures. The order and economy of a house are as honorable to the mistress as those of the farm to the master, and if either be neglected, ruin follows, and children destitute of the means of living.—Ford 10:106. (1818.)

ECONOMY, Ignorance of Political. —I transmit for M. Tracy ... a translation of his *Economie Politique,* which we have made and published here in the hope of advancing our countrymen somewhat in that science, the most profound ignorance of which threatened irreparable disaster during the late war, and by the parasite institutions of banks is now consuming the public industry.—Ford 10:116. (1818.)

ECONOMY, New Loans vs.—I learn with great satisfaction that wholesome economies have been found, sufficient to relieve us from the ruinous necessity of adding annually to our debt by new loans. The deviser of so salutary a relief deserves truly well of his country.—Ford 10:251. (1823.)

ECONOMY, And Honesty.—A rigid economy of the public contributions, and absolute interdiction of all useless expenses, will go far towards keeping the government honest and unoppressive.—Ford 10:280. (1823.)

EDUCATION, Freedom Guarded by Public.—Laws will be wisely formed and honestly administered in proportion as those who form and administer them are wise and honest; whence it becomes expedient for promoting the public happiness that those persons whom nature hath endowed with genius and virtue should be rendered by liberal education worthy to receive, and able to guard, the sacred deposit of the rights and liberties of their fellow citizens; and that they should be called to that charge without regard to wealth, birth, or other accidental condition or circumstance; but the indigence of the greater number disabling them from so educating, at their own expense,

those of their children whom nature hath fitly formed and disposed to become useful instruments for the public, it is better that such should be sought for and educated at the common expense of all than that the happiness of all should be confined to the weak or wicked.—Boyd 2:526. (1779.)

No other sure foundation can be devised for the preservation of freedom and happiness.... Preach, my dear sir, a crusade against ignorance; establish and improve the law for educating the common people. Let our countrymen know that the people alone can protect us against these evils [of misgovernment], and that the tax which will be paid for this purpose is not more than the thousandth part of what will be paid to kings, priests, and nobles who will rise up among us if we leave the people in ignorance.—To George Wythe. Bergh 5:396. (1786.)

If the legislature would add to the literary fund a perpetual tax of a cent a head on the population of the state, it would set agoing at once, and forever maintain, a system of primary or ward schools, and a university where might be taught, in its highest degree, every branch of science useful in our time and country; and it would rescue us from the tax of Toryism, fanaticism, and indifferentism to their own state which we now send our youth to bring from those of New England.—Ford 10:4. (1816.)

EDUCATION, Essential to Preservation of Liberty.—Say... whether peace is best preserved by giving energy to the government, or information to the people. This last is the most certain and the most legitimate engine of government. Educate and inform the whole mass of the people. Enable them to see that it is their interest to preserve peace and order, and they will preserve them. And it requires no very high degree of education to convince them of this. They are the only sure reliance for the preservation of our liberty.—To James Madison. Bergh 6:392. (1787.)

If a nation expects to be ignorant and free, in a state of civilization, it expects what never was and never will be.—Bergh 14:384. (1816.)

EDUCATION, Managed Best by the Private Sector.—It [should not] be proposed to take [the] ordinary branches [of education] out of the hands of private enterprise, which manages so much better all the concerns to which it is equal.—Sixth Annual Message to Congress. Bergh 3:423. (1806.)

EDUCATION, Large Cities and.—I am not a friend to placing young men in populous cities, because they acquire there habits and partialities which do not contribute to the happiness of their after life.—Ford 9:79. (1807.)

EDUCATION, Rising Generation and.—[Correct principles] ought to be instilled into the minds of our youth on their first opening. The boys of the rising generation are to be the men of the next, and the sole guardians of the principles we deliver over to them.—Bergh 12:360. (1810.)

EDUCATION, Military Instruction.—We must...make military instruction a regular part of collegiate education. We can never be safe till this is done.—To James Monroe. Bergh 13:261. (1813.)

EDUCATION, Suffrage and.—There is one provision [in the new constitution of Spain] which will immortalize its inventors. It is that which, after a certain epoch, disfranchises every citizen who cannot read and write. This is new, and is the fruitful germ of the improvement of everything good and the correction of everything imperfect in the present constitution. This will give you an enlightened people, and an energetic public opinion which will control and enchain the aristocratic spirit of the government.—Bergh 14:130. (1814.)

In the constitution of Spain, as proposed by the late Cortes, there was a principle entirely new to me,...that no person born after that day should ever acquire the rights of citizenship until he could read and write. It is impossible sufficiently to estimate the wisdom of this provision. Of all those which have been thought of for securing fidelity in the administration of the government, constant ralliance to the principles of the Constitution, and progressive amendments with the progressive advances of the human mind, or changes in human affairs, it is the most effectual. Enlighten the people generally, and tyranny and oppressions of body and mind will vanish like evil spirits at the dawn of day.—Bergh 14:491. (1816.)

It is better to tolerate the rare instance of a parent refusing to let his child be educated than to shock the common feelings and ideas by the forcible asportation and education of the infant against the will of the father. What is proposed here is to remove the objection of expense by offering education gratis, and to strengthen parental excitement by the disfranchisement of his child while uneducated. Society has certainly a right to disavow him whom they offer, and are not permitted, to qualify for the duties of a citizen. If we do not force instruction, let us at least strengthen the motives to receive it when offered.—Bill for Establishing Elementary Schools. Bergh 17:423. (1817.)

EDUCATION, Need for Rigorous Study.—Our post-Revolutionary youth are born under happier stars than you and I were. They acquire all learning in their mother's womb, and bring it into the world ready made. The information of books is no longer necessary; and all knowledge which is not innate is in contempt, or neglect at least. Every folly must run its round; and so, I suppose, must that of self-learning and self-sufficiency; of rejecting the knowledge acquired in past ages, and starting on the new ground of intuition. When sobered by experience, I hope our successors will turn their attention to the advantages of education. I mean of education on the broad scale, and

not that of the petty *academies,* as they call themselves, which are starting up in every neighborhood, and where one or two men possessing Latin and sometimes Greek, a knowledge of the globes, and the first six books of Euclid imagine and communicate this as the sum of science. They commit their pupils to the theater of the world with just taste enough of learning to be alienated from industrious pursuits, and not enough to do service in the ranks of science.... I hope the necessity will at length be seen of establishing institutions here, as in Europe, where every branch of science useful at this day may be taught in its highest degree.—To John Adams. Bergh 14:150. (1814.)

EDUCATION, Improves the Human Condition.—Enlighten the people generally, and tyranny and oppressions of body and mind will vanish like evil spirits at the dawn of day. Although I do not, with some enthusiasts, believe that the human condition will ever advance to such a state of perfection as that there shall no longer be pain or vice in the world, yet I believe it susceptible of much improvement, and most of all in matters of government and religion; and that the diffusion of knowledge among the people is to be the instrument by which it is to be effected.—Bergh 14:491. (1816.)

If the condition of man is to be progressively ameliorated, as we fondly hope and believe, [education] is to be the chief instrument in effecting it.—Bergh 15:172. (1818.)

I look to the diffusion of light and education as the resource most to be relied on for ameliorating the condition, promoting the virtue, and advancing the happiness of man. That every man shall be made virtuous, by any process whatever, is indeed no more to be expected than that every tree shall be made to bear fruit, and every plant nourishment. The brier and bramble can never become the vine and olive; but their asperities may be softened by culture, and their properties improved to usefulness in the order and economy of the world. And I do hope that, in the present spirit of extending to the great mass of mankind the blessings of instruction, I see a prospect of great advancement in the happiness of the human race. —Bergh 15:399. (1822.)

Jefferson in 1789 (age 46). Bust by Jean Antoine Houdon.

EDUCATION, Jefferson's Plan for Public.—I have sketched and put into the hands of a member a bill, delineating a practicable plan, entirely within the means they [the Virginia legislature] already have on hand, destined to this object. My bill proposes: 1. Elementary schools in every county, which shall place every householder within three miles of a school. 2. District colleges, which shall place every father within a day's ride of a college where he may dispose of his son. 3. A university in a healthy and central situation, with the offer of the lands, buildings, and funds of the Central College, if they will accept that place for their establishment.

In the first will be taught reading, writing, common arithmetic, and general notions of geography. In the second, ancient and modern languages, geography fully, a higher degree of numerical arithmetic, mensuration [measuring, as in geometry], and the elementary principles of navigation. In the third, all the useful sciences in their highest degree. To all of which is added a selection from the elementary schools of subjects of the most promising genius, whose parents are too poor to give them further education, to be carried at the public expense through the colleges and university.

The object is to bring into action that mass of talents which lies buried in poverty in every country, for want of the means of development, and thus give activity to a mass of mind which, in proportion to our population, shall be the double or treble of what it is in most countries. The expense of the elementary schools for every county is proposed to be levied on the wealth of the county, and all children rich and poor to be educated at these three years gratis.... This is, in fact and substance, the plan I proposed in a bill forty years ago, but accommodated to the circumstances of this instead of that day.—Bergh 15:155. (1817.)

EDUCATION, Societal Duties vs. Parental Rights.—A question of some doubt might be raised... as to the rights and duties of society towards its members, infant and adult. Is it a right or a duty in society to take care of their infant members in opposition to the will of the parent? How far does this right and duty extend? To guard the life of the infant, his property, his instruction, his morals? The Roman father was supreme in all these; we draw a line, but where? Public sentiment does not seem to have traced it precisely. Nor is it necessary in the present case. It is better to tolerate the rare instance of a parent refusing to let his child be educated than to shock the common feelings and ideas by the forcible asportation and education of the infant against the will of the father.—Bill for Establishing Elementary Schools. Bergh 17:423. (1817.)

EDUCATION, For All Citizens.—A system of general instruction, which

shall reach every description of our citizens from the richest to the poorest, as it was the earliest, so will it be the latest of all the public concerns in which I shall permit myself to take an interest. Nor am I tenacious of the form in which it shall be introduced. Be that what it may, our descendants will be as wise as we are, and will know how to amend and amend it, until it shall suit their circumstances. Give it to us then in any shape, and receive for the inestimable boon the thanks of the young and the blessings of the old, who are past all other services but prayers for the prosperity of their country, and blessings for those who promote it.—Ford 10:102. (1818.)

EDUCATION, A Family Responsibility.—A plan of female education has never been a subject of systematic contemplation with me. It has occupied my attention so far only as the education of my own daughters occasionally required. Considering that they would be placed in a country situation, where little aid could be obtained from abroad, I thought it essential to give them a solid education, which might enable them, when [they] become mothers, to educate their own daughters, and even to direct the course for sons, should their fathers be lost, or incapable, or inattentive. —Ford 10:104. (1818.)

EDUCATION, Abuses of Power and.—Education is the true corrective of abuses of constitutional power.—Ford 10:161. (1820.)

EDUCATION. See also GENIUS; KNOWLEDGE; SCHOOLS; SCIENCE; UNIVERSITY; UNIVERSITY OF VIRGINIA.

ELECTIONS, Intermeddling with. —From a very early period of my life I determined never to intermeddle with elections of the people, and have invariably adhered to this determination. In my own country, where there have been so many elections in which my inclinations were enlisted, I yet never interfered. I could the less do it in the present instance, your people so very distant from me, utterly unknown to me, and to whom I also am unknown; and above all, I a stranger, to presume to recommend one who is well known to them. The people could not but put this question to me: "Who are you, pray?"—Ford 6:111. (1792.)

ELECTIONS, Should Be Held at Short Intervals.—A government by representatives, elected by the people at *short* periods, was our object; and our maxim at that day was, "Where annual election ends, tyranny begins"; nor have our departures from it been sanctioned by the happiness of their effects.—Ford 7:425. (1800.)

ELECTIONS, Federal Interference with.—Till the event of the [presidential] election is known, it is too soon for me to say what should be done in such atrocious cases as those you mention of federal officers obstructing the operation of the state governments. One thing I will say, that, as to the future, interferences with elections, whether of the state

or general government, by officers of the latter, should be deemed cause of removal, because the Constitutional remedy by the elective principle becomes nothing if it may be smothered by the enormous patronage of the general government.—Ford 7:486. (1801.)

I proposed soon after coming into office to enjoin the executive officers from intermeddling with elections, as inconsistent with the true principles of our Constitution. It was laid over for consideration, but late occurrences prove the propriety of it, and it is now under consideration.—Ford 8:322. (1804.)

ELECTIONS. See also SUFFRAGE.

EMBARGO, Alternative of War.—The alternative was between that and war, and in fact it is the last card we have to play short of war.—Bergh 12:21. (1808.)

We have to choose between the alternatives of embargo and war. There is indeed one and only one other, that is, submission and tribute; for all the Federalist propositions for trading to the places permitted by the edicts of the belligerents result in fact in submission, although they do not choose to pronounce the naked word.—Bergh 12:191. (1808.)

Could the alternative of war, or the embargo, have been presented to the whole nation as it occurred to their representatives, there could have been but the one opinion that it was better to take the chance of one year by the embargo, within which the orders and decrees producing it may be repealed, or peace take place in Europe, which may secure peace to us.—Ford 9:194. (1808.)

EMBARGO, Public Approval of.—I see with satisfaction that this measure of self-denial is approved and supported by the great body of our real citizens, that they meet with cheerfulness the temporary privations it occasions.—Bergh 16:307. (1808.)

EMBARGO, Positive Results of.— We have the satisfaction to reflect that in return for the privations by the measure, and which our fellow citizens in general have borne with patriotism, it has had the important effects of saving our mariners and our vast mercantile property, as well as of affording time for prosecuting the defensive and provisional measures called for by the occasion. It has demonstrated to foreign nations the moderation and firmness which govern our councils, and to our citizens the necessity of uniting in support of the laws and the rights of their country, and has thus long frustrated those usurpations and spoliations which, if resisted, involve war; [or] if submitted to, sacrifice a vital principle of our national independence.— Ford 9:219. (1808.)

EMBARGO, Weapon for Peace.— The great leading object of the [Congress] was, and ours in execution of it ought to be, to give complete effect to the embargo laws. They have bidden agriculture, commerce, navigation, to bow before that object, to be nothing when in competition with it. Finding all their endeavors at general rules to be evaded, they finally gave us the power of detention as the panacea, and I am clear we ought to use it freely that we may, by a fair experiment, know the power of this great weapon, the embargo.—To Albert Gallatin. Bergh 12:52. (1808.)

EMBARGO, Violations of.—The Tories of Boston openly threaten insurrection if their importation of flour is stopped. The next post will stop it. I fear your Governor is not up to the tone of these parricides, and I hope, on the first symptom of an open opposition to the law by force, you will fly to the scene and aid in suppressing any commotion. —To Henry Dearborn (Secretary of War). Bergh 12:119. (1808.)

This embargo law is certainly the most embarrassing one we have ever had to execute. I did not expect a crop of so sudden and rank growth of fraud and open opposition by force could have grown up in the United States.—To Albert Gallatin. Bergh 12:122. (1808.)

The pressure of the embargo, although sensibly felt by every description of our fellow citizens, has yet been cheerfully borne by most of them under the conviction that it was a temporary evil, and a necessary one to save us from greater and more permanent evils— the loss of property and surrender of rights. But it would have been more cheerfully borne but for the knowledge that, while honest men were religiously observing it, the unprincipled along our seacoast and frontiers were fraudulently evading it; and that in some parts they had even dared to break through it openly, by an armed force too powerful to be opposed by the collector and his assistants. To put an end to this scandalous insubordination to the laws, the [Congress] has authorized the President to empower proper persons to employ militia, for preventing or suppressing armed or riotous assemblages of persons resisting the customhouse officers in the exercise of their duties, or opposing or violating the embargo laws.—Ford 9:237. (1809.)

EMBARGO, Letters of Marque and Reprisal to Follow Repeal of.—The House of Representatives passed last night a bill for the meeting of Congress on the 22nd of May. This substantially decides the course they mean to pursue; that is, to let the embargo continue till then, when it will cease, and letters of marque and reprisal be issued against such nations as shall not then have repealed their obnoxious edicts.—Ford 9:238. (1809.)

EMBARGO. See also NONIMPORTATION.

EMIGRATION, Rights Not Affected by.—Our emigration from England to this country gave her no more rights over us than the emigrations of the Danes and Saxons gave to the present authorities of the mother country over England.—Autobiography. Bergh 1:11. (1821.)

EMIGRATION. See also EXPATRIATION; IMMIGRATION.

ENEMIES, Political.—In public life, a man whose political principles have any decided character, and who has energy enough to give them effect, must always expect to encounter political hostility from those of adverse principles.—Bergh 12:9. (1808.)

Men of energy of character must have enemies, because there are two sides to every question; and [when such men take] one with decision, and [act] on it with effect, those who take the other will, of course, be hostile in proportion as they feel that effect.—To John Adams. Bergh 15:109. (1817.)

Dr. [Benjamin] Franklin had many political enemies, as every character must which, with decision enough to have opinions, has energy and talent to give them effect on the feelings of the adversary opinion.—Ford 10:116. (1818.)

ENGLAND, Constitution of.—The first principle of a good government is, certainly, a distribution of its powers into executive, judiciary, and legislative, and a subdivision of the latter into two or three branches. It is a good step gained when it is proved that the English constitution, acknowledged to be better than all which have preceded it, is only better in proportion as it has approached nearer to this distribution of powers. From this, the last step is easy, to show by a comparison of our constitutions with that of England how much more perfect they are.—Ford 4:454. (1787.)

ENGLAND, Influence of, in the United States.—Our laws, language, religion, politics, and manners are so deeply laid in English foundations that we shall never cease to consider their history as a part of ours, and to study ours in that as its origin.— Bergh 12:405. (1810.)

[The English] can do us, as enemies, more harm than any other nation; and in peace and in war, they have more means of disturbing us internally. Their merchants established among us, the bonds by which our own are chained to their feet, and the banking combinations interwoven with the whole have shown the extent of their control, even during a war with her. They are the workers of all the embarrassments our finances have experienced during the war. Declaring themselves bankrupt, they have been able still to chain the government to a dependence on them, and had the war continued they would have reduced us to the inability to command a single dollar. . . . This is the British influence to which I am an enemy, and which we must subject to our government, or it will subject us to that of Britain.—Bergh 14:286. (1815.)

ENGLAND, Friendship with.— There is not a nation on the globe with whom I have more earnestly wished a friendly intercourse on equal conditions. On no other [conditions] would I hold out the hand of friendship to any. I know that their creatures represent me as personally an enemy to England. But fools only can believe this, or those who think me a fool. I am an enemy to her insults and injuries. I am an enemy to the flagitious principles of her administration, and to those which govern her conduct towards other nations. But would she give to morality some place in her political code, and especially would she exercise decency, and at least neutral passions towards us, there is not, I repeat it, a people on earth with whom I would sacrifice so much to be in friendship.—Bergh 14:285. (1815.)

No two nations on earth can be so helpful to each other as friends, nor so hurtful as enemies. And in spite of their insolence, I have ever wished for an honorable and cordial amity with them as a nation.—Ford 10:155. (1820.)

ENGLAND, Kindred Ties with.— Were [the English people] under a government which should treat us with justice and equity, I should myself feel with great strength the ties which bind us together, of origin, language, laws, and manners; and I am persuaded the two people would become in future as it was with the ancient Greeks, among whom it was reproachful for Greek to be found fighting against Greek in a foreign army.—To John Adams. Bergh 15:85. (1816.)

ENGLAND, Reform in.—I am in hopes a purer nation will result and a purer government be instituted, one which, instead of endeavoring to make us their natural enemies, will see in us what we really are, their natural friends and brethren, and more interested in a fraternal connection with them than with any other nation on earth.—To John Adams. Bergh 15:86. (1816.)

ENGLAND, Influence of George III on U.S. Relations with.—Circumstances have nourished between our kindred countries angry dispositions which both ought long since to have banished from their bosoms. I have ever considered a cordial affection as the first interest of both. No nation on earth can hurt us so much as yours, none be more useful to you than ours. The obstacle, we have believed, was in the obstinate and unforgiving temper of your late King, and a continuance of his prejudices kept up from habit after he was withdrawn from power. I hope I now see symptoms of sounder views in your government, in which I know it will be cordially met by ours, as it would have been by every administration which has existed under our present Constitution. None desired it more cordially than myself, whatever different opinions were impressed on your government by a party who wishes to have its weight in their scale as its exclusive friends.—Bergh 15:303. (1820.)

ENGLAND. See also COLONIES (American); GEORGE III.

ENTAIL, Preamble to Bill Abolishing.—Whereas the perpetuation of property in certain families by means of gifts made to them in fee simple is contrary to good policy, tends to deceive fair traders who give credit on the visible possession of such estates, discourages the holder thereof from taking care and improving the same, and sometimes does injury to the morals of youth by rendering them independent of, and disobedient to, their parents; and whereas the former method of docking such estates tail by special act of assembly, formed for every particular case, employed very much the time of the legislature, was burdensome to the public, and also to the individual who made application for such acts, Be it enacted, [etc.]—Ford 2:103. (1776.)

ENTAIL, Abolition of, in Virginia. —On the 12th [of October, 1776], I obtained leave [in the Virginia legislature] to bring in a bill declaring tenants in tail to hold their lands in fee simple. In the earlier times of the colony, when lands were to be obtained for little or nothing, some provident individuals procured large grants; and, desirous of founding great families for themselves, settled them on their descendants in fee tail. The transmission of this property from generation to generation, in the same name, raised up a distinct set of families who, being privileged by law in the perpetuation of their wealth, were thus formed into a patrician order, distinguished by the splendor and luxury of their establishments. From this order, too, the King habitually selected his counsellors of state; the hope of which distinction devoted the whole corps to the interests and will of the Crown.

To annul this privilege, and instead of an aristocracy of wealth, of more harm and danger than benefit to society, to make an opening for the aristocracy of virtue and talent, which nature has wisely provided for the direction of the interests of society, and scattered with equal hand through all its conditions, was deemed essential to a well-ordered republic. To effect it, no violence was necessary, no deprivation of natural right, but rather an enlargement of it by a repeal of the law. For this would authorize the present holder to divide the property among his children equally, as his affections were divided, and would place them, by natural generation, on the level of their fellow citizens.—Autobiography. Bergh 1:53. (1821.)

ENTAIL, Repeal of, Beneficial.— The repeal of the laws of entail would prevent the accumulation and perpetuation of wealth in select families, and preserve the soil of the country from being daily more and more absorbed in mortmain [property held in perpetuity].— Autobiography. Bergh 1:73. (1821.)

ENTAIL. See also INHERITANCES; PRIMOGENITURE.

EPICURUS, His Genuine Teachings Misrepresented.—I am an Epicurean. I consider the genuine (not the imputed) doctrines of Epicurus as containing everything rational in moral philosophy which Greece and Rome have left us. Epictetus, indeed, has given us what was good of the Stoics, all beyond of their dogmas being hypocrisy and grimace. Their great crime was in their calumnies of Epicurus and misrepresentations of his doctrines, in which we lament to see the candid character of Cicero engaging as an accomplice.—Ford 10:143. (1819.)

EPICURUS, Syllabus of His Doctrines.—[I send you] a syllabus of the doctrines of Epicurus:

Physical.—The Universe eternal.

Its parts, great and small, interchangeable.

Matter and Void alone.

Motion inherent in matter which is weighty and declining.

Eternal circulation of the elements of bodies.

Gods, an order of beings next superior to man, enjoying in their sphere their own felicities; but not meddling with the concerns of the scale of beings below them.

Moral.—Happiness the aim of life.

Virtue the foundation of happiness.

Utility the test of virtue.

Pleasure active and indolent.

Indolence is the absence of pain, the true felicity.

Active, consists in agreeable motion; it is not happiness, but the means to produce it.

Thus the absence of hunger is an article of felicity; eating the means to obtain it.

The *summum bonum* is to be not pained in body, nor troubled in mind —i.e., indolence of body, tranquility of mind.

To procure tranquility of mind we must avoid desire and fear, the two principal diseases of the mind.

Man is a free agent.

Virtue consists in: 1. Prudence. 2. Temperance. 3. Fortitude. 4. Justice.

To which are opposed: 1. Folly. 2. Desire. 3. Fear. 4. Deceit.
                                   —Ford 10:146. (1819.)

EQUAL RIGHTS, Aggression on.— No man has a natural right to commit aggression on the equal rights of another; and this is all from which the laws ought to restrain him.—Bergh 15:24. (1816.)

EQUAL RIGHTS, And Republican Government.— The true foundation of republican government is in the equal right of every citizen, in his person and property and in their management.—Ford 10:39. (1816.)

The equal rights of man and the happiness of every individual are now acknowledged to be the only legitimate objects of government. Modern times have the signal advantage, too, of having discovered the only device by which these rights can be secured, to wit, government by the people, acting not in person but by representatives chosen by themselves, that is to say, by every man of ripe years and sane mind who either contributes by his purse or person to the support of his country.—Bergh 15:482. (1823.)

EQUAL RIGHTS, Violated by Special Legislation.— To special legislation we are generally averse, lest a principle of favoritism should creep in and pervert that of equal rights. It has, however, been done on some occasions where a special national advantage has been expected to overweigh that of adherence to the general rule.—Bergh 15:139. (1817.)

EQUAL RIGHTS, Should Be Extended to All Men.— The basis of our [Virginia] constitution is in opposition to the principle of equal political rights, refusing to all but freeholders any participation in the natural right of self-government.... However nature may by mental or physical disqualifications have marked infants and the weaker sex for the protection rather than the direction of government, yet among the men who either pay or fight for their country, no line of right can be drawn.—Ford 10:303. (1824.)

EQUAL RIGHTS. See also NATURAL RIGHTS; RIGHTS; RIGHTS OF MAN.

EQUALITY, Constitutions and.— The foundation on which all [our constitutions] are built is the natural equality of man, the denial of every preeminence but that annexed to legal office, and particularly the denial of a preeminence by birth.— To George Washington. Ford 3:466. (1784.)

EQUALITY, Among American Citizens.— In America, no other distinction between man and man had ever been known but that of persons in office, exercising powers by authority of the laws, and private individuals. Among these last, the poorest laborer stood on equal ground with the wealthiest millionaire, and generally on a more favored one whenever their rights seemed to jar. It has been seen that a shoemaker or other artisan, removed by the voice of his country from his workbench into a chair of office, has instantly commanded all the respect and obedience which the laws ascribe to his office. But of distinction by birth or badge, they had no more idea than they had of the mode of existence in the moon or planets.

They had heard only that there were such, and knew that they must be wrong.—Bergh 17:88. (1786.)

ERROR, Truth vs.—Error has often prevailed by the assistance of power or force. Truth is the proper and sufficient antagonist to error.—Ford 2:102. (1776?)

Truth . . . is the proper and sufficient antagonist of error, and has nothing to fear from the conflict unless by human interposition disarmed of her natural weapons, free argument and debate; errors ceasing to be dangerous when it is permitted freely to contradict them.—Bill for Establishing Religious Freedom. Ford 2:239. (1779.)

ERROR, Value of Pointing Out.—I would be glad to know when any individual member [of Congress] thinks I have gone wrong in any instance. If I know myself, it would not excite ill blood in me, while it would assist to guide my conduct, perhaps to justify it, and to keep me to my duty, alert.—To James Madison. Ford 4:474. (1787.)

ERROR, The People and.—I am persuaded myself that the good sense of the people will always be found to be the best army. They may be led astray for a moment, but will soon correct themselves. The people are the only censors of their governors; and even their errors will tend to keep these to the true principles of their institution. To punish these errors too severely would be to suppress the only safeguard of the public liberty. The way to prevent these irregular interpositions of the people is to give

them full information of their affairs through the channel of the public papers, and to contrive that those papers should penetrate the whole mass of the people. The basis of our governments being the opinion of the people, the very first object should be to keep that right. . . . Cherish, therefore, the spirit of our people, and keep alive their attention. Do not be too severe upon their errors, but reclaim them by enlightening them.—Bergh 6:57. (1787.)

The people . . . will err sometimes and accidentally, but never designedly and with a systematic and persevering purpose of overthrowing the free principles of the government.—Bergh 15:483. (1823.)

ERROR, Toleration of.—Here [at the University of Virginia] we are not afraid to follow truth wherever it may lead, nor to tolerate any error so long as reason is left free to combat it.—Bergh 15:303. (1820.)

ETHICS, Jefferson's System of.—I have but one system of ethics for men and for nations—to be grateful, to be faithful to all engagements and under all circumstances, to be open and generous, promoting in the long run even the interests of both; and I am sure it promotes their happiness.—Ford 5:153. (1790.)

ETHICS, Supplements Law.—[I consider] ethics, as well as religion, as supplements to law in the government of man.—Bergh 16:19. (1824.)

ETHICS. See also MORALITY.

EUROPE, Jefferson's Estimate of.—Behold me at length on the vaunted scene of Europe! ... You are perhaps curious to know how this new scene has struck a savage of the mountains of America. Not advantageously, I assure you. I find the general fate of humanity here most deplorable. The truth of Voltaire's observation offers itself perpetually, that every man here must be either the hammer or the anvil. It is a true picture of that country to which they say we shall pass hereafter, and where we are to see God and his angels in splendor, and crowds of the damned trampled under their feet.

While the great mass of the people are thus suffering under physical and moral oppression, I have endeavored to examine more nearly the condition of the great, to appreciate the true value of the circumstances in their situation which dazzle the bulk of spectators, and especially to compare it with that degree of happiness which is enjoyed in America by every class of people. Intrigues of love occupy the younger, and [intrigues] of ambition the elder part of the great. Conjugal love having no existence among them, domestic happiness, of which that is the basis, is utterly unknown. In lieu of this are substituted pursuits which nourish and invigorate all our bad passions, and which offer only moments of ecstasy amidst days and months of restlessness and torment. Much, very much inferior, this, to the tranquil, permanent felicity with which domestic society in America blesses most of its inhabitants; leaving them to follow steadily those pursuits which

health and reason approve, and rendering truly delicious the intervals of those pursuits.

In science, the mass of the people are two centuries behind ours; their literati, half a dozen years before us. Books, really good, acquire just reputation in that time, and so become known to us, and communicate to us all their advances in knowledge. Is not this delay compensated by our being placed out of the reach of that swarm of nonsensical publications which issues daily from a thousand presses, and perishes almost in issuing?

With respect to what are termed polite manners, without sacrificing too much the sincerity of language, I would wish my countrymen to adopt just so much of European politeness as to be ready to make all those little sacrifices of self which really render European manners amiable, and relieve society from the disagreeable scenes to which rudeness often subjects it. Here it seems that a man might pass a life without encountering a single rudeness. In the pleasures of the table they are far before us, because with good taste they unite temperance. They do not terminate the most sociable meals by transforming themselves into brutes. I have never yet seen a man drunk in France, even among the lowest of the people.

Were I to proceed to tell you how much I enjoy their architecture, sculpture, painting, music, I should want words. It is in these arts they shine. The last of them, particularly, is an enjoyment, the deprivation of which, with us, cannot be calculated. I am almost ready to say it is the only thing which from my heart I envy them, and which, in spite of all the authority of the Decalogue, I do covet.—Bergh 5:152. (1785.)

EUROPE, Ignorance in.—Ignorance, superstition, poverty, and oppression of body and mind, in every form, are so firmly settled on the mass of the people that their redemption from them can never be hoped. If all the sovereigns of Europe were to set themselves to work to emancipate the minds of their subjects from their present ignorance and prejudices, and that as zealously as they now endeavor the contrary, a thousand years would not place them on that high ground on which our common people are now setting out. Ours could not have been so fairly placed under the control of the common sense of the people had they not been separated from their parent stock, and kept from contamination, either from them or the other people of the old world, by the intervention of so wide an ocean. To know the worth of this, one must see the want of it here.—To George Wythe. Bergh 5:396. (1786.)

EUROPE, Eventually to Enjoy Representative Government.—That same light from our West seems to have spread and illuminated the very engines employed to extinguish it [i.e., the nations of Europe]. It has given them a glimmering of their rights and their power. The idea of representative government has taken root and

growth among them. Their masters feel it, and are saving themselves by timely offers of this modification of their own powers. Belgium, Prussia, Poland, Lombardy, etc. are now offered a representative organization—illusive, probably, at first, but it will grow into power in the end.—To John Adams. Bergh 14:395. (1816.)

The light which has been shed on the mind of man through the civilized world has given it a new direction, from which no human power can divert it. The sovereigns of Europe who are wise, or have wise counsellors, see this, and bend to the breeze which blows; the unwise alone stiffen and meet its inevitable crush.—To Marquis de Lafayette. Bergh 15:299. (1820.)

The appeal to the rights of man which had been made in the United States was taken up by France first of the European nations. From her the spirit has spread over those of the south. The tyrants of the north have allied against it, but it is irresistible. Their opposition will only multiply its millions of human victims; their own satellites will catch it, and the condition of man through the civilized world will be finally and greatly ameliorated.— Autobiography. Bergh 1:158. (1821.)

A first attempt to recover the right of self-government may fail; so may a second, a third, etc. But as a younger and more instructed race comes on, the sentiment becomes more and more intuitive, and a fourth, a fifth, or some subsequent one of the ever-renewed attempts will ultimately succeed. In France, the first effort was defeated by Robespierre, the second by Bonaparte, the third by Louis XVIII and his holy allies; another is yet to come, and all Europe, Russia excepted, has caught the spirit, and all will attain representative government, more or less perfect.... To attain all this, however, rivers of blood must yet flow, and years of desolation pass over; yet the object is worth rivers of blood and years of desolation. For what inheritance so valuable can man leave to his posterity? You and I shall look down from another world on these glorious achievements to man, which will add to the joys even of heaven. —To John Adams. Ford 10:270. (1823.)

EUROPE, Political Doctrines of.— The doctrines of Europe [in the eighteenth century] were that men in numerous associations cannot be restrained within the limits of order and justice but by forces physical and moral, wielded over them by authorities independent of their will. Hence their organization of kings, hereditary nobles, and priests. Still further to constrain the brute force of the people, they deem it necessary to keep them down by hard labor, poverty, and ignorance, and to take from them, as from bees, so much of their earnings as that unremitting labor shall be necessary to obtain a sufficient surplus barely to sustain a scanty and miserable life. And these earnings they apply to maintain their privileged orders in splendor and idleness, to fascinate

the eyes of the people and excite in them a humble adoration and submission, as to an order of superior beings.—Bergh 15:440. (1823.)

EUROPE. See also FOREIGN AFFAIRS; FRANCE.

EVILS, Good from.—When great evils happen, I am in the habit of looking out for what good may arise from them as consolations to us, and Providence has in fact so established the order of things as that most evils are the means of producing some good.—Ford 7:458. (1800.)

EVILS, Choice of.—It is the melancholy law of human societies to be compelled sometimes to choose a great evil in order to ward off a greater.—Bergh 14:213. (1814.)

EXCISE LAW, Odious.—[The] accumulation of debt ... [created by the federal government's assumption of states' debts] has obliged [us] ... to resort to an excise law of odious character with the people, partial in its operation, unproductive unless enforced by arbitrary and vexatious means, and committing the authority of the government in parts where resistance is most probable, and coercion least practicable.—To President Washington. Ford 6:2. (1792.)

EXCISE LAW, Resisted.—The people in the western parts of this state [Pennsylvania] have been to the excise officer and threatened to burn his house, etc. They were blackened and otherwise disguised, so as to be unknown. He has resigned, and [Alexander Hamilton] says there is no possibility of getting the law executed there, and that

probably the evil will spread. A proclamation is to be issued, and another
instance of my being forced to
appear to approve what I have condemned uniformly from its first
conception.—To James Madison.
Ford 6:261. (1793.)

EXCISE LAW, Infernal.—The excise law is an infernal one. The first
error was to admit it by the Constitution; the second, to act on that
admission; the third and last will be
to make it the instrument of dismembering the Union, and setting
us all afloat to choose which part of
it we will adhere to.—Ford 6:518.
(1794.)

EXCISE LAW, Unnecessary.—The
excise system, which I considered
as prematurely and unnecessarily
introduced, I was ...glad to see fall.
It was evident that our existing
taxes were *then* equal to our existing
debts. It was clearly foreseen also
that the surplus from excise would
only become aliment for useless
offices, and would be swallowed in
idleness by those whom it would
withdraw from useful industry.—
Ford 10:251. (1823.)

EXECUTIVE, Tyranny of the.—The
executive in our governments is not
the sole, it is scarcely the principal,
object of my jealousy. The tyranny
of the legislatures is the most
formidable dread at present and will
be for many years. That of the
executive will come in its turn, but it
will be at a remote period.—To
James Madison. Ford 5:83. (1789.)

EXECUTIVE, And the People.—
The people...are not qualified to

exercise themselves the executive
department, but they are qualified
to name the person who shall
exercise it. With us, therefore, they
choose this officer every four
years.—Bergh 7:422. (1789.)

EXECUTIVE, Control over the.—
The executive [branch of the gov-
ernment], possessing the rights of
self-government from nature,
cannot be controlled in the exercise
of them but by a law, passed in the
forms of the Constitution.—Ford
5:209. (1790.)

EXECUTIVE, Preeminent in War.—
In times of peace the people look
most to their representatives; but in
war, to the executive solely.—Ford
9:272. (1810.)

EXECUTIVE, Single vs. Plural.—
When our present government was
first established we had many
doubts on this question, and many
leanings towards a supreme executive council. It happened that at that
time the experiment of such a one
was commenced in France, while a
single executive was under trial
here. We watched the motions and
effects of these two rival plans....
The experiment in France failed
after a short course, and not from
any circumstances peculiar to the
times or nation, but from those
internal jealousies and dissensions
in the Directory which will ever
arise among men equal in power,
without a principal to decide and
control their differences.

We had tried a similar experiment
in 1784 by establishing a committee
of the states, composed of a member
from every state, then thirteen, to

exercise the executive functions during the recess of Congress. They fell immediately into schisms and dissensions, which became at length so inveterate as to render all co-operation among them impracticable; they dissolved themselves, abandoning the helm of government, and it continued without a head until Congress met the ensuing winter. This was then imputed to the temper of two or three individuals, but the wise ascribed it to the nature of man.

The failure of the French Directory, and from the same cause, seems to have authorized a belief that the form of a plurality, however promising in theory, is impracticable with men constituted with the ordinary passions; while the tranquil and steady tenor of our single executive, during a course of twenty-two years of the most tempestuous times the history of the world has ever presented, gives a rational hope that this important problem is at length solved. Aided by the counsels of a cabinet of heads of departments, originally four but now five, with whom the President consults, either singly or altogether, he has the benefit of their wisdom and information, brings their views to one center, and produces a unity of action and direction in all the branches of the government.—Ford 9:306. (1811.)

EXECUTIVE. See also FEDERAL GOVERNMENT; PRESIDENCY; PRESIDENT; VETO.

EXECUTIVE ORDERS, Danger of. —I told [President Washington] ...

that if the equilibrium of the three great bodies, legislative, executive, and judiciary, could be preserved, if the legislature could be kept independent, I should never fear the result of such a government; but that I could not but be uneasy when I saw that the executive had swallowed up the legislative branch.— The Anas. Bergh 1:318. (1792.)

EXERCISE, Recommendations for Physical.—Give about two [hours] every day to exercise, for health must not be sacrificed to learning. A strong body makes the mind strong. As to the species of exercise, I advise the gun. While this gives a moderate exercise to the body, it gives boldness, enterprise, and independence to the mind. Games played with the ball, and others of that nature, are too violent for the body, and stamp no character on the mind. Let your gun, therefore, be the constant companion of your walks. Never think of taking a book with you. The object of walking is to relax the mind. You should therefore not permit yourself even to think while you walk, but divert yourself by the objects surrounding you. Walking is the best possible exercise. Habituate yourself to walk very far. The Europeans value themselves on having subdued the horse to the uses of man; but I doubt whether we have not lost more than we have gained by the use of this animal. No one has occasioned so much the degeneracy of the human body. An Indian goes on foot nearly as far in a day, for a long journey, as an enfeebled white does on his horse;

and he will tire the best horses. There is no habit you will value so much as that of walking far without fatigue. I would advise you to take your exercise in the afternoon; not because it is the best time for exercise, for certainly it is not, but because it is the best time to spare from your studies; and habit will soon reconcile it to health, and render it nearly as useful as if you gave to that the more precious hours of the day. A little walk of half an hour in the morning, when you first rise, is advisable also. It shakes off sleep, and produces other good effects in the animal economy. Rise at a fixed and an early hour, and go to bed at a fixed and early hour also. Sitting up late at night is injurious to the health, and not useful to the mind.—Bergh 5:85. (1785.)

EXERCISE, Walking the Best.—Of all exercises, walking is the best.... No one knows, till he tries, how easily a habit of walking is acquired. A person who never walked three miles will, in the course of a month, become able to walk fifteen or twenty without fatigue. I have known some great walkers, and had particular accounts of many more, and I never knew or heard of one who was not healthy and long-lived. —Ford 4:293. (1786.)

EXERCISE, Health and.—You are not to consider yourself as un-employed while taking exercise. That is necessary for your health, and health is the first of all objects. —Ford 4:372. (1787.)

Exercise and recreation are as necessary as reading; I will say

rather more necessary, because health is worth more than learning. —Ford 5:180. (1790.)

EXERCISE. See also HEALTH.

EXPATRIATION, Great Britain and.—Every attempt of Great Britain to enforce her principle of "Once a subject, always a subject" beyond the case of *her own subjects* ought to be repelled.—Ford 8:251. (1803.)

EXPATRIATION, A Natural Right. —I hold the right of expatriation to be inherent in every man by the laws of nature, and incapable of being rightfully taken from him even by the united will of every other person in the nation. If the laws have pro-vided no particular mode by which the right of expatriation may be exercised, the individual may do it by any effectual and unequivocal act or declaration. The laws of Virginia have provided a mode; Mr. Cooper is said to have exercised his right solemnly and exactly according to that mode, and to have departed from the commonwealth, where-upon the law declares that "he shall henceforth be deemed no citizen." Returning afterward he returns an alien, and must proceed to make himself a citizen, if he desires it, as every other alien does.... The general government has nothing to do with this question. Congress may, by the Constitution, "establish an uniform rule of naturalization," that is, by what rule an alien may become a citizen; but they cannot take from a citizen his natural right of divesting himself of the character of a citizen by expatriation.—Ford 8:458. (1806.)

EXPATRIATION. See also EMI-GRATION.

F

FAMILY, Handling Difficult Relationships in.—If the lady [your father-in-law's new wife] has anything difficult in her dispositions, avoid what is rough and attach her good qualities to you. Consider what are otherwise as a bad stop in your harpsichord; do not touch on it, but make yourself happy with the good ones. Every human being, my dear, must thus be viewed according to what it is good for, for none of us, no not one, is perfect; and were we to love none who had imperfections, this world would be a desert for our love. All we can do is to make the best of our friends, love and cherish what is good in them, and keep out of the way of what is bad; but no more think of rejecting them for it than of throwing away a piece of music for a flat passage or two. Your situation will require peculiar attentions and respect to both parties. Let no proof be too much for either your patience or acquiescence. Be you, my dear, the link of love, union, and peace for the whole family. The world will give you the more credit for it in proportion to the difficulty of the task; and your own happiness will be the greater as you perceive that you promote that of others.— To Martha Jefferson Randolph. Betts & Bear, p. 60. (1790.)

FAMILY, Children a Blessing.— [Children are] undoubtedly the keystone of the arch of matrimonial happiness.—To Martha Jefferson Randolph. Betts & Bear, p. 71. (1791.)

I sincerely congratulate you on the addition to your family. The good old book [i.e., the Bible], speaking of children, says, "Happy is the man that hath his quiver full of them" [Psalms 127:5].—Ford 9:144. (1807.)

FAMILY, Necessary for Happiness. —It is in the love of one's family only that heartfelt happiness is known.— To Mary Jefferson Eppes. Betts & Bear, p. 210. (1801.)

By a law of our nature, we cannot be happy without the endearing connections of a family.—Bergh 12:311. (1809.)

FAMILY. See also GRANDCHILDREN; HAPPINESS, Domestic; HOME; MARRIAGE.

FARMERS, Virtue of.—Those who labor in the earth are the chosen people of God, if ever He had a chosen people, whose breasts He has made His peculiar deposit for substantial and genuine virtue. It is the focus in which he keeps alive that sacred fire which otherwise might escape from the face of the earth. Corruption of morals in the mass of cultivators is a phenomenon of which no age nor nation has furnished an example.—*Notes on Virginia.* Bergh 2:229. (1782.)

FARMERS, Valuable Citizens.— Cultivators of the earth are the most valuable citizens. They are the most vigorous, the most independent, the

428   *The Real Thomas Jefferson*

most virtuous, and they are tied to their country, and wedded to its liberty and interests, by the most lasting bonds. As long, therefore, as they can find employment in this line, I would not convert them into mariners, artisans, or anything else.—To John Jay. Bergh 5:93. (1785.)

FARMERS. See also AGRICULTURE.

FAST DAY, Appointment of a.— [After the promulgation of the Boston Port Bill in 1774] we [the young leaders in the Virginia House of Burgesses] were under the conviction of the necessity of arousing our people from the lethargy into which they had fallen as to passing events; and thought that the appointment of a day of general fasting and prayer would be most likely to call up and alarm their attention. No example of such a solemnity had existed since the days of our distresses in the war of 1755, since which a new generation had grown up....

We cooked up a resolution...for appointing the 1st day of June, on which the port bill was to commence, for a day of fasting, humiliation, and prayer, to implore Heaven to avert from us the evils of civil war, to inspire us with firmness in support of our rights, and to turn the hearts of the King and Parliament to moderation and justice....

We returned home, and in our several counties invited the clergy to meet assemblies of the people on the 1st of June, to perform the ceremonies of the day and to address

to them discourses suited to the occasion. The people met generally, with anxiety and alarm in their countenances, and the effect of the day through the whole colony was like a shock of electricity, arousing every man and placing him erect and solidly on his center.—Autobiography. Bergh 1:9. (1820.)

FAVORITISM, Justice and.—Deal out justice without partiality or favoritism.—Ford 5:492. (1792.)

FAVORITISM, Equal Rights vs.— To special legislation we are generally averse, lest a principle of favoritism should creep in and pervert that of equal rights.—Bergh 15:139. (1817.)

FEDERAL AID, Evils of.—Have you considered all the consequences of your proposition respecting post roads? I view it as a source of boundless patronage to the executive, jobbing to members of Congress and their friends, and a bottomless abyss of public money. You will begin by only appropriating the surplus of the post office revenues; but the other revenues will soon be called into their aid, and it will be a source of eternal scramble among the members, who can get the most money wasted in their state; and they will always get most who are meanest. We have thought, hitherto, that the roads of a state could not be so well administered even by the state legislature as by the magistracy of the county, on the spot. How will they be when a member of New Hampshire is to mark out a road for Georgia? Does the power to *establish* post roads, given you by the

Constitution, mean that you shall *make* the roads, or only *select* from those already made, those on which there shall be a post? If the term be equivocal (and I really do not think it so), which is the safest construction? —To James Madison. Bergh 9:324. (1796.)

FEDERAL GOVERNMENT, Coercion of States by.—There never will be money in the treasury till the confederacy shows its teeth. The states must see the rod; perhaps it must be felt by some of them. I am persuaded all of them would rejoice to see every one obliged to furnish its contributions. It is not the difficulty of furnishing them which beggars the treasury, but the fear that others will not furnish as much. Every rational citizen must wish to see an effective instrument of coercion.—Ford 4:265. (1786.)

The coercive powers supposed to be wanting in the federal head, I am of opinion they possess by the law of nature, which authorizes one party to an agreement to compel the other to performance. A delinquent state makes itself a party against the rest of the confederacy.—Bergh 6:219. (1787.)

It has been so often said as to be generally believed, that Congress have no power by the [Articles of] Confederation to enforce anything; for example, contributions of money. It was not necessary to give them that power expressly; they have it by the law of nature. When two parties make a compact, there results to each a power of compelling the other to execute it. Compulsion was never so easy as in our case, where a single frigate would soon levy on the commerce of any state the deficiency of its contributions; nor more safe than in the hands of Congress, which has always shown that it would wait, as it ought to do, to the last extremities before it would execute any of its powers which are disagreeable.—Bergh 6:227. (1787.)

Some peaceable means should be contrived for the federal head to force compliance on the part of the states.—To George Wythe. Bergh 6:300. (1787.)

FEDERAL GOVERNMENT, Jefferson's Proposals for Reorganizing.—To make us one nation as to foreign concerns, and keep us distinct in domestic ones, gives the outline of the proper division of powers between the general and particular governments. But to enable the federal head to exercise the powers given it to best advantage, it should be organized, as the particular ones are, into legislative, executive, and judiciary. The first and last are already separated. The second should also be. When last with Congress, I often proposed to members to do this by making of the committee of the states an executive committee during the recess of Congress, and during its sessions to appoint a committee to receive and dispatch all executive business, so that Congress itself should meddle only with what should be legislative. But I question if any Congress (much less all successively) can have self-denial enough to go through with this distribution. The distribution, then, should be imposed on them.—To James Madison. Bergh 6:9. (1786.)

You ask me in your letter what ameliorations I think necessary in our federal constitution.... My own general idea [is] that the states should severally preserve their sovereignty in whatever concerns themselves alone, and that whatever may concern another state, or any foreign nation, should be made a part of the federal sovereignty; that the exercise of the federal sovereignty should be divided among three several bodies, legislative, executive, and judiciary, as the state sovereignties are; and that some peaceable means should be contrived for the federal head to force compliance on the part of the states.—To George Wythe. Bergh 6:299. (1787.)

FEDERAL GOVERNMENT, Watchfulness over.—Our political machine is now pretty well wound up; but are the spirits of our people sufficiently wound down to let it work glibly? I trust it is too soon for that, and that we have many centuries to come yet before my countrymen cease to bear their government hard in hand.—Bergh 7:99. (1788.)

We, I hope, shall adhere to our republican government, and keep it to its original principles by narrowly watching it.—Bergh 9:45. (1793.)

FEDERAL GOVERNMENT, Constitutional Limitations on.—I consider the foundation of the Constitution as laid on this ground: That "all powers not delegated to the

United States by the Constitution, nor prohibited by it to the states, are reserved to the states or to the people."... To take a single step beyond the boundaries thus specially drawn around the powers of Congress is to take possession of a boundless field of power, no longer susceptible of any definition.— Bergh 3:146. (1791.)

FEDERAL GOVERNMENT, Has No Authority to Exceed Constitution.—The several states composing the United States of America are not united on the principle of unlimited submission to their general government; but ... by a compact under the style and title of a Constitution for the United States, and of amendments thereto, they constituted a general government for special purposes [and] delegated to that government certain definite powers, reserving, each state to itself, the residuary mass of right to their own self-government; and ... whensoever the general government assumes undelegated powers, its acts are unauthoritative, void, and of no force.... To this compact each state acceded as a state, and is an integral party, its co-states forming, as to itself, the other party.... The government created by this compact was not made the exclusive or final judge of the extent of the powers delegated to itself, since that would have made its discretion, and not the Constitution, the measure of its powers; but ... as in all other cases of compact among powers having no common judge, each party has an equal right to judge for itself, as well of infractions as of the mode and measure of redress.—Kentucky Resolutions. Bergh 17:379. (1798.)

The construction applied by the general government (as is evidenced by sundry of their proceedings) to those parts of the Constitution of the United States which delegate to Congress a power "to lay and collect taxes, duties, imposts, and excises, to pay the debts and provide for the common defense and general welfare of the United States," and "to make all laws which shall be necessary and proper for carrying into execution the powers vested by the Constitution in the government of the United States, or in any department or officer thereof," goes to the destruction of all limits prescribed to their power by the Constitution. ...Words meant by the instrument to be subsidiary only to the execution of limited powers ought not to be so construed as themselves to give unlimited powers, nor a part to be so taken as to destroy the whole residue of that instrument.—Kentucky Resolutions. Bergh 17:385. (1798.)

To take from the states all the powers of self-government and transfer them to a general and consolidated government, without regard to the special delegations and reservations solemnly agreed to in that compact, is not for the peace, happiness, or prosperity of these states; and...therefore this commonwealth [Kentucky] is determined, as it doubts not its co-states are, to submit to undelegated, and consequently unlimited, powers in

no man or body of men on earth.... Where powers are assumed which have not been delegated, a nullification of the act is the rightful remedy. ...Every state has a natural right in cases not within the compact...to nullify of their own authority all assumptions of power by others within their limits.... Without this right, they would be under the dominion, absolute and unlimited, of whosoever might exercise this right of judgment for them.—Kentucky Resolutions. Bergh 17:386. (1798.)

FEDERAL GOVERNMENT, Borrowing by, Should Be Unconstitutional.—I wish it were possible to obtain a single amendment to our Constitution. I would be willing to depend on that alone for the reduction of the administration of our government to the genuine principles of its Constitution; I mean an additional article taking from the federal government the power of borrowing.—Bergh 10:64. (1798.)

FEDERAL GOVERNMENT, Should Be Frugal and Simple.—I am for a government rigorously frugal and simple, applying all the possible savings of the public revenue to the discharge of the national debt; and not for a multiplication of officers and salaries merely to make partisans, and for increasing by every device the public debt.—To Elbridge Gerry. Bergh 10:77. (1799.)

Let the general government be reduced to foreign concerns only, and let our affairs be disentangled from those of all other nations, except as to commerce, which the merchants will manage the better the more they are left free to manage for themselves, and our general government may be reduced to a very simple organization, and a very inexpensive one; a few plain duties to be performed by a few servants.—Bergh 10:168. (1800.)

What . . . is necessary to make us a happy and prosperous people? . . . A wise and frugal government, which shall restrain men from injuring one another, which shall leave them otherwise free to regulate their own pursuits of industry and improvement, and shall not take from the mouth of labor the bread it has earned. This is the sum of good government, and this is necessary to close the circle of our felicities.— First Inaugural Address. Bergh 3:320. (1801.)

The multiplication of public offices, increase of expense beyond income, [and] growth and entailment of a public debt are indications soliciting the employment of the pruning knife.—Bergh 15:325. (1821.)

FEDERAL GOVERNMENT, Danger of Transferring States' Functions to.—Our country is too large to have all its affairs directed by a single government. Public servants at such a distance, and from under the eye of their constituents, must, from the circumstance of distance, be unable to administer and overlook all the details necessary for the good government of the citizens; and the same circumstance, by rendering detection impossible to their constituents, will invite the public agents to corruption, plunder, and waste. And I do verily believe that if the principle were to prevail of a common law being in force in the United States (which principle possesses the general government at once of all the powers of the state governments, and reduces us to a single consolidated government), it would become the most corrupt government on the earth. . . . What an augmentation of the field for jobbing, speculating, plundering, office-building and office-hunting would be produced by an assumption of all the state powers into the hands of the general government! The true theory of our Constitution is surely the wisest and best, that the states are independent as to everything within themselves, and united as to everything respecting foreign nations.—Bergh 10:167. (1800.)

When all government, domestic and foreign, in little as in great things, shall be drawn to Washington as the center of all power, it will render powerless the checks provided of one government on another, and will become as venal and oppressive as the government from which we separated.—Bergh 15:332. (1821.)

If ever this vast country is brought under a single government, it will be one of the most extensive corruption, indifferent and incapable of a wholesome care over so wide a spread of surface. This will not be borne, and you will have to choose between reformation and revolution. If I know the spirit of this country, the one or the other is inevitable.—Bergh 15:389. (1822.)

FEDERAL GOVERNMENT, Guiding Principles of.—About to enter, fellow citizens, on the exercise of duties which comprehend everything dear and valuable to you, it is proper that you should understand what I deem the essential principles of our government, and consequently those which ought to shape its administration. I will compress them within the narrowest compass they will bear, stating the general principle but not all its limitations. Equal and exact justice to all men, of whatever state or persuasion, religious or political; peace, commerce, and honest friendship with all nations, entangling alliances with none; the support of the state governments in all their rights, as the most competent administrations for our domestic concerns and the surest bulwark against anti-republican tendencies; the preservation of the general government in its whole Constitutional vigor, as the sheet anchor of our peace at home and safety abroad; a jealous care of the right of election by the people—a mild and safe corrective of abuses, which are lopped by the sword of revolution where peaceable remedies are unprovided; absolute acquiescence in the decisions of the majority—the vital principle of republics, from which there is no appeal but to force, the vital principle and immediate parent of despotism; a well-disciplined militia —our best reliance in peace and for the first moments of war, till regu-

lars may relieve them; the supremacy of the civil over the military authority; economy in the public expense, that labor may be lightly burdened; the honest payment of our debts and sacred preservation of the public faith; encouragement of agriculture, and of commerce as its handmaid; the diffusion of information, and the arraignment of all abuses at the bar of public reason; freedom of religion; freedom of the press; freedom of person under the protection of the *habeas corpus;* and trial by juries impartially selected. These principles form the bright constellation which has gone before us and guided our steps through an age of revolution and reformation. The wisdom of our sages and the blood of our heroes have been devoted to their attainment. They should be the creed of our political faith, the text of civil instruction, the touchstone by which to try the services of those we trust; and should we wander from them in moments of error or alarm, let us hasten to retrace our steps and to regain the road which alone leads to peace, liberty, and safety.—First Inaugural Address. Bergh 3:321. (1801.)

To cultivate peace and maintain commerce and navigation in all their lawful enterprises; to foster our fisheries and nurseries of navigation and for the nurture of man, and protect the manufactures adapted to our circumstances; to preserve the faith of the nation by an exact discharge of its debts and contracts, expend the public money with the

Jefferson in December 1791 (age 48).
Portrait by Charles Willson Peale.

same care and economy we would practice with our own, and impose on our citizens no unnecessary burden; to keep in all things within the pale of our Constitutional powers, and cherish the federal union as the only rock of our safety—these are the landmarks by which we are to guide ourselves in all our proceedings. By continuing to make these our rule of action, we shall endear to our countrymen the true principles of their Constitution, and promote a union of sentiment and of action equally auspicious to their happiness and safety.—Second Annual Message to Congress. Bergh 3:348. (1802.)

FEDERAL GOVERNMENT, Its Proper Relationship with State Governments.—It is a fatal heresy to suppose that either our state governments are superior to the federal, or the federal to the states. The people, to whom all authority belongs, have divided the powers of government into two distinct departments, the leading characters of which are foreign and domestic; and they have appointed for each a distinct set of functionaries. These they have made coordinate, checking and balancing each other, like the three cardinal departments in the individual states; each equally supreme as to the powers delegated to itself, and neither authorized ultimately to decide what belongs to itself or to its coparcener in government; as independent, in fact, as different nations.—Bergh 15:328. (1821.)

With respect to our state and federal governments, I do not think their relations correctly understood by foreigners. They generally suppose the former subordinate to the latter. But this is not the case. They are coordinate departments of one simple and integral whole. To the state governments are reserved all legislation and administration in affairs which concern their own citizens only, and to the federal government is given whatever concerns foreigners, or the citizens of other states; these functions alone being made federal. The one is the domestic, the other the foreign branch of the same government; neither having control over the other, but within its own department.—Bergh 16:47. (1824.)

FEDERAL GOVERNMENT, Anticipated Course to Destruction of.—Our government is now taking so steady a course as to show by what road it will pass to destruction, to wit, by consolidation first, and then corruption, its necessary consequence. The engine of consolidation will be the federal judiciary; the two other branches the corrupting and corrupted instruments.—Bergh 15:341. (1821.)

FEDERAL GOVERNMENT. See also CENTRALIZATION; CONGRESS; CONSTITUTION (U.S.); EXECUTIVE; GOVERNMENT; JUDICIARY; LEGISLATURES; PRESIDENCY; PRESIDENT; SENATE; SEPARATION OF POWERS; STATES; STATES' RIGHTS; SUPREME COURT.

FEDERALIST PARTY, British Influence on.—A party has risen among us, or rather has come among us, which is endeavoring to separate us from all friendly connection with France, to unite our destinies with those of Great Britain, and to assimilate our government to theirs. Our lenity [leniency] in permitting the return of the old Tories gave the first body to this party; they have increased by large importations of British merchants and factors, by American merchants dealing on British capital, and by stock dealers and banking companies who, by the aid of a paper system, are enriching themselves to the ruin of the country, and swaying the government by their possession of the printing presses, which their wealth commands, and by other means, not always honorable to the character of our countrymen. Hitherto, their influence and their system have been irresistible, and they have raised up an executive power which is too strong for the [Congress]. But I flatter myself they have passed their zenith. The people, while these things were doing, were lulled into rest and security from a cause which no longer exists. No prepossessions now will shut their ears to truth. They begin to see to what part their leaders were steering during their slumbers, and there is yet time to haul in, if we can avoid a war with France.—Ford 7:169. (1797.)

FEDERALIST PARTY, Divisions Within.—I have spoken of the Federalists as if they were a homogeneous body, but this is not the truth. Under that name lurks the heretical sect of monarchists. Afraid to wear their own name, they creep under the mantle of Federalism; and the Federalists, like sheep, permit the fox to take shelter among them when pursued by the dogs. These men have no right to office. If a monarchist be in office anywhere, and it be known to the President, the oath he has taken to support the Constitution imperiously requires the instantaneous dismission of such officer; and I should hold the President criminal if he permitted such to remain. To appoint a monarchist to conduct the affairs of a republic is like appointing an atheist to the priesthood. As to the real Federalists, I take them to my bosom as brothers. I view them as honest men, friends to the present Constitution.—Ford 8:237. (1803.)

FEDERALIST PARTY, Contrasted with Jeffersonian Republicans.— Both of our political parties, at least the honest part of them, agree conscientiously in the same object—the public good; but they differ essentially in what they deem the means of promoting that good. One side believes it best done by one composition of the governing powers; the other, by a different one. One fears most the ignorance of the people; the other, the selfishness of rulers independent of them. Which is right, time and experience will prove.—To Abigail Adams. Bergh 11:52. (1804.)

The Federalists wished for everything which would approach our new government to a monarchy; the Republicans to preserve it essentially republican. This was the true origin of the division, and remains still the essential principle of difference between the two parties.—Ford 9:263. (1809.)

At the formation of our government, many had formed their political opinions on European writings and practices, believing the experience of old countries, and especially of England, abusive as it was, to be a safer guide than mere theory. The doctrines of Europe were that men in numerous associations cannot be restrained within the limits of order and justice but by forces physical and moral, wielded over them by authorities independent of their will. Hence their organization of kings, hereditary nobles, and priests. ... And in the convention which formed our government [i.e., the Constitutional Convention of 1787], they endeavored to draw the cords of power as tight as they could obtain them, to lessen the dependence of the general functionaries on their constituents, to subject to them those of the states, and to weaken their means of maintaining the steady equilibrium which the majority of the convention had deemed salutary for both branches, general and local. To recover, therefore, in practice the powers which the nation had refused, and to warp to their own wishes those actually given, was the steady object of the Federalist party. Ours, on the contrary, was to maintain the will of the majority of the convention, and of the people themselves. We believed, with them, that man was a rational animal, endowed by nature with rights, and with an innate sense of justice; and that he could be restrained from wrong and protected in right by moderate powers, confided to persons of his own choice and held to their duties by dependence on his own will. We believed that the complicated organization of kings, nobles, and priests was not the wisest nor best to effect the happiness of associated man.... We believed that men, enjoying in ease and security the full fruits of their own industry, enlisted by all their interests on the side of law and order, habituated to think for themselves, and to follow their reason as their guide, would be more easily and safely governed than with minds nourished in error, and vitiated and debased as in Europe by ignorance, indigence, and oppression. The cherishment of the people, then, was our principle; the fear and distrust of them that of the other party.... The original objects of the Federalists were, first, to warp our government more to the form and principles of monarchy, and, second, to weaken the barriers of the state governments as coordinate powers. In the first they have been so completely foiled by the universal spirit of the nation that they have abandoned the enterprise, shrunk from the odium of their old appellation, taken to themselves a participation of ours, and under the pseudo-Republican mask are now aiming at their second object; and, strengthened by unsuspecting or apostate recruits from our ranks, are advancing fast towards an ascendancy. —Bergh 15:440. (1823.)

FEDERALIST PARTY, Shift of Tactics.—The name of Federalist was extinguished in the battle of New Orleans; and those who wear it now call themselves Republicans. Like the fox pursued by the dogs, they take shelter in the midst of the sheep. They see that monarchism is a hopeless wish in this country, and are rallying anew to the next best point, a consolidated government. They are therefore endeavoring to break down the barriers of the state rights, provided by the Constitution against a consolidation.—To Marquis de Lafayette. Ford 10:233. (1822.)

FEDERALIST PARTY, And Centralized Government.—Consolida-

tion becomes the fourth chapter of the next book of their history. But this opens with a vast accession of strength from their younger recruits, who, having nothing in them of the feelings or principles of '76, now look to a single and splendid government of an aristocracy, founded on banking institutions and moneyed incorporations under the guise and cloak of their favored branches of manufactures, commerce, and navigation, riding and ruling over the plundered ploughman and beggared yeomanry. This will be to them a next-best blessing to the monarchy of their first aim, and perhaps the surest stepping stone to it.—Ford 10:356. (1825.)

FEDERALIST PARTY, Jefferson's Struggles Against Excesses of.—[I regard one of my public services as] the most important, in its consequences, of any transaction in any portion of my life; to wit, the head I personally made against the Federalist principles and proceedings during the administration of Mr. [John] Adams. Their usurpations and violations of the Constitution at that period, and their majority in both houses of Congress, were so great, so decided, and so daring that after combating their aggressions inch by inch without being able in the least to check their career, the Republican leaders thought it would be best for them to give up their useless efforts there, go home, get into their respective legislatures, embody whatever of resistance they could be formed into, and, if ineffectual, to perish there as in the last ditch. All, therefore, retired, leaving Mr. Gallatin alone in the House of Representatives, and myself in the Senate, where I then presided as Vice President. Remaining at our posts, and bidding defiance to the brow-beatings and insults by which they endeavored to drive us off also, we kept the mass of Republicans in phalanx together until the legislatures could be brought up to the charge; and nothing on earth is more certain than that if myself particularly, placed by my office of Vice President at the head of the Republicans, had given way and withdrawn from my post, the Republicans throughout the Union would have given up in despair, and the cause would have been lost forever. By holding on, we obtained time for the legislatures to come up with their weight; and those of Virginia and Kentucky particularly, but more especially the former, by their celebrated resolutions, saved the Constitution at its last gasp.— Bergh 17:459. (1826.)

FEDERALIST PARTY. See also REPUBLICAN PARTY; WASHINGTON (George), And the Federalist Party.

FINANCES, Need for Simplification of National.—I do not at all wonder at the condition in which the finances of the United States are found. [Alexander] Hamilton's object from the beginning was to throw them into forms which should be utterly undecipherable. I ever said he did not understand their condition himself, nor was [he] able to give a clear view of the excess of our debts beyond our credits, nor whether we were diminishing or increasing the debt. My own opinion was that, from the commencement of this government to the time I ceased to attend to the subject, we had been increasing our debt about a million of dollars annually. If Mr. Gallatin [Congressman Albert Gallatin, later Secretary of the Treasury] would undertake to reduce this chaos to order, present us with a clear view of our finances, and put them into a form as simple as they will admit, he will merit immortal honor. The accounts of the United States ought to be, and may be, made as simple as those of a common farmer, and capable of being understood by common farmers.—To James Madison. Bergh 9:323. (1796.)

I think it an object of great importance... to simplify our system of finance, and bring it within the comprehension of every member of Congress.... We might hope to see the finances of the Union as clear and intelligible as a merchant's books, so that every member of Congress, and every man of any mind in the Union, should be able to comprehend them, to investigate abuses, and consequently to control them.—To Albert Gallatin. Bergh 10:306. (1802.)

FINANCES, Sound System Not Through Banks.—Let us be allured by no projects of banks, public or private, or ephemeral expedients which, enabling us to gasp and flounder a little longer, only increase, by protracting, the agonies of death.—To James Monroe. Ford 9:492. (1814.)

The British ministers found some hopes [of success in the war] on the state of our finances. It is true that the excess of our banking institutions, and their present discredit, have shut us out from the best source of credit we could ever command with certainty. But the foundations of credit still remain to us, and need but skill, which experience will soon produce, to marshal them into an order which may carry us through any length of war.—To Marquis de Lafayette. Ford 9:508. (1815.)

FINANCES. See also HAMILTON (Alexander).

FISHERIES, British Rivalry in.— [England] fears no rivals in the whale fishery but America; or rather, it is the whale fishery of America of which she is endeavoring to possess herself. It is for this object she is making the present extraordinary efforts, by bounties and other encouragements; and her success, so far, is very flattering. Before the war, she had not one hundred vessels in the whale trade, while America employed three hundred and nine. In 1786, Great Britain employed one hundred and fifty-one vessels; in 1787, two hundred and eighty-six; in 1788, three hundred and fourteen, nearly the ancient American number; while the latter has fallen to about eighty. They have just changed places, then, England having gained exactly what America has lost. France, by her ports and markets, holds the balance between the two contending parties, and gives the victory, by opening and shutting them, to which she pleases.—Bergh 7:209. (1788.)

The encouragement of our fishery abridges that of a rival nation, whose power on the ocean has long threatened the loss of all balance on that element.—Bergh 3:125. (1791.)

FLORIDA, Acquisition of.— Governor Quesada, by order of his court, is inviting foreigners to go and settle in Florida. This is meant for our people.... I wish a hundred thousand of our inhabitants would accept the invitation. It will be the means of delivering to us peaceably what may otherwise cost us a war. In the meantime, we may complain of this seduction of our inhabitants just enough to make them believe we think it very wise policy for them, and confirm them in it.—To President Washington. Ford 6:316. (1791.)

[It was agreed at a Cabinet meeting that] Monroe be instructed to endeavor to purchase both Floridas if he can, West [Florida] if he cannot [buy] East, at the prices before agreed on; but if neither can be procured, then to stipulate a plenary right to use all the rivers rising within our limits and passing through theirs.... We are more indifferent about pressing the purchase of the Floridas because of the money we have to provide for Louisiana, and because we think they cannot fail to fall into our hands.—Ford 1:300. (1803.)

FOREIGN AFFAIRS, National Character Can Prevent War.—It

should ever be held in mind that insult and war are the consequences of a want of respectability in the national character.—To James Madison. Ford 4:192. (1786.)

FOREIGN AFFAIRS, Avoid the Quarrels of Europe.—I know that it is a maxim with us, and I think it a wise one, not to entangle ourselves with the affairs of Europe.—Ford 4:483. (1787.)

As to everything except commerce, we ought to divorce ourselves from them all. But this system would require time, temper, wisdom, and occasional sacrifice of interest; and how far all of these will be ours, our children may see, but we shall not. The passions are too high at present to be cooled in our day.—Ford 7:154. (1797.)

Better keep together as we are, haul off from Europe as soon as we can, and from all attachments to any portions of it.—Ford 7:265. (1798.)

The Constitution thought it wise to restrain the executive and Senate from entangling and embroiling our affairs with those of Europe.— *Manual of Parliamentary Practice.* Bergh 2:442. (1800.)

Determined as we are to avoid, if possible, wasting the energies of our people in war and destruction, we shall avoid implicating ourselves with the powers of Europe, even in support of principles which we mean to pursue. They have so many other interests different from ours that we must avoid being entangled in them. We believe we can enforce these principles, as to ourselves, by peaceable means, now that we are

likely to have our public councils detached from foreign views.—To Thomas Paine. Ford 8:18. (1801.)

It ought to be the very first object of our pursuits to have nothing to do with the European interests and politics. Let them be free or slaves at will, navigators or agriculturists, swallowed into one government or divided into a thousand; we have nothing to fear from them in any form.... To take part in their conflicts would be to divert our energies from creation to destruction.—Ford 8:23. (1801.)

I have ever deemed it fundamental for the United States never to take part in the quarrels of Europe. Their political interests are entirely distinct from ours. Their mutual jealousies, their balance of power, their complicated alliances, their forms and principles of government are all foreign to us. They are nations of eternal war. All their energies are expended in the destruction of the labor, property, and lives of their people. On our part, never had a people so favorable a chance of trying the opposite system of peace and fraternity with mankind, and the direction of all our means and faculties to the purposes of improvement instead of destruction.—To President James Monroe. Bergh 15:436. (1823.)

FOREIGN AFFAIRS, Self-Interest in.—I think ... that nations are to be governed with regard to their own interest, but I am convinced that it is their interest, in the long run, to be grateful, faithful to their engagements even in the worst of circumstances, and honorable and generous always.—To Marquis de Lafayette. Ford 5:152. (1790.)

FOREIGN AFFAIRS, Citizens Restrained from Violence in Foreign Countries.—The interests of a nation, when well understood, will be found to coincide with their moral duties. Among these it is an important one to cultivate habits of peace and friendship with our neighbors. To do this we should make provisions for rendering the justice we must sometimes require from them. I recommend, therefore, to your consideration whether the laws of the Union should not be extended to restrain our citizens from committing acts of violence within the territories of other nations which would be punished were they committed within our own.—Ford 6:119. (1792.)

FOREIGN AFFAIRS, Rule for Recognizing National Governments.—It accords with our principles to acknowledge any government to be rightful which is formed by the will of the nation substantially declared. —To Gouverneur Morris. Bergh 8:437. (1792.)

We surely cannot deny to any nation that right whereon our own government is founded, that every one may govern itself according to whatever form it pleases, and change these forms at its own will; and that it may transact its business with foreign nations through whatever organ it thinks proper, whether king, convention, assembly, committee, president, or anything else it may choose. The will of the nation is the only thing essential to be regarded. —To Gouverneur Morris. Bergh 9:36. (1793.)

FOREIGN AFFAIRS, Do Not Acquiesce to Insult.—It is an eternal truth that acquiescence under insult is not the way to escape war.—Ford 7:31. (1793.)

FOREIGN AFFAIRS, Commerce with All, Alliances with None.—I am for free commerce with all nations, political connection with none, and little or no diplomatic establishment. And I am not for linking ourselves by new treaties with the quarrels of Europe, entering that field of slaughter to preserve their balance, or joining in the confederacy of kings to war against the principles of liberty.—To Elbridge Gerry. Bergh 10:77. (1799.)

Commerce with all nations, alliance with none, should be our motto.—Ford 7:374. (1799.)

I deem [one of] the essential principles of our government, and consequently [one] which ought to shape its administration, . . . peace, commerce, and honest friendship with all nations, entangling alliances with none.—First Inaugural Address. Bergh 3:321. (1801.)

FOREIGN AFFAIRS, Trade Between Neutrals and Belligerents.—What is contraband by the law of nature? Either everything which may aid or comfort an enemy, or nothing. Either all commerce which would accommodate him is unlawful, or none is. The difference between articles of one or another description is a difference in degree only. No line between them can be drawn. Either all intercourse must cease between neutrals and belligerents or all be permitted. Can the world hesitate to say which shall be the rule? Shall two nations, turning tigers, break up in one instant the peaceable relations of the whole world? Reason and nature clearly pronounce that the neutral is to go on in the enjoyment of all its rights, that its commerce remains free, not subject to the jurisdiction of another, nor consequently its vessels to search or to inquiries whether their contents are the property of an enemy, or are of those which have been called contraband of war.—Ford 8:90. (1801.)

FOREIGN AFFAIRS, Liberality in. —I am in all cases for a liberal conduct towards other nations, believing that the practice of the same friendly feelings and generous dispositions which attach individuals in private life will attach societies on the larger scale, which are composed of individuals.—Ford 8:222. (1803.)

FOREIGN AFFAIRS, America's Policy Toward Other Nations.—We think that peaceable means may be devised of keeping nations in the path of justice towards us by making justice their interest, and injuries to react on themselves. Our distance enables us to pursue a course which the crowded situation of Europe renders, perhaps, impracticable there.—Bergh 10:405. (1803.)

Let it be our endeavor . . . to merit the character of a just nation.—Ford 8:272. (1803.)

FOREIGN AFFAIRS, Moral Basis of Sound Relations.—In the transaction of your foreign affairs, we have endeavored to cultivate the friendship of all nations, and especially of those with which we have the most important relations. We have done them justice on all occasions, favored where favor was lawful, and cherished mutual interests and intercourse on fair and equal terms. We are firmly convinced, and we act on that conviction, that with nations, as with individuals, our interests, soundly calculated, will ever be found inseparable from our moral duties; and history bears witness to the fact that a just nation is taken on its word, when recourse is had to armaments and wars to bridle others. —Second Inaugural Address. Bergh 3:375. (1805.)

FOREIGN AFFAIRS, Mid-Atlantic Meridian.—When our strength will permit us to give the law of our hemisphere, it should be that the meridian of the mid-Atlantic should be the line of demarcation between war and peace, on this side of which no act of hostility should be committed, and the lion and the lamb will lie down in peace together.—Bergh 13:119. (1812.)

FOREIGN AFFAIRS, Need for a Coalition of American Nations.— From many conversations with him [M. Correa], I hope he sees, and will promote in his new situation [in Brazil], the advantages of a cordial fraternization among all the American nations and the importance of their coalescing in an American system of policy, totally independent of and unconnected with that of Europe. The day is not distant when we may formally require a meridian or partition through the ocean which separates the two hemispheres, on the hither side of which no European gun shall ever be heard, nor an American on the other; and when, during the rage of the eternal wars of Europe, the lion and the lamb, within our regions, shall lie down together in peace.... I wish to see this coalition begun.—Bergh 15:262. (1820.)

FOREIGN AFFAIRS, No Kings in American Hemisphere.—I rejoice to learn that Iturbide is a mere usurper, and slenderly supported. Although we have no right to intermeddle with the form of government of other nations, yet it is lawful to wish to see no emperors nor kings in our hemisphere, and that Brazil as well as Mexico will homologize with us.—To President James Monroe. Ford 10:244. (1822.)

FOREIGN AFFAIRS. See also COMMERCE; DIPLOMATS; GOOD FAITH; MONROE DOCTRINE; NEUTRALITY; TREATIES; WAR.

FOREIGN AGENTS, Only with Our Consent.—It is a general rule that no nation has a right to keep an agent within the limits of another without the consent of that other, and we are satisfied it would be best for both Spain and us to abstain from having agents or other persons in our employ, or pay, among the savages inhabiting our respective territories, whether as subjects or

independent. You are therefore desired to propose and press a stipulation to that effect. Should they absolutely decline it, it may be proper to let them perceive that, as the right of keeping agents exists on both sides, or on neither, it will rest with us to reciprocate their own measures.—Ford 6:119. (1792.)

FOREIGN AGENTS, Duty of.—The President of the United States being the only channel of communication between this country and foreign nations, it is from him alone that foreign nations or their agents are to learn what is or has been the will of the nation, and whatever he communicates as such they have a right and are bound to consider as the expression of the nation; and no foreign agent can be allowed to question it, to interpose between him and any other branch of government under the pretext of either's transgressing their functions, nor to make himself the umpire and final judge between them. I am therefore not authorized to enter into any discussions with you on the meaning of our Constitution in any part of it, or to prove to you that it has ascribed to him alone the admission or interdiction of foreign agents. I inform you of the fact by authority from the President.—Ford 6:451. (1793.)

FOREIGN AGENTS, Intermeddling by.—For a foreign agent, addressed to the executive, to embody himself with the lawyers of a faction whose sole object is to embarrass and defeat all the measures of the country, and by their opinions, known to be always in opposition, to endeavor to influence our proceedings, is a conduct not to be permitted.—To Albert Gallatin. Bergh 12:168. (1808.)

FOREIGN INTERVENTION, Evils of.—Wretched, indeed, is the nation in whose affairs foreign powers are once permitted to intermeddle.—Bergh 6:153. (1787.)

FOREIGN INTERVENTION, Should Be Avoided.—Our young Republic . . . [should] never . . . call on foreign powers to settle their differences.—Bergh 6:279. (1787.)

What a crowd of lessons do the present miseries of Holland teach us? . . . Never to call in foreign nations to settle domestic differences.—To John Adams. Ford 4:455. (1787.)

FOREIGN INTERVENTION, United States and.—We wish not to meddle with the internal affairs of any country, nor with the general affairs of Europe.—Bergh 9:56. (1793.)

FOURTH OF JULY, Despotism and the.—The flames kindled on the Fourth of July, 1776, have spread over too much of the globe to be extinguished by the feeble engines of despotism; on the contrary, they will consume these engines and all who work them.—To John Adams. Bergh 15:334. (1821.)

FOURTH OF JULY, Celebration of, to Renew Devotion to the Rights of Man.—May it be to the world what I believe it will be (to some parts sooner, to others later, but finally to all), the signal of arousing men to burst the chains under which monkish ignorance and superstition had persuaded them to bind themselves, and to assume the blessings

and security of self-government. That form which we have substituted restores the free right to the unbounded exercise of reason and freedom of opinion. All eyes are opened, or opening, to the rights of man. The general spread of the light of science has already laid open to every view the palpable truth that the mass of mankind has not been born with saddles on their backs, nor a favored few booted and spurred, ready to ride them legitimately by the grace of God. These are grounds of hope for others. For ourselves, let the annual return of this day forever refresh our recollections of these rights, and an undiminished devotion to them.—Bergh 16:181. (1826.)

FRACTIONAL BANKING, Should Be Outlawed.—It will be asked, are we to have no banks? Are merchants and others to be deprived of the resource of short accommodations, found so convenient? I answer, let us have banks; but let them be such as are alone to be found in any country on earth except Great Britain. There is not a bank of discount on the continent of Europe (at least there was not one when I was there) which offers anything but cash in exchange for discounted bills. No one has a natural right to the trade of a money lender but he who has the money to lend. Let those, then, among us who have a moneyed capital, and who prefer employing it in loans rather than otherwise, set up banks and give cash or national bills for the notes they discount. Perhaps, to encourage them, a larger interest than is legal in the other cases might be allowed them, on the condition of their lending for short periods only.

It is from Great Britain we copy the idea of giving paper in exchange for discounted bills; and while we have derived from that country some good principles of government and legislation, we unfortunately run into the most servile imitation of all her practices, ruinous as they prove to her, and with the gulf yawning before us into which these very practices are precipitating her. The unlimited emission of bank paper has banished all her specie, and is now, by a depreciation acknowledged by her own statesmen, carrying her rapidly to bankruptcy, as it did France, as it did us, and will do us again, and every country permitting paper to be circulated other than that by public authority, rigorously limited to the just measure for circulation. Private fortunes, in the present state of our circulation, are at the mercy of those self-created money lenders, and are prostrated by the floods of nominal money with which their avarice deluges us.—To John W. Eppes. Bergh 13:277. (1813.)

FRACTIONAL BANKING, Ruinous Effects of.—It is said that our paper is as good as silver, because we may have silver for it at the bank where it issues. This is not true. One, two, or three persons might have it; but a general application would soon exhaust their vaults, and leave a ruinous proportion of their paper in its intrinsic worthless

form. It is a fallacious pretense.... Owing to the support its credit receives from the small reservoirs of specie in the vaults of the banks, it is impossible to say at what point their notes will stop. Nothing is necessary to effect it but a general alarm; and that may take place whenever the public shall begin to reflect on and perceive the impossibility that the banks should repay this sum.... Let us suppose [a] panic.... Notes are refused. Cash is called for. The inhabitants of the banking towns will get what is in the vaults, until a few banks declare their insolvency; when, the general crush becoming evident, the others will withdraw even the cash they have, declare their bankruptcy at once, and leave an empty house and empty coffers for the holders of their notes. In this scramble of creditors, the country gets nothing, the towns but little. What are they to do? Bring suits?... Nonsense. The loss is total. And a [large] sum is thus swindled from our citizens.... All this they will justly charge on their legislatures; but this will be poor satisfaction for the two or three hundred millions they will have lost. It is time, then, for the public functionaries to look to this.—To John W. Eppes. Bergh 13:426. (1813.)

The banks themselves were doing business on capitals, three-fourths of which were fictitious; and to extend their profit they furnished fictitious capital to every man who, having nothing and disliking the labors of the plow, chose rather to call himself a merchant, to set up a house of $5,000 a year expense, [and] to dash into every species of mercantile gambling; and if that ended as gambling generally does, a fraudulent bankruptcy was an ultimate resource of retirement and competence. This fictitious capital, probably of one hundred millions of dollars, is now to be lost, and to fall on somebody; it must take on those who have property to meet it, and probably on the less cautious part who, not aware of the impending catastrophe, have suffered themselves to contract or to be in debt, and must now sacrifice their property of a value many times the amount of their debt. We have been truly sowing the wind, and are now reaping the whirlwind. If the present crisis should end in the annihilation of these penniless and ephemeral interlopers only, and reduce our commerce to the measure of our own wants and surplus productions, it will be a benefit in the end. But how to effect this, and give time to real capital and the holders of real property to back out of their entanglements by degrees, requires more knowledge of political economy than we possess. I believe it might be done, but I despair of its being done. The eyes of our citizens are not sufficiently open to the true cause of our distresses. They ascribe them to everything but their true cause, the banking system; a system which, if it could do good in any form, is yet so certain of leading to abuse as to be utterly incompatible with the public safety and prosperity. At present, all is confusion, uncertainty, and panic.—Ford 10:133. (1819.)

FRACTIONAL BANKING, Based on a False Principle.—Like a dropsical man calling out for water, water, our deluded citizens are clamoring for more banks, more banks. The American mind is now in that state of fever which the world has so often seen in the history of other nations. We are under the bank bubble, as England was under the South Sea bubble, France under the Mississippi bubble, and as every nation is liable to be under whatever bubble, design, or delusion may puff up in moments when [they are] off their guard. We are now taught to believe that legerdemain tricks upon paper can produce as solid wealth as hard labor in the earth. It is vain for common sense to urge that *nothing* can produce but *nothing;* that it is an idle dream to believe in a philosopher's stone which is to turn everything into gold, and to redeem man from the original sentence of his Maker, "In the sweat of his brow shall he eat his bread."—Bergh 14:381. (1816.)

FRACTIONAL BANKING. See also BANKS; PAPER MONEY.

FRANCE, Government of.—France ...is the wealthiest but worst governed country on earth.—Bergh 5:23. (1785.)

FRANCE, Home Life in.—The domestic bonds here [France] are absolutely done away, and where can their compensation be found? Perhaps they may catch some moments of transport above the level of the ordinary tranquil joy we experience, but they are separated by long intervals during which all the passions are at sea without rudder or compass. Yet, fallacious as the pursuits of happiness are, they seem on the whole to furnish the most effectual abstraction from a contemplation of the hardness of their government.—Bergh 5:80. (1785.)

FRANCE, Its People Oppressed by Monarchy.—It is difficult to conceive how so good a people, with so good a king, so well-disposed rulers in general, so genial a climate, so fertile a soil, should be rendered so ineffectual for producing human happiness by one single curse—that of a bad form of government. But it is a fact, in spite of the mildness of their governors, the people are ground to powder by the vices of the form of government. Of twenty millions of people supposed to be in France, I am of opinion there are nineteen millions more wretched, more accursed in every circumstance of human existence, than the most conspicuously wretched individual of the whole United States.—Bergh 5:81. (1785.)

If anybody thinks that kings, nobles, or priests are good conservators of the public happiness, send him here. It is the best school in the universe to cure him of that folly. He will see here, with his own eyes, that these descriptions of men are an abandoned confederacy against the happiness of the mass of the people.—To George Wythe. Bergh 5:396. (1786.)

FRANCE, A Day in the Life of a Parisienne.—At eleven o'clock it is day, *chez madame*. The curtains are drawn. Propped on bolsters and pillows, and her head scratched into a little order, the bulletins of the sick are read, and the billets of the well. She writes to some of her acquaintance, and receives the visits of others. If the morning is not very thronged, she is able to get out and hobble round the cage of the Palais Royal; but she must hobble quickly, for the *coiffeur's* turn is come; and a tremendous turn it is! Happy if he does not make her arrive when dinner is half over!

The torpitude of digestion a little passed, she flutters half an hour through the streets by way of paying visits, and then to the spectacles. These finished, another half hour is devoted to dodging in and out of the doors of her very sincere friends, and away to supper. After supper, cards; and after cards, bed; to rise at noon the next day and to tread, like a mill horse, the same trodden circle over again.

Thus the days of life are consumed, one by one, without an object beyond the present moment; ever flying from the ennui of that, yet carrying it with us; eternally in pursuit of happiness, which keeps eternally before us. If death or bankruptcy happens to trip us out of the circle, it is a matter for the buzz of the evening and is completely forgotten by the next morning.—Bergh 6:81. (1787.)

FRANCE, America's Friendship for.—Nothing should be spared on our part to attach this country to us. It is the only one on which we can rely for support under every event. Its inhabitants love us more, I think, than they do any other nation on earth. This is very much the effect of the good dispositions with which the French officers returned.—To James Madison. Ford 4:367. (1787.)

FRANCE, America's Debt of Gratitude to.—It is impossible to desire better dispositions towards us than prevail in [the French National] Assembly. Our proceedings have been viewed as a model for them on every occasion; and though in the heat of debate men are generally disposed to contradict every authority urged by their opponents, ours has been treated like that of the Bible, open to explanation but not to question. I am sorry that in the moment of such a disposition anything should come from us to check it. The placing them on a mere footing with the English will have this effect. When of two nations the one has engaged herself in a ruinous war for us, has spent her blood and money to save us, has opened her bosom to us in peace, and received us almost on the footing of her own citizens; while the other has moved heaven, earth, and hell to exterminate us in war, has insulted us in all her councils in peace, shut her doors to us in every part where her interests would admit it, libelled us in foreign nations, [and] endeavored to poison them against the reception of our most precious commodities— to place these two nations on a footing is to give a great deal more to one than to the other.—To James Madison. Bergh 7:448. (1789.)

Every American owes her [gratitude], as our sole ally during the War of Independence.—Bergh 15:177. (1818.)

FRANCE, Importance of Establishing Republican Government in.—I look with great anxiety for the firm establishment of the new government in France, being perfectly convinced that if it takes place there it will spread sooner or later all over Europe. On the contrary, a check there would retard the revival of liberty in other countries.—To George Mason. Bergh 8:123. (1791.)

FRANCE, Sins Under Napoleon.— In the desolation of Europe to gratify the atrocious caprices of Bonaparte, France sinned much; but she has suffered more than retaliation. Once relieved from the incubus of her late oppression, she will rise like a giant from her slumbers. Her soil and climate, her arts and eminent sciences, her central position and free constitution will soon make her greater than she ever was.— Bergh 15:177. (1818.)

FRANCE, Warmth and Hospitality of Its People.—A more benevolent people I have never known, nor greater warmth and devotedness in their select friendships. Their kindness and accommodation to strangers is unparalleled, and the hospitality of Paris is beyond anything I had conceived to be practicable in a large city.... The politeness of the general manners [and] the ease and vivacity of their conversation give a charm to their society to be found nowhere else.—Autobiography. Bergh 1:159. (1821.)

FRANCE. See also EUROPE; FRENCH REVOLUTION; LOUIS XVI; MARIE ANTOINETTE.

FRANKLIN (Benjamin), America's "Ornament."—Dr. Franklin [was] long the ornament of our country and, I may say, of the world.—Bergh 8:24. (1790.)

There appeared to me more respect and veneration attached to the character of Dr. Franklin in France than to that of any other person in the same country, foreign or native. —Bergh 8:129. (1791.)

Dr. Franklin [was] the greatest man and ornament of the age and country in which he lived.—Bergh 10:55. (1798.)

FRANKLIN (Benjamin), Greatness of.—The succession to Doctor Franklin at the court of France was an excellent school of humility. On being presented to anyone as the minister of America, the commonplace question used in such cases was, *"C'est vous, Monsieur, qui remplace le Docteur Franklin?"*—"It is you, sir, who replace Doctor Franklin?" I generally answered, "No one can replace him, sir; I am only his successor."—Bergh 8:130. (1791.)

FRANKLIN (Benjamin), Defense of.—I have seen, with extreme indignation, the blasphemies lately vended against the memory of the father of American philosophy. But his memory will be preserved and venerated as long as the thunder of heaven shall be heard or feared.— Bergh 9:348. (1796.)

FRANKLIN (Benjamin), Death of.—On the death of Dr. Franklin, the King and Convention of France went into mourning. So did the House of Representatives of the United States. The Senate refused. I proposed to General Washington that the executive department should wear mourning. He declined it, because he said he should not know where to draw the line if he once began that ceremony.... I told him the world had drawn so broad a line between himself and Dr. Franklin on the one side, and the residue of mankind on the other, that we might wear mourning for them and the question still remains new and undecided as to all others. He thought it best, however, to avoid it.—Ford 8:264. (1803.)

FREE ENTERPRISE, Leads to Prosperity.—Agriculture, manufactures, commerce, and navigation, the four pillars of our prosperity, are the most thriving when left most free to individual enterprise.—First Annual Message to Congress. Bergh 3:337. (1801.)

FREE ENTERPRISE. See also COMMERCE; MARKETS.

FREEDOM. See LIBERTY; PRESS; RELIGIOUS FREEDOM; SPEECH.

FRENCH REVOLUTION, Jefferson's Hopes for the.—The [French] nation has been awakened by our Revolution. They feel their strength, they are enlightened, their lights are spreading, and they will not retrograde.—To George Washington. Bergh 7:227. (1788.)

I look with great anxiety for the firm establishment of the new government of France, being perfectly convinced that if it takes place there it will spread sooner or later all over

Europe. On the contrary, a check there would retard the revival of liberty in other countries. I consider the establishment and success of their government as necessary to stay up our own, and to prevent it from falling back to that kind of a halfway house, the English constitution.—To George Mason. Bergh 8:123. (1791.)

I still hope the French Revolution will issue happily. I feel that the permanence of our own leans in some degree on that, and that a failure there would be a powerful argument to prove there must be a failure here.—To Edward Rutledge. Bergh 8:234. (1791.)

I was a sincere well-wisher to the success of the French Revolution, and still wish it may end in the establishment of a free and well-ordered republic.—To Elbridge Gerry. Bergh 10:78. (1799.)

FRENCH REVOLUTION, Influence of Women in the.—In my opinion, a kind of influence which none of their plans of reform take into account will elude them all; I mean the influence of women in the government. The manners of the nation allow them to visit, alone, all persons in office; to solicit the affairs of the husband, family, or friends; and their solicitations bid defiance to laws and regulations. This obstacle may seem less to those who, like our countrymen, are in the precious habit of considering right as a barrier against all solicitation. Nor can such an one, without the evidence of his own eyes, believe in the desperate state to which things are reduced in this country from the omnipotence of an influence which, fortunate for the happiness of the sex itself, does not endeavor to extend itself in our country beyond the domestic line. —To George Washington. Bergh 7:227. (1788.)

FRENCH REVOLUTION, Excesses of the.—Like the rest of mankind, [President Washington] was disgusted with [the] atrocities of the French Revolution.—The Anas. Bergh 1:283. (1818.)

The society of Jacobins was instituted on principles and views as virtuous as ever kindled the hearts of patriots. It was the pure patriotism of their purposes which extended their association to the limits of the nation, and rendered their power within it boundless; and it was this power which degenerated their principles and practices to such enormities as never before could have been imagined.—Ford 10:205. (1822.)

FRENCH REVOLUTION. See also LOUIS XVI; MARIE ANTOINETTE.

FRIENDS, Should Be Loved Despite Imperfections.—Every human being, my dear, must...be viewed according to what it is good for, for none of us, no not one, is perfect; and were we to love none who had imperfections, this world would be a desert for our love. All we can do is to make the best of our friends; love and cherish what is good in them, and keep out of the way of what is bad; but no more think of rejecting them for it than of throwing away a piece of music for a flat passage or two.—To Martha Jefferson Randolph. Betts & Bear, p. 61. (1790.)

FRIENDSHIP, Comforts of.—What an ocean is life! And how our barks get separated in beating through it! One of the greatest comforts of the retirement to which I shall soon withdraw will be its rejoining me to my earliest and best friends and acquaintances.—Ford 6:425. (1793.)

FRIENDSHIP, Enduring.—I never considered a difference of opinion in politics, in religion, [or] in philosophy as cause for withdrawing from a friend.—Ford 7:441. (1800.)

Difference of opinion was never, with me, a motive of separation from a friend. In the trying times of Federalism, I never left a friend. Many left me, [and] have since returned and been received with open arms.—To President James Monroe. Ford 10:298. (1824.)

FUGITIVES, Political.—However desirable it be that the perpetrators of crimes, acknowledged to be such by all mankind, should be delivered up to punishment, yet it is extremely difficult to draw the line between those and acts rendered criminal by tyrannical laws only; hence the first step always is a convention defining the cases where a surrender shall take place.—To President Washington. Ford 5:386. (1791.)

FUGITIVES, Protection of.—The laws of this country take no notice of crimes committed out of their jurisdiction. The most atrocious offender, coming within their pale, is received by them as an innocent man, and they have authorized no one to seize or deliver him. The evil of protecting malefactors of every dye is sensibly felt here, as in other countries; but

until a reformation of the criminal codes of most nations, to deliver fugitives from them would be to become their accomplices; the former, therefore, is viewed as the lesser evil.—Ford 6:426. (1793.)

FUTURE LIFE, Jefferson's Views on.—The laws of nature have withheld from us the means of physical knowledge of the country of spirits, and revelation has, for reasons unknown to us, chosen to leave us in the dark as we were. When I was young I was fond of the speculations which seemed to promise some insight into that hidden country, but observing at length that they left me in the same ignorance in which they had found me, I have for very many years ceased to read or to think concerning them, and have reposed my head on that pillow of ignorance which a benevolent Creator has made so soft for us, knowing how much we should be forced to use it. I have thought it better, by nourishing the good passions and controlling the bad, to merit an inheritance in a state of being of which I can know so little, and to trust for the future to Him who has been so good for the past.—Bergh 10:299. (1801.)

FUTURE LIFE, Jefferson's Belief in a.—Our next meeting must . . . be in the country to which [our past years] have flown—a country for us not now very distant. For this journey we shall need neither gold nor silver in our purse, nor scrip, nor coats, nor staves. Nor is the provision for it more easy than the preparation has been kind. Nothing proves more than this that the Being who presides over the world is essentially benevolent.—To Abigail Adams. Bergh 15:96. (1817.)

The public papers, my dear friend, announce the fatal event of which your letter of October the 20th had given me ominous foreboding [i.e., the death of Abigail Adams]. Tried myself in the school of affliction by the loss of every form of connection which can rive the human heart, I know well and feel what you have lost, what you have suffered, are suffering, and have yet to endure. The same trials have taught me that for ills so immeasurable, time and silence are the only medicine. I will not, therefore, by useless condolences, open afresh the sluices of your grief, nor, although mingling sincerely my tears with yours, will I say a word more where words are vain, but that it is of some comfort to us both that the term is not very distant at which we are to deposit in the same cerement our sorrows and suffering bodies, and to ascend in essence to an ecstatic meeting with the friends we have loved and lost, and whom we shall still love and never lose again. God bless you and support you under your heavy affliction.—To John Adams. Bergh 15:174. (1818.)

FUTURE LIFE. See also DEATH.

G

GAMBLING, Evils of.—Gaming . . . corrupts our dispositions, and teaches us a habit of hostility against all mankind.—To Martha Jefferson. Betts & Bear, p. 41. (1787.)

GAMBLING. See also CHANCE; LOTTERIES; SPECULATION.

GENERAL WELFARE CLAUSE, Interpretation of.—[The Constitution authorizes Congress] to lay taxes to provide for the general welfare of the United States, that is to say, "to lay taxes for *the purpose* of providing for the general welfare." For the laying of taxes is the *power,* and the general welfare the *purpose* for which the power is to be exercised. They are not to lay taxes *ad libitum for any purpose they please;* but only *to pay the debts or provide for the welfare of the Union.* In like manner, they are not *to do anything they please* to provide for the general welfare, but only to *lay taxes* for that purpose. To consider the latter phrase, not as describing the purpose of the first, but as giving a distinct and independent power to do any act they please which might be for the good of the Union, would render all the preceding and subsequent enumerations of power completely useless. It would reduce the whole instrument to a single phrase, that of instituting a Congress with power to do whatever would be for the good of the United States; and as they would be the sole judges of the good or evil, it would be also a power to do whatever evil they please. It is an established rule of construction, where a phrase will bear either of two meanings, to give it that which will allow some meaning to the other parts of the instrument, and not that which would render all the others useless. Certainly no such universal power was meant to be given them. It was intended to lace them up strictly within the enumerated powers, and those without which, as means, these powers could not be carried into effect.—Bergh 3:147. (1791.)

The Constitution says, "Congress shall have power to lay and collect taxes, duties, imposts, and excises, to pay the debts, etc., provide for the common defense and *general welfare* of the United States." ...I suppose its meaning to be that Congress may collect taxes for the purpose of providing for the *general welfare*, in those cases wherein the Constitution empowers them to act for the general welfare. To suppose that it was meant to give them a distinct, substantive power to do *any act* which might tend to the *general welfare* is to render all the enumerations useless, and to make their powers unlimited. —Bergh 3:213. (1792.)

The construction applied by the general government (as is evidenced by sundry of their proceedings) to those parts of the Constitution of the United States which delegate to Congress a power "to lay and collect taxes, duties, imposts, and excises, to pay the debts and provide for the common defense and general welfare of the United States," and "to make all laws which shall be necessary and proper for carrying into execution the powers vested by the Constitution in the government of the United States, or in any department or officer thereof," goes to the destruction of all limits prescribed to their power by the

Constitution.... Words meant by the instrument to be subsidiary only to the execution of limited powers ought not to be so construed as themselves to give unlimited powers, nor a part to be so taken as to destroy the whole residue of that instrument.—Kentucky Resolutions. Bergh 17:385. (1798.)

GENERAL WELFARE CLAUSE, Manufactures and the.—[I told President Washington] that they [the Hamilton party in Congress] had now brought forward a proposition far beyond every one ever yet advanced, and to which the eyes of many were turned as the decision which was to let us know whether we live under a limited or an unlimited government. He asked me to what proposition I alluded. I answered, to that in the Report on Manufactures which, under color of giving *bounties* for the encouragement of particular manufactures, meant to establish the doctrine that the power given by the Constitution to collect taxes to provide for the *general welfare* of the United States permitted Congress to take everything under their management which *they* should deem for the *public welfare,* and which is susceptible of the application of money; consequently, that the subsequent enumeration of their powers was not the description to which resort must be had, and did not at all constitute the limits of their authority; that this was a very different question from that of the Bank [of the United States], which was thought an incident to an enumerated power; that

therefore this decision was expected
with great anxiety; that, indeed, I
hoped the proposition would be rejected, believing there was a majority in both houses against it, and that
if it should be it would be considered
as a proof that things were returning into their true channel.—The
Anas. Bergh 1:291. (1792.)

**GENERAL WELFARE CLAUSE,
Not a Grant of Universal Power.**—
An act for internal improvement,
after passing both houses [of Con-
gress], was [vetoed] by the President.
The act was founded, avowedly, on
the principle that the phrase in the
Constitution which authorizes Congress "to lay taxes, to pay the debts
and provide for the general welfare"
was an extension of the powers specifically enumerated to whatever
would promote the general welfare;
and this, you know, was the Federalist doctrine. Whereas, our tenet ever
was, and indeed it is almost the only
landmark which now divides the
Federalists from the Republicans,
that Congress had not unlimited
powers to provide for the general
welfare, but were restrained to those
specifically enumerated; and that, as
it was never meant they should provide for that welfare but by the
exercise of the enumerated powers,
so it could not have been meant they
should raise money for purposes
which the enumeration did not place
under their action; consequently,
that the specification of powers is a
limitation of the purposes for which
they may raise money.... This
phrase,...by a mere grammatical
quibble, has countenanced the gen-

eral government in a claim of universal power. For in the phrase, "to
lay taxes, to pay the debts and provide for the general welfare," it is
a mere question of syntax whether
the two last infinitives are governed
by the first or are distinct and coordinate powers; a question unequivocally decided by the exact
definition of powers immediately
following.—To Albert Gallatin.
Bergh 15:133. (1817.)

[We] disavow, and declare to be
most false and unfounded, the doctrine that the [Constitution], in
authorizing its federal branch to lay
and collect taxes, duties, imposts,
and excises to pay the debts and provide for the common defense and
general welfare of the United States,
has given them thereby a power to
do whatever *they* may think, or pretend, would promote the general
welfare—which construction would
make that of itself a complete government, without limitation of
powers.... The plain sense and obvious meaning were that they might
levy the taxes necessary to provide
for the general welfare by the various acts of power therein specified
and delegated to them, and by no
others.—Bergh 17:444. (1825.)

GENERAL WELFARE CLAUSE.
See also CONSTITUTION (U.S.).

GENIUS, And Public Service.—
Though...I am duly impressed with
a sense of the arduousness of government, and the obligation those
are under who are able to conduct it,
yet I am also satisfied there is an
order of geniuses above that obligation, and therefore exempted from

it. Nobody can conceive that nature ever intended to throw away a Newton upon the occupations of a crown.... Cooperating with nature in her ordinary economy, we should dispose of and employ the geniuses of men acording to their several orders and degrees.—Ford 2:163. (1778.)

It becomes expedient for promoting the public happiness that those persons whom nature hath endowed with genius and virtue should be rendered by liberal education worthy to receive, and able to guard, the sacred deposit of the rights and liberties of their fellow citizens; and they should be called to that charge without regard to wealth, birth, or other accidental condition or circumstance.—Boyd 2:526. (1779.)

GENIUS. See also ARISTOCRACY; DUTY; TALENTS.

GEORGE III, Our Bitterest Enemy. —It is an immense misfortune to the whole empire to have a King of such a disposition at such a time. We are told, and everything proves it true, that he is the bitterest enemy we have. His minister is able, and that satisfies me that ignorance or wickedness somewhere controls him. In an earlier part of this contest, our petitions told him that from our King there was but one appeal. The admonition was despised, and that appeal forced on us. To undo his empire, he has but one truth more to learn—that after the colonies have drawn the sword, there is but one step more they can take. That step is now pressed upon us by the

measures adopted, as if they were afraid we would not take it.—To John Randolph. Bergh 4:32. (1775.)

GEORGE III, Injuries and Usurpations of.—The history of the present King of Great Britain is a history of unremitting injuries and usurpations, among which appears no solitary fact to contradict the uniform tenor of the rest, but all have in direct object the establishment of an absolute tyranny over these states. To prove this, let facts be submitted to a candid world, for the truth of which we pledge a faith yet unsullied by falsehood.—Declaration of Independence as drafted by Jefferson. Bergh 1:30. (1776.)

GEORGE III, Lunacy of.—The lunacy of the King of England...is a decided fact, notwithstanding all the stuff the English papers publish about his fevers, delirium, etc. The truth is that the lunacy declared itself almost at once, and with as few concomitant complaints as usually attend the first development of that disorder.—To George Washington. Bergh 7:225. (1788.)

GOD, Delights in Man's Happiness. —Providence...delights in the happiness of man here and his greater happiness hereafter.—First Inaugural Address. Bergh 3:320. (1801.)

GOD, Material Nature of.—To talk of *immaterial* existences is to talk of *nothings*. To say that the human soul, angels, God, are immaterial is to say they are *nothings*, or that there is no God, no angels, no soul. I cannot reason otherwise; but I believe I am

supported in my creed of materialism by the Lockes, the Tracys, and
the Stewarts. At what age of the
Christian church this heresy of
immaterialism, or masked atheism,
crept in, I do not exactly know. But
a heresy it certainly is. Jesus taught
nothing of it.—To John Adams.
Bergh 15:274. (1820.)

GOD, Man's Relationship to.—The
relations which exist between man
and his Maker, and the duties resulting from those relations, are the
most interesting and important to
every human being, and the most
incumbent on his study and investigation.—Bergh 19:414. (1822.)

GOD, Existence of.—I think that
every Christian sect gives a great
handle to atheism by their general
dogma that without a revelation
there would not be sufficient proof
of the being of a God.... On the
contrary, I hold (without appeal to
revelation) that when we take a view
of the universe in its parts, general
or particular, it is impossible for the
human mind not to perceive and feel
a conviction of design, consummate
skill, and indefinite power in every
atom of its composition. The movements of the heavenly bodies, so
exactly held in their course by the
balance of centrifugal and centripetal
forces; the structure of our earth
itself, with its distribution of lands,
waters, and atmosphere; animal and
vegetable bodies, examined in all
their minutest particles; insects,
mere atoms of life, yet as perfectly
organized as man or mammoth; the
mineral substances, their genera-

tion and uses—it is impossible, I say,
for the human mind not to believe
that there is, in all this, design,
cause, and effect, up to an ultimate
cause, a Fabricator of all things from
matter and motion, their Preserver
and Regulator while permitted to
exist in their present forms, and
their regeneration into new and
other forms.

We see, too, evident proofs of the
necessity of a superintending power
to maintain the universe in its
course and order. Stars, well known,
have disappeared, new ones have
come into view; comets, in their incalculable courses, may run foul of
suns and planets, and require reno-
vation under other laws; certain
races of animals are become extinct;
and were there no restoring power,
all existences might extinguish
successively, one by one, until all
should be reduced to a shapeless
chaos.

So irresistible are these evidences
of an intelligent and powerful Agent
that, of the infinite numbers of men
who have existed through all time,
they have believed, in the proportion of a million at least to a unit, in
the hypothesis of an eternal pre-
existence of a Creator, rather than
in that of a self-existent universe.
Surely this unanimous sentiment
renders this more probable than
that of the few in the other hypothesis. Some early Christians, indeed,
have believed in the co-eternal pre-
existence of both the Creator and
the world, without changing their
relation of cause and effect.—To
John Adams. Bergh 15:425. (1823.)

GOD. See also DEITY; PROVIDENCE; RELIGION.

GOOD FAITH, Should Govern Public and Private Acts.—Good faith ought ever to be the rule of action in public as well as in private transactions.—Ford 8:489. (1806.)

GOOD FAITH, Of U.S. Government.—It is a great consolation to me that our government, as it cherishes most its duties to its own citizens, so is it the most exact in its moral conduct towards other nations. I do not believe that in the four administrations which have taken place, there has been a single instance of departure from good faith towards other nations. We may sometimes have mistaken our rights, or made an erroneous estimate of the actions of others, but no voluntary wrong can be imputed to us.—Ford 10:68. (1816.)

GOOD FAITH. See also FOREIGN AFFAIRS; HONESTY; LIES; TRUTH.

GOVERNMENT, Honesty in.—The whole art of government consists in the art of being honest.—*Summary View of the Rights of British America.* Bergh 1:209. (1774.)

GOVERNMENT, People's Right to Abolish Oppressive.—We hold these truths to be self evident: that all men are created equal; that they are endowed by their Creator with certain inalienable rights; that among these are life, liberty, and the pursuit of happiness; that to secure these rights, governments are instituted among men, deriving their just powers from the consent of the governed; that whenever any form of government becomes destructive of these ends, it is the right of the people to alter or to abolish it, and to institute new government, laying its foundation on such principles, and organizing its powers in such form, as to them shall seem most likely to effect their safety and happiness.

Prudence, indeed, will dictate that governments long established should not be changed for light and transient causes; and, accordingly, all experience hath shown that mankind are more disposed to suffer, while evils are sufferable, than to right themselves by abolishing the forms to which they are accustomed.

But when a long train of abuses and usurpations, pursuing invariably the same object, evinces a design to reduce them under absolute despotism, it is their right, it is their duty, to throw off such government and to provide new guards for their future security.—Declaration of Independence. Bergh 1:29. (1776.)

GOVERNMENT, Perversion of.—[While] certain forms of government are better calculated than others to protect individuals in the free exercise of their natural rights, and are at the same time themselves better guarded against degeneracy, yet experience hath shown that, even under the best forms, those entrusted with power have, in time, and by slow operations, perverted it into tyranny.—Ford 2:220. (1779.)

GOVERNMENT, Corruption and.—In every government on earth is some trace of human weakness, some germ of corruption and degeneracy, which cunning will discover and wickedness insensibly open, cultivate, and improve.—*Notes on Virginia.* Bergh 2:207. (1782.)

GOVERNMENT, People the Source of All Power.—Every government degenerates when trusted to the rulers of the people alone. The people themselves, therefore, are its only safe depositories. And to render even them safe, their minds must be improved to a certain degree.—*Notes on Virginia.* Bergh 2:207. (1782.)

The influence over government must be shared among all the people. If every individual which composes their mass participates of the ultimate authority, the government will be safe because the corrupting the whole mass will exceed any private resources of wealth, and public ones cannot be provided but by levies on the people. In this case, every man would have to pay his own price. The government of Great Britain has been corrupted because but one man in ten has a right to vote for members of Parliament. The sellers of the government, therefore, get nine-tenths of their price clear.—*Notes on Virginia.* Bergh 2:207. (1782.)

I consider the people who constitute a society or nation as the source of all authority in that nation; as free to transact their common concerns by any agents they think proper; to change these agents individually, or the organization of them in form or function whenever they please; that all the acts done by these agents under the authority of the nation are the acts of the nation, are obligatory to them and inure to their use, and can in nowise be annulled or affected by any change in the form of the government, or of the persons administering it.—Ford 6:220. (1793.)

GOVERNMENT, Fallibility of.—[Were] the government to prescribe to us our medicine and diet, our bodies would be in such keeping as our souls are now. Thus in France the emetic was once forbidden as a medicine, and the potato as an article of food. Government is just as infallible, too, when it fixes systems in physics. Galileo was sent to the Inquisition for affirming that the earth was a sphere; the government had declared it to be as flat as a trencher [wooden platter for serving food], and Galileo was obliged to abjure his error. This error, however, at length prevailed, the earth became a globe, and Descartes declared it was whirled round its axis by a vortex. The government in which he lived was wise enough to see that this was no question of civil jurisdiction, or we should all have been involved by authority in vortices. In fact, the vortices have been exploded, and the Newtonian principle of gravitation is now more firmly established, on the basis of reason, than it would be were the government to step in and to make it an article of necessary faith. Reason and experiment have been indulged, and error has fled before them. It is error alone which needs the support of government. Truth can stand by itself.—*Notes on Virginia.* Bergh 2:222. (1782.)

GOVERNMENT, Hereditary Branches of.—Experience has shown that the hereditary branches of modern governments are the patrons of privilege and prerogative, and not of the natural rights of the people, whose oppressors they generally are.—To George Washington. Ford 3:467. (1784.)

GOVERNMENT, To Protect Citizens.—Every government [is obligated] to yield protection to [its] citizens as the consideration of their obedience.—To John Jay. Bergh 5:172. (1785.)

The persons and property of our citizens are entitled to the protection of our government in all places where they may lawfully go.—Bergh 3:244. (1793.)

GOVERNMENT, Should Not Be Too Energetic.—It has been said ... that our governments, both federal and [state], want energy; that it is difficult to restrain both individuals and states from committing wrong. This is true, and it is an inconvenience. On the other hand, that energy which absolute governments derive from an armed force, which is the effect of the bayonet constantly held at the breast of every citizen, and which resembles very much the stillness of the grave, must be admitted also to have its inconveniences. We weigh the two together, and like best to submit to the former. Compare the number of wrongs committed with impunity by citizens among us with those committed by the sovereign in other countries, and the last will be found most numerous, most oppressive on the

Jefferson in 1797 (age 54). Portrait by James Sharples.

mind, and most degrading of the dignity of man.—Bergh 17:122. (1786.)

I am not a friend to a very energetic government. It is always oppressive. It places the governors, indeed, more at their ease, at the expense of the people.—To James Madison. Bergh 6:391. (1787.)

GOVERNMENT, Danger of Inattention to.—If once [the people] become inattentive to the public affairs, you and I, ... Congress and assemblies, judges and governors shall all become wolves. It seems to be the law of our general nature, in spite of individual exceptions; and experience declares that man is the only animal which devours his own kind; for I can apply no milder term to the governments of Europe, and to the general prey of the rich on the poor.—Bergh 6:58. (1787.)

GOVERNMENT, Three Forms of, in Society.—Societies exist under three forms, sufficiently distinguishable: 1. Without government, as among our Indians. 2. Under governments wherein the will of everyone has a just influence, as is the case in England in a slight degree, and in our states in a great one. 3. Under governments of force, as is the case in all other monarchies, and in most of the other republics.

To have an idea of the curse of existence under these last, they must be seen. It is a government of wolves over sheep. It is a problem, not clear in my mind, that the first condition is not the best. But I believe it to be inconsistent with any great degree of population. The second state has a great deal of good in it. The mass of mankind under that enjoys a precious degree of liberty and happiness. It has its evils, too; the principle of which is the turbulence to which it is subject. But weigh this against the oppressions of monarchy, and it becomes nothing. . . . Even this evil is productive of good. It prevents the degeneracy of government, and nourishes a general attention to the public affairs. I hold it that a little rebellion now and then is a good thing, and as necessary in the political world as storms are in the physical. Unsuccessful rebellions, indeed, generally establish the encroachments on the rights of the people which have produced them.

An observation of this truth should render honest republican governors so mild in their punishment of rebellions as not to discourage them too much. It is a medicine necessary for the sound health of government. —To James Madison. Bergh 6:64. (1787.)

GOVERNMENT, Principles of Good.—The first principle of a good government is, certainly, a distribution of its powers into executive, judiciary, and legislative, and a subdivision of the latter into two or three branches.—To John Adams. Ford 4:454. (1787.)

I do, . . . with sincere zeal, wish an inviolable preservation of our present federal Constitution, according to the true sense in which it was adopted by the states, that in which it was advocated by its friends, and not that which its enemies apprehended, who therefore became its enemies; and I am opposed to the monarchizing its features by the forms of its administration, with a view to conciliate a first transition to a President and Senate for life, and from that to an hereditary tenure of these offices, and thus to worm out the elective principle. I am for preserving to the states the powers not yielded by them to the Union, and to the legislature of the Union [i.e., Congress] its Constitutional share in the division of powers; and I am not for transferring all the powers of the states to the general government, and all those of that government to the executive branch. I am for a government rigorously frugal and simple, applying all the possible savings of the public revenue to the discharge of the national debt; and not for a multiplication of officers and salaries merely to make partisans, and for increasing by every device the public debt, on the principle of its being a public blessing. I am for relying, for internal defense, on our militia solely till actual invasion, and for such a naval force only as may protect our coasts and harbors from such depredations as we have experienced; and not for a standing army in time of peace, which may overawe the public sentiment; nor for a navy which, by its own expenses and the eternal wars in which it will implicate us, will grind us with public burdens and sink us under them. I am for free commerce with all nations, political connection with none, and little or no diplomatic establishment. And I am not for linking ourselves by new treaties with the quarrels of Europe, entering that field of slaughter to preserve their balance, or joining in the confederacy of kings to war against the principles of liberty. I am for freedom of religion, and against all maneuvers to bring about a legal ascendancy of one sect over another; for freedom of the press, and against all violations of the Constitution to silence by force and not by reason the complaints or criticisms, just or unjust, of our citizens against the conduct of their agents.—To Elbridge Gerry. Bergh 10:76. (1799.)

A wise and frugal government, which shall restrain men from injuring one another, which shall leave them otherwise free to regulate their own pursuits of industry and improvement, and shall not take from the mouth of labor the bread it has earned—this is the sum of good government.... It is proper that you should understand what I deem the essential principles of our government, and consequently those which ought to shape its administration.... Equal and exact justice to all men, of whatever state or persuasion, religious or political; peace, commerce, and honest friendship with all nations, entangling alliances with none; the support of the state governments in all their rights, as the most competent administrations for our domestic concerns and the surest bulwarks against anti-republican tendencies; the preservation of the general government in its whole Constitutional vigor, as the sheet anchor of our peace at home and safety abroad; a jealous care of the right of election by the people—a mild and safe corrective of abuses which are lopped by the sword of revolution where peaceable remedies are unprovided; absolute acquiescence in the decisions of the majority—the vital principle of republics, from which there is no appeal but to force, the vital principle and immediate parent of despotism; a well-disciplined militia, our best reliance in peace and for the first moments of war till regulars may relieve them; the supremacy of the civil over the military authority;

economy in the public expense, that labor may be lightly burdened; the honest payment of our debts and sacred preservation of the public faith; encouragement of agriculture, and of commerce as its handmaid; the diffusion of information, and the arraignment of all abuses at the bar of public reason; freedom of religion; freedom of the press; freedom of person under the protection of the *habeas corpus;* and trial by juries impartially selected. These principles form the bright constellation which has gone before us and guided our steps through an age of revolution and reformation. The wisdom of our sages and the blood of our heroes have been devoted to their attainment. They should be the creed of our political faith, the text of civil instruction, the touchstone by which to try the services of those we trust; and should we wander from them in moments of error or alarm, let us hasten to retrace our steps and to regain the road which alone leads to peace, liberty, and safety.—First Inaugural Address. Bergh 3:320. (1801.)

GOVERNMENT, Liberty vs.—The natural progress of things is for liberty to yield and government to gain ground.—Ford 5:20. (1788.)

GOVERNMENT, Limitations on Popular Control of.—We think, in America, that it is necessary to introduce the people into every department of government, as far as they are capable of exercising it; and that this is the only way to insure a long-continued and honest administration of its powers.

1. They are not qualified to exercise themselves the executive department, but they are qualified to name the person who shall exercise it. With us, therefore, they choose this officer every four years.

2. They are not qualified to legislate. With us, therefore, they only choose the legislators.

3. They are not qualified to judge questions of *law,* but they are very capable of judging questions of *fact.* In the form of juries, therefore, they determine all matters of fact, leaving to the permanent judges to decide the law resulting from those facts.—Bergh 7:422. (1789.)

GOVERNMENT, Recommended Books on.—In political economy, I think [Adam] Smith's *Wealth of Nations* the best book extant; in the science of government, [Baron Charles de] Montesquieu's *Spirit of Laws* is generally recommended. It contains, indeed, a great number of political truths; but also an equal number of heresies, so that the reader must be constantly on his guard.... [John] Locke's little book on government is perfect as far as it goes. Descending from theory to practice, there is no better book than *The Federalist.* [Edmund] Burke's political disquisitions are good also, especially after reading [Jean Louis] Delolme. Several of [David] Hume's *Political Essays* are good. There are some excellent books of theory written by [Anne Robert Jacques] Turgot and the economists of France. For parliamentary knowledge, the *Lex Parliamentaria* is the best book.—Bergh 8:31. (1790.)

I think there does not exist a good elementary work on the organization of society into civil government; I mean a work which presents in one full and comprehensive view the system of principles on which such an organization should be founded, according to the rights of nature. For want of a single work of that character, I should recommend [John] Locke on government, [Algernon] Sidney, [Joseph] Priestley's *Essay on the First Principles of Government,* Chipman's *Principles of Government,* and *The Federalist;* adding, perhaps, [Cesare] Beccaria on *Crimes and Punishments,* because of the demonstrative manner in which he has treated that branch of the subject. If your views of political inquiry go further to the subjects of money and commerce, [Adam] Smith's *Wealth of Nations* is the best book to be read, unless [Jean Baptiste] Say's *Political Economy* can be had, which treats the same subjects on the same principles, but in a shorter compass and more lucid manner.—Ford 9:71. (1807.)

GOVERNMENT, Individual Right of Self-Government.—Every man, and every body of men on earth, possesses the right of self-government. They receive it with their being from the hand of nature. Individuals exercise it by their single will; collections of men by that of their majority, for the law of the *majority* is the natural law of every society of men. When a certain description of men are to transact together a particular business, the times and places of their meeting and separating depend on their own will; they make a part of the natural right of self-government. This, like all other natural rights, may be abridged or modified in its exercise by their own consent, or by the law of those who depute them if they meet in the right of others; but as far as it is not abridged or modified, they retain it as a natural right and may exercise it in what form they please, either exclusively by themselves, or in association with others, or by others altogether, as they shall agree.—Ford 5:205. (1790.)

GOVERNMENT, Created to Secure Citizens' Rights.—It is to secure our rights that we resort to government at all.—Ford 7:4. (1795.)

GOVERNMENT, A Painful and Thankless Task.—I have no ambition to govern men. It is a painful and thankless office.—Ford 7:98. (1796.)

GOVERNMENT, Need for Simplicity and Economy in.—I am for a government rigorously frugal and simple.—To Elbridge Gerry. Bergh 10:77. (1799.)

The multiplication of public offices, increase of expense beyond income, [and] growth and entailment of a public debt are indications soliciting the employment of the pruning knife.—Bergh 15:325. (1821.)

I think, myself, that we have more machinery of government than is necessary, too many parasites living on the labor of the industrious. I believe it might be much simplified to the relief of those who maintain it.—Bergh 16:76. (1824.)

GOVERNMENT, Need for Public Confidence in.—In a government like ours, it is necessary to embrace in its administration as great a mass of confidence as possible by employing those who have a character with the public, of their own, and not merely a secondary one through the executive.—Ford 1:312. (1806.)

GOVERNMENT, Inefficient and Costly.—Having always observed that public works are much less advantageously managed than the same are by private hands, I have thought it better for the public to go to market for whatever it wants which is to be found there; for there competition brings it down to the minimum of value.... I think it material, too, not to abstract the high executive officers from those functions which nobody else is charged to carry on, and to employ them in superintending works which are going on abundantly in private hands.—Bergh 12:107. (1808.)

GOVERNMENT, Legitimate Purposes of.—The care of human life and happiness, and not their destruction, is the first and only legitimate object of good government.—Bergh 16:359. (1809.)

The freedom and happiness of man... [are] the sole objects of all legitimate government.—Bergh 12:369. (1810.)

The only orthodox object of the institution of government is to secure the greatest degree of happiness possible to the general mass of those associated under it.—Bergh 13:135. (1812.)

Our legislators are not sufficiently apprised of the rightful limits of their power; that their true office is to declare and enforce only our natural rights and duties, and to take none of them from us.—Bergh 15:24. (1816.)

The equal rights of man and the happiness of every individual are now acknowledged to be the only legitimate objects of government. —Bergh 15:482. (1823.)

GOVERNMENT, Need for Control of.—Unless the mass retains sufficient control over those entrusted with the powers of their government, these will be perverted to their own oppression, and to the perpetuation of wealth and power in the individuals and their families selected for the trust. Whether our Constitution has hit on the exact degree of control necessary is yet under experiment; and it is a most encouraging reflection that, distance and other difficulties securing us against the brigand governments of Europe in the safe enjoyment of our farms and firesides, the experiment stands a better chance of being satisfactorily made here than on any occasion yet presented by history. —Bergh 13:136. (1812.)

GOVERNMENT. See also CENTRALIZATION; CONSTITUTION (U.S.); FEDERAL GOVERNMENT; MONARCHY; PEOPLE; POLITICS; POWER; REPRESENTATION; REPUBLICAN GOVERNMENT; SELF-GOVERNMENT; SEPARATION OF POWERS.

GRANDCHILDREN, Jefferson's Love for His.—I long to be in the midst of the children, and have more pleasure in their little follies than in the wisdom of the wise.—To Martha Jefferson Randolph. Betts & Bear, p. 191. (1801.)

GREAT BRITAIN. See COLONIES (American); ENGLAND.

GREENE (General Nathanael), Abilities of.—Greene was truly a great man. He had not, perhaps, all the qualities which so peculiarly rendered General Washington the fittest man on earth for directing so great a contest under so great difficulties.... But Greene was second to no one in enterprise, in resource, in sound judgment, promptitude of decision, and in every other military talent.—Ford 10:222. (1822.)

H

HABEAS CORPUS, Suspension of. —By a declaration of rights, I mean one which shall stipulate ... no suspensions of the habeas corpus. —Bergh 6:425. (1788.)

I sincerely rejoice at the acceptance of our new Constitution by nine states. It is a good canvas, on which some strokes only want retouching. What these are, I think are sufficiently manifested by the general voice from north to south, which calls for a bill of rights. It seems pretty generally understood that this should go to juries, habeas corpus, standing armies, printing, religion, and monopolies.... Why suspend the habeas corpus in insurrections and rebellions? The parties who may be arrested may be

charged instantly with a well-defined crime; of course, the judge will remand them. If the public safety requires that the government should have a man imprisoned on less probable testimony in those than in other emergencies, let him be taken and tried, retaken and retried, while the necessity continues, only giving him redress against the government for damages.—To James Madison. Bergh 7:96. (1788.)

HABEAS CORPUS, In England.— Examine the history of England. See how few of the cases of the suspension of the habeas corpus law have been worthy of that suspension. They have been either real treason, wherein the parties might as well have been charged at once, or sham plots, where it was shameful they should ever have been suspected. Yet for the few cases wherein the suspension of the habeas corpus has done real good, that operation is now become habitual, and the minds of the nation almost prepared to live under its constant suspension.—To James Madison. Bergh 7:97. (1788.)

HAMILTON (Alexander), His View of the U.S. Constitution.—I told [President Washington] that though the people were sound, there were a numerous sect who had monarchy in contemplation; that the Secretary of the Treasury was one of these. That I had heard him say that this Constitution was a shilly-shally thing of mere milk and water, which could not last, and was only good as a step to something better. That when we reflected that he had endeavored in the convention [of 1787] to make an English constitution of it, and when failing in that we saw all his measures tending to bring it to the same thing, it was natural for us to be jealous.—The Anas. Bergh 1:318. (1792.)

Hamilton frankly avowed that he considered the British constitution, with all the corruptions of its administration, as the most perfect model of government which had ever been devised by the wit of man; professing, however, at the same time that the spirit of this country was so fundamentally republican that it would be visionary to think of introducing monarchy here, and that therefore it was the duty of its administrators to conduct it on the principles their constituents had elected.—To Martin Van Buren. Bergh 16:66. (1824.)

HAMILTON (Alexander), His Management of the Treasury.— Alexander Hamilton's [Treasury] system flowed from principles adverse to liberty, and was calculated to undermine and demolish the Republic by creating an influence of his department over the members of the [Congress]. I saw this influence actually produced, and its first fruits to be the establishment of the great outlines of his project by the votes of the very persons who, having swallowed his bait, were laying themselves out to profit by his plans; and that had these persons withdrawn, as those interested in a question ever should, the vote of the disinterested majority was clearly the reverse of what they had made it. These were no longer

the votes, then, of the representatives of the people, but of deserters from the rights and interests of the people; and it was impossible to consider their decisions, which had nothing in view but to enrich themselves, as the measures of the fair majority, which ought always to be respected.—To President Washington. Ford 6:102. (1792.)

I do not at all wonder at the condition in which the finances of the United States are found. Hamilton's object from the beginning was to throw them into forms which should be utterly undecipherable. I ever said he did not understand their condition himself, nor was able to give a clear view of the excess of our debts beyond our credits, nor whether we were diminishing or increasing the debt.—To James Madison. Bergh 9:323. (1796.)

I think it an object of great importance ... to simplify our system of finance, and bring it within the comprehension of every member of Congress. Hamilton set out on a different plan. In order that he might have the entire government of his machine, he determined so to complicate it as that neither the President nor Congress should be able to understand it, or to control him. He succeeded in doing this, not only beyond their reach, but so that he at length could not unravel it himself. He gave to the debt in the first instance, in funding it, the most artificial and mysterious form he could devise. He then molded up his appropriations of a number of scraps and remnants, many of which were nothing at all, and applied them to different objects in reversion and remainder, until the whole system was involved in impenetrable fog; and while he was giving himself the airs of providing for the payment of the debt, he left himself free to add to it continually, as he did in fact, instead of paying for it.—To Albert Gallatin. Bergh 10:306. (1802.)

HAMILTON (Alexander), Jefferson's Reaction to His Slanders.—To a thorough disregard of the honors and emoluments of office, I join as great a value for the esteem of my countrymen; and conscious of having merited it by an integrity which cannot be reproached, and by an enthusiastic devotion to their rights and liberty, I will not suffer my retirement to be clouded by the slanders of a man whose history, from the moment at which history can stoop to notice him, is a tissue of machinations against the liberty of the country which has not only received and given him bread, but heaped its honors on his head.—To President Washington. Ford 6:109. (1792.)

HAMILTON (Alexander), Subservient to England.—Hamilton is panic-struck if we refuse our breech to every kick which Great Britain may choose to give it. He is for proclaiming at once the most abject principles, such as would invite and merit habitual insults; and indeed every inch of ground must be fought in our councils [Cabinet meetings] to desperation in order to hold up the face of even a sneaking neutrality, for our votes are generally two

and a half against one and a half. Some propositions have come from him which would astonish Mr. Pitt himself with their boldness. If we preserve even a sneaking neutrality, we shall be indebted for it to the President, and not to his counsellors. —To James Monroe. Bergh 9:76. (1793.)

His mind was really powerful, but chained by native partialities to everything English. He had formed exaggerated ideas of the superior perfection of the English constitution, the superior wisdom of their government, and sincerely believed it for the good of this country to make them its model in everything; without considering that what might be wise and good for a nation essentially commercial, and entangled in complicated intercourse with numerous and powerful neighbors, might not be so for one essentially agricultural, and insulated by nature from the abusive governments of the old world.—Ford 10:34. (1816.)

HAMILTON (Alexander), Monarchical Principles of.—Another incident took place on the same occasion [at Jefferson's Philadelphia apartment in 1791] which will further delineate Mr. Hamilton's political principles. The room being hung around with a collection of the portraits of remarkable men, among them were those of Bacon, Newton, and Locke. Hamilton asked me who they were. I told him they were my trinity of the three greatest men the world had ever produced, naming them. He paused for some time. "The greatest man," said he, "that ever lived was Julius Caesar." Mr. [John] Adams was honest as a politician as well as a man; Hamilton [was] honest as a man, but, as a politician, believing in the necessity of either force or corruption to govern men.—To Dr. Benjamin Rush. Bergh 13:4. (1811.)

Hamilton was not only a monarchist, but for a monarchy bottomed on corruption. In proof of this I will relate an anecdote, for the truth of which I attest the God who made me. Before the President [Washington] set out on his southern tour in April 1791, he addressed a letter of the fourth of that month from Mount Vernon to the Secretaries of State, Treasury, and War, desiring that if any serious and important cases should arise during his absence they would consult and act on them. And he requested that the Vice President should also be consulted. This was the only occasion on which that officer was ever requested to take part in a Cabinet question. Some occasion for consultation arising, I invited those gentlemen (and the Attorney General as well, as I remember) to dine with me in order to confer on the subject. After the cloth was removed, and our question agreed and dismissed, conversation began on other matters, and by some circumstance was led to the British constitution, on which Mr. Adams observed, "Purge that constitution of its corruption, and give to its popular branch equality of representation, and it would be the most perfect constitution ever devised by the wit of man." Hamilton paused

and said, "Purge it of its corruption, and give to its popular branch equality of representation, and it would become an *impracticable* government; as it stands at present, with all its supposed defects, it is the most perfect government which ever existed." And this was assuredly the exact line which separated the political creeds of these two gentlemen. The one was for two hereditary branches and an honest elective one; the other for a hereditary king, with a House of Lords and Commons corrupted to his will, and standing between him and the people.—The Anas. Bergh 1:278. (1818.)

HAMILTON (Alexander), Favored Money Brokers.—It is well known that during the [Revolutionary] war the greatest difficulty we encountered was the want of money or means to pay our soldiers who fought, or our farmers, manufacturers, and merchants who furnished the necessary supplies of food and clothing for them. After the expedient of paper money had exhausted itself, certificates of debt were given to the individual creditors, with assurance of payment so soon as the United States should be able. But the distresses of the people often obliged them to part with these for the half, the fifth, and even a tenth of their value, and speculators had made a trade of cozening [cheating] them from the holders by the most fraudulent practices, and [by] persuasions that they would never be paid.

In the bill for funding and paying these, Hamilton made no difference between the original holders and the fraudulent purchasers of this paper. Great and just repugnance arose at putting these two classes of creditors on the same footing, and great exertions were used to pay the former the full value, and to the latter the price only which they had paid, with interest. But this would have prevented the game which was to be played, and for which the minds of greedy members [of Congress] were already tutored and prepared. When the trial of strength on these several efforts had indicated the form in which the bill would finally pass, this being known within doors sooner than without, and especially than to those who were in distant parts of the Union, the base scramble began. Couriers and relay horses by land, and swift-sailing pilot boats by sea, were flying in all directions. Active partners and agents were associated and employed in every state, town, and country neighborhood, and this paper was bought up at five shillings, and often as low as two shillings in the pound, before the holder knew that Congress had already provided for its redemption at par. Immense sums were thus filched from the poor and ignorant, and fortunes accumulated by those who had themselves been poor enough before. Men thus enriched by the dexterity of a leader would follow, of course, the chief who was leading them to fortune, and become the zealous instruments of all his enterprises.—The Anas. Bergh 1:271. (1818.)

HAMILTON (Alexander), His Efforts to Corrupt Congress.—Hamilton's financial system...had two objects. First, as a puzzle to exclude popular understanding and inquiry. Second, as a machine for the corruption of the [Congress]; for he avowed the opinion that man could be governed by one of two motives only, force or interest. Force, he observed, in this country was out of the question; and the interests, therefore, of the members must be laid hold of to keep the [Congress] in unison with the executive. And with grief and shame it must be acknowledged that his machine was not without effect; that even in this, the birth of our government, some members were found sordid enough to bend their duty to their interests, and to look after personal rather than public good.... [Hamilton's financial system] added to the number of votaries to the Treasury, and made its chief the master of every vote in the [Congress] which might give to the government the direction suited to his political views.—The Anas. Bergh 1:271. (1818.)

HAMILTON (Alexander), Character of.—Hamilton was indeed a singular character. Of acute understanding, disinterested, honest and honorable in all private transactions, amiable in society, and duly valuing virtue in private life, yet so bewitched and perverted by the British example as to be under thorough conviction that corruption was essential to the government of a nation.—The Anas. Bergh 1:279. (1818.)

HAMILTON (Alexander). See also FINANCES.

HAPPINESS, Not to Be Perfect in This Life.—Perfect happiness, I believe, was never intended by the Deity to be the lot of one of His creatures in this world; but that He has very much put in our power the nearness of our approaches to it is what I have steadfastly believed. —To John Page. Bergh 4:10. (1763.)

HAPPINESS, Pursuit of, an Inalienable Right.—We hold these truths to be self-evident: that all men are created equal; that they are endowed by their Creator with certain inalienable rights; that among these are life, liberty, and the pursuit of happiness.—Declaration of Independence. Bergh 1:29. (1776.)

HAPPINESS, True Basis of.— Happiness . . . does not depend on the condition of life in which chance has placed [us], but is always the result of a good conscience, good health, occupation, and freedom in all just pursuits.—*Notes on Virginia.* Bergh 2:205. (1782.)

Be assiduous in learning, take much exercise for your health, and practice much virtue. Health, learning, and virtue will insure your happiness; they will give you a quiet conscience, private esteem, and public honor. Beyond these we want nothing but physical necessaries, and they are easily obtained.— Bergh 7:44. (1788.)

HAPPINESS, God and.—The Giver of life . . . gave it for happiness and not for wretchedness.—To James Monroe. Ford 3:59. (1782.)

HAPPINESS, Domestic.—The happiest moments of my life have been the few which I have passed at home in the bosom of my family.— Ford 5:157. (1790.)

The motion of my blood no longer keeps time with the tumult of the world. It leads me to seek for happiness in the lap and love of my family, in the society of my neighbors and my books, in the wholesome occupations of my farm and my affairs, in an interest or affection in every bud that opens, in every breath that blows around me, in an entire freedom of rest, of motion, of thought, owing account to myself alone of my hours and actions.—To James Madison. Bergh 9:119. (1793.)

HAPPINESS, Peace and.—The happiness of mankind is best promoted by the useful pursuits of peace.—Bergh 16:324. (1808.)

HAPPINESS, Education and.—In the present spirit of extending to the great mass of mankind the blessings of instruction, I see a prospect of great advancement in the happiness of the human race.—Bergh 15:400. (1822.)

HARMONY, Sacrifices for.—I see the necessity of sacrificing our opinions sometimes to the opinions of others for the sake of harmony.— Ford 5:194. (1790.)

HARMONY, Public Good and.— The greatest good we can do our country is to heal its party divisions, and make them one people.—Ford 8:76. (1801.)

HARMONY, Dissension vs.—I hope . . . the good sense and patriotism of the friends of free government of every shade will spare us the painful, the deplorable spectacle of brethren sacrificing to small passions the great, the immortal and immutable rights of men.—Ford 8:77. (1801.)

HARMONY, Restoration of National.—To restore that harmony which our predecessors so wickedly made it their object to break up, to render us again one people, acting as one nation, should be the object of every man really a patriot. I am satisfied it can be done, and I own that the day which should convince me of the contrary would be the bitterest of my life.—Ford 8:78. (1801.)

HARMONY. See also DISPUTES.

HEALTH, Necessary for Happiness. —Without health there is no happiness. An attention to health, then, should take [the] place of every other object. The time necessary to secure this by active exercises should be devoted to it in preference to every other pursuit. I know the difficulty with which a studious man tears himself from his studies at any given moment of the day, but his happiness and that of his family depend on it. The most uninformed mind, with a healthy body, is happier than the wisest valetudinarian [person of a weak or sickly constitution].—Ford 4:406. (1787.)

HEALTH. See also EXERCISE.

HENRY (Patrick), Ambition of.— Your character of Patrick Henry is precisely agreeable to the idea I had formed of him. I take him to be of unmeasured ambition.—To James Madison. Ford 4:35. (1785.)

HENRY (Patrick), Foe of the Constitution.—Henry is the avowed foe of the new Constitution. He stands higher in public estimation [in Virginia] than he ever did, yet he was so often in the minority in the present assembly that he has quitted it, never more to return unless an opportunity offers to overturn the new Constitution.—Ford 5:136. (1789.)

HENRY (Patrick), Political Alertness of.—The people of Virginia are beginning to call for a new constitution for their state. This symptom of their wishes will probably bring over Mr. Henry to the proposition. He has been the great obstacle to it hitherto; but you know he is always alive to catch the first sensation of the popular breeze, that he may take the lead of that which in truth leads him.—Ford 6:122. (1792.)

HENRY (Patrick), Results of His Political Apostasy.—As to the effect of Mr. Henry's name among the people, I have found it crumbled like a dried leaf the moment they became satisfied of his apostasy.—Ford 7:381. (1799.)

[Alexander] Hamilton . . . became his idol, and, abandoning the republican advocates of the Constitution, the federal government on Federalist principles became his political creed. . . . His apostasy sank him to nothing in the estimation of his country. He lost at once all that influence which Federalism had hoped, by cajoling him, to transfer with him to itself, and a man who through a long and active life had been the idol of his country, beyond anyone that ever lived, descended to the grave with less than its indifference, and verified the saying of the philosopher that no man must be called happy till he is dead.—Ford 9:344. (1811?)

HENRY (Patrick), His Innate Love of Liberty.—No man ever more undervalued chartered titles than himself. He drew all natural rights from a purer source—the feelings of his own breast.—Ford 10:60. (1816.)

HENRY (Patrick), Oratorical Powers of.—When the famous resolutions of 1765 against the Stamp Act were proposed, I was yet a student of law in Williamsburg. I attended the debate, however, at the door of the lobby of the House of Burgesses, and heard the splendid display of Mr. Henry's talents as a popular orator. They were great, indeed; such as I have never heard from any other man. He appeared to me to speak as Homer wrote.—Autobiography. Bergh 1:5. (1821.)

[I] never heard anything that deserved to be called by the same name with what flowed from him; and where he got that torrent of language is inconceivable.... He was truly a great man.—Quoted from a conversation with Leavit Harris. Henry S. Randall, *The Life of Thomas Jefferson*, 3 vols. (New York: Derby & Jackson, 1858), 1:40. (1824.)

HENRY (Patrick), Literary Indolence of.—He was the laziest man in reading I ever knew.—Autobiography. Bergh 1:12. (1821.)

HISTORY, Value of Studying.—The most effectual means of preventing the perversion of power into tyranny are to illuminate, as far

as practicable, the minds of the people at large, and more especially to give them knowledge of those facts which history exhibits, that possessed thereby of the experience of other ages and countries, they may be enabled to know ambition under all its shapes, and prompt to exert their natural powers to defeat its purposes.—Ford 2:221. (1779.)

History, by apprising [the American people] of the past, will enable them to judge of the future; it will avail them of the experience of other times and other nations; it will qualify them as judges of the actions and designs of men; it will enable them to know ambition under every disguise it may assume; and, knowing it, to defeat its views.—*Notes on Virginia*. Bergh 2:207. (1782.)

HISTORY, Recommended Readings in Morality and.—I advise you to begin a course of ancient history, reading everything in the original and not in translations. First read Goldsmith's history of Greece. This will give you a digested view of that field. Then take up ancient history in the detail, reading the following books in the following order: Herodotus, Thucydides, Xenophontis Anabasis, Arrian, Quintus Curtius, Diodorus Siculus, Justin. This shall form the first stage of your historical reading, and is all I need mention to you now. The next will be of Roman history.* From that we will come down to modern history. In Greek and Latin poetry you have read, or will read at school, Virgil, Terence, Horace, Anacreon, Theocritus, Homer, Euripides,

Sophocles. Read also Milton's "Paradise Lost," Shakespeare, Ossian, [and] Pope's and Swift's works in order to form your style in your own language. In morality, read Epictetus, Xenophontis Memorabilia, Plato's Socratic dialogues, Cicero's philosophies, Antoninus, and Seneca.—To Peter Carr. Bergh 5:84. (1785.)

> *Livy, Sallust, Caesar, Cicero's epistles, Suetonius, Tacitus, Gibbon.—Footnote by Jefferson.

In all cases I prefer original authors to compilers. For a course of ancient history, therefore, of Greece and Rome especially, I should advise the usual suite of Herodotus, Thucydides, Xenophon, Diodorus, Livy, Caesar, Suetonius, Tacitus, and Dion, in their originals if understood, and in translations if not. For its continuation to the final destruction of the empire we must then be content with Gibbon, a compiler, and with Segur, for a judicious recapitulation of the whole. After this general course, there are a number of particular histories filling up the chasms, which may be read at leisure in the progress of life. Such is Arrian, [Quintus] Curtius, Polybius, Sallust, Plutarch, Dionysius, Halicarnassus, Micasi, etc. The ancient *Universal History* should be on our shelves as a book of general reference, the most learned and most faithful perhaps that ever was written. Its style is very plain but perspicuous.—Bergh 16:124. (1825.)

HISTORY, Public Officials Should Keep Records.—It is truly unfortunate that those engaged in public affairs so rarely make notes of transactions passing within their knowledge. Hence history becomes fable instead of fact. The great outlines may be true, but the incidents and coloring are according to the faith or fancy of the writer.—Bergh 14:172. (1814.)

HOME, No Happiness Outside the.—Abstracted from home, I know no happiness in this world.—Ford 2:374. (1780.)

HOME, Independence of.—I am savage enough to prefer the woods, the wilds, and the independence of Monticello to all the brilliant pleasures of this gay capital [Paris].—Bergh 5:128. (1785.)

HOME, Longing for.—I am never a day without wishing myself with you, and more and more as the fine sunshine comes on, which was made for all the world but me.—Bergh 8:324. (1792.)

HOME. See also FAMILY; HAPPINESS, Domestic; MONTICELLO.

HONESTY, Government and.—The whole art of government consists in the art of being honest.—*Summary View of the Rights of British America.* Bergh 1:209. (1774.)

HONESTY, An Exhortation to Practice.—If ever you find yourself environed with difficulties and perplexing circumstances, out of which you are at a loss how to extricate yourself, do what is right, and be assured that that will extricate you the best out of the worst situations. Though you cannot see, when you take one step, what will be the next, yet follow truth, justice, and plain dealing, and never fear their leading you out of the labyrinth in the easiest manner possible. The knot which you thought a Gordian one will untie itself before you. Nothing is so mistaken as the supposition that a person is to extricate himself from a difficulty by intrigue, by chicanery, by dissimulation, by trimming, by an untruth, by an injustice. This increases the difficulties tenfold; and those who pursue these methods get themselves so involved at length that they can turn no way but their infamy becomes more exposed. It is of great importance to set a resolution, not to be shaken, never to tell an untruth. There is no vice so mean, so pitiful, so contemptible; and he who permits himself to tell a lie once finds it much easier to do it a second and third time, till at length it becomes habitual; he tells lies without attending to it, and truths without the world's believing him. This falsehood of the tongue leads to that of the heart, and in time depraves all its good dispositions.—To Peter Carr. Bergh 5:83. (1785.)

HONESTY, Individual.—I know but one code of morality for men, whether acting singly or collectively. He who says I will be a rogue when I act in company with a hundred others, but an honest man when I act alone, will be believed in the former assertion, but not in the latter.... If the morality of one man produces a just line of conduct in him, acting individually, why should not the morality of one hundred men produce a just line of conduct in them, acting together?—Ford 5:111. (1789.)

HONESTY, Wealth Not Conducive to.—I have not observed men's

honesty to increase with their riches. —Ford 7:454. (1800.)

HONESTY. See also GOOD FAITH; LIES; TRUTH.

HONORS, Hostile to Happiness. —There are minds which can be pleased by honors and preferments; but I see nothing in them but envy and enmity. It is only necessary to possess them to know how little they contribute to happiness, or rather how hostile they are to it.—Bergh 6:427. (1788.)

I have seen enough of political honors to know that they are but splendid torments.—To Martha Jefferson Randolph. Betts & Bear, p. 146. (1797.)

HOSPITALITY, Practice of.—You know our practice of placing our guests at their ease by showing them we are so ourselves, and that we follow our necessary vocations instead of fatiguing them by hanging unremittingly on their shoulders.—Ford 10:33. (1816.)

HOUSE OF REPRESENTATIVES. See CONGRESS; LEGISLATURES.

I

IDLENESS, Ill Effects of.—Of all the cankers of human happiness, none corrodes it with so silent yet so baneful a tooth as indolence. Body and mind both unemployed, our being becomes a burden, and every object about us loathsome, even the dearest. Idleness begets ennui, ennui the hypochondria, and that a diseased body. No laborious person was ever yet hysterical. Exercise and application produce order in our affairs, health of body, cheerfulness of mind, and these make us precious to our friends. It is while we are young that the habit of industry is formed. If not then, it never is afterwards. The fortune of our lives therefore depends on employing well the short period of youth. If at any moment, my dear, you catch yourself in idleness, start from it as you would from the precipice of a gulf.—To Martha Jefferson. Betts & Bear, p. 34. (1787.)

Ennui [is] the most dangerous poison of life. A mind always employed is always happy. This is the true secret, the grand recipe for felicity. The idle are the only wretched.—To Martha Jefferson. Betts & Bear, p. 41. (1787.)

IDLENESS. See also TIME.

IGNORANCE, And Misgovernment.—Preach, my dear sir, a crusade against ignorance; establish and improve the law for educating the common people. Let our countrymen know that the people alone can protect us against these evils [of misgovernment], and that the tax which will be paid for this purpose [public education] is not more than the thousandth part of what will be paid to kings, priests, and nobles who will rise up among us if we leave the people in ignorance.—To George Wythe. Bergh 5:397. (1786.)

IGNORANCE, Preferable to Degeneracy.—If science produces no better fruits than tyranny, murder, rapine, and destitution of national morality, I would rather wish our country to be ignorant, honest, and estimable, as our neighboring savages are.—Ford 9:334. (1812.)

IGNORANCE. See also KNOWLEDGE.

ILLUMINATI, Order of.— I have lately by accident got a sight of a single volume (the third) of the Abbe Barruel's *Antisocial Conspiracy*, which gives me the first idea I have ever had of what is meant by the illuminatism against which "Illuminate Morse," as he is now called, and his ecclesiastical and monarchical associates have been making such a hue and cry. Barruel's own parts of the book are perfectly the ravings of a bedlamite. But he quotes largely from Wishaupt, whom he considers as the founder of what he calls the order. As you may not have had an opportunity of forming a judgment of this cry of "mad dog" which has been raised against his doctrines, I will give you the idea I have formed from only an hour's reading of Barruel's quotations from him, which, you may be sure, are not the most favorable.

Wishaupt seems to be an enthusiastic philanthropist. He is among those (as you know the excellent Price and Priestley also are) who believe in the infinite perfectability of man. He thinks he may be able to govern himself in every circumstance so as to injure none, to do all the good he can, to leave government no occasion to exercise their powers over him, and, of course, to render political government useless. This, you know, is Godwin's doctrine, and this is what Robinson, Barruel, and Morse had called a conspiracy against all government. Wishaupt believes that to promote this perfection of the human character was the object of Jesus Christ; that his intention was simply to reinstate natural religion and, by diffusing the light of his morality, to teach us to govern ourselves. His precepts are the love of God and love of our neighbor. And by teaching innocence of conduct, he expected to place men in their natural state of liberty and equality. He says no one ever laid a surer foundation for liberty than our grand master, Jesus of Nazareth. He believes the Freemasons were originally possessed of the true principles and objects of Christianity, and have still preserved some of them by tradition, but much disfigured. The means he proposes to effect this improvement of human nature are "to enlighten men, to correct their morals and inspire them with benevolence."

As Wishaupt lived under the tyranny of a despot and priests, he knew that caution was necessary even in spreading information and the principles of pure morality. He proposed, therefore, to lead the Freemasons to adopt this object, and to make the objects of their institution the diffusion of science and virtue. He proposed to initiate new members into his body by gradations proportioned to his fears of the thunderbolts of tyranny. This had given an air of mystery to his views, was the foundation of his banishment [and] the subversion of the Masonic Order, and is the color for the ravings against him of Robinson, Barruel, and Morse, whose real fears are that the craft would be endangered by the spreading of information, reason, and natural

morality among men. This subject being new to me, I imagine that if it be so to you also, you may receive the same satisfaction in seeing which I have had in forming the analysis of it; and I believe you will think with me that if Wishaupt had written here, where no secrecy is necessary in our endeavors to render men wise and virtuous, he would not have thought of any secret machinery for that purpose; as Godwin, if he had written in Germany, might probably also have thought secrecy and mysticism prudent.—Ford 7:419. (1800.)

IMMATERIALISM. See MATTER.

IMMIGRANTS, Protection of.—It has been the wise policy of these states to extend the protection of their laws to all those who should settle among them, of whatsoever nation or religion they might be, and to admit them to a participation of the benefits of civil and religious freedom; and the benevolence of this practice, as well as its salutary effects, renders it worthy of being continued in future times.—Ford 2:445. (1781.)

IMMIGRANTS, Colonization by.—The best [tenants]...are foreigners who do not speak the language. Unable to communicate with the people of the country, they confine themselves to their farms and families, compare their present state to what it was in Europe, and find great reason to be contented. Of all foreigners, I should prefer Germans. They are the easiest got, the best for their landlords, and do best for themselves.—Bergh 6:253. (1787.)

As to other |than English| foreigners, it is thought better to discourage their settling together in large masses, wherein, as in our German settlements, they preserve for a long time their own languages, habits, and principles of government, and that they should distribute themselves sparsely among the natives for quicker amalgamation. ...English emigrants are without this inconvenience. They differ from us little but in their principles of government, and most of those (merchants excepted) who come here are sufficiently disposed to adopt ours.—Bergh 15:140. (1817.)

IMMIGRATION, Too Rapid.—The present desire of America is to produce rapid population by as great importations of foreigners as possible. But is this founded in good policy? The advantage proposed is the multiplication of numbers.... Civil government being the sole object of forming societies, its administration must be conducted by common consent. Every species of government has its specific principles. Ours, perhaps, are more peculiar than those of any other in the universe. It is a composition of the freest principles of the English constitution, with others derived from natural right and natural reason. To these, nothing can be more opposed than the maxims of absolute monarchies. Yet from such we are to expect the greatest number of emigrants. They will bring with them the principles of the governments they leave, imbibed in their early youth, or, if able to throw them off, it will be in exchange for

an unbounded licentiousness, passing, as is usual, from one extreme to another. It would be a miracle were they to stop precisely at the point of temperate liberty. These principles, with their language, they will transmit to their children. In proportion to their numbers, they will share with us the legislation. They will infuse into it their spirit, warp and bias its directions, and render it a heterogeneous, incoherent, distracted mass.—*Notes on Virginia*. Bergh 2:118. (1782.)

IMMIGRATION, Free.—Our country is open to all men to come and go peaceably when they choose.—Ford 6:459. (1793.)

The first Congress convened since republicanism has recovered its ascendancy...are opening the doors of hospitality to fugitives from the oppressions of other countries.—Bergh 10:309. (1802.)

IMMIGRATION. See also EMIGRATION; NATURALIZATION.

IMMORTALITY. See FUTURE LIFE.

IMPEACHMENT, The Judiciary and.—Having found from experience that impeachment is an impracticable thing, a mere scarecrow, they [the judiciary] consider themselves secure for life.—Ford 10:170. (1820.)

In the general government, in this instance, we have gone even beyond the English caution by requiring a vote of two-thirds in one of the houses for removing a judge; a vote so impossible, where any defense is made before men of ordinary prejudices and passions, that our judges are effectually independent of the nation. But this ought not to be.—Autobiography. Bergh 1:120. (1821.)

Our different states have differently modified their several judiciaries as to the tenure of office. Some appoint their judges for a given term of time; some continue them *during good behavior,* and that to be determined on by the concurring vote of *two-thirds* of each legislative house. In England they are removable by a *majority* only of each house. The last is a practicable remedy; the second is not. The combination of the friends and associates of the accused, the action of personal and party passions, and the sympathies of the human heart will forever find means of influencing one-third of either the one or the other house, will thus secure their impunity, and establish them in fact for life. The first remedy is the best, that of appointing for a term of years only, with a capacity of reappointment if their conduct has been approved.—Bergh 15:486. (1823.)

IMPEACHMENT, Inefficiency of. —Experience has proved that impeachment in our forms is completely inefficient.—Bergh 16:114. (1825.)

IMPRESSMENT, Embargo and.— The stand which has been made on behalf of our seamen enslaved and incarcerated in foreign ships, and against the prostration of our rights on the ocean under laws of nature acknowledged by all civilized nations, was an effort due to the protection of our commerce, and to that portion of our fellow citizens engaged in the pursuits of naviga-

tion. The opposition of the same portion to the vindication of their peculiar rights has been as wonderful as the loyalty of their agricultural brethren in the assertion of them has been disinterested and meritorious.—Bergh 16:351. (1809.)

INCORPORATION, Enumerated Powers and.—[It has been] proposed to Congress to incorporate an agricultural society. I am against that because I think Congress cannot find in all the enumerated powers any one which authorizes the act, much less the giving the public money to that use. I believe, too, if they had the power it would soon be used for no other purpose than to buy with sinecures [offices or positions that require little or no work] useful partisans.—Ford 7:493. (1801.)

INDEMNIFICATION, National Usage of.—The usage of nations requires that we shall give the offender an opportunity of making reparation and avoiding war.—Ford 9:100. (1807.)

INDEMNIFICATION, Great Britain and.—One thousand ships taken, six thousand seamen impressed, savage butcheries of our citizens, and incendiary machinations against our Union declare that [the British] and their allies, the Spaniards, must retire from the Atlantic side of our continent as the only security or indemnification which will be effectual.—Bergh 13:185. (1812.)

INDEPENDENCE. See AMERICAN REVOLUTION; COLONIES (American); DECLARATION OF INDEPENDENCE; ENGLAND;

FOURTH OF JULY; REVOLUTIONARY WAR.

INDIANS, As Allies.—They are a useless, expensive, ungovernable ally.—Ford 2:88. (1776.)

INDIANS, Genius of.—It is in North America we are to seek their [the Indians'] original character. And I am safe in affirming that the proofs of genius given by the Indians of North America place them on a level with whites in the same uncultivated state. The north of Europe furnishes subjects enough for comparison with them, and for a proof of their equality, I have seen some thousands myself, and conversed much with them, and have found in them a masculine, sound understanding. . . . I believe the Indian to be in body and mind equal to the white man.—Ford 3:137. (1785.)

INDIANS, Rights of.—The want of [attention to the Indians' rights] is a principal source of dishonor to the American character.—Bergh 5:390. (1786.)

I am of opinion that . . . the Indians have a right to the occupation of their lands, independent of the states within whose chartered lines they happen to be; that until they cede them by treaty or other transaction equivalent to a treaty, no act of a state can give a right to such lands; that neither under the present Constitution, nor the ancient confederation, had any state or person a right to treat with the Indians without the consent of the general government; . . . that the government is determined to exert all its energy for the patronage and protection of the rights of the Indians, and the preservation of peace between the United States and them; and that if any settlements are made on lands not ceded by them, *without the previous consent of the United States,* the government will think itself bound, not only to declare to the Indians that such settlements are without the authority or protection of the United States, but to remove them also by the public force.—To General Henry Knox. Bergh 8:226. (1791.)

INDIANS, Justice to.—The two principles on which our conduct towards the Indians should be founded are justice and fear. After the injuries we have done them, they cannot love us, which leaves us no alternative but that of fear to keep them from attacking us. But justice is what we should never lose sight of, and in time it may recover their esteem.—Bergh 5:390. (1786.)

I am myself alive to the obtaining lands from the Indians by all *honest* and *peaceable means,* and I believe that the honest and peaceable means adopted by us will obtain them as fast as the expansion of our settlements, with due regard to compactness, will require.—To General Andrew Jackson. Bergh 10:359. (1803.)

Nothing must be spared to convince [the Indians] of the justice and liberality we are determined to use towards them, and to attach them to us indissolubly.—Bergh 11:81. (1805.)

INDIANS, Early Origins in America.—I suppose the settlement of our continent is of the most remote antiquity. The similitude between its inhabitants and those of the eastern parts of Asia renders it probable that ours are descended from them, or they from ours. The latter is my opinion, founded on this single fact: among the red inhabitants of Asia there are but a few languages radically different, but among our Indians the number of languages is infinite which are so radically different as to exhibit at present no appearance of their having been derived from a common source. The time necessary for the generation of so many languages must be immense.—Boyd 10:316. (1786.)

INDIANS, American Nations and.—[It is] an established principle of public law among the white nations of America that while the Indians included within their limits retain all other natural rights, no other white nations can become their patrons, protectors, or mediators, nor in any shape intermeddle between them and those within whose limits they are.—Ford 1:210. (1792.)

INDIANS, Brotherhood of.—Made by the same Great Spirit, and living in the same land with our brothers, the red men, we consider ourselves as of the same family; we wish to live with them as one people, and to cherish their interests as our own.— Address to Indians. Bergh 16:390. (1802.)

INDIANS, Jefferson's Policy Toward.—The Indian tribes residing within the limits of the United States have, for a considerable time, been growing more and more uneasy at the constant diminution of the territory they occupy, although effected by their own voluntary sales; and the policy has long been gaining strength with them of refusing absolutely all further sale on any conditions; insomuch that, at this time, it hazards their friendship and excites dangerous jealousies and perturbations in their minds to make any overture for the purchase of the smallest portions of their land. A very few tribes only are not yet obstinately in these dispositions. In order peaceably to counteract this policy of theirs, and to provide an extension of territory which the rapid increase of our numbers will call for, two measures are deemed expedient. First: to encourage them to abandon hunting, to apply to the raising stock, to agriculture and domestic manufactures, and thereby prove to themselves that less land and labor will maintain them in this better than in their former mode of living. The extensive forests necessary in the hunting life will then become useless, and they will see advantage in exchanging them for the means of improving their farms and of increasing their domestic comforts. Secondly: to multiply trading houses among them, and place within their reach those things which will contribute more to their domestic comfort than the possession of extensive and uncultivated wilds. Experience and reflection will develop to them the wisdom of exchanging what they can spare, and we want, for what we can spare and they want. In leading them thus to agriculture, to manufactures, and civilization, in bringing together their and our settlements, and in preparing them ultimately to participate in the benefits of our government, I trust and believe we are acting for their greatest good.—Confidential Message to Congress. Bergh 3:489. (1803.)

Our system is to live in perpetual peace with the Indians, to cultivate an affectionate attachment from them by everything just and liberal which we can do for them within the bounds of reason, and by giving them effectual protection against wrongs from our own people.—To Governor William Henry Harrison. Bergh 10:369. (1803.)

INDIANS, Adapting to Domestic Pursuits.—The decrease of game rendering their subsistence by hunting insufficient, we wish to draw them to agriculture, to spinning and weaving. The latter branches they take up with great readiness because they fall to the women, who gain by quitting the labors of the field for those which are exercised within doors. When they withdraw themselves to the culture of a small piece of land, they will perceive how useless to them are their extensive forests, and will be willing to pare them off from time to time in exchange for necessaries for their farms and families.—To Governor William Henry Harrison. Bergh 10:369. (1803.)

I consider the business of hunting as already become insufficient to furnish clothing and subsistence to the Indians. The promotion of agriculture, therefore, and household manufacture are essential in their preservation, and I am disposed to aid and encourage it liberally.—Ford 8:213. (1803.)

INDIANS, Amalgamation of.—The ultimate point of rest and happiness for them is to let our settlements and theirs meet and blend together, to intermix and become one people, incorporating themselves with us as citizens of the United States. This is what the natural progress of things will of course bring on, and it will be better to promote than to retard it.—Ford 8:214. (1803.)

Our settlements will gradually circumscribe and approach the Indians, and they will in time either incorporate with us as citizens of the United States or remove beyond the Misssissippi. The former is certainly the termination of their history most happy for themselves, but in the whole course of this it is essential to cultivate their love.—To Governor William Henry Harrison. Bergh 10:370. (1803.)

I shall rejoice to see the day when the red men, our neighbors, become truly one people with us, enjoying all the rights and privileges we do, and living in plenty and peace as we do, without anyone to make them afraid, to injure their persons, or to take their property without being punished for it according to fixed laws.—To the Cherokee chiefs. Bergh 16:434. (1808.)

INDIANS, Efforts to Improve Condition of.—Philanthropic motives have directed the public endeavors to ameliorate the condition of the Indian natives by introducing among them a knowledge of agriculture and

Jefferson in about 1799 (age 56?). Pencil drawing by Benjamin Henry Latrobe.

some of the mechanic arts, by encouraging them to resort to these as more certain and less laborious resources for subsistence than the chase, and by withholding from them the pernicious supplies of ardent spirits. They are our brethren, our neighbors; they may be valuable friends, and troublesome enemies. Both duty and interest, then, enjoin that we should extend to them the blessings of civilized life, and prepare their minds for becoming useful members of the American family.—Bergh 16:289. (1807.)

Our endeavors are to impress on them all profoundly temperance, peace, and agriculture; and I am persuaded they begin to feel profoundly the soundness of the advice.—Bergh 12:219. (1808.)

INDIANS, Schools for.—Teaching the Indian boys and girls to read and write, agriculture and mechanic trades to the former, spinning and weaving to the latter, may perhaps be acceded to by us advantageously for the Indians.—Bergh 12:40. (1808.)

INDIANS, Civilizing of.—The plan of civilizing the Indians is undoubtedly a great improvement on the ancient and totally ineffectual one of beginning with religious missionaries. Our experience has shown that this must be the last step of the process. The following is what has been successful: 1st, to raise cattle, etc., and thereby acquire a knowledge of the value of property; 2nd, arithmetic, to calculate that value; 3rd, writing, to keep accounts, and here they begin to enclose farms, and the men to labor, the women to spin and weave; 4th, to read *Aesop's Fables* and *Robinson Crusoe* are their first delight. The Creeks and Cherokees are advanced thus far, and the Cherokees are now instituting a regular government.—Bergh 12:270. (1809.)

INDIANS, Great Britain and.—You know the benevolent plan we were pursuing here for the happiness of the aboriginal inhabitants in our vicinities. We spared nothing to keep them at peace with one another, to teach them agriculture and the rudiments of the most necessary arts, and to encourage industry by establishing among them separate property. In this way they would have been enabled to subsist and multiply on a moderate scale of landed possession. They would have mixed their blood with ours, and been amalgamated and identified with us within no distant period of time. On the commencement of the present war [with Great Britain], we pressed on them the observance of peace and neutrality, but the interested and unprincipled policy of England has defeated all our labors for the salvation of these unfortunate people. They have seduced the greater part of the tribes within our neighborhood to take up the hatchet against us, and the cruel massacres they have committed on the women and children of our frontiers taken by surprise will oblige us now to pursue them to extermination, or drive them to new seats beyond our reach. . . . The confirmed brutalization, if not the extermination of this race in our America, is therefore to form an additional chapter in the English history of the same colored man in Asia, and of the brethren of their own color in Ireland, and wherever else Anglo-mercantile cupidity can find a two-penny interest in deluging the earth with human blood.—Ford 9:431. (1813.)

INDIANS. See also MURDER, Indians and.

INDUSTRY, Taxing.—Sound principles will not justify our taxing the industry of our fellow citizens to accumulate treasure for wars to happen we know not when, and which might not perhaps happen but from the temptations offered by that treasure.—First Annual Message to Congress. Bergh 3:331. (1801.)

INDUSTRY, People's Right to Fruits of.—Our wish . . . is that the public efforts may be directed honestly to the public good, that . . . equality of rights [be] maintained, and that state of property, equal or unequal, which results to every man from his own industry or that of his fathers.—Second Inaugural Address. Bergh 3:382. (1805.)

[The] rights [of the people] . . . to the exercise and fruits of their own industry can never be protected against the selfishness of rulers not subject to their control at short periods.—Bergh 15:66. (1816.)

INDUSTRY, Taking from the "Haves."—To take from one because it is thought that his own industry and that of his fathers has acquired too much, in order to spare to others who, or whose fathers, have not exercised equal industry and skill, is to violate arbitrarily the first principle of association, "the *guarantee* to everyone of a free exercise of his industry, and the fruits acquired by it."—Bergh 14:466. (1816.)

INDUSTRY. See also LABOR; PROPERTY; REDISTRIBUTION OF WEALTH.

INFLATION, Produced by Excess Paper Money.—Paper . . . is liable to be abused, has been, is, and forever will be abused, in every country in which it is permitted . . . , We are already at ten or twenty times the due quantity of medium, insomuch that no man knows what his property is now worth because it is bloating while he is calculating.... It is a palpable falsehood to say we can have specie for our paper whenever demanded. Instead, then, of yielding to the cries of scarcity of medium set up by speculators, projectors, and commercial gamblers, no endeavors should be spared to begin the work of reducing it by such gradual means as may give time to private fortunes to preserve their poise.—To John W. Eppes. Bergh 13:430. (1813.)

We have no metallic measure of values at present, while we are overwhelmed with bank paper. The depreciation of this swells nominal prices without furnishing any stable index of real value.—Bergh 14:264. (1815.)

We are now without any common measure of the value of property, and private fortunes are up or down at the will of the worst of our citizens. Yet there is no hope of relief from the legislatures who have immediate control over this subject. As little seems to be known of the principles of political economy as if nothing had ever been written or practiced on the subject.... It is an evil, therefore, which we must make up our minds to meet and to endure, as those of hurricanes, earthquakes, and other casualties.—To Albert Gallatin. Bergh 14:357. (1815.)

The flood with which the banks are deluging us of nominal money has placed us completely without any certain measure of value, and, by interpolating a false measure, is deceiving and ruining multitudes of our citizens.—Ford 10:116. (1818.)

INFLATION. See also MONEY; PAPER MONEY.

INHERITANCES, Legislation by States Only.—The [federal] government is incompetent to legislate on the subject of inheritances.—To President Washington. Ford 6:133. (1792.)

INHERITANCES, Equal.—If the overgrown wealth of an individual be deemed dangerous to the state, the best corrective is the law of equal inheritance to all in equal degree; and the better, as this enforces a law of nature, while extra taxation violates it.—Bergh 14:466. (1816.)

Equal partition of inheritances... [is] the best of all agrarian laws.—Autobiography. Bergh 1:73. (1821.)

INHERITANCES. See also ENTAIL; PRIMOGENITURE.

INSURRECTION, Cannot Be Prevented by Force.—[No] degree of power in the hands of government [will] prevent insurrections. In England, where the hand of power is heavier than with us, there are seldom half a dozen years without an insurrection. In France, where it is still heavier,... and where there are always two or three hundred thousand men ready to crush insurrections, there have been three in the course of the three years I have been here.... In Turkey, where the sole nod of the despot is death, insurrections are the events of every day.—To James Madison. Bergh 6:391. (1787.)

INSURRECTION, Precautions Against.—In a country whose Constitution is derived from the will of the people, directly expressed by their free suffrages; where the principal executive functionaries, and those of the legislature, are renewed by them at short periods; where under the character of jurors they exercise in person the greatest portion of the judiciary powers; where the laws are consequently so framed and administered as to bear with equal weight and favor on all, restraining no man in the pursuits of honest industry, and securing to everyone the property which that acquires, it would not be supposed that any safeguards could be needed against insurrection or enterprise on the public peace or authority. The laws, however, aware that these should not be trusted to moral restraints only, have wisely provided punishments for these crimes when committed. But would it not be salutary to give also the means of preventing their commission?—Ford 8:490. (1806.)

INSURRECTION, Suppressing.— I hope, on the first symptom of an open opposition to the [embargo] law by force, you will fly to the scene and aid in suppressing any commotion.—To Henry Dearborn (Secretary of War). Bergh 12:119. (1808.)

INSURRECTION, American People Not Inclined to.—My long and intimate knowledge of my countrymen satisfies me that, let there be occasion to display the banners of the law, and the world will see how few and pitiful are those who shall array themselves in opposition.—Ford 9:211. (1808.)

INSURRECTION. See also REBELLION; RESISTANCE; REVOLUTION; SHAYS'S REBELLION.

INTEGRITY. See GOOD FAITH; HONESTY; LIES; TRUTH.

INTEMPERANCE, The Greatest Calamity.—Mr. B's habitual intoxication will destroy himself, his fortune and family. Of all calamities this is the greatest.—To Mary Jefferson Eppes. Betts & Bear, p. 151. (1798.)

INTEMPERANCE, Should Be Restricted.—The drunkard, as much as the maniac, requires restrictive measures to save him from the fatal infatuation under which he is destroying his health, his morals, his family, and his usefulness to society. One powerful obstacle to his ruinous self-indulgence would be a price beyond his competence.—Ford 10:252. (1823.)

INTEMPERANCE. See also ALCOHOLIC BEVERAGES; WINE.

INTEREST, Right to Collect.— There is not a single title to debt so formal and sacred as to give a right to interest under all possible circumstances, either there [in England] or here [in America].—Bergh 16:274. (1792.)

INTEREST, Sacred Obligation to Pay.—A sacred payment of interest is the only way to make the most of [the people's] resources, and a sense of that renders [the government's] income from our funds more certain.—Bergh 14:217. (1814.)

INTOLERANCE, Defiance of.— I never will, by any word or act, bow to the shrine of intolerance, or admit a right of inquiry into the religious opinions of others.—Bergh 10:378. (1803.)

INTOLERANCE. See also BIGOTRY.

INTOXICATION. See ALCOHOL-
IC BEVERAGES; INTEMPER-
ANCE; WINE.

INTRIGUE, Abhorrence of.—[In
France] I . . . practiced no subleties,
meddled in no intrigues, pursued no
concealed object.—Autobiography.
Bergh 1:96. (1821.)

INVENTIONS, Phosphoric Matches.
—I should have sent you a specimen
of the phosphoric matches, but . . .
I am told Mr. [David] Rittenhouse
has had some of them. They are a
beautiful discovery and very useful,
especially to heads which, like yours
and mine, cannot at all times be got
to sleep. The convenience of lighting
a candle without getting out of bed,
of sealing letters without calling a
servant, of kindling a fire without
flint, steel, punk, etc., is of value.
—To Charles Thomson. Ford 4:14.
(1784.)

INVENTIONS, Air-Screw Propel-
ler.—I went some time ago to see a
machine which offers something
new. A man had applied to a light
boat a very large screw, the thread
of which was a thin plate, two feet
broad, applied by its edge spirally
around a small axis. It somewhat
resembled a bottle brush, if you will
suppose the hairs of the bottle brush
joining together and forming a spiral
plane. This, turned on its axis in the
air, carried the vessel across the
Seine. It is, in fact, a screw which
takes hold of the air and draws itself
along by it; losing, indeed, much of
its effort by the yielding nature of
the body it lays hold of to pull itself
on by. I think it may be applied in the
water with much greater effect and
to very useful purposes. Perhaps it

may be used also for the balloon.—
Bergh 5:157. (1785.)

INVENTIONS, Copying Press.—
When I was in England, I formed a
portable copying press on the principle of the large one they make here
[in Paris] for copying letters. I had a
model made there, and it has
answered perfectly. A workman
here has made several from that
model. . . . You must do me the favor
to accept of one.—Ford 4:347. (1786.)

INVENTIONS, Preserving Flour.—
Every discovery which multiplies
the subsistence of man must be a
matter of joy to every friend of
humanity. As such, I learn with great
satisfaction that you have found the
means of preserving flour more
perfectly than has been done hitherto. But I am not authorized to avail
my country of it by making any offer
for its communication. Their policy
is to leave their citizens free, neither
restraining nor aiding them in their
pursuits.—Bergh 6:255. (1787.)

INVENTIONS, Pedometer.—I send
your pedometer. To the loop at the
bottom of it you must sew a tape,
and at the other end of the tape a
small hook. . . . Cut a little hole in the
bottom of your left watch pocket,
pass the hook and tape through it,
and down between the breeches and
drawers, and fix the hook on the
edge of your knee band, an inch
from the knee buckle; then hook the
instrument itself, by its swivel hook,
on the upper edge of the watch
pocket. Your tape being well ad-
justed in length, your double steps
will be exactly counted by the instrument.—To James Madison.
Bergh 6:460. (1788.)

INVENTIONS, Threshing Machine.
—My threshing machine has arrived at New York. Mr. Pinckney writes me word that the original from which this is copied threshes one hundred and fifty bushels of wheat in eight hours, with six horses and five men. It may be moved either by water or horses. Fortunately the workman who made it (a millwright) is come in the same vessel to America. I have written to persuade him to go on immediately to Richmond, offering him the use of my model to exhibit, and to give him letters to get him into immediate employ in making them.—To James Madison. Ford 6:403. (1793.)

INVENTIONS, Seed Box.—The seed box described in the agricultural transactions of New York reduces the expense of seeding from six shillings to two shillings and three pence the acre, and does the business better than is possible to be done by the human hand.—To James Madison. Ford 7:11. (1795.)

INVENTIONS, Polygraph.—A Mr. Hawkins of Frankford, near Philadelphia, has invented a machine which he calls a polygraph, and which carries two, three, or four pens. That of two pens, with which I am now writing, is best; and is so perfect that I have laid aside the copying press for a twelvemonth past, and write always with the polygraph.—Bergh 11:67. (1805.)

It is for copying with one pen while you write with the other, and without the least additional embarrassment or exertion to the writer. I think it the finest invention of the present age.... As a secretary which copies for us what we write without the power of revealing it, I find it a most precious possession to a man in public business.—Bergh 11:118. (1806.)

INVENTIONS, Jefferson's Model Plow.—I have received ... the medal of gold by which the Society of Agriculture at Paris have been pleased to mark their approbation of a form of the moldboard which I had proposed; also ... the information that they had honored me with the title of foreign associate to their society. I receive with great thankfulness these testimonies of their favor, and should be happy to merit them by greater services.—Bergh 11:212. (1807.)

I shall with great pleasure attend to the construction and transmission to the Society [Agricultural Society of Paris] of a plow with my moldboard. This is the only part of that useful instrument to which I have paid any particular attention. But knowing how much the perfection of the plow must depend, 1st, on the line of traction; 2nd, on the direction of the share; 3rd, on the angle of the wing; [and] 4th, on the form of the moldboard; and persuaded that I shall find the three first advantages eminently exemplified in [the plow] which the Society sends me, I am anxious to see combined with these a moldboard of my form, in the hope it will still advance the perfection of that machine.—Bergh 12:89. (1808.)

INVENTIONS, Stylograph.—The apparatus for stylographic writing ...is certainly very ingenious.... I had never heard of the invention till your letter announced it, for these novelties reach us very late.—Bergh 12:42. (1808.)

INVENTORS, Rights of.—It has been pretended by some (and in England especially) that inventors have a natural and exclusive right to their inventions, and not merely for their own lives, but inheritable to their heirs. But while it is a moot question whether the origin of any kind of property is derived from nature at all, it would be singular to admit a natural and even a hereditary right to inventors.... Inventions then cannot, in nature, be a subject of property. Society may give an exclusive right to the profits arising from them, as an encouragment to men to pursue ideas which may produce utility; but this may or may not be done, according to the will and convenience of the society, without claim or complaint from anybody. Accordingly, it is a fact, as far as I am informed, that England was, until we copied her, the only country on earth which ever, by a general law, gave a legal right to the exclusive use of an idea. In some countries it is sometimes done in a great case, and by a special and personal act, but generally speaking, other nations have thought that these monopolies produce more embarrassment than advantage to society; and it may be observed that the nations which refuse monopolies of invention are as fruitful as England in new and useful devices. —Bergh 13:333. (1813.)

INVENTORS. See also PATENTS.

J

JACKSON (Andrew), Faithful to the Union.—Be assured that Tennessee and particularly General Jackson are faithful.—Ford 9:2. (1807.)

JACKSON (Andrew), Invitation to. —In your passages to and from Washington, should your travelling convenience ever permit a deviation to Monticello, I shall receive you with distinguished welcome.... I recall with pleasure the remembrance of our joint labors while in [the] Senate together in times of great trial and of hard battling. Battles, indeed, of words, not of blood, as those you have since fought so much for your own glory, and that of your country.—To Andrew Jackson. Ford 10:286. (1823.)

JACKSON (Andrew), Passionate.— I feel much alarmed at the prospect of seeing General Jackson [elected as] President. He is one of the most unfit men I know of for such a place. He has had very little respect for laws or constitutions, and is, in fact, an able military chief. His passions are terrible. When I was president of the Senate he was a Senator, and he could never speak on account of the rashness of his feelings. I have seen him attempt it repeatedly, and as often choke with rage. His passions are no doubt cooler now; he has been much tried since I knew him, but he is a dangerous man.—Quoted by Daniel Webster from his interview with Jefferson. Ford 10:331. (1824.)

JAY (John), Monarchical Principles of.—Jay, covering the same [monarchical] principles under the veil of silence, is rising steadily on the ruins of his friends.—To James Monroe. Ford 5:352. (1791.)

JAY (John), Chief Justice.—Jay [has been] nominated Chief Justice. We were afraid of something worse.—Ford 7:471. (1800.)

JAY TREATY, Censured by Most Americans.—No man in the United States has had the effrontery to affirm that the treaty with England was not a very bad one except A.H. [Alexander Hamilton] under the signature of *Camillus*. Its most zealous defenders only pretended that it was better than war, as if war was not invited, rather than avoided, by unfounded demands. I have never known the public pulse beat so full and in such universal union on any subject since the Declaration of Independence.—To James Monroe. Ford 7:58. (1796.)

JAY TREATY, Anticipated Results of.—The campaign of Congress has closed. Though the Anglomen have in the end got their treaty through, and so have triumphed over the cause of republicanism, yet it has been to them a dear-bought victory. It has given the most radical shock to their party which it has ever received; and there is no doubt they would be glad to be replaced on the ground they possessed the instant before Jay's nomination extraordinary. They see that nothing can support them but the colossus of the President's merits with the people, and, the moment he retires, that his successor, if a monocrat, will be overborne by the republican sense

of his constituents; if a republican, he will, of course, give fair play to that sense, and lead things into the channel of harmony between the governors and the governed. In the meantime, patience.—To James Monroe. Bergh 9:348. (1796.)

JEALOUSY, Government and.—Free government is founded in jealousy, and not in confidence; it is jealousy, and not confidence, which prescribes limited constitutions to bind down those whom we are obliged to trust with power.—Kentucky Resolutions. Bergh 17:388. (1798.)

JEFFERSON (Thomas), Family of.—Jane Jefferson, born 1740, June 17; died 1765, Oct. 1.

Mary Jefferson, born 1741, Oct. 1; married 1760, June 24.

Thomas Jefferson, born 1743, Apr. 2;* married 1772, Jan. 1.

Elizabeth Jefferson, born 1744, Nov. 4; died 1773, Jan. 1.

Martha Jefferson, born 1746, May 29; married 1765, July 20.

Peter Field Jefferson, born 1748, Oct. 16; died 1748, Nov. 29.

A son, born 1750, March 9; died 1750, March 9.

Lucy Jefferson, born 1752, Oct. 10; married 1769, Sep. 12.

Anna Scott Randolph Jefferson, born 1755, Oct. 1; married 1788, October.—Ford 1:3.

* After Great Britain's adoption of the Gregorian calendar in 1752, Jefferson's birthday was celebrated on April 13.—Editor.

JEFFERSON (Thomas), His Desire for a Tranquil Life.—There are minds which can be pleased by honors and preferments; but I see nothing in them but envy and enmity. It is only necessary to possess them to know how little they contribute to happiness, or rather how hostile they are to it. . . . I had rather be shut up in a very modest cottage with my books, my family, and a few old friends, dining on simple bacon and letting the world roll on as it liked, than to occupy the most splendid post which any human power can give.—Bergh 6:427. (1788.)

JEFFERSON (Thomas), His Openness in Expressing Opinions.—I never had an opinion in politics or religion which I was afraid to own. A costive reserve on these subjects might have procured me more esteem from some people, but less from myself.—Bergh 7:302. (1789.)

I have not been in the habit of mysterious reserve on any subject, nor of buttoning up my opinions within my own doublet. On the contrary, while in public service especially, I thought the public entitled to frankness, and intimately to know whom they employed.—Ford 10:37. (1816.)

JEFFERSON (Thomas), His Desire to Avoid Public Notice.—My great wish is to go on in a strict but silent performance of my duty, to avoid attracting notice, and to keep my name out of newspapers, because I find the pain of a little censure, even when it is unfounded, is more acute than the pleasure of much praise.—Bergh 7:302. (1789.)

JEFFERSON (Thomas), As a Farmer.—When I first entered on the stage of public life (now twenty-four years ago), I came to a resolution never to . . . wear any other character than that of a farmer.—Bergh 9:44. (1793.)

I return to farming with an ardor which I scarcely knew in my youth, and which has got the better entirely of my love of study.—To George Washington. Bergh 9:283. (1794.)

I have often thought that if heaven had given me [the] choice of my position and calling, it should have been on a rich spot of earth, well watered and near a good market. . . . No occupation is so delightful to me as the culture of the earth.—Bergh 13:79. (1811.)

To keep a Virginia estate together requires in the owner both skill and attention. Skill I never had, and attention I could not have; and, really, when I reflect on all circumstances, my wonder is that I should have been so long as sixty years in reaching the result to which I am now reduced.—Ford 10:383. (1826.)

JEFFERSON (Thomas), His Devotion to the United States.—The first object of my heart is my own country. In that is embarked my family, my fortune, and my own existence. I have not one farthing of interest nor one fiber of attachment out of it.—To Elbridge Gerry. Bergh 10:78. (1799.)

JEFFERSON (Thomas), Had No Secrets to Hide.—I can conscientiously declare that, as to myself, I wish that not only no act but no thought of mine should be unknown.—Bergh 12:175. (1808.)

JEFFERSON (Thomas), At the Crossroads of Decision in His Youth.—When I recollect that at fourteen years of age the whole care and direction of myself was thrown on myself entirely, without a relation or friend qualified to advise or guide me, and recollect the various sorts of bad company with which I associated from time to time, I am astonished I did not turn off with some of them and become as worthless to society as they were. I had the good fortune to become acquainted very early with some characters of very high standing, and to feel the incessant wish that I could ever become what they were. Under temptations and difficulties I would ask myself, what would Dr. [William] Small, Mr. [George] Wythe, [or] Peyton Randolph do in this situation? What course in it will ensure me their approbation? I am certain that this mode of deciding on my conduct tended more to correctness than any reasoning powers I possessed. Knowing the even and dignified line they pursued, I could never doubt for a moment which of two courses would be in character for them; whereas, seeking the same object through a process of moral reasoning, and with the jaundiced eye of youth, I should often have erred.

From the circumstances of my position I was often thrown into the society of horse racers, card players, fox hunters, scientific and professional men, and of dignified men; and many a time have I asked myself in the enthusiastic moment of the death of a fox, the victory of a favorite horse, the issue of a question eloquently argued at the bar or in the great council of the nation, well, which of these kinds of reputations should I prefer? That of a horse jockey? a fox hunter? an orator? or the honest advocate of my country's rights? Be assured, my dear Jefferson, that these little returns into ourselves, this self-catechizing habit, is not trifling nor useless, but leads to the prudent selection and steady pursuit of what is right.—To Thomas Jefferson Randolph. Bergh 12:197. (1808.)

JEFFERSON (Thomas), His Feelings upon Retirement from the Presidency.—Within a few days I retire to my family, my books and farms; and having gained the harbor myself, I shall look on my friends still buffeting the storm with anxiety indeed, but not with envy. Never did a prisoner released from his chains feel such relief as I shall on shaking off the shackles of power. Nature intended me for the tranquil pursuits of science by rendering them my supreme delight. But the enormities of the times in which I have lived have forced me to take a part in resisting them, and to commit myself on the boisterous ocean of political passions. I thank God for the opportunity of retiring from them without censure, and carrying with me the most consoling proofs of public approbation.—Bergh 12:259. (1809.)

JEFFERSON (Thomas), Activities in Old Age.—I am retired to Monticello, where, in the bosom of my family, and surrounded by my books, I enjoy a repose to which I have been long a stranger. My mornings are devoted to correspondence. From breakfast to dinner I am in my shops, my garden, or on horseback among my farms; from dinner to dark I give to society and recreation with my neighbors and friends; and from candlelight to early bedtime I read. My health is perfect, and my strength considerably reinforced by the activity of the course I pursue; perhaps it is as great as usually falls to the lot of near sixty-seven years of age. I talk of plows and harrows, of seeding and harvesting, with my neighbors, and of politics, too, if they choose, with as little reserve as the rest of my fellow citizens, and feel, at length, the blessing of being free to say and do what I please, without being responsible for it to any mortal. A part of my occupation, and by no means the least pleasing, is the direction of the studies of such young men as ask it. They place themselves in the neighboring village [Charlottesville], and have the use of my library and counsel, and make a part of my society.— Bergh 12:369. (1810.)

My present course of life admits less reading than I wish. From breakfast, or noon at latest, to dinner, I am mostly on horseback, attending to my farm or other concerns, which I find healthful to my body, mind, and affairs; and the few hours I can pass in my cabinet are devoured by correspondences; not those with my intimate friends, with whom I delight to interchange sentiments, but with others who, writing to me on concerns of their own in which I have had an agency, or from motives of mere respect and approbation, are entitled to be

answered with respect and a return of good will. My hope is that this obstacle to the delights of retirement will wear away with the oblivion which follows that, and that I may at length be indulged in those studious pursuits from which nothing but Revolutionary duties would ever have called me.—To Dr. Benjamin Rush. Ford 9:294. (1811.)

I am on horseback three or four hours of every day; [and I] visit three or four times a year a possession I have ninety miles distant [Poplar Forest], performing the winter journey on horseback. I walk little, however, a single mile being too much for me, and I live in the midst of my grandchildren, one of whom has lately promoted me to be a great-grandfather.—To John Adams. Ford 9:334. (1812.)

I have for fifty years bathed my feet in cold water every morning, ... and having been remarkably exempted from colds (not having had one in every seven years of my life on an average), I have supposed it might be ascribed to that practice.— Bergh 14:319. (1815.)

JEFFERSON (Thomas), Had a Clear Conscience.—During a long life, as much devoted to study as a faithful transaction of the trusts committed to me would permit, no subject has occupied more of my consideration than our relations with all the beings around us, our duties to them, and our future prospects. After reading and hearing everything which probably can be suggested respecting them, I have formed the best judgment I could as to the course they prescribe, and in the due observance of that course I have no recollections which give me uneasiness.—Bergh 13:376. (1813.)

JEFFERSON (Thomas), A "Real Christian."—I...have made a wee little book...which I call the Philosophy of Jesus; it is a paradigma of His doctrines, made by cutting the texts out of the [New Testament] and arranging them on the pages of a blank book, in a certain order of time or subject. A more beautiful or precious morsel of ethics I have never seen; it is a document in proof that *I am a real Christian*, that is to say, a disciple of the doctrines of Jesus, very different from the Platonists, who call *me* infidel and *themselves* Christians and preachers of the gospel, while they draw all their characteristic dogmas from what its Author never said nor saw. They have compounded from the heathen mysteries a system beyond the comprehension of man, of which the great Reformer of the vicious ethics and deism of the Jews, were He to return on earth, would not recognize one feature.—To Charles Thomson. Bergh 14:385. (1816.)

JEFFERSON (Thomas), Physical Condition in His Final Years.—I retain good health, am rather feeble to walk much, but ride with ease, passing two or three hours a day on horseback, and every three or four months taking in a carriage a journey of ninety miles to a distant possession, where I pass a good deal of my time [Poplar Forest]. My eyes need the aid of glasses by night, and with small print in the day also; my

hearing is not quite so sensible as it used to be; no tooth shaking yet, but shivering and shrinking in body from the cold we now experience, my thermometer having been as low as 12 degrees this morning. My greatest oppression is a correspondence afflictingly laborious, the extent of which I have been long endeavoring to curtail. This keeps me at the drudgery of the writing table all the prime hours of the day, leaving for the gratification of my appetite for reading only what I can steal from the hours of sleep.—To Charles Thomson. Bergh 14:386. (1816.)

Your...request of the history of my physical habits would have puzzled me not a little had it not been for the model with which you accompanied it, of Doctor [Benjamin] Rush's answer to a similar inquiry. I live so much like other people that I might refer to ordinary life as the history of my own.... I have lived temperately, eating little animal food, and that not as an aliment so much as a condiment for the vegetables which constitute my principal diet. I double, however, the doctor's glass and a half of wine, and even treble it with a friend; but halve its effects by drinking the weak wines only. The ardent wines I cannot drink, nor do I use ardent spirits in any form. Malt liquors and cider are my table drinks, and my breakfast is of tea and coffee. I have been blessed with organs of digestion which accept and concoct, without ever murmuring, whatever the palate chooses to consign to them, and I have not yet lost a tooth by age. I was a hard student until I entered on the business of life, the duties of which leave no idle time to those disposed to fulfil them; and now, retired and at the age of seventy-six, I am again a hard student. Indeed, my fondness for reading and study revolts me from the drudgery of letter writing. And a stiff wrist, the consequence of an early dislocation, makes writing both slow and painful. I am not so regular in my sleep as the Doctor says he was, devoting to it from five to eight hours, according as my company or the book I am reading interests me; and I never go to bed without an hour or half hour's previous reading of something moral whereon to ruminate in the intervals of sleep. But whether I retire to bed early or late, I rise with the sun. I use spectacles at night, but not necessarily in the day unless in reading small print. My hearing is distinct in particular conversation, but confused when several voices cross each other, which unfits me for the society of the table. I have been more fortunate than my friend in the article of health, so free from catarrhs that I have not had one (in the breast, I mean) on the average of eight or ten years through life. I ascribe this exemption partly to the habit of bathing my feet in cold water every morning for sixty years past. A fever of more than twenty-four hours I have not had above two or three times in my life. A periodical headache has afflicted me occasionally, once perhaps in six or eight years, for two or three weeks at a time, which now seems to have left me; and except on a late occasion of indisposition, I enjoy good health; too feeble, indeed, to walk much, but riding without fatigue six or eight miles a day, and sometimes thirty or forty.—To Dr. Vine Utley. Bergh 15:186. (1819.)

I am like an old watch, with a pinion worn out here and a wheel there, until it can go no longer.— Quoted by Thomas Jefferson Randolph. Henry S. Randall, *The Life of Thomas Jefferson*, 3 vols. (New York: Derby & Jackson, 1858), 3:543. (1826.)

JEFFERSON (Thomas), His Attitude Toward Political Opponents.—It is true, as you say, that we have differed in political opinions; but I can say with equal truth that I never suffered a political to become a personal difference. I have been left on this ground by some friends whom I dearly loved, but I was never the first to separate. With some others of politics different from mine, I have continued in the warmest friendship to this day, and to all, and to yourself particularly, I have ever done moral justice.—To Timothy Pickering. Bergh 15:322. (1821.)

JEFFERSON (Thomas), Modesty of.—I have sometimes asked myself whether my country is the better for my having lived at all. I do not know that it is. [Those things which] I have been the instrument of doing ... would have been done by others; some of them, perhaps, a little better. —Bergh 1:256. (1821?)

JEFFERSON (Thomas), Epitaph, Written by Jefferson.—
HERE WAS BURIED
THOMAS JEFFERSON,
AUTHOR OF THE
DECLARATION
OF
AMERICAN INDEPENDENCE,
OF THE
STATUTE OF VIRGINIA
FOR
RELIGIOUS FREEDOM,
AND FATHER OF THE
UNIVERSITY OF VIRGINIA.
—Bergh 1:262. (1826.)

JESUS CHRIST, Superiority of His Moral Precepts.—His system of morality was the most benevolent and sublime probably that has been ever taught, and consequently more perfect than those of any of the ancient philosophers.... [He was] the most innocent, the most benevolent, the most eloquent and sublime character that ever has been exhibited to man.—To Dr. Joseph Priestley. Bergh 10:375. (1803.)

I concur with the author [of a recent sermon] in considering the moral precepts of Jesus as more pure, correct, and sublime than those of the ancient philosophers; yet I do not concur with him in the mode of proving it. He thinks it necessary to libel and decry the doctrines of the philosophers; but a man must be blinded, indeed, by prejudice who can deny them a great degree of merit. I give them their just due, and yet maintain that the morality of Jesus as taught by himself, and freed from the corruptions of latter times, is far superior. Their philosophy went chiefly to the government of our passions, so far as respected ourselves, and the procuring our own tranquility. In our duties to others they were short and deficient. They extended their cares scarcely beyond our kindred and friends individually, and our country in the abstract. Jesus embraced with charity and philanthropy our neighbors, our countrymen, and the whole family of mankind. They confined themselves to actions; he pressed his sentiments into the region of our thoughts, and called for purity at the fountainhead.—Bergh 10:376. (1803.)

[His] system of morals,... if filled up in the style and spirit of the rich fragments he left us, would be the most perfect and sublime that has ever been taught by man.... 1. He corrected the deism of the Jews, confirming them in their belief of one only God, and giving them juster notions of His attributes and government. 2. His moral doctrines relating to kindred and friends were more pure and perfect than those of the most correct of the philosophers, and greatly more so than those of the Jews; and they went far beyond both in inculcating universal philanthropy, not only to kindred and friends, to neighbors and countrymen, but to all mankind, gathering all into one family under the bonds of love, charity, peace, common wants, and common aids. A development of this head will evince the peculiar superiority of the system of Jesus over all others. 3. The precepts of philosophy, and of the Hebrew code, laid hold of actions only. He pushed his scrutinies into the heart of man, erected his tribunal in the region of his thoughts, and purified the waters at the fountainhead. 4. He taught emphatically the doctrines of a future state, which was either doubted or disbelieved by the Jews, and wielded it with efficacy as an important incentive, supplementary to the other motives to moral conduct.—To Dr. Benjamin Rush. Bergh 10:384. (1803.)

JESUS CHRIST, Description of.— His parentage was obscure; his condition poor; his education null; his natural endowments great; his life correct and innocent; he was meek, benevolent, patient, firm, disinterested, and of the sublimest eloquence.... According to the ordinary fate of those who attempt to enlighten and reform mankind, he fell an early victim to the jealousy and combination of the altar and the throne, at about thirty-three years of age.—To Dr. Benjamin Rush. Bergh 10:383. (1803.)

JESUS CHRIST, His Original Doctrines Pure and Simple.—The doctrines of Jesus are simple, and tend all to the happiness of man:

1. That there is one only God, and He all perfect.

2. That there is a future state of rewards and punishments.

3. That to love God with all thy heart, and thy neighbor as thyself, is the sum of religion.... Had the doctrines of Jesus been preached always as pure as they came from his lips, the whole civilized world would

now have been Christian.—Bergh 15:383. (1822.)

JESUS CHRIST. See also BIBLE; CHRISTIANITY; RELIGION.

JONES (John Paul), Disinterestedness of.—Captain John Paul Jones ... refuses to accept any indemnification for his expenses [connected with Peyrouse's expedition], which is an additional proof of his disinterested spirit, and of his devotion to the service of America.—To John Jay. Bergh 5:166. (1785.)

JONES (John Paul), Confidence in. —I am [pleased] with the promotion of our countryman, Paul Jones. He commanded the right wing in the first engagement between the Russian and Turkish galleys; his absence from the second proves his superiority over the Captain Pacha, as he did not choose to bring his ships into the shoals in which the Pacha ventured and lost those entrusted to him. I consider this officer as the principal hope of our future efforts on the ocean.—Bergh 7:125. (1788.)

JUDGES, Qualifications of.—The judges ... should always be men of learning and experience in the laws, of exemplary morals, great patience, calmness, and attention; their minds should not be distracted with jarring interests.—To George Wythe. Bergh 4:259. (1776.)

JUDGES, Seeking Power.—We have seen, too, that, contrary to all correct example, [the judges] are in the habit of going out of the question before them, to throw an anchor ahead and grapple further hold for future advances of power.—Autobiography. Bergh 1:121. (1821.)

JUDGES, Impeachment of.—Our different states have differently modified their several judiciaries as to the tenure of office. Some appoint their judges for a given term of time; some continue them *during good behavior*, and that to be determined on by the concurring vote of *two-thirds* of each legislative house. In England they are removable by a *majority* only of each house. The last is a practicable remedy; the second is not. The combination of the friends and associates of the accused, the action of personal and party passions, and the sympathies of the human heart will forever find means of influencing one-third of either the one or the other house, will thus secure their impunity, and establish them in fact for life. The first remedy is the best, that of appointing for a term of years only, with a capacity of reappointment if their conduct has been approved.—Bergh 15:486. (1823.)

JUDICIAL INTERPRETATION, Should Preserve Original Meaning of the Constitution.—On every question of construction, [let us] carry ourselves back to the time when the Constitution was adopted, recollect the spirit manifested in the debates, and instead of trying what meaning may be squeezed out of the text, or invented against it, conform to the probable one in which it was passed.—Bergh 15:449. (1823.)

JUDICIAL REVIEW, Unconstitutional.—You seem to think it devolved on the judges to decide on the validity of the sedition law. But nothing in the Constitution has given them a right to decide for the executive, more than to the executive to decide for them. Both magistrates are equally independent in the sphere of action assigned to them. The judges, believing the law Constitutional, had a right to pass a sentence of fine and imprisonment, because the power was placed in their hands by the Constitution. But the executive, believing the law to be unconstitutional, were bound to remit the execution of it, because that power has been confided to them by the Constitution. That instrument meant that its coordinate branches should be checks on each other. But the opinion which gives to the judges the right to decide what laws are Constitutional and what not, not only for themselves in their own sphere of action, but for the legislature and executive also in their spheres, would make the judiciary a despotic branch.—To Abigail Adams. Bergh 11:50. (1804.)

The Constitution intended that the three great branches of the government should be coordinate, and independent of each other. As to acts, therefore, which are to be done by either, it has given no control to another branch.... It did not intend to give the judiciary ... control over the executive.... I have long wished for a proper occasion to have the gratuitous opinion in *Marbury* v. *Madison* brought before the public, and denounced as not law.—Bergh 11:213. (1807.)

The question whether the judges

are invested with exclusive authority to decide on the Constitutionality of a law has been heretofore a subject of consideration with me in the exercise of official duties. Certainly there is not a word in the Constitution which has given that power to them more than to the executive or legislative branches. Questions of property, of character, and of crime being ascribed to the judges through a definite course of legal proceeding, laws involving such questions belong, of course, to them; and as they decide on them ultimately and without appeal, they of course decide *for themselves*. The Constitutional validity of the law or laws again prescribing executive action, and to be administered by that branch ultimately and without appeal, the executive must decide for *themselves* also whether, under the Constitution, they are valid or not. So also as to laws governing the proceedings of the legislature, that body must judge *for itself* the Constitutionality of the law, and equally without appeal or control from its coordinate branches. And, in general, that branch which is to act ultimately and without appeal on any law is the rightful expositor of the validity of the law, uncontrolled by the opinions of the other coordinate authorities.—Ford 9:517. (1815.)

We find the judiciary, on every occasion, still driving us into consolidation. [I deny] the right they usurp of exclusively explaining the Constitution.... Intending to establish three departments coordinate and independent, that they might check and balance one another, [the

Constitution] has given, according to this opinion [i.e., the notion of judicial review], to one of them alone the right to prescribe rules for the government of the others, and to that one, too, which is unelected by and independent of the nation; for experience has already shown that the impeachment it has provided is not even a scarecrow.... The Constitution, on this hypothesis, is a mere thing of wax in the hands of the judiciary, which they may twist and shape into any form they please. ... My construction of the Constitution ... is that each department is truly independent of the others, and has an equal right to decide for itself what is the meaning of the Constitution in the cases submitted to its action; and especially where it is to act ultimately and without appeal. —To Judge Spencer Roane. Bergh 15:212. (1819.)

JUDICIAL REVIEW, A Dangerous Doctrine.—You seem ... to consider the judges as the ultimate arbiters of all Constitutional questions; a very dangerous doctrine indeed, and one which would place us under the despotism of an oligarchy. Our judges are as honest as other men, and not more so. They have, with others, the same passions for party, for power, and the privilege of their corps.... Their power [is] the more dangerous as they are in office for life, and not responsible, as the other functionaries are, to the elective control. The Constitution has erected no such single tribunal, knowing that to whatever hands confided, with the corruptions of time and party, its members would become despots.

It has more wisely made all the departments co-equal and co-sovereign within themselves.

If the [Congress] fails to pass laws for a census, for paying the judges and other officers of government, for establishing a militia, for naturalization as prescribed by the Constitution, or if they fail to meet in Congress, the judges cannot issue their mandamus to them; if the President fails to supply the place of a judge, to appoint other civil or military officers, to issue requisite commissions, the judges cannot force him. They can issue their mandamus or distringas to no executive or legislative officer to enforce the fulfillment of their official duties, any more than the President or [Congress] may issue orders to the judges or their officers. Betrayed by English example, and unaware, as it should seem, of the control of our Constitution in this particular, they have at times overstepped their limit by undertaking to command executive officers in the discharge of their executive duties; but the Constitution, in keeping three departments distinct and independent, restrains the authority of the judges to judiciary organs, as it does the executive and legislative to executive and legislative organs....

When the legislative or executive functionaries act unconstitutionally, they are responsible to the people in their elective capacity. The exemption of the judges from that is quite dangerous enough. I know no safe depository of the ultimate powers of the society but the people themselves; and if we think them not enlightened enough to exercise their control with a wholesome discretion, the remedy is not to take it from them but to inform their discretion by education. This is the true corrective of abuses of Constitutional power.

Pardon me, sir, for this difference of opinion. My personal interest in such questions is entirely extinct, but not my wishes for the longest possible continuance of our government on its pure principles; if the three powers maintain their mutual independence [of] each other it may last long, but not so if either can assume the authorities of the other. —To William Charles Jarvis. Bergh 15:277. (1820.)

JUDICIAL REVIEW. See also CONSTITUTION (U.S.); MARBURY v. MADISON; SEPARATION OF POWERS; SUPREME COURT.

JUDICIARY, Relationship with Legislative and Executive Branches. —The dignity and stability of government in all its branches, the morals of the people, and every blessing of society depend so much upon an upright and skillful administration of justice that the judicial power ought to be distinct from both the legislative and executive, and independent [of] both,...so it may be a check upon both, as both should be checks upon [the judiciary]. —To George Wythe. Bergh 4:258. (1776.)

JUDICIARY, People Need Protection from.—The new Constitution has secured these [individual rights] in the executive and legislative departments, but not in the judiciary.

It should have established trials by the people themselves, that is to say, by jury. There are instruments so dangerous to the rights of the nation, and which place them so totally at the mercy of their governors, that those governors, whether legislative or executive, should be restrained from keeping such instruments on foot but in well-defined cases. Such an instrument is a standing army. We are now allowed to say such a declaration of rights, as a supplement to the Constitution where that is silent, is wanting to secure us in these points. The general voice has legitimated this objection.—Ford 5:89. (1789.)

JUDICIARY, Monopoly of.—It is the self-appointment [of the county courts] I wish to correct; to find some means of breaking up a cabal, when such a one gets possession of the bench. When this takes place, it becomes the most afflicting of tyrannies because its powers are so various, and exercised on everything most immediately around us. And how many instances have you and I known of these monopolies of county administration?—Ford 10:52. (1816.)

JUDICIARY, Consolidating Federal Power.—After twenty years' confirmation of the federal system by the voice of the nation, declared through the medium of elections, we find the judiciary on every occasion still driving us into consolidation.—To Judge Spencer Roane. Bergh 15:212. (1819.)

The great object of my fear is the federal judiciary. That body, like gravity, ever acting with noiseless foot and unalarming advance, gaining ground step by step and holding what it gains, is engulfing insidiously the [state] governments into the jaws of that which feeds them.—Ford 10:189. (1821.)

It has long...been my opinion, and I have never shrunk from its expression (although I do not choose to put it into a newspaper, nor like a Priam in armor [to] offer myself [as] its champion), that the germ of dissolution of our federal government is in the constitution of the federal judiciary; an irresponsible body (for impeachment is scarcely a scarecrow), working like gravity by night and by day, gaining a little today and a little tomorrow, and advancing its noiseless step like a thief over the field of jurisdiction, until all shall be usurped from the states, and the government of all be consolidated into one. To this I am opposed, because when all government, domestic and foreign, in little as in great things, shall be drawn to Washington as the center of all power, it will render powerless the checks provided of one government on another, and will become as venal and oppressive as the government from which we separated. It will be as in Europe, where every man must be either pike or gudgeon, hammer or anvil. Our functionaries and theirs are wares from the same workshop, made of the same materials and by the same hand. If the states look with apathy on this silent descent of their government into the gulf which is to swallow all, we have only to weep over the human character formed uncontrollable but by a rod of iron, and the blasphemers of man, as incapable of self-government, become his true historians.— Bergh 15:331. (1821.)

Our government is now taking so steady a course as to show by what road it will pass to destruction, to wit, by consolidation first, and then corruption, its necessary consequence. The engine of consolidation will be the federal judiciary; the two other branches the corrupting and corrupted instruments.—Bergh 15:341. (1821.)

We already see the power, installed for life, responsible to no authority (for impeachment is not even a scarecrow), advancing with a noiseless and steady pace to the great object of consolidation. The foundations are already deeply laid by their decisions for the annihilation of Constitutional state rights, and the removal of every check, every counterpoise to the engulfing power of which themselves are to make a sovereign part. If ever this vast country is brought under a single government, it will be one of the most extensive corruption, indifferent and incapable of a wholesome care over so wide a spread of surface. This will not be borne, and you will have to choose between reformation and revolution. If I know the spirit of this country, the one or the other is inevitable. Before the canker is become inveterate, before its venom has reached so much of the body politic as to get beyond control, remedy should be applied.—Bergh 15:388. (1822.)

There is no danger I apprehend so much as the consolidation of our government by the noiseless, and therefore unalarming, instrumentality of the Supreme Court. This is the form in which Federalism now arrays itself, and consolidation is the present principle of distinction between Republicans and the pseudo-Republicans but real Federalists. —Bergh 15:421. (1823.)

JUDICIARY, Federal, Undermining the Constitution.—The judiciary of the United States is the subtle corps of sappers and miners constantly working underground to undermine the foundations of our confederated fabric. They are construing our Constitution from a coordination of a general [i.e., federal] and special [i.e., state] government to a general and supreme one alone. This will lay all things at their feet.... Having found from experience that impeachment is an impracticable thing, a mere scarecrow, they consider themselves secure for life; they skulk from responsibility to public opinion.... A judiciary independent of a king or executive alone is a good thing; but independence of the will of the nation is a solecism, at least in a republican government.—Bergh 15:297. (1820.)

At the establishment of our constitutions, the judiciary bodies were supposed to be the most helpless and harmless members of the government. Experience, however, soon showed in what way they were to become the most dangerous; that the insufficiency of the means provided for their removal gave them a freehold and irresponsibility in office; that their decisions, seeming to concern individual suitors only, pass silent and un-heeded by the public at large; that these decisions nevertheless become law by precedent, sapping by little and little the foundations of the Constitution, and working its change by construction, before any-one has perceived that that invisible and helpless worm has been busily employed in consuming its sub-stance. In truth, man is not made to be trusted for life if secured against all liability to account.—Bergh 15:486. (1823.)

One single object, if your [pro-posed code of laws] attains it, will entitle you to the endless gratitude of society: that of restraining judges from usurping legislation. And with no body of men is this restraint more wanting than with the judges of what is commonly called our general government, but what I call our foreign department. They are prac-ticing on the Constitution by in-ferences, analogies, and sophisms as they would on an ordinary law. They do not seem aware that it is not even a *Constitution,* formed by a single authority and subject to a single superintendence and control; but that it is a compact of many inde-pendent powers, every single one of which claims an equal right to understand it, and to require its observance.... They imagine they can lead us into a consolidate gov-ernment, while their road leads directly to its dissolution. This member of the government was at first considered as the most harm-less and helpless of all its organs. But it has proved that the power of

declaring what the law is *ad libitum,* by sapping and mining, slyly and without alarm, the foundations of the Constitution, can do what open force would not dare to attempt.— To Edward Livingston. Bergh 16:113. (1825.)

JUDICIARY, Amendment Needed to Control Federal.—There was another amendment of which none of us thought at the time [when the Constitution was framed], and in the omission of which lurks the germ that is to destroy this happy combination of national powers in the general government for matters of national concern, and indepen-dent powers in the states for what concerns the states severally. In England, it was a great point gained at the Revolution that the com-missions of the judges, which had hitherto been during pleasure, should thenceforth be made during good behavior. A judiciary depen-dent on the will of the King had proved itself the most oppressive of all tools in the hands of that magis-trate. Nothing, then, could be more salutary than a change there to the tenure of good behavior; and the question of good behavior left to the vote of a simple majority in the two houses of Parliament. Before the [American] Revolution we were all good English Whigs, cordial in their free principles and in their jealousies of their executive magistrate. These jealousies are very apparent in all our state constitutions; and in the general government in this instance, we have gone even beyond the English caution by requiring a vote of two-thirds in one of the houses for removing a judge; a vote so impossible, where any defense is made before men of ordinary prejudices and passions, that our judges are effectually independent of the nation. But this ought not to be. I would not, indeed, make them dependent on the executive authority, as they formerly were in England; but I deem it indispensable to the continuance of this government that they should be submitted to some practical and impartial control; and that this, to be impartial, must be compounded of a mixture of state and federal authorities. It is not enough that honest men are appointed judges. All know the influence of interest on the mind of man, and how unconsciously his judgment is warped by that influence. To this bias add that of the *esprit de corps*, of their peculiar maxim and creed that "it is the office of a good judge to enlarge his jurisdiction," and the absence of responsibility; and how can we expect impartial decision between the general government, of which they are themselves so eminent a part, and an individual state, from which they have nothing to hope or fear? We have seen, too, that, contrary to all correct example, they are in the habit of going out of the question before them to throw an anchor ahead and grapple further hold for future advances of power. They are, then, in fact, the corps of sappers and miners steadily working to undermine the independent rights of the states, and to consolidate all

power in the hands of that government in which they have so important a freehold estate.... I repeat that I do not charge the judges with willful and ill-intentioned error; but honest error must be arrested where its toleration leads to public ruin. As, for the safety of society, we commit honest maniacs to bedlam, so judges should be withdrawn from their bench whose erroneous biases are leading us to dissolution. It may, indeed, injure them in fame or in fortune; but it saves the Republic, which is the first and supreme law.—Autobiography. Bergh 1:120. (1821.)

Let the future appointments of judges be for four or six years, and renewable by the President and Senate. This will bring their conduct, at regular periods, under revision and probation, and may keep them in equipoise between the [federal] and [state] governments. We have erred in this point by copying England, where certainly it is a good thing to have the judges independent of the King. But we have omitted to copy their caution also, which makes a judge removable on the address of both legislative houses. That there should be public functionaries independent of the nation, whatever may be their demerit, is a solecism in a republic, of the first order of absurdity and inconsistency.—Bergh 15:389. (1822.)

JUDICIARY. See also CENTRALIZATION; FEDERAL GOVERNMENT; SEPARATION OF POWERS; SUPREME COURT.

JURY, A Check on Permanent Judges.—The people ... are not qualified to judge questions of *law*, but they are very capable of judging questions of *fact*. In the form of juries, therefore, they determine all matters of fact, leaving to the permanent judges to decide the law resulting from those facts. But we all know that permanent judges acquire an *esprit de corps;* that, being known, they are liable to be tempted by bribery; that they are misled by favor, by relationship, by a spirit of party, by a devotion to the executive or legislative power; that it is better to leave a cause to the decision of [a game of] cross and pile than to that of a judge biased to one side; and that the opinion of twelve honest jurymen gives still a better hope of right than cross and pile does. It is in the power, therefore, of the juries, if they think permanent judges are under any bias whatever in any cause, to take on themselves to judge the law as well as the fact. They never exercise this power but when they suspect partiality in the judges; and by the exercise of this power they have been the firmest bulwarks of English liberty. Were I called upon to decide whether the people had best be omitted in the legislative or judiciary department, I would say it is better to leave them out of the legislative. The execution of the laws is more important than the making [of] them.—Bergh 7:422. (1789.)

JURY, Trial by, an Essential Principle.—I deem [one of] the essential principles of our government, and consequently [one] which ought to shape its administration, ... trial by juries impartially selected.—First Inaugural Address. Bergh 3:321. (1801.)

JUSTICE, Delayed, Is Justice Denied.—Before the Revolution, a judgment could not be obtained under eight years in the Supreme Court [of Virginia] where the suit was in the department of the common law, which department embraces about nine-tenths of the subjects of legal contestation. In that of the chancery, from twelve to twenty years were requisite. This did not proceed from any vice in the laws, but from the indolence of the judges appointed by the King; and these judges holding their office during his will only, he could have reformed the evil at any time. This reformation was among the first works of the legislature after our independence. A judgment can now be obtained in the Supreme Court in one year at the common law, and in about three years in the chancery.—Ford 4:126. (1785.)

JUSTICE, International.—We must make the interest of every nation stand surety for their justice, and their own loss to follow injury to us, as effect follows its cause.—Ford 7:154. (1797.)

We think that peaceable means may be devised of keeping nations in the path of justice towards us, by making justice their interest, and injuries to react on themselves.—Bergh 10:405. (1803.)

We are firmly convinced, and we act on that conviction, that with nations, as with individuals, our interests, soundly calculated, will ever be found inseparable from our moral duties; and history bears witness to the fact that a just nation is trusted on its word, when recourse is had to armaments and wars to bridle others.—Second Inaugural Address. Bergh 3:375. (1805.)

JUSTICE, Equal and Exact.—I deem [one of] the essential principles of our government, and consequently [one] which ought to shape its administration,...equal and exact justice to all men, of whatever state or persuasion, religious or political.—First Inaugural Address. Bergh 3:321. (1801.)

JUSTICE, Must Be Even-Handed.— When one undertakes to administer justice, it must be with an even hand, and by rule; what is done for one must be done for everyone in equal degree.—Ford 8:264. (1803.)

JUSTICE, The Fundamental Law of Society.—I believe...that justice is the fundamental law of society.— Bergh 14:490. (1816.)

JUSTICE, Foundation of.—I believe ...that [justice] is instinct and innate, that the moral sense is as much a part of our constitution as that of feeling, seeing, or hearing; as a wise Creator must have seen to be necessary in an animal destined to live in society; that every human mind feels pleasure in doing good to another; that the nonexistence of justice is not to be inferred from the fact that the same act is deemed virtuous and right in one society which is held vicious and wrong in another; because, as the circumstances and opinions of different societies vary, so the acts which may do them right or wrong must vary

also; for virtue does not consist in the act we do, but in the end it is to effect. If it is to effect the happiness of him to whom it is directed, it is virtuous, while in a society under different circumstances and opinions, the same act might produce pain, and would be vicious. The essence of virtue is in doing good to others, while what is good may be one thing in one society, and its contrary in another.—To John Adams. Bergh 15:76. (1816.)

JUSTICE, Man's Instinct for.—Man was created for social intercourse, but social intercourse cannot be maintained without a sense of justice; then man must have been created with a sense of justice.— Ford 10:32. (1816.)

K

KINGS, Absolutism and.—There is no king who, with sufficient force, is not always ready to make himself absolute.—To George Wythe. Ford 4:270. (1786.)

KINGS, Stupidity of.—No race of kings has ever presented above one man of common sense in twenty generations.—Ford 4:426. (1787.)

There is not a crowned head in Europe whose talents or merits would entitle him to be elected a vestryman by the people of any parish in America.—To George Washington. Ford 5:8. (1788.)

KINGS, Natural Degeneration of European.—The practice of kings marrying only in the families of kings has been that of Europe for some centuries. Now, take any race of animals, confine them in idleness and inaction, whether in a sty, a stable, or a state room, pamper them with high diet, gratify all their sexual appetites, immerse them in sensualities, nourish their passions, let everything bend before them, and banish whatever might lead them to think, and in a few generations they become all body and no mind; and this, too, by a law of nature, by that very law by which we are in the constant practice of changing the characters and propensities of the animals we raise for our own purposes. Such is the regimen in raising kings, and in this way they have gone on for centuries.

While in Europe, I often amused myself with contemplating the characters of the then reigning sovereigns of Europe. Louis the XVI was a fool, of my own knowledge, and in spite of the answers made for him at his trial. The King of Spain was a fool, and of Naples the same. They passed their lives in hunting, and dispatched two couriers a week, one thousand miles, to let each other know what game they had killed the preceding days. The King of Sardinia was a fool. All these were Bourbons. The Queen of Portugal, a Braganza, was an idiot by nature. And so was the King of Denmark. Their sons, as regents, exercised the powers of government. The King of Prussia, successor to the great Frederick, was a mere hog in body as well as in mind. Gustavus of Sweden and Joseph of Austria were really crazy, and George of England, you know, was in a straight waistcoat. There

remained, then, none but old Catherine, who had been too lately picked up to have lost her common sense.

In this state Bonaparte found Europe; and it was this state of its rulers which lost it with scarce a struggle. These animals had become without mind and powerless; and so will every hereditary monarch be after a few generations. Alexander, the grandson of Catherine, is as yet an exception. He is able to hold his own. But he is only of the third generation. His race is not yet worn out. And so endeth the book of kings, from all of whom the Lord deliver us.—Bergh 12:377. (1810.)

KINGS, Unwanted in America.—It is lawful to wish to see no emperor or king in our hemisphere.—To James Monroe. Ford 10:244. (1822.)

KINGS. See also GEORGE III; LOUIS XVI; MONARCHY.

KNOWLEDGE, Freedom Preserved by Diffusion of.—The most important bill in our whole [Virginia] code is that for the diffusion of knowledge among the people. No other sure foundation can be devised for the preservation of freedom and happiness.—To George Wythe. Bergh 5:396. (1786.)

KNOWLEDGE, Encouraging Future Advances in.—I am for encouraging the progress of science in all its branches; and not for raising a hue and cry against the sacred name of philosophy; for awing the human mind by stories of raw-head and bloody bones to a distrust of its own vision, and to repose implicitly on that of others; to go backwards instead of forwards to look for improvement; to believe that government, religion, morality, and every other science were in the highest perfection in ages of the darkest ignorance, and that nothing can ever be devised more perfect than what was established by our forefathers.—To Elbridge Gerry. Bergh 10:78. (1799.)

I am among those who think well of the human character generally. I consider man as formed for society, and endowed by nature with those dispositions which fit him for society. I believe also, with Condorcet,... that his mind is perfectible to a degree of which we cannot as yet form any conception. It is impossible for a man who takes a survey of what is already known not to see what an immensity in every branch of science yet remains to be discovered.... Great fields are yet to be explored to which our faculties are equal, and that to an extent of which we cannot fix the limits. I join you, therefore, in branding as cowardly the idea that the human mind is incapable of further advances. This is precisely the doctrine which the present despots of the earth are inculcating, and their friends here re-echoing, and applying especially to religion and politics, "that it is not probable that anything better will be discovered than what was known to our fathers." We are to look backwards, then, and not forward for the improvement of science, and to find it amidst feudal barbarians and the fires of Spitalfields. But thank heaven the American mind is already too much opened to listen to these impostures; and

Jefferson in early 1800 (age 56). Portrait by Rembrandt Peale. This is considered by many to be the best oil painting of Jefferson. Frequently copied by other artists and used as a model for etchings and political cartoons during Jefferson's presidency, it was the likeness most familiar to Americans of that era.

while the art of printing is left to us, science can never be retrograde; what is once acquired of real knowledge can never be lost. To preserve the freedom of the human mind, then, and freedom of the press, every spirit should be ready to devote itself to martyrdom; for as long as we may think as we will, and speak as we think, the condition of man will proceed in improvement.—Adrienne Koch, ed., *Jefferson* (Englewood Cliffs, N.J.: Prentice-Hall, 1971), p. 62. (1799.)

KNOWLEDGE, Common Property of Mankind.—The field of knowledge is the common property of mankind, and any discoveries we can make in it will be for the benefit of . . . every other nation as well as our own.—Ford 9:86. (1807.)

KNOWLEDGE. See also EDUCATION; IGNORANCE; PROGRESS; SCIENCE.

KOSCIUSKO (General Thaddeus), A Disinterested Patriot.—May heaven have in store for your country a restoration of these blessings [of freedom and order], and you be destined as the instrument it will use for that purpose. But if this be forbidden by fate, I hope we shall be able to preserve here an asylum where your love of liberty and disinterested patriotism will be forever protected and honored, and where you will find, in the hearts of the American people, a good portion of that esteem and affection which glow in the bosom of the friend who writes this.—To General Kosciusko. Bergh 10:116. (1799.)

KOSCIUSKO (General Thaddeus), And Emancipation of Slaves.—General Kosciusko [was] the brave auxiliary of my country in its struggle for liberty, and from the year 1797, when our particular acquaintance began, my most intimate and much-beloved friend. On his last departure from the United States in 1798, he left in my hands an instrument appropriating after his death all the property he had in our public funds, the price of his military services here, to the education and emancipation of as many of the children of bondage in this country as it should be adequate to.—Bergh 15:173. (1818.)

L

LABOR, Economy and.—I deem [one of] the essential principles of our government, and consequently [one] which ought to shape its administration, . . . economy in the public expense, that labor may be lightly burdened.—First Inaugural Address. Bergh 3:321. (1801.)

LABOR, Government and.—Considering the general tendency to multiply offices and dependencies, and to increase expense to the ultimate term of burden which the citizens can bear, it behooves us to avail ourselves of every occasion which presents itself for taking off the surcharge, that it may never be seen here that, after leaving to labor the smallest portion of its earnings on which it can subsist, government shall itself consume the residue of what it was instituted to guard.—First Annual Message to Congress. Bergh 3:333. (1801.)

If we can prevent the government from wasting the labors of the people, under the pretense of taking care of them, they must become happy.—Bergh 10:342. (1802.)

LABOR, Parasites on.—I think . . . we have more machinery of government than is necessary, too many parasites living on the labor of the industrious.—Bergh 16:76. (1824.)

LABOR. See also INDUSTRY.

LABORERS, America Settled by.—Our ancestors . . . who migrated hither were laborers, not lawyers.— *Summary View of the Rights of British America*. Bergh 1:206. (1774.)

LABORERS, Jefferson's Treatment of His.—I made a point of paying my workmen in preference to all other claimants. I never parted with one without settling with him, and giving him either his money or my note. Every person that ever worked for me can attest this, and that I always paid their notes pretty soon. —Ford 5:34. (1788.)

My first wish is that the [colored] laborers may be well treated; the second, that they may enable me to have that treatment continued by making as much as will admit it.— Ford 5:508. (1792.)

LABORERS, Prosperity of American.—The great mass of our population is of laborers; our rich who can live without labor, either manual or professional, being few and of moderate wealth. Most of the laboring class possess property, cultivate their own lands, have families, and from the demand for their labor are enabled to exact from the rich and the competent such prices as enable them to be fed abundantly, clothed above mere decency, to labor moderately and raise their families. They are not driven to the ultimate resources of dexterity and skill because their wares will sell, although not quite so nice as those of England. The wealthy, on the other hand, and those at their ease, know nothing of what the Europeans call luxury. They have only somewhat more of the comforts and decencies of life than those who furnish them. Can any condition of life be more desirable than this?—Bergh 14:182. (1814.)

LABORERS, Slave vs. English.—Nor in the class of laborers do I mean to withhold from the comparison that portion whose color has condemned them, in certain parts of our Union, to a subjection to the will of others. Even these are better fed in these states, warmer clothed, and labor less than the journeymen or day laborers of England. They have the comfort, too, of numerous families, in the midst of whom they live without want, or fear of it; a solace which few of the laborers of England possess. They are subject, it is true, to bodily coercion; but are not the hundreds of thousands of British soldiers and seamen subject to the same, without seeing, at the end of their career, when age and accident shall have rendered them unequal to labor, the certainty, which the other has, that he will never want? And has not the British seaman, as much as the African, been reduced to this bondage by force, in flagrant violation of his own consent, and of his natural right in his own person? And with the laborers of England generally, does not the moral coercion of want subject their will as despotically to that of their employer, as the physical constraint does the soldier, the seaman, or the slave?

But do not mistake me. I am not advocating slavery. I am not justifying the wrongs we have committed on a foreign people, by the example of another nation committing equal wrongs on their own subjects. On the contrary, there is nothing I would not sacrifice to a practicable plan of abolishing every vestige of this moral and political depravity. But I am, at present, comparing the condition and degree of suffering to which oppression has reduced the man of one color, with the condition and degree of suffering to which oppression has reduced the man of another color; equally condemning both.—Bergh 14:183. (1814.)

LAFAYETTE (Marquis de), Character of.—He has a great deal of sound genius, is well remarked by the King [Louis XVI], and rising in popularity. He has nothing against him but the suspicion of republican principles. I think he will one day be of the ministry. His foible is a canine appetite for popularity and fame; but he will get above this.— Ford 4:366. (1787.)

LAFAYETTE (Marquis de), A Cement Between France and America.—Teach your children to be, as you are, a cement between our two nations.—To Marquis de Lafayette. Ford 5:153. (1790.)

LAFAYETTE (Marquis de), Awarded Land in Louisiana.—The acquisition of Louisiana . . . has enabled us to do a handsome thing for Lafayette. He had received a grant of between eleven and twelve thousand acres north of Ohio, worth perhaps a dollar an acre. We have obtained permission of Congress to locate it in Louisiana. Locations can be found adjacent to the city of New Orleans, in the island of New Orleans and in its vicinity, the value of which cannot be calculated—Bergh 11:40. (1804.)

LAFAYETTE (Marquis de), His Triumphal American Tour of 1824.
—You will have seen by our papers the delirium into which our citizens are thrown by a visit from General Lafayette. He is making a triumphant progress through the states, from town to town, with acclamations of welcome such as no crowned head ever received. It will have a good effect in favor of the General with the people in Europe, but probably a different one with their sovereigns. Its effect here, too, will be salutary as to ourselves, by rallying us together and strengthening the habit of considering our country as one and indivisible, and I hope we shall close it with something more solid for him than dinners and balls. The eclat of this visit has almost merged the presidential question, on which nothing scarcely is said in our papers.—Ford 10:322. (1824.)

LAFAYETTE (Marquis de), In War and Peace.—I joy, my friends, in your joy, inspired by the visit of this our ancient and distinguished leader and benefactor. His deeds in the War of Independence you have heard and read. They are known to you and embalmed in your memories and in the pages of faithful history. His deeds in the peace which followed that war are perhaps not known to you, but I can attest them. When I was stationed in his country for the purpose of cementing its friendship with ours and of advancing our mutual interests, this friend of both was my most powerful auxiliary and advocate. He made our cause his own, as in truth it was that of his native country also. His influence and connections there were great. All doors of all departments were open to him at all times, to me only formally and at appointed times. In truth I only held the nail; he drove it. Honor him, then, as your benefactor in peace as well as in war.—Speech at Charlottesville dinner. Quoted in Sarah N. Randolph, *The Domestic Life of Thomas Jefferson* (New York: Harper and Bros., 1871), p. 391. (1824.)

LAW, Americans' Obedience to.— That love of order and obedience to the laws which so remarkably characterize the citizens of the United States are sure pledges of internal tranquility.—Bergh 10:235. (1801.)

LAW, Original Intent Should Be Preserved.—The true key for the construction of everything doubtful in a law is the intention of the lawmakers. This is most safely gathered from the words, but may be sought also in extraneous circumstances, provided they do not contradict the express words of the law.—Bergh 12:59. (1808.)

Whenever the words of a law will bear two meanings, one of which will give effect to the law, and the other will defeat it, the former must be supposed to have been intended by the [Congress], because they could not intend that meaning which would defeat their intention in passing that law; and in a statute, as in a will, the intention of the party is to be sought after.—Bergh 12:110. (1808.)

Laws are made for men of ordinary understanding, and should therefore be construed by the ordinary rules of common sense. Their meaning is not to be sought for in metaphysical subtleties which may make anything mean everything or nothing, at pleasure.—Bergh 15:450. (1823.)

LAW, Self-Preservation Supersedes Written Laws.—The question you propose, whether circumstances do not sometimes occur which make it a duty in officers of high trust to assume authorities beyond the law, is easy of solution in principle, but sometimes embarrassing in practice. A strict observance of the written laws is doubtless *one* of the high duties of a good citizen, but it is not *the highest*. The laws of necessity, of self-preservation, of saving our country when in danger, are of higher obligation. To lose our country by a scrupulous adherence to written law would be to lose the law itself, with life, liberty, property, and all those who are enjoying them with us; thus absurdly sacrificing the end to the means. When, in the battle of Germantown, General Washington's army was annoyed from Chew's house, he did not hesitate to plant his cannon against it, although the property of a citizen. When he besieged Yorktown he leveled the suburbs, feeling that the laws of property must be postponed to the safety of the nation. While the army was before York, the Governor of Virginia took horses, carriages, provisions, and even men by force to enable that army to stay together till it could master the public enemy; and he was justified. A ship at sea in distress for provisions meets another having abundance, yet refusing a supply; the law of self-preservation authorizes the distressed to take a supply by force. In all these cases, the unwritten laws of necessity, of self-preservation, and of the public safety control the written laws of *meum* and *tuum*. . . .

The *salus populi* [is] supreme over the written law. The officer who is called to act on this superior ground does indeed risk himself on the justice of the controlling powers of the Constitution, and his station makes it his duty to incur that risk. But those controlling powers, and his fellow citizens generally, are bound to judge according to the circumstances under which he acted. They are not to transfer the information of this place or moment to the time and place of his action, but to put themselves into his situation. . . .

From these examples and principles you may see what I think on the question proposed. They do not go to the case of persons charged with petty duties, where consequences are trifling and time allowed for a legal course, nor to authorize them to take such cases out of the written law. In these, the example of overleaping the law is of greater evil than a strict adherence to its imperfect provisions. It is incumbent on those only who accept of great charges to risk themselves on great occasions, when the safety of the nation or some of its very high interests are at stake. An officer is bound to obey orders; yet he would be a bad one who should do it in cases for which they were not intended, and which involved the most important consequences. The line of discrimination between cases may be difficult; but the good officer is bound to draw it at his own peril, and throw himself on the justice of his country and the rectitude of his motives.—Bergh 12:418. (1810.)

[To save] the Republic...is the first and supreme law.—Autobiography. Bergh 1:122. (1821.)

LAW, Complicated Language of British.—Of all the countries on earth of which I have any knowledge, the style of the acts of the British Parliament is the most barbarous, uncouth, and unintelligible. It can be understood by those alone who are in the daily habit of studying such tautologous, involved, and parenthetical jargon. Where they found their model I know not. Neither ancient nor modern codes, nor even their own early statutes, furnish any such example. And, like faithful apes, we copy it faithfully.—Bergh 16:114. (1825.)

LAW. See also ALIEN AND SEDITION ACTS; LAWYERS; SEDITION LAW.

LAWS OF NATURE, Legislation Should Conform to.—It is not only vain but wicked in a legislator to frame laws in opposition to the laws of nature, and to arm them with the terror of death. This is truly creating crimes in order to punish them.—Bergh 1:236. (1779.)

LAWS OF VIRGINIA, Revision of.—When I left Congress in 1776, it was in the persuasion that our whole code [of Virginia] must be reviewed [and] adapted to our republican form of government; and now that we had no negatives [i.e., vetoes] of councils, governors, and kings to restrain us from doing right, it should be corrected in all its parts with a single eye to reason, and the good of those for whose government it was framed. Early, therefore, in the session of 1776, to which I returned, I moved and presented a bill for the revision of the laws, which was passed on the 24th of October.—Autobiography. Bergh 1:62. (1821.)

LAWS OF VIRGINIA, Adapted to Republican Government.—We were employed in this work [revising the Virginia laws] from [January 1777] to February 1779, when we met at Williamsburg, that is to say, Mr. [Edmund] Pendleton, Mr. [George] Wythe, and myself; and meeting day by day, we examined critically our several parts, sentence by sentence, scrutinizing and amending until we had agreed on the whole. We then returned home [and] had fair copies made of our several parts, which were reported to the General Assembly [on] June 18, 1779, by Mr. Wythe and myself, Mr. Pendleton's residence being distant, and he having authorized us by letter to declare his approbation. We had, in this work, brought so much of the common law as it was thought necessary to alter, all the British statutes from *Magna Charta* to the present day, and all the laws of Virginia from the establishment of our legislature . . . to the present time which we thought should be retained, within the compass of one hundred and twenty-six bills, making a printed folio of ninety pages only. Some bills were taken out occasionally, from time to time, and passed; but the main body of the work was not entered on by the legislature until after the general peace, in 1785, when, by the unwearied exertions of Mr. [James] Madison, in opposition to the endless quibbles, chicaneries, perversions, vexations, and delays of lawyers and demi-lawyers, most of the bills were passed by the legislature with little alteration.—Autobiography. Bergh 1:65. (1821.)

LAWYERS, Education of.—Carry on the study of the law with that of politics and history. Every political measure will forever have an intimate connection with the laws of the land, and he who knows nothing of these will always be perplexed and often foiled by adversaries having the advantage of that knowledge over him. Besides, it is a source of infinite comfort to reflect that . . . we [lawyers] have a resource in ourselves from which we may be able to derive an honorable subsistence. —Ford 4:405. (1787.)

LAWYERS, And Politics.—The study of the law qualifies a man to be useful to himself, to his neighbors, and to the public. It is the most certain stepping stone to public preferment in the political line.— Ford 5:172. (1790.)

LAWYERS, Success Requires Knowledge.—It is superiority of knowledge which can alone lift you above the heads of your competitors and ensure you success.—Ford 5:182. (1790.)

Never fear the want of business. A man who qualifies himself well for his calling never fails of employment in it.—Ford 6:92. (1792.)

LAWYERS, Need for More Thorough Preparation of.—I have long lamented the depreciation of law science. The opinion seems to be that [Sir William] Blackstone is to us what the Koran is to the Muhammadans; that everything which is necessary is in him, and what is not in him is not necessary. I still lend my counsel and books to such young students as will fix themselves in the neighborhood. [Sir Edward] Coke's institutes and reports are their first, and Blackstone their last book, after an intermediate course of two or three years. It [Blackstone's *Commentaries*] is nothing more than an elegant digest of what they will then have acquired from the real fountains of the law. Now men are born scholars, lawyers, doctors; in our day this was confined to poets.—Ford 9:276. (1810.)

LAWYERS, Too Many.—Law is quite overdone. It is fallen to the ground, and a man must have great powers to raise himself in it to either honor or profit. The mob of the profession get as little money and less respect than they would by digging the earth.—Bergh 12:356. (1810.)

LAWYERS, In Congress.—If the present Congress errs in too much talking, how can it be otherwise in a body to which the people send one hundred and fifty lawyers, whose trade it is to question everything, yield nothing, and talk by the hour? That one hundred and fifty lawyers should do business together ought not to be expected.—Autobiography. Bergh 1:87. (1821.)

LAWYERS, Suggested Studies for.—Begin with [Sir Edward] Coke's four *Institutes*. These give a complete body of the law as it stood in the reign of the first James, an epoch the more interesting to us as we separated at that point from English legislation, and acknowledge no subsequent statutory alterations.

Then passing over (for occasional reading as hereafter proposed) all the reports and treatises to the time of Matthew Bacon, read his abridgment, compiled about one hundred years after Coke's, in which they are all embodied. This gives numerous applications of the old principles to new cases, and gives the general state of the English law at that period. Here, too, the student should take up the chancery branch of the law by reading the first and second abridgments of the cases in equity. The second is by the same Matthew Bacon, the first having been published some time before. The alphabetical order adopted by Bacon is certainly not as satisfactory as the systematic. But the arrangement is under very general and leading heads, and these, indeed with very little difficulty, might be systematically instead of alphabetically arranged and read.

Passing now in like manner over all intervening reports and tracts, the student may take up [Sir William] Blackstone's *Commentaries*, published about twenty-five years later than Bacon's abridgment, and giving the substance of these new reports and tracts. This review is not so full as that of Bacon by any means, but better digested. Here, too, Woodeson should be read as supplementary to Blackstone, under heads too shortly treated by him. Fonblanque's edition of Francis's *Maxims of Equity* and Bridgman's *Digested Index*, into which the latter cases are incorporated, are also supplementary in the chancery branch, in which Blackstone is very short.

This course comprehends about twenty-six octavo volumes, and reading four or five hours a day would employ about two years. After these, the best of the reporters since Blackstone should be read for the new cases which have occurred since his time....

By way of change and relief for another hour or two in the day should be read the law tracts of merit, which are many, and among them all those of Baron Gilbert are of the first order. In these hours, too, may be read Bracton and Justinian's *Institutes*. The method of these two last works is very much the same, and their language often quite so. Justinian is very illustrative of the doctrines of equity, and is often appealed to, and Cooper's edition is the best on account of the analogies and contrasts he has given of the Roman and English law. After Bracton, Reeves's *History of the English Law* may be read to advantage. During this same hour or two of lighter law reading, select and leading cases of the reporters may be successively read, which the several digests will have pointed out and referred to.

I have here sketched the reading in common law and chancery which I suppose necessary for a reputable practitioner in those courts. But there are other branches of law in which, although it is not expected he should be an adept, yet when it occurs to speak of them, it should be understandingly to a decent degree. These are the admiralty law, ecclesiastical law, and the law of nations. I would name as elementary books in these branches *Molloy de Jure Maritimo;* Brown's *Compend of the Civil and Admiralty Law*, 2 volumes, octavo; the *Jura Ecclesiastica*, 2 volumes, octavo; and *Les Institutions du Droit de la Nature et des Gens de Reyneval*, 1 volume, octavo. Besides these six hours of law reading, light and heavy, and those necessary for the reports of the day, for exercise and sleep, which suppose to be ten or twelve, there will be six or eight hours for reading history, politics, ethics, physics, oratory, poetry, criticism, etc., as necessary as law to form an accomplished lawyer.— Bergh 15:319. (1821.)

LEGISLATURES, Subject to Bribery When Too Small.—In what terms reconcilable to Majesty, and at the same time to truth, shall we speak of a late instruction to his Majesty's Governor of the colony of Virginia, by which he is forbidden to assent to any law for the division of a county unless the new county will consent to have no representative in [the] Assembly?... Does his Majesty seriously wish, and publish it to the world, that his subjects should give up the glorious right of representation, with all the benefits derived from that, and submit themselves the absolute slaves of the sovereign will? Or is it rather meant to confine the legislative body to their present numbers, that they may be the cheaper bargain whenever they

shall become worth a purchase?—
*Summary View of the Rights of British
America*. Bergh 1:202. (1774.)

**LEGISLATURES, Dissolution of
Colonial, Under George III.**—One
of the articles of impeachment
against Tresilian and the other
judges of Westminster Hall in the
reign of Richard the Second, for
which they suffered death as traitors
to their country, was that they had
advised the King that he might dissolve his Parliament at any time; and
succeeding kings have adopted the
opinion of these unjust judges. Since
the establishment, however, of the
British constitution... on its free
and ancient principles, neither his
Majesty nor his ancestors have exercised such a power of dissolution in
the island of Great Britain; and when
his Majesty was petitioned by the
united voice of his people there to
dissolve the present Parliament,
who had become obnoxious to them,
his ministers were heard to declare
in open Parliament that his Majesty
possessed no such power by the constitution. But how different their
language, and his practice, here!—
*Summary View of the Rights of British
America*. Bergh 1:203. (1774.)

**LEGISLATURES, Can Be Danger-
ous.**—When the representative body
have lost the confidence of their
constituents, when they have noto-
riously made sale of their most
valuable rights, when they have
assumed to themselves powers
which the people never put into
their hands, then, indeed, their
continuing in office becomes dangerous to the state, and calls for an
exercise of the power of dissolution.

—*Summary View of the Rights of British
America*. Bergh 1:204. (1774.)

LEGISLATURES, Despotism and.
—All the powers of government,
legislative, executive, and judiciary,
result to the legislative body [under
the first Virginia constitution]. The
concentrating these in the same
hands is precisely the definition of
despotic government. It will be no
alleviation that these powers will be
exercised by a plurality of hands, and
not by a single one. One hundred
and seventy-three despots would
surely be as oppressive as one. Let
those who doubt it turn their eyes
on the republic of Venice.—*Notes on
Virginia*. Bergh 2:162. (1782.)

LEGISLATURES, Tyranny of.—
The executive in our governments
is not the sole, it is scarcely the
principal object of my jealousy. The
tyranny of the legislatures is the
most formidable dread at present,
and will be for many years.—To
James Madison. Ford 5:83. (1789.)

LEGISLATURES, The People and.
—The people... are not qualified
to legislate. With us, therefore, they
only choose the legislators.—Bergh
7:422. (1789.)

**LEGISLATURES, Too Many Mem-
bers Create a Tumult.**—Twelve
hundred men in one room [in the
French National Assembly] are too
many.—Bergh 7:408. (1789.)

The [National] Assembly [of
France] proceeds slowly in...
forming their constitution. The
original vice of their numbers causes
this, as well as a tumultuous manner
of doing business.—To John Jay.
Bergh 7:471. (1789.)

Render the [Virginia] legislature a desirable station by lessening the number of representatives (say to 100) and lengthening somewhat their term, and proportion them equally among the electors.—Ford 5:410. (1791.)

Reduce the legislature to a convenient number for full but orderly discussion.—Ford 10:39. (1816.)

LEGISLATURES, Limitation on Powers of.—Our legislators are not sufficiently apprised of the rightful limits of their power; that their true office is to declare and enforce only our natural rights and duties, and to take none of them from us.—Ford 10:32. (1816.)

LEGISLATURES, Purpose of Two Houses.—In the structure of our legislatures, we think experience has proved the benefit of subjecting questions to two separate bodies of deliberants; but in constituting these, natural right has been mistaken, some making one of these bodies, and some both, the representatives of property instead of persons; whereas the double deliberation might be as well obtained, without any violation of true principle, either by requiring a greater age in one of the bodies or by electing a proper number of representatives of persons, dividing them by lots into two chambers, and renewing the division at frequent intervals in order to break up all cabals.—Bergh 16:45. (1824.)

LEGISLATURES. See also CONGRESS; FEDERAL GOVERNMENT; SENATE.

LETTER WRITING, Sometimes Postponed by Domestic Duties.—Instead of writing ten or twelve letters a day, which I have been in the habit of doing as a thing in course, I put off answering my letters now, farmer-like, till a rainy day, and then find them sometimes postponed by other necessary occupations.—To George Washington. Bergh 9:283. (1794.)

LETTER WRITING, Effect of Presidential Duties on Jefferson's.—The constant pressure of business has forced me to follow the practice of not answering letters which do not necessarily require it.—Ford 9:166. (1807.)

LETTER WRITING, Value of Daily.—I would advise you, as an exercise, to write a letter to somebody every morning, the first thing after you get up. As most of the business of life and all our friendly communications are by way of letter, nothing is more important than to acquire a facility of developing our ideas on paper; and practice alone will give this.—To Thomas Jefferson Randolph. Betts & Bear, p. 397. (1810.)

LETTER WRITING, Drudgery of.—From sunrise to one or two o'clock, and often from dinner to dark, I am drudging at the writing table. And all this to answer letters into which neither interest nor inclination on my part enters; and often from persons whose names I have never before heard. Yet, writing civilly, it is hard to refuse them civil answers. This is the burden of my life, a very grievous one indeed, and one which I must get rid of.—To John Adams. Bergh 15:97. (1817.)

LETTER WRITING, Voluminous in Jefferson's Old Age.—I happened to turn to my letter list some time ago, and a curiosity was excited to count those received in a single year. It was the year before the last. I found the number to be one thousand two hundred and sixty-seven, many of them requiring answers of elaborate research, and all to be answered with due attention and consideration. Take an average of this number for a week or a day, and I will repeat the question . . . is this life? At best it is but the life of a mill-horse, who sees no end to his circle but in death. To such a life, that of a cabbage is paradise. —To John Adams. Bergh 15:386. (1822.)

LEWIS (Meriwether), Eminently Qualified to Lead the Lewis and Clark Expedition. —Meriwether Lewis . . . had lost his father at an early age. He continued some years under the fostering care of a tender mother, of the respectable family of Meriwethers of the same county, and was remarkable even in his infancy for enterprise, boldness, and discretion. When only eight years of age, he habitually went out in the dead of night, alone with his dogs, into the forest to hunt the raccoon and opossum, which, seeking their food in the night, can then only be taken. In this exercise no season or circumstance could obstruct his purpose, plunging through the winter's snows and frozen streams in pursuit of his object. At thirteen he was put to the Latin school, and continued at that until eighteen, when he returned to his mother and entered on the cares of his farm, having . . . been left by his father with a competency for all the correct

and comfortable purposes of temperate life.

His talent for observation, which had led him to an accurate knowledge of the plants and animals of his own country, would have distinguished him as a farmer; but at the age of twenty, yielding to the ardor of youth and a passion for more dazzling pursuits, he engaged as a volunteer in the body . . . called out by General Washington on occasion of the discontents produced by the excise taxes in the western parts of the United States; and from that situation he was removed to the regular service as a lieutenant in the line. At twenty-three he was promoted to a captaincy; and always attracting the first attention where punctuality and fidelity were requisite, he was appointed paymaster to his regiment. . . .

[He was] of courage undaunted, possessing a firmness and perseverance of purpose which nothing but impossibilities could divert from its direction, careful as a father of those committed to his charge, yet steady in the maintenance of order and discipline. Intimate with the Indian character, customs, and principles; habituated to the hunting life; guarded by exact observation of the vegetables and animals of his own country against losing time in the description of objects already possessed; honest, disinterested, liberal, of sound understanding and a fidelity to truth so scrupulous that whatever he should report would be as certain as if seen by ourselves — with all these qualifications, as if selected and implanted by nature in one body for this express purpose, I could have no hesitation in confiding the enterprise to him.

To fill up the measure desired, he wanted nothing but a greater familiarity with the technical language of the natural sciences, and readiness in the astronomical observations necessary for the geography of his route. To acquire these he repaired immediately to Philadelphia, and placed himself under the tutorage of the distinguished professors of that place, who, with a zeal and emulation enkindled by an ardent devotion to science, communicated to him freely the information requisite for the purposes of the journey.

While attending to, at Lancaster, the fabrication of the arms with which he chose that his men should be provided, he had the benefit of daily communication with Mr. Andrew Ellicott, whose experience in astronomical observation and practice of it in the woods enabled him to apprise Captain Lewis of the wants and difficulties he would encounter, and of the substitutes and resources offered by a woodland and uninhabited country.—Bergh 18:142. (1813.)

LEWIS AND CLARK EXPEDITION, President Jefferson's Instructions for.—In 1803, the act for establishing trading houses with the Indian tribes being about to expire, some modifications of it were recommended to Congress by a confidential message of January 18th, and an extension of its views to the Indians on the Missouri. In order to prepare the way, the message proposed the sending an exploring party to trace the Missouri to its source [and] to cross the highlands and follow the best water communication which offered itself from thence to the Pacific Ocean. Congress approved the proposition and voted a sum of money for carrying it into execution. Captain [Meriwether] Lewis, who had then been near two years with me as private secretary, immediately renewed his solicitations to have the direction of the party. I had now had opportunities of knowing him intimately,... [and] I could have no hesitation in confiding the enterprise to him.... Deeming it necessary he should have some person with him of known competence to the direction of the enterprise, and to whom he might confide it in the event of accident to himself, he proposed William Clark, brother of General George Rogers Clark, who was approved, and with that view received a commission of captain.

In April 1803 a draft of his instructions was sent to Captain Lewis, and on the 20th of June they were signed in the following form:

"To Meriwether Lewis, Esquire, Captain of the 1st regiment of infantry of the United States of America....

"The object of your mission is to explore the Missouri River, and such principal streams of it as, by its course and communication with the waters of the Pacific Ocean, whether the Columbia, Oregon, Colorado, or any other river, may offer the most direct and practicable water communication across the continent for the purposes of commerce.

"Beginning at the mouth of the Missouri, you will take observations of latitude and longitude at all remarkable points on the river, and especially at the mouths of rivers, at rapids, at islands, and other places and objects distinguished by such natural marks and characters of a durable kind as that they may with certainty be recognized hereafter. The courses of the river between these points of observation may be supplied by the compass, the logline, and by time, corrected by the observations themselves. The variations of the compass, too, in different places should be noticed.

"The interesting points of the portage between the heads of the Missouri, and of the water offering the best communication with the Pacific Ocean, should also be fixed by observation, and the course of that water to the ocean, in the same manner as that of the Missouri....

"The commerce which may be carried on with the people inhabiting the line you will pursue renders a knowledge of those people important. You will therefore endeavor to make yourself acquainted, as far as a diligent pursuit of your journey shall admit, with the names of the nations and their numbers; the extent of their possessions; their relations with other tribes or nations; their language, traditions, monuments; their ordinary occupations in agriculture, fishing, hunting, war, arts, and the implements for these; their food, clothing, and domestic accommodations; the diseases prevalent among them, and the remedies they use; moral and physical circumstances which distinguish them from the tribes we know; peculiarities in their laws, customs, and dispositions, and articles of commerce they may need or furnish, and to what extent; and, considering the interest which every nation has in extending and strengthening the authority of reason and justice among the people around them, it will be useful to acquire what knowledge you can of the state of morality, religion, and information among them, as it may better enable those who may endeavor to civilize and instruct them to adapt their measures to the existing notions and practices of those on whom they are to operate.

"Other objects worthy of notice will be the soil and face of the country; its growth and vegetable productions, especially those not of the United States; the animals of the country generally, and especially those not known in the United States; the remains and accounts of any which may be deemed rare or extinct; the mineral productions of every kind, but particularly metals, limestone, pit-coal and saltpeter; salines and mineral waters, noting the temperature of the last, and such circumstances as may indicate their character; volcanic appearances; climate, as characterized by the thermometer, by the proportion of rainy, cloudy, and clear days, by lightning, hail, snow, [and] ice, by the access and recess of frost, by the winds prevailing at different seasons, the dates at which particular plants put forth or lose their flower or leaf, [and] times of appearance of particular birds, reptiles, or insects....

"In all your intercourse with the natives, treat them in the most friendly and conciliatory manner which their own conduct will admit; allay all jealousies as to the object of your journey, [and] satisfy them of its innocence; make them acquainted with the position, extent, character, [and] peaceable and commercial dispositions of the United States, of our wish to be neighborly, friendly, and useful to them, and of our dispositions to a commercial intercourse with them; confer with them on the points most convenient as mutual emporiums, and the articles of most desirable interchange for them and us. If a few of their influential chiefs within practicable distance wish to visit us, arrange such a visit with them, and furnish them with authority to call on our officers, on their entering the United States, to have them conveyed to this place at the public expense. If any of them should wish to have some of their young people brought up with us, and taught such arts as may be useful to them, we will receive, instruct, and take care of them. Such a mission, whether of influential chiefs or of young people, would give some security to your own party....

"As it is impossible for us to foresee in what manner you will be received by those people, whether with hospitality or hostility, so is it impossible to prescribe the exact degree of perseverance with which you are to pursue your journey. We value too much the lives of citizens to offer them to probable destruction. Your numbers will be sufficient to secure you against the unauthorized opposition of individuals or of small parties; but if a superior force, authorized or not authorized by a nation, should be arrayed against your further passage, and inflexibly determined to arrest it, you must decline its farther pursuit and return. In the loss of yourselves, we should lose also the information you will have acquired. By returning safely with that, you may enable us to renew the essay with better calculated means. To your own discretion, therefore, must be left the degree of danger you may risk, and the point at which you should decline, only saying we wish you to err on the side of your safety, and to bring us back your party safe, even if it be with less information.

"Should you reach the Pacific Ocean, inform yourself of the circumstances which may decide whether the furs of those parts may not be collected as advantageously at the head of the Missouri...as at Nootka Sound, or any other point of that coast, and that trade be consequently conducted through the Missouri and United States more beneficially than by the circumnavigation now practiced....

"On your arrival on that coast, endeavor to learn if there be any post within your reach frequented by the sea vessels of any nation, and to send two of your trusty people back by sea, in such way as shall appear practicable, with a copy of your notes; and should you be of opinion that the return of your party by the way they went will be imminently dangerous, then ship the whole and return by sea, by the way either of Cape Horn or the Cape of Good Hope, as you shall be able. . . .

"Should you find it safe to return by the way you go after sending two of your party round by sea, or with your whole party if no conveyance by sea can be found, do so; making such observations on your return as may serve to supply, correct, or confirm those made on your outward journey. . . .

"Given under my hand at the city of Washington, this 20th day of June, 1803.

"Thomas Jefferson, President of the United States of America."

While these things were going on here, the country of Louisiana, lately ceded by Spain to France, had been the subject of negotiation between us and this last power; and had actually been transferred to us by treaties executed at Paris on the 30th of April. This information, received about the 1st day of July, increased infinitely the interest we felt in the expedition, and lessened the apprehensions of interruption from other powers. Everything in this quarter being now prepared, Captain Lewis left Washington on the 5th of July, 1803, and proceeded to Pittsburgh, where other articles had been ordered to be provided for him. The men, too, were to be selected from the military stations on the Ohio. Delays of preparation, difficulties of navigation down the Ohio, and other untoward obstructions retarded his arrival at Cahokia until the season was so far advanced as to render it

prudent to suspend his entering the Missouri before the ice should break up in the succeeding spring. From this time his journal, now published, will give the history of his journey to and from the Pacific Ocean until his return to St. Louis on the 23rd of September, 1806. Never did a similar event excite more joy through the United States. . . .

It was the middle of February 1807 before Captain Lewis with his companion Clark reached the city of Washington, where Congress was then in session. That body granted to the two chiefs and their followers the donation of lands which they had been encouraged to expect in reward of their toils and dangers. Captain Lewis was soon after appointed Governor of Louisiana, and Captain Clark a general of its militia and agent of the United States for Indian affairs in that department. —Bergh 18:145. (1813.)

LEWIS AND CLARK EXPEDITION. See also AMERICAN CONTINENT.

LIBEL, Newspaper Publication of.— Printers shall be liable to legal prosecution for printing and publishing false facts, injurious to the party prosecuting; but they shall be under no other restraint.—Ford 5:102. (1789.)

In those states where they do not admit even the truth of allegations to protect the printer, they have gone too far.—Ford 8:311. (1804.)

LIBEL, Jefferson's Reaction to.—At a very early period of my life I determined never to put a sentence into any newspaper. I have religiously adhered to the resolution through my life, and have great reason to be contented with it. Were I to undertake to answer the calumnies of the newspapers, it would be more than all my own time and that of twenty aides could effect. For while I should be answering one, twenty new ones would be invented. I have thought it better to trust to the justice of my countrymen, that they would judge me by what they *see* of my conduct on the stage where they have placed me, and what they knew of me *before* the epoch since which a particular party has supposed it might answer some view of theirs to vilify me in the public eye. Some, I know, will not reflect how apocryphal is the testimony of enemies so palpably betraying the views with which they give it. But this is an injury to which duty requires everyone to submit whom the public think proper to call into its councils.—Bergh 10:58. (1798.)

As to the calumny of atheism, I am so broken to calumnies of every kind...that I entirely disregard it. ...It has been so impossible to contradict all their lies that I have determined to contradict none, for while I should be engaged with one they would publish twenty new ones. [My] thirty years of public life have enabled most of those who read newspapers to judge of one for themselves.—To James Monroe. Ford 7:447. (1800.)

LIBEL, Punishment Either Earthly or Divine.—From the moment that a portion of my fellow citizens looked towards me with a view to one of their highest offices, the floodgates of calumny have been opened upon me.... I know that I might have filled the courts of the United States with actions for these slanders, and have ruined perhaps many persons who are not innocent. But this would be no equivalent to the loss of character. I leave them, therefore, to the reproof of their own consciences. If these do not condemn them, there will yet come a day when the false witness will meet a Judge who has not slept over his slanders.—Bergh 10:171. (1800.)

LIBEL. See also NEWSPAPERS; SLANDER.

LIBERTY, The Gift of God.—The God who gave us life gave us liberty at the same time; the hand of force may destroy but cannot disjoin them. —*Summary View of the Rights of British America.* Bergh 1:211. (1774.)

Can the liberties of a nation be thought secure when we have removed their only firm basis, a conviction in the minds of the people that these liberties are...the gift of God? That they are not to be violated but with His wrath?—*Notes on Virginia.* Bergh 2:227. (1782.)

LIBERTY, Preserve at All Costs.— We do then most solemnly, before God and the world, declare that regardless of every consequence, at the risk of every distress, the arms we have been compelled to assume we will use with...perseverance, exerting to their utmost energies all those powers which our Creator hath given us, to preserve that liberty which He committed to us in sacred deposit, and to protect from every hostile hand our lives and our properties.—Declaration of the

Causes and Necessity for Taking Up Arms. Ford 1:474. (1775.)

LIBERTY, An Inalienable Right.— We hold these truths to be self-evident: that all men are created equal; that they are endowed by their Creator with certain inalienable rights; that among these are life, liberty, and the pursuit of happiness.—Declaration of Independence. Bergh 1:29. (1776.)

LIBERTY, Bloodshed and.—The tree of liberty must be refreshed from time to time with the blood of patriots and tyrants. It is its natural manure.—Ford 4:467. (1787.)

A warm zealot for the attainment and enjoyment by all mankind of as much liberty as each may exercise without injury to the equal liberty of his fellow citizens, I have lamented that in France the endeavors to obtain this should have been attended with the effusion of so much blood.—Ford 7:13. (1795.)

LIBERTY, Resistance and.—What country can preserve its liberties if its rulers are not warned from time to time that the people preserve the spirit of resistance?—Ford 4:467. (1787.)

LIBERTY, Best Preserved by an Informed Electorate.—Say... whether peace is best preserved by giving energy to the government, or information to the people. This last is the most certain and the most legitimate engine of government. Educate and inform the whole mass of the people. Enable them to see that it is their interest to preserve peace and order, and they will preserve them. And it requires no very high degree of education to

convince them of this. They are the only sure reliance for the preservation of our liberty.—To James Madison. Bergh 6:392. (1787.)

LIBERTY, Tends to Yield to Government.—The natural progress of things is for liberty to yield and government to gain ground.—Bergh 7:37. (1788.)

LIBERTY, The Parent of Science and Virtue.—Liberty... is the great parent of science and of virtue; and ...a nation will be great in both, always in proportion as it is free.—Bergh 7:329. (1789.)

LIBERTY, Not Easily Achieved.—The ground of liberty is to be gained by inches, and we must be contented to secure what we can get, from time to time, and eternally press forward for what is yet to get. It takes time to persuade men to do even what is for their own good.—Ford 5:142. (1790.)

We are not to expect to be translated from despotism to liberty in a feather bed.—To Marquis de Lafayette. Bergh 8:13. (1790.)

LIBERTY, Too Much vs. Too Little.—I would rather be exposed to the inconveniences attending too much liberty than those attending too small a degree of it.—Bergh 8:276. (1791.)

LIBERTY, A Hope for Universal.—The ball of liberty is now so well in motion that it will roll round the globe.—Ford 7:22. (1795.)

LIBERTY, France and.—The atrocious proceedings of France towards this country had well nigh destroyed its liberties. The Anglomen and monocrats had so artfully confounded the cause of France with that of freedom that both went down in the same scale.—Ford 7:374. (1799.)

LIBERTY, America and.—The last hope of human liberty in this world rests on us. We ought, for so dear a stake, to sacrifice every attachment and every enmity.—Ford 9:313. (1811.)

When we reflect that the eyes of the virtuous all over the earth are turned with anxiety on us as the only depositories of the sacred fire of liberty, and that our falling into anarchy would decide forever the destinies of mankind and seal the political heresy that man is incapable of self-government, the only contest between divided friends should be who will dare farthest into the ranks of the common enemy.—Bergh 13:58. (1811.)

LIBERTY, Requires a Knowledgeable Citizenry.—If a nation expects to be ignorant and free, in a state of civilization, it expects what never was and never will be. The functionaries of every government have propensities to command at will the liberty and property of their constituents. There is no safe deposit for these but with the people themselves; nor can they be safe with them without information. Where the press is free, and every man able to read, all is safe.—Bergh 14:384. (1816.)

LIBERTY. See also TYRANNY.

LIBRARY, Jefferson's Pains to Acquire His Personal.—You know my collection, its condition and extent. I have been fifty years making it, and have spared no pains, opportunity, or expense to make it

what it is. While residing in Paris, I devoted every afternoon I was disengaged, for a summer or two, in examining all the principal bookstores, turning over every book with my own hand and putting by everything which related to America, and indeed whatever was rare and valuable in every science. Besides this, I had standing orders during the whole time I was in Europe, on its principal book marts, particularly Amsterdam, Frankfort, Madrid, and London, for such works relating to America as could not be found in Paris; so that in that department particularly, such a collection was made as probably can never again be effected.... During the same period, and after my return to America, I was led to procure also whatever related to the duties of those in the high concerns of the nation; so that the collection, which I suppose is of between nine and ten thousand volumes, while it includes what is chiefly valuable in science and literature generally, extends more particularly to whatever belongs to the American statesman. In the diplomatic and parliamentary branches, it is particularly full.—To Samuel H. Smith. Bergh 14:191. (1814.)

LIBRARY, Jefferson's, Offered to Congress.—It is long since I have been sensible it ought not to continue private property, and had provided that at my death Congress should have the refusal of it at their own price. But the loss they have now incurred makes the present the proper moment for their accommodation, without regard to the small remnant of time and the barren use of my enjoying it.* I ask of your friendship, therefore, to make for me the tender of it to the library committee of Congress, not knowing myself of whom the committee consists. I enclose you the catalogue, which will enable them to judge of its contents. Nearly the whole are well bound, [an] abundance of them elegantly, and of the choicest editions existing. They may be valued by persons named by themselves, and the payment made convenient to the public.—To Samuel H. Smith. Bergh 14:192. (1814.)

* The "loss" Jefferson referred to was the burning of public buildings and documents in Washington by the British during the War of 1812. Jefferson's library, which was purchased by the federal government for $23,950 as a result of this timely offer, became the nucleus of today's Library of Congress. —Editor.

LIES, Folly of.—It is of great importance to set a resolution, not to be shaken, never to tell an untruth. There is no vice so mean, so pitiful, so contemptible; and he who permits himself to tell a lie once finds it much easier to do it a second and third time, till at length it becomes habitual; he tells lies without attending to it, and truths without the world's believing him. This falsehood of the tongue leads to that of the heart, and in time depraves all its good dispositions.—To Peter Carr. Bergh 5:84. (1785.)

LIES, Jefferson's Reaction to Political.—There is an enemy somewhere endeavoring to sow discord among us. Instead of listen-

ing first, then doubting, and lastly believing anile [feebleminded] tales handed round without an atom of evidence, if my friends will address themselves to me directly, as you have done, they shall be informed with frankness and thankfulness. —Ford 8:431. (1806.)

Were I to buy off every Federalist lie by a sacrifice of two or three thousand dollars, a very few such purchases would make me as bankrupt in reputation as in fortune. To buy off one lie is to give a premium for the invention of others. From the moment I was proposed for my present office, the volumes of calumny and falsehood issued to the public rendered impracticable every idea of going into the work of finding and proving. I determined, therefore, to go straight forward in what was right, and to rest my character with my countrymen, not on depositions and affidavits, but on what they should themselves witness, the course of my life. I have had no reason to be dissatisfied with the confidence reposed in the public; on the contrary, great encouragement to persevere in it to the end.—Ford 9:229. (1808.)

LIES, Not to Be Feared.—The man who fears no truths has nothing to fear from lies.—Ford 10:27. (1816.)

LIES. See also GOOD FAITH; HONESTY; TRUTH.

LIFE, Liberty and.—The God who gave us life gave us liberty at the same time; the hand of force may destroy but cannot disjoin them.— *Summary View of the Rights of British America.* Bergh 1:211. (1774.)

LIFE, An Inalienable Right.—We hold these truths to be self-evident: that all men are created equal; that they are endowed by their Creator with certain inalienable rights; that among these are life, liberty, and the pursuit of happiness.—Declaration of Independence. Bergh 1:29. (1776.)

LIFE, Meant for Happiness.—The Giver of life . . . gave it for happiness and not for wretchedness.—To James Monroe. Ford 3:59. (1782.)

LIFE, Value of Individual.—In a government bottomed on the will of all, the life . . . of every individual citizen becomes interesting to all.—Fifth Annual Message to Congress. Bergh 3:390. (1805.)

LIFE, A Prayer for All.—I sincerely pray . . . that all the members of the human family may, in the time prescribed by the Father of us all, find themselves securely established in the enjoyment of life, liberty, and happiness.—Bergh 16:290. (1807.)

LIFE, Public Order and.—The life of a citizen is never to be endangered but as the last melancholy effort for the maintenance of order and obedience to the laws.—Ford 9:238. (1809.)

LIFE, Government and.—The care of human life and happiness, and not their destruction, is the first and only legitimate object of good government.—Bergh 16:359. (1809.)

LIFE, Jefferson's Attitude Toward.—You ask if I would agree to live my seventy, or rather seventy-three, years over again. To which I say, yea. I think, with you, that it is a good world on the whole, that it has been framed on a principle of benevolence, and more pleasure than pain dealt out to us. There are, indeed (who might say nay), gloomy and hypochondriac minds, inhabitants of diseased bodies, disgusted with the present and despairing of the future; always counting that the worst will happen because it may happen. To these I say, how much pain have cost us the evils which have never happened! My temperament is sanguine. I steer my bark with Hope in the head, leaving Fear astern. My hopes, indeed, sometimes fail, but not oftener than the forebodings of the gloomy. There are, I acknowledge, even in the happiest life, some terrible convulsions, heavy set-offs against the opposite page of the account.—To John Adams. Bergh 14:467. (1816.)

LIVINGSTON (Edward), Jefferson's Friendship for.—I receive Mr. Livingston's question through you with kindness and answer it without hesitation. He may be assured I have not a spark of unfriendly feeling towards him. In all the earlier scenes of life, we thought and acted together. We differed in opinion afterwards on a single point. Each maintained his opinion, as he had a right, and acted on it as he ought. But why brood over a single difference and forget all our previous harmonies?—To President James Monroe. Ford 10:298. (1824.)

LOANS, Government Should Not Obtain, from Private Banks.—I wish it were possible to obtain a single amendment to our Constitution. I would be willing to depend on that alone for the reduction of the administration of our government to the genuine principles of its Constitution; I mean an additional article taking from the federal government the power of borrowing. —Bergh 10:64. (1798.)

The question will be asked and ought to be looked at, what is to be the resource if loans cannot be obtained? There is but one.... Bank paper must be suppressed and the circulating medium must be restored to the nation, to whom it belongs. It is the only fund on which they [the government] can rely for loans, it is the only resource which can never fail them, and it is an abundant one for every necessary purpose. Treasury bills bottomed on taxes, bearing or not bearing interest as may be found necessary, [and] thrown into circulation, will take the place of so much gold and silver, which last, when crowded, will find an efflux into other countries, and thus keep the *quantum* of medium at its salutary level.—Ford 9:399. (1813.)

LOANS, Economy vs.—I learn with great satisfaction that wholesome economies have been found, sufficient to relieve us from the ruinous necessity of adding annually to our debt by new loans. The deviser of so salutary a relief deserves truly well of his country.—Ford 10:251. (1823.)

LOANS. See also DEBT.

LONDON, Beauty of.—The city of London, though handsomer than Paris, is not so handsome as Philadelphia.—Ford 4:214. (1786.)

LOTTERIES, Inadvisable.—Having myself made it a rule never to engage in a lottery or any other adventure of mere chance, I can with the less candor or effect urge it on others, however laudable or

desirable its object may be.—Bergh 12:386. (1810.)

LOTTERIES. See also CHANCE; GAMBLING; SPECULATION.

LOUIS XVI, Execution of.—We have just received here [in Philadelphia] the news of the decapitation of the King of France. Should the present foment in Europe not produce republics everywhere, it will at least soften the monarchical governments by rendering monarchs amenable to punishment like other criminals, and doing away [with] that rage of insolence and oppression, the inviolability of the King's person. —Bergh 9:45. (1793.)

The deed which closed the mortal course of these sovereigns [Louis XVI and Marie Antoinette] I shall neither approve nor condemn. I am not prepared to say that the first magistrate of a nation cannot commit treason against his country, or is unamenable to its punishment. ...I should have shut up the Queen in a convent, putting harm out of her power, and placed the King in his station, investing him with limited powers which, I verily believe, he would have honestly exercised according to the measure of his understanding. In this way no void would have been created, courting the usurpation of a military adventurer, nor occasion given for those enormities which demoralized the nations of the world and destroyed, and [are] yet to destroy, millions and millions of its inhabitants.—Autobiography. Bergh 1:151. (1821.)

LOUIS XVI, Character of.—He had not a wish but for the good of the nation; and for that object, no personal sacrifice would ever have cost him a moment's regret; but his mind was weakness itself, his constitution timid, his judgment null, and without sufficient firmness even to stand by the faith of his word. His Queen, too, haughty and bearing no contradiction, had an absolute ascendancy over him.... The resolutions of the morning, formed under [his best ministers'] advice, would be reversed in the evenings by the influence of the Queen and court.—Autobiography. Bergh 1:131. (1821.)

LOUIS XVI. See also MARIE ANTOINETTE.

LOUISIANA, British Designs on.— It is said that Arnold is at Detroit reviewing the militia there. Other symptoms indicate a general design on all Louisiana and the two Floridas. What a tremendous position would success in these two objects place us in! Embraced from the St. Croix to the St. Mary's on the one side by their possessions, on the other by their fleet, we need not hesitate to say that they would soon find means to unite to them all the territory covered by the ramifications of the Mississippi.—Ford 5:199. (1790.)

I am so deeply impressed with the magnitude of the dangers which will attend our government if Louisiana and the Floridas be added to the British empire that, in my opinion, we ought to make ourselves parties in the *general war* expected to take place should this be the only means of preventing the calamity. But I think we should defer this step as long as possible because war is so full

of chances, which may relieve us from the necessity of interfering; and if necessary, still the later we interfere, the better we shall be prepared. It is often, indeed, more easy to prevent the capture of a place than to retake it. Should it be so in the case in question, the difference between the two operations of preventing and retaking will not be so costly as two, three, or four years more of war. So that I am for preserving neutrality as long, and entering into the war as late, as possible.—Ford 5:238. (1790.)

LOUISIANA, The Constitution and U.S. Acquisition of.—There is no Constitutional difficulty as to the acquisition of territory; and whether, when acquired, it may be taken into the Union by the Constitution, as it now stands, will become a question of expediency. I think it will be safer not to permit the enlargement of the Union but by amendment of the Constitution.—Ford 8:241. (1803.)

LOUISIANA, Bonaparte and.—I very early saw that Louisiana was indeed a speck in our horizon which was to burst in a tornado, and the public are unapprised how near this catastrophe was. Nothing but a frank and friendly development of causes and effects on our part, and good sense enough in Bonaparte to see that the train was unavoidable and would change the face of the world, saved us from that storm. I did not expect he would yield till a war took place between France and England, and my hope was to palliate and endure.... Whether, however, the good sense of Bonaparte might not see the course predicted to be

Jefferson in November 1804 (age 61). Profile drawing by Charles Fevret de Saint-Memin.

necessary and unavoidable, even before a war should be imminent, was a chance which we thought it our duty to try; but the immediate prospect of rupture brought the case to immediate decision. The denouement has been happy, and I confess I look to this duplication of area for the extending a government so free and economical as ours as a great achievement to the mass of happiness which is to ensue.—Ford 8:294. (1804.)

LOUISIANA, And Expansion of the Union.—I know that the acquisition of Louisiana has been disapproved by some from a candid apprehension that the enlargement of our territory would endanger its union. But who can limit the extent to which the federative principle may operate

effectively? The larger our association, the less will it be shaken by local passions; and, in any view, is it not better that the opposite bank of the Mississippi should be settled by our own brethren and children than by strangers of another family? With which shall we be most likely to live in harmony and friendly intercourse?—Second Inaugural Address. Bergh 3:377. (1805.)

LOUISIANA PURCHASE, Part of American Destiny.—The future destinies of our country hang on the event of this negotiation, and I am sure they could not be placed in more able or more zealous hands. On our parts we shall be satisfied that what you do not effect cannot be effected.—To Robert R. Livingston. Ford 8:210. (1803.)

LOUISIANA PURCHASE, Blessings Anticipated from.—While the property and sovereignty of the Mississippi and its waters secure an independent outlet for the produce of the western states, and an uncontrolled navigation through their whole course, free from collision with other powers and the dangers to our peace from that source, the fertility of the country, its climate and extent, promise in due season important aids to our treasury, an ample provision for our posterity, and a widespread field for the blessings of freedom and equal laws.—Third Annual Message to Congress. Bergh 3:353. (1803.)

The acquisition of Louisiana, although more immediately beneficial to the western states by securing for their produce a certain market, not subject to interruption by officers over whom we have no control, yet is also deeply interesting to the maritime portion of our country, inasmuch as by giving the exclusive navigation of the Mississippi it avoids the burdens and sufferings of a war which conflicting interests on that river would inevitably have produced at no distant period. It opens, too, a fertile region for the future establishments in the progress of that multiplication so rapidly taking place in all parts.—Bergh 16:284. (1803.)

LOUISIANA PURCHASE, Doubled the Nation's Land Mass.—The acquisition of Louisiana . . . interests every man of the nation. The territory acquired, as it includes all the waters of the Missouri and Mississippi, has more than doubled the area of the United States, and the new part is not inferior to the old in soil, climate, productions, and important communications.—To General Horatio Gates. Bergh 10:402. (1803.)

LOUISIANA PURCHASE, Should Be Ratified by the American People.—This treaty must of course be laid before both houses [of Congress], because both have important functions to exercise respecting it. They, I presume, will see their duty to their country in ratifying and paying for it, so as to secure a good which would otherwise probably be never again in their power. But I suppose they must then appeal to *the nation* for an additional article to the Constitution, approving and confirming an act which the nation had not previously authorized. The Constitution has made no provision for our hold-

ing foreign territory, still less for incorporating foreign nations into our Union. The executive, in seizing the fugitive occurrence which so much advances the good of their country, have done an act beyond the Constitution. The [Congress], in casting behind them metaphysical subtleties and risking themselves like faithful servants, must ratify and pay for it, and throw themselves on their country for doing for them unauthorized what we know they would have done for themselves had they been in a situation to do it. It is the case of a guardian investing the money of his ward in purchasing an important adjacent territory, and saying to him when of age, I did this for your good; I pretend to no right to bind you; you may disavow me, and I must get out of the scrape as I can; I thought it my duty to risk myself for you. But we shall not be disavowed by the nation, and their act of indemnity will confirm and not weaken the Constitution, by more strongly marking out its lines.—Bergh 10:410. (1803.)

LOUISIANA PURCHASE. See also MANIFEST DESTINY; POPULATION; TERRITORY.

LUXURIES, Taxation on.—The government which steps out of the ranks of the ordinary articles of consumption to select and lay under disproportionate burdens a particular one, because it is a comfort, pleasing to the taste, or necessary to health, and will therefore be bought, is, in that particular, a tyranny.—Ford 10:252. (1819.)

LUXURIES. See also TARIFFS.

M

MADISON (James), Jefferson's Estimate of.—To the purest principles of republican patriotism, [Madison] adds a wisdom and foresight second to no man on earth.—Bergh 12:369. (1810.)

MADISON (James), Jefferson's Friendship for.—My friendship for Mr. Madison, my confidence in his wisdom and virtue, and my approbation of all his measures, and especially of his taking up at length the gauntlet against England, is known to all with whom I have ever conversed or corresponded on these measures.—Ford 9:521. (1815.)

The friendship which has subsisted between us, now half a century, and the harmony of our political principles and pursuits, have been sources of constant happiness to me through that long period. And if I remove beyond the reach of attentions to the University [of Virginia], or beyond the bourne of life itself, as I soon must, it is a comfort to leave that institution under your care, and an assurance that it will not be wanting. It has also been a great solace to me to believe that you are engaged in vindicating to posterity the course we have pursued for preserving to them, in all their purity, the blessings of self-government, which we had assisted, too, in acquiring for them. If ever the earth has beheld a system of administration conducted with a single and steadfast eye to the general interest and happiness of those committed to it, one which, protected by truth, can

never know reproach, it is that to which our lives have been devoted. To myself you have been a pillar of support through life. Take care of me when dead, and be assured that I shall leave with you my last affections.—To James Madison. Bergh 16:158. (1826.)

MADISON (James), Abilities of.—Mr. Madison came into the [legislature of Virginia] in 1776, a new member and young; which circumstances, concurring with his extreme modesty, prevented his venturing himself in debate before his removal to the Council of State in November '77. From thence he went to Congress, then consisting of few members. Trained in these successive schools, he acquired a habit of self-possession which placed at ready command the rich resources of his luminous and discriminating mind, and of his extensive information, and rendered him the first of every assembly afterwards of which he became a member. Never wandering from his subject into vain declamation, but pursuing it closely in language pure, classical, and copious, soothing always the feelings of his adversaries by civilities and softness of expression, he rose to the eminent station which he held in the great [Constitutional] Convention of 1787; and in [the ratifying convention] of Virginia which followed, he sustained the new Constitution in all its parts, bearing off the palm against the logic of George Mason and the fervid declamation of Mr. [Patrick] Henry. With these consummate powers were united a pure and spotless virtue which no calumny has ever attempted to sully. Of the powers and polish of his pen, and of the wisdom of his administration in the highest office of the nation, I need say nothing. They have spoken, and will forever speak, for themselves.— Autobiography. Bergh 1:61. (1821.)

MAJORITY, Will of, Safeguards Natural Rights.—The will of the majority, the natural law of every society, is the only sure guardian of the rights of man. Perhaps even this may sometimes err. But its errors are honest, solitary, and short-lived. Let us, then, my dear friends, forever bow down to the general reason of the society. We are safe with that, even in its deviations, for it soon returns again to the right way.—Boyd 16:179. (1790.)

MAJORITY, Must Be Reasonable.—Bear in mind this sacred principle, that though the will of the majority is in all cases to prevail, that will, to be rightful, must be reasonable; that the minority possess their equal rights, which equal laws must protect, and to violate which would be oppression.—First Inaugural Address. Bergh 3:318. (1801.)

MAJORITY, Force vs.—I deem [one of] the essential principles of our government, and consequently [one] which ought to shape its administration, . . . absolute acquiescence in the decisions of the majority—the vital principle of republics, from which is no appeal but to force, the vital principle and immediate parent of despotism.—First Inaugural Address. Bergh 3:321. (1801.)

MAJORITY, Law of, Essential to Government.—Where the law of the majority ceases to be acknowledged, there government ends; the law of the strongest takes its place, and life and property are his who can take them.—Bergh 16:337. (1809.)

MAJORITY. See also MINORITY; PEOPLE; REPRESENTATION; REPUBLICAN GOVERNMENT; SELF-GOVERNMENT.

MAN, All Men Are Created Equal.—We hold these truths to be self-evident: that all men are created equal; that they are endowed by their Creator with certain inalienable rights; that among these are life, liberty, and the pursuit of happiness.—Declaration of Independence. Bergh 1:29. (1776.)

MAN, Government's Responsibility Toward.—The freedom and happiness of man . . . [are] the sole objects of all legitimate government.—Bergh 12:369. (1810.)

MAN, Innately Good.—I believe . . . that morality, compassion, [and] generosity are innate elements of the human constitution.—Bergh 14:490. (1816.)

MAN, His Condition Improved by Education.—Enlighten the people generally, and tyranny and oppressions of body and mind will vanish like evil spirits at the dawn of day. Although I do not, with some enthusiasts, believe that the human condition will ever advance to such a state of perfection as that there shall no longer be pain or vice in the world, yet I believe it susceptible of much improvement, and most of all in matters of government and religion; and that the diffusion of knowledge among the people is to be the instrument by which it is to be effected.—Bergh 14:491. (1816.)

I look to the diffusion of light and education as the resource most to be relied on for ameliorating the condition, promoting the virtue, and advancing the happiness of man. That every man shall be made virtuous, by any process whatever, is indeed no more to be expected than that every tree shall be made to bear fruit and every plant nourishment. The brier and bramble can never become the vine and olive; but their asperities may be softened by culture, and their properties improved to usefulness in the order and economy of the world. And I do hope that, in the present spirit of extending to the great mass of mankind the blessings of instruction, I see a prospect of great advancement in the happiness of the human race. —Bergh 15:399. (1822.)

MANIFEST DESTINY, God's Plan of Liberty for All.—The ball of liberty is now so well in motion that it will roll round the globe.—Ford 7:22. (1795.)

I sincerely pray that all the members of the human family may, in the time prescribed by the Father of us all, find themselves securely established in the enjoyment of life, liberty, and happiness.—Bergh 16:290. (1807.)

That we should wish to see the people of other countries free is as natural, and at least as justifiable, as that one king should wish to see the kings of other countries maintained in their despotism.—Ford 10:90. (1817.)

MANIFEST DESTINY, Commonwealth of Freedom to Cover the Western Hemisphere.—However our present interests may restrain us within our own limits, it is impossible not to look forward to distant times, when our rapid multiplication will expand itself beyond those limits and cover the whole northern, if not the southern, continent with a people speaking the same language, governed in similar forms, and by similar laws; nor can we contemplate with satisfaction either blot or mixture on that surface. Spain, France, and Portugal hold possessions on the southern continent, as to which I am not well enough informed to say how far they might meet our views. But ... I will have the dispositions of those powers sounded in the first instance.—To James Monroe. Bergh 10:296. (1801.)

MANIFEST DESTINY, Ages of Prosperity.—Retiring from the charge of their affairs, I carry with me the consolation of a firm persuasion that Heaven has in store for our beloved country long ages to come of prosperity and happiness. —Ford 9:225. (1808.)

MANIFEST DESTINY, The Constitution and.—No constitution was ever before so well calculated as ours for extensive empire and self-government.—To President James Madison. Bergh 12:277. (1809.)

MANIFEST DESTINY, To Spread Freedom Worldwide.—The preservation of the holy fire is confided to us by the world, and the sparks which will emanate from it will ever serve to rekindle it in other quarters of the globe.—Bergh 12:361. (1810.)

MANIFEST DESTINY, America the World's Last Hope.—The last hope of human liberty in this world rests on us. We ought, for so dear a stake, to sacrifice every attachment and every enmity.—Ford 9:313. (1811.)

MANIFEST DESTINY, America to Be a Barrier Against Human Degradation.—We are destined to be a barrier against the returns of ignorance and barbarism.—To John Adams. Bergh 15:58. (1816.)

And even should the cloud of barbarism and despotism again obscure the science and liberties of Europe, this country remains to preserve and restore light and liberty to them.—To John Adams. Bergh 15:334. (1821.)

MANIFEST DESTINY, A Day of Power Coming.—The day is not distant when we may formally require a meridian of partition through the ocean which separates the two hemispheres, on the hither side of which no European gun shall ever be heard, nor an American on the other; and when, during the rage of the eternal wars of Europe, the lion and the lamb within our regions shall lie down together in peace.—Bergh 15:263. (1820.)

MANIFEST DESTINY, America Must Set the Example.—We exist, and are quoted, as standing proofs that a government so modeled as to rest continually on the will of the whole society is a practicable government. Were we to break to pieces, it would damp the hopes and the efforts of the good, and give triumph to those of the bad through the whole enslaved world. As members, therefore, of the universal society of mankind, and standing in high and responsible relation with them, it is our sacred duty to suppress passion among ourselves, and not to blast the confidence we have inspired of proof that a government of reason is better than one of force. —Bergh 15:284. (1820.)

MANIFEST DESTINY, Westward Expansion Necessary.—I still believe that the western extension of our confederacy will ensure its duration by overruling local factions which might shake a smaller association. —Ford 10:192. (1821.)

MANIFEST DESTINY. See also AMERICA; POPULATION; TERRITORY; UNITED STATES.

MANSLAUGHTER, Punishment for.—Manslaughter is the killing a man with design, but in a sudden gust of passion, and where the killer has not had time to cool. The first offense is not punished capitally, but the second is. This is the law of England and of all the American states, and is not now a new proposition. Those laws have supposed that a man whose passions have so much dominion over him as to lead him to repeated acts of murder is unsafe to society; that it is better he should be put to death by the law than others more innocent than himself on the movements of his impetuous passions.—Bergh 17:79. (1786.)

MANSLAUGHTER. See also MURDER.

MANUFACTURES, Wisdom of Domestic.—The risk of hanging our prosperity on the fluctuating counsels and caprices of others renders it wise in us to turn seriously to manufactures; and if Europe will not let us carry our provisions to their manufactures, we must endeavor to bring their manufactures to our provisions.—Ford 5:344. (1791.)

I see with satisfaction that . . . our . . . citizens . . . are preparing with spirit to provide for themselves those comforts and conveniences of life for which it would be unwise evermore to recur to distant countries.—Bergh 16:307. (1808.)

The prohibiting duties we lay on all articles of foreign manufacture which prudence requires us to establish at home, with the patriotic determination of every good citizen to use no foreign article which can be made within ourselves, without regard to difference of price, secures us against a relapse into foreign dependency.—Bergh 14:259. (1815.)

MANUFACTURES, In Balance with Agriculture and Commerce.— I trust the good sense of our country will see that its greatest prosperity depends on a due balance between agriculture, manufactures, and commerce.—Ford 9:239. (1809.)

MARBURY v. MADISON, Case of. —I observe that the case of *Marbury v. Madison* has been cited [in the trial of Aaron Burr], and I think it material to stop at the threshold the citing that case as authority, and to have it denied to be law. 1. Because the judges in the outset disclaimed all cognizance of the case, although they then went on to say what would have been their opinion had they had

cognizance of it. This, then, was confessedly an extrajudicial opinion, and as such of no authority. 2. Because, had it been judicially pronounced, it would have been against the law; for to a commission, a deed, a bond, *delivery* is essential to give validity. Until, therefore, the commission is delivered out of the hands of the executive and his agents, it is not his deed. He may withhold or cancel it at pleasure, as he might his private deed in the same situation.

The Constitution intended that the three great branches of the government should be coordinate and independent of each other. As to acts, therefore, which are to be done by either, it has given no control to another branch. A judge, I presume, cannot sit on a bench without a commission, or a record of a commission; and the Constitution having given to the judiciary branch no means of compelling the executive either to *deliver* a commission or to make a record of it, shows that it did not intend to give the judiciary that control over the executive, but that it should remain in the power of the latter to do it or not.

Where different branches have to act in their respective lines, finally and without appeal, under any law, they may give to it different and opposite constructions. Thus, in the case of William Smith, the House of Representatives determined he was a citizen; and in the case of William Duane (precisely the same in every material circumstance), the judges determined he was no citizen. In the cases of Callender and some others, the judges determined the Sedition

Act was valid under the Constitution, and exercised their regular powers of sentencing them to fine and imprisonment. But the executive determined that the Sedition Act was a nullity under the Constitution, and exercised his regular power of prohibiting the execution of the sentence, or rather of executing the real law, which protected the acts of the defendants.

From these different constructions of the same act by different branches, less mischief arises than from giving to any one of them a control over the others. The executive and Senate act on the construction that, until delivery from the executive department, a commission is in their possession, and within their rightful power; and in cases of commissions not revocable at will where, after the Senate's approbation and the President's signing and sealing, new information of the unfitness of the person has come to hand before the *delivery* of the commission, new nominations have been made and approved, and new commissions have issued.

On this construction I have hitherto acted; on this I shall ever act, and maintain it with the powers of the government against any control which may be attempted by the judges, in subversion of the independence of the executive and Senate within their peculiar department. I presume, therefore, that in a case where our decision is by the Constitution the supreme one, and that which can be carried into effect, it is the constitutionally authoritative one, and that that by the judges was *coram non judice,* and unauthoritative, because it cannot be carried into effect.

I have long wished for a proper occasion to have the gratuitous opinion in *Marbury* v. *Madison* brought before the public, and denounced as not law; and I think the present a fortunate one because it occupies such a place in the public attention. I should be glad, therefore, if in noticing that case you could take occasion to express the determination of the executive that the doctrines of that case were given extrajudicially and against law, and that their reverse will be the rule of action with the executive.—Bergh 11:213. (1807.)

MARBURY v. MADISON. See also JUDICIAL REVIEW; JUDICIARY; SUPREME COURT.

MARIE ANTOINETTE, Character of.—She is capricious, like her brother, and governed by him; devoted to pleasure and expense; and not remarkable for any other vices or virtues.—To James Madison. Ford 4:393. (1787.)

This angel, as gaudily painted in the rhapsodies of Burke, with some smartness of fancy but no sound sense, was proud, disdainful of restraint, indignant at all obstacles to her will, eager in the pursuit of pleasure, and firm enough to hold to her desires or perish in their wreck. —Autobiography. Bergh 1:150. (1821.)

MARIE ANTOINETTE, And the French Revolution.—Her inordinate gambling and dissipations...had been a sensible item in the exhaustion of the treasury, which called into action the reforming hand of the nation; and her opposition to it, her inflexible perverseness and dauntless spirit, led herself to the guillotine, drew the King on with her, and plunged the world into crimes and calamities which will forever stain the pages of modern history. I have ever believed that had there been no Queen, there would have been no revolution. No force would have been provoked nor exercised. The King would have gone hand in hand with the wisdom of his sounder counsellors, who, guided by the increased lights of the age, wished only with the same pace to advance the principles of their social constitution.—Autobiography. Bergh 1:150. (1821.)

MARIE ANTOINETTE. See also LOUIS XVI.

MARKETS, Foreign.—Our commerce is certainly of a character to entitle it to favor in most countries. The commodities we offer are either necessaries of life, or materials for manufacture, or convenient subjects of revenue; and we take in exchange either manufactures, when they have received the last finish of art and industry, or mere luxuries. Such customers may reasonably expect welcome and friendly treatment at every market. Customers, too, whose demands, increasing with their wealth and population, must very shortly give full employment to the whole industry of any nation whatever, in any line of supply they may get into the habit of calling for from it.— Ford 6:479. (1793.)

MARKETS, Access to.—It is not to the moderation and justice of others we are to trust for fair and equal access to market with our productions, or for our due share in the transportation of them; but to our own means of independence, and the firm will to use them.—Ford 6:483. (1793.)

MARKETS, Home.—There can be no question, in a mind truly American, whether it is best to send our citizens and property into certain captivity, and then wage war for their recovery, or to keep them at home and to turn seriously to that policy which plants the manufacturer and the husbandman side by side, and establishes at the door of everyone that exchange of mutual labors and comforts which we have hitherto sought in distant regions, and under perpetual risk of broils with them.—Bergh 16:302. (1808.)

MARKETS. See also COMMERCE; FREE ENTERPRISE.

MARQUE AND REPRISAL, Letters of, Should Not Be Issued by State Governors.—The administrator [Governor] shall not possess the prerogative...of issuing letters of marque or reprisal.—Proposed Virginia Constitution. Ford 2:19. (1776.)

MARRIAGE, Happiness in.—The happiness of your life now depends on [your] continuing to please a single person [i.e., your new husband]. To this all other objects must be secondary—even your love [for] me, were it possible that that could ever be an obstacle. But this it can never be. Neither of you can ever have a more faithful friend than myself, nor one on whom you can count for more sacrifices. My own is become a secondary object to the happiness of you both. Cherish, then, for me, my dear child, the affection of your husband, and continue to love me as you have done, and to render my life a blessing by the prospect it may hold up to me of seeing you happy.—To Martha Jefferson Randolph. Betts & Bear, p. 51. (1790.)

MARRIAGE, Motherhood and.— [Motherhood] is undoubtedly the keystone of the arch of matrimonial happiness.—To Martha Jefferson Randolph. Betts & Bear, p. 71. (1791.)

MARRIAGE, How to Maintain Harmony in.—Harmony in the marriage state is the very first object to be aimed at. Nothing can preserve affections uninterrupted but a firm resolution never to differ in will, and a determination in each to consider the love of the other as of more value than any object whatever on which a wish has been fixed. How light, in fact, is the sacrifice of any other wish when weighed against the affections of one with whom we are to pass our whole life. And though opposition in a single instance will hardly of itself produce alienation, yet everyone has [his] pouch into which all these little oppositions are put. While that is filling, the alienation is insensibly going on, and when filled it is complete. It would puzzle either to say why, because no one difference of opinion has been marked enough to produce a serious effect by itself. But he finds his affections wearied out by a constant string of little checks and obstacles. Other sources of discontent, very common indeed, are the little cross purposes of husband and wife in common conversation, a disposition [in] either to criticize and question whatever the other says, a desire always to demonstrate and make him feel himself in the wrong, and especially in company. Nothing is so goading. Much better, therefore, if our companion views a thing in a light different from what we do, to leave him in quiet possession of his view. What is the use of rectifying him if the thing be unimportant; and if important, let it pass for the present and wait a softer moment and more conciliatory occasion of revising the subject together. It is wonderful how many persons are rendered unhappy by inattention to these little rules of prudence.—To Mary Jefferson Eppes. Betts & Bear, p. 151. (1798.)

MARRIAGE. See also FAMILY; HOME.

MARSHALL (John), A Mischief Maker.—He has been hitherto able to do more mischief acting under the mask of republicanism than he will be able to do throwing it plainly off. His lax, lounging manners have made him popular with the bulk of the people of Richmond, and a profound hypocrisy with many thinking men of our country. But [by his] having come forth in the full plenitude of his English principles, the latter will see that it is high time to make him known.—To James Madison. Ford 7:37. (1795.)

MARSHALL (John), Crafty.—[He is] a crafty Chief Judge, who sophisticates the law to his mind by the turn of his own reasoning.—Ford 10:171. (1820.)

MARSHALL (John), Moot Cases and. —The practice of Judge Marshall, of traveling out of his case to prescribe what the law would be in a moot case not before the court, is very irregular and very censurable.—Bergh 15:447. (1823.)

MARTIAL LAW, Recourse to.— There are extreme cases where the laws become inadequate even to their own preservation, and where the universal resource is a dictator, or martial law.—Ford 9:211. (1808.)

MASON (George), Abilities of.— George Mason [was] a man of the first order of wisdom among those who acted on the theater of the Revolution, of expansive mind, profound judgment, cogent in argument, learned in the lore of our former constitution, and earnest for the republican change on democratic principles. His elocution was neither flowing nor smooth, but his language was strong, his manner most impressive, and strengthened by a dash of biting cynicism when provocation made it seasonable.—Autobiography. Bergh 1:60. (1821.)

MASON (George), Bill of Rights and.—The fact is unquestionable that the Bill of Rights and the constitution of Virginia were drawn originally by George Mason, one of our really great men, and of the first order of greatness.—Ford 10:341. (1825.)

MASSACHUSETTS, Republicanism in.—I sincerely congratulate you on the triumph of Republicanism in Massachusetts. The hydra of Federalism has now lost all its heads but two [Connecticut and Delaware]. —Bergh 11:114. (1806.)

MASSACHUSETTS, Apostasy of. —Oh, Massachusetts! How have I lamented the degradation of your apostasy! Massachusetts, with whom I went in pride in 1776, whose vote was my vote on every public question, and whose principles were then the standard of whatever was free or fearless. But she was then under the counsels of the two Adamses; while [Caleb] Strong, her present leader, was promoting petitions for submission to British power and British usurpation. While under her present counsels, she must be contented to be nothing; as having a vote, indeed, to be counted, but not respected. But should the state once more buckle on her republican harness, we shall receive her again as a sister.—Bergh 14:288. (1815.)

MATHEMATICS, Jefferson's Favorite Study.—Having to conduct my grandson through his course of mathematics, I have resumed that study with great avidity. It was ever my favorite one. We have no theories there, no uncertainties remain on the mind; all is demonstration and satisfaction. I have forgotten much, and recover it with more difficulty than when in the vigor of my mind I originally acquired it.—Ford 9:328. (1811.)

MATTER, Demonstrated by Senses, Has Power of Thought.—Let me turn to your puzzling letter...on matter, spirit, motion, etc. Its crowd of skepticisms kept me from sleep. I read it and laid it down, read it and laid it down, again and again; and to give rest to my mind I was obliged to recur ultimately to my habitual anodyne, "I feel, therefore I exist." I feel bodies which are not myself; there are other existences then. I call them *matter*. I feel them changing place. This gives me *motion*. Where there is an absence of matter, I call it *void*, or *nothing*, or *immaterial space*. On the basis of sensation, of matter and motion, we may erect the fabric of all the certainties we can have or need. I can conceive *thought* to be an action of a particular organization of matter, formed for that purpose by its Creator, as well as that *attraction* is an action of matter, or *magnetism* of lodestone.

When he who denies to the Creator the power of endowing matter with the mode of action called *thinking* shall show how He could endow the sun with the mode of action called *attraction*, which reins the planets in the track of their orbits, or how an absence of matter can have a will, and by that will put matter into motion, then the materialist may be lawfully required to explain the process by which matter exercises the faculty of thinking. When once we quit the basis of sensation, all is in the wind.

To talk of *immaterial* existences is to talk of *nothings*. To say that the human soul, angels, God, are immaterial is to say they are *nothings*, or that there is no God, no angels, no soul. I cannot reason otherwise; but I believe I am supported in my creed of materialism by the Lockes, the Tracys, and the Stewarts. At what age of the Christian church this heresy of *immaterialism*, or masked atheism, crept in, I do not exactly know. But a heresy it certainly is. Jesus taught nothing of it.—To John Adams. Bergh 15:273. (1820.)

MEDICINE, Theories vs. Clinical Observations.—I have no doubt that some diseases not yet understood may in time be transferred to the table of those known. But were I a physician, I would rather leave the transfer to the slow hand of accident than hasten it by guilty experiments on those who put their lives into my hands. The only sure foundations of medicine are an intimate knowledge of the human body and observation on the effects of medicinal substances on that. The anatomical and clinical schools, therefore, are those in which the young physician should be formed. If he enters with innocence that of the theory of medicine, it is scarcely possible he should come out untainted with error. His mind must be strong indeed if, rising above juvenile credulity, it can maintain a wise infidelity against the authority of his instructors.... I wished to give a confession of my faith to a friend; and the rather as I had perhaps, at times, to him as well as others, expressed my skepticism in medicine without defining its extent or foundation. At any rate, it has permitted me for a moment to abstract myself from the dry and dreary waste of politics, into which I have been impressed by the times on which I happened, and to indulge in the rich fields of nature, where alone I should have served as a volunteer if left to my natural inclinations and partialities.—Ford 9:81. (1807.)

MEDICINE, Advancements in.—Theories and systems of medicine... have been in perpetual change from the days of the good Hippocrates to the days of the good Rush, but which of them is the true one? The present, to be sure, as long as it is the present; but to yield its place in turn to the next novelty, which is then to become the true system, and is to mark the vast advance of medicine since the days of Hippocrates. Our situation is certainly benefited by the discovery of some new and very valuable medicines; and substituting those for some of his with the treasure of facts, and of sound observations recorded by him (mixed, to be sure, with anilities of his day), ... we shall have nearly the present sum of the healing art.—Bergh 15:210. (1819.)

MERCHANTS, Reproved for Lack of Patriotism.—I join in your reprobation of our merchants, priests, and lawyers for their adherence to England and monarchy in preference to their own country and its Constitution. But merchants have no country. The mere spot they stand on does not constitute so strong an attachment as that from which they draw their gains.—Bergh 14:119. (1814.)

MILITIA, Crimes and Punishments.—Any officer or soldier guilty of mutiny, desertion, disobedience of command, absence from duty or quarters, neglect of guard, or cowardice shall be punished at the discretion of a court-martial by degrading, cashiering, drumming out of the army, whipping not exceeding twenty lashes, fine not exceeding [his pay for] two months, or imprisonment not exceeding one month.—Ford 2:127. (1777.)

MILITIA, Classification of.—Consider whether it would not be expedient, for a state of peace as well as of war, so to organize or class the militia as would enable us, on a sudden emergency, to call for the services of the younger portions, unencumbered with the old and those having families. Upward of three hundred thousand able-bodied men between the ages of eighteen and twenty-six years, which the last census shows we may now count within our limits, will furnish a competent number for offense or defense in any point where they may be wanted, and will give time for raising regular forces after the necessity of them shall become certain.... I cannot, then, but earnestly recommend to your early consideration the expediency of so modifying our militia system as, by a separation of the more active part from that which is less so, we may draw from it, when necessary, an efficient corps fit for real and active service, and to be called to it in regular rotation.—Fifth Annual Message to Congress. Bergh 3:389. (1805.)

MILITIA, Compulsory Service in.—We must train and classify the whole of our male citizens, and make military instruction a regular part of collegiate education. We can never be safe till this is done.—To James Monroe. Bergh 13:261. (1813.)

I think the truth must now be obvious that our people are too happy at home to enter into regular service, and that we cannot be defended but by making every citizen a soldier, as the Greeks and Romans who had no standing armies; and that in doing this all must be marshalled [and] classed by their ages, and every service ascribed to its competent class.—Ford 9:484. (1814.)

MILITIA, Importance of Good Leaders.—Our militia are heroes when they have heroes to lead them on.—Ford 9:504. (1815.)

MILITIA. See also ARMY; DEFENSE; DRAFT.

MIND, Freedom of the.—Almighty God hath created the mind free, and manifested His supreme will that free it shall remain by making it altogether insusceptible of restraint.—Bill for Establishing Religious Freedom. Ford 2:237. (1779.)

MIND, Should Be Influenced by Reason, Not Force.—All attempts to influence [the mind] by temporal punishments or burdens, or by civil incapacitations, tend only to beget habits of hypocrisy and meanness, and are a departure from the plan of the Holy Author of our religion, who, being Lord both of body and mind, yet chose not to propagate it by coercions on either, as was in his Almighty power to do, but to extend it by its influence on reason alone.—Bill for Establishing Religious Freedom. Ford 2:238. (1779.)

MIND, Best Qualities of the.—I estimate the qualities of the mind [to be]: 1, good humor; 2, integrity; 3, industry; 4, science [i.e., knowl-

edge]. The preference of the first to the second quality may not at first be acquiesced in; but certainly we had all rather associate with a good-humored, light-principled man than with an ill-tempered rigorist in morality.—To Dr. Benjamin Rush. Bergh 11:413. (1808.)

MINES, Avoid Government Ownership of.—I received duly your [letter] ...covering an offer of Mr. McDonald of an iron mine to the public.... But having always observed that public works are much less advantageously managed than the same are by private hands, I have thought it better for the public to go to market for whatever it wants which is to be found there; for there competition brings it down to the minimum of value. I have no doubt we can buy brass cannon at market cheaper than we could make iron ones.—Bergh 12:107. (1808.)

MINORITY, Equal Rights of, Must Be Protected.—All...will bear in mind this sacred principle, that though the will of the majority is in all cases to prevail, that will, to be rightful, must be reasonable; that the minority possess their equal rights, which equal laws must protect, and to violate which would be oppression.—First Inaugural Address. Bergh 3:318. (1801.)

The majority, oppressing an individual, is guilty of a crime, abuses its strength, and, by acting on the law of the strongest, breaks up the foundations of society.—Bergh 14:490. (1816.)

MINORITY, Censorship by.—A respectable minority [in Congress] is useful as censors. The present one is not respectable, being the bitterest remains of the cup of Federalism, rendered desperate and furious by despair.—Ford 8:149. (1802.)

MINORITY. See also MAJORITY.

MISSOURI, Its Admission as a Slave State Threatens to Divide the Union.—The Missouri question, . . . like a fire-bell in the night, awakened and filled me with terror. I considered it at once as the knell of the Union. It is hushed, indeed, for the moment. But this is a reprieve only, not a final sentence. A geographical line coinciding with a marked principle, moral and political, once conceived and held up to the angry passions of men, will never be obliterated; and every new irritation will mark it deeper and deeper.

I can say with conscious truth that there is not a man on earth who would sacrifice more than I would to relieve us from this heavy reproach [i.e., slavery] in any *practicable* way. The cession of that kind of property, for so it is misnamed, is a bagatelle which would not cost me a second thought, if in that way a general emancipation and *expatriation* could be effected; and gradually, and with due sacrifices, I think it might be. But as it is, we have the wolf by the ears, and we can neither hold him nor safely let him go. Justice is in one scale, and self-preservation in the other.

Of one thing I am certain, that as the passage of slaves from one state to another would not make a slave of a single human being who would not be so without it, so their diffusion over a greater surface would

make them individually happier and [would] proportionally facilitate the accomplishment of their emancipation by dividing the burden on a greater number of coadjutors. An abstinence, too, from this act of power would remove the jealousy excited by the undertaking of Congress to regulate the condition of the different descriptions of men composing a state. This certainly is the exclusive right of every state, which nothing in the Constitution has taken from them and given to the general government. . . .

I regret that I am now to die in the belief that the useless sacrifice of themselves by the generation of 1776, to acquire self-government and happiness [for] their country, is to be thrown away by the unwise and unworthy passions of their sons, and that my only consolation is to be that I live not to weep over it. If they would but dispassionately weigh the blessings they will throw away against an abstract principle more likely to be effected by union than by scission, they would pause before they would perpetrate this act of suicide on themselves, and of treason against the hopes of the world.—Bergh 15:249. (1820.)

MISSOURI, And Westward Expansion.—I rejoice with you that the state of Missouri is at length a member of our Union. Whether the [slavery] question it excited is dead or only sleepeth, I do not know. . . . I still believe that the western extension of our confederacy will insure its duration by overruling local factions which might shake a smaller association.—To General Henry Dearborn. Bergh 15:329. (1821.)

MOBS, Destroy Sound Government.—The mobs of great cities add just so much to the support of pure government as sores do to the strength of the human body.—*Notes on Virginia*. Bergh 2:230. (1782.)

MOBS, False Reports of American.—It is in the London newspapers only that exist those mobs and riots which are fabricated to deter strangers from going to America. Your person will be sacredly safe and free from insult.—Ford 4:66. (1785.)

MONARCHY, Evils of.—If anybody thinks that kings, nobles, or priests are good conservators of the public happiness, send him here [France]. It is the best school in the universe to cure him of that folly. He will see here, with his own eyes, that these descriptions of men are an abandoned confederacy against the happiness of the mass of the people. The omnipotence of their effect cannot be better proved than in this country particularly, where, notwithstanding the finest soil upon the earth, the finest climate under heaven, and a people of the most benevolent, the most gay and amiable character of which the human form is susceptible—where such a people, I say, surrounded by so many blessings from nature, are loaded with misery by kings, nobles, and priests, and by them alone.—To George Wythe. Bergh 5:396. (1786.)

I am astonished at some people's considering a kingly government as a refuge [from the evils of the confederation]. Advise such to read the fable of the frogs who solicited Jupiter for a king. If that does not put them to rights, send them to Europe to see something of the trappings of monarchy, and I will undertake that every man shall go back thoroughly cured. If all the evils which can arise among us from the republican form of government from this day to the day of judgment could be put into a scale against what this country [France] suffers from its monarchical form in a week, or England in a month, the latter would predominate. Consider the... Almanac Royale of France, and say what a people gain by monarchy. No race of kings has ever presented above one man of common sense in twenty generations. The best they can do is to leave things to their ministers, and what are their ministers but a committee, badly chosen? If the king ever meddles, it is to do harm.—Ford 4:426. (1787.)

MONARCHY, Republican Government vs.—With all the defects of our constitution[s], whether [federal] or [state], the comparison of our governments with those of Europe is like a comparison of heaven and hell. England, like the earth, may be allowed to take the intermediate station.—Bergh 6:274. (1787.)

MONARCHY, Jefferson's Opposition to.—I was much an enemy to monarchies before I came to Europe. I am ten thousand times more so since I have seen what they are.—To George Washington. Ford 5:8. (1788.)

MONARCHY, Advocates of, in the United States.—I know there are some among us who would now establish a monarchy. But they are inconsiderable in number and weight of character.—To James Madison. Ford 5:83. (1789.)

It cannot be denied that we have among us a sect who believe that the English constitution contains whatever is perfect in human institutions; that the members of this sect have, many of them, names and offices which stand high in the estimation of our countrymen. I still rely that the great mass of our community is untainted with these heresies, as [is] its head. On this I build my hope that we have not labored in vain, and that our experiment will still prove that men can be governed by reason. —To George Mason. Ford 5:275. (1791.)

The ultimate object of all this increase of public debt, establishment of a paper money system, corruption of Congress, etc., is, it is charged, to prepare the way for a change from the present republican form of government to that of a monarchy, of which the English constitution is to be the model. That this was contemplated in the [Constitutional] Convention is no secret, because its partisans have made none of it. To effect it then was impracticable, but they are still eager after their object, and are predisposing everything for its ultimate attainment. So many of them have got into the [Congress] that, aided by the corrupt squadron of paper dealers who are at their devotion, they make a majority in both houses. The republican party, who wish to preserve the government in its present form, are fewer in number. They are fewer even when joined by the two, three, or half dozen anti-Federalists who, though they dare not avow it, are still opposed to any general government; but, being less so to a republican than a monarchical one, they naturally join those whom they think pursuing the lesser evil.—To President Washington. Ford 6:3. (1792.)

The aspect of our politics has wonderfully changed since you left us. In place of that noble love of liberty and republican government which carried us triumphantly through the war, an Anglican monarchical party has sprung up, whose avowed object is to draw over us the substance, as they have already done the forms, of the British government. The mass of our citizens, however, remain true to their republican principles; the whole landed interest is republican, and so is a great mass of talents. Against us are the executive, the judiciary, two out of three branches of the legislature, all the officers of the government, all who want to be officers, all timid men who prefer the calm of despotism to the boisterous sea of liberty, British merchants and Americans trading on British capitals, [and] speculators and holders in the banks and public funds—a contrivance invented for the purposes of corruption, and for assimilating us in all things to the rotten as well as the sound parts of the British model. It would give you a fever were I to name to you the apostates who have gone over to these heresies, men who were Samsons in the field and Solomons in the council, but who have had their heads shorn by the harlot England. In short, we are likely to preserve the liberty we have obtained only by unremitting labors and perils. But we shall preserve it. —Bergh 9:335. (1796.)

When, on my return from Europe, I joined the [federal] government in March 1790 at New York, I was much astonished, indeed, at the mimicry I found established of royal forms and ceremonies, and more alarmed at the unexpected phenomenon by the monarchical sentiments I heard expressed and openly maintained in every company, and among others by the high members of the government, executive and judiciary (General Washington alone excepted), and by a great part of the legislature, save only some members who had been of the old Congress, and a very few of recent introduction.—To Martin Van Buren. Bergh 16:59. (1824.)

MONARCHY, Jefferson's Fears of, Exceeded Washington's.—[President Washington said] that as to the idea of transforming this government into a monarchy, he did not believe there were ten men in the United States, whose opinions were worth attention, who entertained such a thought. I told him there were many more than he imagined. . . . I told him that though the people were sound, there were a numerous sect who had monarchy in contemplation; that the Secretary of the Treasury [Alexander Hamilton] was

one of these; that I had heard him say that this Constitution was a shilly-shally thing of mere milk and water, which could not last, and was only good as a step to something better.—The Anas. Bergh 1:317. (1792.)

MONARCHY, Theory and Effects of European.—The doctrines of Europe were that men in numerous associations cannot be restrained within the limits of order and justice but by forces physical and moral, wielded over them by authorities independent of their will. Hence their organization of kings, hereditary nobles, and priests. Still further to constrain the brute force of the people, they deem it necessary to keep them down by hard labor, poverty, and ignorance, and to take from them, as from bees, so much of their earnings as that unremitting labor shall be necessary to obtain a sufficient surplus barely to sustain a scanty and miserable life. And these earnings they apply to maintain their privileged orders in splendor and idleness, to fascinate the eyes of the people and excite in them a humble adoration and submission, as to an order of superior beings.—Bergh 15:440. (1823.)

MONARCHY. See also KINGS; TYRANNY.

MONEY, Coinage Recommended by Jefferson.—If we adopt the dollar for our unit, we should strike four coins, one of gold, two of silver, and one of copper, [namely]: 1. a golden piece, equal in value to ten dollars; 2. the unit or dollar itself, of silver; 3. the tenth of a dollar, of silver also; 4. the hundredth of a dollar, of copper.*—Notes on the Establishment of a Money Unit. Bergh 1:241. (1784.)

*Jefferson later added the five-dollar gold coin to his proposal. —Editor.

Perhaps it would not be amiss to coin three more pieces of silver: one of the value of five-tenths, or half a dollar; one of the value of two-tenths, which would be equal to the Spanish pistareen; and one of the value of five coppers, which would be equal to the Spanish half bit. We should then have five silver coins, [namely]:

1. The unit or dollar;
2. The half dollar or five-tenths;
3. The double-tenth, equal to .2, or one-fifth of a dollar, or to the pistareen;
4. The tenth, equal to a Spanish bit;
5. The five-copper piece, equal to .5, or one-twentieth of a dollar, or the half bit.—Notes on the Establishment of a Money Unit. Bergh 1:244. (1784.)

MONEY, History of American Currency Under the Confederation. —Previous to the Revolution, most of the states were in the habit, whenever they had occasion for more money than could be raised immediately by taxes, to issue paper notes or bills in the name of the state, wherein they promised to pay to the bearer the sum named in the note or bill. In some of the states no time of payment was fixed, nor tax laid to enable payment. In these the bill depreciated. But others of the states named in the bill the day when it should be paid, laid taxes to bring

in money enough for that purpose, and paid the bills punctually, on or before the day named. In these states, paper money was in as high estimation as gold and silver.

On the commencement of the late Revolution, Congress had no money. The external commerce of the states being suppressed, the farmer could not sell his produce, and of course could not pay a tax. Congress had no resource then but in paper money. Not being able to lay a tax for its redemption, they could only promise that taxes should be laid for that purpose so as to redeem the bills by a certain day. They did not foresee the long continuance of the war, the almost total suppression of their exports, and other events which rendered the performance of their engagement impossible. The paper money continued for a twelvemonth equal to gold and silver. But the quantities which they were obliged to emit for the purpose of the war exceeded what had been the usual quantity of the circulating medium. It began, therefore, to become cheaper, or, as we expressed it, it depreciated, as gold and silver would have done had they been thrown into circulation in equal quantities. But not having, like them, an intrinsic value, its depreciation was more rapid and greater than could ever have happened with them. In two years it had fallen to two dollars of paper money for one of silver; in three years, to four for one; in nine months more it fell to ten for one; and in the six months following, that is to say, by September 1779, it had fallen to twenty for one.

Congress, alarmed at the consequences which were to be apprehended should they lose this resource altogether, thought it necessary to make a vigorous effort to stop its further depreciation. They therefore determined, in the first place, that their emissions should not exceed two hundred millions of dollars, to which term they were then nearly arrived; and though they knew that twenty dollars of what they were then issuing would buy no more for their army than one silver dollar would buy, yet they thought it would be worthwhile to submit to the sacrifice of nineteen out of twenty dollars if they could thereby stop further depreciation. They therefore published an address to their constituents, in which they renewed their original declarations that this paper money should be redeemed at dollar for dollar. They proved the ability of the states to do this, and that their liberty would be cheaply bought at that price. The declaration was ineffectual. No man received the money at a better rate; on the contrary, in six months more, that is, by March 1780, it had fallen to forty for one.

Congress then tried an experiment of a different kind. Considering their former offers to redeem this money at par as relinquished by the general refusal to take it but in progressive depreciation, they required the whole to be brought in, declared it should be redeemed at its present value of forty for one, and that they would give to the holders new bills, reduced in their denomination to the sum of gold or silver,

which was actually to be paid for them. This would reduce the nominal sum of the mass in circulation to the present worth of that mass, which was five millions; a sum not too great for the circulation of the states, and which, they therefore hoped, would not depreciate further as they continued firm in their purpose of emitting no more.

This effort was as unavailing as the former. Very little of the money was brought in. It continued to circulate and to depreciate till the end of 1780, when it had fallen to seventy-five for one, and the money circulated from the French army being, by that time, sensible in all the states north of the Potomac, the paper ceased its circulation altogether in those states. In Virginia and North Carolina it continued a year longer, within which time it fell to one thousand for one, and then expired, as it had done in the other states, without a single groan. Not a murmur was heard on this occasion among the people. On the contrary, universal congratulations took place on seeing this gigantic mass, whose dissolution had threatened convulsions which should shake their infant confederacy to its center, quietly interred in its grave.—Bergh 17:54. (1786.)

MONEY, Inflation a Hidden Tax.— It will be asked, how will the two masses of Continental and state money have cost the people of the United States seventy-two millions of dollars, when they are to be redeemed now with about six millions? I answer that the difference, being sixty-six millions, has been lost on the paper bills, separately, by the successive holders of them. Everyone through whose hands a bill passed lost on that bill what it lost in value during the time it was in his hands. This was a real tax on him; and, in this way, the people of the United States actually contributed those sixty-six millions of dollars during the war, and by a mode of taxation the most oppressive of all, because the most unequal of all.—Ford 4:165. (1786.)

MONEY, Should Be Issued by Government, Not Banks.—It is not easy to estimate the obstacles which, in the beginning, we should encounter in ousting the banks from their possession of the circulation; but a steady and judicious alternation of emissions and loans would reduce them in time. But while this is going on, another measure should be pressed to recover ultimately our right to the circulation. The states should be applied to, to transfer the right of issuing circulating paper to Congress exclusively, *in perpetuum* if possible, but during the war at least, with a saving of charter rights. ... Congress would, of course, begin by obliging unchartered banks to wind up their affairs within a short time, and the others as their charters expired, forbidding the subsequent circulation of their paper. This they would supply with their own, bottomed, every emission, on an adequate tax, and bearing or not bearing interest, as the state of the public pulse should indicate. Even in the non-complying states, these bills would make their way, and supplant the unfunded paper of their banks

by their solidity, by the universality of their currency, and by their receivability for customs and taxes. It would be in their power, too, to curtail those banks to the amount of their actual specie by gathering up their paper and running it constantly on them. The national paper might thus take place even in the non-complying states. In this way, I am not without a hope that this great, this sole resource for loans in an agricultural country might yet be recovered for the use of the nation during war; and, if obtained *in perpetuum,* it would always be sufficient to carry us through any war, provided that in the interval between war and war all the outstanding paper should be called in, coin be permitted to flow in again, and to hold the field of circulation until another war should require its yielding place again to the national medium.—To John W. Eppes. Bergh 13:275. (1813.)

The circulating fund is the only one we can ever command with certainty. It is sufficient for all our wants; and the impossibility of even defending the country without its aid as a borrowing fund renders it indispensable that the nation should take and keep it in their own hands, as their exclusive resource.—Ford 9:491. (1814.)

From the establishment of the United States Bank to this day, I have preached against this system, and have been sensible no cure could be hoped but in the catastrophe now happening. The remedy was to let banks drop [gradually] at the expiration of their charters, and for the state governments to relinquish the power of establishing others. This would not, as it should not, have given the power of establishing them to Congress. But Congress could then have issued treasury notes payable within a fixed period, and founded on a specific tax, the proceeds of which, as they came in, should be exchangeable for the notes of that particular emission only. —Bergh 14:188. (1814.)

Although a century of British experience has proved to what a wonderful extent the funding on specific redeeming taxes enables a nation to anticipate in war the resources of peace, and although the other nations of Europe have tried and trodden every path of force or folly in fruitless quest of the same object, yet *we* still expect to find in juggling tricks and banking dreams that money can be made out of nothing, and in sufficient quantities to meet the expenses of a heavy war by sea and land. It is said, indeed, that money cannot be borrowed from our merchants as from those of England. But it can be borrowed from our people. They will give you all the necessaries of war they produce, if, instead of the bankrupt trash they are now obliged to receive for want of any other, you will give them a paper promise funded on a specific pledge, and of a size for common circulation. But you say the merchants will not take this paper. What the people take the merchants must take, or sell nothing. All these doubts and fears prove only the extent of the dominion which the banking institutions have obtained

over the minds of our citizens, and especially of those inhabiting cities or other banking places; and this dominion must be broken or it will break us. But ... we must make up our minds to suffer yet longer before we can get right. The misfortune is that in the meantime we shall plunge ourselves in unextinguishable debt, and entail on our posterity an inheritance of eternal taxes, which will bring our government and people into the condition of those of England, a nation of pikes and gudgeons, the latter bred merely as food for the former.—Ford 9:497. (1815.)

MONEY, Importance of Gold and Silver.—One of the great advantages of specie as a medium is that, being of universal value, it will keep itself at a general level.... This is agreed to by [Adam] Smith, ... the principal advocate for a paper circulation, but advocating it on the sole condition that it be strictly regulated. He admits, nevertheless, that "the commerce and industry of a country cannot be so secure when suspended on the Daedalian wings of paper money as [when] on the solid ground of gold and silver." —To John W. Eppes. Bergh 13:412. (1813.)

MONEY, Supply Should Match Productivity.—It would be best that our medium should be so proportioned to our produce as to be on a par with that of the countries with which we trade, and whose medium is in a sound state.—To John W. Eppes. Bergh 13:430. (1813.)

MONEY, Precious Metals the Best Form of.—Specie is the most perfect medium, because it will preserve its own level; because, having intrinsic and universal value, it can never die in our hands; and it is the surest resource of reliance in time of war. ... The trifling economy of paper as a cheaper medium, or its convenience for transmission, weighs nothing in opposition to the advantages of the precious metals.... [Paper money] is liable to be abused, has been, is, and forever will be abused, in every country in which it is permitted.—To John W. Eppes. Bergh 13:430. (1813.)

MONEY, Inflation Produced by Excess Paper Money.—We have no metallic measure of values at present, while we are overwhelmed with bank paper. The depreciation of this swells nominal prices without furnishing any stable index of real value.—Bergh 14:264. (1815.)

MONEY, Need to Provide Sound.— Treasury notes of small as well as high denomination, bottomed on a tax which would redeem them in ten years, would place at our disposal the whole circulating medium of the United States; a fund of credit sufficient to carry us through any probable length of war. A small issue of such paper is now commencing. It will immediately supersede the bank paper, nobody receiving that now but for the purposes of the day, and never in payments which are to lie by for any time. In fact, all the banks having declared they will not give cash in exchange for their own notes, these circulate merely because there is no other medium of exchange. As soon as the treasury notes get into circulation, the others

will cease to hold any competition with them. I trust that another year will confirm this experiment and restore this fund to the public, who ought never more to permit its being filched from them by private speculators and disorganizers of the circulation.—Ford 9:503. (1815.)

[One] great measure necessary to ensure us permanent prosperity should ensure resources of money by the suppression of all paper circulation during peace, and licensing that of the nation alone during war. The metallic medium of which we should be possessed at the commencement of a war would be a sufficient fund for all the loans we should need through its continuance; and if the national bills issued be bottomed (as is indispensable) on pledges of specific taxes for their redemption within certain and moderate epochs, and be of proper denominations for circulation, no interest on them would be necessary or just because they would answer to everyone the purposes of the metallic money withdrawn and replaced by them.—Ford 10:36. (1816.)

MONEY. See also BANKS; FRACTIONAL BANKING; INFLATION; PAPER MONEY; WEALTH.

MONOPOLY, Bill of Rights Should Protect Against.—By a declaration of rights, I mean one which shall stipulate ... freedom of commerce against monopolies.—Bergh 6:425. (1788.)

A bill of rights ... should go to ... monopolies.... It is better ... to abolish ... monopolies in all cases than not to do it in any.—To James Madison. Bergh 7:96. (1788.)

MONOPOLY, Banking and.—The bill for establishing a national bank undertakes . . . to form the subscribers into a corporation . . . [and] to give them the sole and exclusive right of banking under the national authority; and so far is against the laws of monopoly.—Bergh 3:145. (1791.)

These foreign and false citizens . . . are advancing fast to a monopoly of our banks and public funds, thereby placing our finances under their control.—To Elbridge Gerry. Ford 7:121. (1797.)

MONOPOLY. See also BANK OF THE UNITED STATES; BANKS.

MONROE (James), Purity of.—He is a man whose soul might be turned wrong side outwards without discovering a blemish to the world. —Bergh 5:313. (1786.)

MONROE (James), Jefferson's Friendship for.—I have ever viewed Mr. [James] Madison and yourself as two principal pillars of my happiness. Were either to be withdrawn, I should consider it as among the greatest calamities which could assail my future peace of mind.—To James Monroe. Bergh 11:445. (1808.)

MONROE (James), Ability of.—I clearly think . . . the competence of Monroe to embrace great views of action. The decision of his character, his enterprise, firmness, industry, and unceasing vigilance would, I believe, secure, as I am sure they would merit, the public confidence, and give us all the success which our means can accomplish.—Ford 9:368. (1812.)

MONROE DOCTRINE, Exclusion of European Influence in America.—We consider [Cuba's and Mexico's] interests and ours as the same, and that the object of both must be to exclude all European influence from this hemisphere.—Bergh 12:187. (1808.)

MONROE DOCTRINE, Europe and America Separate Systems.—The European nations constitute a separate division of the globe; their localities make them part of a distinct system; they have a set of interests of their own in which it is our business never to engage ourselves. America has a hemisphere to itself. It must have its separate system of interests, which must not be subordinated to those of Europe. The insulated state in which nature has placed the American continent should so far avail it that no spark of war kindled in the other quarters of the globe should be wafted across the wide oceans which separate us from them.—Bergh 14:22. (1813.)

MONROE DOCTRINE, Need for an American Coalition.—I hope . . . [to see] all the American nations . . . coalescing in an American system of policy, totally independent of and unconnected with that of Europe. The day is not distant when we may formally require a meridian of partition through the ocean which separates the two hemispheres, on the hither side of which no European gun shall ever be heard, nor an American on the other.—Bergh 15:262. (1820.)

Nothing is so important as that America shall separate herself from the systems of Europe and establish one of her own. Our circumstances, our pursuits, our interests are distinct; the principles of our policy should be so also. All entanglements with that quarter of the globe should be avoided if we mean that peace and justice shall be the polar stars of the American societies.... [This] would be a leading principle with me had I longer to live.—Bergh 15:285. (1820.)

MONROE DOCTRINE, Jefferson's Recommendations on Formation of.—The question presented by the letters you have sent me is the most momentous which has been offered to my contemplation since that of independence. That made us a nation; this sets our compass and points the course which we are to steer through the ocean of time opening on us. And never could we embark on it under circumstances more auspicious.

Our first and fundamental maxim should be never to entangle ourselves in the broils of Europe. Our second, never to suffer Europe to intermeddle with cis-Atlantic affairs. America, North and South, has a set of interests distinct from those of Europe, and peculiarly her own. She should therefore have a system of her own, separate and apart from that of Europe. While the last is laboring to become the domicile of despotism, our endeavor should surely be to make our hemisphere that of freedom....

I could honestly, therefore, join in the declaration proposed, that we aim not at the acquisition of any of [the Spanish] possessions, [and] that we will not stand in the way of any amicable arrangement between them and the mother country; but that we will oppose, with all our means, the forcible interposition of any other power, as auxiliary, stipendiary, or under any other form or pretext, and most especially their transfer to any power by conquest, cession, or acquisition in any other way. I should think it therefore advisable that, ... as it may lead to war, the declaration of which requires an act of Congress, the case shall be laid before them for consideration at their first meeting.—To President James Monroe. Bergh 15:477. (1823.)

MONROE DOCTRINE. See also FOREIGN AFFAIRS; TREATIES.

MONTESQUIEU (Baron Charles de), Writings of.—The history of [Montesquieu's *Spirit of Laws*] is well known. He had been a great reader and had commonplaced everything he read. At length he wished to undertake some work into which he could bring his whole commonplace book in a digested form. He fixed on the subject of his *Spirit of Laws,* and wrote the book. He consulted his friend Helvetius about publishing it, who strongly dissuaded it. He published it, however, and the world did not confirm Helvetius's opinion.—Bergh 12:407. (1810.)

I had, with the world, deemed Montesquieu's work of much merit; but saw in it, with every thinking man, so much of paradox, of false principle and misapplied fact, as to render its value equivocal on the whole.—Ford 9:305. (1811.)

MONTICELLO, Jefferson's Fondness for.—It is worth a voyage across the Atlantic to see ... our own dear

Monticello. Where has nature spread so rich a mantle under the eye? Mountains, forests, rocks, rivers. With what majesty do we there ride above the storms! How sublime to look down into the workhouse of nature, to see her clouds, hail, snow, rain, thunder, all fabricated at our feet! And the glorious sun, when rising as if out of a distant water, just gilding the tops of the mountains and giving life to all nature!—To Maria Cosway. Bergh 5:436. (1786.)

I am as happy nowhere else, and in no other society, and all my wishes end where I hope my days will end, at Monticello. Too many scenes of happiness mingle themselves with all the recollections of my native woods and fields to suffer them to be supplanted in my affection by any other.—Bergh 6:265. (1787.)

MONTICELLO. See also HOME.

MORAL LAW, Evidence of a.— Man has been subjected by his Creator [to the moral law], ... of which his feelings, or conscience as it is sometimes called, are the evidence with which his Creator has furnished him.—Bergh 3:228. (1793.)

MORAL LAW, Duties a Divine Responsibility.—The moral duties which exist between individual and individual in a state of nature accompany them into a state of society, and the aggregate of the duties of all the individuals composing the society constitutes the duties of that society towards any other; so that between society and society the same moral duties exist as did between the individuals composing them while in an un-associated state, ... their Maker not

Jefferson in January 1805 (age 61). Portrait by Rembrandt Peale.

having released them from those duties on their forming themselves into a nation.—Bergh 3:228. (1793.)

MORAL SENSE, Implanted in Man by the Creator.—I think it lost time to attend lectures on moral philosophy. He who made us would have been a pitiful bungler if He had made the rules of our moral conduct a matter of science [i.e., knowledge acquired by systematic study]. For one man of science there are thousands who are not. What would have become of them? Man was destined for society. His morality, therefore, was to be formed to this object. He was endowed with a sense of right and wrong, merely relative to this. This sense is as much a part of his nature as the sense of hearing, seeing, feeling; it is the true foundation of morality.... The moral sense, or conscience, is as much a part of man as his leg or arm. It is given to all human beings in a stronger or weaker degree, as force of members is given them in a greater or less degree. It may be strengthened by exercise, as may any particular limb of the body. This sense is submitted, indeed, in some degree, to the guidance of reason, but it is a small stock which is required for this, even a less one than what we call common sense. State a moral case to a plowman and a professor. The former will decide it as well and often better than the latter, because he has not been led astray by artificial rules. In this branch, therefore, read good books, because they will encourage as well as direct your feelings.—To Peter Carr. Bergh 6:257. (1787.)

Nature hath implanted in our breasts a love of others, a sense of duty to them, a moral instinct, in short, which prompts us irresistibly to feel and to succor their distresses.... The Creator would indeed have been a bungling artist had He intended man for a social animal without planting in him social dispositions.... I sincerely, then, believe ... in the general existence of a moral instinct. I think it the brightest gem with which the human character is studded, and the want of it as more degrading than the most hideous of the bodily deformities.—Bergh 14:141. (1814.)

I believe ... that the moral sense is as much a part of our constitution as that of feeling, seeing, or hearing; as a wise Creator must have seen to be necessary in an animal destined to

live in society.—To John Adams. Bergh 15:76. (1816.)

MORAL SENSE, Seldom Lacking. —It is true [that social dispositions] are not planted in every man, because there is no rule without exceptions; but it is false reasoning which converts exceptions into the general rule. Some men are born without the organs of sight, or of hearing, or without hands. Yet it would be wrong to say that man is born without these faculties, and sight, hearing, and hands may with truth enter into the general definition of man. The want or imperfection of the moral sense in some men, like the want or imperfection of the senses of sight and hearing in others, is no proof that it is a general characteristic of the species.—Bergh 14:142. (1814.)

MORAL SENSE, Can Be Cultivated.—When [the moral sense] is wanting, we endeavor to supply the defect by education; by appeals to reason and calculation; by presenting to the being so unhappily conformed other motives to do good and to eschew evil, such as the love or the hatred or rejection of those among whom he lives, and whose society is necessary to his happiness and even existence; demonstrations by sound calculation that honesty promotes [his own] interest in the long run; the rewards and penalties established by the laws; and ultimately the prospects of a future state of retribution for the evil as well as the good done while here. These are the correctives which are supplied by education, and which exercise the functions of the moralist, the preacher, and [the] legislator; and they lead into a course of correct action all those whose [depravity] is not too profound to be eradicated. —Bergh 14:142. (1814.)

MORAL SENSE. See also CONSCIENCE.

MORALITY, An Exhortation to Practice.—When your mind shall be well improved with science, nothing will be necessary to place you in the highest points of view but to pursue the interests of your country, the interests of your friends, and your own interests also, with the purest integrity, the most chaste honor. The defect of these virtues can never be made up by all the other acquirements of body and mind. Make these, then, your first object. Give up money, give up fame, give up science, give the earth itself and all it contains rather than do an immoral act. And never suppose that in any possible situation, or under any circumstances, it is best for you to do a dishonorable thing, however slightly so it may appear to you. Whenever you are to do a thing, though it can never be known but to yourself, ask yourself how you would act were all the world looking at you, and act accordingly. Encourage all your virtuous dispositions, and exercise them whenever an opportunity arises, being assured that they will gain strength by exercise, as a limb of the body does, and that exercise will make them habitual. From the practice of the purest virtue, you may be assured you will derive the most sublime comforts in every moment of life, and in the moment of death.—To Peter Carr. Bergh 5:82. (1785.)

MORALITY, Universal Aspect of All Religion.—Reading, reflection, and time have convinced me that the interests of society require the observation of those moral precepts only in which all religions agree (for all forbid us to murder, steal, plunder, or bear false witness), and that we should not intermeddle with the particular dogmas in which all religions differ, and which are totally unconnected with morality. In all of them we see good men, and as many in one as another. The varieties in the structure and action of the human mind, as in those of the body, are the work of our Creator, against which it cannot be a religious duty to erect the standard of uniformity. The practice of morality being necessary for the well-being of society, He has taken care to impress its precepts so indelibly on our hearts that they shall not be effaced by the subtleties of our brain. We all agree in the obligation of the moral precepts of Jesus, and nowhere will they be found delivered in greater purity than in his discourses. It is, then, a matter of principle with me to avoid disturbing the tranquility of others by the expression of any opinion on the innocent questions on which we schismatize.—Bergh 12:315. (1809.)

MORALITY, And Christianity.—There never was a more pure and sublime system of morality delivered to man than is to be found in the four Evangelists.—Bergh 14:81. (1814.)

MORALITY, Foundations of.—It is really curious that, on a question so fundamental, such a variety of opinions should have prevailed among men, and those, too, of the most exemplary virtue and first order of understanding. It shows how necessary was the care of the Creator in making the moral principle so much a part of our constitution as that no errors of reasoning or of speculation might lead us astray from its observance in practice. Of all the theories on this question, the most whimsical seems to have been that of Wollaston, who considers *truth* as the foundation of morality. The thief who steals your guinea does wrong only inasmuch as he acts a lie in using your guinea as if it were his own. Truth is certainly a branch of morality, and a very important one to society; but presented as its foundation, it is as if a tree taken up by the roots had its stem reversed in the air, and one of its branches planted in the ground.—Bergh 14:139. (1814.)

MORALITY. See also ETHICS; HONESTY; SELFISHNESS; VIRTUE.

MURDER, Indians and.—When a murder has been committed on one of our stragglers, the murderer should be demanded. If not delivered, give time, and still press the demand. We find it difficult, with our regular government, to take and punish a murderer of an Indian. Indeed, I believe we have never been able to do it in a single instance. They [the Indian tribes] have their difficulties also, and require time. In fact, it is a case where indulgence of both

sides is just and necessary to prevent the two nations from being perpetually committed in war by the acts of the most vagabond and ungovernable of their members. When the refusal to deliver the murderer is permanent, and proceeds from the want of will and not of ability, we should then interdict all trade and intercourse with them till they give us complete satisfaction.—Bergh 142. (1808.)

MURDER, Degrees of.—In 1796, [the Virginia] legislature...passed the law for amending the penal laws of the commonwealth.... Instead of the settled distinctions of murder and manslaughter, preserved in my bill, they introduced the new terms of murder in the first and second degree. Whether these have produced more or fewer questions of definition, I am not sufficiently informed of our judiciary transactions to say.—Autobiography. Bergh 1:70. (1821.)

MURDER. See also CAPITAL PUNISHMENT; MANSLAUGHTER.

MUSIC, Jefferson's "Favorite Passion."—If there is a gratification which I envy any people in this world, it is to your country [France] its music. This is the favorite passion of my soul, and fortune has cast my lot in a country where it is in a state of deplorable barbarism.—Bergh 4:40. (1778.)

MUSIC, Negroes and.—In music [the blacks] are more generally gifted than the whites with accurate ears for tune and time, and they have been found capable of imagining a small catch. Whether they will be equal to the composition of a more extensive run of melody, or of complicated harmony, is yet to be proved.—*Notes on Virginia*. Bergh 2:195. (1782.)

MUSIC, Requires Natural Ability. —Music is invaluable where a person has an ear. Where [he has] not, it should not be attempted.—Ford 10:105. (1818.)

MYSTERIES, Better Left Alone.— When I meet with a proposition beyond finite comprehension, I abandon it as I do a weight which human strength cannot lift, and I think ignorance in these cases is truly the softest pillow on which I can lay my head.—To John Adams. Bergh 15:241. (1820.)

N

NATIONAL DEFENSE. See ARMY; DEFENSE; MILITIA; PEACE; WAR.

NATIONS, Integrity and Self-Interest of.—I think, with others, that nations are to be governed according to their own interest; but I am convinced that it is their interest in the long run to be grateful, faithful to their engagements, even in the worst of circumstances, and honorable and generous always.— To Marquis de Lafayette. Ford 5:152. (1790.)

NATIONS, Morality and.—A nation, as a society, forms a moral person, and every member of it is personally responsible for his society.—Ford 6:59. (1792.)

NATIONS, Sovereignty of.—It is true that nations are to be judges for themselves, since no one nation has a right to sit in judgment over another.—Ford 6:221. (1793.)

The presumption of dictating to an independent nation the form of its government is so arrogant, so atrocious, that indignation as well as moral sentiment enlists all our partialities and prayers in favor of [a nation so violated], and our equal execrations against the [aggressor].—Ford 10:257. (1823.)

NATIONS, History and.—Wars and contentions, indeed, fill the pages of history.... But more blessed is that nation whose silent course of happiness furnishes nothing for history to say. This is what I ambition for my own country.—Bergh 11:181. (1807.)

NATIONS, Good Faith of.—A character of good faith is of as much value to a nation as to an individual.—Ford 1:332. (1808.)

NATIONS, Cannot Be Free in Ignorance.—If a nation expects to be ignorant and free, in a state of civilization, it expects what never was and never will be.—Bergh 14:384. (1816.)

NATURAL LAW. See LAWS OF NATURE; MORAL LAW.

NATURAL RIGHTS, Authority over.—Our rulers can have no authority over [our] natural rights, only as we have submitted to them. —*Notes on Virginia*. Bergh 2:221. (1782.)

NATURAL RIGHTS, Self-Government and.—Every man, and every body of men on earth, possesses the right of self-government. They receive it with their being from the hand of nature. Individuals exercise it by their single will, collections of men by that of their majority; for the law of the *majority* is the natural law of every society of men. When a certain description of men are to transact together a particular business, the times and places of their meeting and separating depend on their own will; they make a part of the natural right of self-government. This, like all other natural rights, may be abridged or modified in its exercise by their own consent, or by the law of those who depute them if they meet in the right of others; but as far as it is not abridged or modified they retain it as a natural right, and may exercise them in what form they please, either exclusively by themselves, or in association with others, or by others altogether, as they shall agree.—Ford 5:205. (1790.)

NATURAL RIGHTS, Abridgment of.—All natural rights may be abridged or modified in their exercise by law.—Ford 5:206. (1790.)

Laws...abridging the natural right of the citizen should be restrained by rigorous constructions within their narrowest limits.—Bergh 13:327. (1813.)

NATURAL RIGHTS, Must Not Violate Another's Equal Rights.— No man has a natural right to commit aggression on the equal rights of another; and this is all from which the laws ought to restrain him.—Bergh 15:24. (1816.)

NATURAL RIGHTS, Retention of, in Society.—The idea is quite unfounded that on entering into society we give up any natural right. —Bergh 15:24. (1816.)

NATURAL RIGHTS, Choice of Vocation.—Everyone has a natural

right to choose that [vocation in life] which he thinks most likely to give him comfortable subsistence. —Bergh 17:456. (1826.)

NATURAL RIGHTS. See also EQUAL RIGHTS; RIGHTS; RIGHTS OF MAN.

NATURALIZATION, Laws of.—I cannot omit recommending a revisal of the laws on the subject of naturalization. Considering the ordinary chances of human life, a denial of citizenship under a residence of fourteen years is a denial to a great proportion of those who ask it, and controls a policy pursued from their first settlement by many of these states, and still believed of consequence to their prosperity. And shall we refuse the unhappy fugitives from distress that hospitality which the savages of the wilderness extended to our fathers arriving in this land? Shall oppressed humanity find no asylum on this globe?—First Annual Message to Congress. Bergh 3:338. (1801.)

NATURALIZATION. See also IMMIGRANTS; IMMIGRATION.

NAVIGATION, Rights of, on a Nation's Rivers.—What sentiment is written in deeper characters on the heart of man than that the ocean is free to all men, and their rivers to all their inhabitants? Is there a man, savage or civilized, unbiased by habit, who does not feel and attest this truth? Accordingly, in all tracts of country united under the same political society, we find this natural right universally acknowledged and protected by laying the navigable rivers open to all their inhabitants. —Ford 5:468. (1792.)

NAVIGATION. See also OCEAN.

NAVY, Necessity of an American. —A land army would be useless for offense, and not the best nor safest instrument of defense. For either of these purposes, the sea is the field on which we should meet a European enemy. On that element it is necessary we should possess some power.—*Notes on Virginia*. Bergh 2:241. (1782.)

We ought to begin a naval power if we mean to carry on our own commerce.—To James Monroe. Ford 4:10. (1784.)

NEGROES, Bravery of.—They are at least as brave [as white men], and more adventuresome. But this may perhaps proceed from a want of forethought, which prevents their seeing a danger till it be present. When present, they do not go through it with more coolness or steadiness than the whites.—*Notes on Virginia*. Bergh 2:193. (1782.)

NEGROES, And Music.—In music, they are more generally gifted than the whites with accurate ears for tune and time, and they have been found capable of imagining a small catch. Whether they will be equal to the composition of a more extensive run of melody, or of complicated harmony, is yet to be proved.—*Notes on Virginia*. Bergh 2:195. (1782.)

NEGROES, Integrity of.—That disposition to theft with which they have been branded must be ascribed to their situation, and not to any depravity of the moral sense. The man in whose favor no laws of property exist probably feels himself less bound to respect those made in favor of others.... Notwithstand-

ing these considerations, which must weaken their respect for the laws of property, we find among them numerous instances of the most rigid integrity, and as many as among their better instructed masters of benevolence, gratitude, and unshaken fidelity.—*Notes on Virginia*. Bergh 2:199. (1782.)

NEGROES, Equal in Talents.— Nobody wishes more than I do to see such proofs as you exhibit, that nature has given to our black brethren talents equal to those of the other colors of men, and that the appearance of a want of them is owing merely to the degraded condition of their existence, both in Africa and America.—To Benjamin Banneker. Bergh 8:241. (1791.)

Be assured that no person living wishes more sincerely than I do to see a complete refutation of the doubts I have myself entertained and expressed on the grade of understanding allotted to the Negroes by nature, and to find that in this respect they are on a par with ourselves.... On this subject, they are gaining daily in the opinions of nations, and hopeful advances are making towards their reestablishment on an equal footing with the other colors of the human family. I pray you, therefore, to accept my thanks for the many instances you have enabled me to observe of respectable intelligence in that race of men, which cannot fail to have effect in hastening the day of their relief.—Ford 9:246. (1809.)

NEGROES, Elevation of.—Nobody wishes more ardently [than I do] to see a good system commenced for raising the condition both of their body and mind to what it ought to be, as fast as the imbecility of their present existence, and other circumstances which cannot be neglected, will admit.—To Benjamin Banneker. Bergh 8:242. (1791.)

NEGROES. See also SLAVERY.

NEUTRALITY, Guiding Principle in Foreign Affairs.—We should take no part in European quarrels, but cultivate peace and commerce with all.—To George Washington. Bergh 7:224. (1788.)

We wish not to meddle with the internal affairs of any country, nor with the general affairs of Europe. Peace with all nations, and the right which that gives us with respect to all nations, are our object.—Bergh 9:56. (1793.)

NEUTRALITY, A Lever for Opening New Markets.—If the new government wears the front which I hope it will, I see no impossibility in the availing ourselves of the wars of others to open the other parts of America [i.e., the West Indies] to our commerce, as the price of our neutrality.—Ford 5:57. (1788.)

NEUTRALITY, And Violations of Sovereignty.—It is the *right* of every nation to prohibit acts of sovereignty from being exercised by any other within its limits; and the *duty* of a neutral nation to prohibit such as would injure one of the warring powers.—Ford 6:283. (1793.)

NEUTRALITY, And Armed Vessels.—[The arming of foreign] vessels within our ports, ... of whatever nation, while within the limits of the protection of the United States, will be pointedly forbidden; the government being firmly determined to enforce a peaceable demeanor among all the parties within those limits, and to deal to all the same impartial measure. —Bergh 9:99. (1793.)

NEUTRALITY, Rights of.—Reason and usage have established that when two nations go to war, those who choose to live in peace retain their natural right to pursue their agriculture, manufactures, and other ordinary vocations; to carry the produce of their industry for exchange to all nations, belligerent or neutral, as usual; to go and come freely, without injury or molestation; and, in short, that the war among others shall be, for them, as if it did not exist.—Ford 6:413. (1793.)

The doctrine that the rights of nations remaining quietly under the exercise of moral and social duties are to give way to the convenience of those who prefer plundering and murdering one another is a monstrous doctrine, and ought to yield to the more rational law that "the wrongs which two nations endeavor to inflict on each other must not infringe on the rights or conveniences of those remaining at peace."—Ford 8:90. (1801.)

NEUTRALITY. See also FOREIGN AFFAIRS; TREATIES.

NEWSPAPERS, Essential to Free Government.—The basis of our governments being the opinion of the people, the very first object should be to keep that right; and were it left to me to decide whether we should have a government without newspapers, or newspapers without a government, I should not hesitate a moment to prefer the latter.—Bergh 6:57. (1787.)

NEWSPAPERS, Power of.—Freneau's paper has saved our Constitution, which was galloping fast into monarchy and has been checked by no means so powerfully as by that paper. It is well and universally known that it has been that paper which has checked the career of the monocrats.—Ford 1:231. (1793.)

NEWSPAPERS, Freedom of.—Considering the great importance to the public liberty of the freedom of the press, and the difficulty of submitting it to very precise rules, the laws have thought it less mischievous to give greater scope to its freedom than to the restraint of it. The President has, therefore, no authority to prevent publications of the nature of those you complain of.—Ford 6:350. (1793.)

NEWSPAPERS, Jefferson Attacked by.—I have been for some time used as the property of the newspapers, a fair mark for every man's dirt. Some, too, have indulged themselves in this exercise who would not have done it had they known me otherwise than through these impure and injurious channels. It is hard treatment, and for a singular kind of offense, that of having obtained by the labors of a life the indulgent opinions of a part of one's fellow citizens. However, these moral evils must be submitted to, like the physical scourges of tempest, fire, etc. —Bergh 10:1. (1798.)

NEWSPAPERS, Attacks Unanswered.—Were I to undertake to answer the calumnies of the newspapers, it would be more than all my own time and that of twenty aides could effect. For while I should be answering one, twenty new ones would be invented.... But this is an injury to which duty requires everyone to submit whom the public think proper to call into its councils. —Bergh 10:58. (1798.)

As to the calumny of atheism, I am so broken to calumnies of every kind...that I entirely disregard it.... It has been so impossible to contradict all their lies that I have determined to contradict none, for while I should be engaged with one they would publish twenty new ones. [My] thirty years of public life have enabled most of those who read newspapers to judge of one for themselves.—To James Monroe. Ford 7:447. (1800.)

NEWSPAPERS, Thrive on Controversy.—A coalition of sentiments is not for the interest of the printers. They...live by the zeal they can kindle and the schisms they can create. It is contest of opinion in politics...which makes us take great interest in them, and bestow our money liberally on those who furnish aliment to our appetite.... The printers can never leave us in a state of perfect rest and union of opinion. They would be no longer useful, and would have to go to the plow.—To Elbridge Gerry. Bergh 10:254. (1801.)

NEWSPAPERS, Filled with Falsehoods.—To your request of my opinion of the manner in which a newspaper should be conducted so as to be most useful, I should answer, "by restraining it to true facts and sound principles only." Yet I fear such a paper would find few subscribers. It is a melancholy truth that a suppression of the press could not more completely deprive the nation of its benefits than is done by its abandoned prostitution to falsehood. Nothing can now be believed which is seen in a newspaper. Truth itself becomes suspicious by being put into that polluted vehicle. The real extent of this state of misinformation is known only to those who are in situations to confront facts within their knowledge with the lies of the day. I really look with commiseration over the great body of my fellow citizens, who, reading newspapers, live and die in the belief that they have known something of what has been passing in the world in their time.... The man who never looks into a newspaper is better informed than he who reads them, inasmuch as he who knows nothing is nearer to truth than he whose mind is filled with falsehoods and errors. He who reads nothing will still learn the great facts, and the details are all false.

Perhaps an editor might begin a reformation in some such way as this: Divide his paper into four chapters, heading the 1st, Truths; 2nd, Probabilities; 3rd, Possibilities; 4th, Lies. The first chapter would be very short, as it would contain little more than authentic papers, and information from such sources as the editor would be willing to risk his own reputation for their truth. The second would contain what, from a mature consideration of all circumstances, his judgment should con-

clude to be probably true. This, however, should rather contain too little than too much. The third and fourth should be professedly for those readers who would rather have lies for their money than the blank paper they would occupy. —Bergh 11:224. (1807.)

NEWSPAPERS, Classics vs.—I read one or two newspapers a week, but with reluctance give even that time from Tacitus and Horace and so much other more agreeable reading. —Bergh 12:436. (1810.)

I read but a single paper, and that hastily. I find Horace and Tacitus so much better writers than the champions of the gazettes that I lay those down to take up these with great reluctance.—To James Monroe. Ford 10:256. (1823.)

NEWSPAPERS, Degeneration of American.—I deplore ... the putrid state into which our newspapers have passed, and the malignity, the vulgarity, and mendacious spirit of those who write for them; and I enclose you a recent sample, the production of a New England judge, as a proof of the abyss of degradation into which we are fallen. These ordures are rapidly depraving the public taste, and lessening its relish for sound food. As vehicles of information, and a curb on our functionaries, they have rendered themselves useless by forfeiting all title to belief.—Bergh 14:46. (1814.)

NEWSPAPERS, Proper Functions of.—This formidable censor of the public functionaries, by arraigning them at the tribunal of public opinion, produces reform peaceably which must otherwise be done by revolution. It is also the best instrument for enlightening the mind of man, and improving him as a rational, moral, and social being.—Bergh 15:489. (1823.)

NEWSPAPERS. See also LIBEL; PRESS; PUBLICITY.

NONIMPORTATION, Principle of.—To yield the principle of the Nonimportation Act would be yielding the only peaceable instrument for coercing all our rights.—Ford 1:322. (1807.)

NONIMPORTATION. See also EMBARGO.

NORTH CAROLINA, Political Conditions in.—North Carolina is, at present, in the most dangerous state. The lawyers [are] all Tories, the people substantially republican but uninformed and deceived by the lawyers, who are elected of necessity because [there are] few other candidates. The medicine for that state must be very mild and secretly administered. But nothing should be spared to give them true information.—Ford 7:440. (1800.)

NOTES ON VIRGINIA, Enduring Principles in.—The experience of nearly forty years additional in the affairs of mankind has not altered a single principle [in the *Notes on Virginia*].—Ford 3:79. (1814.)

NOTES ON VIRGINIA, History of.—Before I had left America, that is to say, in the year 1781, I had received a letter from M. de Marbois, of the French legation in Philadelphia, informing me he had been instructed by his government to obtain such statistical accounts of the different states of our Union as might be useful for their informa-

tion; and addressing to me a number of queries relative to the state of Virginia.

I had always made it a practice, whenever an opportunity occurred of obtaining any information of our country which might be of use to me in any station, public or private, to commit it to writing. These memoranda were on loose papers, bundled up without order, and difficult of recurrence, when I had occasion for a particular one. I thought this a good occasion to embody their substance, which I did in the order of Mr. Marbois' queries, so as to answer his wish, and to arrange them for my own use.

Some friends, to whom they were occasionally communicated, wished for copies; but their volume rendering this too laborious by hand, I proposed to get a few printed for their gratification. I was asked such a price, however, as exceeded the importance of the object. On my arrival at Paris, I found it could be done for a fourth of what I had been asked here. I therefore corrected and enlarged them, and had two hundred copies printed under the title of *Notes on Virginia*. I gave a very few copies to some particular friends in Europe, and sent the rest to my friends in America.

A European copy, by the death of the owner, got into the hands of a bookseller, who engaged its translation, and when [it was] ready for the press [he] communicated his intentions and manuscript to me, suggesting that I should correct it, without asking any other permission for the publication. I never had seen so wretched an attempt at translation. Interverted, abridged, mutilated, and often reversing the sense of the original, I found it a blotch of errors from beginning to end. I corrected some of the most material, and in that form it was printed in French. A London bookseller, on seeing the translation, requested me to permit him to print the English original. I thought it best to do so, to let the world see that it was not really so bad as the French translation had made it appear. And this is the true history of that publication.—Autobiography. Bergh 1:90. (1821.)

O

OCCUPATIONS, Governmental Regulation of.—The greatest evils of populous society have ever appeared to me to spring from the vicious distribution of its members among the occupations called for. I have no doubt that those nations are essentially right which leave this to individual choice, as a better guide to an advantageous distribution than any other which could be devised. But when, by a blind concourse, particular occupations are ruinously overcharged and others left in want of hands, the national authorities can do much towards restoring the equilibrium.—Bergh 10:428. (1803.)

OCCUPATIONS, Choice of, a Natural Right.—Everyone has a natural right to choose that [vocation in life] which he thinks most likely to give him comfortable subsistence.—Bergh 17:456. (1826.)

OCEAN, Freedom of the.—I join you ... in a sense of the necessity of restoring freedom to the ocean. But I doubt, with you, whether the United States ought to join in an armed confederacy for that purpose; or rather, I am satisfied they ought not. It ought to be the very first object of our pursuits to have nothing to do with the European interests and politics. Let them be free or slaves at will, navigators or agriculturists, swallowed into one government or divided into a thousand, we have nothing to fear from them in any form.... To take part in their conflicts would be to divert our energies from creation to destruction. Our commerce is so valuable to them that they will be glad to purchase it when the only price we ask is to do us justice. I believe we have in our own hands the means of peaceable coercion; and that the moment they see our government so united as that they can make use of it, they will, for their own interest, be disposed to do us justice. In this way you shall not be obliged by any treaty of confederation to go to war for injuries done to others.—Ford 8:23. (1801.)

OCEAN, Common Property.—Nature has not subjected the ocean to the jurisdiction of any particular nation, but has made it common to all for the purposes to which it is fitted.—Ford 8:89. (1801.)

The ocean, ... like the air, is the common birthright of mankind.—Bergh 16:302. (1808.)

OCEAN, British Claim to.—The intention which the British now formally avow of taking possession of the ocean as their exclusive domain, and of suffering no commerce on it but through their ports, makes it the interest of all mankind to contribute their efforts to bring such usurpations to an end.—Ford 9:330. (1811.)

OCEAN. See also NAVIGATION.

OFFICES. See HONORS; POLITICAL OFFICES.

OLD AGE, Change and.—I am now of an age which does not easily accommodate itself to new manners and new modes of living.—Bergh 5:128. (1785.)

OLD AGE, Jefferson's.—My health has been always so uniformly firm that I have for some years dreaded nothing so much as...living too long. I think, however, that a flaw has appeared which ensures me against that, without cutting short any of the period during which I could expect to remain capable of being useful. It will probably give me as many years as I wish, and without pain or debility. Should this be the case, my most anxious prayers will have been fulfilled by Heaven. ...My florid health is calculated to keep my friends as well as foes quiet, as they should be.—Ford 8:128. (1801.)

OLD AGE, Awareness of Its Effects. —Being very sensible of bodily decays from advancing years, I ought not to doubt their effect on the mental faculties. To do so would evince either great self-love or little observation of what passes under our eyes; and I shall be fortunate if I am the first to perceive and to obey this admonition of nature.—Bergh 11:220. (1807.)

OLD AGE, Duty in.—Nothing is more incumbent on the old than to know when they should get out of the way and relinquish to younger successors the honors they can no longer earn, and the duties they can no longer perform.—Bergh 14:239. (1815.)

OLD AGE, A Kind Preparation for Death.—A decline of health at the age of seventy-six was naturally to be expected, and is a warning of an event which cannot be distant, and whose approach I contemplate with little concern; for indeed, in no circumstance has nature been kinder to us than in the soft gradations by which she prepares us to part willingly with what we are not destined always to retain. First one faculty is withdrawn and then another; sight, hearing, memory, affections, and friends, filched one by one, till we are left among strangers, the mere monuments of times, facts, and specimens of antiquity for the observation of the curious.—Bergh 15:189 (1819.)

OLD AGE, Greatest Desire in.— Tranquility is the *summum bonum* of old age.—Bergh 15:242. (1820.)

OLD AGE, Deformity in.—Man, like the fruit he eats, has his period of ripeness. Like that, too, if he continues longer hanging to the stem, it is but a useless and unsightly appendage.—Ford 10:191. (1821.)

OLD AGE, And Declining Health. —When all our faculties have left, or are leaving us, one by one, sight, hearing, memory, every avenue of pleasing sensation is closed, and athumy, debility, and malaise left in their places; when friends of our youth are all gone, and a new generation is risen around us whom we know not, is death an evil? . . . I have ever dreaded a doting old age; and my health has been generally so good, and is now so good, that I dread it still.—To John Adams. Bergh 15:371. (1822.)

OLD AGE. See also DEATH.

OPINION, Sacredness of Individual.—I never submitted the whole system of my opinions to the creed of any party of men whatever, in religion, in philosophy, in politics, or in anything else where I was capable of thinking for myself. Such an addiction is the last degradation of a free and moral agent. If I could not go to heaven but with a party, I would not go there at all.—Bergh 7:300. (1789.)

OPINION, Differences of.—In every country where man is free to think and to speak, differences of opinion will arise from difference of perception and the imperfection of reason; but these differences, when permitted as in this happy country to purify themselves by free discussion, are but as passing clouds overspreading our land transiently, and leaving our horizon more bright and serene.—Bergh 10:235. (1801.)

I have never thought that a difference in political, any more than in religious, opinions should disturb the friendly intercourse of society. —Bergh 12:356. (1810.)

OPINION, Sacrifices of.—If we do not learn to sacrifice small differences of opinion, we can never act together. Every man cannot have his way in all things. If his own opinion prevails at some times, he should acquiesce on seeing that of others preponderate at other times. With-

out this mutual disposition we are disjointed individuals, but not a society.—Ford 8:76. (1801.)

To the principles of union I sacrifice all minor differences of opinion. These, like differences of face, are a law of our nature and should be viewed with the same tolerance. —Bergh 13:67. (1811.)

OPINION, Jefferson's Tolerance of Differing.—I tolerate with the utmost latitude the right of others to differ from me in opinion without imputing to them criminality. I know too well the weakness and uncertainty of human reason to wonder at its different results.—To Abigail Adams. Bergh 11:52. (1804.)

OPINION. See also DISPUTES; PUBLIC OPINION.

ORATORY, Art in.—In a republican nation, whose citizens are to be led by reason and persuasion, and not by force, the art of reasoning becomes of first importance. In this line antiquity has left us the finest models for imitation, and he who studies and imitates them most nearly will nearest approach the perfection of the art. Among these I should consider the speeches of Livy, Sallust, and Tacitus as preeminent specimens of logic, taste, and that sententious brevity which, using not a word to spare, leaves not a moment for inattention to the hearer. Amplification is the vice of modern oratory. It is an insult to an assembly of reasonable men, disgusting and revolting instead of persuading. Speeches measured by the hour die with the hour.—Bergh 16:30. (1824.)

ORDER, Preservation of.—Every man being at his ease feels an interest in the preservation of order, and comes forth to preserve it at the first call of the magistrate.—Bergh 10:356. (1803.)

ORDER, Maintenance of, vs. Protection of Life.—The life of the citizen is never to be endangered but as the last melancholy effort for the maintenance of order and obedience to the laws.—Ford 9:238. (1809.)

ORDER, Liberty and.—Possessing ourselves the combined blessing of liberty and order, we wish the same to other countries.—Bergh 15:481. (1823.)

P

PAGE (John), Tribute to.—I have known Mr. Page from the time we were boys and classmates together, and love him as a brother, but I have always known him the worst judge of men existing. He has fallen a sacrifice to the ease with which he gives his confidence to those who deserve it not.... I am very anxious to do something useful for him; and so universally is he esteemed in [Virginia] that no man's promotion would be more generally approved. He has not an enemy in the world.—Ford 8:85. (1801.)

PAINE (Thomas), Welcomed Back to America.—I am in hopes you will [on your return from France] find us returned generally to sentiments worthy of former times. In these it will be your glory to have steadily labored, and with as much effect as any man living.—To Thomas Paine. Ford 8:19. (1801.)

PAINE (Thomas), Effect of His 1776 Pamphlet.—Paine's *Common Sense* [electrified] us.—Autobiography. Bergh 1:136. (1821.)

PAINE (Thomas), His Writing Style.—No writer has exceeded Paine in ease and familiarity of style, in perspicuity of expression, happiness of elucidation, and in simple and unassuming language. In this he may be compared with Dr. Franklin; and indeed his *Common Sense* was, for a while, believed to have been written by Dr. Franklin and published under the borrowed name of Paine, who had come over with him from England.—Bergh 15:305. (1821.)

PAPER MONEY, Causes Bankruptcy in New York and Elsewhere.—At length our paper bubble is burst. The failure of Duer in New York soon brought on others, and these still more, till at that place the bankruptcy is become general. Every man concerned in paper [is] broke, and most of the tradesmen and farmers who had been laying down money, having been tempted by these speculators to lend it to them at an interest of from 3 to 6 percent a month, have lost the whole. It is computed there is a dead loss at New York of about five millions of dollars, which is reckoned the value of all the buildings of the city; so that if the whole town had been burned to the ground it would have been just the measure of the present calamity, supposing goods to have been saved. In Boston, the dead loss is about a million of dollars.... It is conjectured that the loss in Philadelphia will be about equal to that of Boston. —Ford 5:509. (1792.)

PAPER MONEY, Evils of.—Stock dealers and banking companies, by the aid of a paper system, are enriching themselves to the ruin of our country and swaying the government by their possession of the printing presses, which their wealth commands, and by other means not always honorable to the character of our countrymen.—Ford 7:170. (1797.)

PAPER MONEY, Bills of Exchange Preferable to.—There is, indeed, a convenience in paper: its easy transmission from one place to another. But this may be mainly supplied by bills of exchange so as to prevent any great displacement of actual coin. Two places trading together balance their dealings, for the most part, by their mutual supplies, and the debtor individuals of either may, instead of cash, remit the bills of those who are creditors in the same dealings, or may obtain them through some third place with which both have dealings. The cases would be rare where such bills could not be obtained, either directly or circuitously, and too unimportant to the nation to overweigh the train of evils flowing from paper circulation.—Bergh 13:416. (1813.)

PAPER MONEY, Abuses of.—Paper . . . is liable to be abused, has been, is, and forever will be abused, in every country in which it is permitted. . . . We are already at ten or twenty times the due quantity of medium, insomuch that no man knows what his property is now worth because it is bloating while he is calculating. . . . It is a palpable falsehood to say we can have specie

for our paper whenever demanded. Instead, then, of yielding to the cries of scarcity of medium set up by speculators, projectors, and commercial gamblers, no endeavors should be spared to begin the work of reducing it by such gradual means as may give time to private fortunes to preserve their poise.—To John W. Eppes. Bergh 13:430. (1813.)

PAPER MONEY, Continental.—When I speak comparatively of the paper emission of the old Congress and the present banks, let it not be imagined that I cover them under the same mantle. The object of the former was a holy one; for if ever there was a holy war, it was that which saved our liberties and gave us independence. The object of the latter is to enrich swindlers at the expense of the honest and industrious part of the nation.—Bergh 13:430. (1813.)

PAPER MONEY, Redeeming Taxes Needed for Each Issue of.—[Jean Baptiste] Say will be surprised to find that forty years after the development of sound financial principles by Adam Smith and the economists, and a dozen years after he has given them to us in a corrected, dense, and lucid form, there should be so much ignorance of them in our country; that instead of funding issues of paper on the hypothecation of specific redeeming taxes (the only method of anticipating in a time of war the resources of times of peace, tested by the experience of nations), we are trusting to the tricks of jugglers on the cards, to the illusions of banking schemes, for the resources of the war, and for the cure of colic to inflations of more wind.—Bergh 14:224. (1814.)

PAPER MONEY, Tricks with.—We are now taught to believe that legerdemain tricks upon paper can produce as solid wealth as hard labor in the earth. It is vain for common sense to urge that *nothing* can produce but *nothing;* that it is an idle dream to believe in a philosopher's stone which is to turn everything into gold, and to redeem man from the original sentence of his Maker, "In the sweat of his brow shall he eat his bread."—Bergh 14:381. (1816.)

PAPER MONEY, Need for Constitutional Veto on.—That paper money has some advantages is admitted. But that its abuses also are inevitable, and [that] by breaking up the measure of value [it] makes a lottery of all private property, cannot be denied. Shall we ever be able to put a Constitutional veto on it?—Bergh 15:113. (1817.)

PAPER MONEY. See also BANKS; FRACTIONAL BANKING; IN-FLATION; MONEY.

PARASITES, In Government.—I think . . . we have more machinery of government than is necessary, too many parasites living on the labor of the industrious.—Bergh 16:76. (1824.)

PARDONS, Review of Petitions for.—In all cases I have referred these petitions [for pardons] to the judges and prosecuting attorney, who, having heard all the circumstances of the case, are the best judges whether any of them were of such a nature as ought to obtain for the criminal a remission or abridg-

ment of the punishment.—Bergh 11:254. (1807.)

PARDONS, For Victims of Unconstitutional Punishments.—The power of pardon committed to executive discretion [can] never be more properly exercised than where citizens [are] suffering without the authority of law, or,˙ which [is] equivalent, under a law unauthorized by the Constitution, and therefore null.—Ford 10:141. (1819.)

PARLIAMENT (British). See COLONIES (American).

PASSIONS, Must Be Enlisted in Rightful Causes.—We must keep the passions of men on our side, even when we are persuading them to do what they ought to do.—Bergh 17:92. (1786.)

PASSIONS, Suppression of.—It is our sacred duty to suppress passion among ourselves, and not to blast the confidence we have inspired of proof that a government of reason is better than one of force.—Bergh 15:284. (1820.)

PATENTS, And Lawsuits.—I found it more difficult than I had on first view imagined to draw the clause you wish to have introduced in the enclosed bill. Will you make the first trial against the patentee conclusive against all others who might be interested to contest his patent? If you do, he will always have a conclusive suit brought against himself at once. Or will you give everyone a right to bring actions separately? If you do, besides running him down with the expenses and vexations of lawsuits, you will be sure to find some jury in the long run who, from motives of partiality or ignorance, will find a verdict against him, though a hundred should have been before found in his favor. I really believe that less evil will follow from leaving him to bring suits against those who invade his right.—Ford 5:392. (1791.)

PATENTS, Duration of.—Certainly an inventor ought to be allowed a right to the benefit of his invention for some certain time. It is equally certain it ought not to be perpetual; for to embarrass society with monopolies for every utensil existing, and in all the details of life, would be more injurious to them than had the supposed inventors never existed. —Bergh 11:201. (1807.)

PATENTS, Abuses of.—The abuse of ... frivolous patents is likely to cause more inconvenience than is countervailed by those really useful. We know not to what uses we may apply implements which [were] in our hands before the birth of our government, and even the discovery of America.—Bergh 14:62. (1814.)

If a new application of our old machines be a ground of monopoly, the patent law will take from us much more good than it will give.— Bergh 14:66. (1814.)

PATENTS. See also INVENTORS.

PATRIOTISM, Inspirations to.—To come here [France] ... will make you adore your own country, its soil, its climate, its equality, liberty, laws, people, and manners. My God! how little do my countrymen know what precious blessings they are in possession of, and which no other people on earth enjoy.... While we shall see multiplied instances of Europeans going to live in America, I will

venture to say no man now living will ever see an instance of an American removing to settle in Europe, and continuing there.—To James Monroe. Bergh 5:21. (1785.)

PATRIOTISM, Effects of Genuine. —The man who loves his country on its own account, and not merely for its trappings of interest or power, can never be divorced from it, can never refuse to come forward when he finds that she is engaged in dangers which he has the means of warding off.—To Elbridge Gerry. Ford 7:151. (1797.)

PATRIOTISM, My Country First.—The first object of my heart is my own country. In that is embarked my family, my fortune, and my own existence.—To Elbridge Gerry. Bergh 10:78. (1799.)

Let the love of our country soar above all minor passions.—Bergh 13:59. (1811.)

My affections are first for my own country, and then, generally, for all mankind.—Ford 9:293. (1811.)

PATRIOTISM, Sacrifices for.—To preserve the peace of our fellow citizens, promote their prosperity and happiness, reunite opinion, [and] cultivate a spirit of candor, moderation, charity, and forbearance toward one another are objects calling for the efforts and sacrifices of every good man and patriot. Our religion enjoins it, our happiness demands it, and no sacrifice is requisite but of passions hostile to both.—Bergh 10:262. (1801.)

PATRIOTISM. See also TREASON.

PATRONAGE, Distribution of.—I am sensible of the necessity as well as justice of dispersing employments over the whole of the United States. But this is difficult as to the smaller offices, which require to be filled immediately as they become vacant and are not worth coming for from the distant states. Hence they will unavoidably get into the sole occupation of the vicinities of the seat of government, a reason the more for removing that seat to the true center.—Ford 5:163. (1790.)

PATRONAGE, Corruption and.— Bad men will sometimes get in [the Presidency], and with such an immense patronage may make great progress in corrupting the public mind and principles. This is a subject with which wisdom and patriotism should be occupied.—Bergh 10:237. (1801.)

PATRONAGE, And Representative Government.—The elective principle becomes nothing if it may be smothered by the enormous patronage of the [federal] government. —Ford 7:487. (1801.)

PATRONAGE, Creates Enmity When Properly Used.—A person who wishes to make [the bestowal of office] an engine of self-elevation may do wonders with it; but to one who wishes to use it conscientiously for the public good, without regard to the ties of blood or friendship, it creates enmities without number, many open, but more secret, and saps the happiness and peace of his life.—Bergh 12:3. (1808.)

PATRONAGE. See also AP- POINTMENT; POLITICAL OF- FICES.

PEACE, Cultivating.—It should be our endeavor to cultivate the peace and friendship of every nation, even of that which has injured us most [i.e., England], when we shall have carried our point against her.—*Notes on Virginia.* Bergh 2:240. (1782.)

PEACE, Ensured by Military Strength.—The power of making war often prevents it, and...would give efficacy to our desire of peace. —To George Washington. Bergh 7:224. (1788.)

PEACE, Love of.—I love peace, and am anxious that we should give the world still another useful lesson by showing to them other modes of punishing injuries than by war, which is as much a punishment to the punisher as to the sufferer.— Ford 6:508. (1794.)

PEACE, Blessings of.—Wars and contentions, indeed, fill the pages of history.... But more blessed is that nation whose silent course of happiness furnishes nothing for history to say. This is what I ambition for my own country.—Bergh 11:181. (1807.)

PEACE, National Reputation and.— I am so far...from believing that our reputation will be tarnished by our not having mixed in the mad contests of the rest of the world that, setting aside the ravings of pepper-pot politicians, of whom there are enough in every age and country, I believe it will place us high in the scale of wisdom to have preserved our country tranquil and prosperous during a contest which prostrated the honor, power, independence, laws, and property of every country on the other side of the Atlantic. Which of them have

better preserved their honor?—
Bergh 13:93. (1811.)

PEACE, Cherishing.—Having seen
the people of all other nations bowed
down to the earth under the wars
and prodigalities of their rulers, I
have cherished their opposites,
peace, economy, and riddance of
public debt, believing that these
were the high road to public as well
as private prosperity and happiness.—Bergh 13:202. (1813.)

PEACE. See also WAR.

**PENDLETON (Edmund), Abilities
and Character of.**—Mr. Pendleton,
. . . taken all in all, was the ablest man
in debate I have ever met with. He
had not, indeed, the poetical fancy of
Mr. [Patrick] Henry, his sublime
imagination, his lofty and over-
whelming diction; but he was cool,
smooth, and persuasive; his language flowing, chaste, and embellished; his conceptions quick, acute,
and full of resource. [He was] never
vanquished; for if he lost the main
battle, he returned upon you and
regained so much of it as to make it
a drawn one by dexterous maneuvers, skirmishes in detail, and the
recovery of small advantages which,
little singly, were important all
together. You never knew when you
were clear of him, but were harassed
by his perseverance until the patience was worn down of all who had
less of it than himself. Add to this
that he was one of the most virtuous
and benevolent of men, the kindest
friend, [and] the most amiable and
pleasant of companions, which ensured a favorable reception to whatever came from him.—Autobiography. Bergh 1:54. (1821.)

**PEOPLE, Government Should Be
Controlled by.**—Every government
degenerates when trusted to the
rulers of the people alone. The
people themselves, therefore, are its
only safe depositories. And to
render even them safe, their minds
must be improved to a certain
degree.—*Notes on Virginia.* Bergh
2:207. (1782.)

The influence over government
must be shared among all the people.
If every individual which composes
their mass participates of the
ultimate authority, the government
will be safe, because the corrupting
the whole mass will exceed any
private resources of wealth, and
public ones cannot be provided but
by levies on the people.—*Notes on
Virginia.* Bergh 2:207. (1782.)

Unless the mass retains sufficient
control over those entrusted with
the powers of their government,
these will be perverted to their own
oppression, and to the perpetuation
of wealth and power in the
individuals and their families
selected for the trust. Whether our
Constitution has hit on the exact
degree of control necessary is yet
under experiment. . . . The experiment stands a better chance of being
satisfactorily made here than on any
occasion yet presented by history.—
Bergh 13:136. (1812.)

No government can continue
good, but under the control of the
people.—Ford 10:152. (1819.)

PEOPLE, Can Lose Their Rights.—
The spirit of the times may alter, will
alter. Our rulers will become corrupt, our people careless. . . . They
will be forgotten, . . . and their rights

disregarded. They will forget themselves but in the sole faculty of making money, and will never think of uniting to effect a due respect for their rights.—*Notes on Virginia.* Bergh 2:224. (1782.)

PEOPLE, Republics Preserved by Spirit of.—It is the manners and spirit of a people which preserve a republic in vigor. A degeneracy in these is a canker which soon eats to the heart of its laws and constitution.—*Notes on Virginia.* Bergh 2:230. (1782.)

PEOPLE, American vs. European.— If all the sovereigns of Europe were to set themselves to work to emancipate the minds of their subjects from their present ignorance and prejudices, and that as zealously as they now endeavor the contrary, a thousand years would not place them on that high ground on which our common people are now setting out. Ours could not have been so fairly put into the hands of their own common sense had they not been separated from their parent stock, and kept from contamination either from them or the other people of the old world, by the intervention of so wide an ocean.—Ford 4:268. (1786.)

PEOPLE, Errors of.—I am persuaded myself that the good sense of the people will always be found to be the best army. They may be led astray for a moment, but will soon correct themselves. The people are the only censors of their governors; and even their errors will tend to keep these to the true principles of their institution. To punish these errors too severely would be to suppress the only safeguard of the public liberty. The way to prevent these irregular interpositions of the people is to give them full information of their affairs through the channel of the public papers, and to contrive that those papers should penetrate the whole mass of the people. The basis of our governments being the opinion of the people, the very first object should be to keep that right.... Cherish, therefore, the spirit of our people, and keep alive their attention. Do not be too severe upon their errors, but reclaim them by enlightening them. If once they become inattentive to the public affairs, you and I, ... Congress and assemblies, judges and governors shall all become wolves.—Bergh 6:57. (1787.)

The people, especially when moderately instructed, are the only safe, because the only honest, depositories of the public rights, and should therefore be introduced into the administration of them in every function to which they are sufficient. They will err sometimes and accidentally, but never designedly and with a systematic and persevering purpose of overthrowing the free principles of the government. —Bergh 15:483. (1823.)

PEOPLE, Duty of Rulers Toward.— To inform the minds of the people and to follow their will is the chief duty of those placed at their head.— Bergh 6:342. (1787.)

PEOPLE, Secure If Well Informed. —Say ... whether peace is best preserved by giving energy to the government, or information to the people. This last is the most certain and the most legitimate engine of government. Educate and inform the whole mass of the people. Enable them to see that it is their interest to preserve peace and order, and they will preserve them. And it requires no very high degree of education to convince them of this. They are the only sure reliance for the preservation of our liberty.—To James Madison. Bergh 6:392. (1787.)

Whenever the people are well informed, they can be trusted with their own government.—Bergh 7:253. (1789.)

To open the doors of truth, and to fortify the habit of testing everything by reason, are the most effectual manacles we can rivet on the hands of our successors to prevent their manacling the people with their own consent.—Bergh 11:34. (1804.)

If a nation expects to be ignorant and free, in a state of civilization, it expects what never was and never will be. The functionaries of every government have propensities to command at will the liberty and property of their constituents. There is no safe deposit for these but with the people themselves; nor can they be safe with them without information. Where the press is free, and every man able to read, all is safe.—Bergh 14:384. (1816.)

PEOPLE, Extent of Participation in Government.—We think, in America, that it is necessary to introduce the people into every department of government as far as they are capable of exercising it; and that this is the only way to insure a long-continued and honest

administration of its powers. 1. They are not qualified to exercise themselves the executive department, but they are qualified to name the person who shall exercise it. With us, therefore, they choose this officer every four years. 2. They are not qualified to legislate. With us, therefore, they only choose the legislators. 3. They are not qualified to judge questions of *law*, but they are very capable of judging questions of *fact*. In the form of juries, therefore, they determine all matters of fact, leaving to the permanent judges to decide the law resulting from those facts.—Bergh 7:422. (1789.)

The people, being the only safe depository of power, should exercise in person every function which their qualifications enable them to exercise, consistently with the order and security of society.—Ford 9:447. (1814.)

Modern times have the signal advantage . . . of having discovered the only device by which [man's equal] rights can be secured, to wit: government by the people, acting not in person but by representatives chosen by themselves, that is to say, by every man of ripe years and sane mind who either contributes by his purse or person to the support of his country. . . . With us, all the branches of the government are elective by the people themselves except the judiciary, of whose science and qualifications they are not competent judges. Yet even in that deparment we call in a jury of the people to decide all controverted matters of fact, because to that investigation they are entirely competent, leaving thus as little as possible, merely the law of the case, to the decision of the judges.—Bergh 15:482. (1823.)

PEOPLE, Authority of.—I consider the people who constitute a society or nation as the source of all authority in that nation.—Bergh 3:227. (1793.)

Leave no authority existing not responsible to the people.—Bergh 15:66. (1816.)

All authority belongs to the people.—Ford 10:190. (1821.)

PEOPLE, Can Be Deceived.—The spirit of 1776 is not dead. It has only been slumbering. The body of the American people is substantially republican. But their virtuous feelings have been played on by some fact with more fiction; they have been the dupes of artful maneuvers, and made for a moment to be willing instruments in forging chains for themselves. But time and truth have dissipated the delusion and opened their eyes.—Ford 7:373. (1799.)

The lesson we have had [i.e., from Federalist excesses] will probably be useful to the people at large by showing to them how capable they are of being made the instruments of their own bondage.—To John Dickinson. Bergh 10:301. (1801.)

PEOPLE, Discernment of.—The firmness with which the people have withstood the late abuses of the press, the discernment they have manifested between truth and falsehood, show that they may safely be trusted to hear everything true and false, and to form a correct judgment between them.—Bergh 11:33. (1804.)

PEOPLE, Jefferson's Confidence in. —My confidence ... in my countrymen generally leaves me without much fear for the future.—Bergh 12:314. (1809.)

We both consider the people as our children, and love them with parental affection. But you love them as infants whom you are afraid to trust without nurses; and I as adults whom I freely leave to self-government.—To Pierre Samuel DuPont de Nemours. Bergh 14:489. (1816.)

I am not among those who fear the people. They, and not the rich, are our dependence for continued freedom.—Bergh 15:39. (1816.)

PEOPLE, Self-Reliance of.—A people having no king to sell them for a mess of pottage for himself, no shackles to restrain their powers of self-defense, find resources within themselves equal to every trial. This we did during the Revolutionary War, and this we can do again, let who will attack us, if we act heartily with one another.—Bergh 13:67. (1811.)

PEOPLE, Stability of Government by the.—Lay down true principles and adhere to them inflexibly. Do not be frightened into their surrender by the alarms of the timid, or the croakings of wealth against the ascendancy of the people. If experience be called for, appeal to that of our fifteen or twenty governments for forty years, and show me where the people have done half the mischief in these forty years that a single despot would have done in a single year; or show half the riots and rebellions, the crimes and the

Jefferson in June 1805 (age 62). Portrait by Gilbert Stuart.

punishments, which have taken place in any single nation under kingly government during the same period.—Ford 10:39. (1816.)

PEOPLE, The Safest Depository of Rights.—The mass of the citizens is the safest depository of their own rights.—Bergh 15:23. (1816.)

PEOPLE, Independent of All But Moral Law.—Independence can be trusted nowhere but with the people in mass. They are inherently independent of all but moral law.—Bergh 15:213. (1819.)

PEOPLE, Knowledge and Virtue in, Required for Good Government.—[A] people [can become] so demoralized and depraved as to be incapable of exercising a wholesome control. ... Their minds [are] to be informed by education what is right and what

wrong, to be encouraged in habits of virtue and deterred from those of vice by the dread of punishments, proportioned, indeed, but irremissible; in all cases, to follow truth as the only safe guide and to eschew error, which bewilders us in one false consequence after another in endless succession. These are the inculcations necessary to render the people a sure basis for the structure of order and good government.—Ford 10:152. (1819.)

PEOPLE, The Only Safe Depository of Power.—I know no safe depository of the ultimate powers of the society but the people themselves; and if we think them not enlightened enough to exercise their control with a wholesome discretion, the remedy is not to take it from them, but to inform their discretion by education. This is the true corrective of abuses of constitutional power. —Bergh 15:278. (1820.)

PEOPLE. See also GOVERNMENT; MAJORITY; PUBLIC OPINION; PUBLICITY; REPRESENTATION; REPUBLICAN GOVERNMENT; SELF-GOVERNMENT.

PETITION, Right of.—The executive of the Union is, ... by the Constitution, made the channel of communication between *foreign* powers and the United States. But citizens, whether individually or in bodies corporate or associated, have a right to apply directly to any department of their government, whether legislative, executive, or judiciary, the exercise of whose powers they have a right to claim; and neither of these can regularly offer its intervention in a case belonging to the other.—Bergh 11:381. (1807.)

The people have a right to petition, but not to use that right to cover calumniating insinuations.—To James Madison. Ford 9:209. (1808.)

PHILOSOPHY, Ancient.—The moral principles inculcated by the most esteemed of the sects of ancient philosophy, or of their individuals, particularly Pythagoras, Socrates, Epicurus, Cicero, Epictetus, Seneca, [and] Antoninus,... related chiefly to ourselves, and the government of those passions which, unrestrained, would disturb our tranquility of mind. In this branch of philosophy they were really great. In developing our duties to others, they were short and defective. They embraced, indeed, the circles of kindred and friends, and inculcated patriotism, or the love of our country in the aggregate, as a primary obligation; towards our neighbors and countrymen they taught justice, but scarcely viewed them as within the circle of benevolence. Still less have they inculcated peace, charity, and love to our fellow men, or embraced with benevolence the whole family of mankind.—To Dr. Benjamin Rush. Bergh 10:381. (1803.)

PLATO, Whimsies of.—Plato... only used the name of Socrates to cover the whimsies of his own brain.—To Dr. Benjamin Rush. Bergh 10:383. (1803.)

PLATO, Nonsense of His Writings. —I amused myself [recently] with reading seriously Plato's *Republic.* I am wrong, however, in calling it amusement, for it was the heaviest task-work I ever went through. I had occasionally before taken up some of his other works, but scarcely ever had patience to go through a whole dialogue. While wading through the whimsies, the puerilities, and unintelligible jargon of this work, I laid it down often to ask myself how it could have been that the world should have so long consented to give reputation to such nonsense as this. How the... Christian world, indeed, should have done it is a piece of historical curiosity. But how could the Roman good sense do it? And particularly, how could Cicero bestow such eulogies on Plato?...With the moderns, I think, it is rather a matter of fashion and authority. Education is chiefly in the hands of persons who, from their profession, have an interest in the reputation and the dreams of Plato. They give the tone while at school, and few in their after years have occasion to revise their college opinions. But fashion and authority apart, and bringing Plato to the test of reason, take from him his sophisms, futilities, and incomprehensibilities, and what remains? In truth, he is one of the race of genuine sophists who has escaped the oblivion of his brethren, first by the eloquence of his diction, but chiefly by the adoption and incorporation of his whimsies into the body of artificial Christianity. His foggy mind is forever presenting the semblances of objects which, half seen through a mist, can be defined neither in form nor dimensions. Yet this, which should have consigned him to early oblivion, really procured his immortality of fame and reverence. ... It is fortunate for us that Platonic republicanism has not obtained the same favor as Platonic Christianity, or we should now have been all living, men, women, and children, pell-mell together like beasts of the field or forest.... Socrates had reason, indeed, to complain of the misrepresentations of Plato, for in truth his dialogues are libels on Socrates.—To John Adams. Bergh 14:147. (1814.)

No writer, ancient or modern, has bewildered the world with more *ignis fatui* than this renowned philosopher, in ethics, in politics, and physics.—Bergh 15:258. (1820.)

PLEASURE, Bait of.—Do not bite at the bait of pleasure till you know there is no hook beneath it.—Ford 4:317. (1786.)

PLEASURE, And Pain.—We have no rose without its thorn; no pleasure without alloy. It is the law of existence, and we must acquiesce. It is the condition annexed to all our pleasures, not by us who receive, but by him who gives them.—Ford 4:321. (1786.)

POLITENESS, Value of.—I have mentioned good humor as one of the preservatives of our peace and tranquility. It is among the most effectual, and its effect is so well imitated and aided, artificially, by politeness, that this also becomes an acquisition of first-rate value. In truth, politeness is artificial good humor; it covers the natural want of it, and ends by rendering habitual a substitute nearly equivalent to the real virtue. It is the practice of sacrificing to those whom we meet in society all

the little conveniences and preferences which will gratify them, and [which] deprive us of nothing worth a moment's consideration; it is the giving a pleasing and flattering turn to our expressions which will conciliate others, and make them pleased with us as well as themselves. How cheap a price for the good will of another! When this is in return for a rude thing said by another, it brings him to his senses, it mortifies and corrects him in the most salutary way, and places him at the feet of your good nature in the eyes of the company.—Bergh 12:198. (1808.)

POLITICAL OFFICES, Training for.—Laws will be wisely formed and honestly administered in proportion as those who form and administer them are wise and honest; whence it becomes expedient for promoting the public happiness that those persons whom nature hath endowed with genius and virtue should be rendered by liberal education worthy to receive, and able to guard, the sacred deposit of the rights and liberties of their fellow citizens; and that they should be called to that charge without regard to wealth, birth, or other accidental condition or circumstance.— Boyd 2:526. (1779.)

POLITICAL OFFICES, Only "Honorable Exile."—Public employment contributes neither to advantage nor happiness. It is but honorable exile from one's family and affairs.—Ford 5:157. (1790.)

POLITICAL OFFICES, Basis for Appointments to.—Talents and science [i.e., knowledge] are sufficient motives with me in appointments to which they are fitted.—To President Washington. Ford 6:107. (1792.)

Exercising that discretion which the Constitution has confided to me in the choice of public agents, I have been sensible, on the one hand, of the justice [due] to those who have been systematically excluded from the service of their country [i.e., because of partisan politics under the previous administration], and attentive, on the other, to restore justice in such a way as might least affect the sympathies and the tranquility of the public mind.—Bergh 16:282. (1802.)

My usage is to make the best appointment my information and judgment enable me to do, and then fold myself up in the mantle of conscience and abide unmoved the peltings of the storm. And oh! for the day when I shall be withdrawn from it; when I shall have leisure to enjoy my family, my friends, my farm and books!—Bergh 11:412. (1808.)

POLITICAL OFFICES, Need for Honorable Persons in.—I love to see honest and honorable men at the helm, men who will not bend their politics to their purses, nor pursue measures by which they may profit, and then profit by their measures.—Ford 7:95. (1796.)

POLITICAL OFFICES, Appointees Retained According to Merit.—Should I be placed in office,...no man who has conducted himself according to his duties would have anything to fear from me, as those who have done ill would have nothing to hope, be their political

principles what they might.—Ford 7:489. (1801.)

POLITICAL OFFICES, Confirming Power of the Senate.—I have always considered the control of the Senate as meant to prevent any bias or favoritism in the President towards his own relations, his own religion, towards particular states, etc., and perhaps to keep very obnoxious persons out of offices of the first grade. But in all subordinate cases, I have ever thought that the selection made by the President ought to inspire a general confidence that it has been made on due inquiry and investigation of character, and that the Senate should interpose their [veto] only in those particular cases where something happens to be within their knowledge against the character of the person, and unfitting him for the appointment.—Ford 8:211. (1803.)

POLITICAL OFFICES, Should Not Be Given to Monarchists.—Monarchists...have no right to office. If a monarchist be in office anywhere, and it be known to the President, the oath he has taken to support the Constitution imperiously requires the instantaneous dismission of such officer; and I should hold the President criminal if he permitted such to remain. To appoint a monarchist to conduct the affairs of a republic is like appointing an atheist to the priesthood.—Ford 8:237. (1803.)

POLITICAL OFFICES. See also ACCOUNTABILITY; APPOINTMENT; GENIUS; HONORS; PATRONAGE; SALARIES.

POLITICAL PARTIES, Jefferson's Independence from.—I never submitted the whole system of my opinions to the creed of any party of men whatever, in religion, in philosophy, in politics, or in anything else where I was capable of thinking for myself. Such an addiction is the last degradation of a free and moral agent. If I could not go to heaven but with a party, I would not go there at all.—Bergh 7:300. (1789.)

POLITICAL PARTIES, Republican vs. Monarchical.—Where a constitution, like ours, wears a mixed aspect of monarchy and republicanism, its citizens will naturally divide into two classes of sentiment according to their tone of body or mind. Their habits, connections, and callings induce them to wish to strengthen either the monarchical or the republican features of the Constitution. Some will consider it as an elective monarchy which had better be made hereditary, and therefore endeavor to lead towards that all the forms and principles of its administration. Others will view it as an energetic republic turning in all its points on the pivot of free and frequent elections. The great body of our native citizens are unquestionably of the republican sentiment.—Ford 7:117. (1797.)

POLITICAL PARTIES, Have Existed in All Societies.—Men have differed in opinion, and been divided into parties by these opinions, from the first origin of societies, and in all governments where they have been permitted freely to think and to speak. The same political parties which now agitate the United States have existed through all time. Whether the power of the people or that of the [aristocracy] should prevail were questions which kept the states of Greece and Rome in eternal convulsions, as they now schismatize every people whose minds and mouths are not shut up by the gag of a despot. And in fact, the terms of Whig and Tory belong to natural as well as to civil history. They denote the temper and constitution of mind of different individuals.—To John Adams. Bergh 13:279. (1813.)

POLITICAL PARTIES, Differences Based on Conflicting Principles.—That each party endeavors to get into the administration of the government and exclude the other from power is true, and may be stated as a motive of action; but this is only secondary, the primary motive being a real and radical difference of political principle. I sincerely wish our differences were but personally who should govern, and that the principles of our Constitution were those of both parties. Unfortunately it is otherwise; and the question of preference between monarchy and republicanism, which has so long divided mankind elsewhere, threatens a permanent division here.—Ford 9:374. (1813.)

POLITICAL PARTIES, Amalgamation of.—What do you think of the state of parties at this time? An opinion prevails that there is no longer any distinction, that the Republicans and Federalists are completely amalgamated; but it is not so. The amalgamation is of name only, not of principle. All, indeed, call themselves by the name of Republicans because that of the Federalists was extinguished in the battle of New Orleans. But the truth is that, finding that monarchy is a desperate wish in this country, they [the old Federalists] rally to the point which they think next best, a consolidated government. Their aim is now, therefore, to break down the rights reserved by the Constitution to the states as a bulwark against that consolidation, the fear of which produced the whole of the opposition to the Constitution at its birth. Hence new Republicans in Congress preaching the doctrines of the old Federalists, and the new nicknames of "Ultras" and "Radicals." But I trust they will fail under the new, as the old, name, and that the friends of the real Constitution and Union will prevail against consolidation as they have done against monarchism. I scarcely know myself which is most to be deprecated, a consolidation or dissolution of the states. The horrors of both are beyond the reach of human foresight.—Ford 10:225. (1822.)

POLITICAL PARTIES, Watchmen for the Public.—I am no believer in the amalgamation of parties, nor do I consider it as either desirable or useful for the public; but only that, like religious differences, a difference in politics should never be permitted to enter into social intercourse, or to disturb its friendship, its charities, or justice. In that form they are censors of the conduct of each other, and useful watchmen for the public.—To Henry Lee. Bergh 16:73. (1824.)

POLITICAL PARTIES, Natural Division of Citizens into.—Men by their constitutions are naturally divided into two parties: 1. Those who fear and distrust the people, and wish to draw all powers from them into the hands of the higher classes. 2. Those who identify themselves with the people, have confidence in them, [and] cherish and consider them as the most honest and safe, although not the most wise, depository of the public interests. In every country these two parties exist, and in every one where they are free to think, speak, and write, they will declare themselves. Call them, therefore, liberals and serviles, Jacobins and Ultras, Whigs and Tories, Republicans and Federalists, aristocrats and democrats, or by whatever name you please, they are the same parties still, and pursue the same object. The last appellation of aristocrats and democrats is the true one expressing the essence of all.—To Henry Lee. Bergh 16:73. (1824.)

POLITICAL PARTIES. See also FEDERALIST PARTY; REPUBLICAN PARTY.

POLITICS, Ignorance and.—I think it is Montaigne who has said that ignorance is the softest pillow on which a man can rest his head. I am sure it is true as to everything political, and shall endeavor to estrange myself to everything of that character.—Ford 6:498. (1794.)

POLITICS, Conversations on.—Political conversations I really dislike, and therefore avoid where I can without affectation. But when urged by others, I have never conceived that having been in public life requires me to belie my sentiments or even to conceal them. When I am led by conversation to express them, I do it with the same independence here which I have practiced everywhere, and which is inseparable from my nature.—To President Washington. Ford 7:83. (1796.)

POLITICS, Passions and.—You and I have formerly seen warm debates and high political passions. But gentlemen of different politics would then speak to each other and separate the business of the Senate from that of society. It is not so now. Men who have been intimate all their lives cross the streets to avoid meeting, and turn their heads another way lest they should be obliged to touch their hats. This may do for young men, with whom passion is enjoyment, but it is afflicting to peaceable minds.—To Edward Rutledge. Ford 7:154. (1797.)

POLITICS, Destructive of Happiness.—Politics and party hatreds destroy the happiness of every being here [in Philadelphia]. They seem, like salamanders, to consider fire as their element.—To Martha Jefferson Randolph. Betts & Bear, p. 162. (1798.)

POLITICS, Taxation and.—The purse of the people is the real seat of sensibility. It is to be drawn upon largely, and they will then listen to truths which could not excite them through any other organ.—Ford 7:281. (1798.)

Excessive taxation...will carry reason and reflection to every man's door, and particularly in the hour of election.—Ford 7:310. (1798.)

POLITICS, Moral Right and.—Political interest can never be separated in the long run from moral right.—To James Monroe. Ford 8:477. (1806.)

POLITICS, Differences in.—I never suffered a political to become a personal difference.—To Timothy Pickering. Bergh 15:322. (1821.)

POLITICS. See also GOVERNMENT.

POLYGRAPH. See INVENTIONS, Polygraph.

POOR, In Early America.—The poor [who are] unable to support themselves are maintained by an assessment on the tithable persons in their parish. This assessment is levied and administered by twelve persons in each parish, called vestrymen.... The poor who have neither property, friends, nor strength to labor are boarded in the houses of good farmers, to whom a stipulated sum is annually paid. To those who are able to help themselves a little, or have friends from whom they derive some succors, inadequate however to their full maintenance, supplementary aids are given which enable them to live comfortably in their own houses, or in the houses of their friends. Vagabonds without visible property or vocation are placed in work houses, where they are well clothed, fed, lodged, and made to work. Nearly the same method of providing for the poor prevails through all our states; and from Savannah to Portsmouth you will seldom meet a beggar. In the large towns, indeed, they sometimes present themselves. These are usually foreigners who have never obtained a settlement in any parish. I never yet saw a native American begging in the streets or highways. —*Notes on Virginia.* Bergh 2:183. (1782.)

POOR, Government Should Keep Hands Off.—If we can prevent the government from wasting the labors of the people, under the pretense of taking care of them, they must become happy.—Bergh 10:342. (1802.)

POOR. See also CHARITY; REDISTRIBUTION OF WEALTH.

POPULATION, America's Capacity for.—The territory of the United States contains about a million of square miles, English. There is in them a greater proportion of fertile lands than in the British dominions in Europe. Suppose the territory of the United States, then, to attain an equal degree of population with the British European dominions; they will have an hundred millions of inhabitants. Let us extend our views to what may be the population of North and South America, supposing them divided at the narrowest part of the Isthmus of Panama. Between this line and that of 50° of north latitude, the northern continent contains about five millions of square miles, and south of this line of division the southern continent contains about seven millions of square miles. . . . Here are twelve millions of square miles which, at the rate of population before assumed, will nourish twelve hundred millions of inhabitants, a

greater number than the present population of the whole globe is supposed to amount to. If those who propose medals for the resolution of questions about which nobody makes any question, those who have invited discussion on the pretended problem, "Whether the discovery of America was for the good of mankind"—if they, I say, would have viewed it only as doubling the numbers of mankind, and of course the quantum of existence and happiness, they might have saved the money and the reputation which their proposition has cost them.— Ford 4:179. (1786.)

POPULATION, Growth of American.—Our growth is now so well established by regular enumerations through a course of forty years, and the same grounds of continuance so likely to endure for a much longer period, that, speaking in round numbers, we may safely call ourselves twenty millions in twenty years, and forty millions in forty years.—Bergh 15:51. (1816.)

POPULATION. See also MANIFEST DESTINY; TERRITORY.

POST OFFICE, Foreign Mails.— The person at the head of the post office here [in Paris] says he proposed to Dr. [Benjamin] Franklin a convention to facilitate the passage of letters through their office and ours. . . . The one proposed here was that, for letters passing hence into America, the French postage should be collected by our post officers and paid every six months, and for letters coming from America here, the American postage should be collected by the post officers here and paid to us in like manner. A second plan, however, presents itself: that is, to suppose the sums to be thus collected on each side will be equal, or so nearly equal that the balance will not pay for the trouble of keeping accounts and for the little bickerings that the settlement of accounts and demands of the balances may occasion; and therefore to make an exchange of postage. This would better secure our harmony, but I do not know that it would be agreed to here. If not, the other might then be agreed to.—To John Jay. Bergh 5:103. (1785.)

POST OFFICE, Expediting Mails.— I am now on a plan with the Postmaster General to make the posts go from Philadelphia to Richmond in two days and a half instead of six, which I hope to persuade him is practicable.—Ford 5:456. (1792.)

POST OFFICE, Political Spies in.— The interruption of letters is becoming so notorious that I am forming a resolution of declining correspondence with my friends through the channels of the post office altogether.—Ford 7:156. (1797.)

A want of confidence in the post office deters me from writing to my friends on the subject of politics.— Ford 7:368. (1799.)

POSTERITY, Historical Judgment of.—It is fortunate for those in public trust that posterity will judge them by their works, and not by the malignant vituperations and invectives of the Pickerings and Gardiners of their age.—To John Adams. Bergh 15:109. (1817.)

POSTERITY, Sacrifices for.—It is from posterity we are to expect remuneration for the sacrifices we are making for their service, of time, quiet, and good will.—Bergh 16:100. (1825.)

It has . . . been a great solace to me to believe that you are engaged in vindicating to posterity the course we have pursued for preserving to them, in all their purity, the blessings of self-government, which we had assisted, too, in acquiring for them.—To James Madison. Bergh 16:159. (1826.)

POWER, Corrupts.—Mankind soon learn to make interested uses of every right and power which they possess, or may assume. The public money and public liberty, intended [in the Virginia constitution] to have been deposited with three branches of magistracy, but found inadvertently to be in the hands of one only, will soon be discovered to be sources of wealth and dominion to those who hold them; distinguished, too, by this tempting circumstance, that they are the instrument as well as the object of acquisition. With money we will get men, said Caesar, and with men we will get money.— *Notes on Virginia.* Bergh 2:164. (1782.)

[We] should look forward to a time, and that not a distant one, when a corruption in this [country], as in the country from which we derive our origin, will have seized the heads of government and be spread by them through the body of the people; when they will purchase the voices of the people and make them pay the price. Human nature is the same on every side of the

Atlantic, and will be alike influenced by the same causes.—*Notes on Virginia*. Bergh 2:164. (1782.)

The time to guard against corruption and tyranny is before they shall have gotten hold of us. It is better to keep the wolf out of the fold than to trust to drawing his teeth and claws after he shall have entered.—*Notes on Virginia*. Bergh 2:165. (1782.)

In every government on earth is some trace of human weakness, some germ of corruption and degeneracy, which cunning will discover and wickedness insensibly open, cultivate, and improve. Every government degenerates when trusted to the rulers of the people alone. The people themselves, therefore, are its only safe depositories. And to render even them safe, their minds must be improved to a certain degree. This, indeed, is not all that is necessary, though it be essentially necessary. An amendment [to] our [Virginia] constitution must here come in aid of the public education. The influence over government must be shared among all the people. If every individual which composes their mass participates of the ultimate authority, the government will be safe, because the corrupting [of] the whole mass will exceed any private resources of wealth, and public ones cannot be provided but by levies on the people. In this case, every man would have to pay his own price. The government of Great Britain has been corrupted because but one man in ten has a right to vote for members of Parliament. The sellers of the government, therefore, get nine-tenths of their price clear. It has been thought that corruption is restrained by confining the right of suffrage to a few of the wealthier of the people; but it would be more effectually restrained by an extension of that right to such [numbers] as would bid defiance to the means of corruptions.—*Notes on Virginia*. Bergh 2:207. (1782.)

The functionaries of public power rarely strengthen in their dispositions to abridge it.—Ford 10:31. (1816.)

POWER, Need for Limitations on.—In a free country, every power is dangerous which is not bound up by general rules.—Ford 4:116. (1785.)

POWER, Exercise of.—I have never been able to conceive how any rational being could propose happiness to himself from the exercise of power over others.—Ford 9:308. (1811.)

POWER, Danger of Independent.—It should be remembered, as an axiom of eternal truth in politics, that whatever power in any government is independent is absolute also; in theory only at first, while the spirit of the people is up, but in practice as fast as that relaxes. Independence can be trusted nowhere but with the people in mass. They are inherently independent of all but moral law.—Bergh 15:213. (1819.)

POWER, Only Safe Depository of.—I know no safe depository of the ultimate powers of the society but the people themselves; and if we think them not enlightened enough to exercise their control with a wholesome discretion, the remedy is not to take it from them, but to inform their discretion by education. This is the true corrective of abuses of constitutional power.—Bergh 15:278. (1820.)

POWER, Origin of.—[David] Hume, the great apostle of Toryism, says [in his *History of England*], "The Commons established a principle which is noble in itself and seems specious, but is belied by all history and experience, *that the people are the origin of all just power.*" And where else will this degenerate son of science, this traitor to his fellow men, find the origin of *just* power if not in the majority of the society? Will it be in the minority? Or in an individual of that minority?—Bergh 16:44. (1824.)

POWER. See also GOVERNMENT; PEOPLE.

PRAYER. See DEITY; FAST DAY; PROVIDENCE; REVELATION.

PRESIDENCY, Jefferson's Attitude Toward.—I shall, from the bottom of my heart, rejoice at escaping [the presidency]. I know well that no man will ever bring out of that office the reputation which carries him into it. The honeymoon would be as short in that case as in any other, and its moments of ecstasy would be ransomed by years of torment and hatred.—To Edward Rutledge. Bergh 9:353. (1796.)

Neither the splendor, nor the power, nor the difficulties, nor the fame or defamation, as may happen, attached to the first magistracy, have any attractions for me. The helm of a free government is always arduous.—Bergh 9:377. (1797.)

I feel no impulse from personal ambition to the office now proposed to me, but... I feel a sincere wish indeed to see our government brought back to its republican principles, to see that kind of government firmly fixed to which my whole life has been devoted. I hope we shall now see it so established as that when I retire it may be under full security that we are to continue free and happy.—To Mary Jefferson Eppes. Betts & Bear, p. 197. (1801.)

PRESIDENCY, A "Splendid Misery."—The second office of the government [Vice President] is honorable and easy; the first is but a splendid misery.—To Elbridge Gerry. Bergh 9:381. (1797.)

PRESIDENCY, Corruption and the.—I sincerely wish... we could see our government so secured as to depend less on the character of the person in whose hands it is trusted. Bad men will sometimes get in, and with such an immense patronage may make great progress in corrupting the public mind and principles. This is a subject with which wisdom and patriotism should be occupied.—Bergh 10:237. (1801.)

PRESIDENT, Reelection of the.—I dislike strongly [in the new Constitution] the perpetual reeligibility of the President. This, I fear, will make that an office for life, first, and then hereditary.... However, I shall hope that before there is danger of this change taking place in the office of President, the good sense and free spirit of our countrymen will make the changes necessary to prevent it.

—To George Washington. Ford 5:8. (1788.)

PRESIDENT, The Senate and the.— The transaction of business with foreign nations is executive altogether. It belongs, then, to the head of that department, except as to such portions of it as are specially submitted to the Senate. Exceptions are to be construed strictly.—Bergh 3:16. (1790.)

PRESIDENT, The Judiciary and the.—The interference of the executive can rarely be proper where that of the judiciary is so.—Ford 6:298. (1793.)

The leading principle of our Constitution is the independence of the legislature, executive, and judiciary of each other, and none are more jealous of this than the judiciary. But would the executive be independent of the judiciary if he were subject to the *commands* of the latter, and to imprisonment for disobedience; if the several courts could bandy him from pillar to post, keep him constantly trudging from north to south and east to west, and withdraw him entirely from his Constitutional duties? The intention of the Constitution, that each branch should be independent of the others, is further manifested by the means it has furnished to each to protect itself from enterprises of force attempted on them by the others, and to none has it given more effectual or diversified means than to the executive.—Ford 9:59. (1807.)

As I do not believe that the district courts have a power of *commanding* the executive government to aban-

don superior duties and attend on them, at whatever distance, I am unwilling, by any notice of the subpoena, to set a precedent which might sanction a proceeding so preposterous. I enclose you, therefore, a letter, public and for the court, covering substantially all they ought to desire.—To George Hay (U.S. Attorney). Bergh 11:365. (1807.)

PRESIDENT, Petitions to the.— The right of our fellow citizens to represent to the public functionaries their opinion on proceedings interesting to them is unquestionably a Constitutional right, often useful, sometimes necessary, and will always be respectfully acknowledged by me.—Ford 8:68. (1801.)

PRESIDENT, Relationship with State Governors.—Comparing the [federal and state] governments together, it is observable that in all those cases where the independent or reserved rights of the states are in question, the two executives, if they are to act together, must be exactly coordinate; they are, in these cases, each the supreme head of an independent government. In other cases, to wit, those transferred by the Constitution to the general government, the general executive is certainly preordinate.—To Governor James Monroe. Bergh 10:267. (1801.)

PRESIDENT, Dangers of a Third Term.—My opinion originally was that the President of the United States should have been elected for seven years, and forever ineligible afterwards. I have since become sensible that seven years is too long to be irremovable, and that there should be a peaceable way of withdrawing a man in midway who is doing wrong. The service for eight years, with a power to remove at the end of the first four, comes nearly to my principle as corrected by experience; and it is in adherence to that that I determine to withdraw at the end of my second term. The danger is that the indulgence and attachments of the people will keep a man in the chair after he becomes a dotard, that reelection through life shall become habitual, and election for life follow that. General Washington set the example of voluntary retirement after eight years. I shall follow it. And a few more precedents will oppose the obstacle of habit to anyone after a while who shall endeavor to extend his term. Perhaps it may beget a disposition to establish it by an amendment of the Constitution. I believe I am doing right, therefore, in pursuing my principle. I had determined to declare my intention, but I have consented to be silent on the opinion of friends, who think it best not to put a continuance out of my power in defiance of all circumstances. There is, however, but one circumstance which could engage my acquiescence in another election; to wit, such a division about a successor as might bring in a monarchist. But that circumstance is impossible.—Bergh 11:56. (1805.)

PRESIDENT, And Retention of Executive Papers.—Reserving the necessary right of the President of the United States to decide, independently of all other authority, what papers coming to him as Presi-

dent the public interests permit to be communicated, and to whom, I assure you of my readiness, under that restriction, voluntarily to furnish on all occasions whatever the purposes of justice may require.— Ford 9:55. (1807.)

The President sends papers to the House [of Representatives] which he thinks the public interest requires they should see. They immediately pass a vote, implying irresistibly their belief that he is capable of having kept back other papers which the same interest requires they should see. They pretend to no direct proof of this. It must, then, be founded in presumption; and on what act of my life or of my administration is such a presumption founded? What interest can I have in leading the [Congress] to act on false grounds? My wish is certainly to take that course with the public affairs which the body of the [Congress] would prefer. It is said, indeed, that such a vote is to satisfy the Federalists and their partisans. But were I to send twenty letters they would say, "You have kept back the twenty-first; send us that." If I sent one hundred they would say, "There were one hundred and one"; and how could I prove the negative? Their malice can be cured by no conduct; it ought, therefore, to be disregarded instead of countenancing their imputations by the sanction of a vote. Indeed, I should consider such a vote as a charge in the face of the nation, calling for a serious and public defense of myself. —Bergh 11:447. (1808.)

PRESIDENT, Term of Office.—My

wish...was that the President should be elected for seven years, and be ineligible afterwards. This term I thought sufficient to enable him, with the concurrence of the [Congress], to carry through and establish any system of improvement he should propose for the general good. But the practice adopted, I think, is better, allowing his continuance for eight years with a liability to be dropped at halfway of the term, making that a period of probation.—Autobiography. Bergh 1:119. (1821.)

PRESIDENT. See also EXECUTIVE; FEDERAL GOVERNMENT; VETO.

PRESS, The Constitution and Freedom of.—It is true as a general principle, and is also expressly declared by one of the amendments to the Constitution, that "the powers not delegated to the United States by the Constitution, nor prohibited by it to the states, are reserved to the states respectively, or to the people"; and,...no power over the freedom of religion, freedom of speech, or freedom of the press being delegated to the United States by the Constitution, nor prohibited by it to the states, all lawful powers respecting the same did of right remain [with], and were reserved to, the states or the people.... Thus was manifested their determination to retain to themselves the right of judging how far the licentiousness of speech and of the press may be abridged without lessening their useful freedom, and how far those abuses which cannot be separated from their use should be tolerated, rather than the use be destroyed....

In addition to this general principle and express declaration, another and more special provision has been made by one of the amendments to the Constitution, which expressly declares that "Congress shall make no law respecting an establishment of religion, or prohibiting the free exercise thereof, or abridging the freedom of speech, or of the press," thereby guarding in the same sentence, and under the same words, the freedom of religion, of speech, and of the press; insomuch that whatever violates either throws down the sanctuary which covers the others, and that libels, falsehood, and defamation, equally with heresy and false religion, are withheld from the cognizance of federal tribunals. —Kentucky Resolutions. Bergh 17:381. (1798.)

PRESS, Freedom of, Abused.—The firmness with which the people have withstood the late abuses of the press, the discernment they have manifested between truth and falsehood, show that they may safely be trusted to hear everything true and false, and to form a correct judgment between them.—Bergh 11:33. (1804.)

Our printers raven on the agonies of their victims, as wolves do on the blood of the lamb.—To James Monroe. Ford 9:324. (1811.)

PRESS, Freedom of, Controlled by States.—While we deny that Congress have a right to control the freedom of the press, we have ever asserted the right of the states, and their exclusive right, to do so. They have accordingly, all of them, made provisions for punishing slander....

In general, the state laws appear to have made the presses responsible for slander as far as is consistent with its useful freedom. In those states where they do not admit even the truth of allegations to protect the printer, they have gone too far. —Ford 8:311. (1804.)

PRESS, Freedom of, Compatible with Orderly Government.—I have lent myself willingly as the subject of a great experiment, which was to prove that an administration conducting itself with integrity and common understanding cannot be battered down even by the falsehoods of a licentious press, and consequently still less by the press as restrained within the legal and wholesome limits of truth. This experiment was wanting for the world to demonstrate the falsehood of the pretext that freedom of the press is incompatible with orderly government.... But the fact being once established that the press is impotent when it abandons itself to falsehood, I leave to others to restore it to its strength by recalling it within the pale of truth. Within that, it is a noble institution, equally the friend of science and of civil liberty.—Ford 9:30. (1807.)

PRESS, Editorial Responsibility of the.—I think an editor should be independent, that is, of personal influence, and not be moved from his opinions on the mere authority of any individual. But with respect to the general opinion of the political section with which he habitually accords, his duty seems very like that of a member of Congress.—Ford 9:315. (1811.)

PRESS, Safety in Freedom of.—Where the press is free and every man able to read, all is safe.—Ford 10:4. (1816.)

PRESS, Its Usefulness to Mankind.—The press...is...the best instrument for enlightening the mind of man and improving him as a rational, moral, and social being. —Bergh 15:489. (1823.)

PRESS. See also LIBEL; NEWSPAPERS; PUBLICITY.

PRIMOGENITURE, Abolition of.—As the law of descents and the criminal law fell...within my portion [in the revision of the Virginia code], I wished the committee to settle the leading principles of these as a guide for me in framing them; and, with respect to the first, I proposed to abolish the law of primogeniture, and to make real estate descendible in parcenary [co-heirship] to the next of kin, as personal property is, by the statute of distribution. Mr. [Edmund] Pendleton wished to preserve the right of primogeniture; but seeing at once that that could not prevail, he proposed we should adopt the Hebrew principle and give a double portion to the elder son. I observed that if the eldest son could eat twice as much, or do double work, it might be a natural evidence of his right to a double portion; but being on a par in his powers and wants with his brothers and sisters, he should be on a par also in the partition of the patrimony; and such was the decision of the other members.— Autobiography. Bergh 1:64. (1821.)

PRIMOGENITURE, Feudal and Unnatural.—The abolition of

primogeniture...removed the feudal and unnatural distinctions which made one member of every family rich and all the rest poor, substituting equal partition [of inheritances], the best of all agrarian laws.—Autobiography. Bergh 1:73. (1821.)

PRIMOGENITURE. See also ENTAIL; INHERITANCES.

PRINCIPLES, Adherence to.—An adherence to fundamental principles is the most likely way to save both time and disagreement [between legislative bodies]; and [as] a departure from them may at some time or other be drawn into precedent for dangerous innovations, ... it is better for both houses, and for those by whom they are entrusted, to correct error while new, and before it becomes inveterate by habit and custom.—Ford 2:135. (1777.)

Lay down true principles and adhere to them inflexibly. Do not be frightened into their surrender by the alarms of the timid, or the croakings of wealth against the ascendancy of the people.—Ford 10:39. (1816.)

PRINCIPLES, America's Future Depends on Preservation of.—If our fellow citizens...will sacrifice favoritism towards men for the preservation of principle, we may hope that no divisions will again endanger a degeneracy in our government.—Bergh 12:10. (1808.)

In the maintenance of...[our] principles...I verily believe the future happiness of our country essentially depends.—Ford 10:143. (1819.)

PRINCIPLES, The Basis of American Independence.—The contest which began with us, which ushered in the dawn of our national existence and led us through various and trying scenes, was for everything dear to free-born man. The principles on which we engaged, of which the charter of our independence is the record, were sanctioned by the laws of our being, and we but obeyed them in pursuing undeviatingly the course they called for. It issued finally in that inestimable state of freedom which alone can ensure to man the enjoyment of his equal rights.—Bergh 16:349. (1809.)

PRINCIPLES, Political Schism and.—We ought not to schismatize on either men or measures. Principles alone can justify that.—Ford 9:313. (1811.)

PRINCIPLES, Departure from.—A departure from principle in one instance becomes a precedent for a second, that second for a third, and so on, till the bulk of the society is reduced to be mere automatons of misery, to have no sensibilities left but for sin and suffering. Then begins indeed the *bellum omnium in omnia* which some philosophers, observing [it] to be so general in this world, have mistaken...for the natural instead of the abusive state of man. And the forehorse of this frightful team is public debt. Taxation follows that, and in its train wretchedness and oppression.—Bergh 15:40. (1816.)

PRINCIPLES, Practice and.—True wisdom does not lie in mere practice without principle.—To John Adams. Bergh 15:75. (1816.)

PRISONERS OF WAR, Retaliation and.—Retaliation is a duty we owe to those engaged in the cause of their country to assure them that if any unlucky circumstance, baffling the efforts of their bravery, shall put them in the power of their enemies, we will use the pledges in our hands to warrant their lives from sacrifice.—Ford 1:495. (1775.)

If the [British] enemy shall put to death, torture, or otherwise ill-treat any of the hostages in their hands, or of the Canadian or other prisoners captivated by them in the service of the united colonies, recourse must be had to retaliation as the sole means of stopping the progress of human butchery, and for that purpose punishments of the same kind and degree shall be inflicted on an equal number of their subjects taken by us till they shall be taught due respect to the violated rights of nations. —Ford 2:34. (1776.)

A uniform exercise of kindness to prisoners on our part has been returned by as uniform severity on the part of our enemies.... It is high time...to teach respect to the dictates of humanity; in such a case retaliation becomes an act of humanity.—Ford 2:251. (1779.)

PRIVILEGES, Aversion to Unequal. —To unequal privileges among members of the same society the spirit of our nation is, with one accord, adverse.—Bergh 10:258. (1801.)

PROGRESS, Comes in Response to Changing Circumstances.—European monarchs, instead of wisely yielding to the general change of circumstances, of favoring progressive accommodation to progressive improvement, have clung to old abuses, entrenched themselves behind steady habits, and obliged their subjects to seek through blood and violence rash and ruinous innovations, which, had they been referred to the peaceful deliberations and collected wisdom of the nation, would have been put into acceptable and salutary forms. Let us follow no such examples, nor weakly believe that one generation is not as capable as another of taking care of itself, and of ordering its own affairs.— Ford 10:42. (1816.)

PROGRESS. See also EDUCATION; KNOWLEDGE; REFORM.

PROPERTY, Unnatural Laws of.— Whenever there [are] in any country uncultivated lands and unemployed poor, it is clear that the laws of property have been so far extended as to violate natural right.—Ford 7:36. (1785.)

PROPERTY, Jurisdiction over Foreigners'.—It is reasonable that everyone who asks justice should do justice; and it is usual to consider the property of a foreigner, in any country, as a fund appropriated to the payment of what he owes in that country exclusively. It is a care which most nations take of their own citizens not to let the property which is to answer their demands be withdrawn from its jurisdiction, and [thus] send them to seek it in foreign countries and before foreign tribunals.—Ford 6:37. (1792.)

PROPERTY, Protection of.—The persons and property of our citizens are entitled to the protection of our government in all places where they may lawfully go.—Bergh 3:244. (1793.)

PROPERTY, Industry and.—Our wish . . . is that . . . equality of rights [may be] maintained, and that state of property, equal or unequal, which results to every man from his own industry or that of his fathers.— Second Inaugural Address. Bergh 3:382. (1805.)

PROPERTY, Recovery of Stolen.— Nature [has given] to all men, individual or associated, [the right] of rescuing their own property wrongfully taken. In cases of forcible entry on individual possessions, special provisions, both of the common and civil law, have restrained the right of rescue by private force and substituted the aid of the civil power. But no law has restrained the right of the nation itself from removing, by its own arm, intruders on its possessions.—Bergh 12:383. (1810.)

By nature's law, every man has a right to seize and retake by force his own property, taken from him by another by force or fraud. Nor is this natural right among the first which is taken into the hands of regular government after it is instituted. It was long retained by our ancestors. It was a part of their common law, laid down in their books, recognized by all the authorities, and regulated as to certain circumstances of practice.—Bergh 18:104. (1812.)

PROPERTY, Free Press and.—The functionaries of every government have propensities to command at will the liberty and property of their constituents. There is no safe deposit for these but with the people themselves, nor can they be safe

with them without information. Where the press is free, and every man able to read, all is safe.—Ford 10:4. (1816.)

PROPERTY, Natural Right to.—A right to property is founded in our natural wants, in the means with which we are endowed to satisfy these wants, and the right to what we acquire by those means without violating the similar rights of other sensible beings.—Bergh 14:490. (1816.)

PROPERTY. See also REDISTRIBUTION OF WEALTH.

PROSPERITY, Pillars of.—Agriculture, manufactures, commerce, and navigation, the four pillars of our prosperity, are the most thriving when left most free to individual enterprise.—First Annual Message to Congress. Bergh 3:337. (1801.)

PROSPERITY, Conditions Needed for.—We remark with special satisfaction those [prosperous circumstances] which, under the smiles of Providence, result from the skill, industry, and order of our citizens, managing their own affairs in their own way and for their own use, unembarrassed by too [many] regulations, unoppressed by fiscal exactions.—Second Annual Message to Congress. Bergh 3:340. (1802.)

I trust the good sense of our country will see that its greatest prosperity depends on a due balance between agriculture, manufactures, and commerce.—Ford 9:239. (1809.)

PROVIDENCE, Human Happiness and.—An overruling Providence, . . . by all its dispensations, proves that it delights in the happiness of man here and his greater happiness here-after.—First Inaugural Address. Bergh 3:320. (1801.)

PROVIDENCE, Supplications to.— I supplicate a protecting Providence to watch over ... our country's freedom and welfare.—Bergh 16:303. (1808.)

I sincerely supplicate that overruling Providence which governs the destinies of men and nations to dispense His choicest blessings on ... our beloved country.—Bergh 16:352. (1809.)

PROVIDENCE. See also DEITY; GOD; RELIGION.

PUBLIC CONFIDENCE, Can Be Dangerous.—It would be a dangerous delusion were a confidence in the men of our choice to silence our fears for the safety of our rights.... Confidence is everywhere the parent of despotism. Free government is founded in jealousy, and not in confidence; it is jealousy, and not confidence, which prescribes limited constitutions to bind down those whom we are obliged to trust with power.... Our Constitution has accordingly fixed the limits to which, and no further, our confidence may go.... In questions of power, then, let no more be heard of confidence in man, but bind him down from mischief by the chains of the Constitution.—Kentucky Resolutions. Bergh 17:388. (1798.)

PUBLIC CONFIDENCE, Perversion of.—What person who remembers the times and tempers we have seen would have believed that within so short a period, not only the jealous spirit of liberty which shaped every operation of our Revolution, but

even the common principles of English Whiggism, would be scouted, and the Tory principle of passive obedience under the new-fangled names of *confidence* and *responsibility* become entirely triumphant? That the Tories, whom in mercy we did not crumble to dust and ashes, could so have entwined us in their scorpion tails that we cannot now move hand or foot?—To Robert R. Livingston. Bergh 10:118. (1799.)

PUBLIC CONFIDENCE, Need for, and Prerequisites of.—In a government like ours it is the duty of the chief magistrate, in order to enable himself to do all the good which his station requires, to endeavor by all honorable means to unite in himself the confidence of the whole people. This alone, in any case where the energy of the nation is required, can produce a union of the powers of the whole and point them in a single direction as if all constituted but one body and one mind; and this alone can render a weaker nation unconquerable by a stronger one. Towards acquiring the confidence of the people, the very first measure is to satisfy them of his disinterestedness, and that he is directing their affairs with a single eye to their good and not to build up fortunes for himself and [his] family.—Ford 9:270. (1810.)

PUBLIC CONFIDENCE, Wisdom and.—It is not wisdom alone, but public confidence in that wisdom, which can support an administration.—To President James Monroe. Ford 10:316. (1824.)

PUBLIC OPINION, Respect for.— There are certainly persons in all the departments who are driving too fast. Government being founded on opinion, the opinion of the public, even when it is wrong, ought to be respected to a certain degree.—Ford 5:282. (1791.)

PUBLIC OPINION, Wisdom of.— It is rare that the public sentiment decides immorally or unwisely, and the individual who differs from it ought to distrust and examine well his own opinion.—Ford 8:27. (1801.)

PUBLIC OPINION. See also MAJORITY; PEOPLE.

PUBLICITY, And Prevention of Public Errors.—The way to prevent these irregular interpositions of the people is to give them full information of their affairs through the channel of the public papers, and to contrive that those papers should penetrate the whole mass of the people.—Bergh 6:57. (1787.)

PUBLICITY, And Executive Support.—No ground of support for the executive will ever be so sure as a complete knowledge of their proceedings by the people; and it is only in cases where the public good would be injured, and *because* it would be injured, that proceedings should be secret. In such cases it is the duty of the executive to sacrifice their personal interests (which would be promoted by publicity) to the public interest.—To President Washington. Ford 6:461. (1793.)

PUBLICITY, Required by Republican Government.—Ours, as you know, is a government which will not tolerate the being kept entirely in the dark.—Ford 9:36. (1807.)

PUBLICITY, The People Entitled to.—I have not been in the habit of mysterious reserve on any subject, nor of buttoning up my opinions within my own doublet. On the contrary, while in public service especially, I thought the public entitled to frankness, and intimately to know whom they employed.— Ford 10:37. (1816.)

PUBLICITY. See also ACCOUNTABILITY; NEWSPAPERS; PEOPLE; PRESS.

PUNISHMENT, Excessive.—It is not only vain but wicked in a legislator to frame laws in opposition to the laws of nature, and to arm them with the terror of death. This is truly creating crimes in order to punish them.—Bergh 1:236. (1779.)

All excess of punishment is a crime.—Ford 5:484. (1792.)

PUNISHMENT. See also CAPITAL PUNISHMENT; CRIME.

R

RANDOLPH (Peyton), Jefferson's Estimate of.—He was indeed a most excellent man; and none was ever more beloved and respected by his friends. Somewhat cold and coy towards strangers, but of the sweetest affability when ripened into acquaintance. Of Attic pleasantry in conversation, always good humored and conciliatory. With a sound and logical head, he was well read in the law; and his opinions, when consulted, were highly regarded, presenting always a learned and sound view of the subject, but generally, too, a listlessness to go into its thorough development; for being heavy and inert in body, he was rather too indolent and careless for business, which occasioned him to get a smaller proportion of it at the bar than his abilities would otherwise have commanded.... Although not eloquent, his matter was so substantial that no man commanded more attention, which, joined with a sense of his great worth, gave him a weight in the House of Burgesses which few ever attained. He was liberal in his expenses, but correct also, so as not to be involved in pecuniary embarrassments; and with a heart always open to the amiable sensibilities of our nature, he did as many good acts as could have been done with his fortune without injuriously impairing his means of continuing them. He left no issue, and gave his fortune to his widow and nephew, the late Edmund Randolph.—Bergh 18:139. (1813 or later.)

REASON, Error vs.—Reason and free inquiry are the only effectual agents against error.—*Notes on Virginia.* Bergh 2:221. (1782.)

REASON, Government and.—I hope that we have not labored in vain, and that our experiment will still prove that men can be governed by reason.—To George Mason. Ford 5:275. (1791.)

REASON, Umpirage of.—We should be most unwise, indeed, were we to cast away the singular blessings of the position in which nature has placed us, the opportunity she has endowed us with...of cultivating general friendship, and of bringing collisions of interest to the umpirage of reason rather than of force.— Ford 8:273. (1803.)

Every man's reason [is] his own rightful umpire. This principle, with that of acquiescence in the will of the majority, will preserve us free and prosperous as long as they are sacredly observed.—Bergh 14:136. (1814.)

REASON, Eternal and Enduring.— Truth and reason are eternal. They have prevailed. And they will eternally prevail; however, in times and places they may be overborne for a while by violence, military, civil, or ecclesiastical.—Bergh 12:361. (1810.)

REASON, Surrender of.—Man, once surrendering his reason, has no remaining guard against absurdities the most monstrous, and like a ship without rudder is the sport of every wind.—Bergh 15:409. (1822.)

REBELLION, Occasionally Necessary.—I hold it that a little rebellion now and then is a good thing, and as necessary in the political world as storms in the physical. Unsuccessful rebellions, indeed, generally establish the encroachments on the rights of the people which have produced them. An observation of this truth should render honest republican governors so mild in their punishment of rebellions as not to discourage them too much. It is a medicine necessary for the sound health of government.—To James Madison. Bergh 6:65. (1787.)

The late rebellion in Massachusetts [Shays's Rebellion] has given more alarm than I think it should have done. Calculate that one rebellion in thirteen states in the course of eleven years is but one for each state in a century and a half. No country should be so long without one.—To James Madison. Bergh 6:391. (1787.)

REBELLION. See also INSURRECTION; RESISTANCE; REVOLUTION; SHAYS'S REBELLION.

REDISTRIBUTION OF WEALTH, A Violation of Fundamental Rights. —Our wish... is that the public efforts may be directed honestly to the public good, ... equality of rights maintained, and that state of property, equal or unequal, which results to every man from his own industry or that of his fathers.—Second Inaugural Address. Bergh 3:382. (1805.)

To take from one because it is thought that his own industry and that of his fathers has acquired too much, in order to spare to others who, or whose fathers, have not exercised equal industry and skill, is to violate arbitrarily the first principle of association, "the *guarantee* to everyone of a free exercise of his industry, and the fruits acquired by it." If the overgrown wealth of an individual be deemed dangerous to the state, the best corrective is the law of equal inheritance to all [his descendants] in equal degree; and the better, as this enforces a law of nature, while extra taxation violates it.—Bergh 14:466. (1816.)

REDISTRIBUTION OF WEALTH. See also POOR; PROPERTY.

REFORM, Constitutional.—Happily for us, ... when we find our constitutions defective and insufficient to secure the happiness of our people, we can assemble with all the coolness of philosophers and set [them] to rights, while every other nation on earth must have recourse to arms to amend or to restore their constitutions.—Bergh 6:295. (1787.)

REFORM, Peaceable.—Go on doing with your pen what in other times was done with the sword; show that reformation is more practicable by operation on the mind than on the body of man.—To Thomas Paine. Ford 6:88. (1792.)

REFORM, Difficulty of National.— I am sensible how far I should fall short of effecting all the reformation which reason would suggest, and experience approve, were I free to do whatever I thought best; but when we reflect how difficult it is to move or inflect the great machine of society, how impossible to advance the notions of a whole people suddenly to ideal right, we see the wisdom of Solon's remark that no more good must be attempted than the nation can bear, and that all will be chiefly to reform the waste of public money, and thus drive away the vultures who prey upon it, and improve some little upon old routines. Some new fences for securing Constitutional rights may, with the aid of a good [Congress], perhaps be attainable. —Bergh 10:255. (1801.)

REFORM, Human Progress Requires.—I am certainly not an advocate for frequent and untried changes in laws and constitutions. I think moderate imperfections had better be borne with, because, when once [these are] known, we accommodate ourselves to them and find practical means of correcting their ill effects. But I know also that laws and institutions must go hand in hand with the progress of the human mind. As that becomes more developed, more enlightened, as new discoveries are made, new truths disclosed, and manners and opinions change with the change of circumstances, institutions must advance also, and keep pace with the times. —Bergh 15:40. (1816.)

REFORM, Need for, in Federal Government.—The multiplication of public offices, increase of expense beyond income, [and] growth and entailment of a public debt are indications soliciting the employment of the pruning knife.—Bergh 15:325. (1821.)

REFORM. See also PROGRESS.

RELIGION, No Salvation by Compulsion.—The care of every man's soul belongs to himself. But what if he neglects the care of it? Well, what if he neglects the care of his health or estate, which more nearly relate to the state? Will the magistrate make a law that he shall not be poor or sick? Laws provide against injury from others, but not from ourselves. God Himself will not save men against their wills. —Ford 2:99. (1776?)

Compulsion in religion is distinguished peculiarly from compulsion in every other thing. I may grow rich by art I am compelled to follow, I may recover health by medicines I am compelled to take against my own judgment, but I cannot be saved by a worship I disbelieve and abhor. —Ford 2:102. (1776?)

RELIGION, Perspectives on Investigating.—In the first place, divest yourself of all bias in favor of novelty and singularity of opinion. Indulge them in any other subject rather

than that of religion. It is too important, and the consequences of error may be too serious. On the other hand, shake off all the fears and servile prejudices under which weak minds are servilely crouched. Fix reason firmly in her seat, and call to her tribunal every fact, every opinion. Question with boldness even the existence of a God; because, if there be one, He must more approve of the homage of reason than that of blindfolded fear....

Do not be frightened from this inquiry by any fear of its consequences. If it ends in a belief that there is no God, you will find incitements to virtue in the comfort and pleasantness you feel in its exercise, and the love of others which it will procure you. If you find reason to believe there is a God, a consciousness that you are acting under His eye, and that He approves you, will be a vast additional incitement; if that there be a future state, the hope of a happy existence in that increases the appetite to deserve it; if that Jesus was also a God, you will be comforted by a belief of his aid and love. In fine, I repeat, you must lay aside all prejudice on both sides, and neither believe nor reject anything because any other persons, or description of persons, have rejected or believed it. Your own reason is the only oracle given you by heaven, and you are answerable, not for the rightness, but uprightness of the decision.—To Peter Carr. Bergh 6:258. (1787.)

RELIGION, Emphasis on Universal Principles.—[We are a people] enlightened by a benign religion, professed, indeed, and practiced in various forms, yet all of them inculcating honesty, truth, temperance, gratitude, and the love of man; acknowledging and adoring an over-ruling Providence, which, by all its dispensations, proves that it delights in the happiness of man here and his greater happiness hereafter.—First Inaugural Address. Bergh 3:320. (1801.)

Reading, reflection, and time have convinced me that the interests of society require the observation of those moral precepts only in which all religions agree (for all forbid us to murder, steal, plunder, or bear false witness), and that we should not intermeddle with the particular dogmas in which all religions differ, and which are totally unconnected with morality. In all of them we see good men, and as many in one as another. The varieties in the structure and action of the human mind, as in those of the body, are the work of our Creator, against which it cannot be a religious duty to erect the standard of uniformity. The practice of morality being necessary for the well-being of society, He has taken care to impress its precepts so indelibly on our hearts that they shall not be effaced by the subtleties of our brain. We all agree in the obligation of the moral precepts of Jesus.—Bergh 12:315. (1809.)

I must ever believe that religion substantially good which produces an honest life, and we have been authorized, by One whom you and I equally respect, to judge of the tree by its fruit. Our particular principles of religion are a subject of account-ability to our God alone. I inquire after no man's, and trouble none with mine; nor is it given to us in this life to know whether yours or mine, our friends or foes, are exactly the right. Nay, we have heard it said that there is not a Quaker or a Baptist, a Presbyterian or an Episcopalian, a Catholic or a Protestant in heaven; that, on entering that gate, we leave those badges of schism behind, and find ourselves united in those principles only in which God has united us all. Let us not be uneasy, then, about the different roads we may pursue, as believing them to be the shortest to that, our last abode; but, following the guidance of a good conscience, let us be happy in the hope that by these different paths we shall all meet in the end. And that you and I may there meet and embrace is my earnest prayer.—Bergh 14:198. (1814.)

RELIGION, The Federal Government and.—In matters of religion, I have considered that its free exercise is placed by the Constitution independent of the powers of the [federal] government. I have therefore undertaken on no occasion to prescribe the religious exercises suited to it, but have left them, as the Constitution found them, under the direction and discipline of state or church authorities acknowledged by the several religious societies.—Ford 8:344. (1805.)

Certainly no power to prescribe any religious exercise, or to assume any authority in religious discipline, has been delegated to the general government. It must then rest with the states, as far as it can be in any human authority.—Ford 9:174. (1808.)

RELIGION, Growth of.—To me, no information could be more welcome than that the minutes of the several religious societies should prove, of late, larger additions than have been usual to their several associations.—Bergh 16:332. (1809.)

RELIGION, Differences of Opinion in.—If thinking men would have the courage to think for themselves, and to speak what they think, it would be found they do not differ in religious opinions as much as is supposed.—To John Adams. Ford 9:410. (1813.)

RELIGION, Sermons on Secular Subjects.—I am aware that arguments may be found which may twist a thread of politics into the cord of religious duties. So may they for every other branch of human art or science. Thus, for example, it is a religious duty to obey the laws of our country; the teacher of religion, therefore, must instruct us in those laws, that we may know how to obey them.... A congregation may, if they please, agree with their preacher that he shall instruct them in medicine also, or law, or politics. Then lectures in these, from the pulpit, become not only a matter of right, but of duty also. But this must be with the consent of every individual, because the association being voluntary, the mere majority has no right to apply the contributions of the minority to purposes unspecified in the agreement of the congregation.—Bergh 14:281. (1815.)

RELIGION, Jefferson's Personal.—I have ever thought religion a concern purely between our God and our consciences, for which we were accountable to Him and not to the priests. I never told my own religion, nor scrutinized that of another. I never attempted to make a convert nor wished to change another's creed. I have ever judged of the religion of others by their lives,... for it is in our lives, and not from our words, that our religion must be read. By the same test the world must judge me.—Bergh 15:60. (1816.)

I am of a sect by myself, as far as I know.—Bergh 15:203. (1819.)

An atheist...I can never be.—To John Adams. Bergh 15:425. (1823.)

RELIGION. See also BIBLE; CHRISTIANITY; DEITY; FAST DAY; GOD; JESUS CHRIST; PROVIDENCE; REVELATION.

RELIGIOUS FREEDOM, An Inalienable Right.—The people have not given the magistrate the care of souls because they could not. They could not because no man has the right to abandon the care of his salvation to another.—Ford 2:101. (1776?)

The error seems not sufficiently eradicated that the operations of the mind, as well as the acts of the body, are subject to the coercion of the laws. But our rulers can have no authority over such natural rights, only as we have submitted to them. The rights of conscience we never submitted, we could not submit. We are answerable for them to our God. The legitimate powers of government extend to such acts only as are injurious to others. But it does me no injury for my neighbor to say there are twenty gods, or no God. It neither picks my pocket nor breaks my legs. If it be said his testimony in a court cannot be relied on, reject it, then, and be the stigma on him. Constraint may make him worse by making him a hypocrite, but it will never make him a truer man. It may fix him obstinately in his errors, but will not cure them.—*Notes on Virginia.* Bergh 2:221. (1782.)

RELIGIOUS FREEDOM, Does Not Justify Criminal Acts.—Whatsoever is lawful in the commonwealth or permitted to the subject in the ordinary way cannot be forbidden to him for religious uses; and whatsoever is prejudicial to the commonwealth in their ordinary uses, and therefore prohibited by the laws, ought not to be permitted to churches in their sacred rites. For instance, it is unlawful in the ordinary course of things, or in a private house, to murder a child. It should not be permitted any sect, then, to sacrifice children. It is ordinarily lawful (or temporarily lawful) to kill calves and lambs. They may, therefore, be religiously sacrificed. But if the good of the state required a temporary suspension of killing lambs, as during a siege, sacrifices of them may then be rightfully suspended also. This is the true extent of toleration. —Ford 2:102. (1776?)

The declaration that religious faith shall be unpunished does not give impunity to criminal acts dictated by religious error.—To James Madison. Bergh 7:98. (1788.)

Jefferson in June 1805 (age 62). Medallion profile by Gilbert Stuart. Jefferson wrote to a friend several years later that family members and others had deemed this likeness "the best which has been taken of me."

RELIGIOUS FREEDOM, Part of God's Plan.—Almighty God hath created the mind free, and manifested His supreme will that free it shall remain by making it altogether insusceptible of restraint.... All attempts to influence it by temporal punishments or burdens, or by civil incapacitations, tend only to beget habits of hypocrisy and meanness, and are a departure from the plan of the Holy Author of our religion, who, being Lord both of body and mind, yet chose not to propagate it by coercions on either, as was in His almighty power to do, but to extend it by its influence on reason alone. —Bill for Establishing Religious Freedom. Ford 2:237. (1779.)

RELIGIOUS FREEDOM, Violated by Establishment of State Religions. —The impious presumption of legislators and rulers, civil as well as

The Real Thomas Jefferson

ecclesiastical, who, being themselves but fallible and uninspired men, have assumed dominion over the faith of others, setting up their own opinions and modes of thinking as the only true and infallible, and as such endeavoring to impose them on others, hath established and maintained false religions over the greatest part of the world and through all time.... To compel a man to furnish contributions of money for the propagation of opinions which he disbelieves and abhors, is sinful and tyrannical.... Even the forcing him to support this or that teacher of his own religious persuasion is depriving him of the comfortable liberty of giving his contributions to the particular pastor whose morals he would make his pattern, and whose powers he feels most persuasive to righteousness; and is withdrawing from the ministry those temporary rewards which, proceeding from an approbation of their personal conduct, are an additional incitement to earnest and unremitting labors for the instruction of mankind.—Bill for Establishing Religious Freedom. Ford 2:238. (1779.)

RELIGIOUS FREEDOM, Dangers of Government Intrusion on.—The opinions of men are not the object of civil government, nor under its jurisdiction.... To suffer the civil magistrate to intrude his powers into the field of opinion, and to restrain the profession or propagation of principles on supposition of their ill tendency, is a dangerous fallacy which at once destroys all religious liberty, because he being, of course,

judge of that tendency, will make his opinions the rule of judgment, and approve or condemn the sentiments of others only as they shall square with or suffer from his own.—Bill for Establishing Religious Freedom. Ford 2:238. (1779.)

RELIGIOUS FREEDOM, Advances the "True Religion."—Reason and free inquiry are the only effectual agents against error. Give a loose to them, [and] they will support the true religion by bringing every false one to their tribunal, to the test of their investigation. They are the natural enemies of error, and of error only. Had not the Roman government permitted free inquiry, Christianity could never have been introduced. Had not free inquiry been indulged at the era of the Reformation, the corruptions of Christianity could not have been purged away. If it be restrained now, the present corruptions will be protected, and new ones encouraged. ...Reason and experiment have been indulged, and error has fled before them. It is error alone which needs the support of government. Truth can stand by itself.—*Notes on Virginia*. Bergh 2:221. (1782.)

RELIGIOUS FREEDOM, In Pennsylvania and New York.—Our sister states of Pennsylvania and New York...have long subsisted without any establishment [i.e., state religion] at all. The experiment was new and doubtful when they made it. It has answered beyond conception. They flourish infinitely. Religion is well supported; of various kinds, indeed, but all good enough, all sufficient to preserve peace and order; or if a sect arises whose tenets would subvert morals, good sense has fair play, and reasons and laughs it out of doors, without suffering the state to be troubled with it. They do not hang more malefactors than we do. They are not more disturbed with religious dissensions. On the contrary, their harmony is unparalleled, and can be ascribed to nothing but their unbounded tolerance, because there is no other circumstance in which they differ from every nation on earth. They have made the happy discovery that the way to silence religious disputes is to take no notice of them. —*Notes on Virginia*. Bergh 2:224. (1782.)

RELIGIOUS FREEDOM, Separation of Church and State.—Believing ... that religion is a matter which lies solely between man and his God, that he owes account to none other for his faith or his worship, [and] that the legislative powers of government reach actions only, and not opinions, I contemplate with sovereign reverence that act of the whole American people which declared that their legislature [i.e., Congress] should "make no law respecting an establishment of religion, or prohibiting the free exercise thereof," thus building a wall of separation between church and state. Adhering to this expression of the supreme will of the nation in behalf of the rights of conscience, I shall see with sincere satisfaction the progress of those sentiments which tend to restore to man all his natural rights, convinced he has no natural right in opposition to his

social duties.—Bergh 16:281. (1802.)

RELIGIOUS FREEDOM, Must Be Defended.—I never will, by any word or act, bow to the shrine of intolerance, or admit a right of inquiry into the religious opinions of others. On the contrary, we are bound, you, I, and everyone, to make common cause, even with error itself, to maintain the common right of freedom of conscience. We ought with one heart and one hand to hew down the daring and dangerous efforts of those who would seduce the public opinion to substitute itself into that tyranny over religious faith which the laws have so justly abdicated.—Bergh 10:378. (1803.)

RELIGIOUS FREEDOM, The Best Support of Good Government.—Among the most inestimable of our blessings ... is that of liberty to worship our Creator in the way we think most agreeable to His will; a liberty deemed in other countries incompatible with good government, and yet proved by our experience to be its best support.—Bergh 16:291. (1807.)

RELIGIOUS FREEDOM, Guaranteed by the Constitution.—No provision in our Constitution ought to be dearer to man than that which protects the rights of conscience against the enterprises of the civil authority. It has not left the religion of its citizens under the power of its public functionaries.—Bergh 16:332. (1809.)

REPRESENTATION, Freedom and. —The Constitution of the United States ... has committed to us the important task of proving by example that a government, if organized in all its parts on the representative principle, unadulterated by the infusion of spurious elements, if founded, not in the fears and follies of man, but on his reason, on his sense of right, on the predominance of the social over his dissocial passions, may be so free as to restrain him in no moral right, and so firm as to protect him from every moral wrong.—Bergh 10:292. (1801.)

REPRESENTATION, Human Happiness and.—A representative government, responsible at short intervals of election, is that which produces the greatest sum of happiness to mankind.—Bergh 16:293. (1807.)

REPRESENTATION, Democratic. —The introduction of this new principle of representative democracy has rendered useless almost everything written before on the structure of government.—Bergh 15:66. (1816.)

REPRESENTATION. See also GOVERNMENT; MAJORITY; PEOPLE; REPUBLICAN GOVERNMENT; SELF-GOVERNMENT.

REPRISAL, Congress and.—If the case were important enough to require reprisal, and ripe for that step, Congress must be called on to take it; the right of reprisal being expressly lodged with them by the Constitution, and not with the executive.—Ford 6:259. (1793.)

REPRISAL. See also RETALIATION.

REPUBLICAN GOVERNMENT, Separation of Powers Enables Extension of.—It is hoped that by a due poise and partition of powers between the [federal] and [state] governments we have found the secret of extending the benign blessings of republicanism over still greater tracts of country than we possess, and that a subdivision may be avoided for ages, if not forever.— Ford 5:369. (1791.)

REPUBLICAN GOVERNMENT, The Universal Principle of.—The catholic principle of republicanism is that every people may establish what form of government they please, and change it as they please, the will of the nation being the only thing essential.—Ford 1:214. (1792.)

REPUBLICAN GOVERNMENT, American Commitment to.—We may still believe with security that the great body of the American people must for ages yet be substantially republican.—Ford 7:369. (1799.)

REPUBLICAN GOVERNMENT, Jefferson's Devotion to.—I feel no impulse from personal ambition to the office now proposed to me [i.e., the presidency], but...I feel a sincere wish indeed to see our government brought back to its republican principles, to see that kind of government firmly fixed to which my whole life has been devoted. I hope we shall now see it so established as that when I retire it may be under full security that we are to continue free and happy.—To Mary Jefferson Eppes. Betts & Bear, p. 197. (1801.)

The storm through which we have passed [i.e., the recent Federalist administration] has been tremendous indeed. The tough sides of our argosy have been thoroughly tried. Her strength has stood the waves into which she was steered with a view to sink her. We shall put her on her republican tack, and she will now show by the beauty of her motion the skill of her builders.... A just and solid republican government maintained here will be a standing monument and example for the aim and imitation of the people of other countries; and I join with you in the hope and belief that they will see, from our example, that a free government is of all others the most energetic; that the inquiry which has been excited among the mass of mankind by our Revolution and its consequences will ameliorate the condition of man over a great portion of the globe.—To John Dickinson. Bergh 10:217. (1801.)

REPUBLICAN GOVERNMENT, The Strongest on Earth.—I know ... that some honest men fear that a republican government cannot be strong; that this government is not strong enough. But would the honest patriot, in the full tide of successful experiment, abandon a government which has so far kept us free and firm on the theoretic and visionary fear that this government, the world's best hope, may by possibility want energy to preserve itself? I trust not. I believe this, on the contrary, the strongest government on earth. I believe it is the only one where every man, at the call of the laws, would fly to the standard of the law and would meet invasions of the public order as his own personal concern. Sometimes it is said that man cannot be trusted with the government of himself. Can he, then, be trusted with the govern-

ment of others? Or have we found angels in the forms of kings to govern him? Let history answer this question.—First Inaugural Address. Bergh 3:319. (1801.)

REPUBLICAN GOVERNMENT, Most Secure When Spread over Extensive Territory.—[The] extent [of the Republic] has saved us. While some parts were laboring under the paroxysm of delusion, others retained their senses, and time was thus given to the affected parts to recover their health. Your portion of the Union [New England] is longest recovering, because the deceivers there wear a more imposing form; but a little more time and they too will recover.—Bergh 10:231. (1801.)

The late chapter of our history furnishes ... a new proof of the falsehood of Montesquieu's doctrine, that a republic can be preserved only in a small territory. The reverse is the truth. Had our territory been even a third only of what it is, we were gone.—Ford 8:24. (1801.)

REPUBLICAN GOVERNMENT, Superiority of.—From the moment that to preserve our rights a change of government became necessary, no doubt could be entertained that a republican form was most consonant with reason, with right, with the freedom of man, and with the character and situation of our fellow citizens. To the sincere spirit of republicanism are naturally associated the love of country [and] devotion to its liberty, its rights, and its honor. Our preference to that form of government has been so far justified by its success, and the prosperity with which it has blessed us. In no portion of the earth were life, liberty, and property ever so securely held. —Bergh 16:333. (1809.)

REPUBLIC AN GOVERNMENT, Maintenance of.—Our lot has been cast by the favor of heaven in a country and under circumstances highly auspicious to our peace and prosperity, and where no pretense can arise for the degrading and oppressive establishments of Europe. It is our happiness that honorable distinctions flow only from public approbation; and that finds no object in titled dignitaries and pageants. Let us then...endeavor carefully to guard this happy state of things by keeping a watchful eye over the disaffection of wealth and ambition to the republican principles of our Constitution, and by sacrificing all our local and personal interests to the cultivation of the Union and maintenance of the authority of the laws.—Bergh 16:356. (1809.)

REPUBLICAN GOVERNMENT, And Happiness.—I conscientiously believe that governments founded in [republican principles] are more friendly to the happiness of the people at large, and especially of a people so capable of self-government as ours.—Bergh 12:436. (1810.)

REPUBLICAN GOVERNMENT, Irresistible.—A republican government is slow to move, yet when once in motion its momentum becomes irresistible.—Bergh 14:270. (1815.)

REPUBLICAN GOVERNMENT, Defined.—I believe...that action by the citizens in person in affairs within their reach and competence, and in all others by representatives chosen immediately and removable by themselves, constitutes the essence of a republic; that all governments are more or less republican in proportion as this principle enters more or less into their composition; and that a government by representation is capable of extension over a greater surface of country than one of any other form.—Bergh 14:490. (1816.)

The term *republic* is of very vague application in every language. Witness the self-styled republics of Holland, Switzerland, Genoa, Venice, Poland. Were I to assign to this term a precise and definite idea, I would say, purely and simply, it means a government by its citizens in mass, acting directly and personally, according to rules established by the majority; and that every other government is more or less republican in proportion as it has in its composition more or less of this ingredient of the direct action of the citizens.—Bergh 15:19. (1816.)

Governments are more or less republican as they have more or less of the element of popular election and control in their composition; and believing, as I do, that the mass of the citizens is the safest depository of their own rights, and especially that the evils flowing from the duperies of the people are less injurious than those from the egoism of their agents, I am a friend to that composition of government which has in it the most of this ingredient. —Bergh 15:23. (1816.)

It is a misnomer to call a government republican in which a branch of the supreme power is independent of the nation.—Ford 10:199. (1821.)

REPUBLICAN GOVERNMENT, Based on Equal Representation.— At the birth of our republic, ... the abuses of monarchy had so much filled all the space of political contemplation that we imagined everything republican which was not monarchy. We had not yet penetrated to the mother principle, that "governments are republican only in proportion as they embody the will of their people, and execute it." Hence, our first constitutions had really no leading principles in them. But experience and reflection have but more and more confirmed me in the particular importance of ... equal representation. ...

A government is republican in proportion as every member composing it has his equal voice in the direction of its concerns, not indeed in person, which would be impracticable beyond the limits of a city or small township, but by representatives chosen by himself and responsible to him at short periods; and let us bring to the test of this canon every branch of our [Virginia] constitution. ...

The true foundation of republican government is the equal right of every citizen in his person and property, and in their management. Try by this, as a tally, every provision of our constitution and see if it hangs directly on the will of the people. Reduce your legislature to a convenient number for full but orderly discussion. Let every man who fights or pays exercise his just and equal right in their election. Submit them to approbation or rejection at short intervals. Let the executive be chosen in the same way, and for the same term, by those whose agent he is to be.—Bergh 15:32. (1816.)

REPUBLICAN GOVERNMENT, Understood Only in Modern Times. —So different was the style of society then and with those people [the ancient Greeks] from what it is now and with us that I think little edification can be obtained from their writings on the subject of government. They had just ideas of the value of personal liberty, but none at all of the structure of government best calculated to preserve it. They knew no medium between a democracy (the only pure republic, but impracticable beyond the limits of a town) and an abandonment of themselves to an aristocracy, or a tyranny independent of the people. It seems not to have occurred that where the citizens cannot meet to transact their business in person, they alone have the right to choose the agents who shall transact it, and that in this way a republican or popular government, of the second grade of purity, may be exercised over any extent of country. The full experiment of a government democratical but representative was and is still reserved for us. ... The introduction of this new principle of representative democracy has rendered useless almost everything written before on the structure of government, and in a great measure relieves our regret if the political writings of Aristotle, or of any other ancient, have been lost or are unfaithfully rendered or explained to us.—Bergh 15:65. (1816.)

REPUBLICAN GOVERNMENT, Jefferson's Hopes for Future of.— I have much confidence that we shall proceed successfully for ages to come, and that . . . it will be seen that the larger the extent of country, the more firm its republican structure, if founded not on conquest but in principles of compact and equality. My hope of its duration is built much on the enlargement of the resources of life going hand in hand with the enlargement of territory, and the belief that men are disposed to live honestly if the means of doing so are open to them. With the consolation of this belief in the future result of our labors, I have that of other prophets who foretell distant events, that I shall not live to see it falsified. My theory has always been that if we are to dream, the flatteries of hope are as cheap [as], and pleasanter than, the gloom of despair.—Bergh 15:130. (1817.)

REPUBLICAN GOVERNMENT, Majority Rule the First Principle of.—The first principle of republicanism is that the *lex majoris partis* is the fundamental law of every society of individuals of equal right; to consider the will of the society enounced by the majority of a single vote as sacred as if unanimous is the first of all lessons of importance, yet the last which is thoroughly learned. This law once disregarded, no other remains but that of force, which ends necessarily in military despotism.—Ford 10:89. (1817.)

REPUBLICAN GOVERNMENT, Political Candidates and Adherence to.—It is, indeed, of little consequence who govern us, if they sincerely and zealously cherish the principles of union and republicanism.—Ford 10:192. (1821.)

REPUBLICAN GOVERNMENT, The Only Means of Securing Equal Rights.—Modern times have the signal advantage . . . of having discovered the only device by which [man's equal] rights can be secured, to wit: government by the people, acting not in person but by representatives chosen by themselves, that is to say, by every man of ripe years and sane mind who either contributes by his purse or person to the support of his country.—Bergh 15:482. (1823.)

REPUBLICAN GOVERNMENT. See also GOVERNMENT; MAJORITY; PEOPLE; REPRESENTATION; SELF-GOVERNMENT.

REPUBLICAN PARTY, Its Objective While in Power.—My great anxiety at present is to avail ourselves of our ascendancy to establish good principles and good practices; to fortify republicanism behind as many barriers as possible, that the outworks may give time to rally and save the citadel, should that be again in danger.—To John Dickinson. Bergh 10:301. (1801.)

REPUBLICAN PARTY, Friendly to the Rights of Man.—Whether the principles of the majority of our fellow citizens or of the little minority still opposing them be most friendly to the rights of man, posterity will judge; and to that arbiter I submit my own conduct with cheerfulness.—Bergh 12:333. (1809.)

REPUBLICAN PARTY, Its Confidence in the People.—The steady object [of the Republican party]... was to maintain the will of the majority of the [Constitutional] convention, and of the people themselves. We believed, with them, that man was a rational animal, endowed by nature with rights and with an innate sense of justice; and that he could be restrained from wrong and protected in right by moderate powers, confided to persons of his own choice and held to their duties by dependence on his own will.... We believed that men, enjoying in ease and security the full fruits of their own industry, enlisted by all their interests on the side of law and order, habituated to think for themselves and to follow their reason as their guide, would be more easily and safely governed than with minds nourished in error, and vitiated and debased as in Europe by ignorance, indigence, and oppression. The cherishment of the people, then, was our principle; the fear and distrust of them that of the [Federalist] party. *—Bergh 15:441. (1823.)

> *It should be noted that the political movement known in Jefferson's day as the Republican party was later called the Democratic-Republican party, and eventually the Democratic party. Today's Republican party is of later origin.—Editor.

REPUBLICAN PARTY. See also FEDERALIST PARTY.

RESISTANCE, Need to Maintain Spirit of.—The spirit of resistance to government is so valuable on certain occasions that I wish it to be always kept alive. It will often be exercised when wrong, but better so than not to be exercised at all.—Ford 4:370. (1787.)

RESISTANCE, When Justified.— When patience has begotten false estimates of its motives, when wrongs are pressed because it is believed they will be borne, resistance becomes morality.— Bergh 11:282. (1807.)

RESISTANCE. See also INSURRECTION; REBELLION; REVOLUTION.

RESPONSIBILITY, Free Government and.—Responsibility is a tremendous engine in a free government.—Bergh 8:277. (1791.)

RESPONSIBILITY, Individual.— Responsibility weighs with its heaviest force on a single head.— Ford 10:40. (1816.)

RESPONSIBILITY. See also ACCOUNTABILITY.

RETALIATION, And Moral Restraint.—The English have burned our Capitol and President's House by means of their force. We can burn their St. James's and St. Paul's by means of our money offered to their own incendiaries, of whom there are thousands in London who would do it rather than starve. But it is against the laws of civilized warfare to employ secret incendiaries. Is it not equally so to destroy the works of art by armed incendiaries? Bonaparte, possessed at times of almost every capital of Europe, with all his despotism and power, injured no monument of art. If a nation, breaking through all the restraints of civilized character, uses its means of destruction (power, for example) without distinction of objects, may we not use our means (*our* money and *their* pauperism) to retaliate their barbarous ravages? Are we obliged to use for resistance exactly the weapons chosen by them for aggression? When they destroyed Copenhagen by superior force, against all the laws of God and man, would it have been unjustifiable for the Danes to have destroyed their ships by torpedoes? Clearly not; and they and we should now be justifiable in the conflagration of St. James's and St. Paul's. And if we do not carry it into execution, it is because we think it more moral and more honorable to set a good example than follow a bad one. —Bergh 14:186. (1814.)

To do wrong is a melancholy resource, even where retaliation renders it indispensably necessary. It is better to suffer much from the scalpings, the conflagrations, [and] the rapes and rapine of savages than to countenance and strengthen such barbarisms by retortion. I have ever deemed it more honorable and more profitable, too, to set a good example than to follow a bad one. —Bergh 14:222. (1814.)

RETALIATION. See also PRISONERS OF WAR; REPRISAL.

RETIREMENT, Jefferson's Anxiety for.—As the moment of my retirement [from the presidency] approaches, I become more anxious for its arrival, and to begin at length to pass what yet remains to me of life and health in the bosom of my family and neighbors, and in communication with my friends, undisturbed by political concerns or passions. —Bergh 12:220. (1808.)

RETIREMENT, Jefferson's Feelings About.—Never did a prisoner released from his chains feel such relief as I shall on shaking off the shackles of power. Nature intended me for the tranquil pursuits of science by rendering them my supreme delight. But the enormities of the times in which I have lived have forced me to take a part in resisting them, and to commit myself on the boisterous ocean of political passions. I thank God for the opportunity of retiring from them without censure, and carrying with me the most consoling proofs of public approbation. —Bergh 12:259. (1809.)

REVELATION, Reason and.—When [God] means to make a personal revelation, He carries conviction of its authenticity to the reason He has bestowed as the umpire of truth. You believe you have been favored with such a special communication. Your reason, not mine, is to judge of this; and if it shall be His pleasure to favor me with a like admonition, I shall obey it with the same fidelity with which I would obey His known will in all cases. —Bergh 14:197. (1814.)

REVOLUTION, Right of.—Whenever any form of government becomes destructive of [man's inalienable rights], it is the right of the people to alter or to abolish it, and to institute new government.... Prudence, indeed, will dictate that governments long established should not be changed for light and transient causes; and, accordingly, all experience hath shown that mankind are more disposed to suffer, while evils are sufferable, than to right themselves by abolishing the forms to which they are accustomed. But when a long train of abuses and usurpations, pursuing invariably the same object, evinces a design to reduce them under absolute despotism, it is their right, it is their duty, to throw off such government and to provide new guards for their future security. Such has been the patient sufferance of these colonies; and such is now the necessity which constrains them to alter their former systems of government.—Declaration of Independence. Bergh 1:29. (1776.)

REVOLUTION, Difficult to Complete Successfully.—The generation which commences a revolution rarely completes it. Habituated from their infancy to passive submission of body and mind to their kings and priests, they are not qualified when called on to think and provide for themselves; and their inexperience, their ignorance and bigotry, make them instruments often, in the hands of the Bonapartes and Iturbides, to defeat their own rights and purposes. This is the present situation of Europe and Spanish America.—Ford 10:269. (1823.)

REVOLUTION. See also AMERICAN REVOLUTION; FRENCH REVOLUTION; INSURRECTION; REBELLION; RESISTANCE.

REVOLUTIONARY WAR, Need for Firmness in.—One bloody campaign will probably decide, everlastingly, our future course; and I am sorry to find a bloody campaign is decided on. If our winds and waters should not combine to rescue their shores from slavery, and General Howe's reinforcements should arrive in safety, we have hopes he will be inspirited to come out of Boston and take another drubbing; and we must drub him soundly before the sceptred tyrant will know we are not mere brutes, to crouch under his hand and kiss the rod with which he designs to scourge us.—To John Randolph. Bergh 4:33. (1775.)

REVOLUTIONARY WAR, Losses in.—I think that upon the whole [our loss during the war] has been about one-half the number lost by the British; in some instances more, but in others less. This difference is ascribed to our superiority in taking aim when we fire, every soldier in our army having been intimate with his gun from his infancy.—Ford 2:157. (1778.)

REVOLUTIONARY WAR, Rarity of Treason During.—It may be mentioned as a proof both of the lenity of our government and unanimity of its inhabitants that though this [Revolutionary] war has now raged near seven years, not a single execution for treason has taken place.—*Notes on Virginia.* Bergh 2:216. (1782.)

REVOLUTIONARY WAR, Importance of Establishing People's Rights During.—The time for fixing every essential right on a legal basis is while our rulers are honest, and ourselves united. From the conclusion of this war we shall be going downhill. It will not then be necessary to resort every moment to the people for support. They will be forgotten, therefore, and their rights disregarded. They will forget themselves, but in the sole faculty of making money, and will never think of uniting to effect a due respect for their rights. The shackles, therefore, which shall not be knocked off at the conclusion of this war will remain on us long, [and] will be made heavier and heavier till our rights shall revive or expire in a convulsion. —*Notes on Virginia.* Bergh 2:225. (1782.)

REVOLUTIONARY WAR, Difficult Conditions of.—The circumstances of our war were without example. Excluded from all commerce, even with neutral nations, without arms, money, or the means of getting them abroad, we were obliged to avail ourselves of such resources as we found at home. Great Britain, too, did not consider it as an ordinary war, but a rebellion; she did not conduct it according to the rules of war established by the law of nations, but according to her acts of Parliament, made from time to time, to suit circumstances. She would not admit our title even to the *strict rights* of ordinary war.—Ford 6:16. (1792.)

REVOLUTIONARY WAR, Justified.—The war of the Revolution will be sanctioned by the approbation of posterity through all future ages.—Ford 9:395. (1813.)

If ever there was a holy war, it was that which saved our liberties and gave us independence.—To John W. Eppes. Bergh 13:430. (1813.)

REVOLUTIONARY WAR. See also AMERICAN REVOLUTION; PRISONERS OF WAR.

RIGHT, And Wrong.—The great principles of right and wrong are legible to every reader; to pursue them requires not the aid of many counselors.—*Summary View of the Rights of British America.* Bergh 1:209. (1774.)

RIGHTS, Inalienable.—We hold these truths to be self-evident: that all men are created equal; that they are endowed by their Creator with certain inalienable rights; that among these are life, liberty, and the pursuit of happiness; that to secure these rights, governments are instituted among men, deriving their just powers from the consent of the governed; that whenever any form of government becomes destructive of these ends, it is the right of the people to alter or to abolish it, and to institute new government, laying its foundation on such principles, and organizing its powers in such form, as to them shall seem most likely to effect their safety and happiness.—Declaration of Independence. Bergh 1:29. (1776.)

RIGHTS, Guarded by Educated Citizens.—It becomes expedient for promoting the public happiness that those persons whom nature hath endowed with genius and virtue should be rendered by liberal education worthy to receive, and able to guard, the sacred deposit of the rights and liberties of their fellow citizens; and that they should be called to that charge without regard to wealth, birth, or other accidental condition or circumstance.—Boyd 2:526. (1779.)

RIGHTS, Some Should Not Be Surrendered to Government.—Our rulers can have no authority over [our] natural rights, only as we have submitted to them. The rights of conscience we never submitted, we could not submit. We are answerable for them to our God. The legitimate powers of government extend to such acts only as are injurious to others.—*Notes on Virginia.* Bergh 2:221. (1782.)

There are rights which it is useless to surrender to the government, and which governments have yet always been found to invade. These are the rights of thinking, and publishing our thoughts by speaking or writing; the right of free commerce; the right of personal freedom.—To David Humphreys. Bergh 7:323. (1789.)

RIGHTS, Best Time for Establishing.—It can never be too often repeated that the time for fixing every essential right on a legal basis is while our rulers are honest and ourselves united.—*Notes on Virginia.* Bergh 2:225. (1782.)

RIGHTS, Defense of Nation's.—The justifiable rights of our country ought not to be given up by those... appointed and trusted to defend them where they may be justly defended.—To Alexander Hamilton. Ford 6:9. (1792.)

RIGHTS, Government Exists to Secure.—It is to secure our rights that we resort to government at all.—Ford 7:4. (1795.)

No interests are dearer to men than those which ought to be secured to them by their form of government, and none deserve better of them than those who contribute to the amelioration of that form.—Bergh 12:256. (1809.)

Our legislators are not sufficiently apprised of the rightful limits of their power; that their true office is to declare and enforce only our natural rights and duties, and to take none of them from us.—Ford 10:32. (1816.)

RIGHTS, Prayer for Recovery of Mankind's.—That man may at length find favor with Heaven, and his present struggles issue in the recovery and establishment of his moral and political rights, will be the prayer of my latest breath. —Ford 7:383. (1799.)

RIGHTS, And Social Duties.—Man ... has no natural right in opposition to his social duties.—Bergh 16:282. (1802.)

RIGHTS, People the Safest Depository of.—The mass of the citizens is the safest depository of their own rights.—Ford 10:31. (1816.)

RIGHTS, Laws Should Prevent Aggression on.—No man has a natural right to commit aggression on the equal rights of another; and this is all from which the laws ought to restrain him.—Ford 10:32. (1816.)

RIGHTS, Not Affected by Emigration.—Our emigration from England to this country gave her no more rights over us than the emigrations of the Danes and Saxons gave to the present authorities of the mother country over England.—Autobiography. Bergh 1:11. (1821.)

RIGHTS, Belong Only to Persons. —Rights and powers can only belong to persons, not to things, not to mere matter unendowed with will. —Bergh 16:48. (1824.)

RIGHTS. See also EQUAL RIGHTS; MORAL LAW; NATURAL RIGHTS.

RIGHTS OF MAN, America's Assertion of the.—I hope and firmly believe that the whole world will, sooner or later, feel benefit from the issue of our assertion of the rights of man.—Bergh 13:130. (1812.)

RIGHTS OF MAN, Charter of the.
—The Declaration of Independence [is] the declaratory charter of our rights, and of the rights of man. —Ford 10:131. (1819.)

RIGHTS OF MAN, Secured by Republican Government.—The equal rights of man and the happiness of every individual are now acknowledged to be the only legitimate objects of government. Modern times have...discovered the only device by which these rights can be secured, to wit: government by the people, acting not in person but by representatives chosen by themselves, that is to say, by every man of ripe years and sound mind who contributes either by his purse or person to the support of his country. —Bergh 15:482. (1823.)

RIGHTS OF MAN, Immutable.— Nothing...is unchangeable but the inherent and unalienable rights of man.—Bergh 16:48. (1824.)

S

SALARIES, Of Public Officials.—It ...[is] inconsistent with the principles of civil liberty, and contrary to the natural rights of the other members of the society, that any body of men therein should have authority to enlarge their own powers, prerogatives, or emoluments [i.e., income] without restraint. The General Assembly

[of Virginia] cannot at their own will increase the allowance which their members are to draw from the public treasury for their expenses while in assembly, but to enable them to do so on application to the body of the people...is necessary.—Ford 2:165. (1778.)

It is just that members of [the] General Assembly, delegated by the people to transact for them the legislative business, should, while attending that business, have their reasonable sustenance defrayed, dedicating to the public service their time and labors freely and without account; and it is also expedient that the public councils should not be deprived of the aid of good and able men who might be deterred from entering into them by the insufficiency of their private fortunes to [meet] the extraordinary expenses they must necessarily incur.—Ford 2:165. (1778.)

SCHOOLS, Curriculum in.—At these [Virginia public] schools shall be taught reading, writing, and common arithmetic, and the books which shall be used therein for instructing the children to read shall be such as will, at the same time, make them acquainted with Grecian, Roman, English, and American history.—Ford 2:223. (1779.)

SCHOOLS, Fostering Genius in.
—By that part of our plan [of education in Virginia] which prescribes the selection of the youths of genius from among the classes of the poor, we hope to avail the state of those talents which nature has sown as liberally among the poor as the rich, but which perish without use if not

sought for and cultivated.—*Notes on Virginia*. Bergh 2:206. (1782.)

SCHOOLS, Ill Effects of Attending European.—An American coming to Europe for education loses in his knowledge, in his morals, in his health, in his habits, and in his happiness. I had entertained only doubts on this head before I came to Europe; what I see and hear since I came here proves more than I had even suspected.—Bergh 5:188. (1785.)

SCHOOLS. See also EDUCATION; GENIUS; UNIVERSITY; UNIVERSITY OF VIRGINIA.

SCIENCE, Mother of Freedom.—Freedom [is] the first-born daughter of science [i.e., knowledge].—Ford 7:3. (1795.)

SCIENCE, Jefferson's Delight in.—Nature intended me for the tranquil pursuits of science by rendering them my supreme delight.—Bergh 12:260. (1809.)

SCIENCE, Objects of.—The main objects of all science [are] the freedom and happiness of man.—Bergh 12:369. (1810.)

SCIENCE, Republican Government and.—Science is more important in a republican than in any other government.—Bergh 15:339. (1821.)

Science is important to the preservation of our republican government, and . . . it is also essential to its protection against foreign power.—Bergh 15:340. (1821.)

SCIENCE. See also INVENTIONS; KNOWLEDGE.

SECESSION, Suppression of Attempts at.—What does this English faction with you [in New England] mean? Their newspapers say rebellion, and that they will not remain united with us unless we will permit them to govern the majority. If this be their purpose, their anti-republican spirit, it ought to be met at once. But a government like ours should be slow in believing this, should put forth its whole might when necessary to suppress it, and promptly return to the paths of reconciliation. The extent of our country secures it, I hope, from the vindictive passions of the petty incorporations of Greece.—Ford 9:359. (1812.)

SECESSION, When Justified.—I see . . . with the deepest affliction the rapid strides with which the federal branch of our government is advancing towards the usurpation of all the rights reserved to the states, and the consolidation in itself of all powers, foreign and domestic; and that, too, by constructions which, if legitimate, leave no limits to their power. Take together the decisions of the federal court, the doctrines of the President [John Quincy Adams], and the misconstructions of the Constitutional compact acted on by the legislature of the federal branch [i.e., Congress], and it is but too evident that the three ruling branches of that department are in combination to strip their colleagues, the state authorities, of the powers reserved by them, and to exercise themselves all functions foreign and domestic. . . . And what is our resource for the preservation of the Constitution? Reason and argument? You might as well reason and argue with the marble columns encircling them.

Jefferson in June 1816 (age 73). Portrait by Bass Otis.

The representatives chosen by ourselves? They are joined in the combination, some from incorrect views of government, some from corrupt ones, sufficient voting together to outnumber the sound parts; and with majorities only of one, two, or three, bold enough to go forward in defiance. Are we then *to stand to our arms,* with the hot-headed Georgian? No. That must be the last resource, not to be thought of until much longer and greater sufferings. If every infraction of a compact of so many parties is to be resisted at once, as a dissolution of it, none can ever be formed which would last one year. We must have patience and longer endurance, then, with our brethren while [they are] under delusion; give them time for reflection and experience of consequences; keep ourselves in a situation to profit by the chapter of accidents; and separate from our companions only when the sole alternatives left are the dissolution of our union with them or submission to a government without limitation of powers. Between these two evils, when we must make a choice, there can be no hesitation. But in the meanwhile, the states should be watchful to note every material usurpation on their rights; to denounce them as they occur in the most peremptory terms; to protest against them as wrongs to which our present submission shall be considered, not as acknowledgments or precedents of right, but as a temporary yielding to the lesser evil, until their accumulation shall overweigh that of separation.— Bergh 16:146. (1825.)

[Virginians] know and value too highly the blessings of their Union ... to consider every infraction [of the Constitution] as to be met by actual resistance. They respect too affectionately the opinions of those possessing the same rights under the same instrument to make every difference of construction a ground of immediate rupture. They would, indeed, consider such a rupture as among the greatest calamities which could befall them; but not the greatest. There is yet one greater— submission to a government of unlimited powers. It is only when the hope of avoiding this shall become absolutely desperate that further forbearance could not be indulged. —Bergh 17:445. (1825.)

SECESSION. See also STATES' RIGHTS; UNION.

SECRET SOCIETIES, Government and.—As revolutionary instruments (when nothing but revolution will cure the evils of the state), they [secret societies] are necessary and indispensable, and the right to use them is inalienable by the people; but to admit them as ordinary and habitual instruments as a part of the machinery of the constitution would be to change that machinery by introducing moving powers foreign to it, and to an extent depending solely on local views, and therefore incalculable.—Ford 8:256. (1803.)

SECRET SOCIETIES, Can Be Dangerous.—I acknowledge the right of voluntary associations for laudable purposes and in moderate numbers. I acknowledge, too, the expediency, for revolutionary purposes, of general associations co-extensive with the nation. But where, as in our case, no abuses call for revolution, voluntary associations so extensive as to grapple with and control the government, should such be or become their purpose, are dangerous machines and should be frowned down in every well-regulated government.—To James Madison. Ford 10:207. (1822.)

SEDITION LAW, Nullified Because of Unconstitutionality.—I discharged every person under punishment or prosecution under the sedition law because I considered, and now consider, that law to be a nullity, as absolute and as palpable as if Congress had ordered us to fall down and worship a golden image; and that it was as much my duty to arrest its execution, in every stage, as it would have been to have rescued from the fiery furnace those who should have been cast into it for refusing to worship the image. It was accordingly done in every instance, without asking what the offenders had done or against whom they had offended, but whether the pains they were suffering were inflicted under the pretended sedition law.... [My motive was] the obligation of an oath to protect the Constitution, violated by an unauthorized act of Congress.—To Abigail Adams. Bergh 11:43. (1804.)

SEDITION LAW. See also ALIEN AND SEDITION ACTS.

SELF-GOVERNMENT, Man Is Capable of.—I have no fear but that the result of our experiment will be that men may be trusted to govern themselves without a master. Could the contrary of this be proved, I should conclude either that there is no God or that he is a malevolent being.—Bergh 6:151. (1787.)

Sometimes it is said that man cannot be trusted with the government of himself. Can he, then, be trusted with the government of others? Or have we found angels in the forms of kings to govern him? Let history answer this question.—First Inaugural Address. Bergh 3:320. (1801.)

[It is a] happy truth that man is capable of self-government, and only rendered otherwise by the moral degradation designedly superinduced on him by the wicked acts of his tyrants.—Bergh 15:130. (1817.)

SELF-GOVERNMENT, Education and.—Whenever the people are well informed, they can be trusted with their own government.—Bergh 7:253. (1789.)

SELF-GOVERNMENT, Right of.—Every man, and every body of men on earth, possesses the right of self-government. They receive it with their being from the hand of nature. Individuals exercise it by their single will, collections of men by that of their majority; for the law of the *majority* is the natural law of every society of men.—Ford 5:205. (1790.)

SELF-GOVERNMENT, Limitations on.—The right of self-government does not comprehend the government of others.—Ford 5:208. (1790.)

SELF-GOVERNMENT, Preservation of.—It behooves our citizens to be on their guard, to be firm in their principles, and full of confidence in themselves. We are able to preserve our self-government if we will but think so.—Ford 7:423. (1800.)

SELF-GOVERNMENT, An Important Experiment for Humanity.—We have no interests nor passions different from those of our fellow citizens. We have the same object, the success of representative government. Nor are we acting for ourselves alone, but for the whole human race. The event of our experiment is to show whether man can be trusted with self-government. The eyes of suffering humanity are fixed on us with anxiety as their only hope, and on such a theatre, for such a cause, we must suppress all smaller passions and local considerations.—Ford 8:156. (1802.)

SELF-GOVERNMENT, Local.—My proposition [for public education in Virginia] had for a further object to impart to these wards [small districts of five or six miles square] those portions of self-government for which they are best qualified, by confiding to them the care of their poor, their roads, police, elections, the nomination of jurors, administration of justice in small cases, [and] elementary exercises of militia; in short, to have made them little republics, with a warden at the head of each, for all those concerns which, being under their eye, they would better manage than the larger republics of the county or state. A general call of ward meetings by their wardens on the same day through the state would at any time produce the genuine sense of the people on any required point, and would enable the state to act in mass, as [the New England] people have so often done, and with so much effect, by their town meetings.—To John Adams. Bergh 13:400. (1813.)

These wards, called townships in New England, are the vital principle of their governments, and have proved themselves the wisest invention ever devised by the wit of man for the perfect exercise of self-government and for its preservation. —Ford 10:41. (1816.)

SELF-GOVERNMENT, America Conducive to.—Before the establishment of the American states, nothing was known to history but the man of the old world, crowded within limits either small or overcharged, and steeped in the vices which that situation generates. A government adapted to such men would be one thing, but a very different one that for the man of these states. Here everyone may have land to labor for himself if he chooses; or, preferring the exercise of any other industry, may exact for it such compensation as not only to afford a comfortable subsistence, but wherewith to provide for a cessation from labor in old age. Everyone, by his property or by his satisfactory situation, is interested in the support of law and order. And such men may safely and advantageously reserve to themselves a wholesome control over their public affairs, and a degree of freedom which, in the hands of the *canaille* [rabble] of the cities of Europe, would be instantly perverted to the demolition and destruction of everything public and private. The history of the last twenty-five years of France, and of the last forty years in America, nay of its last two hundred years, proves the truth of both parts of this observation.—To John Adams. Bergh 13:401. (1813.)

SELF-GOVERNMENT, Voluntary Associations and.—If [a society is] merely a voluntary association, the submission of its members will be merely voluntary also, as no act of coercion would be permitted by the general law.—Bergh 15:102. (1817.)

SELF-GOVERNMENT, Patience with Aberrations of.—We owe every ... sacrifice to ourselves, to our federal brethren, and to the world at large to pursue with temper and perseverance the great experiment which shall prove that man is capable of living in [a] society governing itself by laws self-imposed, and securing to its members the enjoyment of life, liberty, property, and peace; and further to show that, even when the government of its choice shall manifest a tendency to degeneracy, we are not at once to despair, but that the will and the watchfulness of its sounder parts will reform its aberrations, recall it to original and legitimate principles, and restrain it within the rightful limits of self-government.—Bergh 17:446. (1825.)

SELF-GOVERNMENT. See also GOVERNMENT; MAJORITY; PEOPLE; REPRESENTATION; REPUBLICAN GOVERNMENT.

SELFISHNESS, Leads Man Away from Moral Duties.—Self-love ... is no part of morality. Indeed it is exactly its counterpart. It is the sole antagonist of virtue, leading us constantly by our propensities to self-gratification in violation of our moral duties to other. Accordingly, it is against this enemy that are erected the batteries of moralists and religionists, as the only obstacle to the practice of morality. Take from man his selfish propensities, and he can have nothing to seduce him from the practice of virtue. Or subdue those propensities by education, instruction, or restraint, and virtue remains without a competitor.—Bergh 14:140. (1814.)

SELF-RELIANCE, Part of the American Character.—It is a part of the American character to consider nothing as desperate; to surmount every difficulty by resolution and contrivance. In Europe there are shops for every want. Its inhabitants therefore have no idea that their wants can be furnished otherwise. Remote from all other aid, we are obliged to invent and execute; to find means within ourselves, and not to lean on others.—To Martha Jefferson. Betts & Bear, p. 35. (1787.)

SENATE (United States), Wisdom and Stability of.—The Senate ... must from its constitution be a wise and steady body.—Bergh 6:443. (1788.)

SENATE (United States), Honorable.—The Senate is the most honorable and independent station in our government, one where you can peculiarly raise yourself in the public estimation.—Ford 5:244. (1790.)

SENATE (United States), Excesses of.—The Senate was intended as a check on the will of the Representatives when too hasty. They are not only that, but completely so on the will of the people also; and in my opinion are heaping coals of fire, not only on their persons, but on their body as a branch of the [Congress]. ... It seems that the opinion is fairly launched into public that they should be placed under the control of a more frequent recurrence to the will of their constituents. This seems requisite to complete the experiment whether they do more harm or good. —To James Madison. Ford 6:511. (1794.)

SENATE (United States), Term of Office in.—The term of office to our Senate, like that of the judges, is too long for my approbation.—Ford 9:420. (1813.)

SENATE (United States), Limitations on Advice and Consent of.—

The Constitution has made [the Senate's] advice necessary to confirm a treaty, but not to reject it. This has been blamed by some, but I have never doubted its soundness. —Bergh 15:215. (1819.)

SENATE (United States). See also CONGRESS; FEDERAL GOVERNMENT; LEGISLATURES; TREATIES.

SEPARATION OF POWERS, The First Principle of Good Government.—The first principle of a good government is, certainly, a distribution of its powers into executive, judiciary, and legislative, and a subdivision of the latter into two or three branches.—To John Adams. Ford 4:454. (1787.)

SEPARATION OF POWERS, Must Be Maintained.—I wish to preserve the line drawn by the federal Constitution between the [federal] and [state] governments as it stands at present, and to take every prudent means of preventing either from stepping over it.—Bergh 8:276. (1791.)

I see with great pleasure every testimony to the principles of pure republicanism, and every effort to preserve untouched that partition of the sovereignty which our excellent Constitution has made between the [federal] and [state] governments.— Ford 5:369. (1791.)

If the three powers [i.e., legislative, executive, and judiciary] maintain their mutual independence [of] each other, [our government] may last long; but not so if either can assume the authorities of the other. —Bergh 15:278. (1820.)

When all government, domestic and foreign, in little as in great things, shall be drawn to Washington as the center of all power, it will render powerless the checks provided of one government on another and will become as venal and oppressive as the government from which we separated.—Bergh 15:332. (1821.)

I believe the states can best govern our home concerns, and the general government our foreign ones. I wish, therefore, to see maintained that wholesome distribution of powers established by the Constitution for the limitation of both; and never to see all offices transferred to Washington, where, further withdrawn from the eyes of the people, they may more secretly be bought and sold as at market.—Bergh 15:450. (1823.)

SEPARATION OF POWERS, Preserved by Strengthening the State Governments.—Though the experiment has not yet had a long enough course to show us from which quarter encroachments are most to be feared, yet it is easy to foresee, from the nature of things, that the encroachments of the state governments will tend to an excess of liberty, which will correct itself,...while those of the general government will tend to monarchy, which will fortify itself from day to day instead of working its own cure, as all experience shows. I would rather be exposed to the inconveniences attending too much liberty than those attending too small a degree of it. Then it is important to strengthen the state governments;

and as this cannot be done by any change in the federal Constitution (for the preservation of that is all we need contend for), it must be done by the states themselves, erecting such barriers at the Constitutional line as cannot be surmounted either by themselves or by the general government. The only barrier in their power is a wise government. A weak one will lose ground in every contest.—Bergh 8:276. (1791.)

SEPARATION OF POWERS, Horizontal, a Leading Principle of the Constitution.—The principle of the Constitution is that of a separation of legislative, executive, and judiciary functions, except in cases specified. If this principle be not expressed in direct terms, it is clearly the spirit of the Constitution, and it ought to be so commented and acted on by every friend of free government.—To James Madison. Ford 7:108. (1797.)

The leading principle of our Constitution is the independence of the legislative, executive, and judiciary of one another.—Ford 9:60. (1807.)

My construction of the Constitution...is that each department is truly independent of the others, and has an equal right to decide for itself what is the meaning of the Constitution in the cases submitted to its action; and especially where it is to act ultimately and without appeal.—Bergh 15:214. (1819.)

SEPARATION OF POWERS, Threatened by the Federal Government.—It is a singular phenomenon that while our state governments are the very *best in the world,* without exception or comparison, our general government has in the rapid course of nine or ten years become more arbitrary, and has swallowed more of the public liberty than even that of England.—Ford 2:311. (1798.)

It is but too evident that the branches of our foreign department of government [i.e., of the federal government], executive, judiciary, and legislative, are in combination to usurp the powers of the domestic branch, all . . . reserved to the states, and [to] consolidate themselves into a single government without limitation of powers. I will not trouble you with details of the instances which are threadbare and unheeded. The only question is, what is to be done? Shall we give up the ship? No, by heavens, while a hand remains able to keep the deck. Shall we, with the hot-headed Georgian, stand at once to our arms? Not yet, nor until the evil, the only greater one than separation, shall be all upon us—that of living under a government of discretion. Between these alternatives there can be no hesitation. But, again, what are we to do? . . . We had better, at present, rest awhile on our oars and see which way the tide will set in Congress and in the state legislatures.—Ford 10:358. (1826.)

SEPARATION OF POWERS, Practicality of.—Our country is too large to have all its affairs directed by a single government. Public servants at such a distance, and from under the eye of their constituents, must, from the circumstance of distance, be unable to administer and overlook all the details necessary for the good

government of the citizens; and the same circumstance, by rendering detection impossible to their constituents, will invite the public agents to corruption, plunder, and waste.—Bergh 10:167. (1800.)

In government, as well as in every other business of life, it is by division and subdivision of duties alone that all matters, great and small, can be managed to perfection. And the whole is cemented by giving to every citizen, personally, a part in the administration of the public affairs.—Ford 10:41. (1816.)

SEPARATION OF POWERS, Constitutional Theory of.—The true theory of our Constitution is surely the wisest and best, that the states are independent as to everything within themselves, and united as to everything respecting foreign affairs. Let the general government be reduced to foreign concerns only, and let our affairs be disentangled from those of all other nations, except as to commerce, which the merchants will manage the better the more they are left free to manage for themselves, and our general government may be reduced to a very simple organization, and a very inexpensive one; a few plain duties to be performed by a few servants.—Bergh 10:168. (1800.)

SEPARATION OF POWERS, Wisdom of.—Our citizens have wisely formed themselves into one nation as to others, and several states as among themselves. To the united nation belong our external and mutual relations; to each state severally the care of our persons, our property, our reputation and religious freedom. This wise distribution, if carefully preserved, will prove, I trust from example, that while smaller governments are better adapted to the ordinary objects of society, larger confederations more effectually secure independence and the preservation of republican government.—Bergh 10:263. (1801.)

SEPARATION OF POWERS, To Aid Education and Local Self-Government.—I have... two great measures at heart, without which no republic can maintain itself in strength: 1. That of general education, to enable every man to judge for himself what will secure or endanger his freedom. 2. To divide every county [of Virginia] into hundreds, of such size that all the children of each will be within reach of a central school in it. But this division looks to many other fundamental provisions. Every hundred, besides a school, should have a justice of the peace, a constable, and a captain of militia. These officers, or some others within the hundred, should be a corporation to manage all its concerns, to take care of its roads, its poor, and its police by patrols, etc. (as the selectmen of the eastern townships). Every hundred should elect one or two jurors to serve where requisite, and all other elections should be made in the hundreds separately, and the votes of all the hundreds be brought together. Our present captaincies might be declared hundreds for the present, with a power to the courts to alter them occasionally. These little republics would be the main

strength of the great one. We owe to them the vigor given to our Revolution in its commencement in the eastern states, and by them the eastern states were enabled to repeal the embargo in opposition to the middle, southern, and western states and their large and lubberly division into counties which can never be assembled. General orders are given out from a center to the foreman of every hundred, as to the sergeants of an army, and the whole nation is thrown into energetic action in the same direction in one instant and as one man, and becomes absolutely irresistible.... But our children will be as wise as we are and will establish in the fulness of time those things not yet ripe for establishment.—Ford 9:277. (1810.)

SEPARATION OF POWERS, The Key to Good and Safe Government.—The way to have good and safe government is not to trust it all to one, but to divide it among the many, distributing to everyone exactly the functions he is competent to. Let the national government be entrusted with the defense of the nation, and its foreign and federal relations; the state governments with the civil rights, laws, police, and administration of what concerns the state generally; the counties with the local concerns of the counties; and each ward direct the interests within itself. It is by dividing and subdividing these republics from the great national one down through all its subordinations until it ends in the administration of every man's farm by himself, by placing under everyone what his own eye may superintend, that all will be done for the best.—Bergh 14:421. (1816.)

It is not by the consolidation or concentration of powers, but by their distribution that good government is effected. Were not this great country already divided into states, that division must be made, that each might do for itself what concerns itself directly, and what it can so much better do than a distant authority. Every state again is divided into counties, each to take care of what lies within its local bounds; each county again into townships or wards, to manage minuter details; and every ward into farms, to be governed each by its individual proprietor.... It is by this partition of cares, descending in gradation from general to particular, that the mass of human affairs may be best managed for the good and prosperity of all.—Autobiography. Bergh 1:122. (1821.)

SEPARATION OF POWERS, Vertical, Provides Checks and Balances. —The elementary republics of the wards, the county republics, the state republics, and the republic of the Union would form a gradation of authorities standing each on the basis of law, holding every one its delegated share of powers, and constituting truly a system of fundamental balances and checks for the government. Where every man is a sharer in the direction of his ward republic, or of some of the higher ones, and feels that he is a participator in the government of affairs, not merely at an election one

day in the year, but every day; when there shall not be a man in the state who will not be a member of some one of its councils, great or small, he will let the heart be torn out of his body sooner than his power be wrested from him by a Caesar or a Bonaparte.—Bergh 14:422. (1816.)

A county of a state...cannot be governed [solely] by its own laws, but must be subject to those of the state of which it is a part.—Bergh 15:102. (1817.)

SEPARATION OF POWERS, Enables the People to Eliminate Corruption.—The article nearest my heart is the division of counties into wards. These will be pure and elementary republics, the sum of all which, taken together, composes the state, and will make of the whole a true democracy as to the business of the wards, which is that of nearest and daily concern. The affairs of the larger sections, of counties, of states, and of the Union, not admitting personal transactions by the people, will be delegated to agents elected by themselves; and representation will thus be substituted where personal action becomes impracticable. Yet even over these representative organs, should they become corrupt and perverted, the division into wards, constituting the people...a regularly organized power, enables them by that organization to crush, regularly and peaceably, the usurpations of their unfaithful agents, and rescues them from the dreadful necessity of doing it insurrectionally. In this way we shall be as republican as a large society can be, and secure the continuance of purity in our government by the salutary, peaceable, and regular control of the people.—Ford 10:45. (1816.)

SEPARATION OF POWERS. See also CENTRALIZATION; CONSTITUTION (U.S.); FEDERAL GOVERNMENT; GOVERNMENT; JUDICIARY; STATES; STATES' RIGHTS; SUPREME COURT.

SERVICE, And Happiness.—Nothing [makes] me more happy than to render any service in my power, of whatever description.—Bergh 5:163. (1785.)

SERVICE, Reward of.—If, in the course of my life, it has been in any degree useful to the cause of humanity, the fact itself bears its full reward.—Ford 9:515. (1815.)

SERVICE. See also DUTY.

SHAYS'S REBELLION, Conduct and Motives of.—Can history produce an instance of rebellion so honorably conducted? I say nothing of its motives. They were founded in ignorance, not wickedness. God forbid we should ever be twenty years without such a rebellion. The people cannot be all, and always, well informed. The part which is wrong will be discontented in proportion to the importance of the facts they misconceive. If they remain quiet under such misconceptions it is a lethargy, the forerunner of death to the public liberty.—Ford 4:467. (1787.)

SIMPLICITY, Governmental.—I am for a government rigorously frugal and simple.—Ford 7:327. (1799.)

SIMPLICITY, Individual.—Let us deserve well of our country by making her interests the end of all our plans, and not our own pomp, patronage, and irresponsibility.—Ford 8:141. (1802.)

SLANDER, By the Federalist Party.—You have indeed received the Federalist unction of lying and slandering. But who has not? Who will ever again come into eminent office unanointed with this chrism? It seems to be fixed that falsehood and calumny are to be their ordinary engines of opposition; engines which will not be entirely without effect.... If we suffer ourselves to be frightened from our post by mere lying, surely the enemy will use that weapon; for what one [is] so cheap to those of whose system of politics morality makes no part?—To Judge James Sullivan. Bergh 11:72. (1805.)

SLANDER, Requires Forbearance of Patriots.—The patriot, like the Christian, must learn that to bear revilings and persecutions is a part of his duty; and in proportion as the trial is severe, firmness under it becomes more requisite and praiseworthy. It requires, indeed, self-command. But that will be fortified in proportion as the calls for its exercise are repeated.—Bergh 11:73. (1805.)

SLANDER, Punishment for.—Slanderers I have thought it best to leave to the scourge of public opinion.—Ford 9:63. (1807.)

SLANDER, Jefferson's Answer to.—As to Federalist slanders, I never wished them to be answered but by the tenor of my life, half a century of which has been on a theater at which the public have been spectators and competent judges of its merit. Their approbation has taught a lesson, useful to the world, that the man who fears no truths has nothing to fear from lies. I should have fancied myself half guilty had I condescended to put pen to paper in refutation of their falsehoods, or drawn to them respect by any notice from myself. —Ford 10:27. (1816.)

I am not afraid to trust to the justice and good sense of my fellow citizens on future as on former attempts to lessen me in their esteem.—Ford 10:211. (1822.)

My rule of life has been never to harass the public with fendings and provings of personal slanders.... I have ever trusted to the justice and consideration of my fellow citizens, and have no reason to repent [of] it or to change my course. At this time of life, too, tranquility is the *summum bonum*. But although I decline all newspaper controversy, yet when falsehoods have been advanced within the knowledge of no one so much as myself, I have sometimes deposited a contradiction in the hands of a friend, which, if worth preservation, may, when I am no more, nor those whom I might offend, throw light on history and recall that into the path of truth. —To Martin Van Buren. Bergh 16:68. (1824.)

SLANDER. See also LIBEL.

SLAVERY, King George III and. —He has waged cruel war against human nature itself, violating its most sacred rights of life and liberty in the persons of a distant people who never offended him, captivating and carrying them into slavery in another hemisphere, or to incur miserable death in their transportation thither. This piratical warfare, the opprobrium of *infidel* powers, is the warfare of the *Christian* king of Great Britain. Determined to keep open a market where *men* should be bought and sold, he has prostituted his negative [i.e., veto] for suppressing every legislative attempt to prohibit or to restrain this execrable commerce.—Declaration of Independence as drafted by Jefferson. Bergh 1:34. (1776.)

SLAVERY, Evils of.—There must doubtless be an unhappy influence on the manners of our people produced by the existence of slavery among us. The whole commerce between master and slave is a perpetual exercise of the most boisterous passions, the most unremitting despotism on the one part, and degrading submissions on the other. Our children see this, and learn to imitate it; for man is an imitative animal. This quality is the germ of all education in him. From his cradle to his grave he is learning to do what he sees others do. If a parent could find no motive either in his philanthropy or his self-love for restraining the intemperance of passion towards his slave, it should always be a sufficient one that his child is present. But generally it is not sufficient. The parent storms, the child looks on, catches the lineaments of wrath, puts on the same airs in the circle of smaller slaves, gives a loose to the worst of passions, and thus nursed, educated, and daily exercised in tyranny, cannot but be stamped by it with odious peculiarities. The man must be a prodigy who can retain his manners and morals undepraved by such circumstances.

And with what execration should the statesman be loaded who, permitting one half the citizens thus to trample on the rights of the other, transforms those into despots and these into enemies, destroys the morals of the one part and the *amor patriae* of the other. For if a slave can have a country in this world, it must be any other in preference to that in which he is born to live and labor for another; in which he must lock up the faculties of his nature, contribute as far as depends on his individual endeavors to the evanishment of the human race, or entail his own miserable condition on the endless generations proceeding from him.

With the morals of the people, their industry also is destroyed. For in a warm climate, no man will labor for himself who can make another labor for him. This is so true that of the proprietors of slaves a very small proportion indeed are ever seen to labor.—*Notes on Virginia.* Bergh 2:225. (1782.)

SLAVERY, Abolition of.—Can the liberties of a nation be thought secure when we have removed their only firm basis, a conviction in the minds of the people that these liberties are ... the gift of God? That they are not to be violated but with His wrath? Indeed, I tremble for my country when I reflect that God is just; that His justice cannot sleep forever; that considering numbers, nature, and natural means only, a revolution of the wheel of fortune, an exchange of situation, is among possible events; that it may become probable by supernatural interference! The Almighty has no attribute which can take side with us in such a contest. But...I think a change already perceptible since the origin of the present Revolution. The spirit of the master is abating, that of the slave rising from the dust, his condition mollifying, the way I hope preparing, under the auspices of heaven, for a total emancipation, and that this is disposed, in the order of events, to be with the consent of the masters rather than by their extirpation.—*Notes on Virginia.* Bergh 2:227. (1782.)

I have long since given up the expectation of any early provision for the extinguishment of slavery among us. There are many virtuous men who would make any sacrifices to effect it, many equally virtuous who persuade themselves either that the thing is not wrong or that it cannot be remedied, and very many with whom interest is morality. The older we grow, the larger we are disposed to believe the last party to be. But interest is really going over to the side of morality. The value of the slave is every day lessening, his burden on his master daily increasing. Interest is therefore preparing the [master's] disposition to be just;

and this will be goaded from time to time by the insurrectionary spirit of the slaves. This is easily quelled in its first efforts; but from being local it will become general, and whenever it does it will rise more formidable after every defeat until we shall be forced, after dreadful scenes and sufferings, to release them in their own way, which, without such sufferings, we might now model after our own convenience.—Ford 8:340. (1805.)

There is nothing I would not sacrifice to a practicable plan of abolishing every vestige of this moral and political depravity.—Bergh 14:184. (1814.)

I can say with conscious truth that there is not a man on earth who would sacrifice more than I would to relieve us from this heavy reproach in any *practicable* way. The cession of that kind of property, for so it is misnamed, is a bagatelle which would not cost me a second thought, if in that way a general emancipation . . . could be effected.—Bergh 15:249. (1820.)

In 1769 I became a member of the [Virginia] legislature. . . . I made one effort in that body for the permission of the emancipation of slaves, which was rejected; and indeed, during the regal government nothing liberal could expect success.—Autobiography. Bergh 1:4. (1821.)

Nothing is more certainly written in the book of fate than that these people are to be free.—Autobiography. Bergh 1:72. (1821.)

At the age of eighty-two, with one foot in the grave and the other uplifted to follow it, I do not permit myself to take part in any new enterprises, even for bettering the condition of man, not even in the great one which is the subject of your letter [i.e., the abolition of slavery], and which has been through life that of my greatest anxieties. The march of events has not been such as to render its completion practicable within the limits of time allotted to me; and I leave its accomplishment as the work of another generation. And I am cheered when I see that on which it is devolved taking it up with so much good will, and such minds engaged in its encouragement. The abolition of the evil is not impossible; it ought never, therefore, to be despaired of. Every plan should be adopted, every experiment tried, which may do something towards the ultimate object.—Bergh 16:119. (1825.)

SLAVERY, May Be Avenged by God.—We must await with patience the workings of an overruling Providence, and hope that that is preparing the deliverance of these, our suffering brethren. When the measure of their tears shall be full, when their groans shall have involved heaven itself in darkness, doubtless a God of justice will awaken to their distress, and by diffusing light and liberality among their oppressors, or, at length, by His exterminating thunder, manifest His attention to the things of this world, and that they are not left to the guidance of a blind fatality.—Ford 4:185. (1786.)

SLAVERY, Hypocrisy of.—What a stupendous, what an incomprehensible machine is man, who can endure toil, famine, stripes, imprisonment, and death itself in vindication of his own liberty, and the next moment be deaf to all those motives whose power supported him through his trial, and inflict on his fellow men a bondage, one hour of which is fraught with more misery than ages of that which he rose in rebellion to oppose!—Ford 4:185. (1786.)

SLAVERY, An Abomination.—This abomination must have an end. And there is a superior bench reserved in heaven for those who hasten it.—Ford 4:410. (1787.)

SLAVERY, A Moral and Political Error.—Whatever may have been the circumstances which influenced our forefathers to permit the introduction of personal bondage into any part of these states, and to participate in the wrongs committed on an unoffending quarter of the globe, we may rejoice that such circumstances, and such a sense of them, exist no longer. It is honorable to the nation at large that their [Congress] availed themselves of the first practicable moment for arresting the progress of this great moral and political error.—Bergh 16:290. (1807.)

SLAVERY, A Moral Reproach.—My sentiments on the subject of slavery have long since been in the possession of the public, and time has only served to give them stronger root. The love of justice and the love of country plead equally the cause of these people; and it is a moral reproach to us that they should have pleaded it so long in vain.... Yet the hour of emancipation is advancing in the march of time. It will come.—Ford 9:477. (1814.)

SLAVERY. See also MISSOURI; NEGROES.

SOCIALISM. See POOR; PROPERTY; REDISTRIBUTION OF WEALTH.

SOCIETY, Ill Effects of Withdrawing from.—I am convinced our own happiness requires that we should continue to mix with the world, and to keep pace with it as it goes; and that every person who retires from free communication with it is severely punished afterwards by the state of mind into which [he gets], and which can only be prevented by feeding our sociable principles. I can speak from experience on this subject. From 1793 to 1797 I remained closely at home, saw none but those who came there, and at length became very sensible of the ill effect it had upon my own mind, and of its direct and irresistible tendency to render me unfit for society and uneasy when necessarily engaged in it. I felt enough of the effect of withdrawing from the world then to see that it led to an antisocial and misanthropic state of mind, which severely punishes him who gives in to it; and it will be a lesson I never shall forget.—To Mary Jefferson Eppes. Betts & Bear, p. 219. (1802.)

SOCIETY. See also COMMUNAL SOCIETIES; SECRET SOCIETIES.

SOCRATES, "Demon" of.—He was too wise to believe, and too honest to pretend, that he had real and familiar converse with a superior and invisible being. He probably considered the suggestions of his conscience, or reason, as revelations or inspirations from the Supreme Mind, bestowed, on important occasions, by a special superintending Providence.—To John Adams. Bergh 13:391. (1813.)

SOVEREIGNTY, Justice and.—The administration of justice is a branch of the sovereignty over a country, and belongs exclusively to the nation inhabiting it. No foreign power can pretend to participate in their jurisdiction, or that their citizens received there are not subject to it.—Ford 6:56. (1792.)

SPANISH LANGUAGE, Utility of.—Bestow great attention on [the Spanish language], and endeavor to acquire an accurate knowledge of it. Our future connections with Spain and Spanish America will render that language a valuable acquisition. The ancient history of that part of America, too, is written in that language.—To Peter Carr. Bergh 6:257. (1787.)

SPECULATION, Agriculture vs.—Though we shall be neutrals, and as such shall derive considerable pecuniary advantages, yet I think we shall lose in happiness and morals by being launched again into the ocean of speculation, led to overtrade ourselves, tempted to become sea-robbers under French colors, and to quit the pursuits of agriculture, the surest road to affluence and best preservative of morals.—Bergh 6:272. (1787.)

A war wherein France, Holland, and England should be parties seems, *prima facie*, to promise much advantage to us. But in the first place, no war can be safe for us which threatens France with an unfavorable issue; and in the next, it will probably embark us again into the ocean of speculation, engage us to overtrade ourselves, convert us into sea-rovers under French and Dutch colors, [and] divert us from agriculture, which is our wisest pursuit because it will in the end contribute most to real wealth, good morals, and happiness. The wealth acquired by speculation and plunder is fugacious in its nature and fills society with the spirit of gambling. The moderate and sure income of husbandry begets permanent improvement, quiet life, and orderly conduct, both public and private.—To George Washington. Bergh 6:277. (1787.)

SPECULATION. See also CHANCE; GAMBLING; LOTTERIES.

SPEECH, Freedom of, Guaranteed by the Constitution.—One of the amendments to the Constitution . . . expressly declares that "Congress shall make no law respecting an establishment of religion, or prohibiting the free exercise thereof, or abridging the freedom of speech, or of the press," thereby guarding in the same sentence, and under the same words, the freedom of religion, of speech, and of the press; insomuch that whatever violates either throws down the sanctuary which covers the others.—Kentucky Resolutions. Bergh 17:382. (1798.)

SPEECH, Freedom of, a Guard to Liberty.—[The] liberty of speaking and writing...guards our other liberties.—Bergh 16:304. (1808.)

SPEECH. See also ORATORY.

SPELLING, Correct, Produces Praise.—Take care that you never spell a word wrong. Always before you write a word, consider how it is spelled; and if you do not remember it, turn to a dictionary. It produces great praise to a lady to spell well.— To Martha Jefferson. Betts & Bear, p. 20. (1783.)

SPELLING. See also WRITING.

STATES, Bulwarks of Republican Government.—The state governments...[are] the most competent administrations for our domestic concerns and the surest bulwarks against anti-republican tendencies. —First Inaugural Address. Bergh 3:321. (1801.)

STATES, Need for Uniform Laws Among the.—Many are the exercises of power reserved to the states wherein uniformity of proceeding would be advantageous to all. Such are quarantines, health laws, regulations of the press, banking institutions, training militia, etc.—Ford 9:76. (1807.)

STATES, Bastions of Liberty.—The. true barriers of our liberty in this country are our state governments; and the wisest conservative power ever contrived by man is that of which our Revolution and present government found us possessed. Seventeen distinct states, amalgamated into one as to their foreign

Jefferson in March 1821 (age 77). Portrait by Thomas Sully.

concerns, but single and independent as to their internal administration, regularly organized with a legislature and governor resting on the choice of the people, and enlightened by a free press, can never be so fascinated by the arts of one man as to submit voluntarily to his usurpation. Nor can they be constrained to it by any force he can possess.—Bergh 13:19. (1811.)

STATES, Equality in Size.—In establishing new states, regard is had to a certain degree of equality in size.—Bergh 15:102. (1817.)

STATES, More Efficient in Domestic Matters.—The extent of our country was so great, and its former division into distinct states so established, that we thought it better to confederate as to foreign affairs only. Every state retained its self-government in domestic matters, as better qualified to direct them to the good and satisfaction of their citizens than a general government so distant from its remoter citizens, and so little familiar with the local peculiarities of the different parts. —Bergh 15:483. (1823.)

STATES. See also CENTRALIZATION; COLONIES (American); FEDERAL GOVERNMENT; SECESSION; SELF-GOVERNMENT; SEPARATION OF POWERS; UNION; UNITED STATES.

STATES' RIGHTS, Fortified by Wise State Government.—I wish to preserve the line drawn by the federal Constitution between the [federal] and [state] governments as it stands at present, and to take every prudent means of preventing either from stepping over it. Though the experiment has not yet had a long enough course to show us from which quarter encroachments are most to be feared, yet it is easy to foresee from the nature of things that the encroachments of the state governments will tend to an excess of liberty, which will correct itself, ... while those of the general government will tend to monarchy, which will fortify itself from day to day instead of working its own cure, as all experience shows. I would rather be exposed to the inconveniences attending too much liberty than those attending too small a degree of it. Then it is important to strengthen the state governments; and as this cannot be done by any change in the federal Constitution (for the preservation of that is all we need contend for), it must be done by the states themselves, erecting such barriers at the Constitutional line as cannot be surmounted either by themselves or by the general government. The only barrier in their power is a wise government. A weak one will lose ground in every contest. To obtain a wise and an able government, I consider the following changes as important: Render the legislature a desirable station by lessening the number of representatives (say to 100) and lengthening somewhat their term, and proportion them equally among the electors. Adopt also a better mode of appointing [state] senators. Render the executive [i.e., governorship] a more desirable post to men of abilities by making it more independent of the legislature; to wit, let him be chosen by other electors, for a longer time, and ineligible forever after. Responsibility is a tremendous engine in a free government. Let him feel the whole weight of it, then, by taking away the shelter of his executive council. Experience both ways has already established the superiority of this measure. Render the judiciary respectable by every possible means; to wit, firm tenure in office, competent salaries, and reduction of their numbers. Men of high learning and abilities are few in every country; and by taking in those who are not so, the able part of the body have their hands tied by the unable. This branch of the government [i.e., the judiciary] will have the weight of the conflict on their hands, because they will be the last appeal of reason. These are my general ideas of amendments; but, preserving the ends, I should be flexible and conciliatory as to the means. —Bergh 8:276. (1791.)

STATES' RIGHTS, Protected by the Constitution.—The several states composing the United States of America are not united on the principle of unlimited submission to their general government; but... by a compact under the style and title of a Constitution for the United States, and of amendments thereto, they constituted a general government for special purposes [and] delegated to that government certain definite powers, reserving, each state to itself, the residuary mass of right to their own self-government; and... whensoever the general government assumes undelegated powers, its acts are unauthoritative, void, and of no force.... To this compact each state acceded as a state, and is an integral party, its co-states forming, as to itself, the other party.... The government created by this compact was not made the exclusive or final judge of the extent of the powers delegated to itself, since that would have made its discretion, and not the Constitution, the measure of its powers; but...as in all cases of compact among powers having no common judge, each party has an equal right to judge for itself, as well of infractions as of the mode and measure of redress.—Kentucky Resolutions. Bergh 17:379. (1798.)

STATES' RIGHTS, Violations of, Harmful.—To take from the states all the powers of self-government and transfer them to a general and consolidated government, without regard to the special delegations and reservations solemnly agreed to in [the federal] compact, is not for the peace, happiness, or prosperity of these' states.—Kentucky Resolutions. Bergh 17:386. (1798.)

STATES' RIGHTS, Dual Sovereignties of Federal Powers and.—It is a fatal heresy to suppose that either our state governments are superior to the federal, or the federal to the states. The people, to whom all authority belongs, have divided the powers of government into two distinct departments, the leading characters of which are *foreign* and *domestic;* and they have appointed for each a distinct set of functionaries. These they have made coordinate, checking and balancing each other, like the three cardinal departments in the individual states; each equally supreme as to the powers delegated to itself, and neither authorized ultimately to decide what belongs to itself, or to its coparcener in government; as independent, in fact, as different nations. A spirit of forbearance and compromise, therefore, and not of encroachment and usurpation, is the healing balm of such a Constitution; and each party should prudently shrink from all approach to the line of demarcation instead of rashly overleaping it, or throwing grapples ahead to haul to hereafter. But finally, the peculiar happiness of our blessed system is that in differences of opinion between these different sets of servants, the appeal is to neither, but to their employers [i.e., the people], peaceably assembled by their representatives in convention. This is more rational than...the cannon's mouth.—Ford 10:190. (1821.)

Maintain the line of power marked by the Constitution between the two coordinate governments, each sovereign and independent in its department; the states as to everything relating to themselves and their state, the general government as to everything relating to things or persons out of a particular state. The one may be strictly called the domestic branch of government, which is sectional but sovereign; the other, the foreign branch of government, coordinate with the... domestic and equally sovereign on its own side of the line.—Ford 10:263. (1823.)

The best general key for the solution of questions of power between our governments is the fact that "every foreign and federal power is given to the federal government, and to the states every power purely domestic." I recollect but one instance of control vested in the federal over the state authorities in a matter purely domestic, which is that of metallic tenders. The federal is, in truth, our foreign government, which department alone is taken from the sovereignty of the separate states.—Bergh 16:15. (1824.)

The radical idea of the character of the Constitution of our government, which I have adopted as a key in cases of doubtful construction, is that the whole field of government is divided into two departments, domestic and foreign (the states in

their mutual relations being of the latter); that the former department is reserved exclusively to respective states within their own limits, and the latter assigned to a separate set of functionaries, constituting what may be called the foreign branch, which, instead of a federal basis, is established as a distinct government *quoad hoc*, acting as the domestic branch does on the citizens, directly and coercively; that these departments have distinct directories, coordinate and equally independent and supreme, each in its own sphere of action. Whenever a doubt arises [as] to which of these branches a power belongs, I try it by this test. I recollect no case where a question simply between citizens of the same state has been transferred to the foreign department, except that of inhibiting tenders of metallic money, and *ex post facto* legislation.—Ford 10:300. (1824.)

With respect to our state and federal governments, I do not think their relations correctly understood by foreigners. They generally suppose the former subordinate to the latter. But this is not the case. They are coordinate departments of one simple and integral whole. To the state governments are reserved all legislation and administration in affairs which concern their own citizens only; and to the federal government is given whatever concerns foreigners or the citizens of other states, these functions alone being made federal. The one is the domestic, the other the foreign branch of the same government; neither having control over the other, but within its own department. There are one or two exceptions only to this partition of power.—Bergh 16:47. (1824.)

STATES' RIGHTS, Attacked in Founders' Day.—I see ... with the deepest affliction the rapid strides with which the federal branch of our government is advancing towards the usurpation of all the rights reserved to the states, and the consolidation in itself of all powers, foreign and domestic; and that, too, by constructions which, if legitimate, leave no limits to their power. Take together the decisions of the federal court, the doctrines of the President [John Quincy Adams], and the misconstructions of the Constitutional compact acted on by the legislature of the federal branch [i.e., Congress], and it is but too evident that the three ruling branches of that department are in combination to strip their colleagues, the state authorities, of the powers reserved by them, and to exercise themselves all functions foreign and domestic. Under the power to regulate commerce they assume indefinitely that also over agriculture and manufactures, and call it regulation to take the earnings of one of these branches of industry, and that, too, the most depressed, and put them into the pockets of the other, the most flourishing of all. Under the authority to establish post roads they claim that of cutting down mountains for the construction of roads, of digging canals, and, aided by a little sophistry on the words "general welfare," a right to do, not only the acts to effect that which are specifically

enumerated and permitted, but whatsoever they shall think or pretend will be for the general welfare.

And what is our resource for the preservation of the Constitution? Reason and argument? You might as well reason and argue with the marble columns encircling them. The representatives chosen by ourselves? They are joined in the combination, some from incorrect views of government, some from corrupt ones, sufficient voting together to outnumber the sound parts; and with majorities only of one, two, or three, bold enough to go forward in defiance. Are we then *to stand to our arms,* with the hot-headed Georgian? No. That must be the last resource, not to be thought of until much longer and greater sufferings. If every infraction of a compact of so many parties is to be resisted at once, as a dissolution of it, none can ever be formed which would last one year.

We must have patience and longer endurance, then, with our brethren while [they are] under delusion, give them time for reflection and experience of consequences, keep ourselves in a situation to profit by the chapter of accidents, and separate from our companions only when the sole alternatives left are the dissolution of our union with them or submission to a government without limitation of powers. Between these two evils, when we must make a choice, there can be no hesitation. But in the meanwhile, the states should be watchful to note every material usurpation on their rights; denounce them as they occur in the most peremptory terms; to protest against them as wrongs to which our present submission shall be considered, not as acknowledgments or precedents of right, but as a temporary yielding to the lesser evil until their accumulation shall overweigh that of separation.—Bergh 16:146. (1825.)

STATES' RIGHTS, Violated by Infractions of the Constitution.—The states in North America . . . entered into a compact (which is called the Constitution of the United States of America), by which they agreed to unite in a single government as to their relations with each other and with foreign nations, and as to certain other articles particularly specified. They retained at the same time, each to itself, the other rights of independent government, comprehending mainly their domestic interests. . . . But the federal branch has assumed in some cases, and claimed in others, a right of enlarging its own powers by constructions, inferences, and indefinite deductions from those directly given, which [are] usurpations of the powers retained to the independent branches, mere interpolations into the compact, and direct infractions of it.—Bergh 17:442. (1825.)

STATES' RIGHTS. See also CENTRLIZATION; CONSTITUTION (U.S.); FEDERAL GOVERNMENT; SEPARATION OF POWERS.

STEUBEN (Baron von), His Military Services in Virginia.—Baron Steuben, a zealous friend, has descended from the dignity of his proper command to direct our smallest movements. His vigilance has, in a great measure, supplied the want of force in preventing the enemy from crossing the [James] river, which might have been fatal. He has been assiduously employed in preparing equipments for the militia as they should assemble, pointing them to a proper object, and other offices of a good commander.—To General Washington. Ford 1:408. (1781.)

SUFFRAGE, Bribery and.—I believe we may lessen the danger of buying and selling votes by making the number of voters too great for any means of purchase; I may further say that I have not observed men's honesty to increase with their riches.—Ford 7:454. (1800.)

SUFFRAGE, Ark of Safety.—The elective franchise, if guarded as the [ark] of our safety, will peaceably dissipate all combinations to subvert a Constitution dictated by the wisdom, and resting on the will, of the people.—Bergh 10:236. (1801.)

SUFFRAGE, Education and.—There is one provision [in the new constitution of Spain] which will immortalize its inventors. It is that which, after a certain epoch, disfranchises every citizen who cannot read and write. This is new, and is the fruitful germ of the improvement of everything good and the correction of everything imperfect in the present constitution. This will give you an enlightened people, and an energetic public opinion which will control and enchain the aristocratic spirit of the government. —Bergh 14:130. (1814.)

In the constitution of Spain, as proposed by the late Cortes, there was a principle entirely new to me,...that no person born after that day should ever acquire the rights of citizenship until he could read and write. It is impossible sufficiently to estimate the wisdom of this provision.—Bergh 14:491. (1816.)

It is better to tolerate the rare instance of a parent refusing to let his child be educated than to shock the common feelings and ideas by the forcible asportation and education of the infant against the will of the father. What is proposed here is to remove the objection of expense by offering education gratis, and to strengthen parental excitement by the disfranchisement of his child while uneducated. Society has certainly a right to disavow him whom they offer, and are not permitted, to qualify for the duties of a citizen. If we do not force instruction, let us at least strengthen the motives to receive it when offered.—Bill for Establishing Elementary Schools. Bergh 17:423. (1817.)

SUFFRAGE, Right of, Belongs to Soldiers and Taxpayers.—Let every man who fights or pays exercise his just and equal right in the election of the legislature.—Ford 10:39. (1816.)

SUFFRAGE. See also ELECTIONS.

SUPREME COURT, And Questions of Constitutionality.—It is a very dangerous doctrine to consider the judges as the ultimate arbiters of all constitutional questions. It is one which would place us under the despotism of an oligarchy.... The Constitution has erected no such

single tribunal, knowing that to whatever hands confided, with the corruptions of time and party, its members would become despots. It has more wisely made all the departments coequal and cosovereign within themselves.—Ford 10:160. (1820.)

The Chief Justice [John Marshall] says, "There must be an ultimate arbiter somewhere." True, there must; but does that prove it is either party? The ultimate arbiter is the people of the Union, assembled by their deputies in convention at the call of Congress or of two-thirds of the states. Let them decide to which they mean to give an authority claimed by two of their organs. And it has been the peculiar wisdom and felicity of our Constitution to have provided this peaceable appeal where that of other nations is at once to force.—Bergh 15:451. (1823.)

SUPREME COURT, Remedy to Violations of States' Rights by.—The legislative and executive branches may sometimes err, but elections and dependence will bring them to rights. The judiciary branch is the instrument which, working like gravity without intermission, is to press us at last into one consolidated mass.... If Congress fails to shield the states from dangers so palpable and so imminent, the states must shield themselves and meet the invader foot to foot.—Ford 10:184. (1821.)

There are two measures which, if not taken, we are undone. First, to check these unconstitutional invasions of state rights by the federal judiciary. How? Not by impeachment in the first instance, but by a strong protestation of both houses of Congress that such and such doctrines advanced by the Supreme Court are contrary to the Constitution; and if afterwards they relapse into the same heresies, impeach and set the whole adrift. For what was the government divided into three branches, but that each should watch over the others and oppose their usurpations?—Ford 10:192. (1821.)

SUPREME COURT. See also CENTRALIZATION; FEDERAL GOVERNMENT; JUDICIAL REVIEW; JUDICIARY; MARSHALL (John); SEPARATION OF POWERS.

T

TALENTS, Republics and.—I hold it to be one of the distinguishing excellences of elective over hereditary successions that the talents which nature has provided in sufficient proportion should be selected by the society for the government of their affairs, rather than that this should be transmitted through the loins of knaves and fools, passing from the debauches of the table to those of the bed.—Ford 6:107. (1792.)

TALENTS. See also ARISTOCRACY; DUTY; GENIUS.

TARIFFS, Paid by the Rich.—The ...revenue on the consumption of foreign articles is paid cheerfully by those who can afford to add foreign luxuries to domestic comforts. Being collected on our seaboards and frontiers only, and incorporated with the transactions of our mercantile citizens, it may be the pleasure and pride of an American to ask, what farmer, what mechanic, what laborer ever sees a tax gatherer of the United States?—Second Inaugural Address. Bergh 3:376. (1805.)

These revenues will be levied entirely on the rich, the business of household manufacture being now so established that the farmer and laborer clothe themselves entirely. The rich alone use imported articles, and on these alone the whole taxes of the general government are levied. The poor man, who uses nothing but what is made in his own farm or family, or within his own country, pays not a farthing of tax to the general government, but on his salt; and should we go into that manufacture also, as is probable, he will pay nothing. Our revenues liberated by the discharge of the public debt, and its surplus applied to canals, roads, schools, etc., the farmer will see his government supported, his children educated, and the face of his country made a paradise by the contributions of the rich alone, without his being called on to spend a cent from his earnings.—Bergh 13:42. (1811.)

TARIFFS, Patriotism and.—Shall we suppress the impost and give that advantage to foreign over domestic manufactures? On a few articles of more general and necessary use, the suppression in due season will doubtless be right, but the great mass of the articles on which impost is paid is foreign luxuries, purchased by those only who are rich enough to afford themselves the use of them. Their patriotism would certainly prefer its continuance and application to the great purposes of the public education, roads, rivers, canals, and such other objects of public improvement as it may be thought proper to add to the Constitutional enumeration of federal powers.—Sixth Annual Message to Congress. Bergh 3:423. (1806.)

TAX GATHERERS, Cost of.—Our tax gatherers in Virginia cost as much as the whole civil list besides. —Ford 4:16. (1784.)

TAXES, Not for Redistribution of Wealth.—We do not mean that our people shall be burdened with oppressive taxes to provide sinecures for the idle or the wicked under color of providing for a civil list.—Ford 1:480. (1775.)

TAXES, Excise Tax Defined. —*Impost* is a duty paid on an imported article in the *moment of its importation,* and of course it is collected in the seaports only. *Excise* is a duty on any article, whether imported or raised at home, and paid in the *hands of the consumer or retailer;* consequently it is collected through the whole country. These are the true definitions of these words as used in England and in the greater part of the United States. But in Massachusetts they have perverted the word excise to mean a tax on all liquors, whether paid in the moment of importation or at a later moment, and on nothing else. So that on reading the debates of the Massachusetts Convention, you must give this last meaning to the word excise.—Bergh 7:329. (1789.)

TAXES, Federal Excise, Divisive.— The excise law is an infernal one.

The first error was to admit it by the Constitution; the second, to act on that admission; the third, and last, will be to make it the instrument of dismembering the Union and setting us all afloat to choose which part of it we will adhere to.—Ford 6:518. (1794.)

TAXES, Reduction of.—The suppression of unnecessary offices, of useless establishments and expenses, enabled us to discontinue our internal taxes. These, covering our land with officers and opening our doors to their intrusions, had already begun that process of domiciliary vexation which, once entered, is scarcely to be restrained from reaching successively every article of produce and property.—Second Inaugural Address. Bergh 3:376. (1805.)

TAXES, Should Be Limited to Necessities.—Every man is under the natural duty of contributing to the necessities of the society; and this is all the laws should enforce on him.—Bergh 15:24. (1816.)

TAXES, Oppressive English.—No earthly consideration could induce my consent to contract such a debt as England has by her wars for commerce, to reduce our citizens by taxes to such wretchedness as that, laboring sixteen of the twenty-four hours, they are still unable to afford themselves bread, or barely to earn as much oatmeal or potatoes as will keep soul and body together. And all this to feed the avidity of a few millinery merchants, and to keep up one thousand ships of war for the protection of their commercial speculations.—Ford 10:35. (1816.)

TAXES, Must Be Uniform.—Taxes on consumption, like those on capital or income, to be just, must be uniform.—Ford 10:252. (1823.)

TAXES. See also LUXURIES; POLITICS, Taxation and; TARIFFS.

TERRITORY, Expansion of.—Our confederacy must be viewed as the nest from which all America, North and South, is to be peopled. We should take care, too, not to think it for the interest of that great continent to press too soon on the Spaniards. Those countries cannot be in better hands. My fear is that they are too feeble to hold them till our population can be sufficiently advanced to gain it from them piece by piece.—Ford 4:188. (1786.)

However our present interests may restrain us within our own limits, it is impossible not to look forward to distant times when our rapid multiplication will expand itself beyond those limits and cover the whole northern, if not the southern, continent with a people speaking the same language, governed in similiar forms and by similar laws.—To James Monroe. Ford 8:105. (1801.)

TERRITORY, Republicanism and.—The late chapter of our history . . . furnishes a new proof of the falsehood of Montesquieu's doctrine that a republic can be preserved only in a small territory. The reverse is the truth. Had our territory been even a third only of what it is, we were gone. But while frenzy and delusion, like an epidemic, gained certain parts, the residue remained sound and untouched, and held on till their brethren could recover from the temporary delusion.—Ford 8:24. (1801.)

TERRITORY, Acquisition of, by the Federal Government.—The Constitution has made no provision for our holding foreign territory, still less for incorporating foreign nations into our Union. The executive, in seizing the fugitive occurrence which so much advances the good of their country [i.e., completing the Louisiana Purchase], have done an act beyond the Constitution. The [Congress], in casting behind them metaphysical subtleties and risking themselves like faithful servants, must ratify and pay for it, and throw themselves on their country for doing for them unauthorized what we know they would have done for themselves had they been in a situation to do it. It is the case of a guardian investing the money of his ward in purchasing an important adjacent territory, and saying to him when of age, I did this for your good; I pretend to no right to bind you; you may disavow me, and I must get out of the scrape as I can; I thought it my duty to risk myself for you. But we shall not be disavowed by the nation, and their act of indemnity will confirm and not weaken the Constitution, by more strongly marking out its lines.—Bergh 10:411. (1803.)

TERRITORY. See also AMERICAN CONTINENT; CUBA; FLORIDA; LEWIS AND CLARK EXPEDITION; LOUISIANA; LOUISIANA PURCHASE; MANIFEST DESTINY; POPULATION; WESTERN TERRITORY.

TIME, Effective Use of.—Determine never to be idle. No person will have occasion to complain of the want of time who never loses any. It is wonderful how much may be done if we are always doing.—To Martha Jefferson. Betts & Bear, p. 40. (1787.)

TIME. See also IDLENESS.

TOBACCO, Wheat vs.—Tobacco ...is a culture productive of infinite wretchedness. Those employed in it are in a continual state of exertion beyond the power of nature to support. Little food of any kind is raised by them, so that the men and animals on these farms are badly fed, and the earth is rapidly impoverished. The cultivation of wheat is the reverse in every circumstance. Besides clothing the earth with herbage and preserving its fertility, it feeds the laborers plentifully, requires from them only a moderate toil except in the season of harvest, raises great numbers of animals for food and service, and diffuses plenty and happiness among the whole. We find it easier to make a hundred bushels of wheat than a thousand weight of tobacco, and they are worth more when made.—*Notes on Virginia.* Bergh 2:232. (1782.)

TOBACCO, Abuses of.—I have received and read with thankfulness and pleasure your denunciation of the abuses of tobacco and wine. Yet, however sound in its principles, I expect it will be but a sermon to the wind. You will find it is...difficult to inculcate these sanative precepts on the sensualities of the present day.—To Dr. Benjamin Waterhouse. Bergh 15:383. (1822.)

TORIES, Desire Anglo-American Reconciliation.—The Tories would

at all times have been glad to see the confederacy dissolved, even by particles at a time, in hopes of their attaching themselves again to Great Britain.—Ford 4:156. (1786.)

TORIES, Favor Centralized Government.—The consolidationists may call themselves republicans if they please; but the school of Venice, and all of this principle, I call at once Tories.—Ford 10:378. (1826.)

Consolidation is but Toryism in disguise.—Ford 10:379. (1826.)

TRADE. See COMMERCE; FREE ENTERPRISE; MARKETS.

TREASON, Patriotism Often Punished as.—Treason, when real, merits the highest punishment. But most codes extend their definitions of treason to acts not really against one's country. They do not distinguish between acts against the government and acts against the oppressions of the government. The latter are virtues, yet have furnished more victims to the executioner than the former. Real treasons are rare, oppressions frequent. The unsuccessful strugglers against tyranny have been the chief martyrs of treason laws in all countries. Reformation of government with our neighbors [being] as much wanting now as reformation of religion is, or ever was anywhere, we should not wish then to give up to the executioner the patriot who fails and flees to us. —Ford 5:483. (1792.)

TREASON, Punishment by Exile. —Exile [is] the most rational of all punishments for meditated treason. —Bergh 13:82. (1811.)

TREASON. See also CAPITAL PUNISHMENT; REVOLUTION-

ARY WAR, Rarity of Treason During.

TREATIES, Infractions of.—On the breach of any article of a treaty by the one party, the other has its election to declare it dissolved in all its articles, or to compensate itself by withholding execution of equivalent articles, or to waive notice of the breach altogether.—Ford 6:33. (1792.)

TREATIES, Nations and.—I consider the people who constitute a society or nation as the source of all authority in that nation; as free to transact their common concerns by any agents they think proper; to change these agents individually, or the organization of them in form or function, whenever they please; that all the acts done by these agents under the authority of the nation are the acts of the nation, are obligatory on them and inure to their use, and can in nowise be annulled or affected by any change in the form of the government, or of the persons administering it.—Bergh 3:227. (1793.)

TREATIES, Opposition to European.—I am not for linking ourselves by new treaties with the quarrels of Europe, entering that field of slaughter to preserve their balance, or joining in the confederacy of kings to war against the principles of liberty.—To Elbridge Gerry. Bergh 10:78. (1799.)

TREATIES, Power to Make, Limited.—By the general power to make treaties, the Constitution must have intended to comprehend only those objects which are usually regulated by treaty and cannot be otherwise regulated.... It must have meant to except out of these the rights reserved to the states, for surely the President and Senate cannot do by treaty what the whole government is interdicted from doing in any way.—*Manual of Parliamentary Practice.* Bergh 2:442. (1801.)

Our peculiar security is in the possession of a written Constitution. Let us not make it a blank paper by construction. I say the same as to the opinion of those who consider the grant of the treaty-making power as boundless. If it is, then we have no Constitution. If it has bounds, they can be no others than the definitions of the powers which that instrument gives. It specifies and delineates the operations permitted to the federal government, and gives all the powers necessary to carry these into execution. Whatever of these enumerated objects is proper for a law, Congress may make the law; whatever is proper to be executed by way of a treaty, the President and Senate may enter into the treaty; whatever is to be done by a judicial sentence, the judges may pass the sentence. Nothing is more likely than that their enumeration of powers is defective. This is the ordinary case of all human works. Let us go on, then, perfecting it by adding, by way of amendment to the Constitution, those powers which time and trial show are still wanting.—Bergh 10:419. (1803.)

TREATIES, Ratification of.—It has been the usage of the executive, when it communicates a treaty to the Senate for their ratification, to communicate also the correspondence of the negotiations.—*Manual of Parliamentary Practice.* Bergh 2:442. (1801.)

The subjects...confided to the House of Representatives, in conjunction with the President and Senate, [are] exceptions to the general treaty power given to the President and Senate alone;...whenever a treaty stipulation interferes with a law of the three branches [i.e., the President, the Senate, and the House of Representatives], the consent of the third branch [the House of Representatives] is necessary to give it effect; and...there is to this but the single exception of the question of war and peace. There the Constitution expressly requires the concurrence of the three branches to commit us to the state of war, but permits two of them, the President and Senate, to change it to that of peace, for reasons as obvious as they are wise.—Bergh 14:445. (1816.)

When the British treaty [negotiated during my presidency] arrived without any provision against the impressment of our seamen, I determined not to ratify it. The Senate thought I should ask their advice. I thought that would be a mockery of them, when I was predetermined against following it should they advise its ratification. The Constitution had made their advice necessary to confirm a treaty, but not to reject it. This has been blamed by some, but I have never doubted its soundness.—Bergh 15:214. (1819.)

TREATIES, Avoidance of.—Our system is to have [no treaties] with

any nation, as far as can be avoided.... We believe that with nations, as with individuals, dealings may be carried on as advantageously, perhaps more so, while their continuance depends on a voluntary good treatment, as if fixed by a contract which, when it becomes injurious to either, is made by forced constructions to mean what suits them, and becomes a cause of war instead of a bond of peace. It is against our system to embarrass ourselves with treaties or to entangle ourselves at all with the affairs of Europe.—Bergh 11:38. (1804.)

TREATIES. See also FOREIGN AFFAIRS; MONROE DOCTRINE.

TRUTH, Can Stand by Itself. —Truth will do well enough if left to shift for herself. She seldom has received much aid from the power of great men, to whom she is rarely known and seldom welcome. She has no need of force to procure entrance into the minds of men.—Ford 2:102. (1776?)

Truth is great and will prevail if left to herself;...she is the proper and sufficient antagonist to error, and has nothing to fear from the conflict unless by human interposition disarmed of her natural weapons, free argument and debate, errors ceasing to be dangerous when it is permitted freely to contradict them.—Bill for Establishing Religious Freedom. Ford 2:239. (1779.)

It is error alone which needs the support of government. Truth can stand by itself.—*Notes on Virginia.* Bergh 2:222. (1782.)

TRUTH, Importance of Telling.—It is of great importance to set a resolution, not to be shaken, never to tell an untruth. There is no vice so mean, so pitiful, so contemptible; and he who permits himself to tell a lie once finds it much easier to do it a second and third time, till at length it becomes habitual; he tells lies without attending to it, and truths without the world's believing him. This falsehood of the tongue leads to that of the heart, and in time depraves all its good dispositions.—To Peter Carr. Bergh 5:84. (1785.)

TRUTH, Propagated by Free Speech.—Freedom of discussion, unaided by power, is ... sufficient for the propagation and protection of truth.—Second Inaugural Address. Bergh 3:381. (1805.)

TRUTH, Eternal and Enduring.—Truth and reason are eternal. They have prevailed. And they will eternally prevail; however, in times and places they may be overborne for a while by violence, military, civil, or ecclesiastical.—Bergh 12:361. (1810.)

TRUTH, The Only Safe Guide.—The people ... [are] to be encouraged in all cases to follow truth as the only safe guide, and to eschew error, which bewilders us in one false consequence after another in endless succession.—To John Adams. Bergh 15:234. (1819.)

TRUTH. See also GOOD FAITH; HONESTY; LIES.

TYRANNY, Fear and.—Fear is the only restraining motive which may hold the hand of a tyrant.—Ford 1:436. (1774.)

TYRANNY, Best Time to Guard Against.—The time to guard against corruption and tyranny is before they shall have gotten hold of us. It is better to keep the wolf out of the fold than to trust to drawing his teeth and claws after he shall have entered.—*Notes on Virginia.* Bergh 2:165. (1782.)

TYRANNY, Eternal Hostility to.—I have sworn upon the altar of God eternal hostility against every form of tyranny over the mind of man.—To Dr. Benjamin Rush. Bergh 10:175. (1800.)

TYRANNY, Insurrection Against.—The general insurrection of the world against its tyrants will ultimately prevail by pointing the object of government to the happiness of the people, and not merely to that of their self-constituted governors.—Ford 10:233. (1822.)

TYRANNY. See also LIBERTY; MONARCHY.

U

UNION, Constitutional Encroachments and the.—When obvious encroachments are made on the plain meaning of the Constitution, the bond of Union ceases to be the equal measure of justice to all its parts.—Ford 5:454. (1792.)

To preserve the republican form and principles of our Constitution and cleave to the salutary distribution of powers which that has established ... are the two sheet anchors of our Union. If driven from either, we shall be in danger of foundering. —Bergh 15:452. (1823.)

UNION, Dissolution of, to Be Feared.—I can scarcely contemplate a more incalculable evil than the breaking of the Union into two or more parts.—Ford 6:4. (1792.)

UNION, Strength of the.—If there be any among us who would wish to dissolve this Union or to change its republican form, let them stand undisturbed as monuments of the safety with which error of opinion may be tolerated where reason is left free to combat it. I know, indeed, that some honest men fear that a republican government cannot be strong, that this government is not strong enough. But would the honest patriot, in the full tide of successful experiment, abandon a government which has so far kept us free and firm, on the theoretic and visionary fear that this government, the world's best hope, may by possibility want energy to preserve itself? I trust not. I believe this, on the contrary, the strongest government on earth. I believe it is the only one where every man, at the call of the laws, would fly to the standard of the law and would meet invasions of the public order as his own personal concern. Sometimes it is said that man cannot be trusted with the government of himself. Can he, then, be trusted with the government of others? Or have we found angels, in the forms of kings, to govern him? Let history answer this question.—First Inaugural Address. Bergh 3:319. (1801.)

UNION, To Be Fostered.—Cherish every measure which may foster our brotherly Union and perpetuate a constitution of government destined to be the primitive and precious model of what is to change the condition of man over the globe.—Ford 10:301. (1824.)

UNION, Preservation of, Requires Forbearance.—[Virginians] know and value too highly the blessings of their Union...to consider every infraction [of the Constitution] as to be met by actual resistance. They respect too affectionately the opinions of those possessing the same rights under the same instrument to make every difference of construction a ground of immediate rupture. They would, indeed, consider such a rupture as among the greatest calamities which could befall them; but not the greatest. There is yet one greater—submission to a government of unlimited powers. It is only when the hope of avoiding this shall become absolutely desperate that further forbearance could not be indulged.... Meanwhile, we will breast every misfortune, save that only of living under a government of unlimited powers. We owe every other sacrifice to ourselves, to our federal brethren, and to the world at large to pursue with temper and perseverance the great experiment which shall prove that man is capable of living in [a] society governing itself by laws self-imposed, and securing to its members the enjoyment of life, liberty, property, and peace; and further, to show that even when the government of its choice shall manifest a tendency to

Jefferson in October 1825 (age 82). Plaster life mask by John Henri Isaac Browere.

degeneracy, we are not at once to despair, but that the will and the watchfulness of its sounder parts will reform its aberrations, recall it to original and legitimate principles, and restrain it within the rightful limits of self-government.—Bergh 17:445. (1825.)

UNION. See also SECESSION.

UNITED STATES, Potential Expansion of.—Our present federal limits are not too large for good government, nor will the increase of votes in Congress produce any ill effect. On the contrary, it will drown the little divisions at present existing there. Our confederacy must be viewed as the nest from which all America, North and South, is to be peopled.—Ford 4:188. (1786.)

UNITED STATES, Tranquil Conditions in.—There is not a country on earth where there is greater tranquility; where the laws are milder, or better obeyed; where everyone is more attentive to his own business, or meddles less with that of others; where strangers are better received, more hospitably treated, and with a more sacred respect.—Ford 4:316. (1786.)

UNITED STATES, An Example to Other Nations.—It is indeed an animating thought that, while we are securing the rights of ourselves and our posterity, we are pointing out the way to struggling nations who wish, like us, to emerge from their tyrannies also. Heaven help their struggles and lead them, as it has done us, triumphantly through them.—Bergh 8:6. (1790.)

UNITED STATES, The Guardian of Liberty.—The station which we occupy among the nations of the earth is honorable, but awful. Trusted with the destinies of this solitary republic of the world, the only monument of human rights and the sole depository of the sacred fire of freedom and self-government, from hence it is to be lighted up in other regions of the earth, if other regions of the earth shall ever become susceptible of its benign influence. All mankind ought, then, with us, to rejoice in its prosperous and sympathize in its adverse fortunes, as involving everything dear to man. And to what sacrifices of interest or convenience ought not these considerations to animate us? To what compromises of opinion and inclination to maintain harmony and union among ourselves, and to preserve from all danger this hallowed ark of human hope and happiness?—Bergh 16:347. (1809.)

The eyes of the virtuous all over the earth are turned with anxiety on us as the only depositories of the sacred fire of liberty.—Bergh 13:58. (1811.)

UNITED STATES, Fewer Difficulties in.—Our difficulties are indeed great if we consider ourselves alone. But when viewed in comparison to those of Europe, they are the joys of Paradise.... Indeed, ours is a bed of roses. And the system of government which shall keep us afloat amidst the wreck of the world will be immortalized in history.—Ford 9:274. (1810.)

UNITED STATES, Future Greatness of.—I do believe we shall continue to grow, to multiply and prosper, until we exhibit an association powerful, wise, and happy beyond what has yet been seen by men. —Ford 9:333. (1812.)

Not in our day, but at no distant one, we may shake a rod over the heads of all [the European nations] which may make the stoutest of them tremble. But I hope our wisdom will grow with our power, and teach us that the less we use our power, the greater will it be.—Ford 9:520. (1815.)

We are destined to be a barrier against the returns of ignorance and barbarism. Old Europe will have to lean on our shoulders, and to hobble along by our side under the monkish trammels of priests and kings as she can. What a colossus shall we be when the southern continent comes up to our mark! What a stand will it secure as a ralliance for the reason

and freedom of the globe!—To John Adams. Bergh 15:58. (1816.)

UNITED STATES, Duration of.—I have much confidence that we shall proceed successfully for ages to come, and that, contrary to the principle of Montesquieu, it will be seen that the larger the extent of country, the more firm its republican structure, if founded not on conquest but in principles of compact and equality. My hope of its duration is built much on the enlargement of the resources of life going hand in hand with the enlargement of territory, and the belief that men are disposed to live honestly if the means of doing so are open to them.—Bergh 15:130. (1817.)

UNITED STATES. See also AMERICA; COLONIES (American); MANIFEST DESTINY; PATRIOTISM; POPULATION; STATES; TERRITORY; UNION.

UNIVERSITY, Proposal for a National.—Education is here placed among the articles of public care; not that it would be proposed to take its ordinary branches out of the hands of private enterprise, which manages so much better all the concerns to which it is equal, but a public institution can alone supply those sciences which, though rarely called for, are yet necessary to complete the circle, all the parts of which contribute to the improvement of the country, and some of them to its preservation.... I suppose an amendment to the Constitution, by consent of the states, necessary, because the objects now recommended are not among those enumerated in the Constitution, and to which it permits the public moneys to be applied.—Sixth Annual Message to Congress. Bergh 3:423. (1806.)

UNIVERSITY OF VIRGINIA, Objectives of.—This institution of my native state, the hobby of my old age, will be based on the illimitable freedom of the human mind to explore and to expose every subject susceptible of its contemplation.—Ford 10:174. (1820.)

Our aim [is] the securing to our country a full and perpetual institution for all the useful sciences, one which will restore us to our former station in the confederacy.... Patience and steady perseverance on our part will secure the blessed end. If we shrink, it is gone forever.—Bergh 15:364. (1822.)

UNIVERSITY OF VIRGINIA, And Theology.—In our university... there is no professorship of divinity. A handle has been made of this to disseminate an idea that this is an institution, not merely of no religion, but against all religion. Occasion was taken at the last meeting of the visitors to bring forward an idea that might silence this calumny, which weighed on the minds of some honest friends to the institution. In our annual report to the legislature, after stating the Constitutional reasons against a public establishment of any religious instruction, we suggest the expediency of encouraging the different religious sects to establish, each for itself, a professorship of their own tenets on the confines of the university, so near as that their students may at-

tend the lectures there, and have the free use of our library and every other accommodation we can give them; preserving, however, their independence of us and of each other. This fills the chasm objected to ours, as a defect in an institution professing to give instruction in *all* useful sciences. I think the invitation will be accepted, by some sects from candid intentions, and by others from jealousy and rivalship. And by bringing the sects together and mixing them with the mass of other students, we shall soften their asperities, liberalize and neutralize their prejudices, and make the general religion a religion of peace, reason, and morality.—Bergh 15:405. (1822.)

UNIVERSITY OF VIRGINIA, Selection of Textbooks.—In most public seminaries textbooks are prescribed to each of the several schools, ...and this is generally done by authority of the trustees. I should not propose this generally in our university, because I believe none of us are so much at the heights of science in the several branches as to undertake this, and therefore that it will be better left to the professors until occasion of interference shall be given. But there is one branch in which we are the best judges, in which heresies may be taught of so interesting a character to our own state and to the United States as to make it a duty in us to lay down the principles which are to be taught. It is that of government.... It is our duty to guard against... principles [of consolidation] being disseminated among our youth, and the diffusion of that poison by a previous prescription of the texts to be followed in their discourses.—Bergh 16:103. (1825.)

UNIVERSITY OF VIRGINIA, To Keep Whiggism Alive.—In the selection of our law professor, we must be rigorously attentive to his political principles. You will recollect that before the Revolution, Coke Littleton was the universal elementary book of law students, and a sounder Whig never wrote, nor of profounder learning in the orthodox doctrines of the British constitution, or in what were called English liberties. You remember also that our lawyers were then all Whigs. But when his black-letter text and uncouth but cunning learning got out of fashion, and the honeyed Mansfieldism of Blackstone became the students' hornbook, from that moment that profession (the nursery of our Congress) began to slide into Toryism, and nearly all the young brood of lawyers now are of that hue. They suppose themselves, indeed, to be Whigs, because they no longer know what Whiggism or republicanism means. It is in our seminary that that vestal flame is to be kept alive; it is thence it is to spread anew over our own and the sister states. If we are true and vigilant in our trust, within a dozen or twenty years a majority of our own legislature will be from one school, and many disciples will have carried its doctrines home with them to their several states, and will have leavened thus the whole mass.—To

James Madison. Bergh 16:156. (1826.)

UNIVERSITY OF VIRGINIA, Term of Studies.—[A] material question is, what is the whole term of time which the students can give to the whole course of instruction? I should say that three years should be allowed to general education, and two, or rather three, to the particular profession for which they are destined.—Bergh 16:169. (1826.)

V

VETO, Checks on Power of.—I like the negative given [in the federal Constitution] to the executive, with a third of either house; though I should have liked it better had the judiciary been associated for that purpose, or invested separately with a similar power.—To James Madison. Bergh 6:387. (1787.)

VETO, Purposes of.—The negative of the President is the shield provided by the Constitution to protect against the invasions of the legislature: 1. The right of the executive. 2. Of the judiciary. 3. Of the states and state legislatures.—Bergh 3:152. (1791.)

The negative of the President can never be used more pleasingly to the public than in the protection of the Constitution.—Ford 5:500. (1792.)

VETO, Discretion in Use of.—If the [arguments for and against a bill] hang so even as to balance [the President's] judgment, a just respect for the wisdom of the [Congress] would naturally decide the balance in favor

652 The Real Thomas Jefferson

of their opinion. It is chiefly for cases where they are clearly misled by error, ambition, or interest that the Constitution has placed a check in the negative of the President. —Bergh 3:153. (1791.)

VICE, Reduced by Diffusion of Knowledge.—Although I do not, with some enthusiasts, believe that the human condition will ever advance to such a state of perfection as that there shall no longer be pain or vice in the world, yet I believe it susceptible of much improvement, and most of all in matters of government and religion; and that the diffusion of knowledge among the people is to be the instrument by which it is to be effected.—Bergh 14:491. (1816.)

VICE, Governmental Regulation of.—We have seen...that every vocation in life is subject to the influence of chance; that so far from being rendered immoral by the admixture of that ingredient, were they abandoned on that account man could no longer subsist; that, among them, everyone has a natural right to choose that which he thinks most likely to give him comfortable subsistence; but that while the greater number of these pursuits are productive of something which adds to the necessaries and comforts of life, others again, such as cards, dice, etc., are entirely unproductive, doing good to none, injury to many, yet so easy and so seducing in practice to men of a certain constitution of mind that they cannot resist the temptation, be the consequences what they may; that in this case, as

in those of insanity, idiocy, infancy, etc., it is the duty of society to take [such people] under its protection, even against their own acts, and to restrain their right of choice of these pursuits by suppressing them entirely.—Bergh 17:456. (1826.)

VICE PRESIDENCY, Jefferson's Acceptance of.—The idea that I would accept the office of President, but not that of Vice President of the United States, had not its origin with me. I never thought of questioning the free exercise of the right of my fellow citizens to marshal those whom they call into their service according to their fitness, nor ever presumed that they were not the best judges of that. Had I indulged a wish in what manner they should dispose of me, it would precisely have coincided with what they have done.—Bergh 9:377. (1797.)

VICE PRESIDENCY, Honorable and Easy.—The second office of the government is honorable and easy; the first is but a splendid misery.— To Elbridge Gerry. Bergh 9:381. (1797.)

VIRTUE, Self-Perpetuating.—Everything is useful which contributes to fix in the principles and practices of virtue. When any original act of charity or of gratitude, for instance, is presented either to our sight or imagination, we are deeply impressed with its beauty and feel a strong desire in ourselves of doing charitable and grateful acts also. —Bergh 4:237. (1771.)

VIRTUE, Public Office and.—It becomes expedient for promoting the public happiness that those persons whom nature hath endowed with genius and virtue should be rendered by liberal education worthy to receive, and able to guard, the sacred deposit of the rights and liberties of their fellow citizens; and that they should be called to that charge without regard to wealth, birth, or other accidental condition or circumstance.—Boyd 2:526. (1779.)

VIRTUE, Essential to Preservation of the Republic.—It is the manners and spirit of a people which preserve a republic in vigor. A degeneracy in these is a canker which soon eats to the heart of its laws and constitution.—*Notes on Virginia.* Bergh 2:230. (1782.)

VIRTUE, Exhortation to Practice. —Encourage all your virtuous dispositions, and exercise them whenever an opportunity arises; being assured that they will gain strength by exercise, as a limb of the body does, and that exercise will make them habitual. From the practice of the purest virtue you may be assured you will derive the most sublime comforts in every moment of life, and in the moment of death. —To Peter Carr. Bergh 5:83. (1785.)

VIRTUE, Happiness and.—Without virtue, happiness cannot be.—Bergh 14:405. (1816.)

VIRTUE, Essence of.—Virtue does not consist in the act we do, but in the end it is to effect. If it is to effect the happiness of him to whom it is directed, it is virtuous, while in a society under different circumstances and opinions the same act might produce pain and would be vicious. The essence of virtue is in doing good to others, while what is good may be one thing in one society and its contrary in another.—To John Adams. Bergh 15:77. (1816.)

VIRTUE, Self-Interest and.—Virtue and interest are inseparable. —Ford 10:69. (1816.)

VIRTUE, Public, Indispensable to Good Government.—No government can continue good but under the control of the people; and... their minds [are] to be informed by education what is right and what wrong; to be encouraged in habits of virtue and deterred from those of vice by the dread of punishments, proportioned indeed, but irremissible; in all cases to follow truth as the only safe guide, and to eschew error, which bewilders us in one false consequence after another in endless succession. These are the inculcations necessary to render the people a sure basis for the structure of order and good government.—To John Adams. Bergh 15:234. (1819.)

VIRTUE, Not Hereditary.—Virtue is not hereditary.—Ford 10:227. (1823.)

VIRTUE. See also MORALITY; SELFISHNESS; VICE.

VOTE. See ELECTIONS; SUFFRAGE.

W

WALKING. See EXERCISE.

WAR, Impractical.—Never was so much false arithmetic employed on any subject as that which has been employed to persuade nations that it is their interest to go to war. Were the money which it has cost to gain, at the close of a long war, a little town or a little territory, the right to cut wood here or to catch fish there, expended in improving what they already possess, in making roads, opening rivers, building ports, improving the arts, and finding employment for their idle poor, it would render them much stronger, much wealthier and happier. This I hope will be our wisdom.—*Notes on Virginia.* Bergh 2:240. (1782.)

WAR, Insult and.—I think it to our interest to punish the first insult, because an insult unpunished is the parent of many others.—Ford 4:89. (1785.)

It is an eternal truth that acquiescence under insult is not the way to escape war.—Ford 7:31. (1795.)

WAR, Unprofitable.—The most successful war seldom pays for its losses.—To Edmund Randolph. Bergh 5:140. (1785.)

WAR, Often Prevented by Military Strength.—The power of making war often prevents it, and . . . would give efficacy to our desire of peace. —To George Washington. Bergh 7:224. (1788.)

Whatever enables us to go to war secures our peace.—Ford 5:198. (1790.)

WAR, Power to Declare.—The question of declaring war is the function equally of both houses [of Congress].—Ford 1:206. (1792.)

As the executive cannot decide the question of war on the affirmative side, neither ought it to do so on the negative side by preventing the [Congress] from deliberating on the question.—Ford 6:192. (1793.)

If Congress are to act on the question of war, they have a right to information [from the executive].— Ford 7:221. (1798.)

We had reposed great confidence in that provision of the Constitution which requires two-thirds of the [Congress] to declare war. Yet it can be entirely eluded by a majority's taking such measures as will bring on war.—Ford 7:222. (1798.)

The power of declaring war being with the [Congress], the executive should do nothing necessarily committing them to decide for war. —Ford 9:100. (1807.)

WAR, America's Opposition to.— No country, perhaps, was ever so thoroughly against war as ours. These dispositions pervade every description of its citizens, whether in or out of office.—Ford 6:217. (1793.)

WAR, Unwanted But Unfeared. —We love and we value peace; we know its blessings from experience. We abhor the follies of war, and are not untried in its distresses and calamities. Unmeddling with the affairs of other nations, we had hoped that our distance and our dispositions would have left us free in the example and indulgence of peace with all the world. . . . We confide in our strength without boasting of it; we respect that of others without fearing it.—Ford 6:337. (1793.)

WAR, One Is Enough.—I have seen enough of one war never to wish to see another.—To John Adams. Ford 6:505. (1794.)

I think one war enough for the life of one man; and you and I have gone through one which at least may lessen our impatience to embark in another. Still, if it becomes necessary we must meet it like men; old men, indeed, but yet good for something.—To John Langdon. Ford 9:201. (1808.)

WAR, Punishes Everyone.—War ... is as much a punishment to the punisher as to the sufferer.—Ford 6:508. (1794.)

WAR, Abhorrent.—I abhor war and view it as the greatest scourge of mankind.—Ford 7:122. (1797.)

WAR, Commerce vs.—War is not the best engine for us to resort to; nature has given us one *in our commerce* which, if properly managed, will be a better instrument for obliging the interested nations of Europe to treat us with justice.—Ford 7:129. (1797.)

WAR, Bankruptcy and.—Bankruptcy is a terrible foundation to begin a war on.—Ford 7:241. (1798.)

WAR, And Enforcement of Principles.—I do not believe war the most certain means of enforcing principles. Those peaceable coercions which are in the power of every nation, if undertaken in concert and in time of peace, are more likely to produce the desired effect.—Ford 8:91. (1801.)

WAR, When Justified.—The lamentable resource of war is not authorized for evils of imagination, but for those actual injuries only which would be more destructive of our well-being than war itself.—Bergh 10:249. (1801.)

When patience has begotten false estimates of its motives, when wrongs are pressed because it is believed they will be borne, resistance becomes morality.—Bergh 11:282. (1807.)

WAR, Avoidance of.—How much better is it for neighbors to help than to hurt one another; how much happier must it make them. If you will cease to make war on one another, if you will live in friendship with all mankind, you can employ all your time in providing food and clothing for yourselves and your families. Your men will not be destroyed in war, and your women and children will lie down to sleep in their cabins without fear of being surprised by their enemies and killed or carried away. Your numbers will be increased instead of diminishing, and you will live in plenty and in quiet.—Address to Mandar Indians. Bergh 16:414. (1806.)

To cherish and maintain the rights and liberties of our citizens, and to ward from them the burdens, the miseries, and the crimes of war by a just and friendly conduct towards all nations, [are] among the most obvious and important duties of those to whom the management of their public interests have been confided.—Bergh 16:290. (1807.)

WAR, Not to Be Waged for Light Causes.—If nations go to war for every degree of injury, there would never be peace on earth.—Bergh 11:282. (1807.)

WAR, Evils of.—The evils of war are great in their endurance, and have a

long reckoning for ages to come.—
Bergh 16:324. (1808.)

WAR, America Insulated from.—
The insulated state in which nature
has placed the American continent
should so far avail it that no spark of
war kindled in the other quarters of
the globe should be wafted across
the wide oceans which separate us
from them.—Ford 9:431. (1813.)

WAR. See also ARMY; DEFENSE;
FOREIGN AFFAIRS; NAVY;
PEACE; PRISONERS OF WAR;
REVOLUTIONARY WAR.

WASHINGTON, D.C., Location of.
—The remoteness of the Falls of
Potomac from the influence of any
overgrown commercial city recom-
mends [that place for the] permanent seat of Congress.—Ford 3:458.
(1784.)

**WASHINGTON, D.C., Building
Line in.**—I doubt much whether the
obligation to build the houses at a
given distance from the street contributes to its beauty. It produces a
disgusting monotony; all persons
make this complaint against Philadelphia. The contrary practice varies
the appearance and is much more
convenient to the inhabitants.
—Ford 5:253. (1790.)

WASHINGTON, D.C., Lots in.—
The lots [should] be sold in breadths
of fifty feet; their depths to extend
to the diagonal of the square.—Ford
5:253. (1790.)

WASHINGTON, D.C., Streets of.
—I should propose the streets to be
at right angles, as in Philadelphia,
and that no street be narrower than
one hundred feet, with footways of
fifteen feet. Where a street is long

and level, it might be one hundred
and twenty feet wide. I should prefer squares of at least two hundred
yards every way.—Ford 5:253.
(1790.)

**WASHINGTON, D.C., New Resi-
dents Solicited.**—I shall send you . . .
two dozen plans of the city of Washington, . . . which you are desired to
display, not for sale but for public
inspection, wherever they may be
most seen by those descriptions of
people worthy and likely to be at-
tracted to it, dividing the plans
among the cities of London and
Edinburgh chiefly, but sending some
also to Glasgow, Bristol, Dublin, etc.
—To Thomas Pinckney. Bergh 9:8.
(1792.)

**WASHINGTON (George), His At-
titude Toward Monarchy.**—[Presi-
dent Washington] said . . . that the
Constitution we have is an excellent
one if we can keep it where it is; that
it was, indeed, supposed there was a
party disposed to change it into a
monarchical form, but that he could
conscientiously declare there was
not a man in the United States who
would set his face more decidedly
against it than himself. Here I interrupted him by saying, "No rational
man in the United States suspects
you of any other disposition; but
there does not pass a week in which
we cannot prove declarations drop-
ping from the monarchical party that
our government is good for nothing,
is a milk-and-water thing which
cannot support itself, [and that] we
must knock it down and set up
something of more energy." He said
if that was the case he thought it a

proof of their insanity, for...the republican spirit of the Union was so manifest and so solid that it was astonishing how anyone could expect to move it.—The Anas. Bergh 1:386. (1793.)

I am satisfied that General Washington had not a wish to perpetuate his authority [after the Revolutionary War].... There was, indeed, a cabal of the officers of the army who proposed to establish a monarchy and to propose it to General Washington. He frowned indignantly at the proposition.—Bergh 17:400. (1807 or later.)

WASHINGTON (George), His Reaction to Personal Attacks.—The President is...extremely affected by the attacks made and kept up on him in the public papers. I think he feels those things more than any person I ever yet met with. I am sincerely sorry to see them.—To James Madison. Bergh 9:120. (1793.)

WASHINGTON (George), Errors of.—He errs as other men do, but errs with integrity.—Ford 7:41. (1795.)

WASHINGTON (George), Influence of.—You will have seen by the proceedings of Congress the truth of what I always observed to you, that one man outweighs them all in influence over the people, who have supported his judgment against their own and that of their representatives.—To James Monroe. Ford 7:80. (1796.)

WASHINGTON (George), Americans' Confidence in.—Without pretensions to that high confidence you reposed in our first and greatest Revolutionary character, whose preeminent services had entitled him to the first place in his country's love and destined for him the fairest page in the volume of faithful history, I ask so much confidence only as may give firmness and effect to the legal administration of your affairs.—First Inaugural Address. Bergh 3:323. (1801.)

WASHINGTON (George), Fame of.—Washington's fame will go on increasing until the brightest constellation in yonder heavens shall be called by his name.—Quoted in Sarah N. Randolph, *The Domestic Life of Thomas Jefferson* (New York: Harper and Bros., 1871), p. 358. (1809 or later.)

WASHINGTON (George), Political Principles of.—You expected to discover the difference of our party principles in General Washington's valedictory and my inaugural address. Not at all. General Washington did not harbor one principle of Federalism. He was neither an Angloman, a monarchist, nor a separatist. He sincerely wished the people to have as much self-government as they were competent to exercise themselves. The only point on which he and I ever differed in opinion was that I had more confidence than he had in the natural integrity and discretion of the people, and in the safety and extent to which they might trust themselves with a control over their government. He has asseverated [earnestly affirmed] to me a thousand times his determination that the existing government should have a fair trial, and that in support of it he would spend the last drop of his blood. He did this the more repeatedly because he knew [Alexander] Hamilton's political bias, and my apprehensions from it. It is a mere calumny, therefore, in the monarchists to associate General Washington with their principles. But that may have happened in this case which has been often seen in ordinary cases, that by oft repeating an untruth men come to believe it themselves. It is a mere artifice in this party to bolster themselves up on the revered name of that first of our worthies. — Bergh 13:212. (1813.)

WASHINGTON (George), Jefferson's Estimate of.—His mind was great and powerful, without being of the very first order; his penetration strong, though not so acute as that of a Newton, Bacon, or Locke; and as far as he saw, no judgment was ever sounder. It was slow in operation, being little aided by invention or imagination, but sure in conclusion.... He was incapable of fear, meeting personal dangers with the calmest unconcern. Perhaps the strongest feature in his character was prudence, never acting until every circumstance, every consideration, was maturely weighed; refraining if he saw a doubt, but, when once decided, going through with his purpose, whatever obstacles opposed. His integrity was most pure, his justice the most inflexible I have ever known, no motives of interest or consanguinity, of friendship or hatred, being able to bias his decision. He was, in-

deed, in every sense of the words, a wise, a good, and a great man.

His temper was naturally irritable and high toned, but reflection and resolution had obtained a firm and habitual ascendancy over it. If ever, however, it broke its bonds, he was most tremendous in his wrath. In his expenses he was honorable but exact; liberal in contributions to whatever promised utility, but frowning and unyielding on all visionary projects and all unworthy calls on his charity. His heart was not warm in its affections, but he exactly calculated every man's value and gave him a solid esteem proportioned to it.

His person, you know, was fine, his stature exactly what one would wish, his deportment easy, erect and noble; [he was] the best horseman of his age, and the most graceful figure that could be seen on horseback.

Although in the circle of his friends, where he might be unreserved with safety, he took a free share in conversation, his colloquial talents were not above mediocrity, possessing neither copiousness of ideas nor fluency of words. In public, when called on for a sudden opinion, he was unready, short, and embarrassed. Yet he wrote readily, rather diffusely, in an easy and correct style. This he had acquired by conversation with the world, for his education was merely reading, writing, and common arithmetic, to which he added surveying at a later day. His time was employed in action chiefly, reading little, and that only in agriculture and English history.

His correspondence became necessarily extensive, and, with journalizing his agricultural proceedings, occupied most of his leisure hours within doors.

On the whole, his character was, in its mass, perfect, in nothing bad, in few points indifferent; and it may truly be said that never did nature and fortune combine more perfectly to make a man great, and to place him in the same constellation with whatever worthies have merited from man an everlasting remembrance. For his was the singular destiny and merit of leading the armies of his country successfully through an arduous war for the establishment of its independence; of conducting its councils through the birth of a government, new in its forms and principles, until it had settled down into a quiet and orderly train; and of scrupulously obeying the laws through the whole of his career, civil and military, of which the history of the world furnishes no other example....

The soundness of [his judgment] gave him correct views of the rights of man, and his severe justice devoted him to them. He has often declared to me that he considered our new Constitution as an experiment on the practicability of republican government, and with what dose of liberty man could be trusted for his own good; that he was determined the experiment should have a fair trial, and would lose the last drop of his blood in support of it. ... I felt on his death, with my countrymen, that "verily a great man

hath fallen this day in Israel." —Bergh 14:48. (1814.)

WASHINGTON (George), And the Federalist Party.—The Federalists, pretending to be the exclusive friends of General Washington, have ever done what they could to sink his character by hanging theirs on it, and by representing as the enemy of Republicans him who, of all men, is best entitled to the appellation of the father of that republic which they were endeavoring to subvert, and the Republicans to maintain. They cannot deny, because the elections proclaimed the truth, that the great body of the nation approved the Republican measures. General Washington was himself sincerely a friend to the republican principles of our Constitution. His faith, perhaps, in its duration might not have been as confident as mine; but he repeatedly declared to me that he was determined it should have a fair chance for success, and that he would lose the last drop of his blood in its support against any attempt which might be made to change it from its republican form. He made these declarations the [more often] because he knew my suspicions that [Alexander] Hamilton had other views, and he wished to quiet my jealousies on this subject....

General Washington, after the retirement of his first Cabinet and the composition of his second, entirely Federalist, and at the head of which was Mr. [Timothy] Pickering himself, had no opportunity of hearing both sides of any question. His measures consequently took more the hue of the party in whose hands he was. These measures were certainly not approved by the Republicans; yet were they not imputed to him, but to the counselors around him; and his prudence so far restrained their impassioned course and bias that no act of strong mark during the remainder of his administration excited much dissatisfaction.

He lived too short a time after, and too much withdrawn from information, to correct the views [regarding the Republican party] into which he had been deluded; and the continued assiduities of the [Federalist] party drew him into the vortex of their intemperate career, separated him still farther from his real friends, and excited him to actions and expressions of dissatisfaction which grieved them, but could not loosen their affections from him. They would not suffer the temporary aberration to weigh against the immeasurable merits of his life; and although they tumbled his seducers from their places, they preserved his memory embalmed in their hearts with undiminished love and devotion; and there it forever will remain embalmed, in entire oblivion of every temporary thing which might cloud the glories of his splendid life.

It is vain, then, for Mr. Pickering and his friends to endeavor to falsify his character by representing him as an enemy to Republicans and republican principles, and as exclusively the friend of those who were so; and had he lived longer, he would have returned to his ancient and unbiased opinions, would have replaced his confidence in those whom the people approved and supported, and would have seen that they were only restoring and acting on the principles of his own first administration. —To Martin Van Buren. Bergh 16:65. (1824.)

WEALTH, Acquisition of.—The wealth acquired by speculation and plunder is fugacious in its nature, and fills society with the spirit of gambling. The moderate and sure income of husbandry begets permanent improvement, quiet life, and orderly conduct, both public and private.—To George Washington. Bergh 6:277. (1787.)

WEALTH, Liberty and.—What a cruel reflection that a rich country cannot long be a free one.—Bergh 17:162. (1787.)

WEALTH, Not Conducive to Honesty.—I have not observed men's honesty to increase with their riches. —Ford 7:454. (1800.)

WEALTH. See also MONEY; PROPERTY; PROSPERITY; REDISTRIBUTION OF WEALTH.

WEIGHTS AND MEASURES, Rates Fixed.—The weight of the pound troy is to that of the pound avoirdupois as...144 to 175. It is remarkable that this is exactly the proportion of the ancient liquid gallon of Guildhall of 224 cubic inches to the corn gallon of 272.... It is further remarkable still that this is also the exact proportion between the specific weight of any measure of wheat and of the same measure of water.... This seems to have been so combined as to render it indifferent whether a thing were dealt out by weight or measure. —Bergh 3:43. (1790.)

WEIGHTS AND MEASURES, English-American System Based on Scientific Calculation.—Another remarkable correspondence is that between weights and measures, for 1,000 ounces avoirdupois of pure water fill a cubic foot with mathematical exactness. What circumstances of the times, or purposes of barter or commerce, called for this combination of weights and measures, with the subjects to be exchanged or purchased, are not now to be ascertained. But a triple set of exact proportionals representing weights, measures, and the things to be weighed or measured, and a relation so integral between weights and solid measures, must have been the result of design and scientific calculation, and not a mere coincidence of hazard.—Bergh 3:44. (1790.)

WEIGHTS AND MEASURES, Basis for.—Let it . . . be established that an ounce is of the weight of a cube of rainwater of one-tenth of a foot; or, rather, that it is the thousandth part of the weight of a cubic foot of rainwater, weighed in the standard temperature; that the series of weights of the United States shall consist of pounds, ounces, pennyweights, and grains; whereof 24 grains shall be one pennyweight, 18 pennyweights one ounce, [and] 16 ounces one pound.—Bergh 3:47. (1790.)

WELFARE, Public.—To preserve the peace of our fellow citizens, promote their prosperity and happiness, reunite opinion, [and] culti-

vate a spirit of candor, moderation, charity, and forbearance toward one another are objects calling for the efforts and sacrifices of every good man and patriot. Our religion enjoins it, our happiness demands it; and no sacrifice is requisite but of passions hostile to both.—Bergh 10:262. (1801.)

If we can prevent the government from wasting the labors of the people, under the pretense of taking care of them, they must become happy.—Bergh 10:342. (1802.)

WELFARE. See also CHARITY; GENERAL WELFARE CLAUSE; POOR; REDISTRIBUTION OF WEALTH.

WESTERN TERRITORY, Proposed Government for.—The committee [of Congress] appointed to prepare a plan for the temporary government of the western territory have agreed to the following resolutions.

Resolved: That the territory ceded or to be ceded by individual states to the United States, whensoever the same shall have been purchased of the Indian inhabitants and offered for sale by the United States, shall be formed into distinct states. . . . That the settlers within the territory so to be purchased and offered for sale shall, either on their own petition or on the order of Congress, receive authority from them, with appointments of time and place, for their free males of full age to meet together for the purpose of establishing a temporary government, to adopt the constitution and laws of any one of these states, so that such laws nevertheless shall be subject to alteration by their ordinary legislature, and to erect, subject to a like alteration, counties or townships for the election of members for their legislature.

That such temporary government shall only continue in force in any state until it shall have acquired 20,000 free inhabitants, when, giving due proof thereof to Congress, they shall receive from them authority, with appointments of time and place, to call a convention of representatives to establish a permanent constitution and government for themselves; provided that both the temporary and permanent governments be established on these principles as their basis: 1. That they shall forever remain a part of the United States of America. 2. That in their persons, property, and territory they shall be subject to the government of the United States in Congress assembled and to the Articles of Confederation in all those cases in which the original states shall be so subject. 3. That they shall be subject to pay a part of the federal debts, contracted or to be contracted, to be apportioned on them by Congress according to the same common rule and measure by which apportionments thereof shall be made on the other states. 4. That their respective governments shall be in republican forms, and shall admit no person to be a citizen who holds any hereditary title. 5. That after the year 1800 of the Christian era there shall be neither slavery nor involuntary servitude in any of the said states, otherwise than in punishment of crimes whereof the

party shall have been duly convicted to have been personally guilty.

That whenever any of the said states shall have of free inhabitants as many as shall then be in any one [of] the least numerous of the thirteen original states, such state shall be admitted by its delegates into the Congress of the United States, on an equal footing with the said original states; after which the assent of two-thirds of the United States in Congress assembled shall be requisite.—Ford 3:407. (1784.)

WESTERN TERRITORY, Division into States.—I find Congress have reversed their division of the western states and proposed to make them fewer and larger. This is reversing the natural order of things. A tractable people may be governed in large bodies; but in proportion as they depart from this character, the extent of their government must be less. We see into what small divisions the Indians are obliged to reduce their societies.—To James Madison. Ford 4:333. (1786.)

WESTERN TERRITORY, Union with Other States.—I wish to see the western country in the hands of people well disposed, who know the value of the connection between that and the maritime states and who wish to cultivate it. I consider their happiness as bound up together, and that every measure should be taken which may draw the bands of union tighter. It will be an efficacious one to receive them into Congress, as I perceive they are about to desire. If to this be added an honest and disinterested conduct in

Congress, as to everything relating to them, we may hope for a perfect harmony.—Ford 5:16. (1788.)

WESTERN TERRITORY. See also TERRITORY.

WHEAT. See TOBACCO, Wheat vs.

WINE, Abuses of.—I have received and read with thankfulness and pleasure your denunciation of the abuses of tobacco and wine. Yet, however sound in its principles, I expect it will be but a sermon to the wind. You will find it is . . . difficult to inculcate these sanative precepts on the sensualities of the present day.—To Dr. Benjamin Waterhouse. Bergh 15:383. (1822.)

WINE. See also ALCOHOLIC BEVERAGES; INTEMPERANCE.

WOMEN, Barbarous Societies and. —The [Indian] women are submitted to unjust drudgery. This, I believe, is the case with every barbarous people. With such, force is law. The stronger sex imposes on the weaker.... Were we in equal barbarism, our females would be equal drudges.—*Notes on Virginia.* Bergh 2:84. (1782.)

WOMEN, Natural Equality of.—It is civilization alone which replaces women in the enjoyment of their natural equality. That first teaches us to subdue the selfish passions, and to respect those rights in others which we value in ourselves.—*Notes on Virginia.* Bergh 2:84. (1782.)

WOMEN, And Hard Labor.—I observe women and children [in France] carrying heavy burdens and laboring with the hoe. This is an unequivocal indication of extreme poverty. Men, in a civilized country, never expose their wives and chil-

dren to labor above their force and sex as long as their own labor can protect them from it.—Bergh 17:154. (1787.)

WOMEN, And Domestic Happiness in America.—American women have the good sense to value domestic happiness above all other, and the art to cultivate it beyond all other. There is no part of the earth where so much of this is enjoyed as in America.—Ford 5:9. (1788.)

WOMEN, Politics and.—All the world is now politically mad. Men, women, [and] children [in France] talk nothing else, and you know that naturally they talk much, loud, and warm. Society is spoiled by it, at least for those who, like myself, are but lookers on. You, too, [in America] have had your political fever. But our good ladies, I trust, have been too wise to wrinkle their foreheads with politics. They are contented to soothe and calm the minds of their husbands returning ruffled from political debate.—Ford 5:9. (1788.)

However nature may by mental or physical disqualifications have marked infants and the weaker sex for the protection rather than the direction of government, yet among the men who either pay or fight for their country no line of right can be drawn.—Ford 10:303. (1824.)

WORK. See IDLENESS; INDUSTRY; LABOR; TIME.

WORLD, End of the.—I hope you will have good sense enough to disregard those foolish predictions that the world is to be at an end soon. The Almighty has never made known to anybody at what time He created it, nor will He tell anybody when He means to put an end to it, if ever He means to do it. As to preparations for that event, the best way is for you to be always prepared for it. The only way to be so is never to do nor say a bad thing.—To Martha Jefferson. Betts & Bear, p. 21. (1783.)

WRITING, Conciseness in.—No style of writing is so delightful as that which is all pith, which never omits a necessary word nor uses an unnecessary one.—To Thomas Jefferson Randolph. Betts & Bear, p. 369. (1808.)

WRITING. See also CORRESPONDENCE; LETTER WRITING; SPELLING.

WRONG, Principles of Right and. —The great principles of right and wrong are legible to every reader; to pursue them requires not the aid of many counselors.—*Summary View of the Rights of British America.* Bergh 1:209. (1774.)

WRONG, Must Be Resisted.— We..owe it to mankind, as well as to ourselves, to restrain wrong by resistance, and to defeat those calculations of which justice is not the basis.—Ford 9:146. (1807.)

WRONG, No Submission to.—[We] love peace, yet spurn at a tame submission to wrong.—Bergh 16:302. (1808.)

Y

YOUNG MEN, Self-Government and.—I rejoice when I hear of young men of virtue and talents, worthy to receive and likely to preserve the splendid inheritance of self-government which we have acquired and shaped for them. —Bergh 11:34. (1804.)

YOUNG MEN, Enthusiasm of.— Bonaparte will conquer the world if [the European powers] do not learn his secret of composing armies of young men only, whose enthusiasm and health enable them to surmount all obstacles.—Bergh 11:116. (1806.)

YOUNG MEN, Education of.—I am not a friend to placing young men in populous cities [for their education], because they acquire there habits and partialities which do not contribute to the happiness of their after life.—Ford 9:79. (1807.)

YOUNG MEN, Responsibility of America's.—Those who [have] labored faithfully in establishing the right of self-government see in the rising generation, into whose hands it is passing, that purity of principle and energy of character which will protect and preserve it through their day, and deliver it over to their sons as they receive it from their fathers.—Bergh 16:323. (1808.)

YOUNG MEN, To Assume Leadership in World Affairs.—I leave the world and its affairs to the young and energetic, and resign myself to their care of whom I have endeavored to take care when young.—Ford 10:162. (1820.)

Bibliography

Adair, Douglass. "The Jefferson Scandals." An essay written in 1960 and published in *Fame and the Founding Fathers: Essays by Douglass Adair*. Edited by Trevor Colbourn. Published for the Institute of Early American History and Culture at Williamsburg, Virginia. New York: W.W. Norton & Co., Inc., 1974.

Bear, James A., Jr., ed. *Jefferson at Monticello*. Charlottesville, Va.: The University Press of Virginia, 1967.

Chinard, Gilbert. *Thomas Jefferson: The Apostle of Americanism*. 2nd ed. rev. Ann Arbor, Mich.: The University of Michigan Press, 1964.

Curtis, William Eleroy. *The True Thomas Jefferson*. Philadelphia: J.B. Lippincott Company, 1901.

Dabney, Virginius. *The Jefferson Scandals: A Rebuttal*. New York: Dodd, Mead & Company, 1981.

Gardner, Joseph L., et al., eds. *Thomas Jefferson: A Biography in His Own Words*. New York: Newsweek, Inc., 1974.

Jefferson, Thomas. *The Family Letters of Thomas Jefferson*. Edited by Edwin Morris Betts and James Adam Bear, Jr. Columbia, Mo.: University of Missouri Press, 1966.

————. *The Papers of Thomas Jefferson*. Edited by Julian P. Boyd. 20 vols. by 1982. Princeton, N.J.: Princeton University Press, 1950–.

————. *The Writings of Thomas Jefferson*. Edited by Paul Leicester Ford. 10 vols. New York: G.P. Putnam's Sons, 1892–99.

————. *The Writings of Thomas Jefferson*. Edited by Albert Ellery Bergh. 20 vols. Washington: The Thomas Jefferson Memorial Association, 1907.

Koch, Adrienne, ed. *Jefferson*. Englewood Cliffs, N.J.: Prentice-Hall, Inc., 1971.

Malone, Dumas. *Jefferson the Virginian*. Jefferson and His Time, vol. 1. Boston: Little, Brown and Company, 1948.

————. *Jefferson and the Rights of Man*. Jefferson and His Time, vol. 2. Boston: Little, Brown and Company, 1951.

————. *Jefferson and the Ordeal of Liberty.* Jefferson and His Time, vol. 3. Boston: Little, Brown and Company, 1962.

————. *Jefferson the President: First Term, 1801–1805.* Jefferson and His Time, vol. 4. Boston: Little, Brown and Company, 1970.

————. *Jefferson the President: Second Term, 1805–1809.* Jefferson and His Time, vol. 5. Boston: Little, Brown and Company, 1974.

————. *The Sage of Monticello.* Jefferson and His Time, vol. 6. Boston: Little, Brown and Company, 1981.

————. "Thomas Jefferson." *Dictionary of American Biography,* 10:17–35. Edited by Allen Johnson and Dumas Malone. 20 vols. Published under the auspices of the American Council of Learned Societies. New York: Charles Scribner's Sons, 1928–36.

Mayo, Bernard, ed. *Jefferson Himself: The Personal Narrative of a Many-Sided American.* Boston: Houghton Mifflin Company, 1942.

Randall, Henry S. *The Life of Thomas Jefferson.* 3 vols. New York: Derby & Jackson, 1858.

Randolph, Sarah N. *The Domestic Life of Thomas Jefferson.* New York: Harper and Bros., 1871.

Rosenberger, Francis Coleman, ed. *Jefferson Reader: A Treasury of Writings About Thomas Jefferson.* New York: E.P. Dutton & Company, Inc., 1953.

Smith, Margaret Bayard. *The First Forty Years of Washington Society in the Family Letters of Margaret Bayard Smith.* Edited by Gaillard Hunt. New York: Charles Scribner's Sons, 1906.

Index

Archaeology, contribution of TJ to, 197

Architecture, TJ's interest in, 37-38, 182-83; TJ's 1771 elevation drawing of Monticello, **38;** TJ's contributions to American, 127-29, 158-59, 297-98; Roman temple Maison Carree, **128;** Virginia state capitol at Richmond, **128;** west front of Monticello, **183;** University of Virginia Rotunda, **298, 299;** ugliness of Virginia's residential, 351; design of Virginia capitol, 351; importance of, 351. *See also* Monticello; University of Virginia

Aristocracy, TJ on need to eradicate, 77, 78-79; public office and natural, 351; artificial vs. natural, 351. *See also* Genius; Talents

Arms, right to bear, 351-52

Army, increase of American, 352; importance of state militia, 352. *See also* Defense; Draft; Militia; Navy

Arnold, Benedict, attacks Richmond, 93-94; TJ considers plan to capture, 94

Articles of Confederation, adopted by Congress, 75; weaknesses of, 139, 352-53. *See also* Constitution of the United States

Arts, TJ's enthusiasm for, 353. *See also* Architecture; Music

Attorneys. *See* Lawyers

Autobiography, written by TJ, 283n

B

Bacon, Edmund (overseer at Monticello), his reminiscences of TJ, 176-77, 178-79, 180-81; on

TJ's involvement in construction of University of Virginia, 298

Banjo, origin of the, 354-54

Bank of the United States, proposed by Alexander Hamilton, 163; opposed by TJ and James Madison, 164-65 and n; created in 1791, 165; unconstitutional, 354; the nation "saddled and bridled" by, 354; produces ruin, 354; hostile to American government, 354-55; opposition to renewal of its charter, 355

Banks, excess of, 355; evils of, 355-56; a challenge to government, 356; more dangerous than standing armies, 356. *See also* Fractional banking; Money; Monopoly

Barbary states, reject TJ's proposals for trade agreement, 124; TJ on American relations with, 124; United States wins naval war against, 237-38

Bayard, James A., Federalist Congressman from Delaware, **212;** turns presidential election with his vote, 212 and n

Bernhard, Duke of Saxe-Weimar Eisenach, describes TJ in old age, 303

Bible, circulation of the, 356; morality in the, 356. *See also* Christianity; Jesus Christ; "Philosophy of Jesus"; Religion

Bigotry, a disease, 356; self-government and, 356. *See also* Intolerance

Bill of Rights, TJ's efforts to secure, in new American Constitution, 141-43 and n; adopted in 1791, 143; the people entitled to, 356-57; TJ's early definition, 357; national demand for, 357; security in, 357-58

Birthday, TJ's reticence about his, 358

Blackstone, Sir William, *Commentaries* by, 358

Bonaparte, Napoleon, desires to establish French empire on American continent, 238; sells Louisiana Territory to United States, 239, 241–42, 529–30; wages war against England, 261

Books, TJ's love for, 306*n*, 525; on government, 462–63; on history and morality, 472–73; on law, 514–15. *See also* Library

Borrowing, Constituion should prohibit federal government from, 431. *See also* Credit; Debt; Loans

Botany, value of, 358

Boyd, Julian P., on TJ's performance as Governor of Virginia, 102; on the Ordinance of 1784, 113*n;* on breadth of TJ's scholarly investigations, 195

Bribery, in elections, 358

Brodie, Fawn M., evaluation of her biography of TJ, x and *n*, 134*n*, 231–32*n*

Browere, John Henri Isaac, produces plaster life mask of TJ, 304–5; photograph of the life mask, **648**

Brown, Mather, his 1786 portrait of TJ, **363**

Burr, Aaron, elected Vice President of the United States, 207–12; sides with Federalists in Senate during TJ's presidency, 255; loses vice-presidential nomination in 1804, 255; loses New York gubernatorial election, 255; kills Alexander Hamilton in a duel, 255; portrait of, **255;** finishes vice-presidential term in exile, 255–56; organizes conspiracy against the United States, 256; captured on Mississippi River, 256; acquitted in federal trial, 256–57; TJ on his treason, 359

Burwell, Rebecca, her romance with young TJ, 21–24; marries Jacquelin Ambler, 24; daughter of, marries John Marshall, 24*n*

Butler, Samuel, on historians' altering of the past, ix

C

Cabinet, advisers to President, 359; need for public confidence in officers of, 359

Calendar, British transition from Julian to Gregorian, 11*n*

Callender, James Thomson, pardoned under Sedition Act by TJ, 227; publishes slanderous attacks against TJ, 228 and *n;* drowns himself in the James River, 231; evaluation of his stories about TJ and Sally Hemings, 231–35

Canada, expected to join American Revolution, 359–60

Capital punishment, advocated for murder and treason, 360; a last resource, 360; Indians and, 360; substitutes for, ineffective, 360

Cards. *See* Playing cards

Carr, Dabney, friend to young TJ, 16; joins TJ and others in proposing a Continental Congress, 48; TJ buried beside, 317*n*

Carr, Peter (nephew of TJ), the real father of Sally Hemings's children, 233

Cartoons, political, of TJ, **220, 262**

Census, TJ's recommendations for perfecting the, 360–61

Central College, becomes University of Virginia, 296

F

I

Loans, government should not obtain, from private banks, 527-28; economy vs., 528. *See also* Borrowing; Credit; Debt; Economy; Finances

London, TJ joins John Adams in, for diplomatic negotiations, 123-25; beauty of, 528

Lotteries, "Jefferson Lottery" approved by Virginia legislature, 307-8; inadvisable, 528. *See also* Chance; Gambling; Speculation

Louis XVI (King of France), execution of, 528; character of, 528-29. *See also* Marie Antoinette

Louisiana, ceded by Spain to France, 238; sold by Napoleon to the United States, 239, 241-42, 529-30; British designs on, 529; the Constitution and U.S. acquisition of, 529; and expansion of the Union, 530

Louisiana Purchase, doubles the nation's land mass, 239, 531; TJ's views on, 239, 248; map of, **240**; favored by most Americans, 248n; part of American destiny, 530; blessings anticipated from, 530-31; should be ratified by the American people, 531. *See also* Manifest Destiny; Population; Territory

Luxuries, taxation on, 531. *See also* Tariffs

Lyon, Matthew (Republican Congressman from Vermont), Federalists attempt to bribe him, 210-11

M

Maclay, William (Senator from Pennsylvania), describes physical

appearance of TJ as Secretary of State, 156

Madison, Dolley (wife of James Madison), serves as hostess at Executive Mansion during TJ's presidency, 223

Madison, James, elected to Virginia legislature, 80; supports TJ's legislative proposals, 80; serves on Virginia's Council of State during TJ's governorship, 93n; his friendship with TJ, 93n, 138, 286-87, 332-33, 532; "father of the Constitution," 137-38; TJ's influence on his role in the Constitutional Convention of 1787, 137-40; portraits of, **139**, **274**; and the Bill of Rights, 141, 143; co-authors *The Federalist*, 142; opposes Alexander Hamilton's fiscal proposals in Congress, 164; urges TJ to enter 1796 presidential race, 188; drafts Virginia Resolutions of 1798, 200; serves as TJ's Secretary of State, 223, 227, 257; succeeds TJ as President, 273; his inaugural ceremonies, 273-75; on TJ's death, 316; TJ's estimate of, 532; abilities of, 532-33

Maison Carree, ancient Roman temple in France, used by TJ as basis of design for Virginia capitol building, 127-29, **128**, 351

Majority, will of, safeguards natural rights, 533; must be reasonable, 533; force vs., 533; law of, essential to government, 533. *See also* Minority; People; Representation; Republican government; Self-government

Malone, Dumas, on TJ's limitations as a public speaker, 45n; on

N

T

Also available from National Center for Constitutional Studies

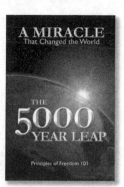

THE 5000 YEAR LEAP
A Miracle That Changed the World

337 pages
$19.95
Bulk discount available at *nccs.net*

The nation the Founders built is now in the throes of a political, economic, social, and spiritual crisis that has driven many to an almost frantic search for modern solutions. The truth is that the solutions have been available for a long time in the writings of our Founding Fathers—carefully set forth in this timely book.

Discover the **28 Principles of Freedom** our Founding Fathers said must be understood and perpetuated by every people who desire peace, prosperity, and freedom. Learn how adherence to these beliefs during the past 200 years has brought about more progress than was made in the previous 5000 years.

> *"This is possibly the most comprehensive treatment of the genius of the American Founding Fathers which has ever been encompassed in a single volume."*
> —Kenneth C. Chatwin, District Judge, Phoenix, Arizona

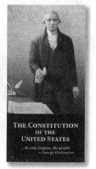

POCKET CONSTITUTION
(Text from the U.S. Bicentennial Commission Edition)

52 pages
$1.00
Bulk discount available at *nccs.net*

Pocket edition of the original *Constitution of the United States* (with Index), and *Declaration of Independence.*

The text is from one produced by the U.S. Bicentennial Commission and was proofed word for word against the original Constitution housed in the Archives in Washington, D.C.—identical in spelling, capitalization and punctuation. This special edition is sized in accordance with one produced by President Thomas Jefferson and includes remarkable quotes from our nation's Founders.

> *"The power under the Constitution will always be in the people."*
> —George Washington

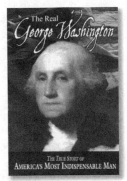

THE REAL GEORGE WASHINGTON
The True Story of America's Most Indispensable Man
928 pages, 119 illustrations.
$24.95
Visit *nccs.net*

"There is properly no history, only biography," wrote Ralph Waldo Emerson. If that is true of the general run of mankind, it is particularly true of George Washington. The story of his life is the story of the founding of America.

Why, after two centuries, does George Washington remain one of the most beloved figures in our history? *The Real George Washington* answers that question by giving us a close look at this man who became the father of our country and the first American President. But rather than focus on the interpretations of historians, much of his exciting story is told in his own words. The second part of this book brings together the most important and insightful passages from Washington's writings, each documented from original sources.

THE REAL BENJAMIN FRANKLIN
The True Story of America's Greatest Diplomat
504 pages, 42 illustrations.
$19.95
Visit *nccs.net*

There are many Benjamin Franklins—or at least he has taken on many different forms in the history books of the last two centuries. Unfounded myths are now being repeated and embellished in school textbooks and educational television programs.

Which of all these Benjamin Franklins, if any, is real? *The Real Benjamin Franklin* seats us across the table from the one person who really knew Benjamin Franklin—that is, Franklin himself—and gives him an opportunity to explain his life and ideas in his own words. Part I of this book details his exciting biography, and Part II includes his most important and insightful writings, all carefully documented from original sources.